*Revised Edition*
*1998*

# *Ornamental*
# *Plants*
# *for*
# *Subtropical*
# *Regions*

*A Handbook for Reference*

*By*

*Roland Stewart Hoyt*

*Livingston Press*

*148 East Orangethorpe Avenue*
*Anaheim, California 92801*

Library of Congress Catalog Card Number: 78-58918

ISBN 0-9601746-1-3


Reprinted 1998
Printed in Hong Kong

## Roland Stewart Hoyt

1890 - 1968

# DEDICATION

Southern California is blessed with a horticulturally benign climate. Naturally a semi-desert, the arrival of water, courtesy of the Mulholland Siphon in the early part of this century, soon transformed the coastal regions to verdant scenes rivaling Eden. Oranges, walnuts, and avocados covered thousands of acres and commercial nurseries proliferated. The introduction of choice ornamentals from around the world sparked a rivalry among the more adventurous growers with the result that it is not an exaggeration to say that serious gardeners have the opportunity to cultivate a greater variety of plants here than anywhere else in the continental United States. It is hoped that among dedicated horticuluralists there will be some who will wish to carry on the great work of plant introduction.

Flowering trees are the most conspicuous of the exotic introductions, yet we see them in our local landscapes all too infrequently. Jacarandas to be sure are well established and their contribution is a refreshing relief to the ubiquitous green blobs which dominate. Where are the Bauhinias, Cassias, and Tabebuias to name a few, which can light up the sky and add a little glamour to the scene? There is no reason why these beautiful trees should be confined to Botanic Gardens. They, together with a wealth of flower shrubs and climbers, belong in our parks and campuses, on avenues and of course in our residential gardens.

I suspect it is largely a matter of education, and the professionals should be leading the way. Landscape architects, garden designers, and park superintendents should inform the general public by example. We are fortunate to have such references as Sunset's Western Garden Book, Mathias' Color in the Landscape, and Perry's Landscape Plants for Western Regions among others, but one such invaluable reference has been missing for years and I am delighted to see its reappearance herewith.

Roland Hoyt's Ornamental Plants for Subtropical Regions is a veritable bible for amateur and professional alike. It was first published in 1938, republished in 1958 but out of print and unavailable since August 1991. Perusing this updated and expanded edition brings back fond memories of discussions with Roland from whom I learned a great deal and much more from his book which I kept on my desk for years.

Landscaping and gardening is a pursuit in which learning never ceases. I have been immersed in this field for sixty years and scarcely a day passes when I fail to learn something new. If we are to educate others we ourselves have to be educated. Young people leaving school to embark upon a career in landscaping are really just beginning the learning process. Horticulture is an engrossing and rewarding pursuit and having the knowledge and experience of Roland Hoyt within arm's reach will not only answer many questions but will boost the thinking process and build confidence.

The organization of the text is quite unlike the aforementioned books and various encyclopedias for that matter. Hoyt's endeavor is to address the entire range of greenscape in all of its various components. He points the way but leaves the final choice to the reader. As a handy reference, this checklist belongs on the desk rather than the bookshelf.

Morgan "Bill" Evans, FASLA

*Morgan 'Bill' Evans*

June 1998

The first volume of the Journal of the California Horticultural Society was published in January 1940. A section of this journal provided book reviews of garden books written by Californians in recognition of their contribution to the knowledge of plants. At the time a copy of Roland Stewart Hoyts' 1938 book, <u>Check Lists for the Ornamental Plants of Subtropical Regions</u>, (a Handbook for Ready Reference) was reviewed. It was noted that this book would "be a most useful compendium for both amateur and professional" because it included so many plants that are not commonly evaluated in other garden books.

It was further noted by the author of this review that "I know of no comparable work." In looking at this book 60 years later, it is still possible to observe how true this is.

The family of Roland Stewart Hoyt and the Livingston Press wish to express their appreciation to Robert Perry, FASLA, who updated the book's plant nomenclature and provided an index for cross referencing. They also wish to thank Courtland Paul, FASLA, for his sustained effort over an extended period to facilitate the reprinting and updating of this very unique reference book. It is the intent of the publisher to continually update the book in the future.

# CHECK LISTS

## FOR

# ORNAMENTAL PLANTS

## OF

# SUBTROPICAL

# REGIONS

A HANDBOOK
FOR
REFERENCE

# FOREWORD

The earlier editions of this book have been the constant companions of a generation of landscape architects and horticulturists. No other manual issued during this period has filled so well the need for a compact guide to the permissible choices of plants for a particular combination of use and site.

The selection of plants is not simple and presents many pitfalls. The exceptional diversity of plant climate zones in the state of California is at once an opportunity and a challenge. The range of plants which can be grown in the climatically favored areas is truly remarkable.

General lists of plants for the various geographical areas are invaluable, but must be used with due consideration for the existence of many micro-climates. We have all seen excellent specimen plants in favorable sites hundreds of miles from the regions in which they are commonly used. Also, the structures of man frequently create considerable modifications in wind currents and in the rate of heat radiation from the soil.

The study of plant ecology opens many new vistas. Many significant additions to knowledge are being made in the Phytotron at the California Institute of Technology, where artificial climates are created at will. The behavior of some plants can now be predicted quite accurately at any given site if adequate information is available concerning the environment. The construction of more accurate plant climate maps and more complete recording of plant behavior in various localities is also under way in the Agricultural Extention Service of the University of California, on both a state and a county basis.

Let us not accept a too limited or stereotyped planting list! Also, perhaps it is even more important that we avoid the costly and unfortunate mistakes of the past in planting design which we see on every hand, particularly in street trees.

This new revision adds to a highly original and useful book much new information gained from many years of observation on the part of the author. We are fortunate to share in the richness of his experience.

Vernon T. Stoutemeyer

Pacific Palisades, California

1958

# PREFACE

There is a growing demand for books on ornamental plants where some appreciable attempt has been made to limit the scope geographically. Almost without exception they are permitted to cover too much territory in view of the limitations imposed by climate and so qualify their value to the layman planter. If a treatise covering California or Florida cannot do complete justice to both the extreme north and southern parts in way of specific and practical information, it cannot be expected that the materials adapted to New England mean anything to the Lower South except incidentally. Yet such are the generalities with which the gardener must cope. He finds himself floundering about in much extraneous matter as best he can, picking and choosing, with sometimes sad experience and certainly loss of time, finally to emerge with the information that should have been available as a starting point.

This work limits itself to what may be termed Sub-Tropical Regions, a logical, if somewhat arbitrary area south of a line drawn through Charleston, Gainsville, Baton Rouge, San Antonio, El Paso, Phoenix and San Francisco. Strictly speaking this is a line only on the map. Projected upon the ground, it becomes a transitional area or belt, its varying width determined by local influences such as soil, topography and prevailing air movement. For the purpose of this book it has been traced in the field as indicated by growing plants found there.

While being descriptive in a degree, it is essentially an attempt to organize and estimate the value of the different plants and place them within the reach and understanding of the average gardener. The thought of limitation is carried beyond climate, where it holds that all plants of landscape value have their place, if used intelligently with reference to culture and the primary uses for which they are fitted. It asserts the intrinsic value of the individual and its singular appeal, but stresses its use as a building material, regarding it as a part of the whole and not conclusive in itself.

It may be observed that the horticulture of much of this country has been laid down over an arid land and depends on the ingenuity of man for its continuance. Water has been conserved or brought in to enhance the ornamental value of the native flora and make possible the growing of new plants from all over the world. This means a high degree of control to suit widely varying needs, while climate throughout allows the development of rare species out of doors which are usually practicable only by articificial means. The seasons progress in but slight modification, punctuated by hot, desiccating winds from the deserts in the west and tropical storms in the east, with frost in very low or very high places. Humidity becomes an important factor, sharply contrasted as between eastern and western portions. Rainfall is abundant in the summer in the east, but is normally the lowest of any thickly populated section of the nation westerly, and comes in the winter or early spring. Air movement is sharp in the east, steady in the west, but sometimes punishing.

Some emphasis may be placed on soils since there will be found all grades and variations from cold heavy clay or adobe to deep warm loams and sand. One universal characteristic in the west is the deficiency in humus or nitrogenous matter, the result of ages of baking out beneath a long-parching sun, with a feeble replenishment by the scant vegetation. Leaching is a problem in the east. The western soils are usually neutral to alkaline, mildly acid in places, with alkali a very real challenge in portions. The eastern soils are better provided in this respect, due to the rank vegetation. They are usually more permeable to water, and generally acid in reaction. However, with-al, good, bad or indifferent, the climate covers most essentials in these regions out of the control of man and one cannot be denied flowers. It but remains to be seen that they are used with understanding and to their full capacity to please.

This is the first of several proposed studies designed to localize the problem of planting to climatic areas, with particular reference to continental United States.

R. S. H.

CONTENTS

EXPLANATORY

Some of these lists will appear to duplicate. On closer examination
it is hoped that a clear dissimilarity will be recognized, especially
in the manner of approach.   It is assumed that the reader will come
to them with a definite quality or circumstance in mind which relates
intimately to his problem. The value of a list, then, will depend in
a measure on the key idea and the way it ties in with these possible
lines of thought.  The matter might well be considered in the nature
of a cross-index, with the usual advantages of getting quickly to the
information sought.  At best it should enable the student to form a
clearer picture of what the plant is and what it will do.


RATINGS
Each list will be divided into three parts roughly, with the individual plants allocated and designated by asterisks (*,**, or ***)in accordance with the desirability in view of the premise of the list
statement, general utility or practicability and whether or not it is
reasonably procurable.  Such a system will always be open to adverse
criticism, yet it is felt here to be of value to the amateur and with
others it may be accepted as the authors appraisal as of the present
time and not final even with him. The amateur will be unquestionably
safe so long as he stays within the first third or those plants marked with a single asterisk (*).   When he goes within the second portion, he should realize he is approaching uncertain ground and properly will seek more information than can be given here, although it may
be said that many plants in this group are there merely because they
are not reasonably intersectional, a matter that may be cleared easily by checking with the COMPENDIUM.   The third portion (***) right-
fully belongs to those who work with some knowledge of plants or who
knowingly enter into the experimental, with all that entails.  It may
not be expected that these ratings are in any way exact.  In the first

## EXPLANATORY

place, the subject matter is arbitrarily divided into three parts which means that some plants will fall in a following group merely because the previous quota has been filled. A plant may merit a place in the first division, yet appears in the third because it is difficult to obtain. The nature of the subject precludes a mathematical accuracy as many plants will fall on the borderline between groups and as logically included in the one as in the other.

## PROCEDURE

Procedure need not be complicated. One ordinarily will go to the list that applies most nearly to the case in question and, consulting the COMPENDIUM, will select the plant which either seems to fit or the one that suits the fancy. Some further degree of accuracy is attainable, if time and care is taken to follow out all leads, and the discussion which follows will suggest possibilities in arriving at the most desirable plant through a process of elimination. But again the fact is disclosed that no great precision obtains; that the material is not subject to more than reasonable manipulation and requires, as always, that some judgement be exercised based on fact available.

## A PROBLEM

As a hypothetical case, assume one wants a woody plant in connection with the lawn, something not so very large, rather floriferous, and of permanent character. The location is partially shaded; is safely removed from the sea, but still subject to considerable salt wind. The soil is on the heavy side. Under LAWN, in the Index, will be found what appears to be a starting point in TREES FOR THE LAWN, a list on page 80. Turning there, we find the single asterisk(*)plants Arbutus unedo, Cedrus deodara, Crinodendron, Buxus microphylla, Hibiscus rosa sinensis, species of Juniperus, Laurus nobilis, Melaleuca styphelioides, Nandina domestica, Pittosporum tobira, Podocarpus elongata, Prunus lyoni, Pyracantha koidzumi, Quercus virginiana, Raphiolepis indica and varieties of Thuja orientalis. Consulting the COMPENDIUM, it is found that Cedrus, Crinodendron, the Melaleuca, Podocarpus and Quercus are large trees, while Juniperus and Thuja have no color and are thereby eliminated. Of the remaining plants only Arbutus, Hibiscus, Pyracantha and Raphiolepis are found in HEAVY SOILS, page 52, all being given the preference of the single asterisk (*). Turning to SEASIDE PLANTING on page 75, Arbutus is not located until the 3rd zone, while Pyracantha and Hibiscus are found in the 2nd zone. Raphiolepis is a strong 1st zone shrub. This appears to give it some preference, but turning to FREE FLOWERING PLANTS on page 153, one finds Hibiscus favored. Again, considering the matter of SHADE, page 38, there must be a three way choice----shade versus flowering----versus salt resistance in a final solution. Go now to the COMPENDIUM and study in detail these three plants and decide on the one that will give the most personal pleasure----anyone of Hibiscus, Pyracantha, Raphiolepis will do. After all this, the planter must have developed something of confidence in the quality of thinking, and of decision which has entered into this choice. There should be much of satisfaction in the processing, with knowledge aquired aside from the prime issue. There should be a feeling of finality in the results. And this is not to mention the profit involved when sound indications are carried out.

## PLANT PORTRAITS

The index should not be overlooked as a feature in the gathering together of information relative to a given plant, because a clear and comprehensive picture of an individual may be formed by tracing the line of treatment back through the list captions. This may be done by means of the page numbering.

Thus, the plant Cytisus canariensis, one of the Brooms, might well be portrayed as a sun-loving shrub, medium in size to some five or eight feet in height according to soil and culture. It is spreading in growth laterally or erect and inclined to stringiness, if seedling grown. It becomes a weighty figure and dense form under light pruning, the stems lightly recurving. Of fairly rapid growth, it is still of some permanence to serve as a filler between shrubs designed for longer life. It submits to some shearing which fits it for a tub, or infrequently hedging. Do not cut into old wood except to remove entire stems. It may be seen appropriate in its various forms against the foundation of a building. The foliage is refined, pale to bright green or of a soft greyish cast, sometimes dense, but always sprightly to relieve harsh lines of construction, or the too heavy texture of a planting and is born rather plentifully on the arching stems which show some interest in way of bark markings.

The flowers come in the spring in showers of bright yellow, with a lesser blooming in the fall or late summer. They are desirable for cutting and may be taken indoors for considerable color. This will dominate and lighten an entire room.

The plant withstands some degree of alkali or salt in the soil and delights in exposure to sea breezes where it takes on and holds characteristic, wind-blown shapes. In the garden it is more subject to defoliation by the genista worm which is very difficult to keep under control. It is less subject to this pest when grown dry and hard or with no fertilizer. It also becomes a choice bit for the snails and serves in their effective baiting, the poisoned mash being placed in the near vicinity or beneath. Drought it withstands to such degree as permits its use generously in arid lands, but always and only in the discipline of harsh surroundings. It is much better adapted to California than to Florida where moisture comes at the wrong time.

The root system is quite vigorous, strong and stringy to fit this plant for a loose or gravelly soil that is sterile and dry. Good use on the face of a fresh fill puts anchorage down to protect against a major slide of earth. There the species tends to naturalize in some permanence and rather freely re-seeding. The better plants, however, are propagated by means of cuttings taken from selected individuals, as used in the garden or other habited place.

It will be seen here, that each plant as it is used may be processed as above, with material available depending on the importance of the individual species. The student may work out his own portraits as a matter of self-instruction or for practical purposes connected with planting. The careful planter will make some attempt to establish in this way and have firmly in mind the range of conditions under which a plant will thrive before he finally decides on form or coloring or anything in way of timing. This is theory in practice that should offer good returns on time spent.

Moreover, it may be observed that the average gardener, after many struggling years, finds he cannot buy beauty for his garden....that illusive and insubstantial fabric of a vision which is to lie implanted in the very essence of his living. Then he comes to know that its attainment is a matter of thought and study and hard personal application. Next is to realize that this is not only a picture, but a place of dimensions which are changing in form from year to year and day by day in light and shadow and color.

There are limitless possibilities for personal accomplishment here and the matter above may suggest a pleasant pastime or diversion and profitable, for anyone sufficiently interested. The stuff of which gargens are made is so basic to all that has gone into the growth of man, that now, when he stands jittery on the threshold of an atomic future, it must be used more freely. It still can compose and restore. It will disburden for better better living, for efficiency and for resource. This is natures great tranquilizer.

# GENERAL LISTS

This section will have to do mainly with plants which are in common use, yet at the same time aims at a reasonably comprehensive and representative treatment of the field of ornamental plants as found in these regions. All will be adequate for service or adaptable for the purposes of the amateur, even in view of the preceding explanation of ratings which still hold in the sense of general utility and applicability. These lists are designed for the casual gardener primarily, but should afford to anyone a birdseye view of the several classifications and their brief application to the landscape or garden. The plants will be grouped in accordance with customary and commonly known or accepted botanical terms where they will be quickly available to those people who desire to cut corners or those who for any other reason will not take time to search out more exactly a species or variety better suited to the handling of their problem. Botanical names are used of necessity since many of the most useful plants have no common name and must rightly go without until the people find one that not only fits but one that persists over time as vernacular.

## TREES
It may be observed that trees are valued universally for the deep emotions they inspire. This has to do with morale, as basic to physical as well as mental health. Sentiment probably does weigh heavily here as laid elsewhere among plants; yet this subjective aspect may be considered as only a part, along with the material look, as a thoro and fair evaluation of both aesthetic and economic properties will show. In the city they deaden noises; tend to purify the atmosphere and in any place afford shade and modify the force of the wind....the good protection embedded so deeply in race consciousness. Special and thorough study should be accorded their selection, use and placing. And they will be considered not only for what they contribute to a picture....what other practical spot do they fill. They become more significant when one realizes their comparative permanence, the fact that they will in all probability not be replaced within a generation or longer. If for no other reason, grow them for the sheer beauty in form, foliage or flower; enjoy and pass on in contribution to the next generation.

PALMS---symbolize grandeur and nobility in nature. They are the aristocrats and carry the impression of tropical magnificence to its further extreme....and as usual are overplanted. They are most effectively grown singly or in groups....not massed, where their purely decorative value is largely lost. Planting in larger sizes becomes important since they do not establish like other trees. New roots originate at the crown and are most active during warm weather. Move in heat for best results. Only a small ball is necessary then; set deeper than the tree stood, the stem wired for wind, most of foliage cut and the basin manured heavily. Ornamentally, they fall into two obvious classes, as follow:

| FAN | FROND |
|---|---|
| * Chamaerops humilis | *** Acrocomia totai |
| * Dracaena australis | *** Actinophloeus macarthuri |
| ** Erythea armata | * Arcontophoenix cunninghamiana |

1

** Erythea edule                  * Arecastrum romanzoffianum
*** Livistona australis            * Butia capitata
*** Rhapidophyllum histrix         *** Caryota urens
** Rhapis excelsa                  ** Chrysalidocarpus lutescens
*** Sabal palmetto                 ** Howea forsteriana
*** Serenoa repens                 * Phoenix canariensis


CONIFERS---with the pine as a popular conception and example. These
trees are evergreen, the leaf in the semblance of a needle, sometimes
flattened, frequently shortened and scale-like.  They carry much refinement in texture and are symmetrically shaped when young, but in
age tend to distort and develop a picturesque quality.  They are at
their best massed in large plantings where low-hanging limbs may sweep
to the ground around the perimeter and conceal bare boles within. With
notable exceptions they do not submit well to pruning and it is well
to do the least possible cutting, especially into heavy wood.  Again
with exceptions, they want the sun, abhore extreme dryness and want
a deep, well drained soil on the acid side. They bear cones or cone-
like berries that find basic uses in decoration.

*** Araucaria bidwilli            ** Juniperus silicicola
*     "    excelsa                 * Libocedrus decurrens
** Casuarina cunninghamiana        ** Pinus canariensis
*     "    equisetifolia           *** "    caribaea
***   "    stricta                 *   "    halepensis
** Cedrus atlantica                *** "    pinea
*** Chamaecyparis lawsoniana       *   "    radiata
** Cupressus arizonica             * Podocarpus elongata
***   "    lusitanica              **  "    macrophylla
**    "    macrocarpa              *** Sequoiadendron giganteum
*     "    sempervirens            *** Taxodium (species)
*** Juniperus chinensis            * Thuja orientalis
***   "    excelsa                 *** Torreya (species)


DWARF CONIFERS---are exemplary, with so many desirable characters
they are often over-used.  This is especially marked at the base of
buildings which stiffen to the belt of cold, unrelated blobs of green,
funeral and monotonous. These are simple things with an artlessness
that attains a kind of dignity and rate a preferred place in plantings of strength and permanence. They are in harmony with the formal
and find an appropriate place in the dominance of entrances, either
architectural or out in the garden. Use them with restraint and purpose, but always relieved and pulled in together with the flow of
of broadleaf types or lightened by spreading deciduous species.

*** Cephalotaxus fortunei          * Juniperus pfitzeriana
** Chamaecyparis allumi            *    "    tamariscifolia
*     "    Rosedale                *    "    torulosa
***   "    wisseli                 ** Pinus mugo
*** Cycas revoluta                 *** Taxus repandens
** Dion edule                      * Thuja beverlyensis
** Juniperus argentea              ***  "    bonita
*     "    conferta                **   "    elegantissima
**    "    excelsa stricta         ** Thujopsis dolobrata


DECIDUOUS TREES---those which drop their leaves to reveal an artistry of branch in winter have been overlooked in a mad scramble for
eternal summer.   Use them for a much needed indication of seasonal
change; in large foliage masses for diversity; for brighter green and
certainly where shade is desirable in the heat of the year and the
warmth of the sun in winter.   A superficial prejudice for the evergreen ignores all these particulars and overlooks the continual clean-
up beneath, together with the more rapid growth.    These will be most
at home with frost to make them quickly and completely leafless.

* Acer floridanum                  ** Betula nigra
***  "    macrophyllum             *** Cercis siliquastrum
* Albizzia julibrissin             * Delonix regia
*** Aleurites moluccana            * Ficus carica

|  |  |  |  |
|---|---|---|---|
| * | Fraxinus velutina | ** | Platanus orientalis |
| ** | Juglans regia | ** | Populus nigra italica |
| ** | Koelreuteria paniculata | ** | Prunus (check species) |
| ** | Liquidambar styraciflua | ** | Quercus lobata |
| *** | Lysiloma latisiliqua | ** | "    virginiana |
| * | Melia azedarach | *** | Robinia pseudacacia |
| *** | Metasequoia glyptostroboides | * | Salix babylonica |
| *** | Morus nigra | *** | Samanea saman |
| *** | Paulownia tomentosa | ** | Sophora japonica |
| ** | Pistacia chinensis | * | Ulmus parvifolia |

BROADLEAF EVERGREEN TREES---as the terms imply, are effective for foliage the year round, the leaf wide in proportion and as compared with the preceding groups. There is also more variation in form and color as well as in texture and structure, so that plantings of this type alone need not be monotonous or tiresome. Generally these trees should be given a fertile moist site to maintain size and color in foliage, and fullness in over-all development.    This is important since chief dependence in subtropical regions will be placed here for the many uses to which trees are put.

### LARGE

|  |  |  |  |
|---|---|---|---|
| ** | Acacia melanoxylon | * | Eugenia myrtifolia |
| *** | Angophora lanceolata | *** | Ficus macrophylla |
| *** | Calophyllum inophyllum | * | Magnolia grandiflora |
| * | Cinnamomum camphora | ** | Pittosporum undulatum |
| *** | Cupania anacardioides | ** | Quercus agrifolia |
| *** | Eucalyptus globulus | ** | "    virginiana |
| * | "    polyanthemos | *** | Quillaja saponaria |
| ** | "    rostrata | * | Schinus molle |
| *** | "    viminalis | *** | Talauma hodgsoni |

### MEDIUM SIZED TREES

|  |  |  |  |
|---|---|---|---|
| * | Acacia decurrens | *** | Fraxinus uhdei |
| ** | Brachychiton acerifolium | * | Grevillea robusta |
| * | Calodendrum capense | ** | Harpephyllum caffrum |
| * | Ceratonia siliqua | * | Jacaranda acutifolia |
| ** | Delonix regia | ** | Macadamia ternifolia |
| *** | Erythrina humeana | *** | Peltophorum inerme |
| * | Eucalyptus ficifolia | *** | Persea borbonia |
| *** | "    leucoxylon | ** | Pittosporum rhombifolium |
| *** | "    rudis | * | Quercus ilex |
| ** | "    sideroxylon | *** | "    suber |
| ** | Eugenia paniculata | *** | Stenocarpus sinuatus |
| ** | Ficus retusa | * | Tristania conferta |

### SMALL

|  |  |  |  |
|---|---|---|---|
| * | Acacia baileyana | ** | Hymenosporum flavum |
| ** | "    floribunda | ** | Lagunaria patersoni |
| *** | "    pendula | *** | Maytenus boaria |
| *** | Acer oblongum | *** | Melaleuca styphelioides |
| * | Brachychiton populneum | * | Metrosideros tomentosa |
| ** | Crinodendrum dependens | * | Olea europaea |
| *** | Dombeya wallichi | ** | Parkinsonia aculeata |
| * | Eriobotrya japonica | *** | Persea indica |
| * | Eucalyptus caesia | * | Pittosporum eugenioides |
| *** | "    erythronema | *** | Quercus douglasi |
| * | "    lehmanni | * | Schinus terebinthifolius |
| *** | "    pyriformis | *** | Ulmus parvifolia (forms) |
| ** | "    torquata | *** | Virgilia capensis |
| ** | Eugenia smithi | ** | Vitex lucens |

SMALL TREES OR LARGE SHRUBS---intermediate  source  plants, on the borderline; the one or the other, as modified by surroundings or the pruning shears.  They may be used as large massed shrubs or as individual specimen trees in the lower element of the shrubbery.  In the main these plants carry an unusual degree of refinement and color to bring out points of special significance.  They are well considered as major elements in any small scale planting.

  * Acacia cultriformis
  ** " longifolia
  *** " verticillata
  * Arbutus unedo
  *** Ceanothus arboreus
  *** Cercis occidentalis
  ** Chilopsis linearis
  *** Chrysobalanus icaco
  ** Datura suaveolens
  * Escallonia montevidensis
  *** Eucalyptus eremophila
  ** " nutans
  * " torquata
  *** Eugenia supraaxillaris
  ** Fuchsia arborescens
  ** Genista monosperma
  * Hakea elliptica
  *** Ilex vomitoria

  *** Illicium anisatum
  * Lagerstroemia indica
  *** Lawsonia inermis
  * Ligustrum lucidum
  ** Magnolia soulangeana
  * Melaleuca nesophila
  ** Michelia fuscata
  * Nerium oleander
  *** Nothopanax arboreum
  ** Pittosporum crassifolium
  *** " tenuifolium
  ** Prunus lyoni
  ** Pyracantha koidzumi
  *** Royena lucida
  *** Sophora secundiflora
  * Stenolobium stans
  *** Umbellularia californica
  * Viburnum japonicum

## EVERGREEN SHRUBS

The shrub, technically, is a woody plant with two or more stems, branching freely or sometimes very remotely.  Principal uses in the landscape are belt, background or boundary planting; the tying in and drawing down of the building mass with foliage to soften harsh lines and sharp angles; functional with walks or the curve of a drive. The wider aesthetic value lies in the mass grouping where interest in the individual plant may be submerged.  Additional to an intrinsic pictorial value, they relate lower herbaceous growth with that of trees in a desirable transition. They furnish a major element in the planting of a garden.    Treat them well and begin by selecting the right plant for its place....soil, exposure, and surely, the purpose which suggests its use.

LARGE SHRUBS---those growing ten to fifteen feet in height, or more when situated favorably for growth or when crowded upward. They will be used of necessity in the background, if the plant is to be allowed its typical shape and spared undue and wasted regulation with the pruning shears. They will want plenty of ground room for rootage.

  ** Acacia longifolia
  *** Acacia cyanophylla
  *** Buddleja asiatica
  * Callistemon lanceolatus
  *** Carissa carandas
  ** Cassia corymbosa
  *** Cestrum diurnum
  ** Cocculus laurifolius
  * Cotoneaster pannosa
  * Duranta repens
  ** Escallonia langleyensis
  *** Fuchsia arborescens
  ** Hakea laurina
  *** " saligna
  ** Jasminum humile
  * Lagerstroemia indica
  ** Laurus nobilis

  * Leptospermum laevigatum
  *** Ligustrum ovalifolium
  *** Malpighia glabra
  * Melaleuca armillaris
  ** " huegeli
  *** Myoporum laetum
  * Nerium oleander
  ** Osmanthus ilicifolius
  * Photinia serrulata
  * Pittosporum crassifolium
  ** Prunus ilicifolia
  * Pyracantha lalandi
  *** Solanum giganteum
  *** Tamarix pentandra
  * Viburnum japonicum
  ** " odoratissimum
  *** Wigandia caracasana

MEDIUM SIZED SHRUBS---growing in the neighborhood of six to ten feet to be used toward the front of the border or back, according to height desired and the function of the plant, as with its neighbor.    This area in shrub sizing shows more clearly than any other that these dimmentions are arbitrary and can be only relative.  An extra fertility or none, plentiful water or scant; any one of several factors can shift the species above or below its natural area of growth.

  * Abelia grandiflora
  *** Acacia vestita
  *** Bauhinia acuminata
  *** Bowkera gerrardiana

  * Buddleja magnifica
  * Camellia japonica
  *** Carpenteria californica
  * Cassia splendida

*** Ceanothus cyaneus
  * Cestrum aurantiacum
 ** Chamaelaucium ciliatum
  * Cotoneaster parneyi
 ** Cytisus canariensis
  * Erica melanthera
  * Escallonia rosea
*** Eugenia uniflora
 ** Euonymus japonicus
*** Gardenia thunbergia
 ** Grevillea thelemanniana
 ** Hakea suaveolens
  * Hibiscus rosa-sinensis
*** Hypericum floribundum
 ** Iochroma lanceolatum
 ** Jasminum rigidum
 ** Ligustrum henryi
*** Malvaviscus grandiflorus

*** Melaleuca decussata
  *     "    hyperiscifolia
 **     "    lateritia
*** Murraea paniculata
  * Nandina domestica
*** Phillyrea media
  * Pittosporum tobira
 ** Poinciana pulcherrima
 ** Pyracantha coccinea varieties
 ** Rondeletia cordata
*** Senecio petasitis
 ** Solanum rantonneti
 ** Spartium junceum
*** Tamarix africana
 ** Tecoma garrocha
 ** Viburnum fragrans
  *     "    tinus
  * Xylosma senticosa

SMALL SHRUBS---sized at three to five feet, more often carry the
qualities suitable to the immediate vicinity of the house and the more
highly developed areas of the garden.    The list, however, must  be
used in this respect advisedly and the COMPENDIUM consulted to elim-
inate questionable species which have been included here on  account
of growth limitation.   As homes are built lower to the ground, this
list will have more meaning and a wider application.

*** Abelia floribunda
 ** Adenocarpus viscosus
*** Aeonium spathulatum
 ** Ardisia crispa
 ** Azalea indica
 ** Berberis darwini
*** Brachysema lanceolatum
 ** Brunfelsia americana
*** Buddleja salvifolia
  * Buxus japonica
  * Cassia artemisoides
*** Ceanothus impressus
 ** Cestrum parqui
  * Cistus ladaniferus
 ** Codiaeum variegatum
 ** Coronilla glauca
  * Correa magnifica
 ** Cotoneaster simonsi
  * Diosma ericoides
 ** Ervatamia coronaria
 ** Escallonia glasniviensis
*** Fabiana imbricata
  * Gardenia jasminoides
*** Grevillea rosmarinifolia
 ** Hamelia erecta
*** Halimium halimifolium
  * Hebe carnea
  * Hydrangea macrophylla
  * Hypericum aureum

 ** Jasminum floridum
  * Lantana camara
*** Ligustrum rotundifolium
*** Lippia citriodora
 ** Lonicera nitida
*** Mahonia pinnata
*** Malvastrum capense
 ** Malvaviscus arboreus
*** Melaleuca thymifolia
  * Myrsine africana
  * Myrtus microphylla
*** Phlomis fruticosa
  * Polygala dalmaisiana
  * Pyracantha crenato-serrata
  * Raphiolepis indica
***     "       "     rosea
*** Salvia greggi
 ** Sarcococca hookeriana
*** Siphonosmanthus delavayi
 ** Sollya heterophylla
 ** Spiraea cantoniensis
  * Streptosolen jamesoni
 ** Tecoma smithi
*** Templetonia retusa
*** Thryallis glauca
*** Thunbergia erecta
*** Viburnum burkwoodi
  *     "    suspensum
  * Westringia rosmarinifolia

DWARF SHRUBS---those which can be expected to grow  not more
than three feet in overall height. Many of them will develop not
to exceed twelve to fifteen inches. Certain sub-shrubby, or what
is frequently termed woody perennials will be found in this group.
This material is becoming more important as gardens become more restricted in area....in-growing-in the economic squeeze.

*** Aster fruticosus
*** Barleria caerulea
*** Berberis gracilis
*** Breynia nivosa
  * Buxus harlandi
 ** Calceolaria integrifolia
  * Carissa compacta
  * Ceratostigma willmottianum

*** Chaenostoma (species)
  * Chorizema cordatum
  * Cistus corbariensis
*** Cneorum tricoccon
 ** Convolvulus cneorum
 ** Coprosma microphylla
*** Correa alba
  * Cotoneaster microphylla

** Cuphea platycentra          ** Malpighia coccigera
 * Diosma reevesi              ** Mesembryanth. aurantiacum
** Euonymus microphyllus      ***    "      browni
*** Euryops pectinatus         **    "      glaucum
** Felicia echinata           ***    "      uncinatum
 * Halimium ocymoides          ** Myrtus minima
** Hebe menziesi              *** Podalyrea sericea
 *    " traversi               * Punica granatum nana
** Hedera arborescens          * Pyracantha yunnanensis
*** Hibiscus diversifolius     * Raphiolepis ovata
*** Hymenanthera crassifolia   ** Russelia equisetiformis
 * Hypericum moserianum       *** Sarcococca humilis
** Ilex cornuta nana          *** Serissa foetida
** Jasminum parkeri            ** Thymus vulgaris
 * Lantana montevidensis       * Turraea obtusifolia
 * Lavandula (species)        *** Vinca rosea
*** Leucophyllum dwarf        *** Zauschneria californica

DECIDUOUS SHRUBS---shed their leaves in winter, but come back in
the spring sparkling with renewed vigor and gloriously alive with
something that is familiar to the northern bred.  Due to the hot and
continuous sun, they are apt to fail early and should be given the
advantage of a cool exposure or slight shade.  The few that follow
are from mild or southern latitudes and will adapt best, with reasonable performance under the comparative monotony of the climate and
torturing length of the season.

** Azalea obtusa               ** Prunus glandulosa
*** Calycanthus occidentalis  ***    "    jaquemonti
*** Caryopteris incana         * Punica granatum
** Ceratostigma griffithi     *** Rhus trilobata
 * Chaenomeles japonica       *** Serissa foetida
** Chilopsis linearis         ** Spiraea cantoniensis
*** Cudrania tricuspidata     ** Syringa persica
 * Erythrina crista-galli      ** Viburnum carlesi
** Hibiscus mutabilis         ***    "      fragrans
 *    " syriacus               * Vitex agnus-castus
 * Philadelphus mexicanus      * Weigela florida

SHRUBBY VINES---plants that partake of the character of both shrub
and vine. Some of them may be used in the shrubbery, with or without
the support of other plants while others will be permitted to scramble
at will over rocks and in the covering of banks or other unfinished
or unsightly areas.  With careful training in pruning, many of them
will carry on as shrubs and at the same time send streamers into the
air, if fastened and held in place.

** Abutilon megapotamicum     *** Lonicera implexa
 * Aloe ciliaris              *** Lycium richi
** Artabotrys uncinata         ** Penstemon cordifolius
*** Capparis spinosa          *** Pereskia aculeata
 * Chorizema cordatum          * Plumbago capensis
*** Clerodendrum thompsonae   *** Rosa laevigata
*** Escallonia franciscana    *** Securidaca diversifolia
** Fuchsia corymbiflora       *** Semele androgyna
 * Holmskioldia sanguinea     ** Solanum rantonneti
*** Jasminum azoricum          * Sollya heterophylla
**    " gracillimum           ** Streptosolen jamesoni
 *    " mesneyi               ** Tecomaria capensis
 * Lantana camara (forms)      * Trachelospermum jasminoides
** Lonicera confusa           *** Vitis arizonica

## VINES

The climber....natures understanding and efficient fingers reaching out to cover and conceal the inelegant or unseemly in all that is decorative and handsome. It will clothe blank spaces with the lovliness of flowers and foliage, the device of shadow and tracery of line gently winding as stem. In the garden they are nearly always additional to a soil already, or soon to be filled with roots to capacity or beyond. In view of this and considering the large production of wood, a generous preparation and fertilization of the soil before planting is urged.  Moisture is another point to have in mind when setting out these lively things, as one is prone to plant close against the wall where little natural moisture reaches.  Herbaceous climbers may be used to bridge the time it takes the slower more permanent vine to become established.

### EVERGREEN

* Bougainvillea (varieties)
*** Cissus hypoglauca
**    "    rhombifolia
** Clematis armandi
*** Clerodendrum thompsonae
** Dolichos lignosus
*** Ficus pumila
* Gelsemium sempervirens
* Hardenbergia comptoniana
** Hedera canariensis

* Jasminum grandiflorum
** Lonicera halliana
*** Muehlenbeckia complexa
*** Pandorea pandorana
** Passiflora caerulea
* Phaedranthus buccinatorius
*** Phaseolus caracalla
** Pyrostegia ignea
** Thunbergia grandiflora
* Trachelospermum jasminoides

### DECIDUOUS

** Ampelopsis brevipedunculata
* Antigonon leptopus
*** Calonyction aculeatum
** Doxantha unguis-cati
* Mandevilla suaveolens

** Parthenocissus tricuspidata
*** Polygonum auberti
* Solanum wendlandi
*** Vitis (species)
*** Wisteria floribunda

### HERBACEOUS

*** Aristolochia elegans
* Boussingaultia baselloides
** Cardiospermum halicacabum
*** Cissus adenopodus
*** Clitoria ternatea
** Cobaea scandens
*** Cucurbita pepo-ovifera
** Eccremocarpus scaber
* Ipomoea purpurea
* Lathyrus odoratus

* Lotus bertheloti
*** Maurandia erubescens
*** Momordica charantia
* Phaseolus coccineus
** Pueraria thunbergiana
* Quamoclit (species)
*** Stizolobium deeringianum
** Thunbergia alata
** Tropaeolum peregrinum
*** Vigna marina

### SUCCULENTS

* Aloe ciliaris
** Hoya carnosa
*** Hylocereus triangularis

** Pereskia aculeata
* Senecio mikanioides
*** Zygocactus truncatus

8

## HERBACEOUS PLANTS

Under this heading will be found the soft, more yielding plants which die down over winter or which tend to do so, returning in the spring either from seed or the crown of a permanent root system. This is the class of plants grown in the garden for flowers to produce color in bed or border rather than for form. They supply the larger portion of cutting material from the garden. The usual subdivisions hold, to include annuals, perennials, bulbs, grasses, ferns and tuberous root- ed plants, a familiar classification that becomes much involved in the far south where many perennials are used as annuals and where many typically annual plants hold over. By degrees and with more time other species from the tropics are becoming known and being made available. They should prove more satisfactory, in the end, than those more fam- iliar names that have been brought down from temperate regions. The planting schedule included later in this work, should be of some as- sistance in handling these plants.

ANNUAL FLOWERS---are used largely for cutting and to supplement the use of perennials in the garden. They should be renewed each year with fresh seed from the seedsman, if high standards of color and size are to be maintained. They are best sown out of doors where they are to stand, the lighter soils almost invariably to be preferred for germ- ination, and warmth for quick growth. An exceptionally heavy clay is best worked over with sand, dug well with strawy manure or compost the year previous. They must have the sun; are rapid in development and soon pass on if neglected or after having gone to seed. Do not plant too early in the fall....heat in California and heavy rains in Florida can be devastating.

Alyssum (Sweet)
  Alyssum maritimum
Amethyst Flower
  Browallia americana
Arctotis
  Arctotis staechadifolia
Aster (China)
  Callistephus chinensis
Baby-blue-eyes
  Nemophila menziesi
Birds-eyes
  Gilia tricolor
Butterfly Flower
  Schizanthus wisetonensis
Calliopsis
  Coreopsis tinctoria
Cape-marigold
  Dimorphotheca aurantiaca
Clarkia
  Clarkia elegans
Cockscomb
  Celosia cristata
Cornflower
  Centaurea cyanus
Cosmos
  Cosmos bipinnatus
Dahlberg Daisy
  Thymophylla tenuiloba
Flax (Scarlet)
  Linum grandiflorum
Flossflower
  Ageratum houstonianum
Kingfisher Daisy
  Felicia bergeriana
Larkspur
  Delphinium ajacis
Lobelia
  Lobelia erinus
Lupine
  Lupinus affinis

Marigold
  Tagetes erecta
Nasturtium
  Tropaeolum majus
Nemesia
  Nemesia strumosa
Painted Daisy
  Chrysanthemum carinatum
Petunia
  Petunia hybrida
Phlox (Annual)
  Phlox drummondi
Pinks
  Dianthus chinensis
Poppy (Shirly)
  Papaver rhoeas
Potmarigold
  Calendula officinalis
Rose-moss
  Portulaca grandiflora
Satinflower
  Godetia grandiflora
Salpiglossis
  Salpiglossis sinuata
Stock (Virginia)
  Malcomia maritima
Swanriver Daisy
  Brachycome iberidifolia
Sweet Scabious
  Scabiosa atropurpurea
Sweet Sultan
  Centaurea moschata
Tahoka Daisy
  Machaeranthera tanacetifolia
Tasselflower
  Emilia sagittata
Tobaccoplant
  Nicotiana alata
Zinnia
  Zinnia elegans

BIENNIAL FLOWERS---plants which require two years to complete the life cycle; building up from seed the one season, to bloom the next year and die. This means that new plants must be coming along with the older ones, or yearlings purchased from the nurseryman. Most of these plants will act in this manner if left alone and they are just as well handled as nature has prescribed. Others are grown as such in order to point for the more difficult times of the year. A tendency to breed this character out is evident in modern strains.

*** Althaea rosea
* Antirrhinum majus
** Bellis perennis
* Campanula medium
*** Ceratotheca triloba
*** Cirsium coulteri
* Cynoglossum amabile
** Echium wildpreti
*** Gilia rubra

** Glaucium flavum
* Mathiola incana
*** Michauxia campanuloides
* Myosotis alpestris
*** Oenothera hookeri
** Papaver nudicaule
* Trachelium caeruleum
** Tragopogon porrifolius
*** Xanthisma texanum

PERENNIAL FLOWERS---plants which live on indefinitely, even to the top in these regions; otherwise renewing in spring from the old crown or root system. The following better known species are taken from the typically and thoroughly perennial kinds best suited by experience for use in subtropical regions. They are more difficult to grow satisfactorily as taken south and those which tend to go off seasonally, or become dilapidated the interim, may be cut back for a second blooming. The time for this will depend on the habits of species....generally as new growth shoots appear at the base. Check the plant against the PLANTING CALENDAR appearing later in this book.

*** Achillea millefolium
* Anemone japonica
*** Angelonia grandiflora
* Aquilegia chrysantha
*** Aristea eckloni
** Armeria maritima
*** Asclepias currassavica
*** Aster amellus
* Bergenia cordifolia
* Campanula poscharskyana
*** Centaurea dealbata
*** Ceratostigma plumbaginoides
* Chrysanthemum maximum
** Convolvulus mauretanicus
** Coreopsis lanceolata
** Dianthus caryophyllus
** Erigeron karvinskyanus
* Felicia amelloides
** Francoa ramosa
** Gaillardia aristata
** Gazania coccinea
* Gerberia jamesoni

** Geum (varieties)
** Heliotropium arborescens
* Heuchera sanguinea
*** Hunnemannia fumariaefolia
** Limonium bellidifolium
*** Linum narbonnense
*** Neomarica gracilis
* Nepeta mussini
** Nierembergia caerulea
* Penstemon gloxinioides
* Primula polyantha
*** Scabiosa columbaria
** Senecio cineraria
*** Sisyrinchium striatum
* Stokesia laevis
* Thalictrum dipterocarpum
*** Tunica saxifraga
** Verbena hortensis
** Veronica incana
** Vinca major
* Viola odorata
*** Wedelia trilobata

ORNAMENTAL GRASSES---including bamboos, may be used in the shrubbery, some forms in bedding, but more satisfactorily in the less intensely cultivated parts of the garden. They require comparatively little attention; dominate their surroundings and fill the soil with roots to the exclusion of less vigorous neighbors. They are best in good moisture, yet with the soil well drained....set during winter. They serve with grace and lightness; are brisk and spirited in wind, with a high point of interest in late summer and fall. Most leaves and seed heads dry out properly for winter boquets if cut before fully matured. See EVERLASTING FLOWERS, which follows.

*** Agrostis nebulosa
* Arrhenatherum tuberosum
** Arundo donax
* Bambusa multiplex
** Briza maxima
* Cortaderia selloana

*** Curculigo capitulata
** Cymbopogan citratus
* Cyperus (species)
** Dactylis glomerata
** Elymus glauca
*** Erianthus ravennae

|   |   |   |   |
|---|---|---|---|
| * | Festuca glauca | * | Phyllostachys aurea |
| *** | Lagurus ovata | ** | Pseudosasa japonica |
| *** | Lamarkia aurea | ** | Sasa disticha |
| ** | Miscanthus sinensis | *** | Setaria palmifolia |
| * | Ophiopogon jaburan | ** | Sinocalamus oldhami |
| *** | Pennisetum ruppeli | *** | Stipa pennata |
| *** | Phalaris picta | * | Tricholaena rosea |

FERNS---are most sensitive to environment and will be grown with
pleasure only where care is given to selection, and requirements for
the individual as to maintenance reasonably observed. Some will take
full sun, but for the most part they want at least partial shade, good
drainage, with leaf mould and protection from the wind.  Light, air,
moisture, all in moderation will cover essentials. Let the leafmould
feed....no active fertilizers.  Allow naturally loose soil, with the
plant set in depth exactly to the old crown. No dryness while maturing fronds. Rock in the ground is to their liking.

|   |   |   |   |
|---|---|---|---|
| *** | Adiantum cuneatum | *** | Lygodium japonicum |
| * | Alsophila australis | * | Nephrolepis exaltata |
| *** | Asplenium flaccidum | *** | Onychium japonicum |
| ** | "      nidus | * | Pellaea andromedaefolia |
| ** | Blechnum occidentale | * | Platycerium bifurcatum |
| ** | Cheilanthes gracillima | ** | Polypodium mandaianum |
| *** | Cibotium schiederi | ** | Polystichum adiantiforme |
| * | Cyrtomium falcatum | *** | Pteris aquilina |
| *** | Davallia canariensis | * | "     tremula |
| ** | Dennstaedtia cicutaria | * | Woodwardia (species) |

BULBS---may be considered the crowning splendor of southern gardens, but not always in the sense nor in the material usually associated with the name. The tulip and hyacinth and other time-honored names
are out so far as continued performance is concerned.   But in their
place comes here, a gathering together of originals; bulbs from far
places....an array of unusuals to match the simple beauty of the natives or  touch a  spot with splendid color, if only for the moment.
Culture is only for the growth period....time of rest is most important, when yellowing leaves will tell.   Set generally two to three
times in depth the diameter of the bulb; as much or more apart. Here
each outdoor season may be gladdened within the range of the following plants. Find more in THE BULB GARDEN which follows.

|   |   |   |   |
|---|---|---|---|
| ** | Amaryllis advena | * | Iris xiphium |
| * | Anemone coronaria | * | Ixia maculata |
| ** | Antholyza aethiopica | ** | Leucojum autumnale |
| ** | Babiana stricta | ** | Lilium longiflorum |
| *** | Bloomeria crocea | * | Narcissus (species) |
| ** | Brodiaea capitata | *** | Ornithogalum arabicum |
| * | Brunsvigia rosea | ** | Oxalis bowieana |
| *** | Chlidanthus fragrans | *** | Polianthes tuberosa |
| ** | Cooperia drummondi | * | Ranunculus asiaticus |
| ** | Crocosmia aurea | ** | Sparaxis tricolor |
| *** | Elisena longipetala | * | Tritonia crocosmaeflora |
| * | Freesia refracta | ** | Vallota speciosa |
| * | Gladiolus hortulanus | ** | Watsonia iridifolia |
| *** | Hymenocallis caribaea | ** | Zephyranthes rosea |

TUBEROUS ROOTED PLANTS---including rhizomes and corms.  These all
are with rather strong-growing tendencies and other dominant points
for the border or for use with shrubs.  They are usually long-lived,
of good foliage, colorful, and may be counted upon  for permanent as
well as important parts to play in the garden.  Depth of planting is
important. Be guided by old earth stains, where top is retained.

|   |   |   |   |
|---|---|---|---|
| * | Acanthus mollis | *** | Begonia ricinifolia |
| ** | Alpinia speciosa | *** | "      tuberhybrida |
| * | Agapanthus africanus | * | Bletilla striata |
| ** | Alstroemeria aurantiaca | ** | Boussingaultia baselloides |
| *** | Arum italicum | ** | Caladium picturatum |

* Clivia miniata
*** Colocasia antiquorum
* Dahlia (varieties)
*** Dianella intermedia
*** Eremurus robustus
** Hedychium coronarium
* Hemerocallis aurantiaca
* Iris (check species)
** Kniphofia uvaria
** Ligularia kaempferi
** Liriope spicata

*** Mirabilis jalapa
* Moraea iridioides
*** Orthrosanthus multiflorus
*** Pasithea caerulea
** Pelargonium echinatum
* Phormium tenax
*** Schizostylis coccinea
** Tulbaghia violacea
*** Ulmaria filipendula
*** Wachendorfia thyrsiflora
* Zantedeschia aethiopica


SUB-TROPICAL FRUITS---the following is submitted for guidance and selection of fruit trees for the home grounds or small family orchard. Many of these plants have considerable ornamental value in one way or another and may be thought of as dual purpose plants.....all will be worth growing. It is well in this situation to consider locale as of paramount importance. Consult with the local nurseryman regarding varieties and species best adapted to local conditions. By all means keep in touch with him for cultural direction. Much of the best general information will be found in state experiment station bulletins.

Akee
  Blighia sapida
Almond
  Prunus amygdalis
Avocado
  Persea americana
Banana
  Musa sapientum
Burdekin-plum
  Pleiogynium solandri
Cherry-apple
  Eugenia edulis
Coco-plum
  Chrysobalanus icaco
Custard-apple
  Annona cherimola
Fig
  Ficus carica
Grape Fruit
  Citrus grandis
Jambolan-plum
  Syzygium cumini
Jujube
  Zizyphus jujuba
Kafir-plum
  Harpephyllum caffrum
Kumquat
  Fortunella japonica
Indian-fig
  Opuntia tuna
Leechee-nut
  Litchi chinensis
Lime
  Citrus aurantifolia
Loquat
  Eribotrya japonica
Mango
  Mangifera indica
Myrobalan
  Terminalia catappa
Mulberry
  Morus nigra

Natal-orange
  Strychnos spinosa
Olive
  Olea europaea
Orange
  Citrus sinensis
Papaya
  Carica papaya
Pecan
  Carya pecan
Persimmon
  Diospyros kaki
Pidgeon-plum
  Coccolobis floridana
Pistachio Nut
  Pistacia vera
Queensland Nut
  Macadamia ternifolia
Rose-apple
  Eugenia Jambos
Sapodilla
  Achras zapota
Sapote
  Casimiroa edulis
Spanish-cherry
  Mimusops elengi
Spanish-lime
  Melicocca bijuga
St Johns Bread
  Ceratonia siliqua
Star-apple
  Chrysophyllum caineto
Surinum-cherry
  Eugenia uniflora
Sweet lime
  Citrus limetta
Tangerine
  Citrus deliciosa
Walnut (English)
  Juglans regia
Walnut (Black)
  Juglans (species)

Wine Palm
Caryota urens

SHRUBBY FRUITS

Barbados-cherry
  Malpighia glabra

Chia
  Salvia columbaria

Chilean-guava                    Pineapple Guava
  Myrtus ugni                      Feijoa sellowiana
Chinese Lemon                    Pomegranate
  Citrus limonia                   Punica granatum
Hill-gooseberry                  Roselle
  Rhodomyrtus tomentosa            Hibiscus sabdariffa
Kei-apple                        Sea-grape
  Dovyalis caffra                  Coccolobis uvifera
Khat                             Strawberry Guava
  Catha edulis                     Psidium cattleianum
Limeberry                        Tree-tomato
  Triphasia trifolia               Cyphomandra betacea
Natal-plum                       Yellow Strawberry Guava
  Carissa grandiflora              Psidium lucidum
Otaheite-gooseberry              Yerba-de-mate
  Phyllanthus acidus               Ilex paraguariensis

                         VINES
Cerimen                          Lemon-vine
  Monstera deliciosa               Pereskia aculeata
Granadilla                       Passion Fruit
  Passiflora quadrangularis        Passiflora edulis
Grape (American)                 Pepino
  Vitis (check species)            Solanum muricatum
               Grape (European)
               Vitis vinifera

SUCCULENTS---an arbitrary classification based on custom that has
grown up in horticultural usage.  Included are all manner of fleshy
and meaty leaved plants, certain types of woody plants with something
in common, culture or aspect, together with so-called airplants that
adapt to soil. One thing in common is striking individuality that may
become fantastic or bizarre. Generally, they want the sun, well drained ground, with little moisture during rest....enter wet seasons as
dry as possible. They belong in collections for the capricious approval of the fancier. Some find a place in the garden as do these.

     * Aeonium decorum            *** Kleinia articulata
   *** Agave attenuata             **    "     ficoides
     * Aloe arborescens             *    "     repens
   ***   "   candelabrum           ** Mesembryanth. anemoniflorum
    **   "   humilis              ***        "       browni
     *   "   variegata              *        "       croceum
    ** Billbergia nutans            *        "       floribundum
     * Byrnesia weinbergi           *        "       roseum
   *** Cephalocereus senilis      ***        "       verruculatum
     * Crassula argentea            * Oliveranthus elegans
    **    "    falcata             ** Opuntia biglovi
   ***    "    lycopodioides        *    "    microdasys
    ** Cyanotis hirsuta            ***    "    tuna
   *** Dasylerion glaucophyllum     * Othonna crassifolia
   *** Doryanthes palmeri          ** Pachyphytum bracteosum
    ** Dyckia sulphurea            ** Pereskia aculeata
    ** Echeveria derenbergi        ** Portulacaria afra
     *    "     pulverulenta      *** Puya alpestris
    **    "     setosa            *** Rochea coccinea
   *** Echinocactus grusoni       *** Sansevieria parva
     * Epiphyllum oxypetalon        *    "     zeylanica
     * Euphorbia splendens        *** Sedum adolphi
    **    "      tirucalli          *   "   brevifolium
    ** Fouquieria splendens        **   "   dasyphyllum
     * Gasteria verrucosa           *   "   sieboldi
   *** Guzmania cardinalis         ** Sempervivum atlanticum
   *** Haworthia reinwardti        ** Senecio mikanioides
   *** Hesperaloe parviflora      *** Stapelia divaricata
     * Hoya carnosa               *** Trichocereus candicans
     * Hylocereus triangularis    *** Yucca aloifolia
   *** Kalanchoe blossfeldiana      *    "   elephantipes
     *    "      flammea           **   "   whipplei
    **    "      marmorata          * Zygocactus truncatus

NATIVE PLANTS---of any land are more sensitive to seasonal change than are the exotic. They have a feeling of belonging, with a charm that the alien plant seldom attains and; being at home, they grow with a marked economy in maintenance. Behavior in the garden should be noted and natural conditions reproduced in so far as is possible. Ordinarily they should be set alone or with their kind, since civilization soon takes from the fine edge of their simplicity....don't force. Some discretion will be necessary in using those from California in Florida and visa versa. Give them drainage in Florida and the driest spot available. In California, the Floridians will be grown best within coast influence and with all the humidity possible. They will be dwarf and compacted under heat. The Arid Southwest and California are more easily reconciled. Occasional cold winter winds from the north into Florida suggest a south exposure for tender material, while high summer winds would indicate strong-rooting trees.

## CALIFORNIA
### TREES

*** Acer macrophyllum
** Alnus rhombifolia
* Cupressus goveniana
** Juglans californica
* Libocedrus decurrens
** Lyonothamnus asplenifolius
*** Pinus coulteri
* " radiata
*** " sabiniana
** " torreyana

* Platanus racemosa
*** Prosopis glandulosa
* Quercus agrifolia
*** " chrysolepis
** " douglasi
** " lobata
*** Salix lasiolepis
** Sequoiadendron giganteum
* Umbellularia californica
*** Torreya californica

### SHRUBS

** Adenostoma fasciculatum
*** " sparcifolium
** Amorpha fruticosa
* Arctostaphylos diversifolia
** " glauca
** " manzanita
*** Artemisia californica
* Baccharis pilularis
*** Beloperone californica
*** Brickellia grandiflora
*** Calliandra californica
* Calycanthus occidentalis
* Carpenteria californica
** Ceanothus (species)
* Cercocarpus betuloides
*** Cneoridium dumosum
** Dendromecon rigida
*** Encelia californica
*** Eriodictyon crassifolium
* Eriogonum (species)
* Fremontia californica
* Galvesia speciosa
*** Hazardia cana
* Heteromeles arbutifolia

*** Juniperus californica
** Lavatera assurgentiflora
** Lupinus arboreus
** Lycium richi
* Mahonia nevini
* Mimulus puniceus
** Penstemon antirrhinoides
*** Pickeringia montana
* Prunus ilicifolia
* " lyoni
*** Quercus dumosa
** Rhamnus (check species)
* Rhus (check species)
** Ribes speciosum
*** " viburnifolium
* Romneya coulteri
*** Rosa californica
*** Sambucus velutina
*** Simmondsia californica
*** Solanum xanti
*** Trichostema lanatum
*** Ungnadia speciosa
*** Vigueria tomentosa
* Zauschneria californica

### VINES

*** Aristolochia californica
** Clematis lasiantha

** Lathyrus splendens
* Lonicera hispidula

*** Vitis girdiana

### HERBACEOUS PLANTS

* Abronia maritima
** Brevoortia ida-maia
** Calochortus weedi
** Centaureum venustum
*** Chorizanthe staticoides
*** Cirsium occidentale
* Coreopsis maritima
*** Corethrogyne californica

* Delphinium cardinale
* Dicentra chrysantha
*** " formosa
** Dodecatheon clevelandi
** Echeveria pulverulenta
** Emmenanthe penduliflora
** Eriogonum nudum
*** Erysimum capitatum

  * Eschscholtzia californica      *** Monardella lanceolata
*** Fritillaria recurva           *** Montia perfoliata
  * Gilia (species)                  * Nemophila menziesi
 ** Godetia bottae                 *** Oenothera cheiranthifolia
*** Hesperocallis undulata          **    "    hookeri
  * Hunnemannia fumariaefolia      *** Orthocarpus purpurascens
 ** Layia elegans                    * Pellaea andromedaefolia
 ** Lotus formosissimus              * Penstemon (check species)
 ** Lupinus affinis                  * Phacelia whitlavia
 ** Malacothrix californica          * Platystemon californicus
  * Mentzelia lindleyi             *** Salvia carduacea
 ** Mesembryanth. aequilaterale     ** Sidalcea malvaeflora
 ** Micromeria chamissonis         *** Silene laciniata
 ** Mimulus brevipes                 * Sisyrinchium bellum
  *    "    cardinalis             *** Styllophyllum orcutti
*** Mirabilis californica            * Yucca whipplei


## FLORIDA AND GULF COAST
### TREES

  * Acer floridanum                  * Magnolia grandiflora
*** Alnus rugosa                    ** Osmanthus americanus
 ** Canella winterana              *** Persea borbonia
*** Cytherexylum spinosum           ** Pinus caribaea
*** Cliftonia monophylla             * Sabal palmetto
  * Coccolobis floridana            ** Torreya taxifolia
 ** Eugenia supraaxillaris         *** Yucca aloifolia


### SHRUBS

*** Ardisia paniculata               * Illicium floridanum
  * Azalea austrina                 ** Lantana camara
  * Baccharis halimifolia           ** Leucothoe axillaris
  * Callicarpa americana          *** Lycium carolinianum
  * Calycanthus floridus             * Magnolia virginiana
*** Ceanothus microphyllus          ** Malpighia glabra
 ** Chiococca alba                  ** Myrica cerifera
 ** Chrysobalanus icaco           *** Pinckneya pubens
  * Coccolobis uvifera             *** Quercus pumila
 ** Cyrilla racemiflora            *** Randia aculeata
  * Duranta repens                 *** Rhapidophyllum histrix
*** Ehretia elliptica              *** Rhus copallina
*** Garberia fruticosa             *** Ribes echinellum
  * Hamelia erecta                  ** Sambucus simpsoni
  * Hypericum aureum                ** Serenoa repens
 ** Ilex vomitoria                   * Stenolobium stans
          ** Zamia floridana


### VINES

*** Decumaria barbara              *** Urechites lutea
  * Gelsemium sempervirens          ** Vitis munsoniana
  * Jaquemontia pentantha           ** Wisteria frutescens

### HERBACEOUS PLANTS
*** Adiantum capillus veneris      *** Heliopsis helianthoides
  * Agave decipiens                 ** Houstonia floridana
 ** Asplenium serratum               * Iris hexagona
*** Befaria racemosa                 * Lilium catesbaei
*** Blechnum serrulatum            *** Peltandra virginica
*** Ceratopteris pteridoides         * Physostegia virginiana
 ** Clematis baldwini              *** Pontederia cordata
  * Coreopsis lanceolata            ** Sabal minor
  * Crinum americanum             *** Sagittaria lancifolia
*** Dyschoriste oblongifolium       ** Stachys floridana
*** Eriogonum tomentosum             * Stokesia laevis
  * Erythrina herbacea              ** Thalia dealbata
  * Eupatorium ageratoides          ** Verbesina encelioides
 ** Euphorbia heterophylla           * Vinca rosea
  * Gilia rubra                    *** Woodwardia virginica
          * Zephyranthes atamasco

## THE ARID SOUTHWEST
### TREES

* Acacia farnesiana
***    " greggi
** Alnus tenuifolia
* Cercidium torreyanum
* Chilopsis linearis
** Ebenopsis flexicaulis
* Fraxinus velutina

*** Juglans rupestris
*** Maclura pomifera
*** Parkinsonia aculeata
*** Prosopis pubescens
*** Pistacia texana
** Sophora secundiflora
** Ulmus crassifolia

### SHRUBS

** Anisacanthus wrighti
*** Atriplex lentiformis
* Beaucarnia recurvata
*** Calliandra eriophylla
** Cordia boissieri
* Cowania mexicana
* Dodonaea viscosa
** Encelia farinosa
* Fallugia paradoxa
* Leucophyllum texanum
*** Lippia ligustrina
*** Loeselia mexicana
** Lycium pallidum
** Mahonia trifoliata

* Malvastrum fasciculatum
*** Philadelphus microphyllus
* Poinciana gilliesi
*** Rhus cismontana
** Rosa stellata
** Salvia columbariae
*    " greggi
** Sambucus neo-mexicana
** Sophora affinis
** Sphaeralcea ambigua
* Thryallis glauca
*** Ungnadia speciosa
*** Yucca tenuistyla
*** Zizyphus obtusifolia

### VINES

** Cardiospermum halicacabum
* Clematis texensis
      ** Vitis arizonica

*** Jaquemontia eastwoodiana
*** Rothrockia cordifolia

### HERBACEOUS PLANTS

*** Abronia villosa
** Aquilegia chrysantha
* Baileya multiradiata
** Callirhoe involucrata
** Calochortus kennedyi
* Cirsium occidentale
* Cooperia drummondi
* Coreopsis tinctoria
** Dasylerion glaucophyllum
*** Dyschoriste linearis
*** Echinocereus rigidissimus
*** Eryngium leavenworthi
* Gaillardia aristata
*** Habranthus andersoni
*** Hesperocallis undulata
*** Hesperaloe parviflora

* Heuchera sanguinea
*** Lilium parryi
** Lupinus texensis
** Milla biflora
*** Nolina parryi
* Oenothera tetraptera
*** Penstemon barbatus
**    " palmeri
* Phlox drummondi
*** Polypteris hookeriana
*** Proboscidea jussieui
* Salvia farinosa
*** Stachys coccinea
** Stanleya pinnata
* Thymophylla tenuiloba
** Xanthisma texanum

# STRUCTURAL FORM

The organic structure of a plant, its shape, the contour of its outline, conformity to type, style or normal method of expression may be examined to determine the part it will perform, either individually or in conjunction with its neighbors. Natural form or habit of growth is one of the more dependable phases with which one works in the landscape. It is permanent, ever present in operation where color is fleeting; forceful, where its accessary, texture, may be only a finishing effect, fortuitous and not at all essential or even important in view of the larger issue. The painter has long had his place in the landscape. The sculptor has always been in evidence there, but too little attended by the average worker. As an element in composition, form ranks as high or higher than either color or texture and may admit of conscious application at the hands of the planter for superior work. Other more practical considerations may not be overlooked in an intense pre-occupation with cultural details. Here one finds the underlying rhythm of nature, in stems as line, in the pattern of or the manner in which a plant climbs; none will be overlooked if the most favorable results are to be secured.

This section may be of more direct interest and assistance to the professional worker; yet for any person with a clear mental picture which he desires to produce substantially on the ground, these aids are submitted with a feeling that they will be of assistance....to any one who will anticipate and seriously direct the future development of their plantings along artistic lines.

## TREE SHAPES

Trees are rich in character that relates to structure, an architectural aspect that should not be overlooked when tree masses are to be seen in some perspective. Note the beauty of line under defoliation; follow that riddle, the pattern of stems; look closely to see the infinitely varied tracery of fine twigs....find verse there. One may be moved from the contemplation of low monotonous lines with the upright tree or soothed into comparative repose of mind by the wistful quality of a weeping willow. The intellectual faculties are susceptible to these influences and the stimulus may be appropriate, pleasing or lost altogether. Each tree has its own expression, a living interpretation of some emotion or thought and each such impression with some place in composition. They are the more important materials in attaining depth or a third dimension.

ERECT TREES---narrow upright, slender or towering forms. The extremes of this composite class are exclamatory and useful as an interjection in normal massing or for vertical accent with architectural detail. They should not be used indiscriminately. The fastigiate is found more often with two or more stems, the tips forming an acute point to emphasize the vertical feeling. Columnar types include certain palms with comparatively small tops, so that a massive stem and thatch carries the impression through to completeness.

## FASTIGIATE COLUMNAR

| | |
|---|---|
| *** Callitris robusta | * Laurus nobilis |
| * Cupressus sempervirens | * Libocedrus decurrens |
| *** Erythea edulis | *** Myrtus communis italica |
| ** Eugenia paniculata | ** Pinus canariensis |
| ** Juniperus excelsa stricta | *** Pittosporum tenuifolium |

16

*** Populus alba pyramidalis        ** Taxus baccata stricta
  *    "    nigra italica           * Thuja orientalis
*** Sequoiadendron giganteum        *** Trachycarpus fortunei
*** Sinocalamus oldhami             ** Washingtonia filifera

### NARROW UPRIGHT

 ** Acacia auriculaeformis          * Melaleuca leucadendra
  *    "    decurrens               *** Michelia champaca
*** Alnus (species)                 * Phoenix reclinata
*** Angophora lanceolata            ***    "    rupicola
  * Araucaria excelsa               *** Pinus sabiniana
*** Bolusanthus speciosus           * Pittosporum eugenioides
*** Celtis australis                * Podocarpus macrophylla
 ** Citherexylum spinosum           ** Populus fremonti
 ** Eucalyptus leucoxylon           * Prunus caroliniana
***    "    rudis                   ** Quercus chrysolepis
  *    "    sideroxylon             *    "    douglasi
 ** Eugenia smithi                  *** Schrebera swietenioides
  * Hymenosporum flavum             ** Sophora secundiflora
*** Lyonothamnus asplenifolius      *** Stenocarpus sinuatus
  * Magnolia grandiflora (forms)    * Tamarix aphylla
***    "    virginiana              ** Ulmus alata
              ** Washingtonia robusta

### BROAD UPRIGHT

 ** Acacia melanoxylon              ** Macadamia ternifolia
***    "    pravissima              * Magnolia grandiflora (forms)
  * Acer floridanum                 *** Melaleuca styphelioides
 **    "    macrophyllum            ** Morus rubra
  * Araucaria bidwilli              * Pittosporum rhombifolium
*** Eucalyptus globulus             ** Platanus orientalis
***    "    tereticornis            ** Prunus amygdalis
***    "    viminalis               *** Quercus lobata
  * Eugenia myrtifolia              *** Terminalia catappa
 ** Ficus retusa                    * Tristania conferta
  * Fraxinus velutina               *** Ulmus parvifolia (forms)


SPREADING TREES---of free natural growth, ultimately requiring considerable space in breadth. Flat tops will be found here and laterally reaching limbs are characteristic.  In some cases, these may suggest the horizontal and  dominate the aspect and  design function of
the tree.  The more pronounced forms are frequently damaged in heavy
storms, so that some protection in an exposed situation will be good
insurance. As these trees come along in growth, retain the feather or
foliage along trunk and stem as long as possible for the thickness
or caliper it produces locally. They tend toward the picturesque in a
mild manner as they come along into age.

### SPREADING

*** Acacia baileyana                * Magnolia grandiflora (forms)
 **    "    saligna                 ** Metrosideros tomentosa
 ** Aleurites moluccana             ** Morus nigra
*** Cupressus funebris              ** Parkinsonia aculeata
 ** Erythrina poeppigiana           * Quercus agrifolia
 ** Eucalyptus cornuta              ***    "    suber
*** Firmiana simplex                * Pinus radiata
  * Harpephyllum caffrum            *** Sapium sebiferum
*** Liquidambar formosana           *** Terminalia catappa
*** Lysiloma latisiliqua            *** Ulmus pumila

### WIDE SPREADING

*** Abbizzia julibrissin            *** Populus alba
  * Cinnamomum camphora             ** Quercus lobata
*** Cupania anacardioides           *    "    virginiana
  * Cupressus macrocarpa            ** Samanea saman
 ** Delonix regia                   ** Schinus molle
 ** Juglans regia                   *** Spathodea campanulata
  * Platanus racemosa               * Tipuana tipu

OPEN HEADED TREES---those that are loose in structure, typically indistinct as to outline, leaving but little impression of form or bulk.
Their attraction lies in the tracery thrown against the sky, or more
bold as an abstract study....delineation in molded limbs.  They will
lay down a  light shadow  for the  ground or one broken by irregular
patches of sunlight, flickering in activity or stable in lazy quies-
cence....a mood to cultivate.  Most trees that are ordinarily termed
irregular,  will be found in this category and will be better used in
group planting and in the larger exposed massing.

|  |  |  |  |
|---|---|---|---|
| * | Acacia floribunda | ** | Juglans regia |
| * | " podalyriaefolia | *** | Lysiloma latisiliqua |
| *** | " pruinosa | *** | Melaleuca styphelioides |
| * | Albizzia julibrissin | * | Melia azedarach |
| *** | Annona cherimola | ** | Morus rubra |
| * | Araucaria imbricata | *** | Ochrosia elliptica |
| *** | Bolusanthus speciosus | * | Parkinsonia aculeata |
| *** | Cassia fistula | ** | Persea americana |
| *** | Castanospermum australe | *** | Pinus halepensis |
| * | Cinnamomum camphora | ** | " pinea |
| *** | Citherexylum spinosum | * | " sabiniana |
| *** | Colvillea racemosa | ** | " torreyana |
| * | Cupressus guadalupensis | * | Pistacia chinensis |
| ** | " lusitanica | * | Platanus racemosa |
| ** | Delonix regia | *** | Pleiogynium solandri |
| *** | Erythrina (check species) | ** | Prunus amygdalus |
| * | Eucalyptus citriodora | ** | Quercus agrifolia |
| * | " cladocalyx | ** | " virginiana |
| ** | " polyanthemos | ** | Salix babylonica |
| *** | Ficus carica | *** | Simaruba amara |
| * | " macrophylla | ** | Stenocarpus sinuatus |
| ** | Fraxinus velutina | ** | Taxodium mucronatum |
| * | Grevillea robusta | * | Tipuana tipu |
| ** | Harpephyllum caffrum | ** | Tristania conferta |
| * | Hymenosporum flavum | * | Ulmus parvifolia |
| ** | Jacaranda acutifolia | *** | Virgilia capensis |

ROUND HEADED TREES---curviform, distinctly rounding in configura-
tion, an arc in outline, either as a unit or in a compound manner as
the limb habit may dictate, but with a definite rendering against the
sky. These trees will be emphatic in following their particular pattern or customary habit of growth and will be found at least moderately close-knit in way of texture. When massed to be seen from a distance, the sequence is that of rolling waves of  unhurried greenery ,
tranquil, soothing, relaxing....look and loosen; slacken speed.

|  |  |  |  |
|---|---|---|---|
| ** | Acacia auriculaeformis | *** | Macadamia ternifolia |
| * | " prominens | * | Magnolia grandiflora |
| *** | " pruinosa | *** | Melaleuca styphelioides |
| ** | Calodendrum capense | ** | Metrosideros tomentosa |
| ** | Casuarina equisetifolia | ** | Morus nigra |
| * | Ceratonia siliqua | * | Olea europaea |
| ** | Cinnamomum camphora | *** | Phytolacca dioica |
| * | Citrus (species) | * | Pinus pinea |
| ** | Coccolobis floridana | * | Pittosporum rhombifolium |
| *** | Colvillea racemosa | ** | " undulatum |
| ** | Crinodendron dependens | *** | Pleiogynium solandri |
| ** | Cupania anacardioides | ** | Podachaenium eminens |
| *** | Cupressus guadalupensis | * | Podocarpus elongata |
| * | Dais cotinifolia | ** | Populus alba |
| * | Eriobotrya japonica | * | Quercus (check species) |
| *** | Eucalyptus cornuta | ** | Quillaja saponaria |
| * | " ficifolia | *** | Salix lasiolepis |
| * | " lehmanni | *** | Sapindus saponaria |
| ** | Ficus retusa | *** | Schinus molle |
| *** | Firmiana simplex | *** | Schrebera swietenioides |
| ** | Harpephyllum caffrum | ** | Ulmus sempervirens |
| *** | Harpullia arborea | * | Umbellularia californica |
| ** | Lysiloma latisiliqua | ** | Vitex lucens |

PYRAMIDAL TREES---rigid and uncompromising; normally with single stems, the branches at right angles to the bole, or drooping with a sweep and frequently whorled, so as to appear in layers. The outline of the tree falls roughly into the plane of a cone with enough regularity to accentuate the peak. They make for strong contrast against the dome, either architectural or as found in other tree forms. This spire is most effective on the skyline and in such perspective, the return is that of rugged strength, restless and suggestive of action rather than repose....pace and repetition important here.

## NARROW PYRAMIDAL

| | |
|---|---|
| \*\*\* Abies venusta | \* Juniperus chinensis |
| \*\*\* Alnus rhombifolia | \*\*\*  "  excelsa |
| \* Araucaria excelsa | \*\* Liquidambar styraciflua |
| \* Brachychiton populneum | \*\*\* Metasequoia glyptostroboides |
| \*\* Casuarina stricta | \*\*\* Pinus halepensis |
| \* Cedrus deodora | \*\* Prunus caroliniana |
| \*\*\* Chamaecyparisus lawsoniana | \*\*\* Sciadopitys verticillata |
| \*\* Cupressus arizonica | \*\* Taxodium distichum |
| \*\*\*  "  benthami | \* Thuja orientalis |

## BROAD PYRAMIDAL

| | |
|---|---|
| \*\*\* Araucaria bidwilli | \*\* Lagunaria patersoni |
| \* Casuarina cunninghamiana | \*\* Pinus radiata |
| \*\* Cupressus lusitanica | \* Pittosporum eugenioides |
| \*  "  macrocarpa | \*\*\* Sapium sebiferum |
| \*\*\* Juniperus silicicola | \*\*\* Sequoiadendron giganteum |

UMBRAGEOUS TREES---round-topped, open-headed types, serving effectually as a canopy and affording shade in the sense of a ward or protection. The term implies more than retirement from the sun; the limb structure and disposition of the leafage may be quite suggestive of the umbrella. Many trees that start life with an entirely different shape, aquire this character in age or may have it forced upon them by the wind.

| | |
|---|---|
| \*\*\* Albizzia julibrissin | \*\* Metrosideros tomentosa |
| \* Alsophila australis | \*\*\* Musa ensete |
| \*\* Bauhinia variegata | \*\*\* Papaya candamarcencis |
| \*\*\* Cercis siliquastrum | \* Phoenix canariensis |
| \* Cinnamomum camphora | \*\*  "  reclinata |
| \*\* Delonix regia | \* Pinus pinea |
| \*\*\* Eucalyptus calophylla | \*\*\* Prosopis glandulosa |
| \*\* Juglans regia | \* Quercus virginiana |
| \*\*\* Ligustrum japonicum | \*\*\* Solanum warscewiczi |
| \* Melia umbraculiformis | \* Tipuana tipu |
| \*\* Ulmus sempervirens | |

WEEPING TREES---with the branches hanging freely.....at times deplored as too well tuned to sentiment and soft ways of life. They are candidly, unnatural and may drip unduly, in a manner of thinking, but have their special places. They go with flat surfaces. Use them in places created artificially; against the hard lines of a structure; to carry off the slope of a steeply pitched roof; with the plane of water or as mild contrast in foliage placement. Suspend as a curtain in concealment, easily thrust aside for an obscured way. They are better used singly and only natural forms since the budded sports are too ridiculous for human comfort and understanding.

| | |
|---|---|
| \*\*\* Acacia pendula | \* Eucalyptus erythrocorys |
| \*\*\* Agonis flexuosa | \*\* Ficus benjamina |
| \*\* Bauhinia tomentosa | \*\*\* Leptospermum citrinum |
| \* Callistemon viminalis | \*\* Maytenus boaria |
| \*\* Callitris robusta (forms) | \* Pittosporum phillyraeoides |
| \* Casuarina equisetifolia | \*\* Salix babylonica |
| \*\*\* Chamaecyparis pendula | \* Schinus molle |
| \* Chilopsis linearis | \*\*\* Taxodium mucronatum |
| \* Crinodendron dependens | \* Ulmus sempervirens |
| \*\*\* Cupressus funebris | \*\*\* Viminaria denudata |
| \*\* Eucalyptus caesia | \*\*\* Zizyphus jujuba |

## SHRUB MASSES

The inherent character of a shrub is one aspect only.  It may be a
thing of special beauty.  Merged with others in the shrubbery it will
become a part of  something else and any outstanding character modified as it is subjected to the influence of its neighbors. This is as
as it should be, since the individual must be submerged in the requirements of  a composition if an effect is to be clear-cut and pleasing
as a whole.  A great variety of  characters to  combine is available
that relate directly to structure and form. This is only the begin-
ing, as a further view of the changing seasons will indicate....that
of budding flowers, their wane and then the waxing berries. Moreover,
beyond this there is the color tone and infinite shaping of leaves,
together with the ramification, color and winter aspect of branch and
twig.  All such will be in the background of thought as the designer
pores over this material for the stuff of which living pictures  are
made....an art surely, for the humanities.


ERECT SHRUBS---plants for emphasis in the border or  any planting
of shrubs, the dominating structural feature being the vertical, manifest in upright mass, rather than line.  These plants are measurably
taller than they are in width; orderly in method of growth and will
tend to discipline in stem.  The definite impression they will give
suggests use at the pivotal points of a planting, with material of
less constraint filling out the effect as desired.   Check with LINE
and COLUMNAR TREES for related material.

|   |   |
|---|---|
| * Acacia cultriformis | *** Illicium anisatum |
| *** Agonis linearifolia | ** Jacobinia carnea |
| ** Arbutus unedo | * Jasminum rigidum |
| *** Brunfeldsia americana | * Lagerstroemia indica |
| ** Buddleja asiatica | *** Lavatera assurgentiflora |
| * Callistemon lanceolatus | * Leptospermum scoparium |
| *** Carissa carandas | * Ligustrum (species) |
| ** Ceanothus verrucosus | * Melaleuca nesophila |
| ** Cestrum diurnum | ** Murraea paniculata |
| *    "    nocturnum | ** Myrsine africana |
| *** Clerodendrum speciosissimum | * Myrtus communis |
| *** Coronilla glauca | *** Osmanthus fortunei |
| *** Cytisus canariensis | **   "    ilicifolius |
| ** Dodonaea viscosa | * Pittosporum crassifolium |
| ** Echium fastuosum | ** Poinciana pulcherrima |
| * Erica melanthera | *** Prunus glandulosa |
| *** Eriogonum giganteum | ***   "    lyoni |
| *** Ervatamia coronaria | ** Psidium cattleianum |
| ** Escallonia langleyensis | ** Pyracantha coccinea |
| * Euonymus japonicus erecta | ** Punica granatum |
| *** Eurya (species) | * Raphiolepis indica |
| *** Euphorbia tirucalli | *** Rhamnus alaternus |
| *** Fremontia californica | *** Rhus integrifolia |
| ** Fuchsia triphylla | ** Rondeletia cordata |
| * Grevillea thelemanniana | ** Senecio petasitis |
| * Hakea (species) | ** Spartium junceum |
| * Hamelia erecta | *** Tecoma smithi |
| * Hibiscus rosa-sinensis | ** Viburnum odoratissimum |
| ** Hypericum aureum | *    "    tinus |
| ** Ilex cornuta | *** Xylosma senticosa |

SPREADING SHRUBS---those expressing lateral mass in their development, wider in sweep than in height. They are more often indeterminate in this respect and will require more than ordinary space in which
to expand. They economize in the filling in of a given area.  They are
amenable to outside influence as growth is directed and normally will
compose the greater portion of the shrubbery, playing to the stronger
elements, as noted above. Check with LINE and SPREADING TREES.

|   |   |
|---|---|
| *** Abelia floribunda | * Calliandra inequilatera |
| * Acacia verticillata | *** Calceolaria integrifolia |
| ***   "    vestita | * Casissa grandiflora |
| ** Berberis darwini | ** Cassia splendida |
| *** Bowkeria gerrardiana | *** Ceanothus grizeus |
| *** Buddleja salvifolia | * Chaenomeles japonica |

** Choisya ternata
* Cistus maculatus
*** Clerodendrum bungei
* Cotoneaster simonsi
*** Deeringia amaranthoides
* Elaeagnus pungens
*** Eriogonum arborescens
** Escallonia rosea
*** Eucalyptus preissiana
** Fabiana imbricata
** Gardenia thunbergia
*** Grevillea rosmarinifolia
** Grewia occidentalis
*** Hakea pugioniformis
*** Halimium halimifolium
* Hypericum henryi
** Ilex paraguariensis
* Jasminum humile
** Lantana camara
** Lippia citriodora
** Lonicera pileata
*** Mahonia nevini

** Malvaviscus grandiflorus
* Melaleuca hyperiscifolia
* Murraea exotica
*** Osmanthus armatus
*** Phillyrea latifolia media
*** Phlomis fruticosa
* Pittosporum tobira
* Polygala dalmaisiana
* Prunus ilicifolia
* Pyracantha crenato-serrata
* Raphiolepis ovata
** Rhamnus californica
** Rhus ovata
*** Ribes malvaceum
** Salvia greggi
* Severinia buxifolia
** Solanum rantonneti
* Streptosolon jamesoni
** Teucrium fruticans
*** Viburnum carlesi
*     "     suspensum
*** Vitex trifolia

SPRAWLING SHRUBS---as distinguished from the preceding group, the lower branches will rest upon the ground with the full weight of herbage. They may be expected to exceed their height considerably in horizontal growth if space is available. They find many special uses in the large rock garden, against boulders of appropriate size and as field cover away under the view, where larger areas may be clothed effectively and permanently with a minimum of plants.

** Acacia armata
***    "    longifolia
*** Araucaria excelsa (forms)
** Atriplex breweri
** Artabotrys uncinatus
** Barleria caerulea
*** Brickellia grandiflora
* Buddleja madagascariensis
** Calocephalis browni
* Carissa prostrata
** Candollea cuneiformis
** Ceratostigma griffithi
** Chamaelaucium ciliatum
*** Chiococca alba
* Chorizema cordatum
** Chrysobalanus icaco
* Cistus corbariensis
* Cotoneaster microphylla
***    "    pannosa nana
* Coprosma prostrata
** Correa pulchella
** Cuphea roezli
*** Eupatorium sordidum
** Euphorbia splendens
* Fuchsia magellanica
** Galvesia speciosa

*** Halimium ocymoides
* Helichrysum petiolatum
*** Hibiscus tiliaceus
** Holmskioldia sanguinea
* Jasminum mesneyi
*** Lonicera etrusca
*** Lycium richi
** Mahernia verticillata
*** Penstemon cordifolius
* Philadelphus mexicanus
*** Pittosporum heterophyllum
* Plumbago capensis
* Pyracantha yunnanensis
*** Quercus dumosa
***    "    pumila
*** Raphiolepis indica (forms)
*** Rhus trilobata
* Rosmarinus officinalis
* Rosa laevigata
**    "    bracteata mermaid
** Santolina chamaecyparissus
*** Schinus dependens (forms)
** Solanum seaforthianum
* Sollya heterophylla
*** Swainsona galegifolia
*** Thryallis glauca

STRAGGLING SHRUBS---erect-irregular to irregular-spreading or just formless shapes that may leave a great deal to be desired for the ordinary border, but useful in rough places....look here for hidden character, something that may be developed. The pruning shears will be used in service of the following and to restrain or correct a stringy growth. There is invariably something worth saving for utility here.

** Acacia greggi
***    "    horrida
*** Adenostoma fasciculatum
** Anisacanthus wrighti
* Arctostaphylos diversifolia

*** Artemisia tridentata
** Bauhinia galpini
* Bouvardia humboldti
* Breynia nivosa
** Callistemon rigidus

|                        |                              |
|------------------------|------------------------------|
| * Carissa edulis       | ** Malvastrum fasciculatum   |
| *** Cassia tomentosa   | * Malvaviscus arboreus       |
| * Calothamnus quadrifidus | ** Penstemon antirrhinoides |
| ** Cercocarpus betuloides | ** Poinciana gilliesi     |
| *** Chilopsis linearis | *** Prostanthera nivea       |
| * Cienfuegosia hakeaefolia | *** Psoralea pinnata     |
| * Clerodendrum myricoides | *** Salvia sessei         |
| * Correa magnifica     | ** Sambucus caerulea         |
| * Dovyalis caffra      | ** Sarcococca hookeriana     |
| ** Encelia californica | * Stenolobium stans          |
| ** Eriogonum fasciculatum | *** Strophanthus speciosus |
| *** Garberia fruticosa | ** Tamarix (species)         |
| *** Grevillea paniculata | * Tecomaria capensis       |
| *** Jacobinia pauciflora | *** Trichostema lanatum    |
| * Leonotis leonurus    | *** Triphasia trifolia       |
| * Leptospermum laevigatum | *** Vitex unifoliolata    |
| * Lonicera nitida      | ** Wigandia caracasana       |
| ** Lycium chilense     | ** Zauschneria californica   |

RECURVING SHRUBS---those which are semi-erect or with arching stems
that may droop to impart roughly to the whole the semblance of an urn
or a vase.    Here is an embodiment of grace in the garden visible to
all and available if handled properly and not ruined by enforced direction or guidance.....don't prune unless to remove entire stems
These are shrubs with a sense of adornment or decoration for a selected spot. They are of the elite and must be studied well for size and
spread, if they are to survive and serve without mutilation.

|                              |                                    |
|------------------------------|------------------------------------|
| * Abelia grandiflora         | ** Iochroma fuchsioides            |
| ** Abutilon hybridum         | * Jasminum floridum                |
| * Azara microphylla          | ** Ligustrum henryi                |
| * Bambusa multiplex          | *** Loeselia mexicana              |
| * Berberis gagnepaini        | ** Lonicera implexa                |
| *** Brachysema lanceolatum   | *** Malvastrum capense             |
| ** Buddleja magnifica        | *** Mimulus puniceus               |
| *** Ceanothus impressus      | *** Phormium colensoi metalica     |
| * Cestrum purpureum          | *** Pickeringia montana            |
| * Cocculus laurifolius       | *** Rhus lancea                    |
| * Cotoneaster pannosa        | **    "   laurina                  |
| *** Dombeya calantha         | ** Ribes speciosum                 |
| ** Entelia arborescens       | ***    "   viburnifolium           |
| ** Escallonia franciscana    | * Russelia equisetiformis          |
| ** Galvesia speciosa         | *** Sambucus simpsoni              |
| *** Gaya lyalli              | * Spirea cantoniensis              |
| * Genista monosperma         | ** Syringa persica                 |
| ** Hebe hulkeana             | ** Tecoma garrocha                 |
| *** Heimia myrtifolia        | * Vitex agnus-castus               |
| *** Hymenanthera crassifolia | ** Weigela florida                 |
| ** Hypericum moserianum      | *** Zamia floridana                |

FACERS---conformable shrubs that will adapt or accomodate in serving the fore-front of the shrubbery; low growth for transition, and
to cover off the base of higher shrubs that do not close in to the
ground of themselves. The following plants may be used independently
or to bring about this union with the minimum amount of pruning or
none at all. Check with sized shrubs....LOW and DWARF.

|                              |                                |
|------------------------------|--------------------------------|
| ** Abelia floribunda         | ** Choisya ternata             |
| * Aster fruticosus           | * Chorizema cordatum           |
| * Berberis darwini           | * Cistus (species)             |
| *** Bowkeria gerrardiana     | * Correa pulchella             |
| ** Buddleja lindleyana       | ** Cotoneaster simonsi         |
| **    "   salvifolia         | ***    "    thymifolia         |
| *** Calceolaria integrifolia | *** Cuphea roezli              |
| ** Calocephalis browni       | ** Cytisus canariensis         |
| *** Candollea cuneiformis    | *** Deeringia amaranthoides    |
| * Carissa grandiflora        | *** Eupatorium sordidum        |
| ** Ceanothus grizeus         | *** Halimium halimifolium      |

* Hypericum moserianum
* Jasminum floridum
* Juniperus pfitzeriana
*** Philadelphus microphyllus
** Ligustrum henryi
** Lonicera confusa
** Myrtus microphylla
*** Phillyrea media
*** Phlomis fruticosa
** Pittosporum heterophyllum
*      "       tobira
** Plumbago capensis
* Polygala dalmaisiana
*** Prostanthera nivea
** Punica granatum nana

* Pyracantha crenato-serrata
** Raphiolepis indica
* Raphiolepis ovata
*** Rosmarinus officinalis
* Sarcococca hookeriana
*** Severinia buxifolia
** Solanum rantonneti
** Sollya heterophylla
*** Swainsona galegifolia
* Streptosolen jamesoni
*** Taxus repandens
** Teucrium fruticans
* Turraea obtusifolia
* Viburnum suspensum
*** Vitex trifolia

SELECT MATERIALS---plants of distinction; those that are choice
within the meaning of restraint, elegant yet not formalized.  These
species have been naturally endowed with and hold certain properties
of cleanliness and neatness that show in manner of growth. Being precise, tidy and self-contained, they bring marked refinement to strategic places. Think of them for intimate and much used areas for living outside....patio or lanai, a breezeway if not too drafty.  Most
of these will be noted as having little tolerance or desire for lime
in the soil, preferring an acid reaction or at least neutral ground.
Determinations· under this heading may become so controversial that
the intention here is to represent each genera when qualified, but
none with more than one species.

## TREES

* Acacia baileyana
*** "      cyanophylla
*** "      pendula
** "       pubescens
** Archontophoenix cunningham.
* Arecastrum romanzoffianum
*** Bauhinia grandiflora
* Calodendrum capense
*** Canella winterana
*** Caryota urens
*** Cassia fistula
* Cedrus atlantica
** Cupressus sempervirens
** Dais cotinifolia
** Delonix regia
** Drimys winteri
** Erythea armata
* Eucalyptus ficifolia
** Ficus benjamina
*** Harpullia arborea

** Harpephyllum caffrum
* Jacaranda acutifolia
* Juniperus torulosa
*** Leucadendron argenteum
** Libocedrus decurrens
* Liquidambar styraciflua
*** Livistona australis
* Magnolia grandiflora
*** Markhamia lutea
* Phoenix reclinata
*** Pinus patula
* Pittosporum rhombifolium
** Prunus amygdalus
*** Pterospermum acerifolium
* Quercus ilex
*** Simaruba amara
* Taxus baccata stricta
** Tristania conferta
*** Tupidanthus calyptratus
** Vitex lucens

## SHRUBS

*** Abelia grandiflora
*** Abutilon palmeri
** Acokanthera spectabilis
* Anthyllis barba-jovis
** Ardisia crispa
* Azalea indica
* Azara microphylla
*** Bambusa multiplex
** Bauhinia acuminata
*** Berberidopsis corallina
* Berberis darwini
* Brunfelsia calycina
*** Bursaria spinosa
* Buxus microphylla
* Calliandra inequalatera
*** Calothamnus quadrifida
* Camellia reticulata
** Candollea cuneiformis

** Carissa grandiflora
** Cassia artemisioides
** Ceanothus gloriosus
** Ceratostigma willmottianum
** Choisya ternata
** Cistus purpureus
*** Citrus myrtifolia
*** Clerodendrum siphonanthus
* Cocculus laurifolius
*** Cordia boissieri
** Correa alba
* Cotoneaster parneyi
*** Damnacanthus indicus
* Daphne odora
** Diosma ericoides
*** Dombeya cayeuxi
** Erica melanthera
** Ervatamia coronaria

** Escallonia glasniviensis
* Euonymus japonicus
*** Eurya emarginata
* Fuchsia triphylla
* Gardenia thunbergia
*** Grevillea sulphurea
*** Griselinia littoralis
*** Hakea elliptica
*** Halimium libanotis
** Hebe hulkeana
*** Hibiscus arnottianus
* Hypericum moserianum
* Ilex cornuta burfordi
*** Illicium anisatum
* Itea ilicifolia
** Jasminum floridum
* Juniperus conferta
* Lagerstroemia indica
*** Ligustrum quihoui
** Lonicera pileata
** Mahonia lomariifolia
*** Malpighia coccigera
*** Melaleuca thymifolia
* Michelia fuscata
*** Mitriostigma axillare
* Myrsine africana
** Myrtus ugni
* Nandina domestica

*** Nerium indicum
*** Ochrosia elliptica
*** Oncoba routledgi
** Osmanthus fortunei
*** Osteomeles anthyllidifolia
*** Phillyrea latifolia media
* Photinia serrulata
*** Pimelia ferruginia
* Pittosporum tobira
*** Prunus lusitanica
* Raphiolepis delacouri
** Rhamnus alaternus
*** Rhus lancea
** Ribes viburnifolium
** Sarcococca hookeriana
* Sasa disticha
** Siphonosmanthus delavayi
** Sollya heterophylla
* Sophora secundiflora
*** Strophanthus speciosus
** Spirea cantoniensis
** Tecoma garrocha
* Ternstroemia japonica
*** Thevetia thevetioides
*** Thryallis glauca
** Turraea obtusifolia
** Viburnum japonicum
* Xylosma senticosa

## VINES

* Ampelopsis brevipedunculata
** Antigonon leptopus
* Arrabidaea magnifica
** Cissus hypoglauca
** Clematis armandi
*** Gloriosa superba
** Hibbertia volubilis
*** Hoya carnosa
*** Jaquemontia eastwoodiana
** Jasminum azoricum
* Hardenbergia comptoniana

* Lonicera confusa
* Mandevilla suaveolens
** Passiflora racemosa
*** Petrea volubilis
* Phaedranthus buccinatorius
*** Rosa banksiae
* Solanum wendlandi
** Stephanotis floribunda
*** Stigmaphyllon ciliatum
** Thunbergia grandiflora
* Trachelospermum jasminoides

## HERBACEOUS PLANTS

** Adiantum cuneatum
* Agapanthus africanus
** Albuca minor
** Allium pulchellum
** Amarcrinum howardi
*** Anigozanthos flavida
** Arthropodium cirrhatum
*** Arum italicum
* Bergenia cordata
*** Bletilla striata
** Brodiaea bridgesi
* Calocephalis browni
* Campanula isophylla mayi
*** Chironia linoides
*** Clitoria ternatea
* Clivia hybrids
** Dianella intermedia
*** Dierama pulcherrima
*** Elisena longipetala
*** Episcia (species)
** Felicia bergeriana
* Francoa ramosa
** Frankenia capitata laevis
* Gerberia jamesoni
** Geum bradshaw
*** Haemanthus katherinae
* Heuchera sanguinea
*** Hymenocallis festalis

*** Iris japonica
** Lavandula officinalis
* Limonium bellidifolium
*** Linum narbonnense
*** Lonas inodora
* Moraea glaucopis
* Nemesia strumosa
*** Neomarica gracilis
*** Nerine fothergilli
* Nierembergia rivularis
** Ornithogalum arabicum
*** Oxalis crassipes
*** Papaver rupifragum
** Pasithea caerulea
* Pelargonium domesticum
*** Pellaea falcata
* Penstemon gloxininioides
*** Pentas coccinea
** Polystichum adiantiforme
* Primula polyantha
** Pteris cretica
*** Putoria calabrica
* Reinwardtia indica
* Rosmarinus Lockwood de Forest
** Salpiglossis sinuata
** Salvia farinacea
*** Satureja intricata
** Schizostylis Hegarty

* Scilla peruviana                    *** Thunbergia cordata
** Sedum sieboldi                      ** Torenia fournieri
* Sternbergia lutea                     * Tricholaena rosea
** Stokesia laevis                      ** Tritonia hyalina
* Strelitzia reginae                    ** Tulbaghia fragrans
*** Streptanthera cuprea                 * Vallota speciosa
*** Teucrium marrum                    *** Veltheimia viridifolia
* Thalictrum dipterocarpum            *** Wahlenbergia saxicola
                ** Zantedeschia elliottiana

## SUCCULENTS

*** Aeonium spathulatum               *** Hylocereus triangularis
** Agave attenuata                     ** Kalanchoe blossfeldiana
*** Aloe plicatilis                    ** Mesembryanth. deltoidea
* Beaucarnea recurvata                  * Oliveranthus elegans
* Byrnesia weinbergi                    ** Opuntia microdasys
** Crassula argentea                   ** Pachyphytum bracteosum
*** Doryanthes palmeri                 ** Pereskia aculeata
** Echeveria setosa                   *** Puya alpestris
** Echinocactus grusoni                 * Yucca whipplei
* Epiphyllum oxypetalum                 * Zygocactus truncatus

## THE VINE FABRIC

The climber is fitted structurally for the purpose of covering, either in the sense of concealment or that of an ornament. Undesirable objects of a necessary nature may be planted out or facilities of our own making, such as a shelter, fence, the pergola or other open overhead softened with foliage, tied in with line or piled with color. The usual error here is over-doing....embellish good architecture; don't conceal it. The mechanics of climbing should be noted and the fact should not be overlooked that a vine, as much or more than any other plant wants consistent and intelligent pruning. This is very important for fitting the subject in degree and manner to carry out accurately the purpose for which selected. Such training should reflect the natural bent of the species as much as possible, after the gardeners requirements have been met. Note that in nature the roots find a place in the shade where the soil is cool while the top seeks light. Many vines tend to become shrubby when grown without support.

VINES FOR MASONRY---climbing plants with special appendages or modified rootlets that permit their clinging to more or less roughened surfaces. Concrete or brick construction will not be impaired by this cover, but the growth should not be allowed to extend onto wood framing and never used on wood construction. Probably half the plants thought necessary for a project will be sufficient, when root space will be conserved. Avoid the driest places beneath overhanging eaves or provide moisture to establish the plant.

*** Anemopoegma chamberlandi          *** Hoya carnosa
** Campsis radicans                     * Hylocereus triangularis
** Cissus striata                      *** Monstera deliciosa
*** Decumaria barbara                   ** Nephthytis afzeli
** Distictis lactiflora                ** Parthenocissus henryana
* Doxantha unguis-cati                  *        "        tricuspidata
*** Ercilla spicata                    *** Philodendron oxycardium
** Fatshedera lizei                    ** Pyrostegia ignea
* Ficus pumila                        *** Scindapsis aureus
* Hedera (species)                    *** Syngonium podophyllum

TWINING VINES---those which raise themselves by winding the stem about other plants or some support provided for them. The stronger growing among these will be throttling to trees and if grown there should be loosened from time to time the first years to prevent binding. Don't expect these plants to work themselves up a wide support. Give them wire in the shade, but use twine in the sun.

LOW CLIMBING VINES---a few unusuals in a class of plants known for vigor and energy in production. They will be available for use where restraint in growth is appropriate or appreciated or an essential requirement. There is little more disconcerting and annoying in garden operations than to have runners of a vine rampant engaging in situations of refinement, with continual reduction necessary.

|  | | | |
|---|---|---|---|
| * | Abrus precatorius | *** | Clerodendrum thompsonae |
| *** | Abutilon megapotamicum (type) | *** | Clianthus puniceus |
| ** | Ampelopsis brevipedunculata | ** | Eccremocarpus scaber |
| ** | Amphicome arguta | ** | Hardenbergia monophylla |
| *** | Araujia sericofera | * | Hibbertia volubilis |
| *** | Aristolochia californica | ** | Jaquemontia (species) |
| * | Asparagus asparagoides | ** | Manettia bicolor |
| *** | Clematis cirrhosa | *** | Momordica charantia |
| ** | "     crispa | *** | Rothrockia cordifolia |
| * | "     texensis | * | Solanum seaforthianum |

VEILING VINES---loosely covering, shielding, or grown for purely decorative purposes.  These will soften rather than conceal, with an interlacing or tangle of stems visible by reason of the lighter foliage cover.   These plants accomplish their purpose gracefully  and bring about a quiet seclusion in a lax, mellowing manner.

|  | | | |
|---|---|---|---|
| ** | Antigonon leptopus | *** | Manettia bicolor |
| * | Asparagus sprengeri | ** | Monstera deliciosa |
| ** | Bomaria caldasiana | * | Parthenocissus lowi |
| * | Boussingaultia baselloides | ** | Passiflora racemosa |
| * | Cissus striata | ** | Phaseolus coccineus |
| *** | Clematis cirrhosa | *** | Philodendron oxycardium |
| * | Cobaea scandens | ** | Pyrostegia ignea |
| ** | Dolichos lignosus | ** | Quamoclit pennata |
| *** | Ficus pumila minima | *** | Securidaca diversifolia |
| ** | Gelsemium sempervirens | * | Solanum jasminoides |
| ** | Hardenbergia comptoniana | ** | Stephanotis floribunda |
| ** | Kennedya rubicunda | ** | Stigmaphyllon ciliatum |
| ** | Ipomoea leari | *** | Thenardia floribunda |
| * | Jasminum dichotomum | ** | Thunbergia fragrans |
| *** | Lapageria rosea | *** | Trachelospermum asiaticum |
| *** | Lonicera aureo-reticulata | *** | Vitis voinieriana |
| * | Mandevilla suaveolens | *** | Wisteria frutescens |

ENVELOPING VINES---generally stronger growing, closely covering, screening, with a more or less compact and complete cover of leafage that should serve in time as a mask. They bring about dense shade and may be used to obscure or thoroughly conceal an area for privacy. They will require space and strong support to carry the weight  of herbage. They will be held in by pinching and with the pruning shears to control and thicken the cover.

|  | | | |
|---|---|---|---|
| ** | Ampelopsis brevipedunculata | ** | Parthenocissus henryana |
| * | Asparagus plumosus | * | "      tricuspidata |
| *** | Aristolochia elegans | * | Passiflora alato-caerulea |
| * | Bougainvillea (varieties) | *** | Pereskia aculeata |
| ** | Campsidium valdivianum | *** | Petrea volubilis |
| * | Cissus capensis | * | Phaedranthus buccinatorius |
| ** | "   hypoglauca | * | Philadelphus mexicanus |
| ** | Clematis armandi | *** | Philodendron erubescens |
| *** | Cryptostegia grandiflora | ** | Podranea ricasoliana |
| * | Ficus pumila | ** | Pueraria thunbergiana |
| * | Hedera helix | * | Solandra guttata |
| ** | Hibbertia volubilis | ** | Sollya heterophylla |
| *** | Jasminum gracile | *** | Stauntonia hexaphylla |
| ** | "    gracillimum | ** | Tecomaria capensis |
| * | Lonicera halliana | * | Thunbergia grandiflora |
| *** | Muehlenbeckia complexa | ** | Trachelospermum jasminoides |
| ** | Oxera pulchella | *** | Vitis munsoniana |
| *** | Pandorea pandorana | * | Wisteria floribunda |

VEILING VINES---loosely covering, shielding, or grown for purely decorative purposes. They will soften rather than conceal, with an inter
lacing of stems that are visible by reason of the lighter foliage
spread. These plants are graceful, lax, mellowing.

*** Abrus precatorius                    * Mandevilla suaveolens
*** Aristolochia elegans                *** Manettia bicolor
  * Asparagus (check species)           ** Muehlenbeckia complexa
*** Boussingaultia baselloides          *** Oxera pulchella
 ** Calonyction aculeatum               *** Petrea volubilis
*** Clerodendrum thompsonae               * Phaseolus (species)
 ** Dolichos lignosus                   *** Podranea ricasoliana
  * Gelsemium sempervirens               ** Polygonum auberti
 " Hardenbergia comptoniana               * Pueraria hirsuta
 ** Hibbertia volubilis                  ** Quamoclit (species)
 ** Ipomoea purpurea                      * Solanum (check species)
*** Jaquemontia (species)               *** Sollya heterophylla
 ** Jasminum (species)                   ** Stephanotis floribunda
 ** Kennedya rubicunda                   ** Stigmaphyllon ciliatum
*** Lapageria rosea                     *** Stizolobium deeringianum
  * Lonicera (check species)             ** Trachelospermum (check species)


TENDRIL CLIMBING VINES---or those which lift themselves by means
of curling tendrils or an adaptation of the leaf tip or stem.  Some
will mount an extremely rough surface such as deeply pitted concrete,
very coarse stucco, or the furrowed bark of a tree.   Any or all may
show a tendency to climb by twining under certain conditions of smoothness or a slippery ascent such as wire....a poor support this, on account of its heat conducting property.

  * Ampelopsis brevipedunculata          ** Doxantha unguis-cati
 ** Anemopoegma chamberlayni            *** Eccremocarpus scaber
  * Antigonon leptopus                  *** Gloriosa superba
*** Arrabidaea magnifica                  * Lathyrus odoratus
 ** Boussingaultia baselloides          *** Maurandia erubescens
  * Cardiospermum halicacabum           *** Momordica charantia
 ** Cissus (species)                     ** Pandorea pandorana
*** Clematis armandi                      * Passiflora caerulea
*** Clytostoma callistegioides           ** Phaedranthus buccinatorius
  * Cobaea scandens                     *** Pithecoctenium cynanchoides
 ** Cydista aequinoctialis               ** Pyrostegia ignea
  * Distictis lactiflora                 ** Vitis voinieriana


HIGH CLIMBING VINES---those with a hearty ambition to surmount and
survive; selected besides for good foliage or flowers that should
carry down from a height effectively. They will be used where a strong
woody stem development is important in arranging an effect at some
distance from place of planting, a roof or high on a cliff. Lift from
time to time off tile or shingles.   Fertility of the soil is significant in view of the large amount of wood to be developed.

*** Arrabidaea magnifica                  * Lonicera hildebrandtiana
*** Asparagus falcatus                   ** Oxera pulchella
  * Beaumontia grandiflora              *** Passiflora racemosa
  * Bougainvillea (varieties)           *** Petrea volubilis
 ** Calonyction aculeatum               *** Phaedranthus buccinatorius
 ** Campsidium valdivianum              *** Phaseolus caracalla
  * Cissus capensis                      ** Polygonum auberti
*** Clematis indivisa                    ** Pyrostegia ignea
 ** Clytostoma callistegioides          *** Rosa bracteata
 ** Cobaea scandens                     *** Scindapsis aureus
 ** Distictis lactiflora                  * Solandra guttata
 ** Doxantha unguis-cati                  * Solanum wendlandi
*** Fatshedera lizei                    *** Stigmaphyllon littorale
  * Gelsemium sempervirens             *** Thunbergia laurifolia
*** Hylocereus triangularis              ** Trachelospermum fragrans
  * Ipomoea leari                      *** Tupidanthus calyptratus
 ** Jasminum officinale                  ** Vitis voinieriana
 ** Kennedya rubicunda                    * Wisteria floribunda

## THE HERBACEOUS MOLD

The cast, organization or form of herbs must be studied if the
most is to be made of such plantings from the standpoint of composition in the garden of flowers, as well as the bearing the herbaceous
species will have on the organization of the landscape.  This material offers even more difficulty in segregation than the fore-going in
way of a clear cut and satisfactory classification, yet is submitted for the the very obvious need when working in this area of the
list and its peculiar bearing on timeliness.

HERBACEOUS FILLERS---plants that are loose, slack or indefinite as
to form and, consequently adjusting easily in growth to surrounding
material that is more decided in character. Their structural function
in the border is to fill in between and tie together the more dominant elements.  As a whole these are flower producing over the longer
period and may be considered as temporary stand-ins or permanent.

| | |
|---|---|
| *** Alonsoa warscewiczi | * Gypsophila elegans |
| ** Anagallis linifolia | ** Lavatera trimestris |
| ** Angelonia grandiflora | ** Limonium bellidifolium |
| *** Aphanostephus skirrobasis | *     "     sinuatum |
| * Artemisia albula | ** Linum grandiflorum |
| *** Asphodelus albus | ***    "    narbonnense |
| * Aster (check species) | ** Lopezia albiflora |
| ** Baileya multiradiata | *** Machaeranthera tanacetifolia |
| * Brachycome iberidifolia | * Myosotis alpestris |
| * Browallia americana | ** Nemophila menziesi |
| ** Calendula officinalis | * Nepeta mussini |
| ** Campanula poscharskyana | *** Nierembergia gracilis |
| *** Chaerophyllum dasycarpum | *** Nolana atriplicifolia |
| *** Chaenostoma hispidum | *** Oxypetalum caeruleum |
| * Charieis heterophylla | ** Papaver (check species) |
| * Chrysanthemum carinatum | *** Pasithea caerulea |
| *** Cladanthus arabicus | * Petunia hybrida |
| ** Clarkia elegans | * Phlox drummondi |
| *** Convolvulus tricolor | ** Piqueria trinervia |
| * Coreopsis lanceolata | *** Polypteris hookeriana |
| * Cynoglossum amabile | ** Rosmarinus Lockwood de Forest |
| *** Dyschoriste linearis | * Salvia farinacea |
| ** Erigeron karvinskyanus | **    "    splendens |
| ** Eschscholtzia californica | ** Scabiosa atropurpurea |
| * Felicia amelloides | * Stokesia laevis |
| * Gaillardia aristata | * Thalictrum dipterocarpum |
| *** Gaura lindheimeri | *** Torenia fournieri |
| ** Gazania uniflora | ** Tunica saxifraga |
| *** Gilia densiflora | *** Venidium (species) |
| ** Gomphrena globosa | *** Viola cornuta |

HERBS FOR FORM---herbaceous plants of marked character and strength
as regards shape, or the body of foliage in mass, or the type of the
inflorescence. These plants will have a predominant influence in the
border or garden bed, or wherever used with other herbaceous growth.
From among them will be chosen material for the core or nucleus of a
planting, about which further and complementary flowering effects will
be built. They are the framework of the composition and may be classified somewhat as follows.

### ROTUND MASS

| | |
|---|---|
| *** Aethionema coridifolium | * Chrysanthemum frutescens |
| ** Aquilegia chrysantha | *** Cuphea platycentra |
| ** Arthropodium cirrhatum | ** Dianella intermedia |
| ** Aster amellus | *** Encelia farinosa |
| * Bergenia (species) | ** Felicia echinata |
| * Calocephalis browni | * Festuca glauca |
| *** Centaurea dealbata | *** Gazania coccinea |
| *** Cheiranthus mutabilis | ** Geum Bradshaw |
| * Chironia linoides | * Heuchera sanguinea |

* Lavandula (species)
** Limonium perezi
*** Ligularia kaempferi
* Liriope spicata
*** Mirabilis jalapa
* Nierembergia caerulea
*** Phormium colensoi

** Reinwardtia indica
* Salvia leucantha
*** Scabiosa columbaria
** Tagetes patula
*** Tulbaghia fragrans
*** Ursinia anthemoides
* Vinca rosea

## SPIRING MASS

* Acanthus (species)
*** Adenophora lilifolia
* Althaea rosea
* Antirrhinum majus
** Asclepias currassavica
*** Camassia leichtlini
* Campanula medium
** Celosia cristata
*** Ceratotheca triloba
** Delphinium ajacis
***        "        grandiflorum
** Dierama pulcherrima
** Echium wildpreti
** Eremurus robustus
** Eryngium amethystinum
* Francoa ramosa
* Hedychium (species)
*** Hesperaloe parviflora
** Hunnemannia fumariaefolia

*** Libertia grandiflora
** Lilium (species)
*** Lupinus longifolius
*** Michauxia campanuloides
* Moraea bicolor
** Nicotiana alata
** Orthrosanthus multiflorus
* Penstemon gloxinioides
** Physostegia virginiana
** Polianthes tuberosa
* Rehmannia angulata
* Salvia farinacea
*** Schizostylis coccinea
*** Sisyrinchium striatum
* Trachelium caeruleum
*** Verbesina encelioides
*** Veronica incana
* Yucca (check species)
*** Zingiber officinalis

## IRREGULAR MASS

*** Acidanthera bicolor
* Agapanthus africanus
* Anemone japonica
*** Albuca minor
*** Anigozanthos flavida
** Aristea eckloni
** Bletilla striata
** Billbergia nutans
* Crinum (species)
*** Crocosmia aurea
** Francoa ramosa
** Galtonia candicans
* Gerberia jamesoni
** Gladiolus tristis

** Godetia grandiflora
*** Guzmania cardinalis
* Hemerocallis aurantiaca
* Iris (check species)
** Kniphofia uvaria
*** Linaria dalmatica
* Mathiola incana
* Moraea (species)
*** Neomarica gracilis
** Pelargonium domesticum
* Tritonia crocosmaeflora
* Tulbaghia violacea
** Vallota speciosa
*** Wachendorfia thyrsiflorus

PROSTRATE PERENNIALS---plants that are completely reclining in habit of growth and so organized as to develop a considerable mat of stems and leafage on the ground. Structurally, the mat may be tight or loose or entirely incoherent to the point of stringiness, while in thickness it may range from a fraction of an inch to the greater part of a foot. Shearing or the wear of traffic is a major influence in the make-up or composition these plants will assume.

## CARPETING

Sod-like in growth; a consolidation of parts to form a close mat immediately against the ground, usually integrating further with the earth in a complicated system of rooting and re-rooting. They have rather special uses apart from the border, such as cover where grass will not grow, and between flagging wherever that may be used; even crawling out laterally into turf.

** Abronia villosa
** Acaena microphylla
*** Achillaea nana
* Ajuga reptans
* Arenaria balearica
* Armeria maritima
** Campanula poscharskyana

*** Chorizanthe staticoides
** Chrysanthemum aureum
** Convolvulus lineatus
*** Cotula squalida
** Crassula impressa
** Cymbalaria aequitriloba
* Dianthus deltoides

*** Erodium cicutarium          ** Nertera depressa
*** Euphorbia truncata          * Nierembergia rivularis
 ** Frankenia capitata laevis   * Ophiopogon japonicus
  * Gazania splendens           ** Origanum dictamnus
*** Gilia dianthoides           *** Paronychia argentea
*** Gypsophila cerastioides     *** Sagina subulata
  * Helxine soleiroli           * Sedum brevifolium
*** Hydrocotyle rotundifolia    **  "    dasyphyllum
*** Jussiaea repens             *** Selaginella denticulata
 ** Linum salsaloides nanum     *** Sempervivum arachnoideum
  * Lotus corniculatus fl. pl.  * Thymus albus
 ** Mesembryanth. aloides       ***  "    coccineus
  *       "      floribundum    * Veronica nummularia
***       "      filicaule      ***  "    repens
 **       "      tuberosum      *** Wahlenbergia saxicola
*** Morisia monantha            * Zoysia tenuifolia

## TRAILING PERENNIALS

These plants are procumbent in habit, but less inclined to
mat together than the preceding. They may be likened to an extremely
open with a more or less exposed warp of long-reaching stout stems
and a woof of observable laterals, or only leaves. They will be
attractive trailing down over rocks or between, and may be thickened
by shearing or by pinching out terminal growth.

  * Abronia maritima            *** Nolana prostrata
 ** Cerastium tomentosum        * Ranunculus repens
*** Clianthus puniceus          ** Saxifraga sarmentosa
*** Clitoria mariana            *** Schizocentron elegans
 ** Crassula monticola          * Sedum lineare
  *      "     perfossa         **   "   sieboldi
*** Cyanotis hirsuta            *    "   spurium
  * Cymbalaria muralis          ***  "   stahli
 ** Felicia petiolata           * Senecio mikanioides
 ** Gypsophila repens           ** Torenia flava
 ** Kleinia radicans            ** Tropaeolum majus
  *     "     repens            * Verbena hortensis
  * Lathyrus splendens          *** Veronica lacinata
  * Lobelia speciosa            **    "    tourneforti
 ** Lotus bertheloti            * Vinca major
*** Mentha gatefossei           *** Viola gracilis
*** Mesembryanth. cordifolium   **    "   pedunculata
  *       "       croceum       *** Wedelia trilobata
 **       "       laeve         *** Zebrina pendula

## BLANKETING

These plants may be trailing, but eventually thicken to form
an interlacing fabric, a smooth or rippling coverlet over the ground
of some depth or thickness and with plenty of nap, so to speak....of
leaves.   They will be used generally in the forepart of the border,
over low garden slopes or in the rock garden in places where their
invading habits will not become a nuisance.

  * Abronia umbellata           ** Mesembryanth. deltoides
*** Acantholimon venustum       *       "       roseum
*** Adiantum caudatum           ***     "       verruculatum
  * Alyssum maritimum           ** Micromeria chamissonis
*** Anacyclus depressus         * Malcomia maritima
*** Arrhenatherum tuberosum     * Nepeta mussini
  * Aubrieta deltoidea          *** Oplismenus hirtellus
*** Campanula fragilis          * Phlox drummondi
 ** Centaureum massoni          *** Potentilla repens fl. pl.
  * Convolvulus mauretanicus    *** Putoria calabrica
 ** Dianthus caesius            *** Reineckia carnea
  * Duchesnea indica            ** Sedum adolphi
 ** Erigeron karvinskyanus      * Teucrium prostratum
  * Fragaria chiloensis         *** Thymus broussoneti
 ** Gypsophila repens           * Tropaeolum minus
  * Lobelia erinus              ** Verbena pulchella
 ** Lysimachia nummularia       *** Veronica pectinata
                *** Viola cornuta

CASUAL PERENNIALS---mostly bulbs and tubers of good constitution, but evanescent character in flower, to be used in the border apparently without design or expectancy. They may be erratic in appearing or regular by the calendar. Some will develop flowers and foliage concurrently, while others will come on separately. They may not be counted upon for more than a pleasing incident additional to the general scheme. Yet even in passing, they serve to spot the monotony of these near tropical lands in line with the hurried bloomings of more temperate regions. Mark where they stand in order that they may not be disturbed out of season, or lost altogether.

| | |
|---|---|
| *** Adiantum emarginatum | *** Hesperantha stanfordiae |
| * Allium triquetrum | *** Homeria collina |
| * Amaryllis (check species) | *** Ionopsidium acaule |
| *** Arrhenatherum tuberosum | * Ixia maculata |
| ** Arum italicum | * Leucojum autumnale |
| * Babiana stricta | *** Lycoris (species) |
| *** Beloperone californica | ** Milla biflora |
| ** Bessera elegans | *** Moraea ramosa |
| * Bletilla striata | ** Muscari armeniacum |
| *** Brevoortia ida-maia | * Narcissus (species) |
| * Brodiaea (species) | *** Nerine (check species) |
| * Brunsvigia rosea | * Ornithogalum (species) |
| ** Calochortus (species) | * Oxalis (check species) |
| *** Calostemma purpurea | *** Oxypetalum caeruleum |
| *** Chlidanthus fragrans | *** Pancratium maritimum |
| ** Colchicum autumnale | ** Papaver orientalis |
| * Cooperia drummondi | *** Pasithea caerulea |
| *** Cyrtanthus obliquus | ** Schizostylis coccinea |
| ** Delphinium cardinale | * Scilla (species) |
| *** " nudicaule | ** Sisyrinchium bellum |
| ** Dicentra spectabilis | ** Sparaxis tricolor |
| *** Dipidax ciliata | *** Sprekelia formosissima |
| ** Elisena longipetala | * Sternbergia lutea |
| ** Eremurus robustus | *** Streptanthera cuprea |
| ** Eucharis grandiflora | * Tigridia pavonia |
| *** Gloriosa superba | ** Tulipa (botanical species) |
| * Habranthus robustus | ** Veltheimia viridifolia |
| *** Haemanthus (check species) | ** Viola pedunculata |
| | * Zephyranthes rosea |

TEXTURAL VALUES---in a foliage survey of woody plants. This relates to the surface aspect and is seldom given enough consideration in laying out a planting. The mass appearance at all times is dull and monotonous or carries interest of a pleasing quality according to whether or not someone has given thought to the admixture of roughness and fineness, not necessarily in the leaf, but in that which may be termed graining. Structurally, the disposition and frequency of parts has an equal bearing on the result, with their relative coarseness.. ..pruning modifies. The texture of plants has a scale relationship against architectural detail, so that with study, a certain unity or integration may be achieved, or completeness lost by want of observation and following thought.

## DENSE TEXTURE

Plants of a coarse-grained texture or those with an observable in-gathering of parts for a suspended, inert feeling that stamps them as if from a mould, have a tendency to stand aside as individuals in a mixed or in a homogeneous planting. They will be most harmonious with heavy construction in mass, and are self-contained rather than expansive. They close actually as of themselves and subconsciously as of the observer. They will seem to dwarf a relative area, particularly when enclosed within walls or in connection with a building group. These plants absorb traffic noise effectively.

### TREES

| | |
|---|---|
| ** Acacia melanoxylon | * Brachychiton populneum |
| *** Acer oblongum | *** Callitris robusta |
| ** Achras zapota | ** Calodendrum capense |
| ** Araucaria bidwilli | * Ceratonia siliqua |

*** Chamaecyparis lawsoniana
  * Citrus (species)
*** Coccolobis floridana
 ** Cupressus forbsi
  *     "      sempervirens
*** Elaeodendron orientale
 ** Eriobotrya japonica
 ** Eucalyptus cornuta
  *     "      ficifolia
  * Ficus retusa
*** Juniperus excelsa
 ** Laurus nobilis
*** Macadamia ternifolia
  * Magnolia grandiflora

 ** Melia umbraculiformis
*** Phytolacca dioica
  * Pinus radiata
 **    "    pinea
*** Pittosporum rhombifolium
  *     "      undulatum
 ** Podocarpus macrophylla
*** Quercus agrifolia
 **    "    virginiana
*** Sapindus saponaria
  * Taxus baccata stricta
 ** Thuja orientalis
 ** Umbellularia californica
*** Vitex lucens

## SHRUBS

*** Abelia grandiflora
 ** Acacia cultriformis
  * Arbutus unedo
*** Aucuba japonica
*** Bougainvillea Temple Fire
  * Buxus japonica
*** Callistemon rigidus
  * Calocephalis browni
*** Canella winterana
  * Carissa grandiflora
  * Cassia splendida
  * Ceanothus verrucosus
*** Choisya ternata
  * Cistus purpureus
*** Cneorum tricoccon
 ** Cocculus laurifolius
 ** Cotoneaster thymifolia
*** Cytisus canariensis
 ** Elaeagnus pungens
 ** Euphorbia tirucalli
 ** Felicia echinata
*** Grevillea rosmarinifolia
  * Hakea laurina
  *    "    saligna
 ** Hebe andersoni
  *    "   buxifolia
*** Hydrangea macrophylla
 ** Hibiscus rosa-sinensis
  * Hydrangea macrophylla

 ** Hypericum moserianum
 ** Ilex cornuta burfordi
***   "  paraguariensis
  * Juniperus argentea
  * Leucophyllum texanum
  * Ligustrum rotundifolium
  * Myrsine africana
  * Myrtus communis
*** Odontospermum sericeum
 ** Osmanthus ilicifolius
*** Phillyrea latifolia
  * Pimelea ferruginea
  * Pittosporum tobira
 ** Plumbago capensis
  * Polygala dalmaisiana
*** Prunus lusitanica
 ** Psidium cattleianum
 ** Pyracantha crenato-serrata
  * Raphiolepis ovata
 ** Rhamnus alaternus
*** Rhus ovata
 ** Rondeletia cordata
  * Santolina chamaecyparissus
*** Severinia buxifolia
 ** Simmondsia californica
 ** Sollya heterophylla
  * Turraea obtusifolia
  * Viburnum tinus
*** Visnea mocanera

## VINES

 ** Asparagus plumosus
 ** Bougainvillea (varieties)
*** Campsidium valdivianum
 ** Cissus hypoglauca
*** Cydista aequinoctialis

  * Lonicera halliana
  * Muehlenbeckia complexa
*** Phaedranthus buccinatorius
  * Thunbergia grandiflora
  * Trachelospermum jasminoides

## TEXTURE OPEN

     These plants are not so definite in form nor as strict in
)utline as the preceding.  There will be a greater dispersion, as of
parts, a scattering of leaves. They will be lighter as regards body
in such away as never to show marked contrast within themselves, highlights or depth of shadow. They will relieve the heaviness of an inert
mass such as concrete or a particularly burdensome stand of foliage
with this flexibility.  For further refinements along this line of
thinking, see ENLIVENING FACTORS following.

## TREES

 ** Acacia decurrens (varieties)
*** Ailanthus altissima
 ** Annona cherimola
 ** Araucaria excelsa
  * Callistemon viminalis

 ** Celtis australis
*** Cupressus arizonica
  * Eucalyptus citriodora
 ** Fraxinus velutina
  * Grevillea robusta

\*\*\* Lysiloma latisiliqua
  \* Hymenosporum flavum
\*\*\* Juglans (species)
  \* Pinus halepensis
\*\*\*    "    sabiniana
 \*\* Pistacia chinensis

 \*\* Pittosporum eugenioides
 \*\* Podocarpus elongata
\*\*\* Prunus amygdalus
\*\*\* Salix babylonica
  \* Tristania conferta
\*\*\* Ulmus parvifolia

## SHRUBS

 \*\* Abelia schumanni
  \* Abutilon hybridum
 \*\* Acacia armata
\*\*\* Aster fruticosus
 \*\* Brachysema lanceolatum
 \*\* Buddleja (species)
  \* Callistemon lanceolatus
 \*\* Candollea cuneiformis
  \* Cassia corymbosa
 \*\* Ceanothus cyaneus
  \* Cercocarpus betuloides
  \* Ceratostigma willmottianum
\*\*\* Cistus maculatus
\*\*\* Coronilla glauca
  \* Cotoneaster (species)
 \*\* Daubentonia (species)
 \*\* Diosma ericoides
\*\*\* Duranta stenostachya
 \*\* Escallonia (species)
  \* Feijoa sellowiana
 \*\* Fremontia californica
 \*\* Grevillea banksi
 \*\* Grewia occidentalis
\*\*\* Halimium ocymoides
 \*\* Hebe hulkeana
 \*\* Hibiscus mutabilis
\*\*\* Hypericum henryi
 \*\* Lawsonia inermis

 \*\* Leonotis leonurus
 \*\* Leptospermum laevigatum
 \*\* Lonicera nitida
  \* Mahonia (species)
 \*\* Murraea exotica
\*\*\* Nuxia floribunda
\*\*\* Olmediella betschleriana
  \* Photinia serrulata
 \*\* Prunus ilicifolia
\*\*\* Punica granatum
\*\*\* Pyracantha koidzumi
\*\*\* Raphiolepis indica
 \*\* Rhamnus crocea
 \*\* Rosmarinus officinalis
\*\*\* Serissa foetida
\*\*\* Siphonosmanthus delavayi
 \*\* Solanum rantonneti
\*\*\* Sparmannia africana
 \*\* Streptosolen jamesoni
  \* Syringa persica
\*\*\* Taxus baccata
 \*\* Tecomaria capensis
 \*\* Teucrium fruticans
\*\*\* Thevetia nereifolia
  \* Vitex agnus-castus
 \*\* Westringia rosmariniformis
\*\*\* Wigandia caracasana
  \* Xylosma senticosa

## VINES

  \* Clematis (species)
 \*\* Gelsemium sempervirens
 \*\* Hardenbergia monophylla
  \* Jasminum (species)
\*\*\* Kennedya rubicunda

 \*\* Mandevilla suaveolens
\*\*\* Passiflora racemosa
 \*\* Pyrostegia ignea
  \* Solanum wendlandi
\*\*\* Wisteria floribunda

## FILAMENTOUS

An extreme in way of texture, a fineness and motility that tends towards sprightliness or vivacity in the foliage mass. In observation of all this, the human faculties react as to cheerfulness and gaiety and the flow of sunniness as opposed to gravity and dejection or the submersion of fog. Line enters into composition with these plants to a greater extent due to their airy nature and possibly the more scantily clad stems, or just that of a feathery foliage.

## TREES

 \*\* Acacia farnesiana
  \*    "    pruinosa
  \* Albizzia (species)
 \*\* Casuarina (species)
\*\*\* Cercidium torreyanum
 \*\* Chilopsis linearis
\*\*\* Cupressus funebris
 \*\* Eucalyptus sideroxylon

\*\*\* Jacaranda acutifolia
\*\*\* Melaleuca styphelioides
  \* Parkinsonia aculeata
\*\*\* Pinus canariensis
\*\*\* Salix crispa
  \* Schinus molle
  \* Tamarix aphylla
\*\*\* Torreya californica

## SHRUBS

\*\*\* Artemisia (species)
\*\*\* Asparagus virgatus
\*\*\* Baeckia virgata
  \* Bambusa multiplex
 \*\* Calliandra portoricensis

\*\*\* Callistemon brachyandrus
\*\*\* Ceanothus impressus
 \*\* Cassia artemisioides
  \* Chamaelaucium ciliatum
  \* Cotoneaster microphylla

** Diosma pulchra
* Erica melanthera
*** Escallonia glasniviensis
** Fabiana imbricata
* Genista monophylla
* Grevillea thelemanniana
** Halimium libanotis
*** Heimia myrtifolia
** Hypericum floribundum
* Lippia citriodora
** Lopezia albiflora
* Melaleuca armillaris
** Melaleuca decussata
*** Melianthus major
*** Myrtus ralphi

* Nandina domestica
*** Osteomeles anthyllidifolia
** Phoenix roebelini
** Phyllostachys aurea
** Pittosporum heterophyllum
* Poinciana gilliesi
*** Prosopis (species)
** Rhapis humilis
*** Rhus lancea
* Russelia equisetiformis
* Sasa disticha
** Swainsona galegifolia
* Tamarix (species)
*** Tecoma garrocha
** Thryallis glauca

## VINES

*** Antigonon leptopus
** Clematis lasiantha
* Hardenbergia comptoniana
** Polygonum auberti
*** Quamoclit pennata

*** Securidaca diversifolia
** Solanum jasminoides
* Stigmaphyllon ciliatum
*** Thenardia floribunda
* Tropaeolum peregrina

LINE---as exemplified in stem and branch or searching liana, plays a part in the off-season aspect of a planting, showing beneath vents in foliation or insistent through a sparse covering.   It is natural for plants to reach for the sun, but man has introduced artificial planes into the landscape that have stressed the horizontal....plants recommended may need help in maturity....following low the earth for space and tranquility.  The perpendicular deals with restriction, agitation, is inspiring; and these plants, aspiring, reach up with resolve....to the restless wind. Then there is an indeterminate ramification, a divergence from either of the above, a deviation in line that can be very attractive in itself, less architectural and not surely predictable.   Look there for the unexpected and unaccountable in unusual character as line.

## THE PERPENDICULAR

* Acanthus mollis
*** " montanus
*** Actinophloeus macarthuri
*** Agonis linearifolia
** Alpinia speciosa
** Anemone japonica
** Anthyllis barba-jovis
* Araucaria excelsa
** Archontophoenix cunningham.
* Arecastrum romanzoffianum
* Bambusa (species)
** Buddleja asiatica
* Brassaia actinophylla
*** Callitris robusta
*** Carnegiea gigantea
*** Cephalocereus senilis
*** Ceratotheca triloba
*** Ceropegia woodi
* Chamaerops humilis (forms)
* Cupressus sempervirens
* Cyperus (check species)
** Dahlia maxoni
** Dianella tasmanica
*** Echium (species)
** Erythea brandigeei
*** Eugenia paniculata
*** Eurya ochnacea
** Fouquieria splendens
* Hedychium (species)

** Hymenosporum flavum
*** Ilex vomitoria
* Jacobinia carnea
*** Lapageria rosea
* Laurus nobilis
** Mahonia lomariifolia
*** Michelia champaca
** Myrsine africana
* Nandina domestica
*** Nothopanax arboreum
*** Osteomeles anthyllidifolia
* Philadelphus mexicanus
*** Phoenix rupicola
* Phormium tenax
* Pinus canariensis
** " sabiniana
*** Pittosporum tenuifolium
* Pyracantha lalandi
** Populus nigra italica
** Rhapis (species)
** Sasa palmata
* Sinocalamus oldhami
*** Stenocarpus sinuatus
** Taxus baccata stricta
** Trachycarpus fortunei
*** Trevesia palmata
** Ulmus alata
** Washingtonia robusta
*** Zingiber officinale

## THE HORIZONTAL

* Acacia baileyana
*** Achras zapota
*** Bauhinia galpini
** Begonia foliosa
*** Calliandra inequilatera
** Ceanothus grizeus
*** Chamaelaucium ciliatum
* Cotoneaster pannosa nana
** Cupressus benthami
* Dion edule
*** Elaeagnus pungens
** Eriogonum giganteum
* Gardenia thunbergia
** Grewia occidentalis
*** Hylocereus triangulata

*** Ilex paraguariensis
*** Lonicera pileata
*** Pereskia aculeata
** Pinus edulis
*** Plumeria emarginata
** Prosopis glandulosa
* Pyracantha crenato-serrata
** Pyrus calleryana
** Russelia equisetiformis
*** Schinus dependens
*** Solanum montana
** Taxus baccata repandens
* Tipuana tipu
*** Ulmus parvifolia (forms)
** Xylosma senticosa

## INDETERMINATE

** Abutilon hybridum
*** Acacia vestita
*** Arctostaphylos diversifolia
*** Calliandra tweedi
** Callistemon rigidus
* Ceratostigma willmottianum
* Cercocarpus betuloides
*** Corokia cotoneaster
*** Cotoneaster microphylla
* Dovyalis caffra
** Dracaena stricta
*** Eucalyptus macrocarpa
* Euphorbia splendens
*** Fallugia paradoxa
* Fatsia japonica
* Fuchsia (varieties)
*** Harpephyllum caffrum
** Holmskioldia sanguinea
*** Ilex cassine
*** Juniperus californica
*         "       torulosa
* Leptospermum laevigatum
*** Leucadendron argenteum
** Lonicera nitida
*** Micropiper excelsum

*** Magnolia stellata
*** Malvastrum fasciculatum
** Medicago arborea
** Melaleuca huegeli
*** Melianthus major
** Metrosideros tomentosa
** Monstera deliciosa
*** Myrtus ralphi
*** Noltea africana
* Olea europaea
** Parkinsonia aculeata
** Phoenix reclinata
** Phyllostachys aurea
*** Pinus attenuata
** Platanus racemosa
* Poinciana gilliesi
** Portulacaria afra
*** Prosopis glandulosa
* Psidium cattleianum
** Pyracantha koidzumi
** Schinus terebinthifolius
*** Tabebuia umbellata
* Tamarix (species)
*** Tetrapanax papyriferum
*** Tithonia rotundifolia

# CULTURAL ASPECTS

The circumstances under which plants thrive and reach their highest expression in form and flowers and fruiting are of manifest importance, with implications that carry widely into the field of hortticulture. A starved, hungry or disease-ridden tree struggling for existence, can never have the ornamental value that may be expected of its full vigor and health. One adverse factor for growth may place the plant under a handicap which it overcomes with difficulty, if at all. That one cause removed or a want supplied may change the entire outlook and the life process goes on unhampered, with its functions in the ornamental scheme unimpaired. Some plants are indifferent to their surroundings or supply. Their likes and dislikes are so vague they may be used at will within reasonable limits. None the less, there are species to accomodate all conditions and desires, natural or artificial or acquired, so that it is incumbent on those who plant to inquire into the suitability of the individual for a given situation if the most is to be expected. These lists will treat generally of conditions of restraint or positive need and specifically of the plants which are either prepared by nature to overcome a case in question or actually require its presence for their well-being. Moreover and above all, they are for planters who accept the conditions of site and move on from there. These are of the elect, the wise and considerate who plant for survival and the adjustments of time.

SUN LOVING PLANTS---or with as much meaning, those which are not tolerant of shade. The following plants are not necessarily resistant to heat and no conclusion as to moisture requirements should be inferred. They are particularly insistent in the matter of full light intensity for proper development of foliage and in many cases, the brightness and purity of coloring in flower and fruit. The tendency in growth is to become more compact. Vines became structurally what they are, seeking light and few will bloom at their best without it. This is a negative list, but of value as a check against plantings that have to cope with overhead shade. These are "must" plants for an open place and for the sun.

## SHRUBS

|   |   |
|---|---|
| * Adenocarpus viscosus | * Cytisus canariensis |
| ** Anisacanthus wrighti | ** Daubentonia (species) |
| * Artemisia (species) | ** Diosma (species) |
| *** Aster fruticosus | *** Dombeya natalensis |
| ** Brachysema lanceolatum | * Erica melanthera |
| ** Buddleja (species) | ** Eriogonum (species) |
| * Callistemon lanceolatus | ** Euphorbia pulcherrima |
| * Calocephalus browni | ** Euryops (species) |
| ** Candollea cuneiformis | ** Fabiana imbricata |
| ** Carissa grandiflora | * Genista monosperma |
| * Cassia (species) | *** Gossypium sturti |
| * Ceanothus (species) | * Grevillea (species) |
| ** Cestrum (species) | *** Greyia sutherlandi |
| * Chamaelaucium ciliatum | * Halimium (check species) |
| *** Cienfuegosia hakeaefolia | *** Holmskioldia sanguinea |
| * Cistus (species) | ** Juniperus (species) |
| * Correa (species) | ** Lagerstroemia indica |
| * Cotoneaster (species) | ** Lantana (species) |
| ** Cuphea (species) | ** Lavandula officinalis |

  * Leucophyllum texanum
*** Mahernia verticillata
*** Odontospermum sericeum
*** Osteomeles anthyllidifolia
  * Penstemon antirrhinoides
*** Phlomis fruticosa
  * Plumbago capensis
 ** Poinciana (species)
 ** Psidium cattleianum
*** Psoralea aphylla
 ** Punica granatum
*** Rondeletia cordata
*** Rhus ovata
  * Spartium junceum
 ** Streptosolen jamesoni
  * Tecoma (species)
  * Teucrium fruticans
  * Thevetia nereifolia
*** Thryallis glauca
*** Vigueria tomentosa
*** Zauschneria californica

## VINES

*** Anemopoegma chamberlayni
  * Antigonon leptopus
*** Beaumontia grandiflora
 ** Bougainvillea (varieties)
 ** Clematis texensis
 ** Hibbertia volubilis
  * Ipomoea (species)
*** Jaquemontia (species)
  * Jasminum (check species)
  * Lonicera (check species)
  * Mandevilla suaveolens
 ** Passiflora (species)
  * Phaseolus (species)
*** Podranea (species)
 ** Pyrostegia ignea
 ** Quamoclit (species)
  * Rosa (varieties)
*** Solandra (species)
  * Solanum wendlandi
*** Thenardia floribunda
  * Thunbergia (species)
*** Wisteria floribunda

## HERBACEOUS PLANTS

 ** Abronia (species)
*** Acantholimon venustum
 ** Agapanthus africanus
  * Alternanthera amoena
  * Alyssum maritimum
  * Amaryllis (species)
 ** Anagallis linifolia
 ** Aphanostephus skirrobasis
  * Arctotis (species)
  * Aster amellus
  * Babiana stricta
*** Baileya multiradiata
*** Brunsvigia rosea
  * Calendula officinalis
*** Centaureum venustum
 ** Chaenostoma (species)
*** Charieis heterophylla
*** Cheilanthes gracillima
 ** Chironia linoides
  * Chrysanthemum (species)
 ** Convolvulus (species)
 ** Cooperia drummondi
  * Coreopsis (species)
*** Cortaderia selloana
  * Dahlia (varieties)
*** Delphinium (check species)
  * Dianthus (species)
*** Dierama pulcherrima
  * Dimorphotheca (species)
*** Erodium (species)
  * Eschscholtzia californica
  * Felicia (species)
*** Frankenia capitata laevis
  * Gaillardia aristata
  * Gazania splendens
  * Gerberia jamesoni
*** Gomphrena globosa
  * Helichrysum (species)
*** Heliophila pilosa
 ** Hesperantha stanfordiae
 ** Iris (check species)
  * Ixia maculata
 ** Kniphofia uvaria
  * Limonium (species)
 ** Lonas inodora
  * Lotus (species)
  * Linum (species)
  * Mesembryanth. (species)
 ** Mirabilis jalapa
 ** Nepeta mussini
*** Nerine (species)
  * Oenothera (species)
*** Pancratium (species)
 ** Papaver (species)
*** Paronychia argentea
 ** Pelargonium (check species)
 ** Penstemon (species)
*** Phacelia whitlavia
  * Phlox drummondi
 ** Polianthes tuberosa
  * Portulaca grandiflora
*** Pterocephalus parnassi
 ** Puya alpestris
 ** Salvia (check species)
*** Sanvitalia procumbens
*** Satureja (species)
 ** Schizostylis coccinea
  * Sparaxis tricolor
  * Stokesia laevis
 ** Tagetes (species)
*** Thymophylla tenuiloba
 ** Tigridia pavonia
*** Tithonia rotundifolia
 ** Tritonia crocosmaeflora
  * Tropaeolum (species)
 ** Tulbaghia violacea
*** Ursinia anthemoides
 ** Vallota speciosa
 ** Venidium (species)
  * Verbena (species)
  * Vinca rosea
*** Wachendorfia thyrsiflora
 ** Watsonia iridifolia
*** Xanthisma texanum
*** Zantedeschia elliottiana
  * Zinnia elegans

PLANTS IN SHADOW---those of a shade-loving disposition and such as
tolerate a low light intensity or the absence of direct sunlight. The
plants listed below will endure dutifully without the sun, but nearly
all should have at least a filtering of rays sometime during the day,
if they are to make their best appearance and development. The typical plant here is not so colorful, but is longer lived.    Shade that
is cast is more easily handled than that which results from overhead.
Stuffiness produced by lack of air circulation, together with a short-
age of light and natural rainfall are bound to tell in time and in
terms of deep-seated decline....in the end, utter hopelessness.

## PARTIAL SHADE
Many plants are on the borderline in this respect. Others
are found growing satisfactorily in the sun, but may be vastly improved with a little shade. Still others cannot survive a burning sun,
yet find themselves in as much difficulty in dense shade. Here is a
place for large leaves that serve with a flourish, shining surfaces
to reflect motes of light, and lush green to absorb such bestowal of
of the sun as may be.

### SHRUBS

*** Abutilon (species)
* Alsophila australis
*** Arctostaphylos diversifolia
*** Ardisia crispa
* Beloperone guttata
** Berberis darwini
*** Breynia nivosa
*** Brunfelsia americana
** Buxus harlandi
* Camellia japonica
** Cantua buxifolia
*** Carpenteria californica
** Ceanothus purpureus
** Ceratostigma willmottianum
** Chaenomeles japonica
** Chorizema cordatum
** Cotoneaster harroviana
** Daphne odora
** Elaeagnus pungens
*** Eurya (species)
** Feijoa sellowiana
* Fuchsia triphylla
*** Gardenia (species)
*** Hamelia erecta
*** Hebe (species)
*** Heterocentron roseum
* Hypericum (species)
* Ilex cornuta burfordi
*** Illicium anisatum

* Iochroma (species)
** Jacobinia pauciflora
*** Leucothoe axillaris
* Ligustrum (species)
** Lonicera nitida
** Mahonia (species)
** Malpighia coccigera
** Malvaviscus arboreus
* Michelia fuscata
** Murraea exotica
* Ochna multiflora
*** Oncoba routledgi
* Osmanthus (species)
*** Photinia serrulata
*** Podocarpus nagi
*** Pimelea ferruginia
** Prunus lusitanica
* Raphiolepis (species)
** Rhamnus alaternus
** Ribes (species)
*** Rondeletia cordata
* Ruellia devosiana
** Severinia buxifolia
*** Strobilanthes dyeriana
* Ternstroemia japonica
** Thea sinensis
* Turraea obtusifolia
* Viburnum (check species)
*** Zamia floridana

### VINES

* Asparagus sprengeri
*** Bomaria caldasiana
*** Clytostoma callistegioides
* Cissus hypoglauca
* Clematis (check species)
** Ficus pumila
* Gelsemium sempervirens
** Hardenbergia (species)

*** Lapageria rosea
* Lonicera (check species)
*** Oxera pulchella
** Solanum seaforthianum
* Stephanotis floribunda
** Tecoma capensis
** Thunbergia (check species)
*** Vitis voinieriana

### HERBACEOUS PLANTS

* Acanthus mollis
** Allium (check species)
** Alstroemeria (species)
* Anemone (species)
** Anigozanthos flavida
*** Antirrhinum majus
* Aquilegia chrysantha
*** Aristea eckloni

*** Arthropodium cirrhatum
** Arum italicum
*** Bletilla striata
*** Browallia americana
*** Calceolaria integrifolia
* Campanula (species)
** Centaurea (species)
*** Centaureum massoni

** Ceratostigma plumbaginoides
* Clarkia elegans
* Coleus blumei
*** Crinum moorei
*** Cymbalaria aequitriloba
** Dianella intermedia
*** Echeveria pulverulenta
*** Epidendrum obrienianum
** Exacum affine
* Fragaria californica
** Freesia refracta
*** Gasteria (species)
* Geum Bradshaw
* Godetia grandiflora
*** Haemanthus (species)
* Hedychium coronarium
* Heliotropium arborescens
*** Helleborus lividus
* Heuchera sanguinea
** Iris (check species)
*** Lilium (species)
** Mimulus luteus
** Nemesia strumosa

* Nemophila menziesi
*** Nertera depressa
* Ophiopogon jaburan
*** Oplismenus hirtellus
** Oxalis hererei
*** Papaver rupifragum
** Pasithea caerulea
*** Pentas lanceolata
* Primula (species)
** Ranunculus (species)
** Rehmannia angulata
** Reinwardtia indica
** Rivina humilis
*** Salvia patens
* Schizanthus wisetonensis
*** Silene schafta
** Strelitzia reginae
** Torenia fournieri
* Thalictrum dipterocarpum
*** Veronica tourneforti
** Viola (species)
*** Wedelia trilobata
** Zephyranthes (species)

## DEEP SHADE

The dark side of a building or other sunless sites find the ordinary plant laboring under abnormal foliage production, with slendering stems straining for light. The soil is cold, with a constant tendency toward sourness and the situation so distressing as to compel the use of willing plants. Reflected light, as from a wall suffusing into this area, will award added tone to the planting and improve the blooming. This list is so comparatively limited in shrubby material, that a few typically small and brush-making trees are suggested, trees that may be pruned, pinched in and held as shrubs for reasonably good service for a time.

### SHRUBS

*** Acanthus montanus
*** Acanthopanax sieboldianum
** Aucuba japonica
* Azalea (species)
** Azara microphylla
*** Berberidopsis corallina
*** Brickellia grandiflora
* Brunfelsia calysina
** Calycanthus floridus
*** Camellia reticulata
** Cocculus laurifolius
*** Coffea arabica
*** Collinia elegans
*** Corynocarpus laevigata
* Dracaena stricta
* Eranthemum nervosum
* Euonymus japonicus
*** Eurya emarginata
* Fatsia japonica
* Fuchsia (varieties)
*** Griselinia lucida
* Hedera arborescens
* Howea belmoreana
* Hydrangea macrophylla
** Hypericum aureum
* Itea ilicifolia
*** Laurus nobilis

** Ligustrum rotundifolium
** Lonicera nitida
* Mackaya bella
* Macropiper excelsum
*** Mahonia lomariifolia
*** Mitriostigma axillare
** Myrsine africana
** Nandina domestica
*** Nothopanax arboreum
*** Osmanthus armatus
** Pachystachys coccinea
** Phillyrea latifolia
*** Pinckneya pubens
* Pittosporum tobira
** Prunus laurocerassus
* Raphiolepis ovata
*** Ribes viburnifolium
** Ruscus aculeatus
** Sarcococca hookeriana
** Siphonosmanthus delavayi
*** Skimmia japonica
*** Strophanthus speciosus
* Taxus baccata
*** Thujopsis dolobrata
*** Torreya (species)
** Viburnum odoratissimum
* Xylosma senticosa

### VINES

** Alseuosmia macrophylla
* Asparagus plumosus
** Cissus rhombifolia

*** Clematis armandi
** Fatshedera lizei
* Hardenbergia comptoniana

* Hedera helix
*** Homalocladium platycladium
* Hoya carnosa
*** Lonicera aureo-reticulata
*** Lygodium japonicum
*** Nephthytis afzeli
* Parthenocissus (species)
** Philodendron (check species)
*** Scindapsis aureus
** Trachelospermum jasminoides
*** Thunbergia laurifolia

## HERBACEOUS PLANTS

*** Acorus gramineus
* Adiantum (species)
* Aglaeonema simplex
*** Agrimonia odorata
** Ajuga reptans
** Allium triquetrum
* Anemone japonica
** Arenaria balearica
* Aspidistra elatior
** Asplenium (check species)
* Begonia (species)
* Bergenia cordifolia
** Billbergia nutans
*** Brunnera myosotidifolia
** Caladium picturatum
*** Calceolaria herbeo-hybrida
*** Carex morrowi
** Ceropegia woodi
*** Chlorophytum elatum
** Cineraria cruenta
* Clivia (species)
*** Curculigo capitulata
* Cyclamen indicum
*** Cymbalaria muralis
*** Dicentra spectabilis
* Dieffenbachia picta
* Epiphyllum oxypetalum
** Francoa ramosa
* Gloxinia speciosa
* Haemanthus puniceus
* Helxine soleiroli
* Impatiens sultani
** Iris foetidissima
* Ligularia kaempferi
* Liriope spicata
** Lobelia erinus
*** Lysimachia nummularia
*** Micromeria chamissonis
* Myosotis alpestris
* Ophiopogon japonicus
** Oxalis crassipes
*** Pilea microphylla
** Polystichum aculeatum
*** Reineckia carnea
*** Rohdea japonica
** Sansevieria (species)
** Saxifraga sarmentosa
*** Selaginella (species)
*** Streptocarpus (hybrids)
** Tolmiea menziesi
** Vinca major
** Viola odorata
*** Woodwardia (species)
* Zantedeschia aethiopica
** Zoysia tenuifolia
*** Zebrina pendula
*** Zygocactus truncatus

THERMAL CONSIDERATIONS---a determination as regards the plant list,
the scope or measure being heat. There are so many nearly related
factors here that it will be necessary for the planter to consider
closely the difference between the dry torture of arid conditions and
the smothering humidity of other regions. An inconvenience in this
respect in either direction can hold back or even prohibit functions
for proper growth and development when serious. There is'nt too much
that can be done about this aspect of planting, so that the lasting
solution must be a willing plant.

### HEAT
Enduring plants which may be depended upon to face high temperature without visible evidence of distress. They will distract the
eye from parched surfaces and absorb sharp reflections from walls or
the cliff. They will survive close canyons, ravines or a pocket in
the garden subject to intensified heat. Sudden blasts that burn or
merely the oppression of close sultry air, hot searing winds; all can
be very devastating to plants not prepared by nature to cope with the
situation. See SUCCULENTS for material peculiarly adapted.

## TREES

* Acacia (check species)
*** Alnus tenuifolia
** Bauhinia variegata
* Brachychiton (species)
*** Carya pecan
*** Castanospermum australe
* Casuarina ( species)
*** Celtis australis
* Ceratonia siliqua
** Cinnamomum camphora
*** Cupressus forbsi
** Erythrina (species)
* Eucalyptus (species)
** Fraxinus uhdei
* Grevillea robusta
* Koelreuteria paniculata
*** Metrosideros tomentosa
** Morus (species)

  * Olea europaea
  * Parkinsonia aculeata
  * Phoenix (species)
*** Phytolacca dioica
 ** Pinus (check species)
*** Pistacia (species)
 ** Prunus amygdalis
***    " campanulata

 ** Quercus (species)
*** Spathodea campanulata
*** Stenocarpus sinuatus
 ** Tamarix aphylla
 ** Tipuana tipu
*** Tristania conferta
  * Washingtonia filifera
*** Zizyphus jujuba

## SHRUBS

*** Abutilon palmeri
  * Adenocarpus viscosus
*** Anthyllis barba-jovis
*** Arctostaphylos manzanita
*** Baeckia virgata
 ** Bauhinia galpini
  * Berberis gagnepaini
*** Brachysema lanceolatum
  * Calliandra inequilatera
  * Callistemon lanceolatus
  * Calocephalis browni
 ** Candollea cuneiformis
  * Carissa grandiflora
 ** Cassia artemisioides
*** Ceanothus cyaneus
 ** Ceratostigma willmottianum
*** Choisya ternata
  * Cistus (species)
 ** Convolvulus cneorum
 ** Correa (species)
*** Cowania mexicana
*** Cycas (species)
*** Daubentonia (species)
  * Diosma ericoides
  * Dodonaea viscosa
 ** Elaeagnus pungens
 ** Euonymus japonicus
 ** Feijoa sellowiana
  * Grevillea (species)
*** Gossypium sturti
  * Hakea (species)
*** Halimium (species)
*** Helianthemum nummularium
 ** Hibiscus (species)

  * Juniperus (species)
  * Lagerstroemia indica
  * Lantana (species)
*** Leonotis leonurus
 ** Ligustrum japonicum
*** Lippia citriodora
*** Mahonia (species)
 ** Malvastrum (species)
  * Melaleuca (species)
 ** Myrsine africana
*** Myrtus communis
  * Nerium oleander
*** Odontospermum sericeum
 ** Phillyrea latifolia
  * Photinia serrulata
  * Pittosporum heterophyllum
 ** Plumbago capensis
 ** Poinciana (species)
*** Prostanthera nivea
 ** Prunus ilicifolia
***    " lusitanica
  * Punica granatum
 ** Rhamnus alaternus
 ** Rhus ovata
  * Rosmarinus officinalis
 ** Senecio petasitis
*** Sophora segundiflora
  * Spartium junceum
 ** Tamarix (species)
*** Templetonia retusa
  * Teucrium fruticans
 ** Thevetia nereifolia
  * Thryallis glauca
 ** Vitex agnus-castus

      * Xylosma senticosa

## VINES

  * Antigonon leptopus
  * Bougainvillea (varieties)
 ** Campsis (radicans)
 ** Cardiospermum halicacabum
 ** Clematis texensis
*** Cryptostegia grandiflora
  * Hedera canariensis
  * Holmskioldia sanguinea

 ** Jasminum officinale
  * Lonicera (check species)
 ** Muehlenbeckia complexa
*** Petrea volubilis
 ** Pueraria thunbergiana
*** Rothrockia cordifolia
 ** Solanum jasminoides
 ** Thunbergia (species)

     *** Vitis arizonica

## HERBACEOUS PLANTS

*** Abronia villosa
*** Acantholimon venustum
*** Aethionema coridifolium
*** Alyssum maritimum
 ** Amaranthus caudatus
 ** Amaryllis (species)
*** Amellus lychnitis
*** Anacyclus depressus
*** Angelonia grandiflora
  * Arctotis (species)
*** Argemone mexicana

*** Arrhenatherum tuberosum
 ** Brachycome iberidifolia
  * Brunsvigia rosea
 ** Ceratostigma plumbaginoides
*** Cheilanthes gracillima
*** Clianthus puniceus
  * Convolvulus (species)
 ** Cooperia drummondi
  * Coreopsis lanceolata
 ** Cortaderia selloana
  * Crinum (check species)

* Dianthus (species)
** Dimorphotheca (species)
*** Erodium (species)
** Eschscholtzia californica
** Euphorbia marginata
* Felicia amelloides
* Gaillardia aristata
* Gerberia jamesoni
*** Gilia capitata
** Gomphrena globosa
** Helichrysum petiolatum
*** Hunnemannia fumariaefolia
** Iresine herbsti
* Iris (check species)
** Lilium regale
** Limonium (species)
*** Lippia canescens
** Mirabilis jalapa
* Moraea (species)
*** Morisia monantha
** Nepeta mussini
* Nicotiana alata
** Oenothera (species)
* Pelargonium (species)

* Pellaea andromedaefolia
* Penstemon (check species)
** Petunia hybrida
* Phlox drummondi
*** Phygelius capensis
** Physostegia virginiana
* Portulaca grandiflora
** Salpiglossis sinuata
* Salvia (species)
*** Sanvitalia procumbens
* Senecio (species)
** Stokesia laevis
*** Thymophylla tenuiloba
* Thymus serpyllum
*** Tithonia rotundifolia
*** Torenia fournieri
** Tropaeolum (check species)
*** Tunica saxifraga
*** Ursinia anthemoides
* Venidium (species)
** Verbena (species)
* Vinca rosea
*** Xeranthemum annuum
* Zinnia elegans

## COOLNESS

This is the lack of heat and in this instance relates back to cold soils primarily. Shade in some degree and especially that of over-head shade has its cooling effect.....partially a by-product of transpiration. A north slope is cool, also an exposure that is bathed in breeze. Here is presented an opportunity and suggestion of place to use these plants that are not up to hard heat. They will like and respond favorably to the acid reaction, high humus content and greater depth of soil generally found under these site conditions.

### TREES

*** Abies venusta
*** Acer macrophyllum
** Alnus (species)
** Annona cherimola
*** Barkleya syringifolia
* Chamaecyparis lawsoniana
** Crinodendron dependens
*** Drimys winteri
*** Embothrium coccineum
** Eucalyptus ficifolia
** Fraxinus dipetala
** Harpullia arborea

*** Lithocarpus densiflora
* Lagunaria patersoni
** Lyonothamnus asplenifolius
*** Markhamia lutea
** Maytenus boaria
* Pinus torreyana
* Podocarpus (species)
*** Quillaja saponaria
*** Sequoia sempervirens
*** Sciadopitys verticillata
*** Talauma hodgsoni
*** Torreya (species)

** Umbellularia californica

### SHRUBS

*** Abelia schumanni
** Aeonium spathulatum
** Acokanthera spectabilis
* Arbutus unedo
*** Arctostaphylos (check species)
* Azalea (species)
** Azara microphylla
*** Berberidopsis corallina
** Berberis darwini
*** Brickellia grandiflora
* Brunfelsia calycina
* Calceolaria integrifolia
** Cantua buxifolia
** Ceanothus arboreus
* Cercocarpus betuloides
** Clethra arborea
* Cocculus laurifolius
* Coprosma baueri

** Cornus capitata
*** Corynocarpus laevigata
*** Daboetia cantabrica
** Daphne odora
* Eranthemum nervosum
* Escallonia (species)
*** Fabiana imbricata
* Fatsia japonica
* Fuchsia (species)
** Galvesia speciosa
** Griselinia littoralis
* Hamelia erecta
*** Hazardia cana
* Hebe (species)
** Heterocentron roseum
* Hydrangea macrophylla
*** Hymenanthera crassifolia
*** Illicium anisatum

** Iochroma (species)                  * Raphiolepis indica
** Itea ilicifolia                    ** Ribes (species)
 * Jacobinia (species)               *** Rondeletia cordata
 * Juniperus conferta                *** Ruellia devosiana
*** Luculia gratissima                 * Sarcococca hookeriana
** Lupinus arboreus                    * Solanum rantonneti
*** Magnolia stellata                  * Ternstroemia japonica
** Michelia fuscata                  *** Thea sinensis
 * Nandina domestica                 *** Trevesia palmata
** Ochna floribunda                    * Turraea obtusifolia
** Olmediella betschleriana          *** Thunbergia erecta
*** Prostanthera nivea                 * Viburnum (species)
 * Prunus lyoni                      *** Visnea mocanera

## VINES

** Ampelopsis brevipedunculata       *** Jasminum azoricum
** Cissus striata                    *** Lapageria rosea
 * Clematis (species)                *** Lygodium japonicum
** Ficus minima                        * Mandevilla suaveolens
 * Hedera helix                      *** Oxera pulchella
*** Hidalgoa wercklei                  * Stephanotis floribunda
** Hoya carnosa                      *** Stigmaphyllon littorale
*** Hylocereus triangularis            * Trachelospermum jasminoides

## HERBACEOUS PLANTS

** Abronia umbellata                   * Lupinus (check species)
*** Achimenes longiflora             *** Mentha requieni
 * Adiantum cuneatum                   * Mimulus luteus
*** Arum italicum                      * Myosotis alpestris
 * Begonia (species)                  ** Narcissus pseudo-narcissus
 * Brodiaea (check species)            * Nemesia strumosa
*** Canarina campanuloides            ** Nemophila menziesi
 * Cineraria cruenta                 *** Nertera depressa
 * Clarkia elegans                    ** Oxalis (species)
** Coleus blumei                      ** Pasithea caerulea
*** Cyrtanthus (species)             *** Pilea microphylla
*** Cymbalaria (species)               * Primula (species)
** Dicentra formosa                  *** Rivina humilis
** Echeveria (species)               *** Rohdea japonica
** Epidendrum obrienianum             ** Saxifraga sarmentosa
** Exacum affine                      ** Sedum (check species)
** Francoa ramosa                     ** Schizanthus wisetonensis
 * Godetia grandiflora               *** Schizocentron elegans
** Hedychium (species)               *** Streptocarpus hybridus
** Helxine soleiroli                  ** Tagetes erecta
 * Heuchera sanguinea                *** Tecophilaea cyanocrocus
** Impatiens sultani                   * Thalictrum dipterocarpum
*** Ionopsidium acaule               *** Tropaeolum speciosum
*** Leucocoryne ixioides               * Viola (species)
 * Ligularia kaempferi               *** Wedelia trilobata
** Lobelia erinus                      * Zantedeschia aethiopica

DROUGHT---and plants notably resistant. This quality is centered largely in the cellular structure and has a bearing on the economy with which the plant functions. Some plants have the ability to carry through extended dry periods because of a happy faculty of closing the pores of the leaf against transpiration, or turn the leaf back or edge-on to the sun. Others root deeply to tap and have available for dry periods, any accumulated moisture of the sub-soil. A garden planted with no thought given to dry spells will give a good account of itself spring and early summer, but without irrigation bogs down the rest of the season. On a small scale, peat or leafmold as a mulch and worked into the soil is effective. Deciduous and near deciduous species are more completely so in dryish ground, which will also favor dormancy and a higher health-tone so vital in the sub-tropics. Check with NATIVE PLANTS for material with this bent built in.

## TREES

  * Acacia (check species)          * Grevillea robusta
 ** Achras zapota                   ** Koelreuteria paniculata
*** Agonis (species)                ** Lagunaria patersoni
 ** Aleurites molucella             ** Lysiloma latisiliqua
  * Brachychiton (species)          ** Melia azedarach
*** Butia capitata                   * Olea europaea
*** Callitris robusta                * Parkinsonia aculeata
  * Casuarina (species)            *** Phytolacca dioica
*** Celtis australis                ** Pinus (check species)
*** Chorisia speciosa               ** Quercus (check species)
 ** Citherexylum spinosum            * Schinus (species)
 ** Coccolobis floridana             * Tamarix aphylla
  * Cupressus (species)             ** Trachycarpus fortunei
*** Delonix regia                  *** Vitex lucens
  * Eucalyptus (check species)     *** Zizyphus jujuba

## SHRUBS

  * Acacia (check species)         *** Hibiscus tiliaceus
  * Adenocarpus viscosus           *** Ilex (check species)
  * Callistemon (species)            * Lantana camara
*** Calothamnus quadrifidus          * Lavandula officinalis
*** Canella winterana                * Leptospermum (species)
 ** Cassia artemisioides             * Ligustrum (species)
  * Chamaelaucium ciliatum        *** Malvastrum (species)
  * Choisya ternata                  * Melaleuca (check species)
*** Cienfuegosia hakeaefolia       *** Myrtus communis
  * Cistus (species)                 * Nerium oleander
  * Correa pulchella               *** Phlomis fruticosa
 ** Cytisus canariensis             ** Pittosporum (check species)
  * Diosma ericoides               *** Polygala apopetala
 ** Dodonaea viscosa                ** Rhamnus alaternus
 ** Dovyalis caffra                *** Rhus lancea
 ** Erica melanthera                ** Rosmarinus officinalis
*** Eugenia jambos                 *** Royena lucida
*** Euryops (species)               ** Sarcococca hookeriana
 ** Genista monosperma               * Spartium junceum
*** Gossypium sturti                ** Tamarix (species)
  * Grevillea (species)             ** Teucrium fruticans
  * Hakea (species)                *** Thryallis glauca
 ** Halimium (check species)        ** Vitex agnus-castus
 ** Hymenanthera crassifolia        ** Westringia rosmariniformis

## VINES

 ** Asparagus (species)              * Lathyrus splendens
*** Boussingaultia baselloides      ** Lonicera halliana
 ** Cissus (check species)          ** Muehlenbeckia complexa
*** Dolichos lignosus              *** Passiflora mollissima
  * Doxantha unguis-cati           *** Podranea (species)
*** Hardenbergia monophylla         ** Polygonum auberti
 ** Jaquemontia eastwoodiana         * Sollya heterophylla
*** Kennedya rubicunda               * Tecomaria capensis

## HERBACEOUS PLANTS

*** Anagallis linifolia              * Dimorphotheca (species)
*** Aquilegia chrysantha             * Erigeron karvinskyanus
  * Arctotis (species)              ** Gaillardia aristata
  * Armeria maritima                 * Gazania (species)
  * Baileya multiradiata            ** Hemerocallis aurantiaca
  * Centaurea cineraria             ** Hyssopus officinalis
*** "        dealbata                * Iris (check species)
*** Chrysanthemum mawi             *** Kalanchoe (species)
*** Chusquea tessellata              * Limonium (species)
  * Cichorium intybus              *** Linum (species)
  * Convolvulus (species)            * Liriope spicata
 ** Coreopsis tinctoria              * Mirabilis jalapa
 ** Cosmos bipinnatus                * Moraea (check species)
 ** Cynoglossum amabile             ** Nepeta mussini
*** Diascea barberae                 * Nephrolepis exaltata

 ** Nicotiana alata                  ** Sedum (check species)
  * Oenothera (species)             ** Stokesia laevis
 ** Ophiopogon japonicus           *** Tanacetum capitatum
*** Oxypetalum caeruleum            ** Thymus (species)
 ** Pancratium (species)            ** Tulbaghia violacea
*** Puya alpestris                 *** Tunica saxifraga
  * Penstemon (species)             ** Vallota speciosa
 ** Petunia hybrida                *** Venidium (species)
*** Phacelia whitlavia               * Vinca major
*** Polypteris hookeriana          *** Xanthisma texanum
 ** Portulaca grandiflora            * Zephyranthes candida
 ** Scabiosa (species)              ** Zinnia linearis


SMOG---smoke, dust or fumes, air contaminants of whatever name or
origin will be a serious menace to plantings. Here are species known
to be resistant to the toxic and clogging effects of industrial or
downtown grime. In such places the plant works under a peculiar dis-
advantage and should be allowed every aid in growth....cultivation,
feeding and especially hosings from time to time. See to drainage
and as the soil becomes impregnated with these myriad impurities add
lime or gypsum as a corrective. Remember that low-lying areas suffer
most and that deciduous plants renew the foliage each spring while
that of the evergreen has to take it....and bear with.

## TREES

  * Acacia melanoxylon             *** Melaleuca leucadendra
 ** Ailanthus altissima             ** Melia azedarach
*** Broussonetia papyrifera         ** Morus (species)
*** Cercis siliquastrum            *** Parkinsonia aculeata
 ** Cupania anacardioides          *** Paulownia tomentosa
 ** Cupressus arizonica              * Phoenix canariensis
  * Dracaena australis               * Pittosporum undulatum
 ** Erythea (species)              *** Podocarpus elongata
  * Eucalyptus (check species)      ** Platanus orientalis
  * Ficus (check species)            * Populus (species)
 ** Ginkgo biloba                  *** Robinia pseudacacia
*** Koelreuteria paniculata        *** Sabal palmetto
*** Libocedrus decurrens            ** Salix babylonica
*** Liquidambar formosana            * Trachycarpus fortunei
 ** Magnolia grandiflora             * Washingtonia robusta

## SHRUBS

*** Acokanthera spectabilis          * Nerium oleander
*** Aeonium spathulatum            *** Olmediella betschleriana
 ** Arundinaria japonica            ** Osmanthus ilicifolius
*** Berberis wilsoni               *** Phillyrea latifolia
  * Buxus microphylla              *** Pittosporum heterophyllum
  * Callistemon lanceolatus          *       "       tobira
  * Cestrum (species)               ** Plumbago capensis
*** Chaenomeles japonica            ** Prunus lyoni
  * Chamaerops humilis             *** Pyracantha (species)
  * Cistus (species)                ** Raphiolepis indica
*** Cotoneaster (check species)      * Rhamnus alaternus
 ** Dodonaea viscosa               *** Rhus integrifolia
 ** Echium fastuosum                ** Rosa bracteata
  * Elaeagnus pungens              *** Sarcococca hookeriana
  * Euonymus japonicus              ** Senecio petasitis
*** Genista monosperma              ** Spartium junceum
 ** Hebe traversi                    * Tamarix (species)
*** Hibiscus rosa-sinensis          ** Tecomaria capensis
  * Juniperus pfitzeriana            ** Viburnum suspensum
  * Lantana (species)              *** Visnea mocanera
  * Laurus nobilis                  ** Vitex agnus-castus
 ** Leptospermum laevigatum        *** Weigela florida
  * Ligustrum ovalifolium           ** Westringia rosmariniformis
  * Melaleuca nesophila              * Wigandia caracasana
 ** Myrsine africana               *** Xylosma senticosa
 ** Myrtus communis                *** Zauschneria californica

## VINES

```
 ** Bougainvillea (varieties)      * Muehlenbeckia complexa
*** Clytostoma callistegioides     * Pandorea pandorana
 ** Doxantha unguis-cati           * Parthenocissus tricuspidata
  * Hedera canariensis            ** Phaedranthus buccinatorius
*** Jasminum officinalis          ** Polygonum auberti
 ** Lonicera halliana            *** Solanum jasminoides
               *** Wisteria floribunda
```

## HERBACEOUS PLANTS

```
 ** Acanthus mollis                * Iris germanica
  * Alyssum maritimum             ** Limonium perezi
  * Arctotis (species)           *** Lysimachia nummularia
 ** Armeria maritima               * Mirabilis jalapa
*** Aristea eckloni              *** Moraea iridioides
*** Baileya multiradiata         *** Nepeta mussini
*** Begonia semperflorens         ** Oenothera tetraptera
*** Bergenia cordifolia           ** Ophiopogon japonicus
*** Campanula isophylla            * Pelargonium (species)
  * Celosia (species)            ** Petunia hybrida
 ** Cichorium intybus            *** Phormium tenax
 ** Ceratostigma plumbaginoides   ** Portulaca grandiflora
  * Chrysanthemum maximum          * Salvia (species)
  * Coreopsis tinctoria          ** Tagetes erecta
 ** Euphorbia marginata          *** Thalictrum dipterocarpum
  * Gaillardia aristata          *** Tradescantia virginiana
  * Gazania (species)             ** Tulbaghia violacea
 ** Hemerocallis aurantiaca      *** Venidium fastuosum
*** Heuchera sanguinea             * Vinca major
```

ALKALI---is an accumulation of salts in the soil detrimental to
plant life. Its presence in topsoils is due primarily to poor drainage and is more often found in the heavier textures. The only rational and lasting solution to this noxious condition lies in drainage..
..and again drainage, although cultivation helps in-so-far as the immediate surface is concerned. Slaked or agricultural lime, sulphur,
gypsum or marl may be added as correctives to bring about beneficial
chemical changes. These reactions relieve the situation, but in the
last analysis, it is again drainage that cleans out the ground. The
concentration of a few or single salts, as found inland, is more virulent to vegetation than the mixed salts or brine of the ocean.

## TREES

```
  * Acacia longifolia            ** Melia azedarach
 **     "    melanoxylon          * Morus rubra
***     "    pycnantha            * Parkinsonia aculeata
*** Ailanthus altissima           * Phoenix (species)
*** Albizzia lophantha            * Pinus halepensis
  * Brachychiton populneum        * Pistacia chinensis
  * Casuarina (species)          ** Platanus racemosa
*** Celtis australis              * Populus fremonti
*** Chilopsis linearis           ** Quercus agrifolia
 ** Cinnamomum camphora         ***     "     lobata
  * Eucalyptus (check species)   **     "     suber
  * Ficus macrophylla           *** Robinia pseudacacia
 ** Fraxinus velutina           *** Sapindus saponaria
 ** Grevillea robusta            ** Schinus molle
 ** Koelreuteria paniculata       * Tamarix aphylla
*** Lagunaria patersoni         *** Ulmus crassifolia
*** Maclura pomifera             **     "    pumila
 ** Melaleuca leucadendra         * Washingtonia filifera
***     "      styphelioides    *** Zizyphus jujuba
               *** Yucca brevifolia
```

## SHRUBS

```
 ** Acacia armata               *** Ceanothus grizeus
  * Atriplex lentiformis        *** Cryptostegia grandiflora
  * Callistemon lanceolatus      ** Cytisus canariensis
 ** Cassia artemisioides          * Dodonaea viscosa
```

* Elaeagnus pungens
** Eriogonum fasciculatum
** Eucalyptus torquata
*** Hibiscus rosa-sinensis
** Juniperus californica
** Lagerstroemia indica
* Lantana (species)
** Lavandula officinalis
*** Lawsonia inermis
*** Leptospermum laevigatum
* Leucophyllum texanum
*** Lippia citriodora
* Lycium (species)
* Melaleuca (species)
** Muehlenbeckia complexa
* Myoporum laetum

** Myrsine africana
* Myrtus communis
* Pittosporum crassifolium
***     "      phillyraeoides
** Poinciana pulcherrima
* Prosopis (species)
** Prunus ilicifolia
** Punica granatum
*** Pyracantha coccinea
* Spartium junceum
* Tamarix (species)
** Thevetia nereifolia
*** Thryallis glauca
*** Triphasia trifolia
*** Viburnum tinus
*** Zizyphus obtusifolia

## HERBACEOUS PLANTS

*** Antigonon leptopus
* Abronia villosa
* Anemopsis californica
* Aloe (species)
** Arundo donax
*** Aster amellus
** Calendula officinalis
** Chrysanthemum frutescens
***     "       maximum
** Cortaderia selloana
*** Cosmos bipinnatus
* Cynodon dactylon
* Cyperus rotundus
** Dimorphotheca (species)
*** Frankenia laevis

** Gazania (species)
*** Gerberia jamesoni
** Grindelia robusta
*** Hesperaloe parviflora
** Iris germanica
* Iris unguicularis
*** Juncus lescuri
*** Lilium regale
** Mesembryanth. (species)
** Oenothera (species)
* Phormium tenax
*** Portulacca grandiflora
* Stanleya pinnata
*** Verbena (species)
* Yucca tenuistyla

SOILS---with various aspects of utmost importance in the growth of
plants. We take ground as it is, preferably, and build up from there,
rather than disturb artificially by import. Loam is a median texture
and for normal garden purposes the most desirable. Good management,
then, means bringing any extreme toward the center by use of amendments, if necessary, but always followed by humus-making materials or
compost....manure gives life. Furnish your soil and you supply your
plants. The chemical fertilizers have their place and can come later.
While fruiting is of secondary importance, the matter of flowering and
general tone of the plant should leave one with the impression of
vigor and enthusiasm. This can be had only when the plant is satisfied with the ground in which it stands. Consideration should be giv-
en to the physical texture, depth, moisture content, fertility and
sometimes the chemical reaction. Attention to any one or all of these
becomes more mandatory as the condition becomes extreme. Plants of
strong growth and otherwise rugged attainments, will more easily surmount a contrary situation in these respects, but even then the natural wants will best be followed for degree and quality of growth.

## FERTILE SOILS

Many plants thrive only in a rich soil. They seem to be of
good assimilative capacity and readily expand in growth where another plant may be thrown off balance by too much available food. The
gross feeders that follow, appear to be agreeable to the fleshpots
and may be depended upon to make the most of exceedingly rich ground
without over-reaching growth or disturbance in blooming.

## TREES

** Acacia pendula
***     "   prominens
*** Barklya syringifolia
* Bauhinia variegata
*** Bocconia frutescens
** Calodendrum capense
*** Cercis siliquastrum

** Diospyros kaki
** Erythrina humeana
*** Eucalyptus caesia
**     "      erythrocorys
*     "      ficifolia
** Fraxinus velutina
* Jacaranda acutifolia

* Juniperus torulosa
* Macadamia ternifolia
* Magnolia grandiflora
*** Paulownia tomentosa
** Persea (species)
** Phoenix reclinata
***    "   rupicola

* Pittosporum rhombifolium
**    "   undulatum
* Quercus (species)
** Sabal palmetto
*** Spathodea campanulata
*** Virgilia capensis
* Vitex lucens

## SHRUBS

* Abelia (check species)
*** Acokanthera spectabilis
*** Artabotrys uncinatus
*** Aucuba japonica
** Azara microphylla
** Bambusa multiplex
* Berberis (species)
* Brunfelsia calycina
** Buddleja lindleyana
*** Cantua buxifolia
* Cestrum (species)
*** Choisya ternata
** Coronilla glauca
* Duranta stenostachya
*** Eranthemum nervosum
*** Ervatamia coronaria
* Erythrina crista-galli
** Fatsia japonica
** Feijoa sellowiana
* Fuchsia (species)
*** Grewia occidentalis
** Hamelia erecta
* Hibiscus rosa-sinensis
* Hydrangea macrophylla
* Hypericum (species)

** Ilex (species)
*** Illicium (species)
*** Iochroma (species)
*** Ixora chinensis
* Jacobinia (species)
* Murraea exotica
* Nandina domestica
** Phoenix roebelini
*** Pimelea ferruginea
** Prunus lyoni
** Raphiolepis (species)
*** Rhapis (species)
** Ribes (species)
** Russelia equisetiformis
** Sambucus (species)
** Sarcococca hookeriana
*** Solanum rantonneti
*** Sollya heterophylla
* Streptosolen jamesoni
** Tecoma (species)
* Thevetia nereifolia
*** Thunbergia erecta
* Viburnum (species)
*** Weigela florida
*** Zamia floridana

## VINES

*** Agdesta clematidea
*** Artabotrys odoratissimus
* Beaumontia grandiflora
*** Bomaria (species)
** Boussingaultia baselloides
* Clematis (species)
*** Clytostoma callistegioides
*** Doxantha unguis-cati
* Gelsemium sempervirens
* Hibbertia volubilis

** Jasminum (species)
* Lathyrus odoratus
*** Lonicera hildebrandtiana
** Mandevilla suaveolens
** Pandorea (species)
** Phaedranthus buccinatorius
** Podranea (species)
*** Stauntonia hexaphylla
*** Tecomaria capensis
** Thunbergia (species)

* Trachelospermum jasminoides

## HERBACEOUS PLANTS

* Acalypha wilksiana
*** Acanthus (species)
* Agapanthus africana
* Ageratum houstonianum
* Alstroemeria (species)
*** Anagallis linifolia
*** Anemone (species)
*** Antirrhinum majus
** Arum italicum
*** Aster amellus
* Bergenia (species)
*** Brunsvigia rosea
*** Calceolaria (species)
*** Callistephus chinensis
* Campanula (species)
* Chrysanthemum morifolium
* Cineraria cruenta
* Clivia (species)
** Collinsia (species)
*** Colocasia antiquorum

* Crinum (species)
*** Cyanella orchidiformis
* Cyclamen indicum
*** Cypella herberti
** Cyperus (species)
* Dahlia pinnata
*** Delphinium grandiflorum
*** Diascia barberae
*** Eucharis grandiflora
*** Eucomis undulata
* Galtonia candicans
* Heuchera sanguinea
** Iris delta hybrids
***    "   japonica
*    "   kaempferi
** Ligularia kaempferi
** Lobelia erinus
** Malcomia maritima
** Mathiola incana
*** Milla biflora

** Narcissus pseudo-narcissus
*** Nemesia strumosa
*** Nerine (species)
* Nicotiana alata
** Petunia hybrida
** Phlox drummondi
** Physostegia virginiana
*** Rehmannia angulata
** Salpiglossis sinuata

* Strelitzia reginae
** Tagetes erecta
** Tigridia pavonia
** Torenia fournieri
*** Tritonia (species)
** Veronica (species)
* Viola (species)
** Zantedeschia (species)
*** Zinnia elegans

## SUCCULENTS

*** Aeonium (species)
* Bernesia weinbergi
** Echeveria (species)
*** Guzmania cardinalis
* Hoya carnosa
*** Hylocereus triangularis

*** Kalanchoe (species)
* Oliveranthus elegans
** Othonna crassifolia
** Pereskia aculeata
** Sansevieria zeylanica
*** Trichocereus candicans

* Zygocactus truncatus

## STERILE SOILS

The lack of a good soil need not be the handicap it may appear at first thought, and fertilizing is not necessarily the happy answer. Many vigorous plants will make the best of ill-furnished ground. Others have accustomed themselves to straightened circumstances over the ages, so that now they more nearly reach their typical form, with longer life and with richer color in bloom, than in a rich soil. Generally these plants will grow more slowly and become more dense in texture. Use tender plants in the poorer soils where they will develop less wood and ripen earlier in autumn to resist cold.

## TREES

*** Agathis robusta
** Albizzia lebbek
** Aleurites moluccana
** Celtis australis
* Ceratonia siliqua
** Cupressus macrocarpa
* Eucalyptus cladocalyx
** "       eremophila
*** "       erythronema
*** "       tereticornis
* Ficus (check species)
* Juniperus (check species)

*** Koelreuteria paniculata
** Melaleuca leucadendra
*** Melia azedarach
* Olea europaea
** Parkinsonia aculeata
* Phoenix (species)
* Pinus (species)
*** Quercus suber
** Schinus (species)
** Trachycarpus fortunei
* Ulmus pumila
*** Zizyphus jujuba

## SHRUBS

*** Arctostaphylos (species)
** Artemisia (species)
*** Calothamnus quadrifidus
** Catha edulis
* Ceratostigma willmottianum
** Chilopsis linearis
* Cistus (species)
* Correa (species)
* Cytisus canariensis
** Diosma ericoides
* Echium fastuosum
* Erica melanthera
** Eriogonum (species)
*** Garberia fruticosa
* Genista monosperma
** Grevillea (species)
** Hakea (species)
** Halimium halimifolium
*** Helichrysum diosmaefolium
** "        petiolatum
** Lavandula officinalis
** Leonotis leonurus
* Leptospermum (species)
** Mahernia verticillata

* Melaleuca (species)
*** Odontospermum sericeum
** Penstemon antirrhinoides
*** Phillyrea latifolia
** Pittosporum crassifolium
*** "        heterophyllum
** "        phillyraeoides
** Poinciana gilliesi
*** Prunus ilicifolia
*** Psidium cattleianum
** Rhus (species)
* Rosmarinus officinalis
*** Ruscus aculeatus
*** Salvia greggi
*** Siphonosmanthus delavayi
* Spartium junceum
** Tamarix (species)
** Teucrium fruticans
*** Thryallis glauca
*** Trichostema lanatum
*** Viburnum suspensum
** Vitex agnus-castus
* Wigandia caracasana
*** Zauschneria californica

## VINES

| | |
|---|---|
| ** Aloe ciliaris | * Lonicera halliana |
| *** Araujia sericofera | *** Muehlenbeckia complexa |
| ** Cissus capensis | ** Passiflora alato-caerulea |
| * Fatshedera lizei | ** Phaseolus caracalla |
| * Ficus pumila | ** Polygonum auberti |
| *** Hedera canariensis | ** Pueraria thunbergiana |
| *** Jasminum azoricum | * Pyrostegia ignea |
| *      "      mesneyi | * Solandra guttata |
| *** Lathyrus splendens | *** Thunbergia grandiflora |
| ** Lonicera confusa | *** Vitis voinieriana |

## HERBACEOUS PLANTS

| | |
|---|---|
| ** Abronia (species) | * Limonium (species) |
| *** Achillea (species) | *** Linum (species) |
| *** Aethionema coridifolium | ** Lippia canescens |
| ** Amaranthus (species) | * Liriope spicata |
| ** Asclepias currassavica | ** Mirabilis jalapa |
| *** Baileya multiradiata | *** Monardella lanceolata |
| *** Browallia americana | * Moraea (species) |
| * Calendula officinalis | *** Morisia monantha |
| * Ceratostigma plumbaginoides | ** Nepeta mussini |
| * Chrysanthemum frutescens | * Nephrolepis exaltata |
| ** Clarkia elegans | *** Oenothera (species) |
| * Coreopsis (species) | *** Papaver (species) |
| ** Cortaderia selloana | * Pelargonium (species) |
| * Cosmos bipinnatus | ** Pellaea andromedaefolia |
| * Cynoglossum amabile | *** Penstemon (species) |
| *** Delphinium ajacis | * Portulaca grandiflora |
| ** Dianthus (species) | *** Reineckia carnea |
| * Dimorphotheca (species) | * Salvia (species) |
| * Erigeron karvinskyanus | ** Santolina chamaecyparissus |
| * Felicia (species) | *** Sparaxis tricolor |
| ** Gaillardia aristata | ** Tagetes patula |
| * Gazania (species) | *** Thalictrum dipterocarpum |
| *** Habranthus (species) | ** Thymus serpyllum |
| * Hemerocallis aurantiaca | *** Tradescantia virginiana |
| ** Helianthemum nummularium | ** Tropaeolum (species) |
| * Iris germanica | ** Vinca (species) |
| **    "    unguicularis | *** Woodwardia radicans |
| ***    "    xiphium | *** Xanthisma texanum |
| ** Kniphofia uvaria | *** Xeranthemum annuum |
| *** Lilium (species) | *** Zephyranthes candida |

## SUCCULENTS

| | |
|---|---|
| ** Agave (species) | ** Opuntia (species) |
| * Aloe (species) | ** Pachyphytum bracteosum |
| * Crassula (species) | *** Portulacaria afra |
| *** Cyanotis hirsuta | *** Sempervivum tectorum |
| ** Mesembryanth. (species) | * Yucca (species) |

## LIGHT SOILS

Blooming is more precipitate and the flower of shorter duration in soils of light texture. Such ground is warm and better able
to support plants making fine roots and those that are inclined to
root more deeply.  Shade is complementary and as a rule, setting out
is better done in the fall to establish before summer heat. Adverse
factors are heat, drought, over-aeration and withering sun. These
soils are less fertile due to leaching. They are formed of larger
particles, with correspondingly larger spaces between; and, strange
as it may seem, have less storage capacity for water than the heavier
soils. Sand enters largely into their structure and the invariably
low humus content may be built up by working in manures or compost.

## TREES

| | |
|---|---|
| * Acacia (species) | *** Cinnamomum camphora |
| *** Acrocomia totai | *** Cupressus (species) |
| ** Araucaria excelsa | ** Dracaena australis |
| * Brachychiton (species) | ** Eucalyptus ficifolia |
| ** Calodendrum capense | * Grevillea robusta |
| * Casuarina (species) | *** Hymenosporum flavum |

```
  * Jacaranda acutifolia          ** Pistacia chinensis
*** Juniperus silicicola         *** Prunus amygdalus
  * Lagunaria patersoni           ** Quercus agrifolia
 ** Libocedrus decurrens          ***    " lobata
*** Melaleuca styphelioides        ** Podocarpus (species)
 ** Metrosideros tomentosa        *** Sapindus saponaria
  * Olea europaea                 *** Samanea saman
 ** Parkinsonia aculeata           ** Tamarix aphylla
 ** Pinus (species)               *** Thespesia populnea
  * Pittosporum crassifolium        * Tristania conferta
 **     " eugenioides              ** Virgilia capensis
***     " rhombifolium            *** Vitex lucens
```

## SHRUBS

```
  * Acacia (check species)         * Genista monosperma
 ** Acokanthera spectabilis        * Grevillea (species)
*** Adenocarpus viscosus         *** Greyia sutherlandi
*** Anthyllis barba-jovis        *** Halimium ocymoides
*** Arctostaphylos glauca        *** Hebe hulkeana
  * Atriplex (species)             * Juniperus conferta
  * Azalea (species)              ** Laurus nobilis
 ** Berberis darwini               * Leptospermum (species)
 ** Breynia nivosa                ** Lycium (species)
  * Callistemon (species)         ** Mahonia nevini
*** Carpenteria californica        * Murraea exotica
  * Cassia artemisioides         *** Pimelea ferruginia
  * Ceanothus (species)            * Plumbago capensis
  * Choisya ternata                * Poinciana gilliesi
 ** Chrysobalanus icaco           ** Polygala dalmaisiana
  * Cistus (species)              ** Prunus (species)
*** Convolvulus cneorum          *** Ribes viburnifolium
 ** Coronilla glauca             *** Romneya coulteri
 ** Correa (species)              ** Solanum rantonneti
*** Cytisus canariensis            * Sollya heterophylla
 ** Datura sanguinea              ** Streptosolen jamesoni
*** Daubentonia (species)          * Tamarix (species)
*** Elaeagnus pungens            *** Templetonia retusa
 ** Fatsia japonica              *** Teucrium fruticans
 ** Feijoa sellowiana            *** Thryallis glauca
           *** Zauschneria californica
```

## VINES

```
 ** Ampelopsis brevipedunculata    * Mandevilla suaveolens
  * Antigonon leptopus           *** Quamoclit (species)
 ** Asparagus (species)          *** Polygonum auberti
  * Clematis (species)           *** Senecio mikanioides
*** Gloriosa superba              ** Solanum wendlandi
 ** Hibbertia volubilis            * Stigmaphyllon ciliatum
*** Jaquemontia eastwoodiana      ** Trachelospermum jasminoides
  * Jasminum (species)           *** Vitis voineriana
```

## HERBACEOUS PLANTS

```
 ** Acaena microphylla           *** Clianthus puniceus
*** Albuca minor                 *** Clitoria ternatea
 ** Alstroemeria (species)         * Convolvulus (species)
  * Alyssum maritimum            *** Cooperia drummondi
 ** Anemone coronaria              * Cosmos bipinnatus
  * Antirrhinum majus              * Cynoglossum amabile
  * Arctotis (species)             * Dimorphotheca (species)
 ** Arenaria balearica            ** Eschscholtzia californica
  * Armeria maritima             *** Francoa ramosa
 ** Asclepias currassavica        ** Gaillardia aristata
  * Aster amellus                 ** Gerberia jamesoni
 ** Babiana stricta                * Gilia (species)
*** Befaria racemosa             *** Heliophila pilosa
  * Calendula officinalis         ** Heliotropium arborescens
  * Callistephus chinensis         * Heuchera sanguinea
  * Campanula isophylla            * Ixia maculata
 ** Centaureum (species)         *** Lagurus ovatus
  * Clarkia (species)             ** Layia elegans
```

  * Lilium (species)                ** Portulaca grandiflora
  * Limonium (species)               * Primula (species)
*** Linum (species)                *** Sanvitalia procumbens
 ** Lupinus (species)              *** Satureja (species)
*** Lycoris radiata                 ** Sparaxis tricolor
  * Mathiola incana                 ** Stokesia laevis
 ** Nemophila menziesi             *** Streptanthera cuprea
*** Nertera depressa                ** Tagetes (species)
*** Nolana atriplicifolia          *** Thymophylla tenuiloba
 ** Oenothera (species)             * Tritonia (species)
  * Oliveranthus elegans           *** Ursinia anthemoides
 ** Ornithogalum (species)         *** Venidium decurrens
*** Pancratium maritimum           *** Wedelia trilobata
  * Papaver (species)              *** Xanthisma texanum
*** Paronychia argentea             ** Zephyranthes rosea

## HEAVY SOILS

Avoid plants in these soils that have difficulty with wet feet, especially where rain comes during the winter. This is cold ground, with deficient aeration and consequent low bacterial count. Full sun is complementary and spring planting desirable for plants that are sensitive to cold. Generally, plants with a shallow rooting habit and those requiring uniform moisture will be used here with more favorable results. The matter of drainage should be watched closely. Sprinkle loose soils for efficient irrigation, but use the open trench wherever practicable in a heavy one, with less frequency in application. These soils are potentially more fertile....use amendments and compost or manures to release and hold nutrients.

### TREES

*** Achras zapota                   * Magnolia grandiflora
*** Annona cherimola              *** Melaleuca leucadendra
 ** Araucaria (species)           *** Michelia champaca
  * Arecastrum romanzoffianum     *** Morus rubra
 ** Blighia sapida                 ** Pinus pinea
*** Casimiroa edulis                *  "   radiata
*** Cassia grandis                 ** Pittosporum undulatum
 ** Cedrus atlantica              ***      "   viridiflorum
 ** Chamaecyparis lawsoniana        * Platanus orientalis
*** Crinodendron dependens          * Prunus caroliniana
  * Eriobotrya japonica             * Pyrus calleryana
*** Eucalyptus polyanthemos        ** Taxus baccata stricta
 **      "      rostrata           ** Thuja orientalis
  *      "      sideroxylon       *** Tipuana tipu
  * Eugenia (species)             *** Torreya taxifolia
  * Ficus (species)                ** Trachycarpus fortunei
 ** Liquidambar styraciflua         * Ulmus parvifolia

### SHRUBS

  * Abelia grandiflora              * Fuchsia (varieties
 ** Acalypha hispida              *** Galvesia speciosa
  * Arbutus unedo                  ** Hamelia erecta
*** Arctostaphylos diversifolia    ** Hebe (species)
*** Bambusa multiplex             *** Heimia myrtifolia
*** Berberis gagnepaini            ** Heteromeles arbutifolia
 ** Buddleja (species)              * Hibiscus rosa-sinensis
 ** Canella winterana              ** Hypericum (species)
 ** Ceanothus arboreus             ** Ilex (species)
  * Ceratostigma (species)         ** Iochroma (species)
  * Cestrum (species)              ** Lagerstroemia indica
 ** Chaenomeles japonica           ** Lavandula officinalis
 ** Chamaerops humilis             ** Mackaya bella
  * Clerodendrum (species)          * Mahonia (species)
*** Cocculus laurifolius          *** Malpighia coccigera
*** Cornus capitata                ** Malvaviscus grandiflorus
  * Cotoneaster (species)         *** Michelia fuscata
*** Datura suaveolens               * Myrsine africana
*** Dovyalis caffra               *** Oncoba routledgi
  * Duranta (species)             *** Osteomeles anthyllidifolia
 ** Escallonia (species             * Phillyrea latifolia

* Photinia serrulata
*** Pittosporum heterophyllum
  *       "     tobira
*** Prunus lusitanica
** Psidium cattleianum
** Punica granatum
* Pyracantha (species)
* Raphiolepis (species)
** Rhus (species)

*** Ribes (species)
* Rosa (species)
*** Senecio petasitis
** Spiraea cantoniensis
* Stenolobium stans
*** Thevetia nereifolia
** Viburnum (species)
** Weigela florida
** Umbellularia californica

*** Zamia floridana

## VINES

*** Bauhinia corymbosa
*** Campsidium valdivianum
** Clerodendrum thompsonae
* Clytostoma callistegioides
** Doxantha unguis-cati
* Ficus pumila
*** Jasminum mesneyi

*** Kennedya rubicunda
* Lonicera (check species)
** Muehlenbeckia complexa
*** Pandorea (species)
* Phaedranthus buccinatorius
*** Pyrostegia ignea
* Thunbergia (species)

** Wisteria floribunda

## HERBACEOUS PLANTS

*** Acidanthera bicolor
* Agapanthus africanus
* Ajuga reptans
* Amaryllis (species)
* Anemone japonica
*** Aristea eckloni
*** Aster gracillimus
*** Aquilegia chrysantha
*** Brodiaea (species)
* Bergenia cordifolia
* Brunsvigia rosea
* Campanula poscharskyana
** Celosia (species)
** Chrysanthemum (species)
*** Cichorium intybus
** Cortaderia selloana
* Crinum (species)
** Cyperus (species)
** Dahlia pinnata
*** Dianella intermedia
** Dianthus (species)
*** Elisena longipetala
** Eupatorium sordidum
** Euphorbia (species)
** Geum (varieties)

*** Gladiolus (species)
*** Hedychium (species)
* Hemerocallis aurantiaca
* Kniphofia uvaria
* Lobelia erinus
* Mentha pulegium
** Nepeta mussini
*** Nerine sarniensis
** Oenothera hookeri
*** Origanum dictamnus
* Penstemon (species)
** Petasitis fragrans
* Petunia hybrida
** Phormium tenax
** Ranunculus (species)
*** Rehmannia angulata
*** Schizanthus wisetonensis
** Senecio cineraria
* Sisyrinchium (species)
*** Sternbergia lutea
* Veronica (species)
* Viola (species)
*** Woodwardia radicans
* Zephyranthes candida
*** Zebrina pendula

## GRAVELLY SOILS

A plant is required here that is equipped to penetrate extremely open, loose, sandy or rocky structures. This suggests a root system of an enquiring, explorative bent, the best being that of such harsh, stringy character as to develop out of all proportion to the top in its search for sustenance and moisture. This is an extreme in the open structure and may be checked back with LIGHT SOILS.

## TREES

*** Acacia greggi
  *    "    melanoxylon
** "    prominens
*** Callitris robusta
*** Cercis (species)
* Chilopsis linearis
** Cupressus (check species)
* Eucalyptus (check species)
** Ficus carica
** Grevillea robusta
** Juglans (species)
* Juniperus (species)

*** Morus rubra
* Parkinsonia aculeata
** Phoenix (species)
* Pinus (species)
*** Pistacia chinensis
* Pittosporum phillyraeoides
** Populus fremonti
* Quercus agrifolia
**   "    ilex
*** "    suber
** Sabal palmetto
* Tamarix aphylla

*** Torreya californica

## SHRUBS

| | | | |
|---|---|---|---|
| * | Acacia armata | ** | Lycium (species) |
| *** | "    horrida | * | Mahonia (species) |
| ** | "    verticillata | ** | Malvastrum (species) |
| ** | Adenocarpus viscosus | *** | Medicago arborea |
| *** | Adenostoma (species) | * | Melaleuca nesophila |
| *** | Arctostaphylos (species) | * | Nerium oleander |
| *** | Artemisia tridentata | ** | Penstemon antirrhinoides |
| * | Baccharis (species) | *** | Phygelius capensis |
| *** | Boronia elatior | *** | Polygala apopetala |
| * | Ceanothus cyaneus | ** | Prosopis (species) |
| ** | "    grizeus | * | Prunus ilicifolia |
| * | Cercocarpus betuloides | ** | "    lyoni |
| * | Chamaelaucium ciliatum | *** | Puya alpestris |
| * | Cistus (species) | ** | Quercus dumosa |
| *** | Coprosma baueri | ** | "    pumila |
| ** | Cytisus canariensis | ** | Rhamnus (species) |
| *** | Daubentonia puniceus | *** | Ribes malvaceum |
| ** | Dovyalis caffra | ** | Rhus laurina |
| * | Echium fastuosum | * | Romneya coulteri |
| ** | Eriogonum (species) | *** | Solanum xanti |
| *** | Fabiana imbricata | * | Spartium junceum |
| ** | Fremontia (species) | *** | Stenolobium stans |
| *** | Garberia fruticosa | * | Tamarix (species) |
| *** | Garrya elliptica | ** | Tecomaria capensis |
| * | Genista monosperma | * | Tetrapanax papyrifera |
| ** | Gossypium sturti | ** | Teucrium fruticans |
| *** | Grevillea rosmarinifolia | *** | Trichostema lanatum |
| * | Hakea (species) | *** | Triphasia trifolia |
| *** | Halimium halimifolium | *** | Ungnadia speciosa |
| *** | Hazardia cana | *** | Vitis arizonica |
| *** | Hymenanthera crassifolia | * | Wigandia caracasana |
| ** | Juniperus conferta | ** | Yucca (species) |
| * | "    pfitzeriana | * | Zauschneria californica |

## HERBACEOUS PLANTS

| | | | |
|---|---|---|---|
| * | Abronia (species) | * | Hunnemannia fumariaefolia |
| *** | Acantholimon venustum | * | Lathyrus splendens |
| *** | Aethionema coridifolium | * | Limonium (species) |
| ** | Aloe (species) | *** | Linum (species) |
| ** | Argemone mexicana | ** | Liriope spicata |
| ** | Centranthus ruber | ** | Lupinus (species) |
| * | Ceratostigma plumbaginoides | * | Mesembryanth. (species) |
| *** | Cheiranthus mutabilis | ** | Monardella lanceolata |
| * | Cichorium intybus | * | Moraea iridioides |
| *** | Cirsium occidentale | ** | Nicotiana alata |
| ** | Cleome spinosa | ** | Oenothera (species) |
| * | Convolvulus (species) | ** | Penstemon australis |
| *** | Dicentra chrysantha | ** | "    heterophyllus |
| * | Glaucium flavum | * | Salvia (species) |
| *** | Hesperaloe parviflora | *** | Tropaeolum speciosum |
| *** | Hesperocallis undulata | *** | Venidium decurrens |

## SHALLOW SOILS

This ground will best be set to trees and shrubs that normally develop a spreading root system naturally or one that adapts readily. It will be found that even with herbaceous materials the flat, matted root systems react best closer to sun and air. They will make the most of a thin layer of soil overlying hardpan or an overburden to a high water table. Examine the matter of blasting carefully. This solution is too easy, and probably indicates that trees or others are to be attempted where they do not belong. Consider whether or not soil importation is cheaper....it will be better. However; to blast, spring a small chamber with quick-acting dynamite, for slow-acting black powder which raises and cracks the formation beneficially to let soil and moisture in and provide foothold.

## TREES

| | | | |
|---|---|---|---|
| * | Acacia (species) | ** | Aleurites moluccana |
| ** | Albizzia julibrissin | * | Arecastrum romanzoffianum |
| *** | "    lophantha | ** | Cassia (check species) |

*** Cedrus atlantica
  * Crinodendron dependens
  * Cupressus forbsi
 **     " goveniana
 ** Erythea (species)
  * Eucalyptus (check species)
 ** Eugenia paniculata
 ** Ficus carica
*** Juniperus silicicola
 ** Melaleuca leucadendra
  * Olea europaea
*** Peltophorum inerme
 ** Phoenix reclinata

*** Pinus attenuata
  *     " edulis
 **     " torreyana
*** Pittosporum viridiflorum
*** Populus alba
 ** Prosopis glandulosa
 ** Robinia pseudacacia
  * Schinus terebinthifolius
*** Torreya taxifolia
 ** Trachycarpus fortunei
 ** Ulmus pumila
*** Virgilia capensis
  * Wigandia caracasana

## SHRUBS

*** Adenostoma fasciculatum
 ** Artemisia (species)
*** Bergerocactus emoryi
*** Ceanothus grizeus
  * Ceratostigma willmottianum
  * Chamaelaucium ciliatum
  * Chamaerops humilis
  * Cistus (species)
*** Clerodendrum myricoides
 ** Cotoneaster decora
  *     " microphylla
***     " pannosa nana
  * Cytisus canariensis
 ** Dovyalis caffra
 ** Encelia (species)
*** Eriodictyon crassifolium
  * Euphorbia splendens
*** Galvesia speciosa
*** Hakea pugioniformis
 ** Heimia myrtifolia
  * Juniperus (check species)
 ** Lavandula officinalis
  * Lycium richi

*** Mahernia verticillata
 ** Mahonia pinnata
  * Melaleuca hyperiscifolia
 ** Mimulus puniceus
  * Muehlenbeckia complexa
  * Myrsine africana
*** Opuntia linguiformis
 ** Penstemon antirrhinoides
 ** Phillyrea latifolia
*** Phlomis fruticosa
 ** Pittosporum heterophyllum
  * Punica granatum
  * Pyracantha (species)
  * Raphiolepis (species)
  * Rhus (check species)
*** Ribes viburnifolium
 ** Rosmarinus officinalis
  * Russelia equisetiformis
 ** Santolina chamaecyparissus
  * Serissa foetida
*** Trichostema lanatum
 ** Zamia floridana
 ** Zauschneria californica

## HERBACIOUS PLANTS

 ** Abronia (species)
  * Ajuga reptans
*** Anacyclus depressus
  * Anemone japonica
  * Aristea eckloni
  * Aster (species)
*** Cheilanthes gracillima
 ** Chlorophytum elatum
  * Chrysanthemum (species)
  * Convolvulus mauretanicus
*** Cyanotis hirsuta
  * Echeveria clavifolia
 ** Erigeron karvinskyanus
  * Felicia (species)
 ** Iris germanica
***     " unguicularis
 ** Kleinia repens
 ** Liriope spicata
 ** Lotus mascaensis
*** Lysimachia nummularia
  * Mentha pulegium
  * Mesembryanth. (species)
*** Muehlenbeckia axillare
 ** Nepeta mussini

*** Oenothera caespitosa
*** Ophiopogon japonica
*** Origanum dictamnus
 ** Othonna crassifolia
 ** Pellaea andromedaefolia
*** Pteris aquilina
 ** Ranunculus repens
  * Reineckia carnea
 ** Salvia farinacea
***     " leucantha
*** Sanvitalia procumbens
  * Sedum altissimum
***     " spurium
  * Sempervivum tectorum
*** Senecio mikanioides
*** Stapelia divaricata
*** Stokesia laevis
 ** Tunica saxifraga
  * Thymus serpyllum
 ** Tropaeolum (check species)
 ** Verbena (check species)
*** Veronica (species)
 ** Vinca major
  * Zebrina pendula

## DEEP SOILS

For trees primarily, an elimination list against which to check a selection for soil footing. This is a great natural advantage if not a necessity for obstinately tapping roots or trees that must have anchorage to stand in storms. Such individuals will stretch out in this place and thrive long, where decline is inevitable and sure over shallow hardpan. This is the place too, for trees that cannot be given enough water in their maturity to keep them going.....let them tap lower sources in order to survive and serve.

| | |
|---|---|
| *** Agathis robusta | *** Juglans regia |
| *** Angophora lanceolata | *** Leucadendron argenteum |
| * Araucaria excelsa | *** Liquidambar styraciflua |
| * Bougainvillea (varieties) | *** Phytolacca dioica |
| * Brachychiton (species) | * Platanus racemosa |
| ** Calodendrum capense | ** Populus fremonti |
| *** Castanospermum australe | ***    "    nigra italica |
| * Cedrus deodara | *** Pterospermum acerifolium |
| ** Chilopsis linearis | * Quercus (species) |
| *** Chorisia speciosa | *** Quillaja saponaria |
| ** Cinnamomum camphora | ** Schinus molle |
| * Cupressus arizonica | ** Sequoia sempervirens |
| **    "    guadalupensis | * Sequoiadendron giganteum |
| ***    "    lusitanica | *** Taxodium (species) |
| ** Dracaena australis | ** Tipuana tipu |
| * Eucalyptus (check species) | *** Torreya californica |
| * Ficus macrophylla | ** Umbellularia californica |
| ** Fraxinus velutina | * Washingtonia filifera |
| *** Harpullia arborea | ** Wisteria floribunda |

SOIL REACTION---or the chemical state or condition of the ground, and as affecting the gardener. The meaning of this is most appreciated after he has worked with it for a time....with notable failures in growth. He will want to know then in the beginning, the reaction of his particular soil and be guided in one of the fundamental factors for high success with soils in gardening. This is basic with many plants and it is not always satisfactory over the long period to change the degree of variance (pH), since it must be held. It is most discouraging, usually useless, to force a plant against its nature when it has sharp demands in this respect.

## ALKALINE SOILS

Soils that are derived from limestone or those overlying marl favor the growth of certain plants. A neutral reaction may be satisfactory for the same plants, yet the addition of plaster refuse, slaked lime or that which has been ground fine, will bring about a basic alkaline condition greatly to be desired for their continued health and well-being, not to mention the service of flowering. Nutrient values are raised with these additions. Check with ALKALI for extremes.

### TREES

| | |
|---|---|
| *** Agonis flexuosa | * Olea europaea |
| * Albizzia lebbek | ** Persea (species) |
| ** Annona cherimola | ** Populus (species) |
| *** Colvillea racemosa | ** Quercus ilex |
| ** Diospyros kaki | *** Phytolacca dioica |
| * Eriobotrya japonica | * Pittosporum (species) |
| * Eucalyptus (species) | ** Schinus (species) |
| ** Ficus (species) | *** Taxodium mucronatum |
| ** Juglans (species) | ** Tipuana tipu |
| * Juniperus (check species) | *** Ulmus crassifolia |

### SHRUBS

| | |
|---|---|
| *** Aloe (species) | * Cistus (species) |
| *** Berberis (species) | * Coronilla glauca |
| * Buxus microphylla | * Cotoneaster (species) |
| * Callistemon (species) | *** Daphniphyllum humile |
| ** Cassia artemisioides | * Elaeagnus pungens |
| ** Chaenomeles japonica | ** Erica melanthera |

** Euonymus japonicus
*** Fallugia paradoxa
** Feijoa sellowiana
*** Fouquieria splendens
*** Gardenia thunbergia
*** Halimium (species)
*** Hebe (species)
*** Ilex vomitoria
 * Juniperus (check species)
** Lantana (species)
 * Laurus nobilis
** Lavandula officinalis
*** Leucophyllum texanum
 * Ligustrum (species)
*** Lippia ligustrina
*** Medicago arborea

** Myrsine africana
 * Myrtus communis
 * Nerium oleander
*** Nyctanthes arbor-tristis
** Poinciana gilliesi
** Prunus ilicifolia
**     "      lyoni
 * Punica granatum
 * Pyracantha (species)
 * Rhus (species)
*** Sophora secundiflora
** Spartium junceum
** Syringa persica
*** Thryallis glauca
** Thevetia nereifolia
 * Viburnum (species)

## VINES

*** Clematis (species)
*** Hardenbergia (species)
 * Lonicera halliana

 * Mandevilla suaveolens
** Phaseolus (species)
** Sollya heterophylla

## HERBACEOUS PLANTS

*** Aethionema coridifolium
*** Anemone japonica
** Arenaria balearica
*** Aster amellus
 * Bouvardia humboldti
 * Calendula officinalis
*** Callistephus chinensis
 * Centaurea (species)
** Chrysanthemum (species)
** Cymbalaria muralis
 * Dianthus (species)
** Erodium chamaedryoides
***    "     chrysanthum
 * Gypsophila elegans
** Hedera helix
*** Heuchera sanguinea
** Hunnemannia fumariaefolia
*** Iris alata
**    "   japonica
 *    "   unguicularis
***    "   xiphium

*** Lathyrus odoratus
** Lilium candidum
***    "    henryi
 *    "    regale
 * Nicotiana alata
** Oenothera (species)
 * Pelargonium (species)
*** Pellaea andromedaefolia
*** Pteris serrulata
 * Salpiglossis sinuata
 * Scabiosa (species)
 * Sempervivum (species)
 * Senecio cineraria
*** Stanleya pinnata
 * Thymus (species)
** Tropaeolum (species)
*** Tulbaghia violacea
** Verbena (species)
 * Vinca (species)
*** Zephyranthes candida
** Zinnia elegans

## ACID SOILS

These are granite soils or the result of much decaying veg-
etatation, such as the mould of rotting leaves found beneath woodland trees....and the end result held against leaching. Such material can be moved into the garden for the betterment of these plants,
or peat may be spaded into the ground for acidity. Chemically, gypsum, powdered sulphur, or aluminum sulphate is effective while light
applications of ammonium sulphate as a fertilizer raises acidity.
Rain or periodic flushings of soft water will tend to remove the accumulated alkaline salts left by irrigation water....in a tub or
planter box or in a small plot of the garden.

## TREES

** Clethra arborea
** Embothrium coccineum
*** Liquidambar (species)
*** Litchi chinensis
 * Magnolia grandiflora
 * Pinus (species)

** Quercus chrysolepis
 *    "    virginiana
*** Sequoia sempervirens
** Sequoiadendron giganteum
*** Stenocarpus sinuatus
*** Taxodium distichum

## SHRUBS

*** Abelia floribunda
** Arbutus unedo
 * Azalea (species)
 * Azara microphylla
*** Berberidopsis corallina

*** Boronia elatior
*** Brunfelsia calycina
 * Camellia (species)
 * Daphne odora
** Entelea arborescens

** Ervatamia nervosa
*** Eurya (species)
** Fabiana imbricata
* Fuchsia (species)
*** Gardenia (species)
** Heterocentron roseum
** Hydrangea macrophylla
*** Illicium floridanum
*** Ixora chinensis
*** Leucothoe axillaris
*** Luculia gratissima

** Mackaya bella
** Magnolia stellata
*** Myrica californica
** Myrtus ugni
** Ochna multiflora
** Osmanthus fragrans
* Pimelea ferruginia
*** Ruellia devosiana
* Ternstroemia japonica
*** Thea sinensis
* Tibouchina (species)

*** Vaccinium virgatum

## VINES

*** Ampelopsis brevipedunculata
* Gelsemium sempervirens
** Lonicera sempervirens
** Philadelphus mexicanus

** Polygonum auberti
** Stizolobium deeringianum
*** Tropaeolum peregrinum
*** Vitis voinieriana

## HERBACEOUS PLANTS

** Acaena microphylla
** Acanthus mollis
* Achimenes longiflora
*** Allium schoenprasm
*** Anemone coronaria
* Aquilegia chrysantha
* Begonia (species)
*** Beloperone guttata
* Bergenia (species)
*** Bessera elegans
** Caladium picturatum
*** Centaureum massoni
* Cineraria cruenta
*** Clitoria ternatea
* Coleus blumei
* Cyclamen indicum
*** Delphinium nudicaule
* Dicentra spectabilis
*** Dodecatheon clevelandi
* Francoa ramosa
** Gladiolus hortulanus
* Gloxinia speciosa

*** Haemanthus (species)
** Helleborus lividus
** Iris delta species
***    "   hexagona
*      "   kaempferi
**     "   pseudacorus
** Leucojum autumnale
* Lilium longiflorum
***    "    testaceum
* Lotus corniculatus
** Miscanthus sinensis
** Nerine (species)
*** Penstemon australis
** Pteris aquilina
* Schizocentron roseum
*** Stachys floridana
** Thalictrum dipterocarpum
*** Tropaeolum speciosum
* Viola (species)
** Watsonia iridifolia
* Zantedeschia (species)
** Zephyranthes (species)

## SOIL MOISTURE

Some plants will stand for only a slight degree of drouth and recover from a major wilt with difficulty. They must have uniformity of moisture in point of time as well as in amount, the latter usually being less important. To use these plants where stark drought, or even seasonal dryness prevails, is to invite trouble all along the line, lowered vitality and attendant disorders, diseases and the ever waiting bugs. Where irrigation is practised, the problem is best solved with some alternation of deep and shallow applications.

## WOODY PLANTS FOR

### DAMP SOILS
will have to do with what is ordinarily called poor drainage.... artificial conditions brought about in the well watered garden or to a mild seepage outside. It is possible with these plants to control or regulate, in a way of thinking, a place that cannot be drained properly.

* Acacia floribunda
*** Acacia pravissima
*** Acalypha hispida
** Aeonium spathulatum
** Adenocalymna alliaceum

### WET SOILS
carries the thought of seasonal extremes. Here the ground may be soggy for a period, possibly with standing water of some depth, yet with drainage to clear the situation up as the season advances into the heat of the year, for a period of time in which the planting may recover.

*** Acacia melanoxylon
* Alnus (species)
*** Amorpha fruticosa
*** Azalea austrina
** Baccharis halimifolia

*** Aucuba japonica
  * Azara microphylla
*** Barklya syringiflora
 ** Buddleja (species)
  * Cassia (check species)
  * Cestrum (species)
*** Clerodendrum (species)
*** Cordia boissieri
  * Crinodendron dependens
 ** Datura (species)
  * Duranta (species)
 ** Erythrina (species)
  * Escallonia (species)
*** Eupatorium sordidum
 ** Fuchsia (varieties)
*** Gaya lyalli
 ** Hamelia erecta
  * Hebe (check species)
  * Hydrangea macrophylla
 ** Hypericum (species)
 ** Illicium floridanum
 ** Iochroma (species)
*** Ixora chinensis
*** Ligustrum japonicum
*** Malvaviscus grandiflorus
 ** Melaleuca (species)
 ** Mimulus puniceus
  * Myoporum laetum
  * Nandina domestica
 ** Philadelphus mexicanus
*** Pinus radiata
 ** Prostanthera nivea
 ** Rhodomyrtus tomentosa
*** Ruellia devosiana
  * Solandra (species)
  * Stenolobium stans
 ** Thevetia nereifolia
  * Weigela florida

  * Bambusa multiplex
*** Befaria racemosa
  * Betula nigra
*** Brunfelsia (species)
 ** Calycanthus floridus
  * Casuarina (species)
*** Chilopsis linearis
  * Coccolobis uvifera
  * Coprosma baueri
*** Cyrilla racemiflora
*** Cliftonia monophylla
 ** Escallonia langleyensis
*** Eucalyptus blakeleyi
 **      "      botryoides
  *      "      globulus
 **      "      robusta
*** Hibiscus rosa-sinensis
 ** Ilex cassine
  *   "   vomitoria
*** Leucothoe axillaris
  * Liquidambar styraciflua
*** Magnolia virginiana
*** Melaleuca ericifolia
  *      "     leucadendra
 ** Metrosideros tomentosa
*** Nerium oleander
 ** Persea borbonia
*** Pinckneya pubens
*** Pinus caribaea
  * Platanus (species)
*** Psoralea pinnata
 ** Sabal minor
  * Salix (species)
 ** Serenoa repens
  * Taxodium distichum
*** Thespesia populnea
 ** Vaccineum virgatum
*** Zamia floridana

## HERBACEOUS PLANTS FOR

### DAMP SOILS
 ** Agapanthus africanus
  * Ajuga reptans
  * Anemone japonica
 ** Arenaria balearica
*** Arthropodium cirrhatum
 ** Asplenium (species)
*** Bergenia crassifolia
 ** Browallia americana
 ** Colocasia antiquorum
  * Crinum (species)
*** Curculigo capitulata
 ** Cymbalaria muralis
  * Cypella herberti
*** Cyrtanthus (species)
 ** Dierama pulcherrima
*** Francoa ramosa
  * Geum (varieties)
 ** Helxine soleiroli
 ** Hemerocallis aurantiaca
  * Hymenocallis (species)
 ** Impatiens sultani
 ** Iris japonica
  * Ligularia kaempferi
 ** Lobelia erinus
  * Malcomia maritima
*** Mentha gatefossei
*** Micromeria chamissonis
  * Mimulus (species)

### WET SOILS
 ** Acorus calamus
*** Anemopsis californica
  * Blechnum serrulatum
 ** Brodiaea lactea
  * Butomus umbellatus
 ** Calla pulustris
*** Calochortus uniflorus
*** Caltha palustris
*** Camassia leichtlini
  * Cortaderia selloana
*** Crinum americanum
 ** Cyanella orchidiformis
  * Cyperus (species)
 ** Dianella intermedia
 ** Dipidax ciliata
*** Frankenia capitata laevis
*** Hymenocallis caribaea
*** Iris delta species
 **   "   hexagona
  *   "   kaempferi
 **   "   pseudacorus
*** Jussiaea (species)
*** Lilium pardalinum
 ** Limnanthes douglasi
 ** Mentha pulegium
  * Nephthytis afzeli
*** Orontium aquaticum
*** Phalaris arundinacea

*** Moraea ramosa                    * Phormium tenax
  * Myosotis alpestris              ** Pontederia cordata
 ** Nierembergia rivularis           * Primula japonica
*** Parochetus communis            *** Saururus cernuus
 ** Pasithea caerulea               ** Senecio mikanioides
*** Pentas lanceolata               ** Schizostylis coccinea
 ** Phormium colensoi              *** Scirpus cernuus
*** Polystichum aculeatum            * Sisyrinchium bellum
  * Schizanthus wisetonensis         * Stenotaphrum secundatum
  * Sisyrinchium (species)          ** Syngonium podophyllum
  * Thalictrum dipterocarpum         * Thalia dealbata
*** Verbesina encelioides          *** Wachendorfia thyrsiflora
  * Viola (check species)            * Woodwardia virginiana
 ** Zephyranthes (species)           * Zephyranthes candida

## SOIL TEMPERATURE

Many plants react measurably to thermal tendencies in the soil. The difference between a warm soil and one that is cold and slow is often that of indifferent success or half failure, a dubious situation that is bound to fall into a mist of error, and of no possible satisfaction to the gardener. Contributing factors are exposure, dampness, shade, the sun, texture of the soil and the result as positive in the growth of a given plant as it may be negative in that of another. Cast a critical eye back over past failures and see how many appear in these lists....on the wrong side of the page. A mulch of dust or one that is applied, is favorable here and rocky ground will be found more even-tempered. North slopes seem to go with the heavier soils and bear down sharply on soil temperature.

## SHRUBS FOR

### WARM SOILS                          ### COOL SOILS

*** Anthyllis barba-jovis          *** Abelia grandiflora
 ** Arbutus unedo                  *** Arctostaphylos diversifolia
*** Brunfelsia calycina              * Azara microphylla
 ** Candollea cuneiformis          *** Berberidopsis corallina
*** Carissa grandiflora              * Berberis (species)
  * Cassia (species)              *** Brachysema lanceolatum
*** Carpenteria californica          * Camellia japonica
  * Ceanothus cyaneus              ** Chaenomeles japonica
*** Cedronella canariensis         *** Chamaecyparis (varieties)
 ** Cibotium schiederi              ** Clematis (species)
  * Cistus (species)              *** Corynocarpus laevigata
 ** Coronilla glauca                 * Cotoneaster (species)
  * Correa (species)               ** Crinodendron dependens
 ** Cuphea hissopifolia              * Daphne odora
  * Cytisus canariensis           *** Fraxinus dipetala
  * Erythrina crista-galli           * Fuchsia (varieties)
 ** Fabiana imbricata                * Galvesia speciosa
  * Gardenia jasminoides           ** Gelsemium sempervirens
*** Garrya elliptica                 * Hardenbergia comptoniana
 ** Genista monosperma               * Hebe (species)
*** Halimium (species)               * Heteromeles arbutifolia
  * Heterocentron roseum          *** Iochroma (species)
 ** Hibiscus (species)              ** Jacobinia (species)
  * Holmskioldia sanguinea          * Juniperus conferta
*** Jaquemontia eastwoodiana        ** Lonicera (species)
 ** Leucophyllum texanum           *** Lupinus arboreus
 ** Myrtus communis                 ** Mimulus puniceus
*** Penstemon antirrhinoides         * Nandina domestica
 ** Phlomis fruticosa              *** Ochna multiflora
  * Poinciana gilliesi              ** Photinia serrulata
 ** Rhus ovata                      ** Raphiolepis indica
*** Ribes malvaceum                 ** Rhus integrifolia
 ** Romneya coulteri               *** Ribes (species)
 ** Rosmarinus officinalis          ** Rosa (species)
*** Salvia greggi                  *** Spiraea cantoniensis
  * Solanum (species)               ** Tibouchina (species)
*** Spartium junceum               *** Torreya (species)

* Streptosolen jamesoni
*** Tecoma garrocha
** Thevetia nereifolia
** Thryallis glauca
*** Zauschneria californica

* Trachelospermum jasminoides
* Turraea obtusifolia
*** Umbellularia californica
* Viburnum (species)
*** Weigela florida

## HERBACEOUS PLANTS FOR

### WARM SOILS

* Ageratum houstonianum
** Anagallis linifolia
* Angelonia grandiflora
* Antigonon leptopus
* Arctotis (species)
** Babiana stricta
** Boussingaultia baselloides
** Browallia americana
** Caladium picturatum
*** Callirhoe involucrata
** Ceratostigma plumbaginoides
** Cheilanthes gracillima
*** Cheiranthes mutabilis
* Convolvulus (species)
*** Dicentra chrysantha
*** Epidendrum obrienianum
*** Eriogonum nudum
** Felicia (species)
* Gerberia jamesoni
** Gladiolus hortulanus
* Helianthemum nummularium
*** Heliophila pilosa
*** Heliotropium arborescens
*** Iresine herbsti
** Ixia maculata
* Limonium (species)
*** Maurandia erubescens
* Nicotiana alata
* Oenothera (species)
** Papaver (species)
* Pellaea (species)
*** Penstemon (species)
** Petunia hybrida
*** Phacelia whitlavia
* Phlox drummondi
*** Polianthes tuberosa
*** Polypteris hookeriana
* Portulaca grandiflora
** Quamoclit (species)
*** Reinwardtia indica
* Salpiglossis sinuata
*** Salvia (species)
* Sempervivum tectorum
** Scabiosa (species)
*** Silene laciniata
** Sparaxis tricolor
*** Stokesia laevis
** Strelitzia reginae
*** Tanacetum capitatum
* Thymus (species)
** Tigridia pavonia
*** Tritonia crocosmaeflora
** Tulbaghia violacea
** Ursinia anthemoides
* Vallota speciosa
** Verbena (species)
* Venidium (species)
* Vinca rosea
*** Viola pedunculata
*** Xanthisma texanum
* Zinnia elegans

### COOL SOILS

* Ajuga reptans
*** Allium (species)
*** Alstroemeria (species)
*** Amphicome arguta
* Anemone japonica
*** Anthriscus cerefolium
* Antirrhinum majus
* Arenaria balearica
* Begonia (species)
** Bergenia (species)
*** Brachycome iberidifolia
** Brodiaea laxa
* Cineraria cruenta
* Clarkia elegans
* Clivia (species)
*** Cosmos bipinnatus
* Cymbalaria (species)
** Delphinium grandiflorum
*** Dianella intermedia
** Dianthus (species)
*** Dicentra formosa
*** Dodecatheon clevelandi
* Echeveria (species)
** Freesia refracta
** Gaura lindheimeri
*** Gazania (species)
* Godetia grandiflora
** Hedychium (species)
* Helxine soleiroli
* Heuchera sanguinea
*** Hidalgoa wercklei
** Impatiens sultani
*** Ionopsidium acaule
* Lilium (species)
*** Ligularia kaempferi
** Lobelia erinus
* Lupinus (species)
*** Mentha requieni
* Mimulus luteus
*** Montia perfoliata
** Myosotis alpestris
** Nemesia strumosa
** Nemophila insignis
*** Nierembergia rivularis
** Oxalis (species)
** Polystichum aculeatum
* Primula (species)
** Ranunculus (species)
*** Rivina humilis
*** Saxifraga sarmentosa
* Sedum dasyphyllum
**       "     lineare
***      "     sieboldi
** Selaginella (species)
*** Sisyrinchium (species)
*** Streptocarpus hybridus
* Thalictrum dipterocarpum
*** Tulbaghia fragrans
*** Tulipa (species)
* Viola (species)
** Zantedeschia aethiopica

WIND WEAR---an evaluation of plants from the standpoint of the warp and impairment of weather and their reaction to extremes. Those with fragile leaves or very early flowers will benefit with a little protection, although entirely hardy in other ways.  Other plants have a fitness for or adapt readily to the open landscape, either because of inherent ruggedness or through structural capacity to withstand the elements at their worst; as storm, or under continual pressure as of a trade wind that blows over a considerable period.

## EXPOSURE

Some plants seem to benefit with stirring air, a trait that may be used here to advantage and relieve the garden of species so often found weak there and subject to disease. Trees with thick stocky stems and deep-anchoring roots or those of pliable, willowy character that will give way are indicated. Quick recovery in growth after damage in a storm should be considered. The following are strong-growing, to thrive and make a more or less characteristic growth in the face of prevailing winds or storms.  Check with SEASIDE lists.

### TREES

| | |
|---|---|
| * Acacia auriculaeforme | *** Koelreuteria paniculata |
| *** " prominens | * Lagunaria patersoni |
| ** " pruinosa | *** Macadamia ternifolia |
| ** Achras zapota | * Maytenus boaria |
| * Araucaria (species) | * Metrosideros tomentosa |
| ** Celtis australis | *** Morus rubra |
| * Cinnamomum camphora | * Olea europaea |
| ** Citherexylum spinosum | *** Peltophorum inerme |
| *** Cupania anacardioides | * Phoenix (species) |
| *** Drimys winteri | * Pinus (species) |
| *** Elaeodendron orientale | ** Sabal palmetto |
| *** Eucalyptus (check species) | ** Samanea saman |
| ** Eugenia supraaxillaris | ** Simaruba amara |
| * Ficus retusa | ** Thespesia populnea |
| ** Juniperus silicicola | *** Tipuana tipu |
| *** Haematoxylon campechianum | ** Trachycarpus fortunei |
| *** Harpephyllum caffrum | *** Ulmus crassifolia |
| * Howea forsteriana | *** Washingtonia robusta |

### SHRUBS

| | |
|---|---|
| * Acacia armata | *** Hymenanthera crassifolia |
| ** " verticillata | * Juniperus (species) |
| *** " vestita | ** Lavandula officinalis |
| ** Acokanthera spectabilis | * Lavatera assurgentiflora |
| *** Agonis linearifolia | * Leptospermum (species) |
| ** Anthyllis barba-jovis | * Ligustrum (species) |
| *** Arctostaphylos glauca | ** Lupinus arboreus |
| * Atriplex breweri | ** Lycium (species) |
| ** Baccharis (species) | * Melaleuca (species) |
| *** Brachysema lanceolatum | ** Myrsine africana |
| *** Calothamnus quadrifidus | *** Ochrosia elliptica |
| *** Corynocarpus laevigata | *** Phillyrea latifolia |
| * Carissa grandiflora | *** Phlomis fruticosa |
| ** Ceanothus verrucosus | * Pittosporum crassifolium |
| * Chamaerops humilis | ** " tobira |
| * Coprosma baueri | *** Poinciana gilliesi |
| * Cotoneaster (species) | ** Polygala dalmaisiana |
| *** Cytisus canariensis | * Raphiolepis (species) |
| ** Dodonaea viscosa | *** Rhamnus alaternus |
| * Echium fastuosum | ** Rhus (species) |
| *** Erica melanthera | ** Rosmarinus officinalis |
| ** Eriogonum (species) | ** Sysigium cumini |
| * Escallonia (species) | *** Spartium junceum |
| *** Medicago arborea | * Tamarix (species) |
| ** Euonymus japonicus | *** Thryallis glauca |
| *** Garrya elliptica | *** Viburnum japonicum |
| ** Genista monosperma | * " suspensum |
| *** Gossypium sturti | ** " tinus |
| * Hakea (species) | * Westringia rosmariniformis |
| * Hebe (check species) | *** Xylosma senticosa |

## PROTECTION

This is a consideration of localities or places of some seclusion....gardens where the air and earth are equably quiet, even, constant; undergoing a minimum of disturbance from the dip of overhead wind. High humidity here is acceptable and may be fostered by fine spray, as of irrigation....no drought. The plants which follow are without exception choice and should reach their fullest expectancy in such a place. This is another negative list to check against when planting under severe conditions of environment.

### TREES

```
**  Acacia pubescens                **  Harpullia arborea
""" Acer palmatum                    **  Howea belmoreana
**  Alsophila australis             **  Hymenosporum flavum
 *  Arcontophoenix cunningham.       *  Jacaranda acutifolia
*** Barklya syringifolia            *** Markhamia lutea
 *  Brachychiton acerifolium         *  Melicocca bijuga
 *  Calodendrum capense             **  Musa ensete
*** Cassia fistula                  **  Peltophorum inerme
 *  Chamaecyparis lawsoniana         *  Pittosporum rhombifolium
**  Chrysalidocarpus lutescens      **  Prunus persica
*** Cibotium schiederi              **  Sequoia sempervirens
 *  Citrus (species)                *** Spathodea campanulata
*** Cochlospermum vitifolium        *** Stenocarpus sinuatus
*** Colvillea racemosa              **  Terminalia catappa
 *  Cryptomeria elegans             *** Tupidanthus calyptratus
**  Eugenia (check species)         *** Virgilia capensis
*** Fraxinus dipetala                *  Vitex lucens
```

### SHRUBS

```
**  Abutilon hybridum               *** Lonicera pileata
 *  Azalea indica                   *** Luculia gratissima
 *  Azara microphylla               *** Malpighia coccigera
*** Bauhinia (check species)        *** Mitriostigma axillare
**  Beloperone guttata              **  Myrtus ugni
*** Berberidopsis corallina         *** Oncoba routledgi
**  Bouvardia humboldti             **  Osmanthus fragrans
 *  Brunfelsia (species)            *** Pachystachys coccinea
*** Bursaria spinosa                **  Pavonia multiflora
*** Calliandra portoricensis         *  Pentas lanceolata
**  Camellia reticulata             **  Pimelea ferruginia
**  Cantua buxifolia                *** Prostanthera nivea
**  Carpenteria californica         **  Reinwardtia indica
**  Cassia (check species)          **  Rhapis excelsa
**  Clerodendrum siphonanthus       *** Robinsonella cordata
**  Codiaeum variegatum              *  Ruellia devosiana
**  Coffea arabica                  **  Siphonosmanthus delavayi
**  Crossandra infundibuliformis    **  Solanum rantonneti
 *  Cuphea (species)                **  Streptosolen jamesoni
 *  Eranthemum nervosum             **  Strobilanthus anisophilus
**  Daphne odora                     *      "        dyerianus
*** Dombeya cayeuxi                 **  Strophanthus speciosus
**  Duranta stenostachya            *** Strychnos spinosa
 *  Ervatamia coronaria              *  Syagrus weddelliana
**  Eurya emarginata                *** Synsepalum dulsificum
 *  Fuchsia (species)               **  Tabernaemontana grandiflora
**  Gardenia jasminoides            **  Tecoma garrocha
**  Hamelia erecta                  *** Tephrosia candida
 *  Heterocentron roseum             *  Ternstroemia japonica
**  Hibiscus arnottianus            **  Thea sinensis
***     "      huegeli               *  Thevetia nereifolia
**  Hypoestis phyllostachys         ***     "      thevetioides
 *  Hypericum (species)             **  Thunbergia erecta
 *  Illicium anisatum               **  Tibouchina elegans
*** Iochroma fuchsioides             *      "      semidecandra
 *  Itea ilicifolia                 *** Tournefortia heliotropinoides
*** Ixora chinensis                  *  Turraea obtusifolia
**  Jacobinia carnea                *** Urera caracasana
*** Jasminum sambac                 **  Visnea mocanera
*** Ligustrum quihoui
```

## VINES

*** Abrus precatorius              * Gloriosa superba
** Allamanda hendersoni            * Hoya carnosa
*** Aristolochia elegans           *** Lapageria rosea
** Artabotrys odoratissimus        ** Oxera pulchella
* Clerodendrum thompsonae          ** Stigmaphyllon ciliatum
*** Cydista equinoctialis          *** Thunbergia laurifolia

UNDERWOOD---plants for more or less willing growth beneath trees, the ground being either moist or dry. These plants must take the drip from the tree, its shade, light to fairly dense, and demonstrate some stamina in competition with its roots....less at the base of the trunk. Roots of the tree are less competitive when left uncut, while to trim low-hanging branches is to defeat the purpose of the planting. A fine point is the estimate of measure or degree to which the tree in question depends upon the topsoil in order that accurate selections may be made for the ground beneath. Check with DROUGHT and SHADOW.

## DRY GROUND

*** Anemone blanda                 * Nephrolepis exaltata
*** Allium triquetrum              ** Oenothera tetraptera
* Asparagus (species)              ** Ophiopogon (species)
** Aspidistra elatior              * Oxalis crassipes
* Brodiaea uniflora                ** Pellaea andromedaefolia
*** Cotoneaster harroviana         *** Petasitis fragrans
** Cyrilla racemiflora             *** Phillyrea latifolia media
*** Danae racemosa                 *** Pteris aquilina
** Euonymus japonicus              *     "    tremula
* Fatsia japonica                  *** Rhus trilobata
*** Galvesia speciosa              *** Ruscus aculeatus
* Hardenbergia monophylla          * Sarcococca hookeriana
* Hedera helix                     ** Sasa pygmaea
** Hypericum calycinum             * Sedum album
* Ligustrum (species)              ***   "    lineare
** Liriope spicata                 **    "    treleasi
* Lonicera halliana                * Vinca major
*** Mahonia pinnata                * Zebrina pendula
** Muehlenbeckia complexa          *** Zephyranthes candida

## MOIST GROUND

** Acaena microphylla              ** Lysimachia nummularia
** Adiantum caudatum               * Mackaya bella
***    "    emarginatum            ** Malvaviscus arboreus
* Ajuga reptans                    *** Micromeria chamissonis
*** Alstroemeria aurantiaca        * Monstera deliciosa
* Anemone japonica                 ** Myosotis alpestris
*** Arenaria balearica             *** Pachystachys coccinea
* Azalea (species)                 * Parthenocissus henryana
** Begonia (species)               * Polystichum aculeatum
** Bergenia cordifolia             ***    "    adiantiforme
** Buxus japonica                  ** Primula malacoides
*** Camellia japonica              *      "    polyantha
*** Carissa prostrata              ***    "    sinensis
*** Cotoneaster microphylla        * Ranunculus repens
** Cymbalaria muralis              * Raphiolepis ovata
* Cyrtomium falcatum               *** Reineckia carnea
** Dicentra formosa                ** Ribes (species)
* Duchesnea indica                 * Saxifraga sarmentosa
* Fuchsia (varieties)              *** Selaginella (check species)
* Gelsemium sempervirens           *** Streptocarpus hybridus
* Hardenbergia comptoniana         *** Swainsona galegifolia
*** Helleborus lividus             ** Thalictrum dipterocarpum
* Helxine soleiroli                *** Tolmiea menziesi
** Hypericum (species)             * Trachelospermum jasminoides
*** Itea ilicifolia                *** Veronica repens
** Jacobinia carnea                * Viburnum suspensum
*** Leucojum autumnale             ** Viola (check species)
** Ligularia kaempferi             ** Weigela florida
*** Lonicera hispidula             * Woodwardia (species)
*     "    nitida                  ** Zoysia tenuifolia

RATE OF INCREASE---is one of the first factors to consider in the selective process. A tree should relate to things or objects with which it functions, along with its own part in the planting scheme. The relative speed or tempo of its growth has a bearing on the length and quality of its service. By all means inquire into the time element in bringing along a plant and know the satisfaction of results in line with a predetermined plan. Nearly all these plants will have a more or less fixed schedule by which they develop and this should not be unduly disturbed if they are to serve typically and well. Do not force them in growth without a considered reason nor permit them the luxury of lagging along without point.

## SLOW GROWTH

Here is material for long continuance of usefulness, plants that are slow to grow and lasting in point of time. Most of these plants will incline toward a more or less fixed formality and convention. They more generally will be found appropriate with architecture or in a situation where a relatively static condition of growth is desirable. The trees should be used only where they will have a long time lease on the ground....a thought for posterity.

### TREES

| | |
|---|---|
| *** Acacia pendula | * Libocedrus decurrens |
| *** Achras zapota | *** Liquidambar styraciflua |
| *** Agathis robusta | *** Livistona australis |
| *** Agonis flexuosa | ** Macadamia ternifolia |
| * Araucaria bidwilli | * Magnolia grandiflora |
| ** Brachychiton populnea | * Metrosideros tomentosa |
| *** Butia capitata | ** Phoenix reclinata |
| * Cedrus atlantica | * Pinus coulteri |
| * Ceratonia siliqua | ** " pinea |
| * Cinnamomum camphora | ** Pittosporum rhombifolium |
| *** Colvillea racemosa | ** Quercus suber |
| *** Cupania anacardioides | *** Sapindus saponaria |
| ** Dracaena australis | *** Sequoiadendron giganteum |
| ** Erythea (species) | * Taxus baccata stricta |
| ** Eucalyptus ficifolia | *** Terminalia catappa |
| ** Ficus (species) | * Thuja orientalis |
| * Juniperus excelsa | *** Torreya (species) |
| ** Howea forsteriana | ** Vitex lucens |

### SHRUBS

| | |
|---|---|
| * Acokanthera spectabilis | *** Michelia fuscata |
| * Arbutus unedo | *** Murraea exotica |
| ** Arctostaphylos (species) | ** Myrtus communis |
| *** Bauhinia acuminata | * Nandina domestica |
| * Buxus microphylla | *** Ochna multiflora |
| *** Callistemon rigidus | *** Odontospermum sericeum |
| * Camellia japonica | ** Osmanthus fragrans |
| *** Canella winterana | *** Phillyrea latifolia |
| * Chamaerops humilis | * Philodendron selloum |
| *** Chrysobalanus icaco | *** Phoenix roebelini |
| * Cocculus laurifolius | * Pittosporum tobira |
| * Cotoneaster pannosa nana | ** Photinia serrulata |
| ** Cycas (species) | ** Prunus ilicifolia |
| *** Entelea arborescens | ** Punica granatum nana |
| *** Erica melanthera | ** Raphiolepis indica |
| ** Euonymus japonicus | ** " ovata |
| *** Fabiana imbricata | *** Rhapis (species) |
| ** Gardenia thunbergia | * Sarcococca hookeriana |
| *** Guaiacum officinale | *** Severinia buxifolia |
| * Hakea laurina | *** Sophora secundiflora |
| *** Hebe cupressoides | * Ternstroemia japonica |
| * Ilex (species) | ** Thuja (varieties) |
| *** Illicium anisatum | *** Triphasia trifolia |
| *** Itea ilicifolia | *** Umbellularia californica |
| ** Jasminum floridum | *** Viburnum odoratissimum |
| * Laurus nobilis | * " tinus |
| ** Ligustrum ovalifolium | *** Visnea mocanera |
| *** Mahonia lomariifolia | *** Yucca brevifolia |
| *** Malpighia coccigera | ** Xylosma senticosa |

## VINES

** Cissus hypoglauca          * Muehlenbeckia complexa
 * Hedera helix              *** Petrea volubilis
** Hibbertia volubilis         * Philodendron (check species)
*** Kennedya rubicunda        *** Thunbergia grandiflora
** Mandevilla suaveolens       * Trachelospermum jasminoides
 * Monstera deliciosa         *** Wisteria floribunda


## MODERATE GROWTH

The matter of speed in reaching an objective is legitimate, and reasonable enough for this fast moving era, but judgement in the choice of materials should not be allowed to become prejudiced by a mere fret for the finished product. The list has been examined here with a view of including some quality along with rapid development; and to reserve something of a lasting nature, reconciled with this desire for haste. Almost without exception, a better tree results if it is not forced....one presses here, too.

## TREES

 * Acacia decurrens          *** Lyonothamnus asplenifolius
***      "    prominens       ** Morus (species)
 * Albizzia julibrissin        * Olea europaea
 * Araucaria excelsa          ** Parkinsonia aculeata
** Betula nigra              *** Peltophorum inerme
 * Callistemon viminalis       * Pinus radiata
*** Callitris robusta          ** Pittosporum undulatum
 * Calodendrum capense       ***      "     viridiflorum
** Casuarina (species)         ** Platanus (species)
 * Cedrus deodara            *** Pleiogynium solandri
*** Citrus aurantium           * Podocarpus elongata
*** Cupressus (species)        ** Populus nigra italica
** Delonix regia             *** Prunus amygdalis
** Drimys winteri            **      "    caroliniana
** Erythrina (check species)   * Quercus (species)
** Eugenia smithi            *** Samanea saman
** Fraxinus velutina          ** Schinus molle
 * Grevillea robusta           *      "    terebinthifolius
 * Jacaranda acutifolia       *** Spathodea campanulata
*** Juniperus silicicola        * Tipuana tipu
 *      "     torulosa        *** Terminalia catappa
 * Lagunaria patersoni         ** Ulmus (species)
*** Ligustrum japonicum       *** Virgilia capensis


## SHRUBS

 * Abelia (species)           ** Hamelia erecta
 * Acacia cultriformis         * Hebe (species)
**      "    verticillata       * Hibiscus rosa-sinensis
***     "    vestita           ** Hypericum (species)
*** Bowkeria gerrardiana       ** Iochroma (species)
 * Camellia sasanqua          ** Jasminum rigidum
** Calliandra (species)       *** Lawsonia inermis
 * Callistemon lanceolatus      * Leptospermum laevigatum
 * Carissa grandiflora          * Ligustrum (species)
*** Ceanothus (species)        ** Lonicera pileata
*** Cestrum aurantiacum        ** Malvaviscus grandiflorus
**      "    purpureum         * Melaleuca (species)
 * Choisya ternata            *** Myrtus ugni
*** Clerodendrum (species)     *** Osmanthus ilicifolius
 * Coprosma baueri            *** Philodendrum evansi
 * Cotoneaster (species)        ** Phlomis fruticosa
*** Duranta stenostachya        * Pittosporum (species)
 * Escallonia (species)         * Plumbago capensis
*** Fremontia californica       ** Prunus lyoni
** Fuchsia arborescens         * Pyracantha (species)
*** Gardenia florida           *** Rhus (species)
** Genista monosperma         ** Ribes (species)
*** Grevillea rosmarinifolia    *** Rondeletia cordata
** Grewia occidentalis         ** Rosa (species)
** Hakea elliptica             ** Solanum rantonneti

** Sollya heterophylla          ** Thevetia nereifolia
*** Sparmannia africana         *** Turraea obtusifolia
** Spiraea cantoniensis          * Viburnum japonicum
** Tecoma smithi                 ** "      suspensum
 * Teucrium fruticans            *** Vitex agnus-castus
                *** Weigela florida

## VINES

*** Anemopoegma chamberlayni     * Lonicera (species)
 ** Antigonon leptopus           *** Pandorea (species)
  * Cissus antarctica            ** Passiflora (species)
*** Distictis lactiflora         ** Phaedranthus buccinatorius
 ** Doxantha unguis-cati         ** Polygonum auberti
  * Hardenbergia (species)       *** Pyrostegia ignea
*** Hylocereus triangularis      ** Solanum jasminoides
  * Jasminum (species)            * Tecomaria capensis
                *** Thunbergia laurifolia


## RAPID GROWTH
These plants will be used in anticipation of the earliest
possible maturity and usefulness for a plan....the flash of a quick-
opening completion....sop to ways and means. Ornamental and cultural
considerations have been submerged in the idea of the nearly immediate, where little, or no thought whatever is given to the long run of
the future. This is a high point in expediency, serving advantage,
rather than principle, but warranted under some circumstances.

### TREES

  * Acacia (species)             * Melia azedarach
 ** Acer floridanum             ** Morus nigra
*** Albizzia lophantha          *** Myoporum laetum
  * Casuarina stricta            * Pinus halepensis
*** Crinodendron dependens      *** Podochaenium eminens
*** Cupressus macrocarpa         * Populus (species)
 ** Erythrina poeppigiana       ** Prunus persica
  * Eugenia myrtifolia           * Salix (species)
*** Harpephyllum caffrum        *** Tamarix aphylla

### SHRUBS

 ** Acacia armata               *** Lavatera assurgentiflora
***    "    longifolia          *** Leonotis leonurus
 ** Atriplex breweri             * Leptospermum scoparium
  * Buddleja (species)          ** Lippia citriodora
*** Calceolaria integrifolia    ** Lonicera nitida
 ** Candollea cuneiformis       ** Mackaya bella
*** Ceanothus grizeus           ** Melaleuca hyperiscifolia
  * Cestrum nocturnum            * Nierembergia frutescens
 ** Chamaelaucium ciliatum      ** Pimelia ferruginea
  * Cistus (species)            *** Psoralea pinnata
*** Crotalaria agatiflora        * Pyracantha koidzumi
*** Cyphomandra betacea         *** Reinwardtia indica
*** Dahlia maxoni               *** Rhus lancea
*** Datura suaveolens            * Ricinus communis
 ** Daubentonia tripeti         ** Rosmarinus officinalis
  * Duranta repens              *** Salvia clevelandi
 ** Echium fastuosum            ***    "    sessei
  * Escallonia langleyensis     ** Sambucus (species)
*** Euryops (species)           ** Senecio petasitis
  * Fuchsia (varieties)          * Solanum laurifolium
 ** Grevillea thelemanniana     **     "    montanum
  * Hakea suaveolens            ***    "    warscewiczi
 ** Hebe carnea                  * Streptosolen jamesoni
*** Helichrysum petiolatum      *** Swainsona galegifolia
  * Holmskioldia sanguinea       * Tamarix (species)
 ** Hypericum floribundum       ** Tecoma garrocha
*** Iochroma lanceolatum        ** Teucrium fruticans
 ** Jasminum mesneyi             * Wigandia caracasana
  * Lantana (species            *** Vitex trifolia

## VINES

*** Agdestis clematidea
* Alseuosmia macrophylla
*** Araujia sericofera
*** Cissus adenopodus
** Cobaea scandens
* Dolichos lignosus
*** Echinocistus macrocarpa
* Fatshedera lizei
** Ipomoea (species)
** Lagenaria leucantha

* Lotus bertheloti
* Passiflora alato-caerulea
*** Phaseolus caracalla
**      "      coccinea
** Pueraria thunbergiana
** Quamoclit lobata
** Solanum wendlandi
*** Stizolobium deeringianum
* Thunbergia gibsoni
** Vitis voinieriana

FROST PROOF PLANTS---for upper subtropical regions or any area liable to frost, especially low spots subject to cold air draining in from higher ground. Many of these plants will thrive and develop the highest tone of health by reason of periodic cold. Conditioning or partial dormancy of the plant is all-important....with-hold water and fertilizer through autumn to ripen wood, but see that the soil is in good moisture at time of probable or expected frost. A loose leaf-mulch may save the crown of a plant in a heavy freeze while a fine spray of water in very early morning will break any hoar-frost so as to prevent or reduce damage. Plants under lath or trees or against walls are less subject. Do not cut out dead or injured wood until new growth indicates extent of impairment. Hard wood and firm leaves or those covered with fine hair are more reliably hardy, while young plants with tender parts close to the ground and those poorly established or in containers are more susceptible. Plants to follow are normally evergreen and will stand some degree of frost without either immediate damage or the drawn out effect of chill; some may drop foliage un-naturally. Hardiest species of a doubtful genera may be included. See BORDERLINE NORTH, DECIDUOUS LISTS and NATIVE PLANTS.

## TREES

* Acacia baileyana
*** Agonis flexuosa
** Araucaria bidwilli
* Brachychiton populnea
*** Butia capitata
* Callistemon viminalis
* Calodendrum capense
* Casuarina cunninghamiana
* Cedrus (species)
** Ceratonia siliqua
*** Chamaecyparis lawsoniana
** Cinnamomum camphora
*** Citrus mitis
*** Cornus capitata
** Crinodendron dependens
*** Cunninghamia lanceolata
* Cupressus (species)
** Cycas (check species)
* Dracaena australis
*** Drimys winteri
*** Embothrium coccineum

* Eriobotrya japonica
* Eucalyptus (check species)
** Firmiana simplex
* Grevillea robusta
*** Lagunaria patersoni
** Laurus nobilis
*** Livistona australis
* Magnolia grandiflora
*** Maytenus boaria
** Olea europaea
** Parkinsonia aculeata
*** Phoenix (check species)
* Pinus (species)
** Pittosporum phillyraeoides
*** Podocarpus (species)
** Sabal palmetto
* Schinus (species)
** Taxus baccata stricta
** Torreya (species)
** Trachycarpus fortunei
*** Umbellularia californica

*** Washingtonia robusta

## SHRUBS

* Abelia grandiflora
*** Adenocarpus viscosus
* Arbutus unedo
*** Arctostaphylos (species)
*** Azara microphylla
*** Bambusa multiplex
* Berberis (species
** Buddleja magnifica
* Buxus japonica
*** Calliandra tweedi
** Callistemon lanceolatus
* Camellia (species)

*** Cassia corymbosa
*** Ceanothus (species)
* Ceratostigma (species)
*** Cestrum parqui
* Chamaerops humilis
* Choisya ternata
* Cistus (species)
* Cocculus laurifolius
*** Cordia boissieri
*** Coronilla glauca
* Cotoneaster (species)
** Daphne odora

** Diosma (species)
** Dodonaea viscosa
*** Dovyalis caffra
** Echium fastuosum
* Elaeagnus pungens
** Erica melanthera
*** Erythrina bidwilli
** Escallonia (species)
* Euonymus japonicus
*** Eurya (species)
** Fabiana imbricata
* Fatsia japonica
** Feijoa sellowiana
* Gardenia jasminoides
*** Grevillea rosmarinifolia
** Grewia occidentalis
*** Hakea saligna
*** Hibiscus arnottianus
* Hypericum (species)
** Illicium anisatum
*** Itea ilicifolia
* Juniperus (species)
** Lavandula officinalis
* Leptospermum (species)
*** Leucophyllum texanum
* Ligustrum (species)
** Mahonia (species)
*** Michelia fuscata
** Myrsine africana
* Myrtus communis

* Nandina domestica
* Nerium oleander
*** Olmediella betschleriana
** Osmanthus (species)
*** Phillyrea latifolia
*** Philodendron selloum
*** Phlomis fruticosa
* Photinia serrulata
* Pittosporum tobira
** Poinciana gilliesi
*** Prunus lusitanica
*** Psidium cattleianum
** Punica granatum nana
* Pyracantha (species)
** Pyrus calleryana
* Raphiolepis (species)
** Rhamnus (species)
** Rhus ovata
*** Romneya coulteri
* Rosmarinus officinalis
** Sarcococca hookeriana
** Sasa palmata
*** Siphonosmanthus delavayi
*** Sophora secundiflora
* Spartium junceum
** Tamarix (species)
** Teucrium (species)
* Viburnum (species)
* Yucca (check species)
*** Xylosma senticosa

## VINES

** Ampelopsis brevipedunculata
* Cissus striata
* Clematis (species)
** Clytostoma callistegioides
*** Fatshedera lizei
** Ficus pumila
* Gelsemium sempervirens

** Hardenbergia monophylla
* Hedera (species)
** Jasminum (check species)
*** Kennedya rubicunda
*** Lonicera (check species)
*** Muehlenbeckia complexa
*** Pandorea pandorana

* Trachelospermum jasminoides

PEST-FREE PLANTS---those able either to resist the inroads of disease organisms and insect pests or which prove unattractive to them.
It has been truly said that vigorous plants are poor meat for bugs
and rarely require the doctor. There will be fewer pests if the soil
is high in humus, the result of rotted or rotting vegetation (compost)
being worked in from time to time. Maintain phosphorus and potassium
at the expense of nitrogen for easier control. Prune out to keep the
body of the plant open to light and air and spray materials. This list
should be of especial value to those who work with an old garden that
is charged with spores and eggs of the generations, and where the addition of another natural or acceptable host merely intensifies the
problem of maintenance.

## TREES

* Acacia (species)
** Albizzia (species)
** Betula nigra
* Brachychiton acerifolium
* Calodendrum capense
* Callistemon viminalis
** Casuarina (species)
*** Celtis australis
** Chamaecyparis lawsoniana
** Cinnamomum camphora
* Crinodendron dependens
*** Eucalyptus (species)
*** Ficus (species)
** Grevillea robusta

*** Harpephyllum caffrum
*** Homalanthus populifolius
* Hymenosporum flavum
* Jacaranda acutifolia
*** Libocedrus decurrens
* Liquidambar styraciflua
*** Lyonothamnus asplenifolius
** Macadamia ternifolia
*** Maytenus boaria
** Metrosideros tomentosa
*** Parkinsonia aculeata
* Podocarpus (species)
** Phoenix (species)
*** Pistacia chinensis

 * Pittosporum undulatum
 * Quercus ilex
** Stenocarpus sinuatus

** Thuja orientalis
*** Ulmus crassifolia
** Vitex lucens

## SHRUBS

 * Abelia (species)
** Acacia (check species)
** Aeonium spathulatum
 * Arbutus unedo
 * Aster fruticosus
** Brachysema lanceolatum
*** Calliandra tweedi
 * Callistemon (species)
*** Calothamnus quadrifidus
*** Candollea cuneiformis
*** Canella winterana
** Carpenteria californica
** Cassia (species)
 * Cocculus laurifolius
 * Diosma ericoides
** Duranta (species)
** Elaeagnus pungens
 * Ervatamia coronaria
*** Escallonia (species)
*** Euphorbia (species)
** Eurya (species)
*** Grevillea (check species)
** Grewia occidentalis
*** Hakea (species)
 * Halimium (species)
 * Hebe (species)
** Hibiscus rosa-sinensis
 * Ilex (species)
*** Iochroma (species)
** Jasminum (check species)

*** Lavandula officinalis
*** Lavatera (species)
*** Leptospermum (species)
*** Ligustrum (species)
*** Malvastrum (species)
*** Melaleuca (species)
 * Murraea exotica
 * Myrsine africana
 * Nierembergia frutescens
** Osmanthus ilicifolius
*** Phillyrea latifolia
 * Pittosporum (check species
*** Plumbago (capensis)
** Polygala dalmaisiana
*** Prunus ilicifolia
** Psidium cattleianum
** Raphiolepis (species)
 * Rosmarinus officinalis
 * Russelia equisetiformis
 * Sarcococca hookeriana
 * Senecio petasitis
*** Serissa foetida
*** Tamarix (species)
 * Tecoma (species)
** Teucrium fruticans
 * Thevetia nereifolia
 * Turraea obtusifolia
*** Vitex agnus-castus
 * Westringia rosmariniformis
** Xylosma senticosa

## VINES

** Ampelopsis brevipedunculata
*** Anemopoegma chamberlayni
*** Arrabidaea magnifica
*** Bomaria (species)
 * Bougainvillea (varieties)
*** Campsidium valdivianum
 * Cissus (species)
 * Distictis lactiflora
 * Gelsemium sempervirens
 * Hardenbergia (species)

 * Lonicera (species)
** Mandevilla suaveolens
*** Muehlenbeckia (species)
** Pandorea (species)
*** Petrea volubilis
** Phaedranthus buccinatorius
*** Pyrostegia ignea
*** Solandra guttata
 * Trachelospermum jasminoides
** Wisteria floribunda

## HERBACEOUS PLANTS

*** Acanthus mollis
 * Ageratum houstonianum
** Alternanthera amoena
 * Alyssum maritimum
** Arctotis (species)
** Armeria maritima
*** Asclepias currassavica
** Bletilla striata
*** Brachycome iberidifolia
** Browallia americana
 * Brunsvigia rosea
 * Calendula officinalis
*** Calocephalis browni
*** Ceratostigma plumbaginoides
 * Chrysanthemum maximum
 * Clarkia elegans
** Convolvulus mauretanicus
 * Coreopsis (species)
** Cynoglossum amabile
** Dimorphotheca (species)
** Erigeron karvinskyanus
 * Felicia (species)

*** Frankenia capitata laevis
** Gaillardia aristata
** Gazania (species)
 * Geum (varieties)
** Godetia grandiflora
*** Helichrysum (species)
** Hemerocallis aurantiaca
 * Heuchera sanguinea
** Kniphofia uvaria
*** Limonium (species)
** Linum (species)
** Moraea (species)
 * Myosotis alpestris
** Nemesia strumosa
 * Nemophila menziesi
*** Nepeta mussini
*** Oenothera (species)
** Oxalis (species)
 * Papaver (species)
*** Pasithea caerulea
 * Pelargonium (species)
 * Penstemon gloxinioides

** Pentas lanceolata
*** Physostegia virginiana
** Portulaca grandiflora
*** Pteris (species)
*** Rehmannia angulata
*** Salpiglossis sinuata
** Salvia (check species)
* Scabiosa (species)
* Schizanthus wisetonensis
** Sedum (species)
*** Sempervivum tectorum
** Senecio cineraria

* Strelitzia reginae
*** Sisyrinchium (species)
* Tagetes (species)
*** Thalictrum dipterocarpum
** Tritonia crocosmaeflora
* Tropaeolum (species)
*** Tunica saxifraga
** Vallota speciosa
*** Veronica (species)
* Vinca (species)
** Watsonia iridifolia
* Zephyranthes (species)

PLANTS TO ABUSE---concerns the hard knocks in the experiance of a planting; the unavoidable roughness or actual violence that comes with certain uses, or the neglect that too often falls to the part of carefully conceived and well executed plantings. This is a negative approach....but knowing, and if unfavorable prospects can be foreseen, these lists may be studied with profit. They carry a message in fellow feeling, as some plants seem to suffer in adversity while others are impatient of the amenities of civilization, the coddling that goes with it, and want to be left strictly on their own. The following own to a wide tolerance in natures struggle and will stand for very hard usage when established. Check closely with the COMPENDIUM to locate the weak link that almost always exists in any chain of hardihood and consider the lists under NATIVE PLANTS and SUCCULENTS.

## TREES

* Acacia (check species)
*** Ailanthus altissima
*** Broussonetia papyrifera
* Butia capitata
* Casuarina equisetifolia
** Citrus aurantium
* Cupressus (species)
*** Dracaena australis
** Erythea (species)
* Eucalyptus (species)
** Eugenia supraaxillaris
* Ficus (check species)
** Grevillea robusta
** Koelreuteria paniculata

*** Maclura pomifera
* Melia azedarach
* Olea europaea
** Phoenix (species)
*** Phytolacca dioica
*** Pittosporum undulatum
*** Quercus douglasi
** "       suber
*** Robinia pseudacacia
** Schinus molle
** Trachycarpus fortunei
*** Tristania conferta
*** Ulmus (check species)
* Washingtonia robusta

## SHRUBS

* Acacia (check species)
** Adenostoma (species)
** Arundo donax
*** Aster fruticosus
* Atriplex (species)
** Baccharis (species)
* Bambusa multiplex
* Callistemon rigidus
*** Candollea cuneiformis
** Catha edulis
* Chamaerops humilis
** Chrysobalanus icaco
* Cistus (species)
** Correa (species)
* Cytisus canariensis
* Dendromecon rigida
** Diosma ericoides
* Dodonaea viscosa
* Echium fastuosum
** Erica melanthera
** Eriogonum (species)
* Euonymus japonicus
** Fatsia japonica
** Fremontia californica
* Genista monosperma

** Grevillea (species)
* Hakea (species)
*** Halimium (check species)
** Heimia myrtifolia
** Jasminum mesneyi
* Juniperus pfitzeriana
* Lavandula officinalis
** Lycium (species)
* Mahonia (species)
** Malvastrum coccineum
* Melaleuca (species)
** Myrsine africana
* Nerium oleander
** Odontospermum sericeum
** Phillyrea latifolia
** Phlomis fruticosa
** Pittosporum heterophyllum
* Prunus ilicifolia
* Punica granatum
** Puya alpestris
** Pyracantha lalandi
* Rhamnus alaternus
* Rhus integrifolia
* Romneya coulteri
** Rosa (check species)

  * Rosmarinus officinalis
*** Royena lucida
 ** Sabal glabra
  * Salvia greggi
 ** Sasa humilis
  * Spartium junceum

 ** Sphaeralcea ambigua
 ** Tetrapanax papyrifera
  * Teucrium fruticans
 ** Ungnadia speciosa
  * Wigandia caracasana
 ** Zauschneria californica

## VINES

*** Araujia sericofera
  * Bougainvillea sanderiana
*** Campsidium valdivianum
  * Cissus capensis
 ** Dolichos lignosus
  * Ficus pumila

 ** Hedera canariensis
 ** Lonicera halliana
*** Muehlenbeckia complexa
 ** Polygonum auberti
*** Sollya heterophylla
  * Tecomaria capensis

## HERBACEOUS PLANTS

*** Adenophora lilifolia
*** Aethionema coridifolium
  * Allium (species)
  * Anemone japonica
 ** Armeria maritima
  * Arrhenatherum tuberosum
*** Arundinaria japonica
  * Aspidistra elatior
  * Bletilla striata
*** Brunsvigia rosea
  * Campanula poscharskyana
 ** Centranthus ruber
 ** Cheilanthes gracillima
 ** Chrysanthemum maximum
*** Chusquea tessellata
  * Cichorium intybus
 ** Cirsium occidentale
*** Cooperia drummondi
 ** Coreopsis lanceolata
  * Cortaderia sellowana
 ** Crinum giganteum
*** Dimorphotheca ecklonis
 ** Erigeron karvinskyanus
  * Freesia refracta
 ** Gazania splendens
*** Hemerocallis aurantiaca
  * Iris germanica
***   " unguicularis
 **   " xiphium
*** Leucojum autumnale
  * Limonium (species)

*** Lysimachia nummularia
 ** Mentha pulegium
  * Mesembryanth. (species)
  * Mirabilis jalapa
  * Moraea iridioides
*** Nepeta mussini
  * Nephrolepis exaltata
  * Oenothera tetraptera
*** Origanum dictamnus
*** Ornithogalum arabicum
  * Oxalis (species)
*** Oxypetalum caeruleum
 ** Pellaea andromedaefolia
  * Pelargonium (check species)
*** Petasitis fragrans
 ** Phormium tenax
*** Physostegia virginiana
 ** Pteris aquilina
 ** Ranunculus repens
*** Reineckia carnea
  * Sedum album
 ** Senecio cineraria
*** Tragopogon porrifolius
*** Tritonia crocosmaeflora
 ** Tropaeolum (check species)
  * Tulbaghia violacea
*** Vallota speciosa
*** Venidium fastuosum
 ** Vinca major
  *   " rosea
*** Xanthisma texanum

       *** Zephyranthes candida

# PURPOSE ADAPTATION

Human demands upon plant life have grown as man progresses and becomes more civilized, with developing liesure and capacity to enjoy;
so that now, wants exist in kind other than the production of food or
other vital service related to survival. In a sense of ministration
we find plants attending our aesthetic and spiritual development, and
in adapting to these further needs, we find them falling into groups
based on special uses. We wish to plant a screen or drape a bank; fill
in the openings in flagging or serve in a tub. We desire a hedge, or
want a tree for the color of its bloom, or it may be those illusive
shades which come to the leaf in autumn. It may be only the shadow it
throws that delights and intrigues. We find that one plant will do
well indoors or that a combination of characters fits another for the
varied and periodic requirements of the garden. When the planter has
come to appreciate thoroughly this functional aspect and act upon it,
he will know the pleasure of working with plants that perform willingly and apparently with a kind of comfort and ease. The more common of
these uses will be found here, with the plants that will most nearly
supply the qualities desired with a minimum of guidance and special
attention. This is a high in the selective process.

GENERAL PURPOSE PLANTS---for the basic and therefore lasting elements of a landscape or garden planting. These species and variety
forms are what tend to remain after the wear of the years, the visi-
tations of time and inattention of people. They can give the garden
that character of permanence and durability so desirable to build a-
round. Here are substantial plants that will adapt to most radical
as well as reasonable conditions required of plantings and serve thru
the year without seasonal time out. It is mainly that they have no
temperament, no waggish whims or unexpected deviations to foil and
beguile the innocent. Availability in the nursery trade is one of the
prime considerations of selection. An elaboration of this theme is a
study of the GENERAL LISTS found earlier in this work.

## TREES

|   |   |
|---|---|
| ** Acacia dealbata | *** Lagunaria patersoni |
| *     "    floribunda | ** Laurus nobilis |
| ** Calodendrum capense | *** Macadamia ternifolia |
| ** Casuarina equisetifolia | * Magnolia grandiflora |
| * Cedrus deodara | ** Olea europaea |
| *** Ceratonia siliqua | *** Olmediella betschleriana |
| *** Cinnamomum camphora | ** Pinus radiata |
| ** Dracaena australis | * Pittosporum undulatum |
| * Eucalyptus (check species) | ** Podocarpus elongata |
| ** Eugenia myrtifolia | ** Populus nigra italica |
| *** Ficus retusa | *** Quercus ilex |
| * Grevillea robusta | * Schinus (species) |
| * Jacaranda acutifolia | *** Ulmus parvifolia |

## SHRUBS

|   |   |
|---|---|
| * Abelia grandiflora | ** Camellia japonica |
| *** Acacia verticillata | * Carissa grandiflora |
| * Arbutus unedo | *** Cassia splendida |
| ** Buddleja magnifica | ** Ceratostigma willmottianum |
| *** Calliandra inequilatera | *** Choisya ternata |
| * Callistemon lanceolatus | * Cistus (species) |

73

** Cytisus canariensis
*** Cocculus laurifolius
* Coprosma baueri
*** Correa magnifica
* Cotoneaster (species)
** Diosma (species)
*** Dodonaea viscosa
* Duranta (species)
** Elaeagnus pungens
** Erica melanthera
*** Escallonia (check species)
** Euonymus japonicus
*** Euphorbia pulcherrima
* Fuchsia (varieties)
** Hibiscus rosa-sinensis
** Hydrangea macrophylla
* Hypericum moserianum
*** Ilex cornuta
*** Jasminum humile
* Juniperus pfitzeriana
** Lantana camara
*** Leptospermum laevigatum
* Ligustrum (species)

** Melaleuca (species)
** Myrsine africana
* Myrtus communis
* Nandina domestica
* Nerium oleander
** Photinia serrulata
* Pittosporum tobira
* Plumbago capensis
** Prunus lyoni
** Psidium cattleianum
** Punica granatum
* Pyracantha (species)
* Raphiolepis (species)
* Rhus integrifolia
*** Rondeletia cordata
*** Sarcococca hookeriana
* Spartium junceum
* Streptosolen jamesoni
*** Tamarix (species)
*** Tecomaria capensis
*** Teucrium fruticans
* Viburnum suspensum
** Xylosma senticosa

## VINES

** Antigonon leptopus
* Bougainvillea (varieties)
** Cissus capensis
*** Doxantha unguis-cati
** Gelsemium sempervirens
* Jasminum officinale
** Hardenbergia comptoniana
* Lonicera halliana

*** Muehlenbeckia complexa
* Parthenocissus tricuspidata
*** Passiflora alato-caerulea
* Phaedranthus buccinatorius
*** Polygonum auberti
** Pyrostegia ignea
** Thunbergia grandiflora
* Trachelospermum jasminoides

*** Wisteria floribunda

## HERBACEOUS PLANTS

* Acanthus mollis
** Agapanthus africanus
* Alyssum maritimum
*** Amarcrinum howardi
* Anemone japonica
* Begonia (species)
*** Beloperone guttata
*** Bletilla striata
* Brunsvigia rosea
* Calendula officinalis
** Campanula poscharskyana
*** Centaurea cineraria
* Chrysanthemum morifolium
** Cineraria cruenta
*** Clivia miniata
** Coreopsis lanceolata
** Cosmos bipinnatus
** Cyperus alternifolius
*** Cyrtomium falcatum
* Dahlia pinnata
** Delphinium ajacis
* Dianthus (species)
*** Erigeron karvinskyanus
** Freesia refracta
* Gaillardia aristata
** Gerberia jamesoni
** Geum (varieties)
* Gladiolus hortulanus
** Heliotropium arborescens
* Hemerocallis aurantiaca
* Heuchera sanguinea
* Iris germanica
*** Ixia maculata
*** Kniphofia uvaria
* Lavandula officinalis

*** Liriope spicata
* Lobelia erinus
** Lotus mascaensis
** Malcomia maritima
*** Mesembryanth. (species)
** Mirabilis jalapa
*** Moraea (check species)
* Myosotis alpestris
** Narcissus pseudo-narcissus
*** Nepeta mussini
*** Nierembergia caerulea
** Oxalis bowieana
* Pelargonium (check species)
* Penstemon gloxinioides
* Phlox drummondi
*** Phormium tenax
** Primula polyantha
** Ranunculus asiaticus
*** Schizanthus wisetonensis
** Sedum album
*** Stokesia laevis
** Tagetes erecta
** Teucrium chamaedrys
*** Thymus serpyllum
* Tritonia crocosmaeflora
** Tropaeolum majus
*** Tulbaghia violacea
** Vallota speciosa
* Verbena hortensis
* Viola tricolor
* Watsonia iridifolia
*** Xeranthemum annuum
** Zantedeschia aethiopica
** Zephyranthes (species)
* Zinnia elegans

SEASIDE PLANTING---is limited in growth as well as in the latitude of choice in materials by the combination of wind and salt. Resistance seems to center in the color and structure of the leaf, with grey foliage or smooth, and particularly shining leaves or those with a waxy coating the more immune to searing. Rough leaves are more susceptible to salt. A small or needle-type leaf of close cellular structure and low in chlorophyll, will wage a long and gratifying struggle with the elements. There should be good drainage here. The marginal area subject to these influences may be fairly, if roughly divided into three belts or zones of exposure, as follows.

## FIRST ZONE OF EXPOSURE

The shoreline must bear up under the most rigorous of conditions, as of salt in the soil and in driven spray. Barriers, whether for shelter or for ornament and permanent or temporary, may be used to intercept the first violence, while some mulching material will prove beneficial. Quick recovery is important here since the plant may be sheltering a neighbor having less resistance. These lusty plants will stand in the teeth of the wind with the minimum of burning and give as much satisfaction as may be had at the shore.

### TREES

*   Acacia longifolia
***   "    pycnantha
**  Albizzia lebbec
***   "     lophantha
*   Araucaria excelsa
**  Casuarina equisetifolia
*** Chrysobalanus icaco
*** Clusia rosea
*** Corynocarpus laevigata
**  Coccolobis floridana
**  Cocos nucifera
*   Cupressus macrocarpa
**  Dracaena (check species)
*** Eucalyptus cornuta
*     "    ficifolia
**    "    lehmanni
***   "    torquata

*   Ficus macrophylla
*** Juniperus barbadensis
*   Lagunaria patersoni
*   Metrosideros tomentosa
*   Myoporum laetum
**  Phoenix canariensis
***   "    reclinata
**  Pinus radiata
***   "    torreyana
**  Pittosporum viridiflorum
*** Populus alba
*   Quercus ilex
*** Ricinus communis
*   Sabal palmetto
*** Thespesia populnea
*** Trachycarpus fortunei
*   Washingtonia robusta

### SHRUBS

**  Acacia armata
**  Acokanthera spectabilis
*   Atriplex breweri
*   Carissa grandiflora
*** Ceratostigma griffithi
*   Coccolobis uvifera
*   Coprosma baueri
**  Correa pulchella
*** Cotoneaster pannosa
**  Dodonaea viscosa
*** Dovyalis caffra
**  Elaeagnus pungens
*** Eriogonum arborescens
*   Escallonia rosea
**  Euonymus japonicus
*** Grevillea banksi
**  Griselinia littoralis
**  Hakea suaveolens
*** Halimium halimifolium
**  Hebe carnea
**  Heteromeles arbutifolia
**  Hibiscus tiliaceus
*** Hymenanthera crassifolia

*** Ilex paraguariensis
*** Jaquinea keyensis
*   Juniperus conferta
*** Lantana camara
*   Lavatera assurgentiflora
*   Leptospermum laevigatum
*   Ligustrum lucidum
**  Lonicera nitida
*   Lycium richi
*** Lotus formosissimus
*** Medicago arborea
*   Melaleuca nesophila
*** Phlomis fruticosa
*   Pittosporum crassifolium
**    "     tobira
*** Podalyrea sericea
*   Raphiolepis (species)
**  Rhamnus alaternus
*   Rhus integrifolia
*** Rosmarinus officinalis
*** Spartium junceum
*** Triphasia trifolia
*   Westringia rosmariniformis

### VINES

*** Asparagus falcatus
**  Cissus incisa
**  Ficus pumila
*** Ipomoea pes-capri
*   Lonicera hildebrandtiana

**  Jasminum gracile
**  Muehlenbeckia complexa
*   Phaedranthus buccinatorius
*   Solandra guttata
**  Rosa banksiae

### HERBACEOUS PLANTS

* Abronia (species)
** Agave (species)
** Aloe (species)
* Alyssum maritimum
** Ammophila arenaria
** Armeria maritima
* Atriplex semibaccata
** Centranthus ruber
*** Ceratostigma plumbaginoides
** Chrysanthemum maximum
** Coreopsis maritima
*** Corethrogyne californica
* Crassula argentea
*** Dimorphotheca ecklonis
** Echeveria pulverulenta
*** Eriophyllum caespitosum
*** Erysimum capitatum
** Fragaria chiloensis
*** Frankenia capitata laevis
* Furcraea gigantea
* Gazania splendens
*** Glaucium flavum
*** Grindelia robusta

* Helichrysum petiolatum
** Iris unguicularis
*** Kalanchoe flammea
* Kleinia repens
** Lavandula officinalis
* Limonium perezi
** Lotus mascaensis
* Mesembryanth. (species)
** Oenothera tetraptera
** Ophiopogon japonica
** Pachyphytum bracteosum
** Phormium tenax
** Portulacaria afra
* Pelargonium domesticum
*** Salvia argentea
* Sedum album
* Sempervivum calcareum
** Senecio cineraria
* Stenotaphrum secundatum
*** Tetragonia expansa
*** Veronica incana
*** Vigna marina
*** Wedelia trilobata

### SECOND ZONE OF EXPOSURE

This area reckons with considerable salt in both the air and soil, but assumes some protection from the wind to materially reduce the infiltration of storms with their sting and lash. The height back of a cliff may suffice; the shelter of an established planting; the leeward side of a building or sufficient distance at least from the surf-line to prevent the actual wetting down by spray. For appropriate plants in a further protection back of this line, see WIND FIGURATION and EXPOSURE that appear earlier in this study.

### TREES

** Acacia pruinosa
** Achras zapota
*** Agathis robusta
** Agonis flexuosa
*** Albizzia julibrissin
* Araucaria bidwilli
*** Bucida bucerus
*** Calophyllum inophyllum
* Callistemon viminalis
* Casuarina (species)
** Crinodendron dependens
* Cupressus (check species)
** Delonix regia
* Eriobotrya japonica
** Erythea edulis
* Eucalyptus (species)
* Ficus (species)

*** Guaiacum officinale
*** Haematoxylon campechianum
** Juniperus torulosa
* Macadamia ternifolia
* Melaleuca leucadendra
*** Melicocca bijuga
*** Lyonothamnus asplenifolius
* Lysiloma siliquastrum
** Maytenus boaria
*** Ochrosia elliptica
*** Olea chrysophylla
** Phoenix (species)
* Pinus (check species)
*** Pittosporum undulatum
** Quercus virginiana
** Schinus terebinthifolius
*** Simaruba amara

*** Ulmus crassifolia

### SHRUBS

* Acacia verticillata
** Aeonium spathulatum
*** Agonis linearifolia
** Anthyllis barba-jovis
* Baccharis (species)
** Berberis darwini
** Brachysema lanceolatum
*** Buddleja salvifolia
* Callistemon (species)
*** Calothamnus quadrifidus
*** Camellia sasanqua
** Cassia splendida
* Ceanothus verrucosus

** Ceratostigma willmottianum
** Cestrum diurnum
** Convolvulus cneorum
* Cistus (species)
** Correa (species)
* Cotoneaster (species)
** Cytisus canariensis
* Echium fastuosum
* Erica melanthera
*** Eriocephalis africanus
*** Eriogonum (check species)
*** Erythrina crista-galli
* Escallonia (species)

** Fatsia japonica
*** Garrya elliptica
** Genista monosperma
*** Gossypium sturti
*** Grevillea rosmarinifolia
* Grewia occidentalis
* Hakea laurina
*** Halimium (species)
* Hebe (species)
*** Hibiscus rosa-sinensis
*** Ilex (species)
* Juniperus (species)
** Lantana (species)
* Laurus nobilis
** Leptospermum scoparium
* Ligustrum (species)
*** Lupinus arboreus
* Melaleuca (species)
** Myrsine africana
** Nerium oleander
*** Noltea africana

** Ochna multiflora
*** Odontospermum sericeum
** Osmanthus fortunei
*** Phillyrea latifolia
* Pittosporum (species)
* Polygala dalmaisiana
* Prunus lyoni
** Pseudopanax lessoni
** Psoralea pinnata
* Pyracantha (species)
** Rhus (species)
*** Ribes viburnifolium
** Romneya coulteri
*** Rondeletia cordata
*** Salvia greggi
** Solanum laurifolium
*** Siphonosmanthus delavayi
* Sollya heterophylla
** Teucrium fruticans
** Viburnum japonicum
***     "     odoratissimum

## VINES

** Anemopoegma chamberlayni
* Bougainvillea (varieties)
** Cissus (species)
*** Clematis indevisa
* Hedera canariensis

** Ipomoea (species)
** Lonicera confusa
*** Oxera pulchella
** Passiflora racemosa
*** Stigmaphyllon littorale

## HERBACEOUS PLANTS

** Agapanthus africanus
* Anemone japonica
* Bergenia cordifolia
* Calendula officinalis
*** Campanula poscharskyana
*** Chrysanthemum maximum
** Coreopsis lanceolata
** Dianthus (species)
*** Echium wildpreti
* Erigeron karvinskyanus
*** Eschscholtzia californica
* Felicia (species)
** Geum Bradshaw
* Hemerocallis aurantiaca
** Heuchera sanguinea
*** Jasminum parkeri
** Iris germanica
*** Kalanchoe fedschenkoi
*** Lavatera olbia
*** Linum narbonnense
** Lippia canescens

** Liriope spicata
* Malcomia maritima
** Mathiola incana
* Moraea (species)
** Nepeta mussini
** Ophiopogon (species)
*** Pancratium maritimum
* Pelargonium peltatum
** Phlox drummondi
*** Reineckia carnea
** Salvia farinacea
*** Scabiosa caucasica
* Sedum (species)
** Senecio (species)
*** Thymus (species)
*** Tulbaghia (species)
** Veronica (species)
* Vinca major
*** Zantedeschia aethiopica
** Zephyranthes candida
*** Zoysia tenuifolia

## THIRD ZONE OF EXPOSURE

Further suggestions for the immediate coastline, plants that will adjust to some degree of salt in the soil and stand up to a reliably baffled wind. They may actually favor the moderating influence of the sea air and fresh humidity, so that the year round appearance may be improved. This is the last step back to normal, with a lot of the refinement and color from more protected gardens. Light soils for warmth and drainage are still advantageous in leaching out the salt that will inevitably filter through.

## TREES

* Acacia (species)
** Butia capitata
* Calodendrum capense
*** Cercis siliquastrum
** Cinnamomum camphora
*** Eugenia paniculata
*** Grevillea robusta

* Jacaranda acutifolia
* Liquidambar styraciflua
* Magnolia grandiflora
*** Mimusops elengi
** Olea europaea
* Pittosporum (species)
** Podocarpus (species)

*** Samanea saman                      *** Umbellularia californica
  * Schinus molle                      *** Vitex lucens
 ** Ulmus parvifolia                    ** Thuja orientalis

## SHRUBS

  * Abelia grandiflora                  ** Jasminum (check species)
  * Arbutus unedo                      *** Magnolia stellata
*** Ardisia (species)                    * Mahonia (species)
 ** Azalea (species)                    ** Michelia fuscata
 ** Berberis (species)                   * Myrtus communis
 ** Buddleja (species)                 *** Osmanthus (species)
*** Calceolaria integrifolia            ** Poinciana (species)
  * Camellia (species)                   * Prunus (check species)
  * Ceanothus (check species)          ** Ribes glutinosum
 ** Cestrum aurantiacum                *** Senecio petasitis
*** Choisya ternata                    *** Serissa foetida
  * Coronilla glauca                    ** Solanum (check species)
 ** Daphne odora                       *** Sophora secundiflora
*** Daphniphyllum humile                 * Streptosolen jamesoni
*** Entelea arborescens                 ** Turraea obtusifolia
  * Grevillea (species)                  * Viburnum (species)
 ** Hypericum moserianum               *** Vitex trifolia
*** Illicium anisatum                  *** Weigela florida
 ** Lippia citriodora                   ** Xylosma senticosa

## VINES

*** Arrabidaea magnifica               *** Jasminum (check species)
  * Boussingaultia baselloides         *** Kennedya rubicunda
  * Distictis lactiflora                ** Passiflora (species)
  * Gelsemium sempervirens               * Polygonum auberti
  * Hardenbergia (species)              ** Rosa (species)
 ** Hibbertia volubilis                *** Solanum wendlandi

## HERBACEOUS PLANTS

 ** Acanthus mollis                    *** Lupinus (species)
*** Albuca minor                        ** Narcissus pseudo-narcissus
 ** Alstroemeria aurantiaca              * Nierembergia (species)
 ** Amaryllis (species)                *** Ornithogalum arabicum
 ** Anagallis linifolia                 ** Oxalis (species)
  * Arenaria balearica                 *** Oxypetalum caeruleum
 ** Aristea ecklonis                   *** Papaver (species)
*** Asclepias currassavica             *** Pellaea andromedaefolia
*** Callistephus chinensis               * Pelargonium (species)
  * Campanula (species)                  * Penstemon gloxinioides
 ** Centaurea cyanus                     * Petunia hybrida
  * Chrysanthemum (species)           *** Pteris tremula
 ** Clivia (species)                    ** Ranunculus (species)
  * Cynoglossum amabile                 ** Salvia (species)
*** Delphinium grandiflorum              * Scabiosa (species)
*** Dianella (species)                 *** Sternbergia lutea
*** Elisena longipetala                 ** Tagetes (species)
 ** Freesia refracta                   *** Tithonia rotundifolia
  * Gaillardia aristata                 ** Tropaeolum majus
  * Gerberia jamesoni                  *** Verbena hortensis
  * Geum (varieties)                   *** Veltheimia iridifolia
 ** Hunnemannia fumariaefolia            * Viola (species)
  * Iris (species)                     *** Zaluzianskya capensis
 ** Kniphofia uvaria                    ** Zantedeschia (species)
*** Ligularia kaempferi                  * Zebrina pendula
*** Linaria dalmatica                   ** Zephyranthes (species

## SUCCULENTS

  * Aeonium decorum                    *** Opuntia linguiforme
 ** Byrnesia weinbergi                    * Othonna crassifolia
*** Echeveria derenbergi                ** Pereskia aculeata
*** Euphorbia tirucalli                 ** Portulacaria afra
*** Hesperaloe parviflora                * Sansevieria (species)
*** Hylocereus triangularis              * Sedum (species)
 ** Kalanchoe (species)                 ** Senecio mikanioides
  * Oliveranthus elegans                ** Yucca elephantipes

STREET TREES---whether set by the municipality or by the citizen should of all plantings be considered in light of service to be expected. When they actually place the sidewalk at the curb, there will be more good trees for this purpose. As it is, the perfect street tree does not exist. A lack of vigor under city conditions will rule out some. Others are too large and require such heavy pruning as to leave likely opening for infections that are difficult to control. They either litter badly or will not accomodate their roots to cramped quarters and vent an ill humour on curb and sidewalk. The following have been found to be the more satisfactory in service and length of life. Give the soil every possible preparation.

### AVENUE

| | |
|---|---|
| \*\*\* Acacia melanoxylon | \* Fraxinus velutina |
| \*\*\* Brachychiton acerifolium | \* Magnolia grandiflora |
| \*\* Calophyllum inophyllum | \*\* Pinus radiata |
| \*\*\* Casuarina equisetifolia | \*\*\* " torreyana |
| \* Cinnamomum camphora | \*\* Pittosporum undulatum |
| \* Cupania anacardioides | \*\* Platanus orientalis |
| \*\* Cupressus benthami | \*\*\* Quercus agrifolia |
| \*\*\* " macrocarpa | \*\* " lobata |
| \* Cedrus (species) | \* " virginiana |
| \* Eucalyptus cornuta | \*\*\* Quillaja saponaria |
| \*\* " rostrata | \* Schinus molle |
| \*\*\* " tereticornis | \*\*\* Washingtonia filifera |
| \*\*\* Ficus retusa | \*\* Ulmus pumila |

### STREET

| | |
|---|---|
| \*\*\* Acacia decurrens | \*\* Ligustrum japonicum |
| \*\*\* Agonis flexuosa | \*\* Liquidambar styraciflua |
| \*\*\* Angophora lanceolata | \*\* Melaleuca leucadendra |
| \*\*\* Arecastrum romanzoffianum | \*\*\* " styphelioides |
| \* Brachychiton diversifolia | \*\* Pinus canariensis |
| \* Calodendrum capense | \*\*\* Pistacia chinensis |
| \*\*\* Cassia grandis | \* Pittosporum rhombifolium |
| \*\*\* Casuarina cunninghamiana | \*\* Podocarpus elongata |
| \*\*\* Celtis australis | \*\* Populus nigra italica |
| \*\* Delonix regia | \* Prunus caroliniana |
| \*\*\* Elaeodendron orientale | \*\*\* Quercus chrysolepis |
| \*\* Erythea edulis | \*\* " laurifolia |
| \*\*\* Eucalyptus calophylla | \* " ilex |
| \* " ficifolia | \* Sapindus saponaria |
| \*\*\* " leucoxylon | \*\*\* Sapium sebiferum |
| \*\* " polyanthemos | \*\*\* Schrebera swietenioides |
| \* " sideroxylon | \*\* Terminalia catappa |
| \*\* Firmiana simplex | \*\*\* Thespesia populnea |
| \* Fraxinus uhdei | \* Tristania conferta |
| \* Harpephyllum caffrum | \*\* Ulmus alata |
| \*\* Jacaranda acutifolia | \*\*\* Vitex lucens |
| \* Lagunaria patersoni | \*\* Washingtonia robusta |

### LANE

| | |
|---|---|
| \*\* Acacia pendula | \* Ligustrum lucidum |
| \*\*\* " prominens | \*\* Maytenus boaria |
| \*\* Arcontophoenix cunningham. | \* Melaleuca nesophila |
| \*\* Bolusanthus speciosus | \*\* Metrosideros tomentosa |
| \*\*\* Cassia fistulosa | \*\*\* Michelia champaca |
| \* Casuarina stricta | \* Nerium oleander |
| \*\*\* Ceanothus arboreus | \*\*\* Olmediella betschleriana |
| \*\*\* Coccolobis floridana | \* Persea indica |
| \*\* Crinodendron dependens | \*\* Pittosporum eugenioides |
| \*\*\* Eucalyptus caesia | \* " viridiflorum |
| \*\*\* " erythrocorys | \*\* Populus simoni |
| \*\* " erythronema | \*\*\* Prunus campanulata |
| \* " torquata | \*\* " lyoni |
| \*\*\* Fraxinus dipetala | \*\*\* Quercus douglasi |
| \*\*\* Homalanthus populifolius | \*\*\* Sophora secundiflora |
| \*\* Hymenosporum flavum | \*\*\* Stenocarpus sinuatus |
| \* Lagerstroemia indica | \* Trachycarpus fortunei |
| \*\*\* Ulmus parvifolia | |

TREES FOR THE HIGHWAY---properly, large, stout-hearted individuals
which may be expected to establish themselves at the roadside and to
be maintained in some permanence at a minimum of expense. They should
be of definite form, spreading, vase-shaped, or clearly erect for a
long-narrowing perspective. Natives may not be so successful, out of
the huddled woodland seclusion, yet on the whole offer good material
if placed to their liking and advantage....cross-check thoroughly.
Monotony, as of regular spacing, may well be avoided in view of increasing speed and too quickly recurring impressions. This leads to
off-way planting where un-used ground or rock wastes might be set to
small groves in the highway scheme, with partial or ultimate use as
woodlots. Deciduous trees have advantages with a bearing on wet pav-
ing....explore this and other safety factors of good planting.

### ARID REGIONS

| | | | |
|---|---|---|---|
| ** | Casuarina equisetifolia | *** | Phoenix dactylifera |
| ** | Cedrus atlantica | *** | Phytolacca dioica |
| * | Cupressus forbsi | *** | Pinus coulteri |
| *** | "      goveniana | ** | "    radiata |
| ** | Eucalyptus maculata | * | "    sabiniana |
| * | "         polyanthemos | *** | Populus fremonti |
| * | "         rostrata | * | "    nigra italica |
| * | "         tereticornis | *** | Prunus amygdalus |
| *** | "         viminalis | ** | Quercus agrifolia |
| *** | Ficus macrophylla | * | "    lobata |
| ** | Fraxinus velutina | *** | "    suber |
| * | Grevillea robusta | *** | Sequoiadendron giganteum |
| *** | Juglans (check species) | * | Schinus molle |
| ** | Libocedrus decurrens | ** | Tipuana tipu |
| ** | Melia azedarach | * | Ulmus pumila |
| *** | Phoenix canariensis | ** | Washingtonia filifera |

### HUMID REGIONS

| | | | |
|---|---|---|---|
| *** | Albizzia julibrissin | * | Grevillea robusta |
| ** | Aleurites moluccana | * | Liquidambar styraciflua |
| *** | Betula nigra | * | Magnolia grandiflora |
| *** | Broussonetia papyrifera | ** | Persea borbonia |
| ** | Casuarina equisetifolia | *** | Phoenix canariensis |
| ** | Cedrus deodara | *** | Pinus caribaea |
| *** | Celtis australis | * | Pittosporum undulatum |
| * | Cinnamomum camphora | ** | Platanus orientalis |
| *** | Cupania anacardioides | ** | Quercus laurifolia |
| * | Cupressus benthami | *** | "    palustris |
| *** | Eugenia paniculata | * | "    virginiana |
| *** | Eucalyptus botryoides | ** | Samanea saman |
| * | "         cornuta | ** | Terminalia catappa |
| ** | "         robusta | ** | Tristanea conferta |
| ** | Fraxinus velutina | * | Ulmus pumila |

TREES FOR THE LAWN---including certain shrubs of individuality and
qualification, since grass is not the most acceptable place for them.
Selections below are for an arborescent character or inclination and
ability to give good service in turf. They may be used formally or at
random or for purely specimen interest. Surprisingly few plants will
adjust happily to turf management and conditions. Either the one or
the other will suffer in the inevitable competition. Those which
follow will tend to meet this want of harmony or agreement and adapt
reasonably. Set them high, rather than low to the soil-line for an
added interest in a buttressed base. Deep irrigation in drouth is indicated as an extra, while the matter of litter and its timing should
be considered....it is important maintenance-wise.

### SHRUBS

| | | | |
|---|---|---|---|
| * | Arbutus unedo | *** | Eucalyptus forrestiana |
| *** | Bauhinia acuminata | ** | Eugenia uniflora |
| *** | Brunfelsia americana | *** | Fuchsia arborescens |
| * | Buxus microphylla | *** | Gaya lyalli |
| ** | Callistemon lanceolatus | * | Hibiscus rosa-sinensis |
| *** | Cycas circinalis | ** | Ilex vomitoria |
| ** | Erythrina crista-galli | ** | Juniperus excelsa stricta |

** Melaleuca huegeli                    * Prunus lyoni
** Michelia fuscata                     ** Psidium cattleianum
** Murraea paniculata                   * Pyracantha koidsumi
* Nandina domestica                     * Raphiolepis indica
** Nerium oleander                      *** Thevetia thevetioides
* Pittosporum tobira                    * Thuja orientalis (varieties)
                    *** Viburnum odoratissimum

## TREES

** Acacia pendula                       *** Homalanthus populifolius
*** Acrocomia totai                     * Juniperus torulosa
*** Agathis robusta                     *** Lagerstroemia indica
** Alnus (species)                      * Laurus nobilis
* Arecastrum romanzoffianum             * Libocedrus decurrens
** Bauhinia variegata                   * Liquidambar styraciflua
** Betula nigra                         *** Macadamia ternifolia
** Brachychiton acerifolium             * Magnolia grandiflora
* Callistemon viminalis                 ** Maytenus boaria
* Cedrus deodara                        ** Melaleuca leucadendra
*** Chamaecyparis lawsoniana            *       "      styphelioides
*** Cornus capitata                     ** Metrosideros tomentosa
* Crinodendron dependens                ** Phoenix reclinata
*** Cupressus lusitanica                *** Pinus radiata
** Erythea armata                       * Pittosporum rhombifolium
** Erythrina humeana                    **      "      viridiflorum
*** Escallonia montevidensis            * Podocarpus elongata
* Eucalyptus citriodora                 ** Prunus amygdalus
**      "      leucoxylon               *** "      caroliniana
**      "      robusta                  * Quercus virginiana
*** Eugenia paniculata                  *** Quillaja saponaria
** Ficus benjamina                      ** Thuja orientalis
** Firmiana simplex                     *** Torreya taxifolia
*** Harpephyllum caffrum                *** Vitex lucens
                    ** Umbellularia californica

SHADE TREES---admit of the most intimate association with every phase of outdoor living. This goes back to the beginning, so that the companionship becomes a thing of substance, of more than physical comfort and of very apparent beauty. This list will include species that take readily to domestication, produce the minimum of litter or such as is easily removed, and which in other ways are least onerous about habitations or public places. A choice must be approached critically from the standpoint of what the tree will do for its surroundings, depth of shadow, stem breakage, and especially the root levy on the soil. Generally these trees should be set south and west of the immediate area to be served.

## LIGHT SHADE

* Acacia floribunda                     *** Juglans rupestris
** Acacia pruinosa                      *** Lysiloma latisiliqua
* Albizzia julibrissin                  * Melia azedarach
* Aleurites moluccana                   ** Morus rubra
**      "      fordi                    ** Olea europaea
*** Alnus cordata                       * Parkinsonia aculeata
*** Angophora lanceolata                *** Peltophorum inerme
*** Barklya syringifolia                ** Pinus halepensis
*** Cassia fistula                      * Pistacia chinensis
**      "      grandis                  *** Pittosporum eugenioides
** Chilopsis linearis                   ** Platanus racemosa
** Delonix regia                        * Podocarpus elongata
*** Ebenopsis flexicaulis               ** Populus alba
*** Erythrina poeppigiana               ** Prosopis glandulosa
* Eucalyptus citriodora                 * Prunus amygdalus
***      "      polyanthemos            ** Pyrus calleryana
**      "      sideroxylon              *** Quercus chrysolepis
*** Ficus carica                        **      "      suber
** Fraxinus velutina                    ** Salix babylonica
** Hymenosporum flavum                  *** Sapindus saponaria
* Jacaranda acutifolia                  ** Schinus molle

*** Simaruba amara              * Tipuana tipu
*** Spathodea campanulata        * Tristania conferta
*** Terminalia catappa         *** Ulmus alata
            *** Virgilia capensis

## HEAVY SHADE

 ** Acacia melanoxylon            * Magnolia grandiflora
*** Acer oblongum                 * Melia umbraculiformis
*** Achras zapota               *** Morus rubra
*** Broussonetia papyrifera     *** Persea americana
*** Celtis australis              * Phoenix canariensis
  * Ceratonia siliqua            ** Phytolacca dioica
  * Cinnamomum camphora          ** Pinus pinea
 ** Cupania anacardioides         *    "    radiata
 ** Cupressus macrocarpa         ** Pittosporum rhombifolium
*** Eucalyptus calophylla         *    "      undulatum
  *     "      cornuta          *** Platanus orientalis
 **     "      ficifolia        *** Pterospermum acerifolium
 ** Ficus benjamina               * Quercus agrifolia
***     "   macrophylla           *    "     virginiana
*** Firmiana simplex            *** Samanea saman
 ** Harpephyllum caffrum         ** Sapium sebiferum
 ** Juglans regia                 * Schinus terebinthifolius
*** Koelreuteria paniculata      ** Ulmus pumila
 ** Liquidambar formosana       *** Umbellularia californica
            *** Vitex lucens


FLOWERING TREES---should be placed to be seen, obviously, and the
more perspective involved, the more complete the showing.  Moreover,
a little distance usually allows the fallen petalage to remain on the
ground as a further relish to the eye. The more spectacular of these
trees are tropical in origin and are finding their way northerly as
they adapt to chill and deeper cold, to light frost. The gardener,
rather than rejecting off-hand, should foster this process in his
handling and help pull their frontier north in orderly progression.
Help this with a warm exposure, good air drainage, and a little protection when young.  Guide them into winter with dry feet, but not too
dry at a critical period of cold.  The matter of propagation, then, is
most important, not only in retaining hardy strains, but in color
selection.  Go to a careful nurseryman who will take bud sticks from
a selected tree and of flowering wood. Minimum, or light pruning of
the growing tree, will encourage flower buds and early production by
retarding vegetative growth....most effective if done just after a
growth flush has started.

  * Acacia baileyana          *** Embothrium coccineum
***    "    decurrens          ** Erythrina (check species)
 **    "    floribunda          * Eucalyptus caesia
  *    "    pubescens         ***    "      erythrocorys
 **    "    pycnantha           *    "      ficifolia
  * Albizzia julibrissin       **    "      sideroxylon rosea
*** Barklya syringifolia      *** Fraxinus dipetala
 ** Bauhinia grandiflora        * Grevillea robusta
  *    "    variegata           * Hymenosporum flavum
 ** Bolusanthus speciosus       * Jacaranda acutifolia
  * Brachychiton acerifolium   ** Lagunaria patersoni
 ** Callistemon viminalis       * Magnolia grandiflora
  * Calodendrum capense       *** Markhamia lutea
*** Cassia fistulosa            * Metrosideros tomentosa
***    "    grandis           *** Paulownia tomentosa
*** Castanospermum australe   *** Peltophorum inerme
 ** Cercis siliquastrum        ** Prunus amygdalus
 ** Chorisia speciosa         ***    "    campanulata
*** Cochlospermum vitifolium    *    "    persica
*** Colvillea racemosa         ** Spathodea campanulata
 ** Crinodendron dependens    *** Stenocarpus sinuatus
  * Dais cotinifolia          *** Tabebuia umbellata
 ** Delonix regia              ** Tipuana tipu
*** Delostoma roseum          *** Virgilia capensis

WALL PLANTS---those adapted for use in some way with a wall; to
break harsh lines; to diminish an expanse of construction; or in general, to modify architectural definition. Sometimes the plant may be
frankly thrown in relief against the mass to bring out some intrinsic grace in its own structure or a potential pattern that may be expected to emerge. Certain vining shrubs may be grown outside to conserve root space within the enclosure, the body of the plant to be
carried over the wall in a flopping manner. Again, the plant may be
set and grown in some form of orniture such as a lyre or repeated hor-
izontals, using an appropriate means of support.  Sun-warmth in the
wall carried into and released at night will reduce chill and foster
flowering in marginal tropical subjects that may otherwise fail under
frost. Study the exposure carefully and fit the plant.

## ESPALIER

Originally the trellis upon which the plant was trained, now
referring to the plant itself as it adapts to the guiding hand against
a wall. Choose a plant with growth disposed in accord with the thought
pattern, erect-rigid with arms that tend to branch with close-held
leaf and flower. Moderate to slow growth is best and a tendency to
make short spurs the more efficient. Start with a young plant, pinch-
out and pruning to desired form. This should be related to growth
periods else the plant gets out of hand.  Support on a wood frame or
carry on wires through eyed lag-bolts cemented or plugged in lead.
Good culture is mandatory for proper dividends on time and expense,
but always, a plant to start with that has something extra in way of
interest and advantage to offer the project.

| | |
|---|---|
| *** Abelia floribunda | *** Itea ilicifolia |
| ** Abutilon megapotamicum | *** Loropetalum chinense |
| * Azara microphylla | *** Magnolia stellata |
| * Bauhinia galpini | * Michelia fuscata |
| * Calliandra inequilatera | * Ochna multiflora |
| ** Calothamnus quadrifidus | *** Oncoba routledgi |
| * Camellia sasanqua | *** Osmanthus armatus |
| ** Ceanothus papillosus | *** Pereskia aculeata |
| *** Cercis siliquastrum | * Photinia serrulata nova |
| ** Chaenomeles japonica | *** Plumeria emarginata |
| *** Chiococca alba | ** Podocarpus nagi |
| * Citrus (check species) | ** Psidium cattleianum |
| ** Coprosma baueri | * Pyracantha (variety forms) |
| ** Correa pulchella | * Pyrus kawakami |
| *** Dendromecon rigida | *** Schinus dependens |
| *** Epiphyllum oxypetalon | *** Solandra longiflora |
| ** Erythrina bidwilli | *** Solanum muricatum |
| *** Eucalyptus macrocarpa | * Sophora secundiflora |
| * Fuchsia (select varieties) | *** Strophanthus speciosus |
| * Gardenia thunbergia | *** Strychnos spinosa |
| ** Garrya elliptica | * Ternstroemia japonica |
| ** Grewia occidentalis | ** Viburnum burkwoodi |
| *** Griselinia lucida | ** Wisteria floribunda |
| ** Hibiscus rosa-sinensis | * Xylosma senticosa |

## WALLTOP TUMBLERS

Here are willing plants that are pliable and active in growth
yet controlable as a straddle to break the too-long line of the free-
standing wall. At the same time they serve to reduce an expanse of
construction.  A tendency to build up wood and herbage out of desirable proportion may be offset by thinning from time to time. Make the
cuts at random and allow to stand until wilting leaves indicate further cuts for smaller sections to be removed.

| | |
|---|---|
| *** Abutilon megapotamicum (type) | * Holskioldia sanguinea |
| ** Antigonon leptopus | *** Homalocladium platycladium |
| * Artabotrys uncinatus | * Jasminum grandiflorum |
| ** Bauhinia corymbosa | ** Lonicera (check species) |
| * Campsidium valdivianum | *** Macropiper excelsum |
| ** Cissus hypoglauca | ** Muehlenbeckia complexa |
| *** Fatshedera lizei | ** Oxera pulchella |
| *** Fuchsia corymbiflora | *** Plumbago capensis alba |
| *** Helichrysum diosmaefolium | ** Podranea ricasoliana |

*** Securidaca diversifolia      * Streptosolen jamesoni
  * Solanum rantonneti          ** Tecomaria capensis
  * Sollya heterophylla          * Trachelospermum jasminoides

## SILHOUETTE

Plants of distinction, those with marked clarity of line or easy gracefulness that will stand of themselves against the wall, where these special characters may be seen in relief. The value of thrown shadow will be brought out here with all the meaning that the moon has for inanimate things....stable enough and coherent by day, but endowed with mysterious abstractions by night.

*** Acanthus montanus           *** Eurya emarginata
*** Adenostoma sparsifolium      *** Fouquieria splendens
 ** Aloe (check species)           * Gardenia thunbergia
  * Bauhinia tomentosa           *** Greyia sutherlandi
*** Berberis gagnepaini           ** Lonicera nitida
 ** Camellia reticulata            * Monstera deliciosa
 ** Caryota mitis                 ** Nandina domestica
 ** Cephalocereus senilis        *** Phillerya latifolia
  * Coccolobis uvifera            ** Philodendron (check species)
 ** Cocculus laurifolius           * Phoenix roebelini
*** Collinia elegans             *** Phygelius capensis
  * Cotoneaster pannosa nana     *** Portulacaria afra
  * Cyperus (check species)        * Rhapis (species)
 ** Dahlia maxoni                 ** Strelitzia (species)
*** Damnacanthus indicus          ** Tibouchina elegans
 ** Dasylirion glaucophyllum     *** Vitis arizonica
  * Echium fastuosum               * Xylosma senticosa
*** Euphorbia tirucalli          *** Yucca (species)

PILLAR PLANTS---vines of restraint or those easily repressed, together with climbing shrubs to use in connection with the pergola, porch post or other slender column. The more formalized the pillar the less import the plant carries and vice versa, until the structural parts may be nearly if not entirely covered. The important consideration is the manner in which the stems mount, as a gracefully winding line is usually of more concern than coverage. This is especially true if wisps of foliage can be coaxed out low on the stem to soften the course.....or grow in two or more strands, reducing one every year or two, thus producing a kind of rotation upwards.

 ** Abrus precatorius             ** Lonicera aureo-reticulata
*** Ampelopsis brevipedunculata   *    "      confusa
*** Araujia sericofera           ** "      etrusca
*** Artabotrys uncinatus         *** "      sempervirens
*** Asparagus falcatus            *.Mandevilla suaveolens
 ** Boussingaultia baselloides   *** Nephthytis afzeli
 ** Clytostoma callistegioides     * Passiflora racemosa
*** Cantua buxifolia             *** Petrea volubilis
*** Cardiospermum halicacabum     ** Philodendron oxycardium
  * Cissus antarctica            *** Plumbago capensis alba
 ** "      hypoglauca            *** Rosa banksiae
 ** "      striata               *** Securidaca diversifolia
*** Clematis cirrhosa              * Solanum jasminoides
 ** "      crispa                 ** "      seaforthianum
 ** "      texensis              *** "      wendlandi
 ** Clerodendrum thompsonae      *** Sollya heterophylla
*** Ercilla spicata                * Stigmaphyllon ciliatum
*** Escallonia franciscana        ** Thunbergia alata
  * Hardenbergia comptoniana     *** "      fragrans
 ** "          monophylla       *** Tecomaria capensis
  * Hibbertia volubilis           ** Trachelospermum asiaticum
 ** Hoya carnosa                 **  "          fragrans
*** Jaquemontia (species)          *  "          jasminoides
  * Jasminum azoricum            *** Tropaeolum peregrinum
*** "      gracile               *** Urechites lutea
 ** "      gracillimum           *** Wisteria frutescens

STANDARDS---result of the training of a plant in the nursery to a single stem with a formalized tuft at the top; a sphere, a cube or other angularity. They will be used in tubs or boxes in a formal way or set in the ground as accents. Some of these plants will be unobtainable in this form and will of necessity be developed on project by pruning and pinching out of terminals. Certain shrubby vines may be used, the stem being rigged or braided of two to three wythe-like stems which pull together in growth for a natural graft or at least for strength and stability to support the top.

| | |
|---|---|
| *** Acacia alata | * Lavatera assurgentiflora |
| *** Aloe ferox | * Ligustrum ovalifolium |
| ** Beaucarnea recurvata | *** Magnolia stellata |
| * Buxus microphylla | *** Malvaviscus arboreus |
| *** Canella winterana | * Michelia fuscata |
| ** Cassia corymbosa | ** Murraea paniculata |
| * Citrus deliciosa | ** Myrtus communis |
| ** Datura suaveolens | * Nerium oleander |
| ** Dracaena stricta | ** Osmanthus ilicifolius |
| ** Eriobotrya japonica | ** Petrea volubilis |
| * Eucalyptus forrestiana | *** Phillyrea latifolia media |
| ** Eugenia uniflora | *** Pittosporum heterophyllum |
| *** Euryops athanasiae | *     "     tobira |
| *** Ficus lyrata | *** Polygala apopetala |
| * Fortunella japonica | * Raphiolepis indica |
| ** Fuchsia arborescens | *** Prunus jaquemonti |
| * Grewia occidentalis | *** Prunus lusitanica |
| ** Guaiacum officinale | * Rose (varieties) |
| *** Hibiscus huegeli | *** Solanum giganteum |
| ** Jasminum humile | **     "     rantonneti |
| * Jasminum rigidum | *** Viburnum tinus |
| ** Ilex cornuta | * Wisteria floribunda |
| * Laurus nobilis | * Xylosma senticosa |

CLIMBERS FOR TREES---are not recommended, but certain plants with an ambition to climb, may be used to accentuate the natural feeling of woodland, to drape a pole, an unwanted, dead or dying tree until steps are taken for removal. It is the stout twiner that is harmful to the living tree and when used, should be kept as loose as possible to prevent strangling. Some of these plants hook their way up. Others are no more than climbing shrubs and may require assistance.

| | |
|---|---|
| ** Anemopoegma chamberlayni | ** Jasminum pubescens |
| *** Arrabidaea magnifica | * Lonicera hildebrandtiana |
| * Beaumontia grandiflora | ** Malvaviscus arboreus |
| * Bougainvillea (varieties) | *** Oxera pulchella |
| ** Campsidium valdivianum | ** Parthenocissus henryana |
| *** Cissus capensis | ** Pereskia aculeata |
| ** Clematis indevisa | *** Petrea volubilis |
| *** Clytostoma callistegioides | * Phaedranthus buccinatorius |
| * Distictis lactiflora | *** Philodendron (check species) |
| ** Elaeagnus reflexa | ** Pyrostegia ignea |
| *** Ercilla spicata | ** Polygonum auberti |
| * Gelsemium sempervirens | * Solanum wendlandi |
| ** Holmskioldia sanguinea | *** Thunbergia laurifolia |
| *** Ipomoea horsfalliae | ** Trachelospermum fragrans |
| ***     "     setosa | * Vitis (species) |

FISSURE PLANTS---a classification for extremely narrow crevices, in rock or as an open seam in concrete or any such place where the foothold is restricted and drainage sure. These plants will fit themselves in satisfactorily under these conditions, in plan or in elevation. They droop gracefully across the face of a wall or mark the opening with greenery. In extremely narrow cracks it may be necessary to use very small plants or sections, or even start with seed.

| | |
|---|---|
| ** Acaena microphylla | ** Cheilanthes gracillima |
| * Alyssum maritimum | *** Convolvulus lineatus |
| * Arenaria balearica | *** Crassula nana |
| ** Campanula fragilis | ** Cymbalaria aequitriloba |

|   |   |
|---|---|
| * Dianthus deltoides | *** Mesembryanth. filicaule |
| *** Euphorbia truncata | **      "      tuberosum |
| *** Gilia dianthoides | ** Muehlenbeckia axillare |
| ** Gypsophila cerastioides | *** Sagina subulata |
| ** Haworthia tessellata | * Sedum brevifolium |
| * Helxine soleiroli | **   "    dasyphyllum |
| ** Kalanchoe uniflora | ***   "    hispanicum |
| *** Linum salsaloides nanum | *** Sempervivum (select forms) |
| ** Lysimachia nummularia | * Thymus serpyllum |
| *** Mentha requieni | ** Veronica nummularia |

PLANTS FOR SUSPENSION---greenery and color to hang or depend from a height. The rawness of a bare cliff may be reduced or an awkward elevation in architecture seemingly lessened by this means. Paved courts or inaccessible interior angles or other, may be treated by leading these plants in from the soil outside. The great difficulty is to find suitable plants of body that will grow downwards with the pull of gravity without climbing back upon themselves and so disarrange and defeat the purpose for which planted.

## CONFINED

Close-growing material, mostly matting herbaceous plants of substance or woody perennials and prostrate shrubs which, in the absence of support, will reach outwards and downward over the face of a wall or low sharp bank. Against the facade of a building, it will be necessary to use a box placed or attached at the strategic spot.

|   |   |
|---|---|
| ** Abutilon megapotamicum (type) | * Lonicera confusa |
| ** Artabotrys uncinatus | **    "    halliana |
| * Asparagus asparagoides | ** Lopezia albiflora |
| ** Baccharis pilularis | * Lotus mascaensis |
| ** Campanula fragilis | *** Lycium richi |
| *** "      isophylla | *** Lysimachia nummularia |
| ** Campsidium valdivianum | * Malvastrum coccineum |
| * Carissa grandiflora (forms) | ** Maurandia erubescens |
| ** Ceropegia browni | ** Mesembryanth. cordifolium |
| * Chorizema cordatum | *      "      croceum |
| * Cissus rhombifolia | *      "      floribundum |
| *** Chlorophytum elatum | ***      "      speciosum |
| *** Clematis crispa | *** Moraea catenulata |
| **   "    lasiantha | * Muehlenbeckia complexa |
| *** Clianthus puniceus | *** Nepeta mussini |
| * Cotoneaster microphylla | *** Origanum dictamnus |
| **   "    pannosa nana | *** Pyracantha yunnanensis |
| ** Cymbalaria muralis | *** Rhus trilobata |
| ** Dolichos lignosus | ** Ribes viburnifolium |
| *** Ercilla spicata | * Rosmarinus prostratus |
| * Eriogonum fasciculatum | *** Senecio confusus |
| **   "    rubescens | * Solanum seaforthianum |
| ** Grevillea obtusifolia | * Sollya heterophylla |
| * Juniperus conferta | * Streptosolen jamesoni |
| *** Kalanchoe uniflora | *** Thymus lanuginosus |
| *** Kleinia radicans | * Thunbergia alata |
| ** Lantana camara | * Trachelospermum jasminoides |
| *   "    montevidensis | *** Verbena hortensis |
| *** Lathyrus splendens | *** Vigueria tomentosa |
| ** Lippia canescens | *** Zauschneria californica |

## RANGING

Here are shrubby vines and vines proper with long-reaching stems to dress the face of a steep declivity in billowing surges of foliage, with the flatness of a screen or the folds of a curtain. Close-clinging vines set at the foot will meet those from above, where the structure is reasonably stable....or is it desirable to leave openings to reveal texture or color of rock or the pattern of eroded soil. Outdoor murals in nature are easily overlooked.

|   |   |
|---|---|
| *** Aloe ciliaris | ** Baccharis pilularis |
| ** Antigonon leptopus | ** Bauhinia corymbosa |
| ** Arrabidaea magnifica | *** Beaumontia grandiflora |

** Bougainvillea (varieties)
** Calonyction aculeatum
** Cissus antarctica
** Elaeagnus reflexa
 * Ficus pumila
** Grewia occidentalis
 * Holmskioldia sanguinea
*** Ipomoea horsfalliae
 * Jasminum officinale
** Lotus bertheloti
*** Oxera pulchella
 * Pandorea (species)
** Passiflora (species)

 * Phaedranthus buccinatorius
 * Phaseolus caracalla
 * Philadelphus mexicanus
** Philodendron erubescens
*** Plumbago capensis alba
*** Polygonum auberti
 * Pyrostegia ignea
*** Rosa bracteata
*** Semele androgyna
 * Solanum wendlandi
*** Vitex unifoliolata
** Vitis voinieriana
 * Wisteria floribunda

FOUNDATION PLANTING---that at the base of a building, should claim
thought equal to that of the interior and this calls for restraint.
Conformity with architectural detail is an obvious corollary, with
due recognition of entrances, and windows underplanted unless to be
deliberately veiled with an open, revealing growth. Neatness and simplicity are of first importance, conditioned with interest over the
year. Consider scale of leaf and association of textures as of the
structure....let this carry to the ground somewhere with only a bead-
ing for transition, or to the grass. Here is a place for the more deeply domesticated species, substantial forms that are slow to out-grow
narrow or restricted quarters, together with more freely growing kinds
that will not become disorderly. Directional exposure must be held
in mind and the soil examined for debris left from building operations. Check with sized shrubs in GENERAL LISTS and further, if necessary, with GENERAL PURPOSE SHRUBS.

## CONDITIONAL

Plants which place emphasis on form and texture, rather than
on color in flower. These are the more absolute in effect and carry
the more consequential parts in a planting, as at the door or to point
up some notion or fancy relative to design. They are the more slowly
growing and may well be set in larger sizes for a kind of timeliness
with the more rapid-growing components.

** Azalea indica
*** Berberis gagnepaini
 * Buxus japonica
 * Camellia japonica
** Carissa compacta
*** Choisya ternata
*** Cneorum tricoccon
** Cocculus laurifolius
** Coprosma baueri
*** Damnacanthus indicus
*** Daphniphyllum humile
 * Diosma ericoides
 * Euonymus japonicus
*** Fuchsia triphylla
 * Hebe (check species)
** Hydrangea macrophylla
 * Hypericum moserianum
 * Ilex cornuta burfordi
*** Itea ilicifolia
** Jasminum floridum

** Ligustrum rotundifolium
*** Lonicera pileata
*** Malpighia coccigera
 * Myrsine africana
 * Myrtus microphylla
***    "        "     minima
** Osmanthus ilicifolius
** Polygala dalmaisiana
*** Raphiolepis delacouri
**     "        indica
 *     "        ovata
** Severinia buxifolia
** Siphonosmanthus delavayi
** Turraea obtusifolia
** Viburnum suspensum
 *    "      tinus
*** Visnea mocanera
** Ternstroemia japonica
** Xylosma senticosa
*** Zamia floridana

## PROVISIONAL

Less affirmative shrubs that are relatively informal, with
less fixed shape and usually more colorful in flower. They brighten
this planting and fill in the lesser spaces with more flowing form,
tying together the heavier points of the composition. Generally they
are less permanent, more rapid-growing, require more space laterally
and are better planted in the smaller sizes.

 * Abelia (species)
*** Aeonium spathulatum
*** Ardisia crispa

*** Aster fruticosus
 * Berberis darwini
 * Camellia sasanqua

** Carissa grandiflora
** Chaenomeles japonica
*** Chorizema cordatum
** Convolvulus cneorum
** Correa pulchella
* Cotoneaster parneyi
** Escallonia glasniviensis
*** Fuchsia (varieties)
** Gardenia (check species)
*** Grevillea rosmarinifolia
**        "        thelemanniana
** Hebe hulkeana
** Hypericum henryi
*** Ilex cassine
** Jasminum humile
* Juniperus pfitzeriana
*** Lantana camara
** Ligustrum henryi
*** Mackaya bella

** Mahonia pinnata
*** Malvastrum capense
*** Melaleuca thymifolia
* Murraea exotica
* Ochna multiflora
*** Phillyrea latifolia media
** Prunus glandulosa
* Pyracantha crenato-serrata
*** Raphiolepis rosea
*** Salvia greggi
* Sarcococca hookeriana
*** Spiraea cantoniensis
** Streptosolen jamesoni
*** Strophanthus speciosus
*** Taxus repandens
** Tecoma garrocha
*** Thryallis glauca
*** Viburnum carlesi
*** Weigela florida

* Westringia rosmariniformis

## SPECIFIC CHARACTER

In view of the generality and wide scope of this planting and in order to complete it with a prudent supplementary touch, consider the vine with its hanging line....its pattern possibilities in ramification of stem and vent in foliage. Look to the lower, tree-like shrub of one or more stems and its value in relating the structure to its surroundings. Find a place for these in a vertical accent either in the shrubbery mass or out alone where the building will carry through to the ground. The vine pulls down....the tree lifts.

## SHRUBS

** Acokanthera spectabilis
** Alsophila australis
* Arbutus unedo
** Bambusa multiplex
** Bauhinia tomentosa
*** Bursaria spinosa
* Callistemon viminalis
*** Canella winterana
* Clethra arborea
* Coccolobis uvifera
*** Cotoneaster parneyi
*** Delostoma roseum
** Dracaena stricta
*** Eucalyptus forrestiana
** Eugenia smithi
*** Eurya japonica
* Fatsia japonica
*** Ilex vomitoria
** Lagerstroemia indica
* Laurus nobilis
** Lawsonia inermis
*** Leptospermum citrinum
** Ligustrum lucidum
*** Loropetalum chinense
* Michelia fuscata
* Murraea paniculata
*** Myrtus ralphi
* Nandina domestica
*** Noltea africana
** Nothopanax arboreum
*** Ochrosia elliptica
*** Oncoba routledgi
** Olmediella betschleriana
* Osmanthus fragrans
* Phoenix roebelini
* Pittosporum phillyraeoides

** Podocarpus totara
*** Prunus jaquemonti
* Pyracantha koidzumi
*** Rhapis excelsa
*** Royena lucida
** Sophora secundiflora
* Strelitzia nicholai
* Taxus baccata stricta
** Trachycarpus fortunei
*** Tupidanthus calyptratus
* Viburnum japonicum

## VINES

** Anemopoegma chamberlayni
** Arrabidaea magnifica
*** Bomaria caldasiana
* Distictus lactiflora
** Hibbertia volubilis
*** Hoya carnosa
** Jasminum azoricum
*** Kennedya rubicunda
*** Lapageria rosea
** Oxera pulchella
*** Petrea volubilis
* Phaedranthus buccinatorius
** Phaseolus caracalla
* Pyrostegia ignea
*** Solandra longiflora
* Solanum wendlandi
** Stephanotis floribunda
*** Stizolobium deeringianum
** Trachelospermum fragrans
*** Vitis voinieriana

GARDEN TREES AND SHRUBS---designed as a short-cut to well behaved woody plants that are consistent with garden development in scale, culture and comeliness. They will be grown for color or fragrance or simply for a background of use there....an abstract notion of felicity and fruition in company with people. These plants will have no serious shabby or unkempt period, no decided off-season, unless in winter. A tree, to qualify, should be of light shadow, free of any inclination to sucker in dug earth, and preferably tap and more or less occupy the topsoil. If shrubs are found that may be discouraged in surface feeding, the topsoil will be left freer for herbaceous growth. This may be utopian, but is attainable in a degree. Irrigation for deep penetration will help this arrangement.

## TREES

| | |
|---|---|
| *** Acacia pendula | * Magnolia grandiflora |
| **  "  pubescens | *** Markhamia elegans |
| ** Bauhinia (check species) | *** Michelia champaca |
| ** Bolusanthus speciosus | ** Ochrosia elliptica |
| * Brachychiton acerifolium | ** Olmediella betschleriana |
| * Callistemon viminalis | ** Peltophorum inerme |
| * Calodendrum capense | ** Pinus patula |
| *** Cassia fistula | ** Pistacia chinensis |
| *** Cercis siliquastrum | * Pittosporum rhombifolium |
| *** Crytomeria elegans | * Podocarpus elongata |
| ** Dais cotinifolia | *** Prunus amygdalus |
| *** Delostoma roseum | **  "  caroliniana |
| *** Drimys winteri | *  "  persica |
| ** Eucalyptus caesia | * Pyrus calleryana |
| ***  "  citriodora | * Quercus ilex |
| **  "  erythrocorys | *  "  virginiana |
| ***  "  torquata | *** Spathodea campanulata |
| *** Fraxinus dipetala | *** Tabebuia umbellata |
| * Hymenosporum flavum | * Taxus baccata stricta |
| * Jacaranda acutifolia | *** Tipuana tipu |
| ** Koelreuteria formosana | ** Vitex lucens |

## SHRUBS

| | |
|---|---|
| * Abelia (species) | ** Lippia citriodora |
| ** Allamanda nereifolia | *** Magnolia stellata |
| *** Anthyllis barba-jovis | ** Melaleuca huegeli |
| * Azalea indica | ***  "  lateritia |
| ** Bauhinia acuminata | * Michelia fuscata |
| * Berberis darwini | * Nandina domestica |
| *** Buddleja lindleyana | *** Nerium indicum |
| * Calliandra inequilatera | * Nierembergia frutescens |
| * Camellia sasanqua | *** Osmanthus fortunei |
| ** Cantua buxifolia | *  "  fragrans |
| *** Ceanothus hybrids | *** Osteomeles anthyllidifolia |
| **  "  impressus | * Pelargonium domesticum |
| * Ceratostigma willmottianum | *** Photinia serrulata |
| * Cocculus laurifolius | *** Pimelea ferruginia |
| *** Coronilla glauca | *** Pittosporum tobira |
| ** Daphne odora | * Poinciana gilliesi |
| ** Diosma (species) | ** Polygala dalmaisiana |
| * Duranta stenostachya | * Pyracantha crenato-serrata |
| ** Ervatamia coronaria | * Raphiolepis (species) |
| *** Fuchsia (check species) | *** Ribes glutinosum |
| ** Gardenia florida | ** Rosmarinus officinalis |
| ***  "  thunbergia | *** Ruellia devosiana |
| ** Halimium halimifolium | *** Salvia greggi |
| ** Hamelia erecta | *** Sasa disticha |
| * Hebe (species) | **  "  palmata |
| * Hibiscus rosa-sinensis | ** Senecio petasitis |
| *** Hypericum henryi | *** Siphonosmanthus delavayi |
| *  "  moserianum | *** Solanum rantonneti |
| *** Iochroma (species) | ** Sollya heterophylla |
| * Jasminum humile | * Spiraea cantoniensis |
| ** Lavandula officinalis | * Streptosolen jamesoni |
| *** Leptospermum citrinum | *** Strobilanthes dyerianus |
| *** Ligustrum quihoui | ** Tecoma (species) |

|       |                          |       |                            |
|-------|--------------------------|-------|----------------------------|
| ** | Thea sinensis | * | Viburnum carlesi |
| ** | Thevetia nereifolia | *** | "   tinus |
| *** | Thryallis glauca | ** | Weigela florida |
| * | Turraea obtusifolia | ** | Westringia rosmariniformis |
| *** | Viburnum burkwoodi | ** | Xylosma senticosa |

## VINES

|       |                            |       |                              |
|-------|----------------------------|-------|------------------------------|
| ** | Ampelopsis brevipedunculata | ** | Jasminum officinale |
| * | Antigonon leptopus | ** | Passiflora alato-caerulea |
| *** | Cissus hypoglauca | *** | Phaedranthus buccinatorius |
| *** | Clematis armandi | *** | Solanum wendlandi |
| * | Gelsemium sempervirens | ** | Stigmaphyllon ciliatum |
| * | Hardenbergia comptoniana | *** | Thunbergia grandiflora |
| ** | Hibbertia volubilis | * | Trachelospermum jasminoides |

SPECIMEN PLANTS---emphatic individuals for accent, each having some peculiar interest inherent in themselves, decisive form or structure, striking growth or distinctive foliage. This over-plus of character will appear to best advantage alone, as against the crowded border where a typically definite outline or precise texture tend to merge with the mass and are lost as such. They stand on parade, a unifying motif for the terrace or other place of some formality and may appear again at strategic spots in the lawn or detached from the bulge of a plant mass to further the indent of a bay. They point the way in contemporary planting. Normally, they should have the support of other plantings or the explanation of a pattern or design of the area.

## TREES

|       |                           |       |                         |
|-------|---------------------------|-------|-------------------------|
| ** | Araucaria (species) | ** | Liquidambar styraciflua |
| ** | Arecastrum romanzoffianum | *** | Lyonothamnus asplenifolius |
| * | Brachychiton populneum | *** | Macadamia ternifolia |
| ** | Callistemon viminalis | ** | Magnolia lanceolata |
| *** | Callitris robusta | *** | Markhamia lutea |
| * | Cedrus (species) | ** | Myrtus communis italica |
| *** | Chamaecyparis lawsoniana | *** | Ochrosia elliptica |
| *** | Chorisia speciosa | ** | Phoenix reclinata |
| *** | Cupressus funebris | ** | Podocarpus macrophylla |
| * | "   guadalupensis | * | Populus nigra italica |
| ** | "   sempervirens | ** | Prunus caroliniana |
| *** | Erythea (species) | *** | Quercus douglasi |
| ** | Eugenia myrtifolia | * | "   ilex |
| * | Eucalyptus ficifolia | ** | Strelitzia nicholai |
| ** | Ficus retusa | * | Trachycarpus fortunei |
| * | Juniperus excelsa stricta | *** | Vitex lucens |
| *** | Leucadendron argenteum | *** | Washingtonia robusta |

## SHRUBS

|       |                         |       |                        |
|-------|-------------------------|-------|------------------------|
| *** | Acanthus montanus | * | Nandina domestica |
| *** | Acer palmatum | *** | Nothopanax arboreum |
| *** | Acokanthera spectabilis | ** | Osmanthus ilicifolius |
| *** | Anthyllis barba-jovis | ** | Phormium tenax |
| * | Arbutus unedo | *** | Pimelea ferruginea |
| *** | Bauhinia acuminata | ** | Pittosporum tenuifolium |
| *** | Bursaria spinosa | *** | Polygala apopetala |
| * | Buxus japonica | ** | Portulacaria afra |
| *** | Camellia reticulata | *** | Prunus lusitanica |
| * | Cocculus laurifolius | ** | Psidium cattleianum |
| ** | Cycas (species) | *** | Puya alpestris |
| ** | Datura suaveolens | *** | Raphiolepis indica |
| ** | Dodonaea viscosa | * | Rhapis excelsa |
| * | Erythrina crista-galli | *** | Rondeletia cordata |
| ** | Gardenia thunbergia | ** | Sasa palmata |
| ** | Hebe (check species) | *** | Spartium junceum |
| * | Hibiscus rosa-sinensis | * | Strelitzia reginae |
| * | Hydrangea macrophylla | * | Ternstroemia japonica |
| ** | Ilex cornuta | * | Thuja (varieties) |
| * | Juniperus argentea | *** | Trevesia palmata |
| *** | Lagerstroemia indica | *** | Trichocereus candicans |
| * | Laurus nobilis | *** | Viburnum odoratissimum |
| *** | Mahonia lomariifolia | ** | "   tinus |
| ** | Murraea paniculata | *** | Yucca (check species) |

THE HEDGE---in the landscape is essentially line in design. These lines appear in the separation of areas, as enclosures or may serve as an ornamental screen. They are allowed to grow naturally or clipped as the case and material may warrant or suggest. They should serve equally in shade or sun and adapt easily to changing soil in the length. They show neglect quickly.  The initial cost is low compared to that of a wall, but the upkeep over the years eats into these savings while the roots take their daily toll of the surrounding ground. Ornamental considerations, however, usually offset any reasonable extraction from purse and soil, and we find the living wall a source of service and much satisfaction. There is a large range of materials available with plenty of latitude for variety and some originality.  Texture, color and proportion are as important in the choice of a plant for this purpose as they are in the building of a wall.

## BOUNDARY HEDGES

Where space is wanting, material to mark the line or to prevent trespass may be limited to a hedge in place of the more expensive fence, belt planting or border.  Plants suggested are all ready growers of some size and will accomodate in way of hedging, grown naturally, kept in line by light selective prunings or sheared more tightly to conserve space.  Keep the body clear of dead wood and debris, open for air circulation, and where tree forms are adapted to this use, special care should be taken in the beginning to break their arborescent habit for the spread and fine wood that makes a hedge.

 ** Acacia longifolia
*** Carissa carandas
  * Casuarina equisetifolia
 ** Chrysobalanus icaco
 ** Coccolobis floridana
*** Cudrania tricuspidata
*** Cupressus macrocarpa
  * Duranta repens
 ** Escallonia langleyensis
*** Euphorbia tirucalli
*** Fouquieria splendens
  * Hakea saligna
 ** Hibiscus rosa-sinensis
 ** Lagerstroemia indica

  * Leptospermum laevigatum
  * Ligustrum japonicum
 ** Malpighia glabra
*** Metrosideros tomentosa
*** Ochrosia elliptica
*** Olmediella betschleriana
 ** Pittosporum tenuifolium
 ** Prunus caroliniana
 ** Psidium cattleianum
  * Punica granatum
  * Rhamnus alaternus
*** Simmondsia californica
 ** Tamarix aphylla
  * Taxus baccata

## BOXING

Here are some plants that will not be reluctant to serve as a glorified edging or hedging in miniature, when they may be used to enclose a garden plot.  They control the herbage of the bed while continuity of the line of a path is improved.  Do not let them out of hand for lack of attention. They will be unusually demanding in the matter of shearing for form and continual restraint.

 ** Breynia nivosa
*** Calocephalis browni
  * Carissa grandiflora minima
 ** Chaenostoma hispidum
*** Cotoneaster thymifolia
  * Euonymus microphyllus
  * Hebe buxifolia
***    "   menziesi
  * Hedera helix (forms)
*** Kochia scoparia
 ** Lavandula stoechas

*** Ligustrum henryi
  * Lonicera nitida
*** Malpighia coccigera
  * Myrtus minima
*** Nierembergia caerulea
*** Punica granatum nana
  * Rosmarinus Lockwood de Forest
 ** Santolina chamaecyparissus
 ** Satureja montana
*** Severinia buxifolia
  * Teucrium chamaedrys

                 ** Thymus vulgaris

## FLOWERING HEDGES

The thought expressed here is that of a casual or less determinate barrier, a living fence or line of flowering shrubs that are not too individualistic and which enter into a whole without too much compulsion. Some may be pruned, but the most effective reduction will be the merest tipping back to induce bushiness and freer flowering....done with knife or sickle when wood is new and tender.
 *** Abelia schumanni              *** Acacia cultriformis

** Azalea indica                    ** Hibiscus rosa-sinensis
** Berberis darwini                 ** Jasminum floridum
 * Buddleja lindleyana              ** Lantana camara
*** Calothamnus quadrifidus         ** Ligustrum rotundifolium
 * Carissa grandiflora               * Mahonia pinnata
** Cassia splendida               *** Malvaviscus arboreus
 * Chaenomeles japonica             ** Murraea exotica
*** Choisya ternata                  * Myrsine africana
*** Correa alba                    *** Myrtus ugni
 * Crassula argentea                 * Nerium oleander
** Diosma ericoides                 ** Osmanthus ilicifolius
*** Escallonia glasniviensis      *** Osteomeles anthyllidifolia
*** Eucalyptus forrestiana          ** Pittosporum tobira
 * Eugenia uniflora               *** Poinciana pulcherrima
** Euphorbia neriifolia              * Punica granatum
 * Feijoa sellowiana              *** Raphiolepis indica
** Fuchsia triphylla                **      "      ovata
*** Grewia caffra                 *** Rosa laevigata
 * Hakea elliptica                  ** Sasa disticha
 * Hebe carnea                      ** Spiraea cantoniensis
 * Heimia myrtifolia               *** Syringa persica
        ** Westringia rosmariniformis

## FORMAL HEDGES

The important thing to consider here is whether the plant will produce foliage under shearing without taking excessive time out to recover, together with the life-span that may be expected under this restraint. Tops should be cut back sharply when the plant is set so that the hedge is started low and brought up uniformly, gradually to become nearly stationary at the height desired. This tends to fill in the body from the ground up, although some vents or imperfections have value....highlight and deep shadow. The better hedge results from frequent shearings regulated or synchronized with growth periods.

 * Abelia grandiflora              * Ligustrum (species)
 * Atriplex breweri              *** Lycium pallidum
*** Bambusa multiplex              * Myrtus communis
 * Buxus japonica                *** Noltea africana
*** Carissa arduina               ** Pittosporum tenuifolium
 * Coprosma baueri                 * Podocarpus nagi
** Cotoneaster simonsi            ** Prunus ilicifolia
** Dodonaea viscosa                * Punica granatum
** Elaeagnus pungens               * Pyracantha (check species)
 * Eugenia myrtifolia             ** Rhamnus crocea
** Euonymus japonicus            *** Simmondsia californica
** Guaiacum officinale           *** Tamarix (species)
** Hakea saligna                   * Tecomaria capensis
** Ilex vomitoria                *** Thea sinensis
** Jasminum humile                 * Triphasia trifolia
*** Juniperus silicicola         *** Turraea obtusifolia
** Lawsonia inermis              *** Umbellularia californica

## HERBACEOUS HEDGES

Usually a plant with a woody base for quick colorful dividing lines within the garden. They are perennial, or at least semipermanent in character and will be improved for this purpose by pinching back the tips from time to time....best done when out of flower and in growth. Close-planting is better than forcing.

 * Acalypha wilksiana              ** Dimorphotheca ecklonis
** Barleria caerulea               * Felicia echinata
*** Breynia nivosa                ** Hedychium coronarium
** Calceolaria integrifolia        * Hibiscus sabdariffa
 * Calocephalis browni           *** Hunnemannia fumariaefolia
** Canna generalis                ** Impatiens sultani
 * Chaenostoma grandiflorum      *** Kochia scoparia
*** Chironia linoides              * Lavandula (species)
 * Chrysanthemum frutescens       ** Mirabilis jalapa
** Clerodendrum siphonanthus       * Nierembergia frutescens
*** Codiaeum (forms)             *** Pachyphytum bracteosum
*** Cynara scolymus                * Pelargonium domesticum

```
*** Pennisetum ruppeli        ** Salvia leucantha
 ** Phormium tenax             * Santolina chamaecyparissus
 ** Physostegia virginiana    *** Tithonia rotundifolia
 ** Rosmarinus officinalis     ** Vinca rosea
              *** Zantedeschia aethiopica
```

MAJOR BARRIERS---plantings, temporary or permanent, designed to check or deflect the course of storm and prevailing winds in the protection of buildings or other planting....orchard or nursery. Too often the protective devices are as harmful as the elements, especially from the standpoint of invasive roots that sap moisture and nutrients. Desirable here, are uniformity in height and in denseness; supple stems and strong roots for anchorage; moderate requirements as to upkeep; a reasonably rapid growing level and durability studied as for the project. They will be set out in such a manner as to give the maximum in masking value, in line, staggered or at random and with enough distance from protected growth to allow for good air circulation. Try only to temper the wind. Double trunks, forks and tenacious leaves that do not break away in a storm are not admissible in view of the stresses involved.

## WINDBREAKS

A combination of forms is usually more effective here than any one in the building of a complete functional mass from the ground to the ultimate height expected. The trees are set to straight lines and more closely together than normal. Width beyond that required for denseness is ineffective and further protection should be arranged in echelon, broadside to heavy wind. Protection horizontally may be expected some twenty times height....a variable.

```
*** Acacia pruinosa           *** Juniperus silicicola
 ** Achras zapota               * Ligustrum japonicum
*** Brachychiton populneum    *** Lysiloma latisiliqua
 ** Callistemon viminalis       * Melaleuca leucadendra
 ** Calophyllum inophyllum     ** Pinus (check species)
  * Casuarina (check species)  ** Pittosporum undulatum
  * Cupressus (check species)  ** Populus nigra italica
  * Eucalyptus (check species) ** Sinocalamus oldhami
 ** Eugenia myrtifolia        *** Syzygium cumini
*** Ficus religiosa             * Tamarix aphylla
  * Hakea laurina             *** Ulmus pumila
```

## SCREENS

It sometimes becomes desirable or necessary to plant out objectionable views or to obscure an area from public observation. Density of leafage is not so important as vigor and uniformity of growth, since the plants may be set in lines staggered to cover off. Thought will be given to ultimate height and whether evergreen or deciduous species will best serve. Where space is wanting, climbing shrubs and close-growing vines may be grown on mesh-wire, to be controlled casually or sheared back to as narrow a buffer as is required or will suffice to screen from observation.

```
          TREES                *** Nuxia floribunda
 ** Acacia decurrens            ** Olmediella betschleriana
 ** Albizzia lophantha          ** Parkinsonia aculeata
  * Bambusa multiplex          *** Photinia serrulata
*** Baeckia virgata              * Pinus halepensis
*** Buddleja asiatica           ** Pittosporum eugenioides
*** Carissa carandas            ** Poinciana pulcherrima
 ** Ceanothus arboreus         *** Populus simoni
 ** Coccolobis floridana         * Prunus caroliniana
  * Dodonaea viscosa           *** Rhus lancea
 ** Eucalyptus erythronema      ** Ricinus communis
  * Feijoa sellowiana           ** Salix crispa
 ** Hakea saligna                * Tamarix (check species)
  * Lagerstroemia indica
  * Laurus nobilis                    CLIMBERS
  * Ligustrum lucidum           ** Abutilon megapotamicum
                                 * Camellia sasanqua
```

** Chorizema cordatum
** Dolichos lignosus
** Eccremocarpus scaber
*** Elaeagnus reflexa
* Hardenbergia monophylla
* Hedera helix
* Ipomoea (check species)
** Jaquemontia (species)
** Jasminum azoricum
*** Kennedya rubicunda
* Lantana montevidensis
** Lonicera ( check species)
* Muehlenbeckia complexa
*** Pereskia aculeata
*** Podranea ricasoliana
** Plumbago capensis alba
** Pueraria thunbergiana
*** Rosa laevigata
*** Securidaca diversifolia
*** Solanum rantonneti
* Sollya heterophylla
** Thunbergia gibsoni
* Trachelospermum jasminoides

## SHELTER BELTS

Mixed plantings along the side of, or about a homestead have a more direct application to the rural in extremely windy sections. The planting is random or along with standing growth and allowed to develop as a woodlot, allowing space for normal development. Sometimes these are considered temporary, but more often not, with soft and hard woods mixed judiciously for ultimate cropping as wood. Protection, however, is the prime consideration below.

** Acacia auriculaeformis
***    "    farnesiana
***    "    melanoxylon
* Achras zapota
** Albizzia lebbek
** Broussonetia papyrifera
* Casuarina equisetifolia
* Celtis australis
*** Cupressus arizonica
** Eucalyptus leucoxylon
*       "       polyanthemos
***     "       rostrata
** Fraxinus velutina
* Grevillea robusta
** Juniperus silicicola
** Libocedrus decurrens
*** Melaleuca styphelioides
* Melia azedarach
** Morus rubra
* Pinus (check species)
** Populus (check species)
*** Prosopis (species)
* Tamarix aphylla
*** Thespesia populnea
** Tipuana tipu
*** Tristania conferta
* Ulmus (species)

GROUND COVERS---defined here as earth-hugging plants for an effect in plan. They may re-root or not and may lift somewhat, but in principal part will handle the flat of a foreground or other area economically, pleasingly and well. Little or no traffic is to be assumed, all walking being between plants or precariously over them. It is important in the management of the planting that species of somewhat like cultural requirements be used together, since all must take essentially the same treatment regardless of likes. With some study of available materials, it will be seen that much can be done in way of texture, color and especially modeling. Check further with PROSTRATE PERENNIALS, SHRUBBY VINES and LAWN SUBSTITUTES.

## SHRUB-LIKE

** Aloe striatula
** Arctostaphylos franciscana
*** Amphycome arguta
* Baccharis pilularis
* Camellia sasanqua
* Carissa prostrata
*** Ceanothus gloriosus
*       "       grizeus horizontalis
** Chorizema cordatum
* Coprosma (check species)
* Cotoneaster decora
*** Ercilla spicata
** Grevillea obtusifolia
***     "       paniculata
** Halimium ocymoides
*** Hebe chathamica
** Helianthemum nummularium
** Hibiscus tiliaceus
** Hymenanthera crassifolia
*** Jasminum parkeri
* Juniperus conferta
* Lantana montevidensis
*** Lonicera pileata
** Lopezia albiflora
** Mahernia verticillata
* Malvastrum coccineum
*** Micromeria piperella
*** Penstemon cordifolius
* Pyracantha yunnanensis
*** Ribes viburnifolium
* Rosmarinus prostratus
** Sabal minor
* Santolina chamaecyparissus
*** Sarcococca humilis
*** Sasa pigmaea
*** Serenoa repens

* Teucrium chamaedrys
*** Thomasia purpurea
* Thymus vulgaris
*** Vitex unifoliolata
** Zauschneria californica

### VINING

** Aloe ciliaris
*** Bougainvillea (varieties)
*** Clianthus puniceus
*** Distictis lactiflora
** Dolichos lignosus
*** Eccremocarpus scaber
* Ficus pumila
* Gelsemium sempervirens
* Hardenbergia comptoniana
* Hedera (species)
** Ipomoea (check species)

*** Jaquemontia (species)
** Lathyrus splendens
* Lonicera halliana
*** Pandorea pandorana
** Parthenocissus henryana
** Philadelphus mexicanus
*** Podranea ricasoliana
*** Pueraria thunbergiana
** Stizolobium deeringianum
* Thunbergia gibsoni
* Trachelospermum jasminoides

### HERBACEOUS COVER

** Acaena microphylla
* Ajuga reptans
*** Anacyclus depressus
** Arenaria balearica
** Arrhenatherum tuberosum
*** Beloperone tomentosa
* Campanula poscharskyana
* Ceratostigma plumbaginoides
*** Chlorophytum elatum
*** Chusquea tessellata
** Cissus incisa
* Convolvulus mauretanicus
*** Cymbalaria (species)
* Dianthus (check species)
** Duchesnea indica
xx Echeveria (check species)
* Erigeron karvinskyanus
*** Eriophyllum caespitosum
*** Felicia petiolata
*** Festuca glauca
* Fragaria chiloensis
** Frankenia capitata laevis
* Gazania (species)
*** Grindelia arenicola
* Helichrysum petiolatum
* Hypericum calycinum
*** Hemigraphis colorata
* Lotus bertheloti
** " mascaensis
*** Mentha gatefossei
*** Micromeria chamissonis
** Muehlenbeckia axillare
* Nepeta hederacea
** " mussini
** Nierembergia rivularis
* Oenothera tetraptera
* Ophiopogon japonicus

*** Oplismenus hirtellus
** Origanum dictamnus
*** Pelargonium alchemilloides
* " peltatum
** Polygonum capitatum
*** " reynoutrya
** Portulaca grandiflora
*** Pterocephalis parnassi
*** Putoria calabrica
** Ranunculus repens
*** Reineckia carnea
* Rosmarinus prostratus
** Satureja intricata
** Saxifraga sarmentosa
*** Schizocentron elegans
* Sedum album
** " altissimum
** " guatemalense
*** " pachyphyllum
** " spurium
*** Selaginella denticulata
* Senecio mikanioides
*** Stachys corsica
*** Tanacetum capitatum
* Teucrium prostratum
*** Thymus broussonetia
* " serpyllum
* Verbena hortensis
*** " peruviana
** " pulchella
** Veronica nummularia
*** " pectinata
* " repens
* Vinca major
*** Viola odorata
*** Wedelia trilobata
*** Zebrina pendula

### SUCCULENTS

*** Aloe distans
* Byrnesia weinbergi
** Crassula multicava
*** " perfossa
* Cyanotis hirsuta
*** Euphorbia truncata
*** Kalanchoe uniflora
** Kleinia repens
*** Mesembryanth. anemoniflorum
** " cordifolium
* " croceum

** Mesembryanth. edule
* " floribundum
* " laeve
*** " roseum
** " verruculatum
* Oliveranthus elegans
*** Opuntia linguiformis
* Othonna crassifolia
*** Pelargonium echinatum
** Sempervivum tectorum
*** Stapelia divaricata

SOIL BINDERS---where the primary purpose is that of holding ground against sand in the wind or water in movement, whether mud at the edge of a stream or the surface of a slope. These plants will prove to be tenacious in manner of rooting, re-rooting in a thorough occupation of the soil, efficient in all ways in slowing up run-off and the erosion that results. The cheapness of the plants and the readiness with which they establish are usually as pertinent to the problem or more so than the ornamental value. This is soil erosion in the garden.

## SLOPES

Moderate grades in or near the garden may be bound down and the soil held in place by plants of strong rooting habits, preferably within the ornamental scheme. Low-lying stems may or may not root, but have their place in retaining the topsoil which banks up against and over them to stabilize. These are all acceptable within gardens.

| | | | |
|---|---|---|---|
| * | Ajuga reptans | * | Mesembryanth. (species) |
| *** | Aloe striatula | ** | Micromeria piperella |
| * | Campanula poscharskyana | ** | Oenothera tetraptera |
| * | Ceratostigma plumbaginoides | ** | Ophiopogon japonicus |
| ** | Chusquea tessellata | * | Origanum dictamnus |
| *** | Davallia canariensis | *** | Parthenocissus henryana |
| ** | Dianthus (check species) | *** | Petasitis fragrans |
| * | Duchesnea indica | *** | Pimelea coarctica |
| ** | Erigeron karvinskyanus | *** | Polygonum reynoutrya |
| ** | Felicia (species) | * | Ranunculus repens |
| ** | Fragaria chiloensis | *** | Sasa pygmaea |
| * | Gazania (species) | * | Sedum (check species) |
| ** | Gypsophila cerastioides | *** | Serissa foetida |
| *** | Hedysarum coronarium | *** | Thomasia purpurea |
| * | Hypericum calycinum | * | Thymus serpyllum |
| *** | Linaria dalmatica | ** | Verbena pulchella |
| *** | Lysimachia nummularia | * | Veronica nummularia |
| *** | Mahernia verticillata | ** | Vinca major |

## SAND DUNES

These plants will find it possible to manage in pure sand, usually further burdened with salt bearing winds. Sand fixing ability depends upon an all-embracing rootage and an absolute refusal to be buried in the piling drifts. A dune may not always be changed in any degree, but it may be restrained and made to become a thing of unusual beauty when supporting appropriate materials. It is obvious that while the forces behind the dune are the same in desert or by the sea, not the plants. These are primarily for the seacoast. Check with the NATIVE PLANTS of an area, especially for annuals that may be adapted.

### WOODY PLANTS

| | | | |
|---|---|---|---|
| | | * | Lycium chilense |
| *** | Acacia armata | ** | Malvastrum fasciculatum |
| * | " farnesiana | ** | Pinus attenuata |
| *** | " horrida | * | Rhus integrifolia |
| * | " pycnantha | *** | Sabal palmetto |
| * | Atriplex (species) | *** | Serenoa repens |
| * | Baccharis (check species) | *** | Sidalcea malvaeflora |
| ** | Casuarina equisetifolia | *** | Scaevola frutescens |
| *** | Ceanothus grizeus | *** | Simmondsia californica |
| ** | " microphyllus | * | Tamarix (species) |
| ** | Coccolobis uvifera | *** | Vitex unifoliolata |
| * | Coprosma baueri | | |
| ** | Echium fastuosum | | HERBACEOUS |
| * | Eriogonum (species) | * | Abronia (species) |
| ** | Eucalyptus eremophila | ** | Ammophila arenaria |
| *** | " macrocarpa | ** | Anthemis tinctoria |
| * | " pulverulenta | * | Argemone mexicana |
| * | Genista monosperma | ** | Armeria maritima |
| ** | Hibiscus tiliaceus | * | Atriplex semibaccata |
| *** | Hymenanthera crassifolia | ** | Corethrogyne californica |
| * | Lavatera assurgentiflora | ** | Elymus arenarius |
| ** | Leptospermum laevigatum | *** | Eremochloa ophiuroides |
| ** | Lotus formosissimus | *** | Eriophyllum caespitosum |
| ** | Lupinus arboreus | * | Eschscholtzia californica |

| | | | |
|---|---|---|---|
| * | Fragaria chiloensis | ** | Malacothrix californica |
| ** | Gilia capitata | * | Mesembryanth. aequilaterale |
| * | Glaucium flavum | *** | "        crystallinum |
| *** | Ipomoea horsfalliae | ** | Monardella lanceolata |
| ** | "    pes-caprae | * | Oenothera cheiranthifolia |
| *** | Lathyrus littoralis | ** | Platystemon californicus |
| * | Limonium sinuatum | ** | Sanvitalia procumbens |
| *** | Lupinus (check species) | *** | Vigna marina |

*** Wedelia trilobata

## MUD BANKS

The proper plants in this place will obscure the periodical-ly slimy aspect of mud and hold it from the swirl of rising waters. A study of these plants will indicate some fitted to drape the bank and others more appropriate to the flat normally found beneath.

| | SLOPES | | THE FLAT |
|---|---|---|---|
| *** | Ajuga reptans | ** | Alisma plantago-aquatica |
| * | Acorus (species) | * | Butomus umbellatus |
| *** | Brasenia schreberi | * | Calla palustris |
| * | Caltha palustris | ** | Crinum americanum |
| ** | Casuarina lepidophloia | *** | Eichornia crassipes |
| ** | Eichornia azurea | *** | Iris hexagona |
| *** | Hottonia palustris | ** | "   pseudacorus |
| ** | Hydrocotyle rotundifolia | ** | Jussiae longifolia |
| *** | Jussiaea repens | *** | Orontium aquaticum |
| ** | Lippia nodiflora | *** | Phalaris arundinacea |
| *** | Marsilea quadrifolia | * | Sagittaria lancifolia |
| * | Mentha pulegium | *** | Thalia dealbata |
| *** | Myriophyllum proserpinacoides | * | Typha latifolia |
| * | Scirpus cernuus | ** | Wachendorfia thyrsiflorus |
| *** | Syngonium podophyllum | *** | Zantedeschia aethiopica |

DIRT FILLS---an assortment of plants prepared by nature in the structure of the root system, or in having a certain pliability and toughness of top, to hold and preserve in place the slope of freshly moved earth. Besides stabilizing the bank, these plants will be expected to cope with drought and sterility of soil usually incident to such a place. A further and important consideration here, is selection and arrangement of the subject plants in such a manner that the artificial plane of the fill may be broken and the whole merged harmoniously with the surroundings. Such a planting will make use of tree, shrub and herbaceous forms in completing the job. Check with COPSE for more large scale plants and with BANK PLANTING for small.

## APRON AND SURFACE OF SLOPE

Here are vines, shrubs and herbaceous material with fibrous roots which are notably tenacious in their rooting to bind and conserve the surface. They will offer resistance to a rush of water over the face of the slope or let it slide harmlessly over and down a path of their yielding tops....a slick that minimizes the carry of soil.

| | | | |
|---|---|---|---|
| ** | Acacia armata | ** | Grevillea paniculata |
| *** | Aloe ciliaris | *** | "   rosmarinifolia |
| * | Atriplex semibaccata | ** | Hedera helix |
| * | Baccharis pilularis | * | Helichrysum petiolatum |
| *** | Buddleja madagascariensis | * | Hypericum calycinum |
| * | Ceratostigma griffithi | *** | Ipomoea horsfalliae |
| ** | "       plumbaginoides | * | Juniperus conferta |
| *** | Chusquea tessellata | * | Lathyrus splendens |
| ** | Cistus corbariensis | *** | Lippia nodiflora |
| * | "    salvifolius | * | Lolium multiflorum |
| *** | Coprosma kirki | ** | Lonicera chinensis |
| ** | "       prostrate | * | "       halliana |
| ** | Correa pulchella | *** | "       hispidula |
| * | Cynodon dactylon | * | Lycium richi |
| * | Eriogonum rubescens | ** | Mahernia verticillata |
| *** | Ficus pumila | ** | Malvastrum coccineum |
| * | Grevillea obtusifolia | * | Mesembryanthemum croceum |

* Mesembryanth. edule
**     "     floribundum
**     "     laeve
***    "     verruculatum
*** Micromeria piperella
** Moraea catenulata
*** Muehlenbeckia axillare
** Nepeta mussini
* Nephrolepis exaltata
* Oenothera tetraptera
*** Opuntia linguiformis
** Penstemon cordifolius
** Pittosporum heterophyllum

*** Polygonum reynoutria
*** Pteris aquilina
*** Reineckia carnea
*** Rhus trilobata
*** Ribes viburnifolium
** Sarcococca hookeriana
* Sasa pigmaea
*** Schinus dependens
** Solanum xanti
* Sollya heterophylla
** Teucrium prostratum
*** Vinca major
** Zauschneria californica

## SUB-FUNCTIONAL

Plants with elongating, stringy rootings of reasonably rapid penetration should be used with those of fibrous character in order that the entire mass of the fill may ultimately be reinforced as with steel against a major slide or other sudden movement. The following shrubs and trees, it will be noted, are well able to root for themselves....actually....literally....figuratively....and do a supreme job of holding. This is a list for the engineer.

*** Adenostoma (species)
*** Arctostaphylos diversifolius
*** Artemisia tridentata
* Atriplex breweri
* Baccharis (species)
*** Cercidium torreyanum
* Ceratostigma willmottianum
** Cercis occidentalis
* Chilopsis linearis
*** Cichorium intybus
* Cistus (species)
* Cytisus canariensis
*** Dendromecon rigida
*** Dicentra chrysantha
** Echium fastuosum
* Eucalyptus (check species)
* Eriogonum fasciculatum
** Fremontia californica
** Genista monosperma
* Grevillea thelemanniana
*** Hakea (check species)
*** Juglans californica
* Juniperus (species)
** Lavatera assurgentiflora
** Leptospermum laevigatum
*** Malvastrum fasciculatum
*** Medicago arborea

** Melaleuca decussata
*     "    nesophila
** Melianthus major
*** Muehlenbeckia complexa
* Parkinsonia aculeata
*** Phillyrea latifolia
*** Phlomis fruticosa
*** Pickeringia montana
* Pinus (species)
** Pittosporum phillyraeoides
*** Polygala apopetala
* Prosopis (species)
** Prunus ilicifolia
**     "    lyoni
*** Quercus dumosa
* Rhus (species)
* Romneya coulteri
** Schinus (species)
** Spartium junceum
* Tamarix (species)
** Tecomaria capensis
*** Teucrium fruticans
*** Ulmus pumila
*** Vitex agnus-castus
* Wigandia caracasana
** Zauschneria californica
*** Ziziphus jujuba

BANK PLANTING---calls in the first place for materials that will warp low in mass in conforming to the ground. Then the question....is the site in the shade on a north slope or does it bake out in the sun on the south. Does the ground structure, if any, slope into the bank or out, an important point with a bearing on moisture. Sunken rocks will conserve moisture and equalize soil temperature. Low-lying stems that root and roots that spread and sucker, aid in the matter of erosion, while sturdy plants at the base of the slope tend to stand against a slide and adapt to the inevitable build-up of soil. The complicated nature of this problem calls for a thorough check across drought, heat, shade, texture and quality of the soil.

### WARM SLOPES

* Acacia armata
** Aloe ciliaris
* Artabotrys uncinatus
*** Atriplex semibaccata
** Baccharis pilularis

* Bougainvillea (varieties)
** Candollea cuneiformis
*** Capparis spinosa
** Carissa prostrata
* Ceratostigma griffithi

** Chamaelaucium ciliatum
* Cistus (species)
*** Clitoria ternatea
* Eriogonum fasciculatum
*** Erythrina bidwilli
*** Euphorbia splendens
** Gilia californica
** Grevillea (check species)
*** Halimium halimifolium
* Helichrysum petiolatum
*** Ipomoea (check species)
* Jasminum mesneyi
*** Jaquemontia eastwoodiana
* Juniperus (check species)
** Lantana (species)
** Lathyrus splendens
* Lonicera (check species)
* Lotus mascaensis
*** Lycium richi
*** Mahernia verticillata
** Mahonia pinnata
* Malvastrum coccineum

** Malvaviscus arboreus
** Melaleuca hyperiscifolia
* Mesembryanth. (species)
** Nepeta mussini
** Opuntia linguiformis
** Penstemon cordifolius
*** Phlomis fruticosa
* Pittosporum heterophyllum
* Plumbago capensis
*** Quercus dumosa
* Rhus ovata
** Rosmarinus officinalis
** Salvia greggi
** Santolina chamaecyparissus
*** Schinus dependens
*** Semele androgyna
*** Solanum xanti
** Teucrium fruticosa
** Thryallis glauca
* Thunbergia gibsoni
*** Trichostoma lanatum
*** Vitis arizonica

* Zauschneria californica

## COOL SLOPES

*** Adiantum emarginatum
*** Amphicome arguta
*** Barleria caerulea
* Beloperone tomentosa
* Camellia sasanqua
* Ceanothus grizeus
** Chaenomeles japonica
*** Chiococca alba
** Chorizema cordatum
* Cissus hypoglauca
** Cotoneaster decora
***       "      microphylla
*** Deeringia amaranthoides
*** Ercilla spicata
*** Fatshedera lizei
* Galvesia speciosa
** Gelsemium sempervirens
*** Hebe hulkeana
* Hedera helix
*** Hedysarum coronarium
*** Hymenanthera crassifolia
* Hypericum reptans
* Juniperus conferta

** Lotus bertheloti
*** Muehlenbeckia complexa
* Philadelphus mexicanus
* Pyracantha yunnanensis
** Rhamnus crocea
* Ranunculus repens
* Rhus integrifolia
*** Ribes viburnifolium
*** Rosa bracteata
**      "   laevigata
*** Securidaca diversifolia
** Serissa foetida
** Severinia buxifolia
* Solanum rantonneti
* Sollya heterophylla
*** Strophanthus speciosus
** Swainsona galegifolia
*** Tetragonia expansa
** Teucrium chamaedrys
* Trachelospermum jasminoides
** Verbena rigida
*** Vitex unifoliolata
* Woodwardia radicans

*** Zamia floridana

MINIATURE FORMS---juvenile types or specimens in the likeness of conventional or well known species; plants that are minute as to size or scale of parts for a small city garden, or patio type of development. The use of these plants in such a place permits of a more complete composition with varied effects and combinations within limited space. Certain plants that are normally shrubs may be whipped up to a single stem and used here as a tree. Pruning is important to keep some of these plants in scale, while cutting down through the root structure will restrict growth and aid where necessary in the lessening process. Check further with DWARF SHRUBS and with SMALL TREES OR LARGE SHRUBS.

## TREES

** Acer palmatum
** Alsophila australis
*** Bolusanthus speciosus
* Canella winterana
* Chamaerops humilis
* Citrus deliciosa
***     "   taitensis

*** Collinia elegans
*** Dracaena fragrans
** Ervatamia coronaria
** Eucalyptus erythronema
*       "      forrestiana
**      "      pyriformis
*** Eurya japonica

* Fortunella japonica
** Guaiacum officinale
* Lavatera assurgentiflora
*** Livistona humilis
* Lawsonia inermis
* Magnolia lanceolata
*** " stellata
** Michelia fuscata

* Murraea paniculata
*** Musa cavendishi
** Myrsine africana
* Phoenix roebelini
** Poinciana gilliesi
*** Prunus jaquemonti
** Rhapis humilis
*** Syagrus weddelliana

*** Viminaria denudata

## SHRUBS

* Abelia schumanni
*** Acalypha godseffiana
* Aeonium decorum
* Azalea obtusa
*** Beloperone longispicua
** Berberis gracilis
** Buxus suffruticosa
** Daboetia cantabrica
* Ceratostigma willmottianum
** Cistus salvifolius
*** Cneorum tricoccon
*** Cotoneaster pannosa nana
** " thymifolia
* Cuphea hissopifolia
** " platycentra
* Diosma reevesi
*** Eriogonum rubescens
* Euonymus microphyllus
* Halimium libanotis
* Hebe buxifolia
*** " chathamica
** " menziesi
* " traversi
* Jasminum floridum
** " parkeri

** Lavandula officinalis
*** Melianthus minor
** Myrtus minima
* Nierembergia caerulea
** " gracilis
*** Pimelea coarctica
*** Prunus cistena
* Punica granatum nana
*** Rhus cismontana
* Rosa chinensis
*** Sabal minor
* Sarcococca humilis
** Sasa disticha
** Satureja montana
* Serissa foetida
** Solanum pseudo-capsicum
* Teucrium chamaedrys
*** " marrum
*** Thomasia purpurea
** Thymus argenteus
* " nitidus
*** " vulgaris
*** Yucca tenuistylis
*** Zamia floridana
*** Zauschneria californica

## VINES

*** Abrus precatorius
** Asparagus asparagoides
** Camellia sasanqua
*** Cissus striata
* Ficus pumila minima
** Fuchsia magellanica (varieties)

** Hedera helix minima
*** Littonia modesta
** Manettia bicolor
* Parthenocissus lowi
* Solanum seaforthianum
* Thunbergia alata

## HERBACEOUS PLANTS

*** Acaena microphylla
* Alyssum (dwarf forms)
*** Anemone hupehensis
* Arctotis acaulis
* Armeria maritima
*** Begonia foliosa
* " gracilis
* " multiflora
*** " semperflorens
*** Briza minor
* Brodiaea uniflora
** Campanula erinus
* " mayi
** Centaureum massoni
*** Chlorophytum picturatum
*** Chrysanthemum mawi
** " parthenium
*** Convolvulus lineatus
** Cymbalaria aequitriloba
** Cyperus gracilis
* Dianthus deltoides
* Erigeron karvinskyanus
*** Fuchsia procumbens

** Gilia lutea
*** Gypsophila cerastioides
** Helxine soleiroli
*** Hesperantha stanfordiae
* Heuchera sanguinea
*** Iris alata
** " delta species)
* " unguicularis
* Lavandula stoechas
*** Lilium elegans
** Linum salsoloides nanum
* Lobelia erinus
* Lupinus affinis
*** Mentha requieni
** Micromeria piperella
** Narcissus cyclamineus
*** Nertera depressa
** Nymphaea chromatella
*** " tetragona
** Ocimum basilicum
* Ophiopogon japonicum
** Oxalis hererei
** Papaver nudicaule

*** Paronychia argentea          ** Sisyrinchium macouni
 ** Pellaea densa                *** Stachys corsica
 ** Petunia dwarf forms)          * Tagetes signata pumila
 ** Phalaris picta               ** Thymus minimus
 ** Pilea microphylla             * Tropaelum minus
  * Primula malacoides           ** Tunica saxifraga
 ** Rivina humilis               ** Viola pedunculata
 ** Scirpus cernuus             *** Wahlenbergia saxicola
  * Sedum (check species)         * Zinnia linearis

## SUCCULENTS

*** Agave victoriae-reginae     *** Kalanchoe uniflora
  * Aloe variegata               ** Kleinia ficoides
  * Byrnesia weinbergi            * Mesembryanth. deltoides
 ** Crassula impressa            ***    " odoratum
*** Cyanotus hirsuta             **    " tuberosum
 ** Dyckia sulphurea             ** Oliveranthus elegans
  * Echeveria amoena             ** Othonna crassifolia
 **     "      derenbergi       *** Sansevieria parva
*** Euphorbia truncata           ** Sempervivum tectorum
  * Gasteria (species           *** Stapelia divaricata
  * Haworthia (species)           * Zygocactus truncatus


NATURALIZING SUBJECTS---alien plants that will take the high spots
and the low of climate without quibbling. They will be found  allied
in principle and possesed in some degree of that intrinsic feeling of
freedom, with tenure born of the wildling.....its simple, unaffected
grace and the capacity to survive.  Some are escapes, foreign plants
that have found places so much to their liking, they settle down. There
they reproduce and go through further adaptation, become naturalized
and frequently take on attractive qualities they never develop under
cultivation. They are sometimes easier to establish than the natives,
especially if viable seed is available. Help them along until able to
take over for themselves, when they will require only nominal attention, if any at all. Rodents are particularly bothersome here. Check
with NATIVE PLANTS and with the COMPENDIUM for preference as to arid
or humid regions. This is frequently a matter of life or death.

## TREES

*** Acacia auriculaeformis        * Melaleuca leucadendra
  *    "     podalyriaefolia     ** Melia azedarach
 **    "     pycnantha            * Parkinsonia aculeata
*** Ailanthus altissima         *** Phyllanthus acidus
 ** Albizzia lophantha          *** Phytolacca dioica
*** Angophora lanceolata         ** Pinus canariensis
 ** Blighia sapida                * Pittosporum phillyraeoides
  * Casuarina equisetifolia      ** Quercus suber
 ** Cinnamomum camphora         *** Robinia pseudacacia
*** Citherexylum spinosum         * Schinus molle
  * Eucalyptus cladocalyx       *** Thespesia populnea
 ** Grevillea robusta             * Ulmus pumila

## SHRUBS

  * Adenocarpus viscosus        *** Doryanthes palmeri
 ** Anthyllis barba-jovis         * Echium fastuosum
*** Aster fruticosus            *** Erica melanthera
 ** Atriplex breweri             ** Euphorbia heterophylla
 ** Bambusa multiplex            ** Genista monosperma
*** Brachysema lanceolatum        * Grevillea (check species)
 ** Callistemon lanceolatus      ** Hakea elliptica
*** Calothamnus quadrifidus       *    "    laurina
 ** Candollea cuneiformis        ** Helichrysum petiolatum
  * Cassia artemisoides         *** Hibiscus mutabilis
 ** Ceratostigma willmottianum    * Lantana camara
*** Clerodendrum fragrans        **    "    montevidensis
 ** Correa magnifica              * Leonotis leonurus
  * Cytisus canariensis          ** Malvastrum capense
  * Daubentonia punicea          ** Opuntia (check species)

*** Phillyrea latifolia          ** Salvia (species)
*** Photinia serrulata           ** Sasa humilis
  * Pittosporum heterophyllum   *** Senecio petasitis
 ** Poinciana gilliesi            * Sollya heterophylla
 ** Polygala apopetala            * Spartium junceum
*** Puya alpestris              *** Swainsona galegifolia
  * Ricinus communis              * Tecomaria capensis
  * Rosa laevigata                * Teucrium fruticans
 ** Russelia equisetiformis     *** Yucca aloifolia

## HERBACEOUS PLANTS

  * Allium (species)             * Limonium (species)
  * Alyssum maritimum            * Linaria (species)
*** Amaryllis rutila           *** Linum narbonnense
*** Anemone blanda             *** Mesembryanth. croceum
 **      "      fulgens          *      "       edule
  * Anthemis tinctoria          ** "       floribundum
  * Arctotis (species)           *      "       roseum
 ** Aristea eckloni             ** Moraea iridioides
 ** Asclepias currassavica     *** Muscari armenaicum
*** Asphodelus albus             * Narcissus pseudo-narcissus
 ** Babiana stricta            *** "       tazetta
*** Cheiranthus mutabilis       ** Nepeta mussini
 ** Chrysanthemum mawi         *** Ornithogalum arabicum
 ** Delphinium ajacis            * Oxalis (species)
 ** Dimorphotheca (species)     ** Primula malacoides
  * Echium wildpreti            ** Rehmannia angulata
  * Felicia amelloides          ** Sanvitalia procumbens
*** Foeniculum vulgare          ** Scilla hispanica
 ** Freesia refracta           *** "       hyacinthoides
  * Gaura lindheimeri           ** Sedum altissimum
*** Hesperantha stanfordiae      * Sparaxis tricolor
*** Homeria collina            *** Streptanthera cuprea
 ** Hunnemannia fumariaefolia    * Tithonia rotundifolia
  * Iris unguicularis          *** Torenia fournieri
  * Ixia maculata              ** Tritonia (species)
 ** Lagurus ovatus             ** Tulipa (botanical species)
 ** Lamarkia aurea             *** Venidium (species)
  * Leucojum autumnale         *** Verbena rigida

FLAGGING---flat stones for the naturalistic garden. Used casually they are free of any suggestion or thought of the formal or of the artificial. They are adapted admirably to level ground or slight slopes as paths or suggested ways for circulation. Grass may be grown between the stones or the following plants used to fill the inter-spacing and alongside. This gives color with greenery and varied interest in low form and a further textural value to the plain or a dead flat. Check with CARPETING PLANTS for more material.

 ** Acaena microphylla         *** Paronychia argentea
  * Ajuga reptans              *** Pilea nummulariaefolia
  * Arenaria balearica          ** Sagina subulata
 ** Armeria maritima             * Sedum brevifolium
 ** Cymbalaria aequitriloba     ** "       dasyphyllum
  * Dianthus deltoides         *** "       hispanicum
  * Erodium chamaedryoides      ** Schizocentron elegans
 ** Gypsophila cerastioides     ** Selaginella denticulata
*** Haworthia tessellata         * Sempervivum (forms)
  * Helxine soleiroli          *** Stachys corsica
*** Mentha requieni              * Thymus albus
 ** Linum salsoloides nanum     ** "       coccineus
*** Mesembryanth. filicaule    *** "       minimus
 **      "       tuberosum     *** Umbilicus chrysanthus
 ** Morisia monantha           ** Veronica nummularia
*** Origanum dictamnus           * "       repens
 ** Nierembergia rivularis     *** Viola gracilis
*** Nertera depressa           *** Wahlenbergia saxicola
              * Zoysia tenuifolia

FILLERS---applied as a term to plants of rapid growth and often temporary nature, to be used for early effect and maturity intermingling with plants of slower growth that are planned to be permanent. The temporary plant will be restrained as found desirable or necessary, but when the whole becomes crowded, and well before any real harm is evident in the slower plant, the filler is grubbed out thoroly to prevent suckering. When these measures are taken, the grouping should be studied with a view to matching types and cultural requirements. Use only one or very few kinds of filler plants. Strong-growing woody perennials, or even rangy, lifting vines or vining shrubs may be used where color is wanted in preference to the larger mass.

## TREES

| | |
|---|---|
| * Acacia floribunda | * Melia azedarach |
| *   "    longifolia | * Myoporum laetum |
| **  "    podalyriaefolia | * Pinus halepensis |
| *** "    pruinosa | *** Podachaenium eminens |
| *** "    pycnantha | *** Populus alba |
| **  "    saligna | * Prunus persica |
| * Albizzia lophantha | * Ricinus communis |
| * Casuarina equisetifolia | *** Robinia pseudacacia |
| *** Dombeya wallichi | * Salyx (species) |
| *** Eucalyptus globulus compacta | * Schinus terebinthifolius |
| *    "      lehmanni | *** Solanum warscewiczi |
| **   "      preissiana | ** Stenolobium stans |
| **   "      pulverulenta | ** Tamarix aphylla |
| ***  "      stricklandi | *** Virgilia capensis |
| ** Grevillea robusta | ** Wigandia caracasana |

## SHRUBS

| | |
|---|---|
| ** Abutilon hybridum | *** Hibiscus sabdariffa |
| *** Acacia alata | * Hypericum floribundum |
| *    "   armata | * Iochroma (species) |
| **   "   verticillata | ** Jasminum humile |
| ***  "   vestita | *    "      officinale |
| * Artemisia albula | *** "      pubescens |
| ** Asparagus virgatus | ** Lantana camara |
| * Atriplex breweri | *** Lavatera assurgentiflora |
| * Buddleja (species) | * Leonotis leonurus |
| ** Candollea cuneiformis | *** Lippia citriodora |
| *** Capparis spinosa | ** Lonicera nitida |
| * Cassia (species) | ** Lupinus arboreus |
| *** Ceanothus cyaneus | ***  "      paynei |
| ***  "      grizeus | *** Lycium (species) |
| * Ceratostigma willmottianum | *** Malvastrum fasciculatum |
| * Cestrum (species) | * Malvaviscus arboreus |
| *** Chorizema cordatum | **   "         grandiflorus |
| ** Cienfuegosia hakeaefolia | * Melaleuca decussata |
| * Cistus (species) | **    "       hyperiscifolia |
| ** Clerodendrum myricoides | ***   "       nesophila |
| *** Coprosma baueri | ** Poinciana (species) |
| ** Coronilla glauca (forms) | ** Psoralea pinnata |
| * Cytisus canariensis | ** Salvia sessei |
| ** Datura suaveolens | * Solanum rantonneti |
| * Daubentonia (species) | * Streptosolen jamesoni |
| *** Deeringia amaranthoides | *** Tamarix (species) |
| *** Dovyalis caffra | * Tecoma garrocha |
| *** Eriogonum giganteum | ** Tecomaria capensis |
| ** Euphorbia pulcherrima | *** Teucrium fruticans |
| ** Fuchsia arborescens | *** Tibouchina semidecandra |
| * Genista monosperma | ** Thevetia nereifolia |
| ** Grewia occidentalis | *** Vitex trifolia |

## VINES

| | |
|---|---|
| ** Alseuosmia macrophylla | ** Lathyrus splendens |
| *** Fatshedera lizei | *** Lycium barbarum |
| *** Fuchsia corymbiflora | * Rosa laevigata |
| * Holmskioldia sanguinea | ** Solandra guttata |
| ** Jasminum mesneyi | *** Vitis arizonica |

## WOODY PERENNIALS

* Acalypha wilksiana
** Alonsoa warscewiczi
*** Beloperone tomentosa
** Breynia nivosa
** Calceolaria integrifolia
* Calocephalis browni
*** Cheiranthus mutabilis
* Chaenostoma grandiflorum
* Chrysanthemum frutescens
*** Cuphea roezli
*** Dahlia maxoni
*** Dicentra chrysantha
** Dimorphotheca ecklonis
* Echium fastuosum
** Erythrina herbacea

* Euphorbia heterophylla
* Felicia amelloides
***      "   echinata
*** Helichrysum petiolatum
*** Hibiscus diversifolius
** Hunnemannia fumariaefolia
** Jacobinia pauciflora
* Lavatera olbia
* Mirabilis jalapa
** Reinwardtia indica
** Rosmarinus officinalis
* Russelia equisetiformis
* Santolina chamaecyparissus
** Senecio confusus
* Swainsona galegifolia

*** Tithonia rotundifolia

COPSE---suckering shrubs and small trees that will more or less naturally develop a many-stemmed woodland in miniature. This can be a distinctive effect in its own right, at the same time holding ground of a broad hillside or other land of oblique or indirect use. It can be in the nature of an environment for an over-looking belvedere or other feature designed as a retreat or overlook. If these plants do not develop the desired multiplicity of stems, cut into the root mass a distance from the base crown of the plant. An under-cover planting in the same conception and field of view will tend to finish off beneath and further stabilize the ground against erosion.

## OVER COVER

** Acacia melanoxylon
*** Casuarina lepidophloia
*** Clerodendrum bungei
**     "    fragrans
* Maytenus boaria
*** Melaleuca ericifolia
**     "    leucadendra
** Pickeringia montana
*** Pittosporum phillyraeoides

* Populus alba
***     nigra italica
*** Rhus cismontana
** Robinia pseudacacia
** Solanum warscewiczi
* Tetrapanax papyriferum
*** Ungnadia speciosa
* Wigandia caracasana
*** Zizyphus jujuba

## UNDER COVER

** Adiantum (check species)
* Anemone japonica
*** Asparagus tenuisissimus
** Blechnum occidentale
*** Corydalis lutea
** Davallia canariensis
** Dicentra formosa
* Duchesnea indica
*** Fuchsia triphylla
* Hypericum calycinum
** Lysimachia nummularia
* Malvastrum coccineum
*** Microlepia platyphylla
** Micromeria chamissonis
* Nephrolepis exaltata
** Oenothera tetraptera

** Parthenocissus henryana
** Pellaea andromedaefolia
*** Petasitis fragrans
** Polygonum reynoutria
*** Polypodium mandaianum
** Pteris aquilina
* Ranunculus repens
*** Reineckia carnea
*** Rhus trilobata
** Sasa pygmaea
*** Sarcococca humilis
** Solanum laurifolium
*** Tolmeia menziesi
* Vinca minor
* Woodwardia (species)
** Zauschneria californica

## VINING

*** Amphicome arguta
*** Araujia sericofera
* Asparagus (check species)
*** Campsidium valdivianum
** Campsis radicans
** Cissus incisa
*** Eccremocarpus scaber
* Fatshedera lizei
* Gelsemium sempervirens

*** Hardenbergia monophylla
* Hedera helix
* Lonicera halliana
** Mandevilla suaveolens
** Muehlenbeckia complexa
** Polygonum auberti
** Solanum seaforthianum
** Sollya heterophylla
*** Thunbergia gibsoni

ARMED SHRUBS---as protective thickets or buffers may forestall
many a heart-ache over trampled plants that are treasured. These solid
and sturdy fellows are provided with thorns, spines, claws or rudimentary spurs which will furnish an effective barrier against encroach-
ing animals or willful people and possibly serve as a sharp reminder
to careless friends or a thoughtless public. Set these plants more
closely together than normal for quick coverage.

|  |  |  |  |
|---|---|---|---|
| * | Acacia farnesiana | ** | Lycium (species) |
| *** | " greggi | * | Opuntia (check species) |
| ** | " horrida | *** | Osmanthus ilicifolius |
| ** | Acrocomia mexicana | *** | Osteomeles anthyllidifolia |
| ** | Artabotrys uncinatus | * | Parkinsonia aculeata |
| *** | Bergerocactus emoryi | *** | Pelargonium echinatum |
| * | Carissa (species) | *** | Pickeringia montana |
| ** | Cercidium torreyanum | ** | Prosopis (species) |
| * | Chaenomeles japonica | * | Pyracantha (species) |
| ** | Colletia cruciata | ** | Rhapidophyllum hystrix |
| * | Dovyalis caffra | * | Rosa (species) |
| * | Duranta repens | ** | Sabal minor |
| ** | Echinocactus (species) | *** | Serenoa repens |
| *** | Echinocereus rigidissimus | * | Severinia buxifolia |
| * | Elaeagnus pungens | ** | Solanum giganteum |
| ** | Euphorbia splendens | *** | " warscewiczi |
| *** | Fourquieria splendens | *** | Strychnos spinosa |
| *** | Guzmania cardinalis | ** | Triphasia trifolia |
| *** | Hakea pugioniformis | *** | Xylosma senticosa |
| ** | Ilex cornuta | *** | Zizyphus obtusifolia |

CUT FLOWERS---may be spared from the garden that has been planned
with that eventuality in mind. Material should be taken from a number
of plants in order that the place appearance may be the least disturbed.
Cut when in poor moisture with the structure and habit of species in
mind....always with a sharp instrument for a clean, untorn cut that
will take water quickly. There are many ways to treat the cut material, and aids to be used in prolonging freshness....cool, clean water
is very good. Weak solutions of corrosive sublimate, formaldehyde or
common table salt have been recommended while sugar is effective. Cut
in late afternoon when sugar content of plant is high.   These plants
may be used in the layout of the home grounds incidental to other
phases of planting and thus with uses beyond cutting. They have been
selected here for length of bloom, keeping qualities and decorative
value, or the manner in which they make up. Women should go over
these lists before making any extensive plans for planting.  Check
further with the CUTFLOWER GARDEN for marginal material.

## WOODY PLANTS

In cutting stems of shrubs, vines or trees, unless pruning
for other purposes, leave no stub without at least one bud for new
growth. A second cut under water, as in a pail or pool, permits of the
conducting tubes filling with water to the exclusion of air. The butt
end of the stem may be slant-cut or split and the sides peeled back to
facilitate absorbtion. Stems with milky juice should be dipped in
melted wax, sealed in boiling water or charred over fire....may be
closed temporarily by thrusting cut end into moist earth.

|  |  |  |  |
|---|---|---|---|
| *** | Acacia alata | ** | Chamaelaucium ciliatum |
| * | " baileyana | *** | Chorizema cordatum |
| *** | " cyanophylla | ** | Cytisus canariensis |
| * | " pubescens | *** | Erica melanthera |
| ** | Antigonon leptopus | ** | Eriogonum giganteum |
| *** | Baeckia virgata | * | Eucalyptus erythrocorys |
| ** | Beaumontia grandiflora | ** | " erythronema |
| ** | Beloperone guttata | ** | " ficifolia |
| *** | Bougainvillea (varieties) | *** | " forrestiana |
| * | Bouvardia humboldti | *** | " preissiana |
| ** | Buddleja magnifica | * | Euphorbia pulcherrima |
| *** | Carpenteria californica | ** | Euryops athanasiae |
| * | Chaenomeles japonica | *** | Fremontia californica |

** Fuchsia (varieties)
** Galvesia speciosa
 * Gardenia (species)
** Genista monosperma
*** Jasminum mesneyi
** Lagerstroemia indica
 * Lavandula (species)
*** Leonotis leonurus
 * Leptospermum scoparium
*** Lonicera confusa
 **     "    hildebrandtiana
** Leucophyllum texanum
*** Luculia gratissima
*** Mitriostigma axillare
 * Nierembergia frutescens
** Peltophorum inerme
*** Podalyria sericea

** Polygonum auberti
 * Prostanthera nivea
** Prunus amygdalus
***    "    glandulosa
 *     "    persica
 * Rose (varieties)
*** Russelia equisetiformis
 * Spartium junceum
 * Spiraea cantoniensis
*** Streptosolen jamesoni
*** Swainsona galegifolia
** Syringa persica
 * Tamarix (species)
** Tecoma (species)
** Trachelospermum jasminoides
*** Viburnum carlesi
 * Weigela florida

## HERBACEOUS PLANTS

Flowers that are not quite fully developed are usually the best to take. Plunge deeply into water for a time before arranging. Renew the water daily, cutting away a bit of stem each change. If this is done in the evening, take out of container and immerse in cool water over night. Vases should be boiled clean from time to time since bacterial growth at the intake tends to choke the tubes against water and salts. Submerged leaves rot to accentuate this. Sharp temperature changes affect adversely, while sudden or continual drafts are most detrimental and should be guarded against.

*** Allium caeruleum
 *     "    neapolitanum
**     "    pulchellum
 * Alstroemeria (species)
 * Anemone (species)
** Angelonia grandiflora
** Arthropodium cirrhatum
 * Aster amellus
*** Befaria racemosa
*** Bletilla striata
** Brodiaea (species)
*** Centaureum venustum
 * Chrysanthemum (species)
 * Coreopsis (species)
*** Crassula multicava
** Cynoglossum amabile
** Eschscholtzia californica
** Felicia amelloides
 * Francoa ramosa
** Gaillardia aristata
 * Gerberia jamesoni
 * Geum (varieties)
 * Godetia grandiflora
** Heliophila pilosa
 * Heuchera sanguinea
*** Hunnemannia fumariaefolia
*** Hymenocallis (species)

** Iris germanica
***    "    japonica
 *     "    xiphium
 * Lathyrus odoratus
*** Leucojum autumnale
** Limonium (species)
** Linaria maroccana
*** Milla biflora
** Ornithogalum (species)
** Papaver (species)
*** Physostegia virginiana
** Rehmannia angulata
 * Salpiglossis sinuata
 * Salvia farinacea
**     "    patens
***    "    sessei
 * Scabiosa caucasica
*** Schizostylis coccinea
** Sparaxis tricolor
*** Tithonia rotundifolia
 * Tritonia (species)
** Tulipa clusiana
*** Venidium (species)
*** Verbesina encelioides
 * Viola odorata
** Watsonia iridifolia
*** Zantedeschia aethiopica

EVERLASTING FLOWERS---immortelles, mostly natural species that retain their shape and color after having been dried out. They are at their best in sunny gardens of light, lean soils. The flower head is taken normally just before or as the florets become full open. Hang in bunches head down in a darkened place for two or three weeks, then pack away in a dry place for future use. They will be most valuable over winter, uplift and lasting remembrance of the brighter season that has been left behind, rare aid in the snuggery of the time.

** Agrostis nebulosa
*** Ammobium alatum
*** Anaphalis margaritacea
 * Armeria maritima

** Briza maxima
** Cardiospermum halicacabum
** Catananche caerulea
** Celosia (species)

* Chaerophyllum dasycarpum
** Chusquea tessellata
*** Coix lachryma-jobi
* Cortaderia selloana
*** Emilia sagittata
** Emmenanthe penduliflora
* Eriogonum (species)
*** Eryngium amethystinum
** Gilia capitata
** Glaucium flavum
* Gomphrena globosa
* Helichrysum (species)

*** Helipterum (species)
*** Lagurus ovatus
*** Lamarkia aurea
* Limonium (species)
*** Lonas inodora
*** Lunaria annua
* Molucella laevis
** Phormium tenax
*** Physalis francheti
** Salvia clevelandi
*** Stipa pennata
* Xeranthemum annuum

FRAGRANT FLOWERS---in the garden have greater significance than is generally realized and now that scent is being lost in the quest for bigger and bloomier blooms, it becomes doubly important. Happy happenings long out of the past will recur vividly with the smell of a flower for a joyful moment....a prod for the mind....resurgence of spirit. And not only is the moment quickened, the projection of the day seems hastened, or lingers in a pleasant glow, as one is disposed. Humidity is conducive to a fuller perfume, while a dry climate inhibits the flow. White flowers are usually the more powerful, followed by red, yellow and blue. Thick, waxy petals indicate a high potential. One should by all means consider this aspect of planting and choose from the list some plant with a particular meaning for one's self....personal gratification that will exalt, probe deep and reach high. Then note the correlation of odor in the garden, the mixture of these above with that of the clean earth in the cool of the evening, again in early morning under the first sun-warmed breeze....that time called June.

## TREES

* Acacia (species)
** Blighia sapida
** Calophyllum inophyllum
** Chilopsis linearis
* Citrus (species)
* Hymenosporum flavum
*** Magnolia virginiana
*** Osmanthus americanus

** Peltophorum inerme
* Pittosporum (check species)
*** Plumeria emarginata
*** Pterospermum acerifolium
* Prunus (species)
*** Robinia pseudacacia
* Sophora secundiflora
*** Talauma hodsoni

## SHRUBS

* Acokanthera spectabilis
* Artabotrys uncinatus
** Azalea (species)
* Azara microphylla
*** Boronia elatior
* Bouvardia humboldti
** Brunfelsia americana
** Buddleja (check species)
*** Calliandra portoricensis
* Calycanthus (species)
** Carissa grandiflora
*** Carpenteria californica
* Cestrum nocturnum
**      "     parqui
* Choisya ternata
** Clerodendrum fragrans
*** Damnacanthus indicus
** Daphne odora
* Elaeagnus pungens
* Ervatamia coronaria
*** Eurya ochnacea
* Gardenia (species)
*** Genista monosperma
*** Hakea suaveolens
*** Hibiscus arnottianus
*** Ixora chinensis
** Jasminum sambac
* Lavandula officinalis

** Lawsonia inermis
*** Lippia ligustrina
* Lonicera (check species)
*** Luculia gratissima
** Magnolia stellata
*** Melianthus major
* Michelia fuscata
* Murraea exotica
** Nerium oleander
** Ochna multiflora
** Oncoba routledgi
*** Osmanthus ilicifolius
* Philadelphus microphyllus
* Pittosporum tobira
*** Rhamnus crocea
* Rose (check varieties)
*** Sarcococca hookeriana
** Severinia buxifolia
*** Siphonosmanthus delavayi
* Spartium junceum
** Syringa persica
** Ternstroemia japonica
*** Triphasia trifolia
* Viburnum carlesi
***      "     fragrans
**      "     odoratissimum
*** Visnea mocanera
* Vitex agnus-castus

## VINES

*** Agdestis clematidea
*** Araujia sericofera
*** Asparagus falcatus
*** Artabotrys odoratissimus
  * Beaumontia grandiflora
  * Boussingaultia baselloides
 ** Calonyction aculeatum
 ** Clematis (check species)
  * Gelsemium sempervirens
 ** Hoya carnosa
  * Jasminum (check species)
  * Lathyrus odoratus

  * Lonicera (check species)
  * Mandevilla suaveolens
 ** Osmanthus fragrans
 ** Passiflora alato-caerulea
*** Podranea brycei
*** Phaseolus caracalla
  * Philadelphus mexicanus
*** Stauntonia hexaphylla
 ** Stephanotis floribunda
*** Thenardia floribunda
*** Thunbergia fragrans
  * Trachelospermum jasminoides

## HERBACEOUS PLANTS

 ** Ageratum houstonianum
  * Alyssum maritimum
 ** Amarcrinum howardi
*** Amaryllis aulica
 ** Centaurea (species)
 ** Cheiranthus mutabilis
*** Chlidanthus fragrans
 ** Cooperia drummondi
*** Crinum americanum
 **    " giganteum
  * Dianthus caryophyllus
 **    " chinensis
 ** Dodecatheon clevelandi
*** Eucharis grandiflora
  * Freesia refracta
  * Hedychium flavum
 ** Heliotropium arborescens
 ** Hymenocallis calathina
 ** Leucocoryne ixioides
*** Lilium (species)

  * Mathiola incana
*** Mentzelia lindleyi
 ** Milla biflora
  * Narcissus (species)
  * Nicotiana alata
*** Nymphaea odorata
 ** Oenothera caespitosa
*** Pancratium illyricum
*** Petasitis fragrans
  * Petunia hybrida
  * Polianthes tuberosa
*** Reseda odorata
*** Saururus cernuus
*** Scilla hispanica
  * Tagetes (species)
  * Tropaeolum (species)
*** Tulbaghia fragrans
 ** Verbena hortensis
  * Viola odorata
*** Zaluzianskya capensis

SCENTED FOLIAGE---urges one on and spurs the passing fancy to explore the farther depths of a garden. Pleasant odors arise from these plants, essential oils becoming gaseous in the warmth of the sun; reacting to coolness or other stimulus. Here is a subtle diffusion of something very real in the individuality of a garden. These plants are particularly intriguing when placed within pinching distance of a path so that a passing mortal may sniff freshly and at will the odor of Eden....and set the very marrow aleaping. Curiously, the scentless leaves seem to go with the more fragrant flowers.

*** Alpinia speciosa
  * Anthriscus cerefolium
  * Artemisia (species)
 ** Buxus microphylla
 ** Calycanthus (species)
*** Canella winterana
*** Cedronella canariensis
 ** Chamaelaucium ciliatum
 ** Choisya ternata
 ** Chrysanthemum balsamita
 ** Cinnamomum camphora
*** Cneoridium dumosum
  * Cupressus (species)
*** Cymbopogon citratus
  * Diosma ericoides
*** Eriocephalis africanus
  * Eucalyptus citriodora
 ** Foeniculum vulgare
 ** Illicium anisatum
 ** Juniperus (species)
*** Lantana camara
  * Laurus nobilis
  * Lavandula (species)

  * Leptospermum citratum
  * Libocedrus decurrens
  * Lippia citriodora
*** Majorana hortensis
*** Melianthus major
 ** Melissa officinalis
  * Mentha (species)
  * Micromeria (species)
  * Myrtus (species)
 ** Nepeta mussini
 ** Ocimum basilicum
*** Origanum dictamnus
  * Pelargonium (species)
 ** Pinus (species)
 ** Prostanthera nivea
  * Rosmarinus officinalis
  * Salvia officinalis
 ** Santolina chamaecyparissus
  * Tagetes (species)
 ** Tanacetum vulgare
  * Thymus (species)
 ** Umbellularia californica
*** Vitex agnus-castus

PLANTS FOR CONTAINERS---where only well mannered chattels will be allowed. These rate sharp selection for color, form, vigor, tidiness and other minor characters that relate to type of container. They must own to a rugged conception of life since they will view it from a hot, sometimes very dry bit of earth encased within a foreign, inorganic material. This mutes and hinders beneficial soil reactions, both physical and chemical that are found in normal ground. Good drainage is a must and the soil neither heavy nor extremely light, as of too much sand. It should be essentially retentive of moisture, with peatmoss most effective. Large leaves or abundant foliage will require more water. Watch the tips of new growth, as irregular irrigation will show up there first,....an over-all dullness indicates a more deeply seated suffering. Keep up fertility and an eternal vigilance for pests. Plants on the borderline of hardiness will have more difficulty here during cold weather and should be covered or taken in cold nights.

## POT PLANTS

To be used inside or out of doors in the decoration of balconies, the terrace or on a low wall where they add dramatic bits of color and diverting greenery to otherwise dead construction....hold for voids that may develop in the garden. It is well to arrange relays in this connection, since growing conditions here are unusually severe, when most plants will benefit with a period of time under lath or in a protected garden hospital for recuperation. These plants are often more satisfactory and come into flower earlier if allowed to bind their roots slightly in the container.

### ANNUALS

*** Amaranthus caudatus
  * Anagallis linifolia
 ** Browallia americana
*** Calceolaria herbeohybrida
  * Calendula officinalis
 ** Capsicum frutescens
  * Cineraria cruenta
*** Clarkia elegans
  * Diascia barberae
 ** Dianthus chinensis
*** Emilia sagittata
*** Godetia grandiflora

 ** Nemesia strumosa
 ** Nicotiana alata
 ** Petunia hybrida
 ** Piqueria trinervia
  * Primula malacoides
*** Salpiglossis sinuata
 ** Schizanthus wisetonensis
*** Schizopetalon walkeri
  * Tagetes signata pumila
 ** Torenia fournieri
*** Tropaeolum minus
*** Ursinia anthemoides

*** Zinnia linearis

### PERENNIALS

 ** Adiantum cuneatum
 ** Alonsoa warscewiczi
*** Aristea eckloni
*** Asclepias currassavica
  * Asplenium nidus
  * Bergenia (species)
*** Blechnum moorei
 ** Calathea roseo-picta
  * Campanula isophylla
*** Chironia linoides
*** Chlorophytum elatum
  * Chrysanthemum frutescens
 ** Cyperus alternifolius
  * Dieffenbachia picta
*** Felicia (check species)
 ** Francoa ramosa
  * Gloxinia speciosa
*** Helleborus lividus
 ** Heuchera sanguinea
 ** Lavandula multifida

*** Limonium perezi
  * Maranta kerchoviana
 ** Mimulus luteus
*** Neomarica gracilis
 ** Ophiopogon jaburan
*** Oxypetalum caeruleum
  * Pelargonium (check species)
 ** Pentas lanceolata
 ** Peperomia sandersi
*** Polystichum tsus-simense
  * Primula obconica
 ** Pteris cretica
  * Rivina humilis
  * Saintpaulia ionantha
*** Scirpus cernuus
 ** Senecio cineraria
  * Solanum pseudocapsicum
*** Streptocarpus hybridus
*** Thunbergia cordata
*** Trachelium caeruleum

### SHRUBS

  * Ardisia crispa
*** Aster fruticosus
  * Azalea (check species)
*** Beloperone longispicua

*** Boronia elatior
  * Bouvardia humboldti
*** Calceolaria integrifolia
 ** Camellia sasanqua

*** Chaenomeles japonica          ** Lavandula officinalis
*** Cistus (check species)        *** Macropiper excelsum
  * Codiaeum (varieties)          ** Malpighia coccigera
  * Convolvulus cneorum           *** Nierembergia gracilis
 ** Cuphea platycentra            *** Mahonia pinnata
 ** Daphne odora                    * Punica granatum nana
 ** Dracaena (check species)      ** Ruellia devosiana
 ** Erica melanthera              ** Russelia equisetiformis
 ** Eurya japonica                *** Salvia greggi
  * Fuchsia (select varieties)    ** Sasa disticha
  * Gardenia veitchi              *** Solanum giganteum
*** Jasminum parkeri              *** Trichosporum pulchrum

### VINES

  * Antigonon leptopus            ** Littonia modesta
*** Aristolochia elegans          ** Manettia bicolor
*** Asparagus (check species)     ** Maurandia erubescens
*** Bomaria caldasiana            ** Momordica charantia
  * Cissus rhombifolia             * Nephthytis afzeli
*** Clerodendrum thompsonae       *** Solanum seaforthianum
 ** Hibbertia volubilis            * Stephanotis floribunda
  * Hoya carnosa                  *** Stigmaphyllon littorale
*** Ipomoea purpurea               * Trachelospermum jasminoides
*** Jaquemontia eastwoodiana      ** Thunbergia alata

### BULBS & TUBEROUS ROOTED PLANTS

  * Achimenes longiflora          *** Iris alata
*** Acidanthera biflora           **   "  unguicularis
 ** Agapanthus africana            *   "  xiphium
  * Allium neapolitanum           *** Lapeirousia cruenta
  * Alstroemeria pulchella        *** Lilium candidum
*** Amaryllis rutila               *   "   longiflorum
 ** Anemone coronaria             **   "   regale
*** Anigozanthos flavida           * Liriope spicata
*** Anthurium andreanum           *** Milla biflora
*** Arum italicum                 ** Moraea catenulata
 ** Babiana stricta                * Narcissus pseudo-narcissus
 ** Beaucarnea recurvata           * Ornithogalum arabicum
  * Begonia (species)              * Oxalis crassipes
  * Caladium picturatum           ***   "  hererei
  * Clivia (species)             ** Polianthes tuberosa
  * Cyclamen indicum              ** Ranunculus asiaticus
 ** Cyrtanthus mackeni            ** Rohdea japonica
*** Dianella intermedia           ** Schizostylis coccinea
*** Eucharis grandiflora          *** Scilla hyacinthoides
*** Eucomis undulata              **   "   peruviana
 ** Freesia refracta              ** Sparaxis tricolor
  * Gloriosa superba              ** Sprekelia formosissima
  * Gloxinia speciosa             *** Sternbergia lutea
 ** Habranthus robustus           ** Streptanthera cuprea
*** Hidalgoa wercklei             *** Tulbaghia fragrans
 ** Hymenocallis calathina         * Veltheimia viridifolia

### SUCCULENTS

  * Aeonium decorum               ** Kleinia tomentosa
  * Aloe variegata                 * Mesembryanth. aurantiacum
*** Billbergia (species)           *     "      deltoides
 ** Crassula falcata              **     "      glaucum
  *   "    tetragona              **     "      maximum
*** Cryptanthus beuckeri          ***     "      puterilli
 ** Dyckia sulphurea               * Oliveranthus elegans
*** Echeveria metalica            ** Opuntia microdasys
  * Euphorbia splendens           *** Rochea coccinea
 ** Gasteria (species)            ** Sedum adolphi
*** Haworthia reinwardti           * Sansevieria zeylanica
 ** Kalanchoe fedtschenkoi        *** Stapelia divaricata
***    "    flammea               ** Stylophyllum orcutti
 ** Kleinia ficoides               * Zygocactus truncatus

## PLANTS FOR TUBS

Most plants used for this purpose must submit to shearing unless naturally trim as to form or structure, with a definite moulding to suit a formalized environment. The tub or box is nothing more than a larger pot to accomodate a larger plant in a larger scale composition and subject in the main to conditions as outlined above. Many of the pot plants will ultimately be graduated into the tub where life expectancy is considerably higher, if life in the pot has been easy.,...geriatrics in its infancy.

### PALMS & RELATED PLANTS

*** Actinophloeus macarthuri
*** Agathis robusta
  * Brassaia actinophylla
  * Butia capitata
  * Canella winterana
  * Caryota mitis
  * Chamaerops humilis
 ** Chrysalidocarpus lutescens
 ** Cibotium schiederi
*** Collinia elegans
*** Curculigo capitulata
 ** Cycas (species)
*** Dion edule
 ** Dracaena stricta
  * Fatsia japonica
  * Howea belmoreana
*** Livistona humilis
  * Monstera deliciosa
 ** Nandina domestica
  * Phoenix roebelini

 ** Phormium tenax
 ** Rhapis excelsa
*** Sabal minor
 ** Sasa humilis
*** Sciadopitys verticillata
*** Setaria palmifolia
 ** Syagrus weddelliana
*** Trevesia palmata
*** Tupidanthus calyptratus

### BULBS & TUBERS

  * Alocasia macrorhiza
 ** Alpinia speciosa
  * Amarcrinum howardi
 ** Asplenium nidus
*** Begonia verschaffeltiana
*** Crinum giganteum
*** Dianella tasmanica
  * Strelitzia reginae
*** Veltheimia viridifolia

### SHRUBS

 ** Abelia floribunda
*** Abutilon palmeri
 ** Acacia alata
 ** Acokanthera spectabilis
  * Aucuba japonica
  * Bougainvillea Temple Fire
  * Buxus macrophylla
  * Camellia japonica
  * Citrus (check species)
 ** Clusia rosea
*** Danae racemosa
 ** Elaeodendron orientale
*** Entelea arborescens
*** Eriobotrya demissa
  * Ervatamia coronaria
*** Eucalyptus forrestiana
 **    "    torquata
  * Eugenia uniflora
 ** Ficus (check species)
  * Fortunella japonica
*** Fuchsia arborescens
  * Gardenia florida
*** Griselinia lucida
  * Guaiacum officinale
*** Hibiscus huegeli
  * Hydrangea macrophylla

 ** Ilex cornuta
 ** Juniperus excelsa
*** Lagerstroemia indica
  * Laurus nobilis
*** Ligustrum lucidum
 **     "     rotundifolium
*** Mahonia lomariifolia
 **     "     pinnata
  * Michelia fuscata
*** Mitriostigma axillare
 ** Murraea paniculata
*** Myrtus communis italica
  * Nerium oleander
*** Odontospermum sericeum
*** Olmediella betschleriana
 ** Osmanthus (check species)
  * Philodendron (species)
*** Phygelius capensis
  * Podocarpus macrophylla
***     "     nagi
*** Prunus lusitanica
 ** Punica granatum
  * Thuja orientale
 ** Umbellularia californica
  * Viburnum odoratissimum
*** Visnea mocanera

### SUCCULENTS

*** Agave (check species)
 ** Aloe arborescens
  *    "    candelabrum
  *    "    plicatilis
***    "    salm-dyckiana
  * Crassula argentea
*** Canarina campanulata
 ** Dasylerion glaucophyllum
 ** Doryanthes palmeri

  * Epiphyllum oxypetalon
*** Furcraea gigantea
*** Guzmania cardinalis
 ** Kalanchoe blossfeldiana
 ** Pachyphytum bracteosum
*** Pedilanthus tithymaloides
 ** Portulacaria afra
  * Puya alpestris
  * Yucca (species)

### THE WINDOW BOX

A stationary container that is exposed to all drying agen-
cies, therefore particularly vulnerable and difficult to maintain over
any considerable period. This can be minimized with quick changes of
the less durable plants or by the use of small pots of established material. Use both erect and trailing species for a complete effect and
note partition of the list based on the plants reaction to sun, heat,
shade and dryness. The south and west fronts are definitely related
culturally, as are the north and the east.

### SOUTH BY WEST EXPOSURES

| | |
|---|---|
| ** Abronia umbellata | ** Mathiola incana |
| * Acalypha (check species) | *** Maurandia erubescens |
| ** Ageratum houstonianum | *** Mesembryanth. (check species) |
| * Alyssum maritimum | * Nepeta mussini |
| ** Antirrhinum majus | *** Nephrolepis exaltata |
| *** Bocconia frutescens | *** Nierembergia gracilis |
| ** Browallia americana | *** Ophiopogon jaburan |
| ** Centaurea cineraria | ** Othonna crassifolia |
| ** Codiaeum (varieties) | ** Oxalis crassipes |
| * Convolvulus cneorum | * Pelargonium hortorum |
| ** " mauretanicus | * " peltatum |
| *** Crassula lycopodioides | * Petunia hybrida |
| *** Cuphea llavia | * Phlox drummondi |
| * Dracaena australis | ** Salvia splendens |
| * Felicia amelloides | *** Sideritis candicans |
| *** Hedera canariensis | *** Solanum seaforthianum |
| *** Jaquemontia (species) | *** Tropaeolum majus |
| * Lantana montevidensis | * Verbena hortensis |
| ** Liriope spicata | * Vinca (species) |
| * Lotus mascaensis | ** Zebrina pendula |
| *** Lysimachia nummularia | ** Zinnia elegans |

### NORTH BY EAST EXPOSURES

| | |
|---|---|
| ** Antirrhinum majus | *** Kleinia ficoides |
| * Asparagus (check species) | ** Lobelia erinus |
| ** Aspidistra elatior | * " speciosa |
| * Begonia (check species) | *** Lonicera aureo-reticulata |
| *** Calathea roseo-picta | ** Lopesia albiflora |
| ** Calceolaria integrifolia | ** Nemophila menziesi |
| *** Campanula fragilis | * Nephrolepis (varieties) |
| ** Cineraria cruenta | * Primula malacoides |
| * Cissus rhombifolia | ** " polyantha |
| ** Clarkia elegans | * Ranunculus asiaticus |
| * Coleus blumei | *** " repens |
| * Cymbalaria muralis | * Schizanthus wisetonensis |
| ** Dracaena fragrans | ** Sedum spurium |
| * Fuchsia (varieties) | *** " stahli |
| ** Godetia grandiflora | *** Torenia fournieri |
| ** Hedera helix (varieties) | *** Tropaeolum major |
| * Heliotropium arborescens | * Vinca major |
| ** Heuchera sanguinea | ** Viola cornuta |
| *** Kalanchoe fedtschenkoi | *** " tricolor |
| ** " uniflora | *** Wedelia trilobata |

### THE PLANTER BOX

A more recent concept in the architectural scheme that rec-
ognizes the planting element as a part of the whole. Control of herbage, the use of line and dappling mass in silhouette, and the playing of parts such as individual or collected leaves against a plain
or textured back, is the aim here. The motif need not be tropical.
Personal preference is still paramount. Consider culture carefully,
as of indoors or outside; also the fact that many of these species
will be used only in the juvenile stage, becoming too large later.

| | |
|---|---|
| ** Acalypha wilksiana | ** Aloe candelabrum |
| * Acanthus (species) | * Alpinia speciosa |
| * Acokanthera spectabilis | * Alsophila australis |
| ** Agave attenuata | ** Amarcrinum howardi |
| *** Albuca minor | ** Amaryllis hybrids |

*** Ampelopsis brevipedunculata
** Arrhenatherum tuberosum
** Asplenium nidus
* Brassaia actinophylla
* Byrnesia weinbergi
*** Calathea roseo-picta
** Caryota mitis
*** Chrysophyllum caineto
* Citrus taitensis
** Clivia hybrids
* Coccolobis uvifera
*** Cneorum tricoccon
** Codiaeum variegatum
* Colocasia antiquorum
* Corynocarpus laevigata
** Crassula argentea
** Curculigo capitulata
** Cycas (species)
* Dieffenbachia picta
*** Dion edule
* Dracaena (check species)
*** Echinocactus grusoni
* Fatsia japonica
*** Ficus elastica
*** Greyia sutherlandi
** Griselinia littoralis
*** Haemanthus katherinae
** Itea ilicifolia
* Juniperus torulosa

* Kalanchoe (check species)
** Laurus nobilis
** Leucadendron argenteum
*** Livistona chinensis
* Melianthus major
*** Nolana atriplicifolia
*** Ochrosia elliptica
** Pedilanthus tithymaloides
*** Pereskia bleo
* Philodendron (species)
** Phoenix roebelini
* Phormium (species)
*** Phygelius capensis
* Rhapis excelsa
** Russelia equisetiformis
** Sasa palmata
** Sedum (check species)
*** Selaginella (species)
*** Serenoa repens
*** Setaria palmifolia
** Solandra longiflora
* Ternstroemia japonica
* Trachelospermum jasminoides
*** Tupidanthus calyptratus
** Veltheimia viridifolia
*** Venidium fastuosum
*** Visnea mocanera
*** Wigandia caracasana
*** Zamia floridana

## BASKETS

This container has no contact except that of the grudging, inhospitable atmosphere. It should be immersed in the pool or other held water from time to time as surety in the matter of thorough moistening. This is especially important during hot weather concurrent with low humidity....use peat moss to line the basket and in the soil mix. These lists contemplate the somewhat darkened interior of the plant house, porch, patio or lanai. Here are erect-growing species, those that will spill over the side and suggestions for the holding wires. There are those which can serve alone with fulfillment and not too much objection on their own part.

### CLIMBING PLANTS

** Abrus precatorius
** Aristolochia elegans
* Asparagus asparagoides
** Bomaria carderi
** Cissus adenopodus
*** Eccremocarpus scaber
*** Gloriosa superba

*** Littonia modesta
* Manettia bicolor
** Maurandia erubescens
*** Parochetus communis
* Thunbergia alata
* Tropaeolum peregrinum
*** Vicia atropurpurea

### UPRIGHT

*** Alonsoa warscewiczi
** Achimines longiflora
* Begonia gracilis
*** Blechnum moorei
** Bletilla striata
* Browallia americana
*** Davallia canariensis
*** Caladium picturatum
*** Centaurea cineraria
* Coleus blumei
** Cuphea platycentra
** Dracaena godseffiana
*** Felicia tenella

*** Lachenalia (species)
* Liriope spicata
* Nephrolepis (varieties)
*** Nierembergia gracilis
** Onychium japonicum
** Oxalis hererei
***    "      hirta
* Pelargonium hortorum
*** Piqueria trinervia
* Primula obconica
** Pteris cretica
* Tropaeolum minus
*** Vinca rosea

### DROOPING

** Abutilon megapotamicum
*** Adiantum caudatum
* Asparagus nanus

** Asplenium flaccidum
* Begonia lloydi
**    "      rubellina

** Campanula fragilis             ** Lotus bertheloti
*       "      isophylla          *** Lysimachia nummularia
** Ceropegia woodi                * Mimulus luteus
* Cissus rhombifolia              ** Nemophila menziesi
** Crassula perfossa              *** Oplismenus hirtellus
*** Cyanotis hirsuta              * Pelargonium peltatum
* Cymbalaria muralis              ** Saxifraga sarmentosa
*** Episcea (species)             * Schizanthus wisetonensis
*** Felicia petiolata             *** Schizocentron elegans
* Fuchsia (select hybrids)        ** Sedum sieboldi
**      "      procumbens         ** Vinca major
*** Kalanchoe uniflora            *** Zebrina pendula
* Lobelia speciosa                *** Zygocactus truncatus

## SINGLE FEATURE PLANTS

* Achimenes longiflora            ** Kalanchoe flammea
** Alonsoa warscewiczi            ** Macropiper excelsum
* Asparagus sprengeri             *** Mahernia verticillata
* Begonia lloydi hybrids          ** Moraea catenulata
** Billbergia saundersi           ** Neomarica gracilis
* Calceolaria integrifolia        *** Oxalis hererei
** Campanula poscharskyana        **    "     hirta
*** Chlorophytum elatum           *** Pellaea falcata
*** Cissus adenopodus             *** Polystichum tsus-simense
** Cuphea llavia                  *** Russelia equisetifolia
*** Epidendrum cochleatum         * Sedum morganianum
* Felicia tenella                 * Senecio confusus
* Fuchsia (varieties)             *** Solanum seaforthianum
** Jaquemontia (species)          ** Trichosporum pulchrum
          * Zygocactus truncatus

## BEDDING PLANTS

As such have little place in the modern garden and the following has reference as much to patches and temporary vacancies in the
border as to typical bedding. These species will be considered  from
the standpoint of color display and duration, together with  massing
tendencies leading up to compactness.  They are more acceptable used
in generous mass or, in case of the more theatrical kinds, in the nature of parterre for public display geometrically within paved areas.
They may be blocked in a contemporary patio floor....and give place to
the fiddle-faddle of painted rock.

## FOLIAGE

** Acalypha ( check species)      *** Euphorbia heterophylla
* Alternanthera amoena            * Festuca glauca
** Amaranthus caudatus            *** Iresine herbsti
** Arrhenatherum tuberosum        ** Kleinia ficoides
* Begonia (check species)         * Ligularia kaempferi
** Calocephalis browni            *** Oplismenus hirtellus
** Centaurea cineraria            *** Phalaris arundinacea picta
*** Chrysanthemum aureum          *** Selaginella (check species)
** Codiaeum variegatum            *** Sedum guatemalense
* Coleus blumei                   **    "    treleasi
** Colocasia antiquorum           * Senecio cineraria
** Crassula monticola             *** Sideritis candicans
*** Dactylis variegata            *** Strobilanthes dyerianus
* Dieffenbachia picta             ** Teucrium marrum
* Euphorbia marginata             *** Xeranthemum annuum

## FOR FLOWERS IN THE SPRING

** Alyssum maritimum              ** Clarkia elegans
** Anemone coronaria              * Cynoglossum amabile
*** Babiana stricta               *** Delphinium ajacis
** Begonia semperflorens          * Dimorphotheca aurantiaca
*** Billbergia nutans             * Freesia refracta
* Calendula officinalis           * Gazania splendens
*** Campanula erinus              ** Godetia grandiflora
*** Centaurea cyanus              *** Iberis umbellata
* Cineraria cruenta               *** Linaria maroccana

*** Linum grandiflorum
** Myosotis alpestris
* Narcissus pseudo-narcissus
** Oxalis bowieana
***   "   crassipes
**   "   hirta
* Nemesia strumosa

** Nemophila menziesi
** Papaver nudicaule
* Petunia hybrida
*** Phacelia whitlavia
* Primula (species)
* Ranunculus asiaticus
* Viola cornuta

### BEDDING FOR SUMMER

* Ageratum houstonianum
** Alyssum maritimum
*** Angelonia grandiflora
* Antirrhinum majus
* Begonia multiflora
**   "   tuberhybrida
** Browallia americana
*** Callistephus chinensis
*** Canna generalis
** Centaurea (species)
*** Charieis heterophylla
** Chrysanthemum carinatum
*** Convolvulus tricolor
*** Cuphea llavia
*** Diascia barberae
* Exacum affine
** Gazania coccinea
* Gloxinia speciosa
*** Gomphrena globosa
*** Heliophila pilosa
* Lobelia erinus
*** Lonas inodora

* Mathiola incana
* Mimulus luteus
* Nierembergia caerulea
*** Nemophila menziesi
** Oliveranthus elegans
*** Oxalis crassipes
* Pelargonium (check species)
* Penstemon heterophyllus
*** Pentas lanceolata
* Petunia hybrida
** Phlox drummondi
*** Portulaca grandiflora
** Salpiglossis sinuata
** Salvia splendens
* Schizanthus wisetonensis
*** Streptocarpus hybridus
* Tagetes signata pumila
*** Thymophylla tenuiloba
*** Tigridia pavonia
** Torenia fournieri
*** Ursinia anthemoides
* Vinca rosea

* Zinnia elegans

### AUTUMN INTO WINTER

** Alonsoa warscewiczi
* Alyssum maritimum
*** Antirrhinum majus
* Begonia semperflorens
** Browallia americana
* Calendula officinalis
*** Callistephus chinensis
** Cineraria cruenta
*** Clianthus puniceus
** Convolvulus tricolor
* Dahlia hybrids
*** Dimorphotheca aurantiaca
** Limonium bellidifolium
* Lobelia erinus
*** Mathiola incana
* Nemesia strumosa

*** Nicotiana alata
** Papaver nudicaule
** Pelargonium (check species)
* Penstemon gloxinioides
***   "   heterophyllus
** Petunia hybrida
*** Piqueria trinervia
** Salpiglossis sinuata
* Salvia splendens
*** Scabiosa atropurpurea
** Sedum sieboldi
*** Torenia fournieri
*** Venidium (species)
* Vinca rosea
* Viola tricolor
** Zinnia elegans

### CARPET BEDDING & RELATED PLANTS

** Acorus gramineus
** Aeonium decorum
* Alternanthera amoena
* Byrnesia weinbergi
*** Celosia (species)
* Coleus blumei
** Crassula impressa
***   "   monticola
**   "   nana
* Echeveria (species)
*** Euphorbia marginata
*** Heliotropium arborescens
*** Helichrysum petiolatum
** Iresine herbsti
*** Kleinia repens

* Lobelia erinus
*** Mesembryanth. aloides
**   "   deltoides
* Othonna crassifolia
*** Paronychia argentea
** Pelargonium Salleroi
** Pentas lanceolata
*** Salvia splendens
** Sedum brevifolium
*   "   dasyphyllum
*   "   hispanicum
**   "   treleasi
* Sempervivum tectorum
*** Stylophyllum orcutti
*** Umbilicus chrysanthus

*** Wahlenbergia saxicola

HOUSE PLANTS---must endure conditions of insufficient light, stale
dry air, drafts and both extremes of temperature, sharply and quickly contrasted. With all this, they are expected to brighten indoors
with something of the garden and present for a time, many intangibles
of virtue....that glowing, viable stuff wrought from sun and rain
and earth. Water them regularly and give an occasional syringing or
actually wash the larger leaves. Air conditioning is a boon and bless-
ing. These plants are for general house purposes rather than for conservatory or window-gardening, yet may serve as such if the COMPENDIUM
or other source is studied for likes and dislikes.

### PALMS & PALMLIKE

*** Butia capitata                *** Pandanus utilis
** Chrysalidocarpus lutescens      * Phoenix roebelini
** Collinia elegans                * Rhapis excelsa
 * Dracaena (check species)      *** Sasa palmata
 * Howea belmoreana              *** Syagrus weddelliana

### WOODY PLANTS

** Abutilon megapotamicum          * Ficus elastica
 * Aglaonema simplex            ***  "   lyrata
*** Anthurium andreanum           ** Fuchsia (varieties)
 * Araucaria excelsa            *** Gynura aurantiaca
** Ardisia crispa                 ** Laurus nobilis
** Aucuba japonica              *** Lippia citriodora
 * Bergenia cordifolia             * Monstera deliciosa
*** Chorizema cordatum             * Philodendron (species)
** Cissus rhombifolia           *** Pittosporum variegatum
 * Codiaeum variegatum          *** Rhoeas discolor
*** Crossandra infundibuliformis  ** Rochea coccinea
*** Damnacanthus indicus          ** Sasa disticha
 * Dieffenbachia picta             * Scindapsis aureus
** Erica melanthera                * Solanum pseudo-capsicum
*** Fabiana imbricata             ** Ternstroemia japonica
 * Fatsia japonica              *** Visnea mocanera

### HERBACEOUS PLANTS

** Anemone coronaria               * Fittonia verschaffelti
*** Asclepias currassavica        ** Freesia refracta
 * Aspidistra elatior              * Gloxinia speciosa
** Asplenium (check species)      ** Impatiens sultani
 * Begonia (species)            *** Haemanthus puniceus
 * Billbergia (species)         *** Kaempferia involucrata
** Blechnum occidentale            * Ligularia kaempferi
** Bletilla striata                * Narcissus pseudo-narcissus
*** Browallia americana         *** Neomarica gracilis
** Calathea roseo-picta            * Nephrolepis (varieties)
*** Calceolaria herbeohybrida      * Pelargonium hortorum
 * Campanula isophylla          *** Penstemon gloxinioides
*** Chrysanthemum frutescens    *** Pilea (species)
 * Cineraria cruenta               * Pteris (check species)
 * Clivia hybrids                  * Rohdea japonica
 * Cyclamen indicum                * Saintpaulia ionantha
** Cyperus alternifolius          ** Selaginella (species)
 * Cyrtomium falcatum             ** Scilla peruviana
*** Diascia barberae            *** Tolmiea menziesi
*** Dicentra spectabilis          ** Torenia fournieri
*** Episcia (species)           *** Veltheimia viridiflora
*** Eucharis grandiflora           * Zebrina pendula
*** Felicia tenella               ** Zephyranthes (check species)

### SUCCULENTS

*** Agave decipiens               ** Gasteria (species)
 * Aloe variegata                 ** Kalanchoe fedtschenkoi
** Byrnesia weinbergi             ** Kleinia ficoides
*** Crassula argentea           *** Phormium colensoi
** Cryptanthus beuckeri            * Rochea coccinea
*** Dyckia sulphurea               * Sansevieria zeylanica
** Epiphyllum oxypetalon        *** Sempervivum tectorum
*** Euphorbia splendens            * Zygocactus truncatus

COVER CROPS---of an ornamental nature, with color that carries or only foliage to offer, may be used over large areas of unfinished ground that grades out into the wild....the foreground of a vista or view. When near at hand, the woody kinds will want to be cut back at times for a presentable appearance. Use a brush scythe to keep low and encourage the production of new wood. All may be economically started with seed broadcast early in the season. Some of these plants will be found adapted to erosion control and either one or several kinds may be used in a planned effect or seasonal color.

## WOODY COVER

Apache Plume
  Fallugia paradoxa
Beach Morning-glory
  Ipomoea pes-caprea
Buddleja
  Buddleja madagascariensis
Buckwheat Wild
  Eriogonum fasciculatum
Bush Sunflower
  Encelia californica
Chamise
  Adenostoma fasciculatum
Chia
  Salvia columbaria
Encienso
  Encelia farinosa
Grounselbush
  Baccharis (species)
Kangaroo-thorn
  Acacia armata
Lord's Candle
  Yucca whipplei
Monkeyflower
  Mimulus puniceus

Nightshade
  Solanum xanti
Palmetto
  Sabal minor
Rainbow Cactus
  Echinocereus rigidissimus
Red Yucca
  Hesperaloe parviflora
Sagebrush
  Artemisia tridentata
Scrub-palmetto
  Serenoa repens
Tree-alfalfa
  Medicago arborea
Tulip-poppy
  Hunnemannia fumariaefolia
Wormwood
  Artemisia californica
Yerba Santa
  Eriodictyon crassifolia
Yucca
  Yucca tenuistylis
  Zauschneria californica
  Hummingbird Trumpet

## HERBACEOUS COVER

Alfilaria
  Erodium cicutarium
Anise
  Pimpinella anisatum
Beachbean
  Vigna marina
Birdsfoot Trefoil
  Lotus corniculatus
Blazingstar
  Mentzelia lindleyi
Bracken
  Pteris aquilina
Bur-clover
  Medicago denticulata
Chilicothe
  Echinocystus macrocarpa
Desert-lily
  Hesperocallis undulata
Dingle-grass
  Briza maxima
Fennel
  Foeniculum vulgare
Fescue-grass
  Festuca elatior
Globe-mallow
  Sphaeralcea ambigua
Horned-poppy
  Glaucium flavum
Hottentot-fig
  Mesembryanthemum edule
Iceplant
  Mesembryanthemum crystallinum

Lupine
  Lupinus (species)
Mallow
  Malvastrum coccinium
Mustard
  Brassica nigra
Natal-grass
  Tricholaena rosea
Nut-grass
  Cyperus rotundus
Owls-clover
  Orthocarpus purpurascens
Poppy (California)
  Eschscholtzia californica
Pride of California
  Lathyrus splendens
Purple Vetch
  Vicia atropurpurea
Reed canary-grass
  Phalaris arundinacea
Rye-grass
  Lolium multiflorum
Salt-grass
  Atriplex semibaccata
Sand Trefoil
  Lotus formosissimus
Sand-verbena
  Abronia (species)
Spinach New Zealand
  Tetragonia expansa
Velvetbean
  Stizolobium deeringianum

NOCTURNAL HABITS---of bloom or fragrance may be used to advantage in places that are occupied in the evening such as a patio, a garden seat or shelter that remains pleasant after sunset. Have an open sky for this experience. Make good use of silhouette and skyline.  Know that artificial lighting usually yields....just that. Prevailing air currents may be studied in order that scented air in dilution may be available at the right place. Water at night weaves its special magic, silent or in movement. The lighter colors make the sharper display at dusk, particularly white, the darker tones tending to merge with the deepening shadows. Silvery and glossy leaves are active under the moon. Some of these plants may be disappointing by day, but on the approach of darkness seem to rise and expand and take on new life for an enchantment that reaches deeply into human emotions that are not for daylight. And this must be experienced, to be true.

## WOODY PLANTS

| | | | |
|---|---|---|---|
| ** | Acacia floribunda | * | Ervatamia coronaria |
| *** | Akebia quinata | ** | Eugenia jambos |
| *** | Bauhinia grandiflora | * | Gardenia thunbergia |
| *** | Brickellia grandiflora | *** | Hebe cupressoides |
| ** | Brunfelsia americana | ** | Hoya carnosa |
| *** | Buddleja nivea | ** | Hylocereus triangularis |
| *** | Calliandra portoricensis | *** | Ixora chinensis |
| * | Calonyction aculeatum | * | Jasminum dichotomum |
| *** | Carnegiea gigantea | ** | Lippia citriodora |
| * | Cephalocereus senilis | * | Magnolia grandiflora |
| * | Cestrum nocturnum | *** | Michelia champaca |
| ** | Choisya ternata | * | Myrtus communis |
| * | Citrus (species) | ** | Nyctanthes arbor-tristis |
| *** | Clerodendrum siphonanthus | *** | Nyctocereus serpentinus |
| ** | Coronilla glauca | *** | Pachira macrocarpa |
| ** | Daphne odora | *** | Pittosporum tenuifolium |
| * | Datura suaveolens | * |    "     undulatum |
| ** | Diosma ericoides | * | Stephanotis floribunda |
| ** | Embothrium coccineum | *** | Yucca (species) |

## HERBACEOUS PLANTS

| | | | |
|---|---|---|---|
| *** | Abronia umbellata | *** | Lilium testaceum |
| * | Alyssum maritimum | ** | Limnanthus douglasi |
| * | Cooperia drummondi | *** | Lunaria annua |
| * | Crinum giganteum | ** | Mathiola bicornis |
| * | Dianthus (species) | ** | Mentzelia lindleyi |
| * | Epiphyllum oxypetalum | *** | Mesembryanth. odoratum |
| * | Freesia refracta | * | Mirabilis jalapa |
| ** | Gazania uniflora | ** | Myosotis alpestris |
| *** | Gilia dichotoma | * | Nicotiana alata |
| * | Gladiolus tristis | *** | Nymphaea rubra |
| ** | Heliotropium arborescens | * | Oenothera hookeri |
| ** | Hemerocallis thunbergi | ** | Petunia axillaris |
| * | Hesperantha stanfordiae | ** | Polianthes tuberosa |
| *** | Hunnemannia fumariaefolia | *** | Salvia clevelandi |
| ** | Ipomoea leari | *** | Schizopetalon walkeri |
| * | Lathyrus odoratus | *** | Silene noctiflora |
| * | Lilium candidum | ** | Trichocereus candicans |
| ** |   "    regale | *** | Zaluzianskya capensis |
| *** |   "    speciosum | *** | Zingiber officinale |

FERN ALLIES---not to be interpreted in a strictly botanical sense, the meaning of the term broadened to include any low plant that may be associated with or that may be grown successfully under the average conditions suitable to ferns. Considerations involved include the introduction of color and supplementary greenery, frequently as cover beneath or low before the frond display of the ferns.

| | | | |
|---|---|---|---|
| *** | Achimenes longiflora | ** | Brodiaea uniflora |
| ** | Arenaria balearica | ** | Caladium picturatum |
| * | Arum italicum | *** | Calochortus albus |
| ** | Asparagus (species) | *** | Chionodoxa luciliae |
| * | Begonia (species) | * | Collinsia grandiflora |

*** Corydalis lutea
 ** Cotula squalida
  * Cyclamen indicum
*** Cyrtanthus obliquus
*** Dicentra formosa
 **    "    spectabilis
 ** Exacum affine
  * Fuchsia (varieties)
*** Gloriosa superba
 ** Gloxinia speciosa
 ** Helleborus lividus
 ** Helxine soleiroli
 ** Iris reticulata
*** Jacobinia carnea
  * Leucojum autumnale
 ** Lilium (species)

 ** Lobelia erinus
*** Lycopodium clavatum
 ** Mentha requieni
  * Mimulus luteus
*** Muscari armeniacum
  * Myosotis alpestris
*** Narcissus cyclamineus
*** Nertera depressa
  * Oxalis (species)
*** Pilea microphylla
 ** Primula malacoides
*** Scilla hispanica
 ** Selaginella (species)
*** Streptocarpus hybridus
  * Thalictrum dipterocarpum
*** Zamia floridana

INDOOR DECORATION---with foliage, flowers, berries or colored twigs brings to mind the following plants which are suited to that end. The Christmas season finds many uses for material to fashion into wreaths or made up as festoons, or just brought in for a general inspiriting of the home. Another time which needs a gladdening touch is that bridging late winter and early spring when stems of precocious flowering shrubs and trees will bloom prematurely if forced indoors in water. These plants may be expected to rate high on the list for material to arrange in the modern manner as well as in the old traditional way. Remove the foliage, if any, from fruiting sprays and the berries will last longer.

## FOLIAGE SPRAYS

 ** Acacia pruinosa
*** Acanthus mollis
*** Agathis robusta
  * Aglaonema simplex
 ** Alnus (species)
  * Asparagus (species)
*** Atriplex lentiformis
 ** Aucuba japonica
  * Azara microphylla
*** Bocconia frutescens
 ** Brachychiton populneum
*** Caryota urens
 ** Casuarina stricta
*** Chrysophyllum caineto
  * Cissus hypoglauca
  * Cocculus laurifolius
  * Corynocarpus laevigata
 ** Crinodendron dependens
 ** Cupania anacardioides
  * Cycas (species)
  * Cyperus (check species)
  * Cyrtomium falcatum
 ** Dennstaedtia cicutaria
*** Dion edule
  * Elaeagnus pungens
  * Eriobotrya japonica
  * Eucalyptus (check species)
  * Fatshedera lizei
 ** Hedera canariensis
*** Hibiscus tiliaceus
 ** Ilex (species)
*** Itea ilicifolia

 ** Leptospermum laevigatum
  * Leucadendron argenteum
 ** Leucothoe axillaris
 ** Lyonothamnus asplenifolius
 ** Maytenus boaria
  * Melianthus major
  * Myrtus communis
*** Noltea africana
*** Osmanthus (species)
*** Phoenix (species)
 ** Pistacia chinensis
 ** Pittosporum tenuifolium
  * Podocarpus (species)
*** Polypodium mandaianum
  * Polystichum adiantiforme
  * Prunus ilicifolia
*** Quercus (check species)
 ** Ricinus communis
*** Ruscus aculeatus
 ** Schinus (species)
 ** Scindapsis aureus
*** Serenoa repens
*** Taxus baccata
*** Trachelospermum fragrans
*** Umbellularia californica
 ** Viburnum japonicum
*** Vitex lucens
 ** Westringia rosmariniformis
*** Woodwardia (species)
  * Xylosma senticosa
*** Zamia floridana
*** Zingiber officinale

## FLOWERING SPRAYS

 ** Acacia (check species)
*** Alnus rhombifolia
  * Aloe (check species)
*** Anigozanthos flavida
 ** Anisacanthus wrighti

  * Antigonon leptopus
  * Bauhinia (check species)
 ** Beaumontia grandiflora
  * Bouvardia humboldti
 ** Buddleja colvillei

** Camelia japonica
*** Calothamnus quadrifidus
*** Carissa carandas
** Ceratostigma willmottianum
*** Cercis siliquastrum
** Chaenomeles japonica
* Chamaelaucium ciliatum
** Chorizema cordatum
** Cytisus canariensis
*** Embothrium coccineum
* Erythrina (check species)
** Eucalyptus caesia
*        "        erythrocorys
***      "        forrestiana
* Euphorbia pulcherrima
** Genista monosperma
** Hibiscus rosa-sinensis
** Holmskioldia sanguinea
** Magnolia soulangeana

** Osmanthus fragrans
*** Osteomeles anthyllidifolia
** Phormium tenax
*** Prunus glandulosa
*       "    persica
*** Puya alpestris
* Rondeletia cordata
*** Ribes (check species)
** Rosa banksiae
** Salix discolor
*** Sophora secundiflora
* Spartium junceum
** Spiraea cantoniensis
* Stenolobium stans
*** Thunbergia grandiflora
* Tricholaena rosea
*** Tipuana tipu
** Viburnum lucidum
*** Wigandia caracasana

## FRUITING SPRAYS

* Acokanthera spectabilis
** Ampelopsis brevipedunculata
* Arbutus unedo
** Artabotrys uncinatus
** Berberis darwini
* Cardiospermum halicacabum
*** Citherexylum spinosum
* Cortaderia selloana
* Cotoneaster (species)
** Cucumis dipsaceus
** Cucurbita pepo ovifera
*** Dovyalis caffra
** Duranta repens
** Elaeagnus fruitlandi
* Eugenia smithi
** Fatsia japonica
*** Harpullia arborea
* Heteromeles arbutifolia

*** Lagenaria leucantha
** Ligustrum (species)
* Mahonia (species)
*** Momordica charantia
** Murraea exotica
* Nandina domestica
* Ochna multiflora
** Papaver (species)
** Persea borbonia
*** Phillyrea latifolia
* Phoradendron flavescens
*** Photinia serrulata
*** Pittosporum rhombifolium
* Pyracantha (species)
*** Rhus laurina
** Sapium sebiferum
*** Triphasia trifolia
*** Typha latifolia

*** Ungnadia speciosa

## DISTINCTION FOR ARRANGEMENTS

### LARGE SUBJECTS

*** Acacia alata
*        "    baileyana
**       "    pubescens
** Adenanthera pavonina
* Antigonon leptopus
*** Atriplex lentiformis
** Azara microphylla
* Beaumontia grandiflora
* Brassaia actinophylla
*** Camellia reticulata
** Canella winterana
* Cedrus atlantica
*** Chiranthodendron platanoides
* Citrus (species)
** Clematis armandi
** Coccolobis uvifera
* Cocculus laurifolius
*** Cornus capitata
*** Corynocarpus laevigata
* Crotalaria agatiflora
*** Dais cotinifolia
** Dovyalis caffra
* Dracaena (check species)
* Echium fastuosum
** Elaeagnus pungens

* Eriobotrya japonica
** Eriogonum giganteum
* Eugenia smithi
*** Gardenia thunbergia
*** Garrya elliptica
*** Greyia sutherlandi
*** Guaiacum officinale
** Hoya carnosa
*** Jasminum azoricum
* Leptospermum laevigatum
** Leucadendron argenteum
* Ligustrum lucidum
** Lyonothamnus asplenifolius
* Magnolia grandiflora
*** Mahonia lomariifolia
*** Meryta sinclairi
*** Muehlenbeckia platyclada
* Nandina domestica
** Ochna multiflora
*** Ochrosia elliptica
** Olmediella betschleriana
** Passiflora racemosa
*** Petrea volubilis
*** Phyllostachys aurea
*** Pinckneya pubens
** Pinus cembroides

```
  *  Pittosporum tobira              ***  Eucomis undulata
 **  Podocarpus totara                 *  Francoa ramosa
***  Prosopis (species)              **  Hymenocallis calathina
 **  Prunus jaquemonti                 *  Iris foetidissima
 **  Pyrus calleryana                **  Lonicera aureo-reticulata
  *  Quercus ilex                   ***  Macropiper excelsum
***  Rhus lancea                      *  Molucella laevis
 **  Salix discolor                 **  Neomarica gracilis
***  Solandra longiflora              *  Nephrolepis exaltata
 **  Strelitzia nicholai            **  Nerine (check species)
  *  Ternstroemia japonica          **  Parthenocissus henryana
  *  Vitex lucens                  ***  Pasithea caerulea
                                   ***  Petasitis fragrans
                                    **  Rivina humilis
          SMALL SUBJECTS            **  Rohdea japonica
  *  Aeonium tabulaeforme             *  Russelia equisetiformis
  *  Agapanthus africanus           ***  Salvia carduacea
***  Albuca minor                  ***  Selaginella uncinata
***  Allium pulchellum               **  Sisyrinchium striata
 **  Alstroemeria (species)         **  Thalia dealbata
  *  Anemone japonica                 *  Trachelospermum jasminoides
***  Arthropodium cirrhatum          **  Tricholaena rosea
  *  Aspidistra elatior              **  Veltheimia viridifolia
 **  Asplenium nidus                 **  Venidium fastuosum
  *  Bambusa multiplex             ***  Wachendorfia thyrsiflorus
  *  Bergenia cordifolia             *  Zantedeschia (species)
  *  Bletilla striata
  *  Calocephalis browni
***  Ceratotheca triloba
 **  Chaerophyllum dasycarpum               SUCCULENTS
***  Cladanthus arabicus             *  Aloe candelabrum
  *  Clivia nobilis                 **  Byrnesia weinbergi
  *  Cotoneaster pannosa nana      ***  Kalanchoe flammea
 **  Dianella intermedia            **  Mesembryanth. deltoides
***  Dicentra chrysantha             *  Oliveranthus elegans
***  Dipidax ciliata                **  Pereskia aculeata
***  Elisena longipetala           ***  Sansevieria parva
```

EDGINGS---for garden bed or border, low plants of more or less precise growth and defining character, either prostrate or erect. They will outline or mark the way of a path and restrict the herbage of the bed or allow limited latitude for expansion to the front. They should allow for any measures necessary in control, clipping along the path side or reduction in height. They may provide color, but surely crowded leaves at all times.

```
***  Acantholimon venustum           *  Mesembryanth. deltoides
  *  Ageratum houstonianum          **       "       lehmanni
  *  Allium schoenprasm            ***       "       tuberosum
 **  Alyssum maritimum (forms)       *  Nierembergia caerulea
***  Anagallis linifolia             *  Ophiopogon japonica
  *  Armeria maritima              ***  Oplismenus hirtellus
***  Arrhenatherum tuberosum       ***  Oxalis crassipes
***  Convolvulus tricolor            *  Pelargonium salleroi
  *  Cuphea hyssopifolia            **  Petroselinum hortense
 **  Dianthus deltoides            ***  Phalaris arundinacea picta
***       "      caesius          ***  Pilea microphylla
  *  Echeveria (check species)    ***  Primula malacoides
***  Erigeron karvinskyanus         **       "     polyantha
 **  Erodium corsicum              ***  Sanvitalia procumbens
 **  Exacum affine                 ***  Scirpus cernuus
  *  Festuca glauca                  *  Sempervivum tectorum
 **  Fuchsia procumbens            ***  Sisyrinchium bermudiana
***  Gazania splendens              **       "      macouni
 **  Heliophila pilosa               *  Tagetes signata pumila
  *  Heuchera sanguinea             **  Thymus nitida
 **  Lagurus ovatus                ***       "     vulgaris
 **  Lobelia erinus                 **  Torenia fournieri
 **  Malcomia maritima            ***  Tropaeolum minus
                 *  Zinnia linearis
```

SUCCESSIONAL SOWINGS---annuals of temporary, extremely transient character, quick in color and as quickly blooming themselves out. They are mostly self-sowing little plants of specific rating which may become more or less naturalized in agreeable spots, to return year after year as a regular re-current motif for the naturalistic garden.....or may be considered cluttering and in any case will be reduced to numbers desired. For a continuing show, seed will be sown at following times and the young plants thinned out as found desirable or necessary. This thinning will be the only control in the operation.

| | |
|---|---|
| ** Ageratum houstonianum | * Linaria maroccana |
| * Alyssum maritimum | *** Linum grandiflorum |
| *** Brachycome iberidifolia | ** Lonas inodora |
| *** Chaerophyllum dasycarpum | * Malcomia maritima |
| * Chrysanthemum carinatum | ** Myosotis alpestris |
| *** Clarkia elegans | ** Nemophila menziesi |
| ** Coreopsis tinctoria | * Papaver rhoeas |
| *** Cosmos bipinnata | *** Phacelia whitlavia |
| * Delphinium ajacis | *** Piqueria trinervia |
| * Dimorphotheca annua | ** Phlox drummondi |
| ** Eschscholtzia californica | *** Reseda odorata |
| *** Geranium robertianum | *** Sanvitalia procumbens |
| *** Gilia lutea | * Scabiosa atropurpurea |
| ** Gilia tricolor | *** Schizopetalon walkeri |
| *** Gladiolus hortulanus | ** Torenia (species) |
| ** Gomphrena globosa | *** Veronica tourneforti |
| * Gypsophila elegans | *** Wahlenbergia saxicola |

                    * Xeranthemum annuum


TURFING FLOWERS---plants that may be used in thin grass and abandoned late season, or in a plot with an especially intimate bearing on family life and use. Some may be grown in the lawn proper and cut along with the grass. Others, especially bulbs that do not start too early in the fall, will go in along the edges where the foliage will ripen better. There should be no promiscuous scattering, but rather, a judicious and well-considered selection and matching of plant and place. Feed the turf only after the insert foliage has failed.

| | |
|---|---|
| * Alyssum maritimum | *** Montia perfoliata |
| ** Anthemis nobilis | *** Muscari armeniacum |
| * Bellis perennis | ** Narcissus cyclamineus |
| * Brodiaea uniflora | * Nierembergia rivularis |
| *** Chionodoxa luciliae | *** Ophiopogon japonica |
| ** Chrysanthemum tchihatchewi | * Oxalis bowieana |
| *** Dodecatheon clevelandi | *** Potentilla cinerea |
| * Freesia refracta | *** Scilla hispanica |
| ** Lapeirousia cruenta | * Sisyrinchium bellum |
| ** Lippia canescens | ** Thymus serpyllum |
| *** Lonas inodora | *** Veronica nummularia |
| ** Malcomia maritima | **    "      repens |


WASTE PLACES---where the one and absorbing thought is to cover over or to blot out of sight ugly or untenable ground of poor suitability for normal planting. Old dumps or tainted soil left from building operations or other past restrictive usage, instead of growing up to weeds, may be set to one or few of the following....with obvious advantage and fulfillment. They will be resolute in handling a situation, spontaneous in growth with spreading stems and covering herbage or vigorously suckering roots to encompass the evil. For a wider range of material, see PLANTS TO ABUSE.

| | |
|---|---|
| * Abronia (species) | ** Asclepias currassavica |
| *** Aethionema coridifolium | * Baileya multiradiata |
| *** Agdestis clematidea | ** Buddleja madagascariensis |
| * Alyssum maritimum | ** Chusquea tessellata |
| *** Amaranthus caudatus | ** Cortaderia selloana |
| ** Anthemis tinctoria | *** Cyperus gracilis |
| * Atriplex semibaccata | * Dimorphotheca (species) |
| ** Argemone mexicana | *** Echinocystus macrocarpa |

*** Encelia (species)
** Eriogonum fasciculatum
** Euphorbia marginata
*** Foeniculum vulgare
** Glaucium flavum
*** Hedera (check species)
** Ipomoea (species)
*** Linaria dalmatica
* Lantana (species)
** Lycium (species)
*** Malvastrum (check species)
* Mentha pulegium
* Mirabilis jalapa
* Nephrolepis exaltata
** Oenothera (species)
* Vinca major

* Papaver (species)
*** Parthenocissus henryana
*** Pteris aquilina
* Ricinus communis
*** Rosa bracteata
*    "  laevigata
* Sasa pygmaea
*** Sedum album
*** Sempervivum atlanticum
** Solanum laurifolium
*** Sphaeralcea ambigua
** Thymus vulgaris
* Tithonia rotundifolia
* Tropaeolum majus
*** Verbena rigida

REMOTE BORDERS---where large, coarse or weedy perennials and near relinquishments may find a proper place to work out their destiny with the minimum of human fuss and interference....expedience, in a way. This will be the better place for bulbs that demand a period of drying out after bloom or those other plants that want special conditions or culture difficult to reconcile with ordinary garden operations. This is a catch-all place where off-season aspects and unseemly color may be buried with some dignity; where resurrection is under control or immaterial and where little care will be given.

* Allium (species)
*** Argemone mexicana
* Asphodelus albus
** Aster gracillima
** Babiana stricta
* Brodiaea (species)
* Brunsvigia rosea
* Centranthus ruber
** Cichorium intybus
** Delphinium nudicaule
** Dimorphotheca (species)
*** Encelia (species)
** Eremurus robustus
** Freesia refracta
*** Hedychium (species)
* Iris germanica
** Ixia maculata
** Kalanchoe (check species)
*** Lachenalia (species)
*** Malvastrum coccineum
** Milla biflora
* Mirabilis jalapa

* Moraea iridioides
*** Nerine (check species)
* Oenothera (check species)
** Ornithogalum (species)
* Oxalis (species)
** Papaver orientale
** Pelargonium crispum
** Petasitis fragrans
*** Phacelia whitlavia
*** Polypteris hookeriana
*** Salpiglossis sinuata
* Sidalcea malvaeflora
*** Sisyrinchium bellum
** Sparaxis tricolor
*** Sprekelia formosissima
*** Stachys coccinea
*** Streptanthera cuprea
* Tithonia rotundifolia
** Tritonia (check species)
*** Tulipa (botanical species)
*** Venidium (species)
** Verbesina encelioides

PERENNIALS WITH SHRUBS---may help in the filling out of an effect in color and serve as a refining influence in texture. Some may find a place in the border itself as a filler and thought of as temporary; others will be rudimentary climbers that may be permanent. The principal application of the idea, however, is that of the ground work or facing down to meet the turf. These plants are in the main colorful and with good foliage mass, but are selected here on the basis of growing qualities that permit of competition.

*** Acanthus mollis
* Amarcrinum howardi
** Amaryllis rutila
* Anemone japonica
*** Arthropodium cirrhatum
** Bletilla striata
*** Calceolaria integrifolia
** Campanula poscharskyana
*** Centranthus ruber

*** Ceratotheca triloba
* Chrysanthemum (check species)
* Cichorium intybus
*** Cynara scolymus
* Dahlia (seedlings)
** Dianella (species)
*** Dierama pulcherrima
** Erythrina herbacea
*** Euryops (species)

* Gladiolus (species)
* Hedychium (species)
* Hemerocallis aurantiaca
** Hibiscus mutabilis
*** " diversifolius
*** Hunnemannia fumariaefolia
* Kniphofia uvaria
** Lathyrus splendens
** Lavatera olbia
* Limonium perezi
*** Linaria dalmatica
*** Littonia modesta
** Lupinus (check species)
* Moraea (species)

** Nicotiana alata
* Penstemon gloxinioides
** Prostanthera nivea
*** Scabiosa columbaria
** Swainsona galegifolia
** Thalictrum dipterocarpum
*** Thunbergia cordata
*** Tragopogon porrifolius
** Trachelium caeruleum
* Tulbaghia violacea
*** Verbena rigida
*** Veronica incana
** Wachendorfia thyrsiflora
** Zamia floridana

** Zantedeschia (check species)


LAWN GRASSES---available do not satisfactorily solve the question of turf in these southern countries. They are not persevering. With the best of care, under the need for almost continuous activity over the year, they ultimately fail. So it is that material should be reviewed for what it has to offer and a mix designed for actual conditions of project. An intelligent approach will take into account the quality, condition and texture of the soil; degree of shade, if any; optimum moisture content; amount of wear to be expected. Since there are no natives suitable for this purpose, the lawn becomes an expensive luxury, which suggests limiting areas to minimum requirements.

Bent (Seaside)
  Agrostis maritima
Bent (Rhode Island)
  Agrostis canina
Bermuda or Devil-grass
  Cynodon dactylon
Blue-grass (Kentucky)
  Poa pratensis
Blue-grass (Wood)
  Poa nemoralis
Blue-grass (Rough-stalked)
  Poa trivialis
Carpet-grass
  Axonopus compressus
Centipede-grass
  Eremochloa ophiuroides
Clover (Bur)
  Medicago denticulata
Clover (White)
  Trifolium repens

Dogstail (Crested)
  Cynosurus cristatus
Fescue (Chewings)
  Festuca rubra
Fescue (Meadow)
  Festuca elatior
Kyllinga-grass
  Cyperus brevifolius
McCoy-grass
  Cyperus gracilis
Orchard-grass
  Dactylis glomerata
Redtop
  Agrostis palustris
Rye-grass
  Lolium multiflorum
St. Augustine-grass
  Stenotaphrum secundatum
Velvet-grass
  Zoysia tenuifolia


LAWN SUBSTITUTES---may be enumerated in view of difficulties encountered with the true grasses. These must be creepers that develop a sod-like mat close to the earth; huggers, with no parts to be held appreciably above the body of growth. The mat must submit to at least casual walking about without showing damage. Actually there are very few of these that subscribe to all requirements indicated in literal use or interpretation.  Use the following in place of, or to augment grass....this where conditions warrant, or merely to develop the flat in a gardenesque manner.

** Abronia villosa
** Acaena microphylla
*** Ajuga reptans
* Anthemis nobilis
* Arenaria balearica
*** Arrhenatherum tuberosum
*** Convolvulus lineatus
** " mauretanicus
** Cotula squalida
* Dichondra repens
*** Duchesnea indica

** Frankenia capitata laevis
* Fragaria chiloensis
* Hedera colchica
** Helxine soleiroli
*** Hydrocotyle rotundifolia
* Lippia canescens
** Lotus corniculatus (forms)
** Mesembryanth. floribundum
*** Morisia monantha
*** Muehlenbeckia axillare
*** Nertera depressa

   * Ophiopogon japonicus      * Sagina subulata
  ** Origanum dictamnus     ** Thymus serpyllum
*** Potentilla repens    *** Veronica nummularia


   DUST ACCRETION---settlement on the foliage will impair the appearance of a planting in open country or along an unpaved road.    This
over-cast can be minimized with high-gloss leaves or by the use of
certain yellowish greys or slate-greens which only neutralize or dark-
en, where a more vivid coloring becomes dirty-looking. This, along with
the structure of the leaf, its disposition or surface texture has a
bearing on the problem to an extent that prompts the following suggestions. Color of the dust should be considered.

   * Acacia cultriformis    *** Eriodictyon crassifolia
  **    "    pendula      * Eriogonum (species)
***    "    verticillata   *** Erythea armata
  ** Anthyllis barba-jovis     * Genista monosperma
   * Artemisia tridentata    ** Juniperus (check species)
  ** Atriplex breweri      * Lagunaria patersoni
   *    "    semibaccata     * Lavandula officinalis
  ** Baccharis (species)    *** Lavatera olbia
  ** Buddleja asiatica      * Leptospermum laevigatum
  ** Callistemon (species)  *** Lonicera confusa
*** Calothamnus quadrifidus  *** Mahonia nevini
*** Caryopteris incana    *** Melaleuca hyperiscifolia
   * Cassia artemisioides    **    "    latertia
   * Casuarina equisetifolia  *** Noltea africana
  ** Ceanothus arboreus    ** Olea europaea
***    "    verrucosus      * Parkinsonia aculeata
  ** Cedrus deodara      * Pinus halepensis
   * Cercocarpus betuloides    **    "    torreyana
*** Chilopsis linearis   *** Plumbago capensis
  ** Coprosma baueri     ** Rhamnus crocea
*** Cornus capitata    *** Populus alba
   * Correa pulchella      * Rhus (species)
*** Cotoneaster microphylla    ** Rosmarinus officinalis
   *    "    pannosa     ** Schinus molle
  **    "    simonsi      * Spartium junceum
  ** Cytisus canariensis      * Tamarix (species)
*** Dasylirion glaucophyllum  *** Ternstroemia japonica
  ** Dendromecon rigida    ** Teucrium fruticans
   * Diosma ericoides    *** Viburnum carlesi
*** Erica melanthera      * Westringia rosmariniformis
        *** Zauschneria californica

# ORNAMENTAL CHARACTERS

The art of landscape design is based in a large way on aesthetic qualities found ready made in nature, so that the intelligent use to which they are put depends on an understanding and knowledge of plant characters. There is an essence behind it all; there is a mode of seeing things, when one comes in tune with nature and not imitative. An attractive garden, as with a classic painting or good music, must reflect the technical equipment of the composer. An orderly arrangement then for a desired effect will consider not only color, but its time of appearance; natural form and comparative textures; habit and kind of fruiting, together with other minor elements that go to make up the picture nature presents. It may be safely said that too much emphasis is placed on flowers and color to the neglect of more stable and continuing effects resulting from other characters, such as found in foliage. The importance of all this becomes more apparent when one realizes that here a policy of trial and error is not admissible; that one cannot judge and digest, study and re-arrange. This phase of ones accomplishment comes into being only with the years, and will be unyielding in its reflection of the thought and information that went into its conception. Moreover, these other characters of foliage and berries take on an increased significance in sunny lands where bloom is hastened in heat to completion and passes quickly. All this will be held closely in the consciousness of any serious student of planting design....and re-examined from time to time.

FOLIAGE CONTRASTS---extremes in greenery and textural qualities of leafage in woody plants for purposes of composition. Here will be found material for more subtle effects and possibly a higher precedence and type of expression than the display of color with its time limitation. An advanced student in planting arrangement will want closely at hand the materials of value for contrast, for he knows of the defining powers they have for his picture when out of flower and berry. Green is, perhaps too obviously, the natural back for color in these relations. Its effective use is the greater art. Primarily it suggests repose and relaxation; release for fleeting moods of exuberance or gaiety exemplified in color. It leads back to tranquility and contentment which is the ultimate in garden expression. The size of a leaf has much to do with scale in composition and should interpret correctly the meaning of the architect. Brightness and sprightliness may be interpolated as intermediate values....leaves are most expressive. In any event and even for the casual planter, a reasonable and conscious mingling of these characters will preclude monotony in a composition and afford interest in variation.

## DARK GREEN LEAVES
The deeper tones carry the feeling of solidity. They are solemn, serious, sober at times to the point of gloom and fall in naturally with formality. They appear best against construction. Values are accepted and blend easily and freely in the dimness of shadow and there they may be thrown into high relief by roving shafts of light.

126

The contrast of the new foliage is highly illuminating, lifting, inspirational and the eye is refreshed.

## TREES

* Acacia dealbata
** " melanoxylon
** Albizzia julibrissin
* Alnus rhombifolia
** Araucaria bidwilli
*** Bauhinia grandiflora
*** Callitris robusta
*** Calophyllum inophyllum
* Cedrus atlantica
* Ceratonia siliqua
** Citrus (species)
*** Crinodendron dependens
*** Cupania anacardioides
** Cupressus macrocarpa
* " sempervirens
** Eriobotrya japonica
* Eucalyptus ficifolia
** " globulus
*** " robusta

** Ficus retusa
*** Fraxinus velutina
** Harpephyllum caffrum
* Jacaranda acutifolia
*** Olea chrysophylla
*** Persea borbonia
*** Pinus pinea
* " radiata
* Pittosporum rhombifolium
*** " viridiflorum
* Podocarpus elongata
** Pyrus calleryana
* Quercus agrifolia
*** Schrebera swietenioides
** Taxus baccata stricta
*** Tipuana tipu
** Torreya taxifolia
* Ulmus parvifolia
** Umbellularia californica

## SHRUBS

*** Acanthus montanus
** Acacia verticillata
* Arbutus unedo
*** Aucuba japonica
* Azara microphylla
*** Berberidopsis corallina
** Berberis darwini
** Bowkeria gerrardiana
*** Brunfelsia calycina
** Camellia japonica
* Carissa grandiflora
** Carpenteria californica
*** Ceanothus cyaneus
** " papillosus
* " verrucosus
** Ceratostigma willmottianum
*** Clerodendrum speciosissimum
*** Cneorum tricoccon
* Cocculus laurifolius
*** Cordia boissieri
* Corynocarpus laevigata
** Duranta stenostachya
* Eurya emarginata
* Euonymus japonicus
* Gardenia thunbergia
*** Grevillea banksi
*** Greyia sutherlandi
* Heteromeles arbutifolia
* Ilex cornuta
** Itea ilicifolia
*** Leucothoe axillaris
* Ligustrum lucidum
** Lonicera nitida
** Mackaya bella

** Mahonia lomariifolia
* Melaleuca armillaris
** " huegeli
*** " nesophila
** Myrtus microphylla
** Nerium oleander
*** Noltea africana
** Ochna floribunda
* Osmanthus ilicifolius
** Phillyrea latifolia
* Photinia serrulata
*** Pimelea ferruginea
* Pittosporum tobira
** Prunus ilicifolia
*** " lusitanica
* Psidium cattleianum
** Pyracantha coccinea
* Raphiolepis ovata
*** Rhamnus alaternus
** " crocea
** Rhus integrifolia
** Ribes viburnifolium
** Sarcococca hookeriana
** Severinia buxifolia
*** Siphonosmanthus delavayi
*** Sophora secundiflora
** Tecomaria capensis
** Ternstroemia japonica
** Thea sinensis
*** Thunbergia erecta
* Turraea obtusifolia
** Viburnum burkwoodi
*** " odoratissimum
** " suspensum

## VINES

* Beaumontia grandiflora
** Cissus striata
* Clematis armandi
** Hardenbergia comptoniana
* Hedera helix
** Jasminum azoricum
*** " pubescens

*** Macropiper excelsum
*** Oxera pulchella
** Phaedranthus buccinatorius
*** Sollya heterophylla
** Stephanotis floribunda
** Thunbergia grandiflora
* Trachelospermum jasminoides

## LIGHT GREEN LEAVES

The higher tones of greenery in foliage will aid in depth perception, with its important bearing on perspective. They will expand the apparent size of relative space. These are happy shades that go with sunny days, lifting spirits and immateriality....light hearts and mirth, rejoicing. This emotional lift may be played upon most effectively in darkened places. Use there in such a way as to catch patches of sunlight that may be served up to the surroundings and bring out the delicate color value of shadow. This all tends to lighten the subconscious being of the observer positively.

### TREES

* Acacia floribunda
** " mollis
*** Alnus cordata
** Bauhinia variegata
** Brachychiton (species)
** Callistemon viminalis
*** Castanospermum australe
*** Cassia fistula
** Cedrus deodara
* Citrus limonia
* Cinnamomum camphora
** Clusia rosea
* Cornus capitata
** Cupressus funebris
* Eucalyptus citriodora
** " cladocalyx
** Eugenia paniculata
*** " supraaxillaris
*** Ficus religiosa

*** Ilex perado
** Illicium anisatum
*** Koelreuteria formosana
*** Markhamia lutea
* Maytenus boaria
* Pinus halepensis
** " patula
* Pittosporum undulatum
** Platanus (species)
** Podocarpus macrophylla
** Populus (species)
* Prunus caroliniana
*** Quercus chrysolepis
*** Sapium sebiferum
* Schinus molle
*** Taxodium distichum
*** Torreya californica
* Tristania conferta
*** Vitex lucens

### SHRUBS

* Acacia armata
*** Actinophloeus macarthuri
*** Arctostaphylos diversifolia
*** Baccharis pilularis
*** Bauhinia acuminata
* " tomentosa
* Brunfelsia americana
** Buxus japonica
* Cassia (species)
** Ceanothus arboreus
** Cercocarpus betuloides
* Cestrum nocturnum
** Coprosma baueri
* Cotoneaster simonsi
** Cytisus canariensis
** Dahlia maxoni
*** Daphniphyllum humile
** Deeringia amaranthoides
*** Dendromecon rigida
** Dodonaea viscosa
* Duranta repens
*** Entelea arborescens
* Ervatamia coronaria
*** Escallonia (species)
** Eurya ochnacea
* Fatsia japonica
*** Galvesia speciosa
* Genista monosperma
** Hakea saligna
* Hydrangea macrophylla
*** Hymenanthera crassifolia
* Hypericum (species)
* Ilex cassine
*** " vomitoria
** Lavatera assurgentiflora
** Lawsonia inermis

*** Leptospermum citratum
** Lycium pallidum
* Malvaviscus arboreus
*** Melaleuca hyperiscifolia
* Murraea exotica
* Myrtus communis
* Nandina domestica
*** Nuxia floribunda
** Olmediella betschleriana
** Osmanthus armatus
*** Phyllanthus acidus
** Pittosporum heterophyllum
* Plumbago capensis
** Polygala dalmaisiana
** Prunus lyoni
** Pyracantha koidzumi
*** Sambucus simpsoni
* Stenolobium stans
*** Strophanthus speciosus
*** Thryallis glauca
** Viburnum japonicum
* Vitex agnus-castus

### VINES

*** Allamanda hendersoni
* Boussingaultia baselloides
** Bauhinia galpini
* Hedera canariensis
** Jasminum officinale
*** Philadelphus mexicanus
*** Podranea ricasoliana
* Pyrostegia ignea
*** Rosa laevigata
** Solandra guttata
* Solanum wendlandi
** Stigmaphyllon ciliatum

## COARSE FOLIAGE

Large leaves and those with harsh rough surface may be used in rustic places and as a touch for emphasis to bring out refinement. They carry the greater pictorial weight, centering the attention and confining it subjectively within a boundary. They go with rough textures in stone, shake shingles or brick, and in shadow. Their use in the ordinary border will better be restricted to the back or in the distance on account of the dwarfing effect. They are nicely scaled to the heavy stone masses of contemporary architecture.

### TREES

*** Acer macrophyllum
*** Bocconia frutescens
 ** Brachychiton acerifolium
  * Brassaia actinophylla
*** Chiranthodendron platanoides
 ** Clusia rosea
 ** Coccolobis floridana
*** Dahlia maxoni
  * Dombeya wallichi
*** Drimys winteri
  * Eriobotrya japonica
 ** Eucalyptus ficifolia
  * Ficus (species)
 ** Macadamia ternifolia

  * Magnolia grandiflora
*** Meryta sinclairi
 ** Musa ensete
 ** Persea borbonia
*** Phytolacca dioica
  * Platanus (species)
*** Podachaenium eminens
 ** Populus (species)
*** Pterospermum acerifolium
 ** Solanum warscewiczi
  * Strelitzia nicholai
*** Talauma hodgsoni
 ** Terminalia catappa
  * Tristania conferta

### SHRUBS

 ** Acokanthera spectabilis
  * Bergenia cordifolia
*** Clerodendrum bungei
  * Coccolobis uvifera
  * Corynocarpus laevigata
  * Datura (species)
*** Dombeya calantha
 **      "    natalensis
*** Entelea arborescens
 ** Ervatamia coronaria
*** Eupatorium sordidum
  * Euphorbia pulcherrima
  * Fatsia japonica
*** Greyia sutherlandi
*** Griselinia littoralis
*** Homalanthus populifolius
*** Hazardia cana
 ** Hedychium (species)
  * Hibiscus tiliaceus
 ** Hydrangea macrophylla
 ** Jacobinia carnea
 ** Ligustrum japonicum
 ** Limonium perezi
*** Macropiper excelsum

*** Magnolia soulangeana
 ** Myoporum laetum
*** Olmediella betschleriana
*** Oncoba routledgi
*** Osmanthus armatus
*** Phlomis fruticosa
  * Phormium tenax
  * Photinia serrulata
 ** Pittosporum tobira
*** Prunus lusitanica
*** Psidium guineense
  * Pyrus calleryana
*** Rhus laurina
  * Ricinus communis
*** Romneya coulteri
*** Rondeletia cordata
 ** Sambucus (species)
  * Senecio petasitis
*** Solanum giganteum
 ** Sparmannia africana
  * Strelitzia reginae
  * Tetrapanax papyrifera
 ** Viburnum japonicum
  * Wigandia caracasana

*** Yucca elephantipes

### VINES

 ** Alseuosmia macrophylla
  * Beaumontia grandiflora
  * Cissus capensis
  * Fatshedera lizei
 ** Ficus pumila
  * Hedera canariensis
  * Monstera deliciosa
*** Petrea volubilis

*** Philodendron erubescens
 **      "      evansi
  *      "      selloum
*** Quamoclit lobata
 ** Solandra guttata
 ** Thunbergia grandiflora
*** Trachelospermum fragrans
*** Vitis (species)

### SUCCULENTS

  * Agave attenuata
 ** Aloe humilis
*** Crassula falcata
 ** Doryanthes palmeri
  * Echeveria metalica

  * Epiphyllum oxypetalon
*** Guzmania cardinalis
 ** Kalanchoe marmorata
 ** Opuntia biglovi
*** Pachyphytum bracteosum

## FOLIAGE REFINED

Leaves that are not necessarily small, but elegant in shape or cast and in fineness of division or serration, will find uses appropriate to their character. They go with smooth surfaces in architecture, delicate mouldings or staff detail and in the light. They increase the apparent size of an area. An excellence in these leaves may be reflected from within as tissue and defined as substance, or it may appear as a pattern in venation for close inspection.

### TREES

* Acacia (species)
* Albizzia (species)
* Casuarina (species)
* Cedrus (species)
*** Chamaccyparis lawsoniana
** Colvillea racemosa
** Cryptomeria elegans
*** Cupania anacardioides
* Cupressus (species)
** Delonix regia
** Ficus benjamina
***    "    retusa
** Grevillea robusta
* Jacaranda acutifolia
* Juniperus (species)

** Libocedrus decurrens
** Lyonothamnus asplenifolius
*** Maytenus boaria
*** Melaleuca styphelioides
** Parkinsonia aculeata
* Pinus (species)
*** Pittosporum phillyraeoides
** Prosopis glandulosa
*** Samanea saman
*** Schinus molle
*** Stenocarpus sinuatus
* Tamarix aphylla
** Taxodium (species)
** Taxus baccata
** Thuja orientalis

*** Tipuana tipu

### SHRUBS

** Acacia verticillata
* Anthyllis barba-jovis
* Azara microphylla
* Berberis darwini
** Buxus microphylla
* Calliandra (species)
** Calothamnus quadrifidus
* Cassia artemisioides
** Cneorum dumosum
*** Cocculus laurifolius
** Collinia elegans
** Cuphea hissopifolia
** Cyperus (species)
** Cytisus canariensis
* Diosma (species)
* Erica melanthera
** Eriocephalis africanus
*** Euonymus japonicus
*** Eurya emarginata
** Genista monosperma
* Grevillea (species)
** Halimium libanotis
*** Hebe (check species)
** Heimia myrtifolia
*** Ilex vomitoria
* Juniperus (species)
** Lavandula officinalis
** Lawsonia inermis
*** Leptospermum citratum
** Lopesia albiflora
** Mahernia verticillata
* Melaleuca armillaris

** Melaleuca decussata
***    "    huegeli
*** Murraea exotica
*** Myrtus microphylla
* Nandina domestica
** Nierembergia frutescens
** Osteomeles anthyllidifolia
** Phoenix roebelini
*** Pimelea ferruginea
** Pittosporum heterophyllum
* Poinciana gilliesi
*** Polygola dalmaisiana
*** Prunus ilicifolia
*** Psidium cattleianum
*** Pyracantha crenato-serrata
** Raphiolepis delacouri
* Rosmarinus Lockwood de Forest
* Sasa disticha
*** Syagrus weddelliana
*** Siphonosmanthus delavayi
* Sollya heterophylla
*** Spiraea cantoniensis
* Streptosolen jamesoni
*** Swainsona galegifolia
* Tamarix (species)
** Tecoma garrocha
** Thevetia nereifolia
* Thryallis glauca
** Turraea obtusifolia
*** Vitex agnus-castus
* Westringia rosmariniformis
*** Xylosma senticosa

### VINES

* Asparagus (species)
*** Cissus hypoglauca
*    "    rhombifolia
**    "    striata
*** Gelsemium sempervirens
* Hardenbergia comptoniana
** Jasminum azoricum

** Manettia bicolor
* Muehlenbeckia complexa
*** Podrania ricasoliana
*** Polygonum auberti
* Quamoclit pennata
*** Stigmaphyllon ciliatum
** Trachelospermum jasminoides

## GLOSSY LEAVES

Shining foliage throws back the sun in a multi-facet reflection and will be in lively contrast with that which absorbs light. They require to be planted with dull livid greenery to bring out full value....one spot or small area therein is usually enough; or a larger infusion will stimulate a lifeless array of greens to surprising animation. There is harmony here in a polished courteous setting and the very sharpest highlight within shadow.

* Abelia grandiflora
* Alseuosmia macrophylla
*** Anisacanthus wrighti
*** Artabotrys uncinatus
*** Asparagus asparagoides
*** Azalea serrulata
* Berberis darwini
***    "    gagnepaini
*** Bergenia cordifolia
* Boussingaultia baselloides
** Brassaia actinophylla
** Buxus japonica
** Camellia japonica
* Carissa grandiflora
** Catha edulis
** Ceanothus cyaneus
***    "    foliosus
** Chrysobalanus icaco
** Cinnamomum camphora
** Cissus rhombifolia
*** Citherexylum spinosum
* Coccolobis uvifera
* Coprosma baueri
** Corynocarpus laevigata
*** Cupania anacardioides
** Dennstaedtia cicutaria
* Ervatamia coronaria
** Eucalyptus grossa
*** Eurya ochnacea
* Fatsia japonica
* Gardenia florida
***    "    thunbergia
*** Griselinia littoralis
* Ilex (species)
*** Jasminum dichotomum
**    "    humile

* Ligustrum ovalifolium
*** Lonicera pileata
*** Malpighia glabra
* Maytenus boaria
* Michelia fuscata
*** Mimusops elengi
** Murraea exotica
*** Nothopanax arboreum
* Olmediella betschleriana
** Oncoba routledgi
** Osmanthus americanus
***    "    armatus
** Pandorea pandorana
** Photinia serrulata
** Pittosporum euginioides
***    "    heterophyllum
***    "    rhombifolium
*    "    tobira
** Polystichum adiantiforme
** Populus (check species)
* Prunus lyoni
** Pyrus calleryana
** Quercus laurifolia
*** Quillaja saponaria
*** Rhamnus alaternus
* Rhus ovata
** Sapium sebiferum
** Terminalia catappa
* Ternstroemia japonica
*** Torreya (species)
*** Tupidanthus calyptratus
** Ulmus sempervirens
* Viburnum japonicum
***    "    odoratissimum
* Vitex lucens
* Xylosma senticosa

## FOLIAGE HOLLY-LIKE

Leaves that are spined in the likeness of the thistle or shaped as in holly will introduce a sprightly quality to the mass that enlivens. This grows on one with a fascination that may break into a moon-raking mood. Value increases in effectiveness directly with the degree of lustre. Such plants will be better used with some restraint. Let them season the border rather than make any material part of it.

** Acacia armata
*** Acanthus montanus
** Argemone mexicana
** Atriplex lentiformis
*** Berberidopsis corallina
* Berberis darwini
** Ceanothus gloriosus
**    "    purpureus
* Chorizema cordatum
*** Cirsium occidentale
** Cyrtomium falcatum
* Ilex aquifolium
**    "    cornuta

*** Ilex perado
** Itea ilicifolia
*** Macadamia ternifolia
* Mahonia (species)
*** Malpighia coccigera
* Osmanthus ilicifolius
* Prunus ilicifolia
***    "    lyoni
** Quercus agrifolia
*    "    ilex
** Rhamnus ilicifolia
*** Salvia carduacea
*** Solanum giganteum

FOLIAGE VARIEGATION---abnormal coloration in the leaves that may appear as stripes, bands, spots, splotches, or as an edging, gives a spicy touch to a mass of leafage. The garden purist finds but little merit here, and a large use of this material is a pretense so far as good taste is concerned and not desirable. Recourse to it will be made sparingly unless for an artificial and temporary effect. The plant is usually less vigorous than its type species and should be given any and all advantage in location and in culture.

### WOODY PLANTS

** Abutilon (varieties)
* Acalypha wilksiana
*** Agave (check species)
*** Aloe variegata
*** Arundo donax variegatum
*** Aucuba japonica (forms)
* Bambusa multiplex (forms)
** Breynia nivosa
* Codiaeum variegatum
* Coprosma baueri variegata
* Daphne odora marginata
** Dracaena godseffiana
* Elaeagnus pungens (varieties)
*** Euphorbia lathyrus
**        "        marginata

* Euonymus japonicus var.
** Hebe andersoni var.
*** Hypoestis phyllostachys
** Juniperus argentea
*** Ligustrum aureum
*        "        variegatum
** Lonicera aureo-reticulata
* Myrtus communis variegata
** Nerium oleander var.
* Osmanthus argenteo-marginatus
**        "        atro-purpureus
**        "        aureo-marginatus
* Pittosporum tobira var.
*** Serissa foetida marginata
** Trachelospermum (varieties)

### HERBACEOUS PLANTS

* Alternanthera amoena
*** Amaranthus caudatus
*** Aphelandra squarrosa
** Arrhenatherum tuberosum
** Arum italicum
* Caladium picturatum
** Calathea roseo-picta
* Chlorophytum elatum
*** Cirsium occidentale
** Cryptanthus beuckeri
*** Dactylis glomerata var.
* Dieffenbachia picta
* Dracaena fragrans
** Euphorbia marginata
* Hedera helix var.
* Ligularia kaempferi
** Maranta leuconeura

*** Miscanthus (varieties)
** Ophiopogon jaburan var.
*** Oplismenus hirtellus
*** Opuntia monacantha var.
*** Phalaris arundinacea picta
*** Pepperomia sandersi
* Phormium veitchianum
*** Rohdea japonica (forms)
*** Salvia officinalis
* Sansevieria zeylanica
** Saxifraga sarmentosa
* Scindapsis aureus
** Sedum lineare var.
* Thymus vulgaris argenteus
* Vinca major variegata
* Zantedeschia elliottiana
** Zebrina pendula

*** Zingiber darceyi

FALL AND WINTER COLOR---pigmentation visible in the leaf on retirement of vital saps and chlorophyll in species that know how to act on approach of cold weather. Brilliant hues of autumn are lacking in the far south, but a little frost will bring on touches of yellow, gold and crimson in some plants, which go hand in hand with berries in the artistry of the season. Yellow appears more commonly, while red seems accented in acid soils, but tinged with violet in alkalinity. It is more often seen far south in a flecking of the individual leaf rather than being uniform in the foliage as a whole. It may be noted that normal to high rainfall of the season will accentuate, as will bright days and cool nights. These points may be kept in mind when calling the following species into use.

** Abelia grandiflora
*** Acalypha musaica
** Berberis darwini
* Buxus japonica
** Carissa grandiflora
** Ceratostigma griffithi
* Catha edulis
* Cissus capensis
** Cneoridium dumosum

** Cotinus coggigria
** Cotoneaster (species)
** Diospyros kaki
*** Eucalyptus ficifolia
**        "        sideroxylon
** Eugenia uniflora
*** Euphorbia tirucalli
** Ginkgo biloba
*** Guzmania cardinalis

** Hedera helix minima
*** Homalanthus populifolius
 * Lagerstroemia indica
*** Ligustrum ovalifolium
 * Liquidambar (species)
** Mahonia pinnata
*** Melaleuca leucadendra
*** Metasequoia glyptostroboides
 * Nandina domestica
** Parthenocissus henryana
 * Persea borbonia
 * Photinia serrulata
 * Pistacia chinensis

** Platanus racemosa
*** Populus nigra italica
** Psidium guineense
** Pyracantha (species)
 * Quercus lobata
*** Raphiolepis ovata
** Rhus trilobata
 * Sapium sebiferum
*** Terminalia catappa
 * Ulmus pumila
*** Ungnadia speciosa
** Vaccinium virgatum
*** Zizyphus jujuba

ORNAMENTAL FRUITS---extend the usefulness of a plant much as a
second crop of flowers in spreading color out over the year. These
lists have to do with plants where the fruit, pod, berry or capsule
becomes an appreciable element in the garden or landscape. They are
not necessarily edible nor are they always long-lasting, yet even in
going, they attract life and movement in the activity of birds. Red
will have the highest visibility and display value, while shriveling
will be less and the effect prolonged, if the plant is maintained in
good moisture. The plants will be grouped generally in way of color,
although it should be noted that some species will pass through two
or more separate colorings. If it is desirable to keep fruits from
the birds, hang bright tops of ordinary tin cans back within the body
of the plant, where they will be inconspicuous but flash false warn-
ings as a deterrent....for the time. Birds seem to reject until the
last, fruits of high acidity and those with punky, indigestible pulp.

WHITE

** Ampelopsis brevipedunculata
 * Baccharis halimifolia
** Caladium picturatum
 * Cestrum nocturnum
 * Chiococca alba
*** Coix lachryma-jobi
 * Coprosma baueri
*** Cordia boissieri

*** Elaeodendron orientale
*** Hymenanthera crassifolia
** Malvaviscus arboreus
** Melia azedarach
 * Muehlenbeckia complexa
*** Nandina domestica alba
 * Phoradendron flavescens
** Sapium sebiferum

*** Solanum warscewiczi

YELLOW AND ORANGE

** Artabotrys uncinatus
*** Cestrum aurantiacum
** Chaenomeles japonica
 * Citrus (species)
 * Cotoneaster francheti
**      "      simonsi
 * Dovyalis caffra
 * Duranta (species)
** Ehretia elliptica
 * Eriobotrya japonica
** Eugenia edulis
**      " jambos
** Feijoa sellowiana
** Fortunella japonica

** Hymenosporum flavum
*** Macropiper excelsum
*** Mimusops elengi
 * Momordica charantia
*** Nertera depressa
*** Passiflora quadrangularis
*** Pereskia aculeata
 * Pittosporum (check species)
*** Psidium guineense
 * Psidium lucidum
 * Pyracantha lalandi
**      "      yunnanensis
 * Rhus integrifolia
*** Solanum muricatum

*** Strychnos spinosa

SCARLET-RED-CRIMSON

** Abrus precatorius
 * Acokanthera spectabilis
*** Ailanthus altissima
 * Arbutus unedo
** Arctostaphylos diversifolia
** Ardisia crispa
** Arum italicum
** Aucuba japonica

 * Canella winterana
 * Capsicum frutescens
 * Carissa (species)
*** Clerodendrum siphonanthus
*** Cneorum tricoccon
*** Cornus capitata
** Cotoneaster pannosa
 *      "      parneyi

*** Cudrania tricuspidata
*** Cyphomandra betacea
*** Damnacanthus indicus
*** Danae racemosa
  * Duchesnea indica
  * Eugenia myrtifolia
 ** Eurya ochnacea
*** Ficus benjamina
 ** Harpephyllum caffrum
*** Harpullia arborea
  * Heteromeles arbutifolia
  * Ilex (species)
*** Iris foetidissima
*** Litchi chinensis
  * Magnolia grandiflora
*** Malpighia (species)
  * Malvaviscus arboreus
 ** Murraea exotica
  * Nandina domestica

  * Ochna multiflora
*** Ochrosia elliptica
 ** Photinia serrulata
 ** Prunus lyoni
*** Psidium cattleianum
  * Punica granatum
*** Putoria calabrica
  * Pyracantha crenato-serrata
 ** Rhamnus crocea
 ** Rhus laurina
 ** Rivina humilis
  * Ricinus communis
*** Rohdea japonica
 ** Schinus (species)
*** Sophora secundiflora
  * Solanum (species)
*** Triphasia trifolia
*** Viburnum odoratissimum
 **     "    suspensum

*** Zamia floridana

## LAVENDER-BLUE-BLACK

*** Ampelopsis brevipedunculata
 ** Ardisia paniculata
  * Berberis darwini
 ** Cinnamomum camphora
  * Cissus (species)
*** Citharexylum spinosum
*** Coprosma petrei
*** Daphniphyllum humile
  * Dianella (species)
 ** Eugenia smithi
 ** Fatsia japonica
 ** Hamelia erecta
  * Juniperus (species)
 ** Lantana camara
  * Ligustrum (species)
 ** Mahonia pinnata
*** Meryta sinclairi
  * Myrtus (species)

  * Olea europaea
*** Ophiopogon jaburan
  * Osmanthus ilicifolius
 ** Parthenocissus (species)
*** Persea borbonia
 ** Phillyrea latifolia
  * Prunus caroliniana
  * Raphiolepis (species)
*** Sarcococca hookeriana
 ** Severinia buxifolia
 ** Siphonosmanthus delavayi
*** Stizolobium deeringianum
*** Ungnadia speciosa
*** Vaccinium virgatum
 ** Viburnum carlesi
***    "   odoratissimum
 ** Vitis (species)
*** Zizyphus obtusifolia

FOLIAGE COLOR---embraces coloring in the leafage where the chlorophyll or greening element of the leaf is partially or entirely suppressed. Many of these forms are not only un-natural, they assume a predominance that is not warranted in ordinary planting and should be used with discretion. Intensity is usually variable and suseptible to seasonable change or may be modified in the sun, or against a shadow. This phenomena may be genetic or only physiological. Is it nutritional or is it the chemical reaction of the soil that is responsible for a degree of coloring....and by which some control may be exerted. In any event, always supply enough green to prevent unpleasant colors in combination and do not be snared into excessive use.

## SILVERY LEAVES
This covers the nearest approach to white, as a general observation, with inclusions that are practically white, but without the reflecting value of silver. Silver will be found closely allied to blue and grey and merges imperceptibly into either. The effect is usually metalic, the result of very fine hairs or tiny scales overlying the surface. Green may in some cases lie behind, but is seldom, if ever, in admixture with the silver. Purple in combination is very striking and often used.

 ** Acacia dealbata
  * Anthyllis barba-jovis
*** Araujia sericofera
  * Artemisia lactiflora
*** Atriplex lentiformis
*** Buddleja nivea

  * Calocephalis browni
  * Convolvulus cneorum
*** Correa alba
 ** Echeveria pulverulenta
  * Elaeagnus pungens
 ** Encelia farinosa

* Eriocephalis africana
** Eucalyptus crucis
*      "      pulverulenta
*** Euryops pectinatus
** Genista monosperma
*** Halimium halimifolium
** Hunnemannia fumariaefolia
* Leucadendron argenteum
* Leucophyllum texanum
* Lotus mascaensis
** Lupinus paynei
*** Odontospermum sericeum

*** Orontium aquaticum
** Pachyphytum bracteosum
*** Pinus sabiniana
*** Podalyrea sericea
* Romneya coulteri
** Senecio cineraria
*** Sideritis candicans
** Solanum montanum
*** Teucrium marrum
*** Thalia dealbata
** Thymus argenteus
* Westringia rosmariniformis

** Xeranthemum annuum

## YELLOW GREEN

May be used to heighten the warmth of a sunny patch in a large area of shadow. It has a cheerful effect on the emotions and may well be used in broad masses, but in harmonious relations rather than contrasted. This makes a good back for a brown motif, with a progressive and natural blending, whether in foliage or in an inorganic substance....of the building or as found in the garden.

*** Abies venusta
** Acacia floribunda
** Adenostoma sparscifolium
*** Arctostaphylos (check species)
*** Atriplex hortensis (forms)
** Brassaia actinophylla
** Candollea cuneiformis
*** Chiranthodendron platanoides
*** Choisya ternata
*** Chrysophyllum caineto
*** Citrus (species)
* Coleus (varieties)
*** Coprosma kirki
*** Correa magnifica
** Dendromecon rigida
* Eucalyptus lehmanni
** Eugenia jambos
* Gelsemium sempervirens
*** Griselinia lucida
** Heimia myrtifolia
* Hymenosporum flavum
* Hypericum (species)
*** Jacobinia pauciflora
* Jasminum humile
** Laurus nobilis
* Ligustrum ovalifolium

** Mahernia verticillata
*** Melaleuca hyperiscifolia
*** Meryta sinclairi
* Michelia fuscata
** Myrsine africana
*** Olmediella betschleriana
** Opuntia microdasys
* Parkinsonia aculeata
*** Petrea volubilis
** Phyllostachys aurea
* Pittosporum eugenioides
*** Populus trichocarpa
*** Quercus chrysolepis
*** Rhus laurina
*** Samanea samen
** Senecio petasitis
** Selaginella brauni
*** Siphonosmanthus delavayi
*** Sophora secundiflora
*** Spathodea campanulata
** Stenolobium stans
** Taxus baccata
* Thevetia nereifolia
* Thuja orientalis
*** Tipuana tipu
* Xylosma senticosa

## RED OR PURPLE LEAFAGE

Hue ranges here through warmth to actual vehemence in red to the fury and violence of some purples. There are tones for pleasure; other notes are arousing, aggressive, but always too exciting for any large masses in foliage. High color is particularly offensive in a natural effect, but may be sprightly as a touch and will stir a sluggish composition into something of life and vitality. Purple can be the darkest color, that of farthest depth in shadow. Deep shade will soften magenta, when cultural points can be reconciled.

** Acacia baileyana purpurea
***      "      pruinosa
* Acokanthera spectabilis
*** Aeonium arboreum
* Ajuga reptans (forms)
* Begonia (check species)
*** Calathea roseo-picta
** Cissus adenopodus
* Codiaeum (varieties)
** Coleus blumei
** Crassula impressa

*** Cyanotis hirsuta
* Dodonaea viscosa purpurea
*** Dracaena terminalis
** Euphorbia heterophylla
** Eurya ochnacea
*** Guzmania cardinalis
* Gynura aurantiaca
** Hamelia erecta
* Hebe imperialis
** Hibiscus sabdariffa
*** Iresine herbsti

*** Jacobinia carnea              *** Ricinus communis
 ** Kalanchoe (check species)       * Ruellia devosiana
  * Leptospermum scoparium hybrids  * Saintpaulia ionantha
*** Oplismenus hirtellus           ** Sapium sebeferum
*** Opuntia basilaris              ** Saxifraga sarmentosa
  * Parthenocissus henryana        ** Sedum pachyphyllum
*** Phormium (varieties)          ***    "    stahli
 ** Portulacaria afra              ** Ternstroemia japonica
  * Prunus pissardi                 * Zebrina pendula

### BLUE-GREEN
Bluish foliage approaches grey in coolness and poise.  It
is psychologically inert, at times to become almost uncourteous. It
is passive and the two will often be found in nature intermingling.
It will react satisfactorily in almost any combination. Blue in foliage is submissive, staid, always unruffled.  It does not appear at
its best in close conjunction with the more extreme yellow greens in
leaves....be very careful.

*** Abutilon palmeri               *** Eucalyptus grossa
  * Acacia baileyana                **    "    polyanthemos
***    "    cyanophylla             * Festuca glauca
*** Acrocomia totai                ** Hebe glaucophylla
 ** Agave attenuata               *** Helleborus lividus
 ** Araucaria excelsa             *** Hesperaloe parviflora
  * Arctostaphylos glauca         *** Juniperus pachyphlaea
 ** Bauhinia variegata             ** Kalanchoe glaucescens
 ** Brachysema lanceolatum         ** Kleinia repens
  * Butia capitata                *** Lepidium sativum (forms)
 ** Carpenteria californica       *** Leptospermum laevigatum
  * Cedrus atlantica glauca         * Limonium perezi
*** Cercidium torreyanum          *** Mahonia nevini
*** Cercis siliquastrum            **    "    trifoliata
  * Chamaecyparis alumi             * Melaleuca decussata
 ** Coronilla glauca                * Melianthus major
  * Crotalaria agatiflora         *** Penstemon centranthifolius
  * Cupressus guadalupensis        ** Pinus canariensis
*** Dasylerion glaucophylla         * Quercus douglasi
*** Elymus glaucus                 ** Sedum dasyphyllum
*** Eriodictyon crassifolia        ** Selaginella uncinata
 ** Erythea armata                  * Strobilanthes dyerianus
  * Eucalyptus globulus compacta  ** Taxus repandens
            *** Trachycarpus fortunei

### GREY
This is cold and impersonal. It goes with the broad sands of
the desert and the narrow reach of the shore. It creates, devises or
improvises distance and brings out the delicate coloring of stone,
either in the rock garden or as used against a building.  Throw strong
color against it in complete safety.  It complements blue and is a
welcome departure from the more vivid greens.  It wants the sun and
the plants that carry it in the leaf are usually found in nature growing in dry to dryish or baked out soils, and in heat.

  * Acacia cultriformis             * Lavandula officinalis
 **    "    pendula                 * Lotus bertheloti
  *    "    podalyriaefolia        ** Metrosideros tomentosa
*** Aloe vera                       * Olea europaea
 ** Atriplex breweri              *** Phlomis fruticosa
 ** Cassia artemisioides            * Pittosporum crassifolium
  * Cistus salvifolius            *** Rosa stellata
  * Correa pulchella               ** Rosmarinus officinalis
  * Cotoneaster pannosa            ** Salvia officinalis
*** Eriogonum arborescens           * Santolina chamaecyparissus
 ** Eugenia edulis                  * Tamarix (species)
  * Feijoa sellowiana              ** Tetrapanax papyrifera
*** Halimium ocymoides              * Teucrium fruticans
*** Hazardia cana                 *** Thymus lanuginosus
 ** Helichrysum petiolatum        *** Vigueria tomentosa
*** Jaquemontia eastwoodiana      *** Zauschneria californica

COLOR AS TO BLOOM---groupings of related color in flowers having
actual floral merit; an arrangement of species in rough working order
for those who will build their planting program on a studied color
effect. Mixed and indifferent or vague values will be omitted and the
lists kept open only for those of reasonably definite character where
coloring can be predicted with some certainty.  Purity is assumed as
a base, working out into modification as indicated by ratings.   The
visible impurity will be less objectionable as it becomes localized.
Use bright color in the sun. Pastels are more effective in shadow.
Warm color reflects light; cool color absorbs it.  In gradation of
color; a shade results from admixture with black; a tint from less
dilution or admixture with white; a tinge from a faint trace of added color that is foreign. Most flowers appear to best advantage against
a neutral or light background and it is also appropriate to show delicate colors with fineness in texture. Color primarily expresses emotion and, as in all nature, is most intense in spring, glimmering fitfully over summer in approaching the tawny shades of fall.

## WHITE

        This involves the total lack of color, with purity very
important. Adulterated, it becomes dirty-looking, unless with enough
color, when it becomes a tint. White dazzles. It is the great harmon-
izer and materially helps to blend doubtful associations.  It serves
to bring out delicate or unusual color quality in neighboring plants
and does not require strong color for contrast.  Comparative whites
become more pure in shadow, while a cold hard white softens against
grey. It suggests breadth and brings about a certain calmness, but can
be over-done, a more deadly monotony resulting than in any other color
in the garden.

### TREES

*** Angophora lanceolata          * Ligustrum japonicum
  * Bauhinia grandiflora           * Magnolia grandiflora
 ** Calophyllum inophyllum       *** Phytolacca dioica
 ** Crinodendron dependens        ** Plumeria emarginata
 ** Escallonia montevidensis       * Prunus persica wh.
*** Eucalyptus globulus          *** Pterospermum acerifolium
 ** Eugenia paniculata             * Pyrus calleryana
 ** Hakea saligna                *** Quillaja saponaria
 ** Lyonothamnus asplenifolius    ** Robinia pseudacacia

### SHRUBS

*** Azalea serrulata               * Lantana camara wh.
*** Bauhinia acuminata             * Leptospermum laevigatum
*** Bowkeria gerrardiana          ** Magnolia stellata
  * Camellia (varieties)          ** Melaleuca armillaris
  * Carissa grandiflora          ***    "     huegeli
*** Carpenteria californica        * Murraea exotica
 ** Ceanothus verrucosus           * Myrtus communis
 ** Cestrum diurnum                * Nandina domestica
*** Chaenostoma hispidum         *** Nerium indicum
  * Choisya ternata              *** Noltea africana
  * Cistus corbariensis           ** Oncoba routledgi
*** Clerodendrum siphonanthus    *** Pereskia aculeata
 ** Clethra arborea              *** Philadelphus microphyllus
 ** Convolvulus cneorum            * Photinia serrulata
*** Cordia boissieri              ** Pittosporum tobira
*** Damnacanthus indicus         *** Prostanthera nivea
  * Diosma ericoides              ** Prunus ilicifolia
 ** Dombeya natalensis           ***    "    lusitanica
*** Entelea arborescens            *    "    lyoni
  * Ervatamia coronaria            * Pyracantha (species)
  * Escallonia organensis         ** Romneya coulteri
  * Gardenia (species)           *** Royena lucida
 ** Gaya lyalli                   ** Siphonosmanthus delavayi
*** Genista monosperma             * Spiraea cantoniensis
 ** Hakea suaveolens               * Turraea obtusifolia
 ** Halimium libanotis           *** Viburnum odoratissimum
  * Hebe glaucophylla              *    "    suspensum
  * Heteromeles arbutifolia       **    "    tinus
 ** Hibiscus arnottianus         *** Visnea mocanera

## VINES

*** Agdestis clematidea
  * Beaumontia grandiflora
 ** Boussingaultia baselloides
 ** Calonyction aculeatum
*** Clerodendrum thompsonae
  * Clematis armandi
 ** Hoya carnosa
*** Hylocereus triangularis
  * Jasminum (check species)

  * Mandevilla suaveolens
 ** Oxera pulchella
 ** Pandorea jasminoides
*** Plumbago capensis alba
  * Polygonum auberti
*** Solanum jasminoides
  * Stephanotis floribunda
*** Thunbergia fragrans
  * Trachelospermum (species)

*** Wisteria floribunda wh.

## HERBACEOUS PLANTS

  * Agapanthus africanus wh.
  * Allium neapolitanum
  * "     triquetrum
  * Alyssum maritimum
*** Amaryllis immaculata
*** Ammobium alatum
  * Anemone japonica wh.
*** Aphanostephus skirrobasis
 ** Aster gracillimus
 ** Brodiaea lactea
  * Chaerophyllum dasycarpum
 ** Callistephus chinensis wh.
*** Calochortus albus
  * Campanula isophylla
  * Chrysanthemum frutescens
  *       "       maximum
*** Crinum americanum
  *       "   giganteum
 ** Cyrtanthus mackeni
 ** Dianthus caryophyllus wh.
*** Elisena longipetala
*** Eucharis grandiflora
*** Eucomis undulata
  * Francoa ramosa
 ** Galtonia candicans
  * Gladiolus (check species)
  * Gypsophila elegans
*** Haemanthus albiflos
  * Hedychium coronarium
*** Helichrysum diosmaefolium

*** Hymenocallis festalis
  * Iris germanica wh.
  * Leucojum autumnale
*** Libertia grandiflora
  * Lilium candidum
***     "    philippinense
 **     "    regale
*** Michauxia campanuloides
 ** Milla biflora
*** Moraea glaucopis
 ** Narcissus (varieties)
  * Nicotiana alata
 ** Oenothera acaulis
 ** Ornithogalum arabicum
*** Pancratium (species)
 ** Petunia hybrida wh.
 ** Piqueria trinervia
  * Polianthes tuberosa
*** Ranunculus asiaticus wh.
*** Satureja intricata
*** Schizopetalon walkeri
 ** Sedum album
***     "    dasyphyllum
*** Ulmaria filipendula
 ** Vinca rosea wh.
  * Viola tricolor wh.
 ** Watsonia iridifolia
*** Yucca whipplei
  * Zantedeschia aethiopica
 ** Zephyranthes candida

## YELLOW

Yellow flowers and orange are of the sun. They dominate and are especially intensified by white. They are the flowers for gladness and give full value out in the open under full exposure and where all is revealed. The typical plant seems to belong there and reaches wistfully for light when placed in shadow. Orange is essentially warm while yellow is the lightest color of all and has the greatest reflecting power. Yellow is illusive, fugitive, as under passing clouds and therefore better used in masses....bedding. It associates more or less agreeably with all other colors.

## TREES

  * Acacia (species)
 ** Barklya syringifolia
 ** Castanospermum australe
*** Cochlospermum vitifolium
 ** Colvillea racemosa
  * Eucalyptus erythrocorys
  * Grevillea robusta
  * Hymenosporum flavum

 ** Koelreuteria paniculata
*** Markhamia lutea
  * Parkinsonia aculeata
*** Peltophorum inerme
*** Pittosporum phillyraeoides
*** Simaruba amara
 ** Stenolobium stans
  * Tipuana tipu

## SHRUBS

 ** Abutilon hybridum
 ** Acacia alata
  *   "   armata

  * Acacia verticillata
***   "   vestita
 ** Adenocarpus viscosus

*** Azalea austrina
** Berberis (species)
*** Bauhinia tomentosa
* Candollea cuneiformis
* Cassia splendida
* Cestrum aurantiacum
* Coronilla glauca
*** Cowania mexicana
** Cytisus canariensis
** Daubentonia tripeti
*** Dendromecon rigida
*** Euryops (species)
*** Fremontia californica
*** Halimium halimifolium
*** Heimia myrtifolia
* Hypericum (species)
** Jasminum floridum
* Jasminum humile

*** Jasminum rigidum
** Leonotis leonurus
*** Lupinus arboreus
** Mahernia verticillata
* Mahonia (species)
** Medicago arborea
** Ochna multiflora
*** Odontospermum sericeum
*** Penstemon antirrhinoides
*** Phlomis fruticosa
* Poinciana gilliesi
*      "      pulcherrima
*** Senecio petasitis
* Spartium junceum
* Streptosolen jamesoni
** Tecoma smithi
* Thevetia (species)
*** Thryallis glauca

## VINES

*** Adenocalymna alliaceum
** Allamanda hendersoni
* Anemopoegma chamberlayni
*** Bougainvillea Praetorius
** Doxantha unguis-cati
* Gelsemium sempervirens
*** Gloriosa superba
* Hibbertia volubilis
*** Jasminum mesneyi

** Lonicera confusa
*       "      halliana
** Pyrostegia ignea
** Senecio confusus
* Solandra guttata
** Stigmaphyllon ciliatum
*** Thunbergia alata
**      "      gibsoni
* Tropaeolum peregrinum

*** Vigna marina

## HERBACEOUS PLANTS

** Aloe eru
* Aquilegia chrysantha
*** Bloomeria crocea
* Calendula officinalis
*** Calochortus weedi
*** Chlidanthus fragrans
* Chrysanthemum morifolium
*** Cladanthus arabicus
* Coreopsis (species)
** Crocosmia aurea
*** Cypella herberti
*** Dicentra chrysantha
* Dimorphotheca aurantiaca
** Duchesnea indica
*** Erodium chrysanthum
* Eschscholtzia californica
* Gazania splendens
***     "     uniflora
* Gerberia hybrids
* Geum stratheden
*** Habranthus andersoni
** Hedychium flavum
* Hemerocallis aurantiaca
*** Hesperantha stanfordiae
** Hunnemannia fumariaefolia
*** Hypericum reptans
* Iris (check species)
* Ixia (select color)
*** Kalanchoe aliciae
* Kniphofia uvaria
** Lilium henryi
*** Linaria dalmatica
*** Littonia modesta
** Lonas inodora
* Lotus mascaensis
*** Lycoris aurea

*** Moraea ramosa
* Mentzelia lindleyi
* Mesembryanth. aurantiacum
***     "     glaucum
**      "     laeve
** Mimulus (species)
* Narcissus pseudo-narcissus
*** Ornithogalum thyrsoides
** Othonna crassifolia
*** Oxalis cernuua
* Papaver nudicaule
* Primula kewensis
** Ranunculus (select color)
** Reinwardtia indica
* Sanvitalia procumbens
** Sedum guatemalense
***     "     pachyphyllum
*      "      prealtum
** Sparaxis (select color)
*** Stanleya pinnata
** Sternbergia lutea
** Sisyrinchium bermudianum
***      "      striatum
* Tagetes erecta
***     "     patula
** Tigridia (select color)
** Torenia flava
*** Tritonia squalida
* Tropaeolum major
** Ursinia anthemoides
** Venidium (species)
*** Verbesina encelioides
* Viola (select color)
*** Wachendorfia thyrsiflorus
*** Xanthisma texanum
** Zantedeschia elliottiana

## RED FLOWERS

From scarlet through crimson to light purple and magenta
are highly emotional.  They are the more primative and virile; they
motivate; they advance.  Rose, and in lesser degree pink, have some
difficulty in combination, while magenta may clash seriously and should
be used alone or in conjunction with white or light blue. These strong
reds are less virulent in shadow. They are not to be discarded care-
lessly and off-hand on account of this violence, since the color frequently is an effectual tactic in bringing out a pallid color scheme.
Use red vigorously. The bold approach is the less painful.

### TREES

| | |
|---|---|
| ** Albizzia julibrissin | * Eucalyptus ficifolia |
| * Brachychiton acerifolium | **    "    sideroxylon rosea |
| * Callistemon viminalis | ** Lagunaria patersoni |
| * Calodendrum capense | *** Magnolia soulangeana |
| *** Cassia grandis | * Metrosideros tomentosa |
| ** Cercis siliquastrum | ** Poinciana regia (Delonix) |
| *** Dais cotinifolia | ** Prunus persica (select color) |
| ** Erythrina (check species) | *** Robinia decaisneana |
| *** Eucalyptus erythronema | ** Stenocarpus sinuatus |

      ** Vitex lucens

### SHRUBS

| | |
|---|---|
| * Abelia (species) | * Hibiscus rosa-sinensis |
| ** Aloe arborescens | *** Holmskioldia sanguinea |
| * Azalea indica | ** Hydrangea macrophylla |
| *** Berberidopsis corallina | ** Iochroma fuchsioides |
| ** Brachysema lanceolatum | * Jacobinia carnea |
| * Calliandra inequilatera | * Lagerstroemia indica |
| ***    "    tweedi | *** Loeselia  mexicana |
| * Callistemon lanceolatus | *** Malvastrum capense |
| *** Calothamnus quadrifidus | * Malvaviscus arboreus |
| * Camellia (species) | ***    "    grandiflorus |
| ** Cantua buxifolia | * Melaleuca hyperiscifolia |
| ** Carissa carandas | ***    "    lateritia |
| * Cestrum purpureum | * Nerium oleander (select color) |
| ** Clerodendrum fragrans | ** Pachystachys coccinea |
| *** Correa ventricosa | ** Penstemon cordifolius |
| ** Daphne odora | *** Phygelius capensis |
| ** Daubentonia punicea | ** Pimelea ferruginea |
| *** Delostoma roseum | *** Podalyrea sericea |
| * Diosma pulchra | *** Polygala apopetala |
| ** Erica melanthera | * Punica granatum |
| *** Erythrina (check species) | ** Ribes (species) |
| * Escallonia langleyensis | ** Rondeletia cordata |
| **    "    rosea | * Rosa (check species) |
| **    "    rubra | * Russelia equisetiformis |
| *** Fouquieria splendens | ** Salvia greggi |
| * Fuchsia triphylla | ***    "    sessei |
| *** Galvesia speciosa | *** Swainsona galegifolia |
| *** Grevillea banksi | * Tamarix (species) |
| **    "    thelemanniana | * Tecoma capensis |
| *** Grewia caffra | **    "    garrocha |
| ** Greyia sutherlandi | *** Templetonia retusa |
| * Hakea laurina | ** Viburnum carlesi |
| * Hebe carnea | *** Weigela florida |
| ** Heterocentron roseum | *** Zauschneria californica |

### VINES

| | |
|---|---|
| ** Alseuosmia macrophylla | ** Manettia bicolor |
| * Antigonon leptopus | ** Pandorea jasminoides |
| *** Arrabidaea magnifica | ** Podranea ricasoliana |
| * Bougainvillea (select color) | ** Passiflora mollissima |
| ** Clematis texensis | **    "    racemosa |
| *** Gloriosa superba | * Phaedranthus buccinatorius |
| *** Hidalgoa wercklei | *** Phaseolus coccineus |
| ** Kennedya rubicunda | *** Quamoclit pennata |

## HERBACEOUS PLANTS

** Alonsoa warscewiczi
** Amaryllis advena
*** Anacyclus depressus
 * Anemone coronaria
*** Antholyza aethiopica
*** Armeria maritima
*** Bessera elegans
 ** Brevoortia ida-maia
 * Brunsvigia rosea
*** Calostemma purpurea
*** Ceratotheca triloba
 ** Chrysanthemum morifolium
 ** Chironia linoides
*** Clianthus puniceus
 ** Cyrtanthus obliquus
 ** Dianthus (species)
*** Dierama pulcherrima
 ** Erodium corsicum
 * Erythrina herbacea
 ** Felicia petiolata
 * Gazania coccinea
 * Gerberia jamesoni
 * Geum bradshaw
 * Godetia grandiflora
*** Habranthus brachyandrus
*** Haemanthus coccineus
 * Heuchera sanguinea
 * Hibiscus mutabilis
 ** Lilium catesbaei
 **    "    pardalinum
 * Linum grandiflorum
 ** Lotus bertheloti
*** Lycoris radiata
*** Malvastrum coccineum

** Mathiola (select color)
*** Moraea pavonia
*** Mesembryanth. amoenum
 **    "    croceum
 **    "    deltoides
 *     "    floribundum
 *     "    roseum
 *     "    speciosum
 ** Nerine sarniensis
 ** Oenothera tetraptera
 * Oliveranthus elegans
 ** Oxalis crassipes
*** "    hirta
*** Papaver rupifragum
 * Penstemon gloxinioides
 * Petunia (select color)
*** Physostegia virginiana
 * Primula (check species)
*** Putoria calabrica
 ** Salvia (splendens
 ** Sparaxis (select color)
 ** Sprekelia formosissima
*** Streptanthera cuprea
*** Streptocarpus hybrids
*** Tagetes patula
*** Thymus broussoneti
 ** Tigridia (select color)
 * Tritonia crocosmaeflora
*** "    hyalina
 * Vallota speciosa
*** Veltheimia viridifolia
 * Vinca rosea
 * Watsonia iridifolia
 ** Zygocactus truncatus

## BLUE

Dark purple, violet and blue are cooling emotionally, soothing in principle. They are not as a rule the most telling in shadow.
They recede. They want a full play of light and the proximity of other
colors to bring out value. Undertones of purple may appear to better
advantage in the shade while violet or lavender is the very essence  of
the coloring of shadow, all much subdued. This series is really of a
retiring nature  as compared  with  the reds and suggestive of repose
and contemplation, not of action.

### TREES

** Bauhinia variegata
 * Bolusanthus speciosus
*** Ceanothus arboreus
 ** Guaiacum officinale

 * Jacaranda acutifolia
 ** Melia azedarach
 ** Paulownia tomentosa
*** Virgilia capensis

### SHRUBS

*** Amorpha fruticosa
*** Amphicome arguta
*** Barleria caerulea
 * Buddleja lindleyana
 **    "    magnifica
 * Ceanothus (species)
 * Ceratostigma (species)
 ** Chaenostoma grandiflorum
*** Clerodendrum myricoides
 ** Cuphea hissopifolia
 ** Dracaena stricta
 * Duranta (species)
 ** Echium fastuosum
 ** Eranthemum nervosum
*** Eupatorium sorditum

*** Gossypium sturti
 ** Grewia occidentalis
 * Hebe andersoni
 **    "    chathamica
*** "    hulkeana
*** Hibiscus huegeli
 * Iochroma lanceolatum
 ** Lantana montevidensis
 ** Lavandula officinalis
 ** Leucophyllum texanum
 ** Limonium perezi
 ** Melaleuca decussata
 * Nierembergia frutescens
 * Plumbago capensis
 ** Polygala dalmaisiana

*** Psoralea pinnata                  *** Sophora secundiflora
*** Puya alpestris                    *** Strobilanthes dyerianus
 ** Rosmarinus officinalis             ** Teucrium fruticans
 *** Salvia leucantha                 *** Thunbergia erecta
*** Solanum giganteum                   * Tibouchina (species)
   *     "     rantonneti              ** Trichostema lanatum
   * Sollya heterophylla                * Vitex agnus-castus
              *** Wigandia caracasana

## VINES

 ** Bauhinia corymbosa                *** Jaquemontia (species)
 ** Clematis crispa                    ** Passiflora caerulea
***    "     jackmani                   * Petrea volubilis
*** Clytostoma callistegioides        *** Phaseolus caracalla
 ** Cobaea scandens                    ** Pueraria thunbergiana
*** Cydista aequinoctialis              * Solanum wendlandi
  * Distictis lactiflora              *** Stizolobium deeringianum
  * Hardenbergia comptoniana            * Thunbergia grandiflora
  * Ipomoea (check species)          *** Wisteria (select color)

## HERBACEOUS PLANTS

*** Acanthus mollis                     * Iris xiphium
*** Adenophora lilifolia               ** Limonium bellidifolium
  * Agapanthus africanus             ***    "     sinuatum
  * Ageratum houstonianum             ** Linum narbonnense
 ** Ajuga reptans                      * Lobelia erinus
*** Allium caeruleum                 *** Machaeranthera tanacetifolia
*** Amellus lychnitis                 ** Lupinus (species)
*** Angelonia grandiflora            *** Moraea polystachya
 ** Aristea eckloni                  *** Muscari armeniacum
 ** Aster amellus                       * Myosotis alpestris
 ** Bletilla striata                  ** Nemophila menziesi
 ** Babiana stricta                     * Nepeta mussini
*** Borago officinalis                  * Nierembergia caerulea
 ** Brodiaea capitata                *** Nolana atriplicifolia
***    "     uniflora                *** Orthrosanthus multiflorus
  * Browallia americana              *** Oxypetalum caeruleum
 ** Callistephus (select color)      *** Parochetus communis
  * Campanula (species)               ** Pasithea caerulea
  * Centaurea cyanus                    * Petunia (select color)
  * Ceratostigma plumbaginoides       ** Phacelia whitlavia
 ** Charieis heterophylla            *** Salvia columbaria
  * Cichorium intybus                   *    "     leucantha
  * Cineraria (select color)          **    "     patens
*** Clitoria ternatea                *** Satureja montana
*** Collinsia (species)              *** Scabiosa columbaria
 ** Convolvulus mauretanicus          ** Scilla (species)
***    "         tricolor             ** Sisyrinchium bellum
*** Cyanella orchidiformis           ***    "         macouni
  * Cynoglossum amabile                 * Stokesia laevis
  * Delphinium ajacis                  ** Streptocarpus (select color)
 ** Dianella intermedia              *** Tecophilaea cyanocrocus
***    "       tasmanica                * Thalictrum dipterocarpum
 ** Dimorphotheca ecklonis            ** Thunbergia cordata
*** Dyschoriste oblongifolia            * Torenia fournieri
*** Eichornia azurea                  ** Trachelium caeruleum
 ** Exacum affine                    *** Tradescantia virginiana
  * Felicia amelloides               *** Tragopogon porrifolius
 **    "     bergeriana               ** Tulbaghia fragrans
***    "     tenella                 ***    "        violacea
  * Gloxinia (select color)            * Verbena (select color)
*** Heliophila pilosa                *** Veronica incana
  * Heliotropium arborescens           *     "     repens
*** Hyssopus officinalis              **     "     tourneforti
*** Iris alata                       *** Viola cornuta
  *   "  germanica (select color)      *    "   odorata
 **   "  japonica                     **    "   tricolor
 **   "  unguicularis                *** Wahlenbergia saxicola

PERIOD OF BLOOM---a grouping together of the more important flowering plants according to a general area of season, where a reasonably
definite period prevails. This disposition should be of service in
planning a reliable succession of bloom or where one wishes to concentrate on a single season. With species available for the entire year,
it can be recommended to use seasonable flowers in their natural time.
To crowd a plant off the course charted on habits of the centuries
may easily throw it off stride. Vagaries of season may carry it over
or cause it to precede its normal time, so that it may lose some of
its identification with the calendar, but not with the season. Note
the deepening of color as the year advances, pastels of spring and a
hardening over summer, to the wild and rich virility of autumn....
the composure, the inexcitability and rest of winter. Period limits
become more vague as the tropics are approached. Double flowers may
be depended upon for a somewhat longer flowering than their single
prototypes. Unusual heat will reduce a period, as coolness will prolong and it will be later, years of drought. One should check further
with FLOWERING HABITS for a more complete understanding.

## SPRING

This bustling and sprightful season is marked by a spontaniety in bloom that is reflected in the young thoughts and freshened
mood of man. Those plants of a herbaceous nature will be generally
lower in stature and the herbage softer and more refined than at any
other time of the year. There will be no difficulty in filling this
season with color, whether with tree, shrub or lower plant.

### TREES

| | |
|---|---|
| * Acacia dealbata | * Eucalyptus sideroxylon |
| ** " longifolia | * Grevillea robusta |
| *** " prominens | *** Magnolia soulangiana |
| *** Aleurites fordi | ** Melia azedarach |
| * Bauhinia variegata | ** Phytolacca dioica |
| xx Calophyllum inophyllum | *** Pittosporum phillyraeoides |
| *** Cassia grandis | *** Prunus campanulata |
| * Cercis siliquastrum | * Prunus persica |
| ** Eriobotrya demissa | * Pyrus calleryana |
| *** Erythrina poeppigiana | *** Virgilia capensis |
| *** Eucalyptus calophylla | ** Vitex lucens |

### SHRUBS

| | |
|---|---|
| * Abelia floribunda | ** Genista monosperma |
| *** Acacia alata | * Grewia occidentalis |
| * " armata | *** Hakea saligna |
| ** Anthyllis barba-jovis | *** Halimium ocymoides |
| *** Azalea austrina | *** Hebe hulkeana |
| *** Berberis gagnepaini | ** Hypericum floribundum |
| *** Boronia elatior | * Jacobinia pauciflora |
| ** Brunfelsia eximia | * Leptospermum laevigatum |
| * Calliandra (species) | *** Magnolia stellata |
| * Callistemon lanceolatus | ** Mahernia verticillata |
| ** Candollea cuneiformis | * Melaleuca armillaris |
| *** Cantua buxifolia | ** Osteomeles anthyllidifolia |
| ** Cassia artemisioides | *** Penstemon antirrhinoides |
| ** Ceanothus verrucosus | * Pittosporum tobira |
| *** Chamaelaucium ciliatum | * Raphiolepis (species) |
| * Choisya ternata | ** Ribes (species) |
| * Chorizema cordatum | ** Rondeletia cordata |
| ** Cytisus canariensis | ** Senecio petasitis |
| ** Daphne odora | ** Siphonosmanthus delavayi |
| ** Dendromecon rigida | *** Solanum giganteum |
| ** Diosma (species) | *** Sparmannia africana |
| ** Eranthemum nervosum | * Spiraea cantoniensis |
| * Escallonia montevidensis | *** Syringa persica |
| *** Eupatorium sordidum | * Tamarix africana |
| ** Fabiana imbricata | ** Tecoma smithi |
| ** Fouquieria splendens | *** Templetonia retusa |
| ** Fremontia californica | *** Thunbergia erecta |
| *** Fuchsia arborescens | * Viburnum tinus |

## VINES

* Beaumontia grandiflora
*** Clytostoma callistegioides
** Clematis armandi
* Distictis lactiflora
* Gelsemium sempervirens
* Hardenbergia comptoniana
*** Jaquemontia pentantha
** Jasminum mesneyi

* Pandorea pandorana
*** Petrea volubilis
** Philadelphus mexicanus
* Solandra guttata
** Solanum jasminoides
** Tecomaria capensis
** Thunbergia gibsoni
*** Wisteria floribunda

## HERBACEOUS PLANTS

** Ajuga reptans
* Anemone coronaria
** Antholyza aethiopica
* Antirrhinum majus
* Armeria maritima
** Babiana stricta
* Bergenia cordifolia
** Bletilla striata
** Bravoa geminiflora
** Brodiaea (species)
* Centaurea cyanus
** Centaureum venustum
* Cineraria cruenta
*** Clematis baldwini
** Clivia nobilis
*** Crinum americanum
** Cuphea roezli
*** Cyanella orchidiformis
*** Cyrtanthus mackeni
* Delphinium ajacis
*** Dodecatheon clevelandi
* Eschscholtzia californica
*** Felicia echinata
** Freesia refracta
* Gazania (species)
** Gladiolus colvillei
*** Hesperantha stanfordiae
*** Hymenocallis caribaea
* Iris (check species)
* Ixia maculata

*** Libertia grandiflora
** Linum grandiflorum
*** Lopezia albiflora
* Lotus mascaensis
** Lupinus (species)
*** Mesembryanth. browni
**            "        glaucum
*            "        laeve
*            "        speciosum
** Muscari armeniacum
** Nemesia strumosa
*** Neomarica gracilis
*** Ornithogalum thyrsoides
*** Oxalis cernua
** Papaver nudicaule
*** Pasithea caerulea
** Phacelia whitlavia
* Primula malacoides
* Ranunculus asiaticus
** Scilla peruviana
** Sisyrinchium bellum
* Sparaxis tricolor
* Strelitzia reginae
*** Streptanthera cuprea
*** Tecophilaea cyanocrocus
*** Tulbaghia fragrans
*** Tulipa (botanical species)
* Viola odorata
** Watsonia iridifolia
*** Zantedeschia rehmanni

## SPRING-SUMMER

Here is an overlapping of bloom which is desirable for continuity in color for the garden....this delightful time that lies in between. The precocious tenderlings of spring will have been discouraged by this first hint of summer with its heat and few will venture far into that season of hazard and risk. The following lists will supply likely materials for late spring and early summer.

## TREES

* Acacia floribunda
*** Bolusanthus speciosus
* Calodendrum capense
*** Cordia boissieri
** Crinodendron dependens
** Delonix regia
*** Drimys winteri

** Hymenosporum flavum
* Jacaranda acutifolia
*** Lagerstroemia speciosa
** Lagunaria patersoni
*** Lyonothamnus asplenifolius
* Magnolia grandiflora
* Metrosideros tomentosa

* Stenolobium velutina

## SHRUBS

* Abelia grandiflora
** Abutilon hybridum
** Adenocarpus viscosus
* Aster fruticosus
*** Buddleja globosa
** Calliandra tweedi
* Callistemon lanceolatus

** Candollea cuneiformis
*** Carpenteria californica
*** Ceanothus cyaneus
* Cestrum aurantiacum
* Cistus (species)
* Cotoneaster (species)
** Cytisus canariensis

* Datura suaveolens
** Daubentonia punicea
* Duranta repens
** Echium fastuosum
* Escallonia langleyensis
* Feijoa sellowiana
*** Fremontia mexicana
** Fuchsia triphylla
*** Gaya lyalli
*** Halimium ocymoides
* Hebe carnea
**    " menziesi
*** Helichrysum diosmaefolium
** Illicium anisatum
** Leonotis leonurus
* Ligustrum (species)
** Melaleuca decussata
*      " hyperiscifolia
***     " huegeli
** Michelia fuscata
*** Mirabilis californica

* Murraea exotica
** Ochna multiflora
*** Oncoba routledgi
** Penstemon antirrhinoides
* Photinia serrulata
*** Pickeringia montana
** Pimelea ferruginia
*** Prostanthera nivea
*** Prunus lusitanica
*** Psoralea pinnata
* Punica granatum
*** Ribes viburnifolium
* Romneya coulteri
** Rondeletia amoena
*** Rosa stellata
* Solanum rantonneti
* Spartium junceum
** Viburnum odoratissimum
** Weigela florida
*** Wigandia caracasana
*** Yucca aloifolia

## VINES

*** Anemopoegma chamberlayni
* Bougainvillea (varieties)
* Distictis lactiflora
** Doxantha unguis-cati
* Hibbertia volubilis
*** Kennedya rubicunda
* Lathyrus odoratus

*** Lonicera confusa
* Passiflora alato-caerulea
*** Petrea volubilis
** Rosa (check species)
** Solandra guttata
*** Solanum jasminoides
*** Thunbergia gibsoni

* Trachelospermum jasminoides

## HERBACEOUS PLANTS

** Abronia umbellata
** Acanthus mollis
*** Albuca minor
* Allium neapolitanum
*** Alstroemeria (species)
*** Amaryllis immaculata
* Antirrhinum majus
* Armeria maritima
* Aquilegia chrysantha
*** Arthropodium cirrhatum
*** Bloomeria crocea
*** Bletilla striata
* Brachycome iberidifolia
*** Breevortia ida-maia
* Campanula medium
** Canna generalis
** Centaurea cyanus
*** Chaenostoma hispidum
** Charieis heterophylla
* Clarkia elegans
* Cynoglossum amabile
*** Cypella lutea
*** Cyrtanthus obliquus
** Dianella (species)
* Dianthus deltoides
*** Dicentra chrysantha
*** Dicranostigma franchettianum
*** Dierama pulcherrima
* Dimorphotheca annua
*** Elisena longipetala
** Erythrina herbacea
** Exacum affine
*** Felicia bergeriana
* Francoa ramosa
*** Frankenia capitata laevis
* Gazania uniflora

** Gladiolus blandus
* Godetia grandiflora
*** Haemanthus katherinae
*** Helianthemum nummularium
* Hemerocallis aurantiaca
* Heuchera sanguinea
** Hymenocallis calathina
* Iris (check species)
*** Lilium elegans
** Lotus bertheloti
*** Mesembryanth. aequilaterale
*       " aurantiacum
**      " deltoides
*       " floribundum
***     " uncinatum
* Mimulus luteus
*** Moraea ramosa
** Nemophila menziesi
*** Neomarica gracilis
* Nepeta mussini
** Ophiopogon jaburan
*** Papaver rupifragum
*** Pasithea caerulea
* Pelargonium domesticum
*** Primula polyantha
*** Putoria calabrica
* Sedum prealtum
** Sidalcea malvaeflora
*** Sisyrinchium striatum
** Sprekelia formosissima
*** Thunbergia cordata
* Tulbaghia violacea
*** Ulmaria filipendula
** Viola gracilis
*** Wachendorfia thyrsiflora
** Xanthisma texanum

## SUMMER

While some bloom will be left over from the exuberance of the recent more temperate period, it is well to point for the devastating heat of midsummer with such plants as may surely be depended upon. A judicious selection from the following should pick up the sequence at near the beginning of the natural slump and care for the high-middle of the year in as good shape as may be expected.

### TREES

** Acacia pruinosa
** Agonis flexuosa
 * Albizzia julibrissin
 * Brachychiton acerifolium
** Castanospermum australe
** Chilopsis linearis
*** Chiranthodendron platanoides
** Clethra arborea
** Dais cotinifolia

*** Eucalyptus eremophila
**   "    erythrocorys
*** Jacaranda acutifolia
** Koelreuteria paniculata
*** Melaleuca genistifolia
 * Parkinsonia aculeata
** Peltophorum inerme
*** Stenocarpus sinuatus
 * Tipuana tipu

*** Virgilia capensis

### SHRUBS

*** Abelia schumanni
** Abutilon megapotamicum
** Azalea serrulata
*** Baeckia virgata
** Bauhinia acuminata
 * Belóperone guttata
** Buddleja magnifica
*** Calliandra porto-ricensis
** Callistemon rigidus
** Ceanothus cyaneus
 * Ceratostigma willmottianum
 * Cestrum nocturnum
*** Cienfuegosia hakeaefolia
 * Cistus (species)
 * Convolvulus cneorum
 * Daubentonia (species)
** Ervatamia coronaria
*** Erythrina bidwilli
 * Escallonia organensis
*** Fallugia paradoxa
*** Felicia echinata
 * Gardenia (species)
*** Halimium halimifolium
 * Hebe (check species)
*** Heimia myrtifolia

 * Hibiscus rosa-sinensis
** Hydrangea macrophylla
 * Hypericum (species)
** Illicium floridanum
 * Lagerstroemia indica
*** Malvastrum capense
*** Malvaviscus grandiflorus
 * Melaleuca decussata
 * Nandina domestica
 * Nerium oleander
** Nierembergia frutescens
** Pachystachys coccinea
 * Poinciana gilliesi
*** Ruellia devosiana
*** Salvia clevelandi
** Solanum rantonneti
 * Sollya heterophylla
*** Swainsona galegifolia
*** Tamarix chinensis
** Tecoma garrocha
*** Ternstroemia japonica
 * Thevetia nereifolia
*** Thryallis glauca
*** Turraea obtusifolia
** Vitex agnus-castus

### VINES

 * Antigonon leptopus
 * Bougainvillea (varieties)
*** Clematis crispa
** Distictis lactiflora
*** Eccremocarpus scaber
*** Hibbertia volubilis
** Hoya carnosa
** Ipomoea (species)
** Jasminum grandiflorum

 * Lonicera halliana
** Mandevilla suaveolens
*** Podranea ricasoliana
 * Passiflora (species)
** Phaseolus coccineus
** Solanum seaforthianum
*** Stigmaphyllon ciliatum
*** Thenardia floribunda
 * Thunbergia (species)

### HERBACEOUS PLANTS

*** Acantholimon venustum
*** Aphanostephus skirrobasis
 * Agapanthus africanus
** Angelonia grandiflora
*** Amellus lychnitis
*** Asclepias currassavica
** Baileya multiradiata
 * Bergenia ligulata
*** Billbergia pyramidalis
** Brodiaea coronaria

 * Brunsvigia rosea
*** Calostemma purpurea
** Campanula fragilis
 * Canna generalis
 * Centaurea (species)
*** Chlidanthus fragrans
 * Chrysanthemum carinatum
***    "    mawi
**     "    parthenium
*** Cladanthus arabicus

*** Clitoria ternatea
  * Clivia hybrids
*** Collinsia (species)
  * Convolvulus mauretanicus
 ** Cooperia drummondi
  * Coreopsis (species)
 ** Crinum (species)
 ** Crocosmia aurea
*** Cypella herberti
 ** Dianthus chinensis
 ** Diascia barberae
*** Emilia sagittata
*** Eucomis undulata
  * Euphorbia marginata
*** Frankenia capitata laevis
  * Gaillardia aristata
  * Gaura lindheimeri
  * Gerberia jamesoni
  * Geum (varieties)
 ** Gladiolus tristus
  * Gloxinia speciosa
 ** Gomphrena globosa
 ** Hedychium (species)
  * Hemerocallis aurantiaca
 ** Hesperaloe parviflora
*** Hymenocallis festalis
 ** Iris kaempferi
 ** Kalanchoe fedtschenkoi
  * Kniphofia uvaria
 ** Lavatera (species)
  * Lilium (species)
 ** Linum narbonnense
*** Littonia modesta
 ** Lonas inodora
*** Mesembryanth. aloides
 **         "         roseum
 ** Milla biflora

  * Mimulus luteus
*** Molucella laevis
*** Monardella lanceolata
 ** Moraea catenulata
  * Nierembergia rivularis
*** Nolana atriplicifolia
  * Oliveranthus elegans
 ** Othonna crassifolia
*** Oxypetalum caeruleum
 ** Pancratium (species)
  * Papaver rhoeas
  * Penstemon (species)
 ** Phormium tenax
 ** Physostegia virginiana
*** Polypteris hookeriana
*** Pterocephalis parnassi
*** Putoria calabrica
*** Rochea coccinea
 ** Santolina chamaecyparissus
*** Scabiosa graminifolia
*** Schizocentron elegans
  * Sedum (check species)
*** Streptocarpus hybridus
  * Thalictrum dipterocarpum
*** Thunbergia cordata
 ** Thymophylla tenuiloba
*** Thymus broussoneti
 ** Tigridia pavonia
  * Tulbaghia violacea
 ** Ursinia anthemoides
*** Verbesina encelioides
*** Veronica incana
  * Vinca rosea
*** Wahlenbergia saxicola
  * Zantedeschia elliottiana
*** Zephyranthes grandiflora
  * Zinnia elegans

## SUMMER-AUTUMN

This is probably the most discouraging time of the entire year in the garden. Most plants that have been working under difficulties through midseason are worn with the struggle, while people have either gone on vacation or have declined in spirit themselves and let up. These are the dog days when all nature seems to pant....if the following have been considered, the gardener blows more easily.

### TREES

*** Acacia greggi
 **      " horrida
  * Albizzia lebbek
 ** Bauhinia grandiflora
 ** Calophyllum inophyllum
*** Colvillea racemosa

  * Erythrina humeana
 **      "      poeppigiana
 ** Eucalyptus caesia
  *      "      ficifolia
  * Parkinsonia aculeata
*** Sophora japonica

### SHRUBS

  * Abelia grandiflora
 ** Alseuosmia macrophylla
*** Anisacanthus wrighti
  * Bauhinia tomentosa
 ** Buddleja lindleyana
***      "      nivea
  * Cassia corymbosa
  * Ceratostigma willmottianum
  * Cestrum nocturnum
 ** Chaenostoma grandiflorum
*** Clerodendrum speciosissimum
 ** Daubentonia tripeti

 ** Ervatamia coronaria
  * Erythrina crista-galli
  * Escallonia langleyensis
*** Eucalyptus preissiana
  * Hamelia erecta
  * Hibiscus rosa-sinensis
  * Holmskioldia sanguinea
*** Itea ilicifolia
 ** Jasminum humile
 ** Leonotis leonurus
*** Ligustrum quihoui
*** Lonicera etrusca

*** Malvastrum capense          ** Tamarix pentandra
** Nierembergia frutescens      ** Tecoma garrocha
* Nerium oleander               *** Teucrium fruticans
** Phlomis fruticosa            * Thevetia nereifolia
*** Phygelius capensis          * Tibouchina semidecandra
* Plumbago capensis             *** Thryallis glauca
*** Salvia greggi               ** Vitex agnus-castus
** Solanum rantonneti           *** Zauschneria californica

### VINES

*** Agdestis clematidea         *** Pandorea jasminoides
* Antigonon leptopus            *** Polygonum auberti
*** Bauhinia corymbosa          ** Pueraria thunbergiana
* Bougainvillea (varieties)     ** Quamoclit (species)
** Boussingaultia baselloides   ** Rosa bracteata
* Calonyction aculeatum         *** Solandra longiflora
*** Clerodendrum thompsonae     * Solanum wendlandi
*** Cryptostegia grandiflora    ** Stephanotis floribunda
* Distictis lactiflora          ** Tecomaria capensis
                * Thunbergia grandiflora

### HERBACEOUS PLANTS

*** Acidanthera bicolor         ** Hedychium (species)
*** Allium pulchellum           ** Hunnemannia fumariaefolia
* Amarcrinum howardi            * Kniphofia uvaria
** Angelonia grandiflora        ** Limonium bellidifolium
** Asclepias currassavica       *** Lycoris (species)
* Begonia tuberhybrida          ** Nepeta mussini
*** Billbergia pyramidalis      *** Nerine filifolia
** Callistephus chinensis       * Nicotiana alata
* Campanula isophylla           ** Papaver rhoeas
* Centaurea cyanus              * Penstemon (species)
* Ceratostigma plumbaginoides   *** Pentas lanceolata
*** Chironia linoides           *** Physostegia virginiana
* Chrysanthemum maximum         ** Polyanthes tuberosa
** Convolvulus mauretanicus     * Salpiglossis sinuata
***     "       tricolor        ** Salvia (species)
*** Cooperia drummondi          ** Sanvitalia procumbens
* Coreopsis lanceolata          * Schizanthus wisetonensis
* Cosmos bipinnatus             *** Sedum sieboldi
* Dahlia pinnata                ** Stokesia laevis
** Dianthus chinensis           ** Trachelium caeruleum
*** Emilia sagittata            * Tritonia crocosmaeflora
** Euphorbia marginata          ** Tulbaghia violacea
** Gaillardia aristata          *** Ursinia anthemoides
*** Galtonia candicans          *** Vallota speciosa
* Gerberia jamesoni             *** Veronica incana
* Gloxinia speciosa             * Vinca rosea
*** Habranthus andersoni        *** Zephyranthes rosea
*** Haemanthus coccineus        * Zinnia elegans

### FALL FLOWERS

Many plants that have been unable to continue bloom through
summer will rise to the occasion again with the freshening influence
of autumn, usually with a lesser display. Those which have taken their
time in coming along are ordinarily tall, very likely to be coarse in
texture and pungent, with other gross habits which place them in the
back of the border. This is not necessarily a season for melancholia.
It may be crisp and fresh, vital in its own right and rich in color.
Sterility at this time will be the result of neglect or poor planning or both.

### TREES

* Acacia podalyriaefolia        ** Eucalyptus ficifolia
** Ceratonia siliqua            ***     "       nutans
** Chorisia speciosa            * Parkinsonia aculeata
*** Colvillea racemosa          *** Peltophorum inerme
* Erythrina humeana             * Stenolobium stans
*** Eucalyptus calophylla       *** Terminalia catappa

## SHRUBS

** Abelia floribunda
*** Ardisia paniculata
* Azalea indica
*** Brachysema lanceolatum
** Buddleja magnifica
* Calliandra inequilatera
* Camellia sasanqua
*** Cassia nairobensis
** " splendida
* Ceratostigma griffithi
*** Chaenostoma grandiflorum
*** Correa pulchella
** Crotalaria agatiflora
** Cytisus canariensis
*** Elaeagnus pungens
*** Ervatamia coronaria
*** Euryops (species)
*** Eucalyptus grossa
** Euphorbia pulcherrima
** Felicia echinata
* Fuchsia triphylla
*** Genista monosperma

*** Hibiscus arnottianus
** " mutabilis
* Iochroma lanceolatum
*** Jacobinia carnea
* Jasminum humile
*** Leonotis leonurus
** Nierembergia frutescens
*** Osmanthus ilicifolius
*** Phlomis fruticosa
* Plumbago capensis
** Salvia greggi
*** " sessei
* Solanum rantonneti
*** Sparmannia africana
* Tecomaria capensis
* Teucrium fruticans
* Thevetia nereifolia
*** Thryallis glauca
* Tibouchina semidecandra
*** Turraea obtusifolia
** Viburnum robustum
* Vitex agnus-castus

## VINES

*** Alseuosmia macrophylla
* Antigonon leptopus
*** Arrabidaea magnifica
* Bougainvillea (varieties)
*** Clematis texensis
* Distictis lactiflora

** Lonicera confusa
* Phaedranthus buccinatorius
*** Polygonum auberti
** Quamoclit (species)
** Rosa laevigata
** Solanum wendlandi

## HERBACEOUS PLANTS

*** Amaryllis advena
*** Anagallis linifolia
* Anemone japonica
** Aster amellus
* Antirrhinum majus
** Bessera elegans
* Callistephus chinensis
** Centaurea cyanus
*** Ceratotheca triloba
* Ceratostigma plumbaginoides
* Chrysanthemum morifolium
*** Cineraria cruenta
*** Cleome spinosa
* Coreopsis lanceolata
* Cosmos bipinnatus
* Dahlia (species)
*** Dimorphotheca aurantiaca
*** Euphorbia marginata
** Gaillardia aristata
* Gerberia jamesoni
*** Haemanthus albiflos
* Hedychium (species)
* Kniphofia uvaria
*** Ligularia kaempferi
* Limonium (species)

*** Machaeranthera tanacetifolia
** Nemesia strumosa
** Nerine bowdeni
*** " fothergilli
** Oxalis bowieana
*** Papaver orientalis
** Pentas lanceolata
* Petunia hybrida
** Polianthes tuberosa
** Salpiglossis sinuata
** Salvia (species)
** Sanvitalia procumbens
** Scabiosa atropurpurea
*** " caucasica
** Sedum sieboldi
*** Sternbergia lutea
* Stokesia laevis
* Strelitzia reginae
** Tigridia pavonia
* Tithonia rotundifolia
** Trachelium caeruleum
*** Tulbaghia (species)
** Ursinia anthemoides
* Vinca rosea
** Zephyranthes rosea

## SUCCULENTS

** Aloe vera
** Billbergia pyramidalis
* Crassula falcata
*** Dyckia sulphurea
* Euphorbia splendens
*** Hesperaloe parviflora

** Kalanchoe aliciae
** Mesembryanth. bolusi
*** " maximum
* Othonna crassifolia
** Puya alpestris
*** Umbillicus chrysanthus

* Zygocactus bicolor

## WINTER BLOOM

Some few plants find it possible to flower sometime during
the winter....although little enthused.  Many of this list, however,
are autumn  blooming  species,  flowers  that  stand  over  in  the  garden.
Others  are  early  types  that  cannot  wait  for  spring.   The  exposure
they must bear with and the severity of the season will have much to
do with the success of the following plants at that time.   They must
never, under any consideration be pruned or divided after midseason,
always in  early  spring,  if  flowering  is  to  be  complete,  or  even  to
fall within the period of winter.

### TREES

* Acacia baileyana
***    "   farnesiana
* Arbutus unedo
** Ceanothus arboreus
*** Chorisia speciosa
* Dombeya (species)
** Dracaena australis
** Erythrina humeana

*** Erythrina poeppigiana
** Eucalyptus stricklandi
*    "    torquata
* Pittosporum undulatum
*** Prosopis glandulosa
** Prunus campanulata
*** Pterospermum acerifolium
* Stenolobium stans

### SHRUBS

*** Agonis linearifolia
*** Arctostaphylos (species)
* Azalea indica
*** Beloperone californica
**          tomentosa
*** Bowkeria gerrardiana
* Calliandra inequilatera
* Camellia japonica
* Cassia artemisioides
***    "   nairobensis
**   "   splendida
* Ceanothus verrucosus
* Cestrum purpureum
* Chaenomeles japonica
* Chamaelaucium ciliatum
*** Colletia cruciata
** Coronilla glauca
** Correa (species)
** Crotalaria agatiflora
** Daphne odora
** Eranthemum nervosum
** Erica melanthera
*** Eriocephalis africanus
** Euphorbia splendens
*** Euryops (species)
** Fatsia japonica
** Fuchsia arborescens
*** Garrya elliptica
* Hakea laurina
** Hakea suaveolens
** Hibiscus arnottianus

*** Hibiscus huegeli
* Jacobinia (species)
** Jasminum floridum
*    "    mesneyi
* Leptospermum scoparium
*** Loeselia mexicana
*** Luculia gratissima
*** Mackaya bella
** Mahernia verticillata
* Medicago arborea
** Melianthus major
*** Nuxia floribunda
* Osmanthus fragrans
*** Phlomis fruticosa
* Pittosporum tobira
*** Podalyria sericea
* Raphiolepis (species)
** Ribes (check species)
** Rondeletia cordata
*** Ruellia devosiana
*** Sarcococca hookeriana
* Senecio petasitis
*** Sparmannia africana
* Tecomaria capensis
** Tecoma smithi
*** Templetonia retusa
** Thea sinensis
* Turraea obtusifolia
* Viburnum burkwoodi
***    "    fragrans
**    "    lucidum

### VINES

** Aloe ciliaris
** Alseuosmia macrophylla
*** Clematis balearica
* Hardenbergia monophylla
** Jasminum gracile
*** Passiflora manicata

** Podranea brycei
* Pyrostegia ignea
*** Securidaca diversifolia
** Solandra longiflora
*** Thunbergia laurifolia
*** Wisteria japonica

### HERBACEOUS PLANTS

** Allium triquetrum
*** Alonsoa warscewiczi
** Amaryllis aulica
** Anagallis linifolia
* Anemone coronaria
***    "    fulgens

* Antholyza aethiopica
* Aristea eckloni
* Bergenia crassifolia
* Billbergia nutans
*** Bravoa geminiflora
* Brodiaea uniflora

*** Canarina campanulata
*** Cheiranthus cheiri
**         "      mutabilis
* Cineraria cruenta
*** Clianthus puniceus
* Clivia miniata
*** Crinum americanum
** Cuphea roezli
* Cyclamen indicum
*** Cyrtanthus mackeni
** Dimorphotheca aurantiaca
** Dipidax ciliata
*** Erysimum perofskianum
* Freesia refracta
*** Galanthus bizantinus
** Helleborus lividus
** Hymenocallis caribaea
*** Iberis sempervirens
** Ionopsidium acaule
*** Iris alata
**    "   japonica
*    "   unguicularis
*** Lachenalia pendula
* Lopezia albiflora
* Malcomia maritima
** Moraea polystachya
** Muscari armeniacum
* Narcissus tazetta
** Nemophila menziesi
** Papaver nudicaule
*** Petasitis fragrans
* Primula kewensis

** Primula malacoides
* Ranunculus asiaticus
* Reinwardtia indica
** Salvia splendens
*** Scabiosa columbaria
*** Scilla hispanica
* Strelitzia reginae
** Tulbaghia fragrans
*** Veltheimia viridifolia
*** Verbena pulchella
* Viola (check species)
* Zantedeschia aethiopica

## SUCCULENTS

** Aeonium arboreum
* Aloe arborescens
*     "   candelabra
***    "   humilis
***    "   plicatilis
**    "   salmdyckiana
* Crassula argentea
**     "      monticola
*** Kalanchoe blossfeldiana
** Mesembryanth. filicaule
*       "      linguiforme
** Othonna crassifolia
** Sedum guatamalense
***    "   pachyphyllum
* Zygocactus truncatus

BLOOMING HABITS---apart from fixed time or color may be taken into consideration and is actually a necessary consideration in completing the picture of the floral year. Knowing the ways of a plant, the gardener will encourage activity at the proper time, recognizing rest periods when they appear and letting up in culture accordingly. Exceptional or untimely offerings in bloom are usually acceptable and can sometimes be assisted into a larger completion. Know which plants are able and willing and place them where they will do the most good. The removal of seed heads, or better, the flowers before the seed has set, has an important bearing on behavior of the plant and on next years crop. This is especially true of herbaceous plants.

## PERPETUAL BLOOM

An ambitious caption perhaps, yet practically possible under suitable conditions of warmth and correct handling. These plants may be expected to flower well over the span of the months and with a reasonable continuity at peak. They may be fairly marked seasonally and appear in the relevant lists, but with flowers in evidence the intervening times. This is really a state or condition where the ranks are inclined to close and where repetition tends to merge as the tropics are neared....few truly everblooming plants here.

## SHRUBS

*** Acalypha californica
** Barleria caerulea
* Berberis darwini
* Brachysema lanceolatum
*** Brunfelsia floribunda
*** Chaenostoma hispidum
* Carissa grandiflora
* Cassia nairobensis
*** Cuphea platycentra
* Duranta repens
** Eucalyptus torquata
* Euphorbia splendens

*** Impatiens sultani
*** Ixora chinensis
*** Jacobinia carnea
*** Jasminum floridum
* Lantana (species)
** Malvaviscus arboreus
** Nierembergia caerulea
*** Parkinsonia aculeata
*** Pavonia multiflora
* Polygala dalmaisiana
** Rosmarinus officinalis
*** Ruellia devosiana

** Galvesia speciosa                 ** Salvia greggi
** Grewia caffra                     * Solanum rantonneti
*** Grevillea paniculata             * Strelitzia nicholai
** Hamelia erecta                    ** Streptosolen jamesoni
*** Heterocentron roseum             * Stenolobium velutina
*** Hibiscus huegeli                 ** Teucrium fruticans
 * Holmskioldia sanguinea            *** Thevetia nereifolia

## VINES

** Alseuosmia macrophylla            * Jasminum dichotomum
*** Allamanda hendersoni             *** Manettia bicolor
** Bauhinia galpini                  * Passiflora alato-caerulea
** Beaumontia grandiflora            * Phaseolus caracalla
 * Bomaria caldasiana                ** Phaedranthus buccinatorius
*** Cardiospermum halicacabum        *** Senecio confusus
*** Jaquemontia eastwoodiana         *** Stigmaphyllon ciliatum
          * Thunbergia gibsoni

## HERBACEUS PLANTS

 * Ageratum houstonianum             ** Lobelia erinus
 * Alonsoa warscewiczi               *** Oenothera tetraptera
 * Alyssum maritimum                 ** Othonna crassifolia
 * Arctotis (species)                *** Oxalis crassipes
 * Begonia semperflorens             ** Pelargonium hortorum
 * Calendula officinalis             **      "     peltatum
 * Chrysanthemum frutescens          * Penstemon gloxinioides
*** Crassula quadrifida              *** Pentas lanceolata
** Cymbalaria muralis                ** Petunia hybrida
*** Epidendrum obrienianum           ** Salvia splendens
** Erigeron karvinskyanus            *** Scabiosa caucasica
** Felicia amelloides                ** Verbena pulchella
*** Heliotropium arborescens         * Vinca rosea
*** Hemerocallis aurantiaca          *** Viola cornuta
** Limonium perezi                   ** Zantedeschia godefreyana

## INTERMITTENT BLOOM

These plants own to more or less well defined periods of
bloom, flurries of flowering recurring usually in response to a cultural stimulus, a marked seasonal impulse or a combination of the two.
The plant may be no more than erratic, with no set notions on the
subject and no fixed time for appearance. The list is composed largely of spring blooming materials that merely relax over the heat and
the cool of the year and become nearly constant during years of optimum weather experience, or as taken south.

## TREES

*** Acacia auriculaeforme            * Callistemon viminalis
 *    "    floribunda                *** Delostoma roseum
**    "    saligna                   ** Eucalyptus caesia
*** Blighia sapida                   *      "     ficifolia
          ** Peltophorum inerme

## SHRUBS

*** Abelia floribunda                ** Escallonia (species)
 * Abutilon (species)                *** Gardenia jasminoides
** Bouvardia humboldti               * Genista monosperma
** Calceolaria integrifolia          *** Grewia occidentale
** Calothamnus quadrifidus           ** Grevillea thelemanniana
 * Cassia tomentosa                  * Jasminum officinale
 * Cestrum (species)                 *** Leucophyllum texanum
 * Choisya ternata                   ** Lippia citriodora
** Cistus purpureus                  *** Mahernia verticillata
** Clerodendrum myricoides           * Murraea exotica
*** Cordia boissieri                 *** Pimelea ferruginia
** Cytisus canariensis               * Plumbago capensis
** Dendromecon rigida                * Poinciana pulcherrima
*** Ehretia elliptica                *** Vitex trifolia

### VINES

*** Arrabidaea magnifica
*** Cydista aequinoctialis
  * Lonicera confusa
 ** Osmanthus fragrans

*** Oxera pulchella
*** Pereskia aculeata
 ** Petrea volubilis
  * Rosa laevigata

### HERBACEOUS PLANTS

*** Adenphora lilifolia
 ** Alpinia speciosa
*** Amaryllis hybrids
  * Armeria maritima
*** Cooperia drummondi
*** Crinum giganteum
*** Dimorphotheca ecklonis
*** Eucharis grandiflora
*** Felicia tenella
  * Gazania uniflora

  * Gerberia jamesoni
 ** Habranthus brachyandrus
 ** Iris unguicularis
  * Moraea iridioides
*** Orthrosanthus multiflorus
 ** Penstemon heterophyllus
 ** Primula obconica
 ** Saintpaulia ionantha
 ** Salvia leucantha
 ** Tulbaghia violacea

 ** Zephyranthes (species)

### FREE FLOWERING

Plants for those who would luxuriate in color and who have
some idea as to how it should be used....the pulling of extremes together. The list is filled with such plants as are marked by an exuberance or profusion of bloom, or which by reason of some striking quality in the coloring of the flower, are conspicuous in the landscape.
They will not be over-planted in deference to good taste, although
there is much less likelihood of color clash out of doors, what with
unseen mists, motility of shadow in flux and especially in infinitely
changing light....palette of values unavailable to the interior.

### TREES

  * Acacia (species)
  * Bauhinia variegata
  * Brachychiton acerifolium
 ** Calodendrum capense
  * Cercis siliquastrum
*** Chorisia speciosa
*** Cochlospermum vitifolium
*** Colvillea racemosa
 ** Delonix regia
 ** Embothrium coccineum
  * Erythrina (species)

  * Eucalyptus ficifolia
 ** Grevillea robusta
  * Jacaranda acutifolia
*** Lagerstroemia speciosa
*** Magnolia soulangeana
  * Metrosideros tomentosa
 ** Prunus persica
 ** Stenolobium stans
*** Spathodea campanulata
*** Tabebuia serratifolia
 ** Tipuana tipu

### SHRUBS

 ** Abelia floribunda
 ** Abutilon megapotamicum
 ** Acacia cultriformis
  * Aster fruticosus
  * Azalea indica
  * Bauhinia galpini
 ** Brunfelsia exemia
  * Buddleja lindleyana
***     "     magnifica
 ** Callistemon lanceolatus
  * Candollea cuneiformis
 ** Cassia (species)
  * Ceanothus cyaneus
 ** Cestrum purpureum
 ** Chorizema cordatum
  * Cistus purpureus
  * Crotalaria agatiflora
  * Daubentonia (species)
  * Echium fastuosum
 ** Erythrina crista-galli
  * Euphorbia pulcherrima
*** Fremontia mexicana
*** Fuchsia arborescens
 **     "     triphylla

*** Gaya lyalli
*** Gilia rubra
 ** Halimium halimifolium
 ** Hebe imperialis
 ** Hibiscus rosa-sinensis
*** Hypericum henryi
  * Lagerstroemia indica
 ** Lantana montevidensis
*** Leptospermum scoparium
*** Luculia gratissima
*** Lupinus paynei
*** Magnolia stellata
*** Mahonia lomariifolia
*** Mahernia verticillata
  * Nerium oleander
  * Nierembergia frutescens
*** Pereskia bleo
*** Pimelea ferruginia
*** Poinciana pulcherrima
*** Polygala apopetala
  * Punica granatum
 ** Raphiolepis delacouri
  * Romneya coulteri
 ** Rondeletia cordata

*** Salvia sessei
*** Senecio petasitis
** Solanum rantonneti
*** Spartium junceum

** Streptosolen jamesoni
* Tibouchina semidecandra
* Turraea obtusifolia
*** Viburnum tinus

*** Weigela florida

## VINES

*** Arrabidaea magnifica
* Bougainvillea (varieties)
*** Clerodendrum thompsonae
** Distictis lactiflora
** Gelsemium sempervirens
** Hardenbergia comptoniana

** Passiflora manicata
*** Petrea volubilis
* Phaedranthus buccinatorius
* Pyrostegia ignea
* Solanum wendlandi
*** Trachelospermum fragrans

## HERBACEOUS PLANTS

*** Agapanthus africanus
* Ageratum houstonianum
** Amaryllis hybrids
*** Anagallis linifolia
** Anemone coronaria
***     "    fulgens
* Antirrhinum majus
*** Aphanostephus skirrobasis
** Asclepias currassavica
** Aster amellus
*** Begonia scharfi hybrids
*     "     semperflorens
**     "     multiflora
*     "     tuberhybrida
* Bouvardia humboldti
* Brunsvigia rosea
*** Calendula officinalis
* Campanula medium
*** Chironia linoides
*** Chrysanthemum carinatum
*       "      morifolium
* Cineraria cruenta
*** Clitoria ternatea
* Clivia hybrids
*** Convolvulus mauretanicus
*** Coreopsis (species)
** Dianthus chinensis
** Dimorphotheca aurantiaca
*** Emilia sagittata
** Erythrina herbacea
* Eschscholtzia californica
** Felicia bergeriana
* Gazania splendens
*** Gloriosa superba
*** Gynura aurantiaca
*** Haemanthus katherinae
** Heliophila pilosa
*** Helleborus lividus
*** Littonia modesta
* Lotus mascaensis

*** Machaeranthera tanacetifolia
** Mentzelia lindleyi
*** Mesembryanth. amoenum
##       "      browni
*       "      speciosum
*** Michauxia campanuloides
** Moraea polystachya
*** Nerine fothergilli
* Nierembergia caerulea
*** Nolana atriplicifolia
*** Oxalis crassipes
** Penstemon (species)
** Petunia hybrida
*** Phygelius capensis
** Polypteris hookeriana
*** Primula malacoides
* Ranunculus asiaticus
** Reinwardtia indica
*** Rochea coccinea
** Rosmarinus Lockwood de Forest
*** Salvia patens
*** Sanvitalia procumbens
* Schizanthus wisetonensis
*** Selaginella uncinata
* Senecio confusus
*** Silene laciniata
*** Sisyrinchium macouni
** Sprekelia formosissima
* Streptanthera cuprea
** Tigridia pavonia
*** Tithonia rotundifolia
* Tritonia hyalina
*** Tropaeolum speciosum
* Vallota speciosa
** Venidium (species)
** Verbena peruviana
***       "     rigida
** Viola cornuta
*     "     tricolor
* Zinnia elegans

# DISTINCTIVE QUALITIES

Individuality in plant life is as marked as it is in other forms of life or modes of expression to one who observes and thinks beneath the surface. Distinction in form or pattern or manner of reaction to natural causes are of subjective value and may be appropriated to the purposes of the planter in advanced phases of garden or landscape design. Inert mass will be relieved by movement, as of the sway of a bough. The play of light and shadow softens harsh lines, interrupts the flatness of a monotonous surface and lends something of zest to the inanimate. Cold concrete then, becomes less impersonal. The contemplation of something that is striking is diverting and tends to focus the attention on a prepared mould emotionally. The picturesque is always stimulating and tends further, to awaken the perceptions through a quicker response of the observer. Then, it is, we see more clearly these other things about us, some with latent meanings, others with implications that dig more deeply than we know. To those conventional and practical minds, all such abstractions may appear overly subtle, if not a circumvention, and possibly a matter of honesty and truth. Yet they become very genuine when a fine effect in the landscape or an exquisite detail in a garden is analyzed, and pleasing emotions traced to known or simple origins. Contemporary thinking in architecture is having much to do with the direction these attitudes are taking in the landscape. There is much in this section for the architect as he views his structure in the abstract, and more as he carries it on to completion.

ARCHITECTURAL SENSE ---as expressed in fixed and frequently rather severe lines sharply delineated, an accent on which the eye will linger. No allusion is implied in the way of the building mass other than that of a comparative simplicity of effect, directness in appeal and the absence of superfluous or confusing detail. The particular uses to which these plants may be put usually involves some formality in feeling, yet not so strictly that some of them will not find value of contrast or accent in a naturalistic setting. It is from among such plants as these that the decorative arts take and conventionalize many of their motifs and artifacts.

| | | | |
|---|---|---|---|
| *** | Acacia cultriformis | * | Chamaerops humilis |
| * | Acanthus mollis | ** | Cirsium occidentale |
| *** | Acer oblongum | * | Cissus antarctica |
| ** | Agathis robusta | *** | "     capensis |
| * | Aeonium (species) | ** | "     striata |
| * | Agave attenuata | * | Cocculus laurifolius |
| *** | Ailanthus altissima | ** | Crassula argentea |
| * | Aloe candelabrum | * | Cupressus guadalupensis |
| *** | "    salmdyckiana | * | "     sempervirens |
| ** | Alpinia speciosa | *** | Dasylerion glaucophyllum |
| * | Anemone japonica | * | Datura sanguinea |
| ** | Anthyllis barba-jovis | *** | Dicentra chrysantha |
| * | Araucaria excelsa | ** | Doryanthes palmeri |
| ** | Arctostaphylos manzanita | * | Dracaena australis |
| * | Azara microphylla | ** | "     fragrans |
| *** | Bocconia frutescens | *** | Echeveria clavifolia |
| *** | Callitris robusta | ** | Epiphyllum oxypetalon |
| ** | Cercocarpus betuloides | * | Eriogonum giganteum |

155

*** Euphorbia lathyrus
  *      "      tirucalli
** Hedera canariensis
** Howea belmoreana
 * Hoya carnosa
** Hylocereus triangularis
 * Ilex cornuta
*** Iris foetidissima
*** Juniperus excelsa stricta
  *      "      torulosa
*** Kalanchoe beharensis
*** Kleinia tomentosa
 * Laurus nobilis
** Libocedrus decurrens
 * Magnolia grandiflora
*** Mahonia lomariifolia
*** Markhamia lutea
*** Melaleuca huegeli
 * Melianthus major
*** Momordica charantia

** Monstera deliciosa
 * Nandina domestica
*** Osmanthus ilicifolius
** Phoenix reclinata
*** Philodendron (species)
 * Phormium tenax
 * Phygelius capensis
*** Pittosporum phillyraeoides
 * Rhapis excelsa
*** Rhus lancea
*** Sansevieria (species)
** Sasa palmata
*** Sempervivum tectorum
** Taxus baccata stricta
 * Ternstroemia japonica
** Trachycarpus fortunei
*** Vitex lucens
** Yucca (species)
*** Xylosma senticosa
 * Zygocactus truncatus

ORIENTAL EFFECTS---plants that are in scale and feeling to suit an occidental conception and appreciation of the oriental in gardening. The symbolism and meaning in the use of materials in the Japanese garden are beyond the comprehension of most western planters, yet the precision and cunning application of detail, the delicate touch as of line and of form, or the whimsical use of the picturesque might well be used more conspicuously in their own gardens. Restraint is paramount. Repose and contemplation seem to be the ultimate in attainment....a lesson in living for the restless nordic. The flower as an object is more or less incidental and possibly to be deplored as a disturbing element, with its concept and any heedfulness of purely subjective significance. The miniature depends upon occasional large scale plants for the full effect in dwarfing. The following is inadequate, but attempts to list some of the more typical plants with which to work in these regions. Check with MINIATURE FORMS.

## TREES

 * Acacia baileyana
*** "      pendula
** Acer palmatum
*** Betula nigra
** Callitris robusta
*** Celtis australis
 * Cercis siliquastrum
*** Cinnamomum camphora
*** Cornus capitata
 * Cryptomeria elegans
*** Cupressus funebris
*** Firmiana simplex
 * Ginkgo biloba
 * Juniperus torulosa
*** Liquidambar formosana
** Pinus attenuata
 *    "    cembroides

*** Pinus patula
** Pinus pinea
 * Pittosporum phillyraeoides
** Podocarpus (species)
*** Prunus jaquemonti
 * Prunus persica
*** Pterospermum acerifolium
 * Salix babylonica
** Sciadopitys verticillata
*** Sinocalamus oldhami
 * Taxodium distichum
** Taxus baccata
*** Torreya taxifolia
*** Trachycarpus fortunei
** Ulmus parvifolia
*** Vitex lucens
** Zizyphus jujuba

## SHRUBS

*** Arctostaphylos glauca
 * Ardisia crispa
*** Artemisia albula
*** Arundinaria japonica
 * Aucuba japonica
 * Azalea obtusa
** Azara microphylla
** Berberis darwini
*** "      wilsoni

 * Camellia sasanqua
*** Ceanothus papillosus
** Cedronella canariensis
 * Chaenomeles japonica
** Clerodendrum speciosissimum
 * Corokia cotoneaster
*** Cotoneaster decora
**    "        microphylla
 *    "        pannosa nana

*** Cuphea platycentra
** Cycas revoluta
*** Damnacanthus indicus
** Dion edule
*** Elaeagnus pungens
* Euonymus japonicus
*** Euphorbia splendens
** Eurya japonica
* Fatsia japonica
*** Fuchsia magellanica
*** Gardenia jasminoides
*** Hibiscus mutabilis
* Hydrangea macrophylla
* Juniperus conferta
** Lagerstroemia indica
*** Ligustrum rotundifolium
** Magnolia stellata
** Mahernia verticillata
*** Mahonia pinnata
** Michelia fuscata
* Nandina domestica
* Osmanthus fragrans
**      "     ilicifolius

*** Osteomeles anthyllidifolia
*** Photinia glabra
* Phyllostachys aurea
*** Pittosporum tobira
** Prunus glandulosa
** Podocarpus totara
** Punica granatum nana
* Raphiolepis (species)
** Rhapis (species)
** Rosa wichuriana
** Russelia equisetiformis
* Sasa disticha
***     "    palmata
** Serissa foetida
** Skimmia japonica
*** Solanum pseudo-capsicum
*** Spiraea cantoniensis
* Ternstroemia japonica
** Thea sinensis
** Thujopsis dolobrata
*** Viburnum japonicum
**     "      odoratissimum
*** Viminaria denudata

*** Vitex agnus-castus


## VINES

** Antigonon leptopus
* Asparagus (species)
** Cissus hypoglauca
***     "    rhombifolia
*     "    striata
** Hardenbergia comptoniana
* Hedera helix
** Ipomoea (species)
** Kadsura japonica

* Lonicera halliana
*** Lygodium japonicum
** Rosa banksiae
* Parthenocissus lowi
*** Passiflora racemosa
*** Pueraria thunbergiana
*** Solanum seaforthianum
** Stauntonia hexaphylla
* Trachelospermum jasminoides

* Wisteria floribunda


## HERBACEOUS PLANTS

*** Achillea millefolium
* Anemone japonica
** Arenaria balearica
** Armeria maritima
* Aspidistra elatior
** Aster gracillimus
*** Begonia foliosa
* Briza maxima
** Calceolaria (species)
* Chrysanthemum morifolium
**      "      parthenium
*** Chusquea tessellata
*** Cichorium intybus
** Cyperus alternifolius
***      "     brevifolius
*      "     papyrus
* Dicentra spectabilis
*** Dicranostigma franchetianum
* Euphorbia marginata
** Hedychium coronarium
** Helxine soleiroli
* Hemerocallis aurantiaca
* Iris japonica
*     "   kaempferi
***     "   pseudacoris
**     "   xiphium
* Lilium auratum
* Liriope spicata
*** Mentha gatefossei

*** Miscanthus sinensis
** Moraea bicolor
*      "    iridioides
***      "    ramosa
* Narcissus tazetta
* Onychium japonicum
** Ophiopogon japonicus
** Papaver orientale
*** Pedilanthus tithymaloides
** Physalis alkekengi
* Primula sinensis
* Pteris serrulata
*** Rivina humilis
* Rohdea japonica
*** Sagina subulata
*** Sanguisorba minor
** Saxifraga sarmentosa
* Schizanthus wisetonensis
*** Scirpus cernuus
*** Selaginella denticulata
** Senecio mikanioides
*** Sisyrinchium striatum
*** Sternbergia lutea
*** Verbena pulchella
** Watsonia iridifolia
*** Zamia floridana
*** Zephyranthes (species)
** Zingiber officinale
* Zoysia tenuifolia

WIND FIGURATION---a list made up of hardy, rugged or self-willed
individuals, species that elect to resist continual or excessive wind
and as a result, take on and hold characteristic wind-blown shapes.
Obviously, this will be sought, and in fact obtained only in exposed
places where surroundings and total environment explains the distor-
tion. A saturation of salt in the air will accentuate and hasten this
development and hold the effect without help from the gardener.

| | |
|---|---|
| *** Acacia horrida | ** Griselinia littoralis |
| " verticillata | ** Hakea suaveolens |
| ** Arctostaphylos glauca | *** Hibiscus tiliaceus |
| ** Calophyllum inophyllum | *** Hymenanthera crassifolia |
| *** Calothamnus quadrifidus | * Juniperus chinensis (var.) |
| * Carissa grandiflora | ** Lagunaria patersoni |
| * Casuarina stricta | * Leptospermum laevigatum |
| ** Ceanothus grizeus | *** Lupinus arboreus |
| * Ceratostigma willmottianum | *** Lycium richi |
| ** Clusia rosea | * Melaleuca armillaris |
| *** Cneoridium dumosum | * Metrosideros tomentosa |
| * Coccolobis uvifera | * Noltea africana |
| * Coprosma baueri | * Pinus pinea |
| ** Cotoneaster pannosa nana | *** " radiata |
| * Cupressus macrocarpa | ** " torreyana |
| ** Cytisus canariensis | * Pittosporum tobira |
| * Dodonaea viscosa | *** Pyracantha coccinea |
| * Dovyalis caffra | * Raphiolepis (species) |
| * Eucalyptus lehmanni | ** Rhus integrifolia |
| *** " preissiana | *** Ribes viburnifolium |

ENGAGING BARK AND TWIGS---as an increment of interest in the open
landscape can be no more than incidental. Where the plant is under
close observation, however, as in the patio or near a path, it may take
some thought and part in composition. A branchy shrub that has been
pruned to develop a twiggy aspect stands out as against one of free
outline and indefinite shape, particularly when out of leaf and if
tinted. The matter of notable shape, color, unusual texture or markings are the considerations in compiling this list. Color in twigs
will be more pronounced in the sun.

| | |
|---|---|
| ** Acacia decurrens | ** Ipomoea setosa |
| ** " pycnantha | ** Libocedrus decurrens |
| * Acokanthera spectabilis | * Liquidambar styraciflua |
| ** Acer floridanum | *** Medicago arborea |
| *** Adenocarpus viscosus | * Melaleuca (check species) |
| ** Adenostoma sparsifolium | *** Melicocca bijuga |
| * Arbutus unedo | *** Myrsine africana |
| * Arctostaphylos (species) | *** Opuntia (check species) |
| ** Bambusa multiplex | *** Osmanthus (check species) |
| *** Bergerocactus emoryi | * Parkinsonia aculeata |
| * Betula nigra | * Pellaea andromedaefolia |
| ** Cercidium torreyanum | *** Pistacia simaruba |
| * Chorisia speciosa | *** Pittosporum eugenioides |
| ** Colletia cruciata | * " tenuifolium |
| ** Colvillea racemosa | * Platanus (species) |
| ** Correa (species) | *** Populus (check species) |
| *** Cudrania tricuspidata | *** Portulacaria afra |
| * Cytisus canariensis | *** Pteris tremula |
| ** Drimys winteri | * Quercus suber |
| *** Ebenopsis flexicaulis | *** Ribes viburnifolium |
| * Elaeagnus pungens | ** Ricinus communis |
| ** Eucalyptus (check species) | *** Rosa muscosa |
| *** Euphorbia grandicornis | ** Salix crispa |
| ** Firmiana simplex | ** Salvia farinacea |
| * Fouquieria splendens | *** Sarcococca hookeriana |
| ** Genista monosperma | * Solanum montanum |
| *** Griselinia lucida | * Spartium junceum |
| * Gynura aurantiaca | *** Tamarix aphylla |
| ** Hibiscus sabdariffa | ** Teucrium fruticans |
| *** Hymenanthera crassifolia | * Tristania conferta |
| *** Ilex vomitoria | ** Vitis voinieriana |

*** Xanthosoma bataviense

TROPICAL EFFECTS---plants of truly tropical feeling as distinguished from the sub-tropical which may be said to stress a more harsh or severe condition together with more aridity. This is usually expressed in terms of line, queer texture, sharp color or an abundancy of succulent growth, as in the exact and delicate bole of a narrow palm; the rank vegetation of a banana or heavy, long-reaching vines....liana like. It has to do with the subtle fascination of the tropics, its strange perfumes and gorgeous flowers. With some exceptions, these plants will want a warm, quiet place with much humus, very rich soil and ample moisture....high ground will be good insurance for chill or frost. Generally, these plants should be moved during warm weather and best just as growth starts in order that quick-rooting may be facilitated. Check with BORDERLINE SOUTH and HUMID REGIONS.

## TREES

| | |
|---|---|
| * Achras zapota | *** Dracaena australis |
| ** Acrocomia (species) | * Erythrina (species) |
| * Alsophila australis | ** Ficus lyrata |
| ** Archontophoenix cunningham. | ** Harpullia arborea |
| *** Bocconia frutescens | *** Homalanthus populifolius |
| * Brachychiton acerifolium | *** Lagerstroemia speciosa |
| * Brassaia actinophylla | *** Mangifera indica |
| *** Carica papaya | * Musa (species) |
| *** Cecropia palmata | ** Nyctanthes arbor-tristis |
| *** Chiranthodendron platanoides | *** Paulownia tomentosa |
| ** Chrysalidocarpus lutescens | ** Phoenix (species) |
| * Cibotium schiederi | * Phytolacca dioica |
| *** Cochlospermum vitifolium | *** Pterospermum acerifolium |
| *** Colvillea racemosa | *** Sabal palmetto |
| ** Delonix regia | *** Sinocalamus oldhami |
| * Dombeya wallichi | *** Spathodea campanulata |
| | * Strelitzia nicholai |

## SHRUBS

| | |
|---|---|
| *** Actinophloeus macarthuri | *** Pachystachys coccinea |
| ** Arundinaria japonica | *** Phyllanthus acidus |
| ** Arundo donax | * Phyllostachys aurea |
| * Bambusa multiplex | * Poinciana pulcherrima |
| * Beloperone guttata | ** Prostanthera nivea |
| ** Cestrum (species) | *** Psidium gwineense |
| * Codiaeum variegatum | ** Punica granatum |
| * Cycas (species) | *** Reinwardtia indica |
| *** Cyphomandra betacea | *** Rhapidophyllum histrix |
| *** Dion edule | ** Rhapis (species) |
| * Dracaena stricta | ** Ricinus communis |
| ** Eranthemum nervosum | * Ruellia devosiana |
| * Erythrina crista-galli | ** Sasa (species) |
| * Euphorbia pulcherrima | * Senecio petasitis |
| ** Fatsia japonica | *** Serenoa repens |
| ** Hamelia erecta | * Solanum montanum |
| ** Heterocentron roseum | *** Sparmannia africana |
| * Hibiscus rosa-sinensis | ** Streptosolen jamesoni |
| *** Ilex paraguariensis | * Tetrapanax papyriferum |
| *** Ixora chinensis | *** Thevetia thevetioides |
| ** Jacobinia (species) | ** Tibouchina semidecandra |
| *** Macropiper excelsum | *** Trevesia palmata |
| * Melianthus major | *** Tupidanthus calyptratus |
| ** Nandina domestica | ** Wigandia caracasana |

## VINES

| | |
|---|---|
| *** Abrus precatorius | * Fatshedera lizei |
| *** Allamanda hendersoni | *** Gloriosa superba |
| ** Aristolochia elegans | ** Hoya carnosa |
| ** Artabotrys odoratissimus | ** Hylocereus triangularis |
| * Beaumontia grandiflora | *** Jasminum dichotomum |
| * Bougainvillea (varieties) | * Monstera deliciosa |
| ** Clerodendrum thompsonae | *** Muehlenbeckia platyclada |
| *** Cydista inequinoctialis | *** Oxera pulchella |

*** Pandorea jasminoides          ** Stephanotis floribunda
  * Philodendron (species)         *** Syngonium podophyllum
 ** Petrea volubilis               *** Tetrastigma harmandi
*** Scindapsis aureus               * Trachelospermum fragrans
  * Solandra guttata               ** Urechitis lutea
  * Solanum wendlandi              *** Vanilla fragrans

## HERBACEOUS PLANTS

*** Acanthus montanus             *** Gynura aurantiaca
 ** Alonsoa warscewiczi           *** Haemanthus katherinae
  * Alpinia speciosa                * Hedychium coronarium
  * Alocasia macrorhiza            ** Helxine soleiroli
  * Amarcrinum howardi              * Kalanchoe (species)
 ** Aglaeonema simplex            ** Levisticum officinale
*** Aphelandra squarrosa           * Maranta leuconeura
*** Beaucarnia recurvata          *** Microlepia platyphylla
  * Bergenia cordifolia            ** Neomarica gracilis
  * Begonia (species)             *** Nephthytis afzeli
*** Bletilla striata              *** Peperomia sandesi
  * Caladium picturatum            ** Phormium tenax
  * Calathea roseo-picta           ** Pilea microphylla
*** Canarina campanulata           ** Polianthes tuberosa
 ** Canna generalis                * Polypodium mandaianum
  * Cineraria cruenta              ** Rheum rhaponticum
  * Colocasia antiquorum           ** Saintpaulia ionantha
*** Cortaderia selloana           *** Sansevieria zeylanica
  * Clivia nobilis                 *** Saururus cernuus
 ** Crinum (species)               ** Sprekelia formosissima
  * Cyperus (species)               * Strelitzia reginae
*** Dracaena terminalis           *** Talinum triangulare
 ** Dieffenbachia picta           *** Thalia dealbata
 ** Epidendrum obrienianum         ** Tigridia pavonia
*** Erythrina herbacea             ** Zamia floridana
 ** Euphorbia heterophylla          * Zantedeschia (species)
*** Guzmania cardinalis           *** Zingiber officinale
              * Zygocactus truncatus

ENLIVENING FACTORS---plants of agreeable natural form or structural composition; either fixed, rigorous, and set to strain the breeze
for a pastoral fantasia; or unrestrained, airy and light as regards
texture, grace in movement or the effect of parts in catching the eye.
In either case a natural attractiveness in the plants which follow
will be heightened in air movement from the standpoint of light, sound
or merely movement in itself. The purl of foliage as it moves in mass
or its flickering reflection of light are positive realities and closely allied as a part of the extrinsic values which one finds in the
landscape. These are basic in ones cantact with the natural.

## LIGHT

A kind of translucence in flowers, multi or two-toned, scaly
and frequently spined leaves in certain lights, bring about a hover-
ing radiance due to the shimmering manner in which light rays are
thrown off. It may be a glandular condition that brings about a minute dispersion that attracts, so as to illumine the area....and inner
thoughts of those who are impressionable and willing and able.

*** Abelia grandiflora             * Cissus hypoglauca
  * Acacia pruinosa                 * Coprosma baueri
*** Araujia sericofera             * Elaeagnus pungens
  * Asparagus asparagoides        *** Elaeodendron chinensis
  * Azara microphylla             *** Embothrium coccineum
 ** Baileya multiradiata           ** Fatsia japonica
 ** Berberis darwini               ** Gynura aurantiaca
 ** Caladium picturatum            ** Holmskioldia sanguinea
 ** Ceanothus cyanus               ** Hunnemannia fumariaefolia
*** "      papillosus             *** Leucadendron argenteum
  * Cercocarpus betuloides          * Lycium pallidum
*** Chrysophyllum caineto         *** Melaleuca nesophila

** Mirabilis californica
** Nerine coruscans
*** Odontospermum sericeum
*** Osmanthus americanus
*** Pasithea caerulea
*** Peltophorum inerme
 * Penstemon heterophyllus
** Pittosporum rhombifolium
 * Populus alba
*** Salix lasiolepis
 * Ternstroemia japonica
** Thuja orientalis
*** Torreya (species)
 * Tritonia hyalina
** Ulmus sempervirens
*** Westringia rosmariniformis

 * Vitex lucens

## SOUND

The soughing, the drift of air through the fineness of a pine tree; the restless twittering of poplar leaves or even the raucous rattling of the segments of a palm leaf, bears a soothing relation to the over-burdened nerves of mortals. To relax there is to open one's mind and sensitivity to muted whisperings, tide-born stirrings of well-being....much in the way one sleeps better with pattering rain.

 * Albizzia lebbek
 * Araucaria excelsa
** Arecastrum romanzoffianum
** Casuarina (species)
 * Cedrus atlantica
** Cupressus (species)
** Ficus religiosa
*** Hakea suaveolens
*** Juniperus silicicola
*** Melaleuca armillaris
*** Phoenix (species)
** Phormium tenax
 * Pinus (species)
 * Populus (species)
** Sapium sebiferum
*** Schinus molle
*** Thuja orientalis
** Torreya (species)

*** Yucca elephantipes

## MOVEMENT

The alternate blur and definition of an olive, due to bend-ing boughs in the wind or fluttering leaves in a lesser blow, make for briskness in the landscape, so that a normally stolid grouping may come to life. Or note the successive waves of rye grass in head, or long-stemmed ivy leaves across the dull face of a wall or high on a building and the meaning they give to blank spaces.

** Acacia pendula
 *     "    pruinosa
 * Agrostis nebulosa
** Albizzia julibrissin
 * Alnus (species)
 * Aquilegia chrysantha
*** Artemisia lactiflora
*** Arundinaria japonica
** Bambusa multiplex
** Betula nigra
 * Briza maxima
*** Bursaria spinosa
 * Callistemon viminalis
*** Chamaecyparis pendula
** Chilopsis linearis
 * Coix lachryma-jobi
** Cupressus funebris
 * Curculigo capitulata
 * Cyperus alternifolius
**     "    papyrus
 * Dahlia maxoni
** Diascia barberae
** Dierama pulcherrima
*** Eriogonum nudum
 * Eucalyptus caesia
 *      "     cladocalyx
**      "     erythrocorys
***     "     globulus
**      "     sepulcralis
***     "     viminalis
*** Eugenia supraaxillaris
*** Ficus religiosa
 * Gaura lindheimeri
** Genista monosperma
*** Hypericum floribundum
*** Jasminum mesneyi
** Leptospermum citrinum
*** Leucocoryne ixioides
** Lippia citriodora
 * Lolium multiflorum
*** Lyonothamnus asplenifolius
 * Maytenus boaria
 * Melianthus major
*** Moraea iridioides
 * Olea europaea
** Parkinsonia aculeata
 * Parthenocissus tricuspidata
*** Phalaris arundinacea
 * Phyllostachys aurea
** Pittosporum phillyraeoides
 * Podocarpus elongata
*** Poinciana gilliesi
*** Polygonum auberti
 * Populus (species)
*** Rhus lancea
** Sasa disticha
** Schinus molle
** Sinocalamus beechyanus
*** Stipa pennata
*** Tamarix aphylla
 * Thalictrum dipterocarpum
*** Thevetia thevetioides
** Ulmaria filipendula
*** Viminaria denudata
*** Virgilia capensis
 * Zizyphus jujuba

STRIKING CHARACTER---as exhibited in plants may be used legitimate-
ly to center attention or to counteract a developing monotony. These
plants are usually related to some vantage point or they may be grown
frankly as oddities....but obscured. This group is made up of plants
that are in some way or other unique, flower, leaf or stem. Some are
so extreme in the fantastic shapes they assume as to become absurdly
incongruous in a normal garden setting or landscape. The beginner may
be drawn to the uncommon or bizarre in materials and need not be discouraged in their use, if qualifications are pointed out and the matter of good taste examined and stressed.

## LARGE PLANTS

** Acacia greggi
* Agave attenuata
** Aloe salmdyckiana
** Amarcrinum howardi
*** Araucaria imbricata
*** Bauhinia variegata
* Beaumontia grandiflora
*** Begonia ricinifolia
** Brachychiton acerifolium
* Brassaia actinophylla
*** Carnegiea gigantea
** Caryota urens
** Chorisia speciosa
*** Clerodendrum siphonanthus
* Datura suaveolens
* Dracaena draco
*** Embothrium coccineum
** Erythrina crista-galli
* Eucalyptus macrocarpa
*** " pulverulenta
* Fatsia japonica
* Ficus lyrata
*** " religiosa
*** Ginkgo biloba
* Kalanchoe beharensis
*** Leucadendron argenteum

*** Liquidambar styraciflua
* Lonicera hildebrandtiana
*** Lyonothamnus asplenifolius
** Maclura pomifera
* Melaleuca leucadendra
** Melia umbraculiformis
** Phyllanthus acidus
*** Prosopis pubescens
*** Pterospermum acerifolium
** Puya alpestris
* Romneya coulteri
** Salix crispa
* Solandra guttata
** Solanum warscewiczi
*** Stenocarpus sinuatus
* Strelitzia (species)
* Strophanthus speciosus
* Tetrapanax papyrifera
*** Thevetia thevetioides
** Trevesia palmata
*** Trichocereus candicans
*** Tupidanthus calyptratus
*** Viburnum rhytidophyllum
** Vitex lucens
*** Wachendorfia thyrsiflorus
** Yucca brevifolia

## SMALL PLANTS

*** Abrus precatorius
** Acacia alata
* " cultriformis
** Acanthus (species)
*** Albuca minor
* Aloe plicatilis
* Anigozanthos flavida
*** Aristolochia elegans
* Beaucarnia recurvata
** Beloperone guttata
*** Billbergia pyramidalis
** Caladium picturatum
** Celosia (species)
* Cephalocereus senilis
* Cladanthus arabicus
** Clerodendrum thompsonae
*** Clianthus puniceus
** Clitoria ternatea
* Colletia cruciata
* Crotalaria agatiflora
* Cycas (species)
* Cynara scolymus
*** Cypella herberti
** Dasylerion glaucophyllum
*** Dion edule
** Eremurus robustus
** Eucomis undulata
** Euphorbia tirucalli
** Fouquieria splendens
** Garrya elliptica

* Gloriosa superba
*** Guzmania cardinalis
*** Haemanthus katherinae
*** Hidalgoa wercklei
** Kleinia articulata
* Kniphofia uvaria
*** Mesembryanth. bolusi
** Michauxia campanuloides
* Molucella laevis
** Momordica charantia
* Monstera deliciosa
*** Muehlenbeckia platyclada
*** Nolina parryi
*** Papaver orientale
* Passiflora (species)
** Phaseolus caracalla
* Philodendron selloum
** Phormium tenax
*** Rhapidophyllum histrix
*** Salvia carduacea
* Sasa palmata
** Senecio petasitis
*** Solanum montanum
* Strelitzia reginae
** Veltheimia viridifolia
*** Venidium fastuosum
** Yucca whipplei
** Zamia floridana
** Zoysia tenuifolia
* Zygocactus truncatus

THE PICTURESQUE---plants with a marked faculty for the vivid portrayal of the unusual. These are of singular import. They are stamped with an intangible something over and above mere beauty or interest, to border on the dramatic without being ostentatious. The thought or quality involved is not only pleasing, it so impresses as to persist in the consciousness to vitalize in memory a fine experience in contacting the natural. Age is necessary in most of these plants to bring out the rich individualism, while some require the discipline of inclement surroundings. Full value in the landscape will depend on a solitary function adjusted to some simple plan or effect.

* Acacia baileyana
ⅱ ⅱ ⅱ Adenostoma sparsifolium
** Alsophila australis
*** Araucaria bidwilli
* Arbutus unedo
** Arctostaphylos manzanita
** Calophyllum inophyllum
*** Carnegiea gigantea
*** Casuarina lepidophloia
* Cedrus libani
** Chamaecyparis lawsoniana
* Chamaerops humilis
** Chorisia speciosa
*** Cissus hypoglauca
* Coccolobis uvifera
* Cocculus laurifolius
** Crassula argentea
*** Cupressus funebris
**    "    guadalupensis
*    "    macrocarpa
** Cycas circinalis
** Delonix regia
* Dracaena australis
** Drimys winteri
*** Epiphyllum oxypetalon
** Erythea armata
* Eucalyptus cladocalyx
***    "    lehmanni
**    "    pulverulenta
* Ficus carica
** Harpephyllum caffrum
** Hylocereus triangularis
*** Ilex paraguariensis

** Juniperus silicicola
*****    "    pachyphlaea
*    "    torulosa
* Leptospermum laevigatum
** Libocedrus decurrens
* Melaleuca armillaris
***    "    genistifolia
** Metrosideros tomentosa
* Nandina domestica
* Olea europaea
*** Opuntia tuna
** Osmanthus fragrans
* Phoenix reclinata
*** Pinus attenuata
*    "    pinea
**    "    torreyana
*** Pistacia chinensis
* Platanus racemosa
*** Plumeria emarginata
* Podocarpus elongata
***    "    totara
** Poinciana gilliesi
* Populus nigra italica
*** Pyracantha koidzumi
* Pyrus calleryana
*** Quercus lobata
*    "    virginiana
* Schinus molle
*** Sophora japonica
** Taxodium (species)
*** Taxus baccata
*** Torreya (species)
*** Trachycarpus fortunei

* Wisteria floribunda

# GARDEN MISCELLANEA

The garden, within its greater meaning and in its highest estate is a retreat and refuge....its conception and execution a living art. It is sanctuary for one's self and friends, associates....and such as flower regardless. It may well represent increasing neatness and order in this disorderly world, so immeasurably bereft of the civilizing influence claimed. It can be a chantry for spiritual lift, and still a place for plants. It is a place of mutual devotion for people, and where simply being, may be tranquil, serene, content. And it is under such conditions, in a return toward nature's setting that the thinking principle of the race may ultimately survive. The gathering together into appropriate groups, plants which normally fall into accepted types and phases of gardening is a study in associational values. These in turn are founded on micro-climatic, structural, and to a lesser extent on cultural considerations. Moreover, such an organization of the plant list to suit these types, calls for an examination of the species along historical and ecological lines. Certain plants do well under similar conditions and together, while another will do better where the demands on the soil, as an instance, are not identical. This adjustment of a plant to its neighbor is a fine point in the ultimate success of a garden and is always met, either with knowledge or by chance in a lasting arrangement. The work which follows does no more than suggest plants of like habits and similar demands, leaving of necessity the finer dispositions for the gardener to work out for himself and his own locality.

THE WILDFLOWER GARDEN---a patch-like place that is inherently weedy and which becomes increasingly unkempt as the summer advances....yet withal, some see visions there among the weeds. It seldom shows time and thought spent on its development. On the contrary, all effort in the direction of polish is misplaced and should be avoided. Follow the spontaneous patterns of nature and be correct. As a place it may have no definite boundary or border. Consider in way of an environment with directives for walking not always premeditated....trails, not paths....and if a vista or other natural feature occurs, it too should happen. This collecting of plants from the wild is always a question; whether of ethics or of the law, the gardener need not be concerned since the most satisfactory source is seed or the nursery. Many of the wildflower mixes will have a generous inclusion of the prototypes of garden species which may be overly generous. Select from the following to minimize untidiness and to rank this place somewhat above what may be termed a native planting. Check with NATIVE PLANTS and NATURALIZING SUBJECTS for further treatment of the subject.

## WOODY PLANTS

| ------EAST------ | ------WEST------ |
|---|---|
| *** Allophyton mexicanum | ** Aster fruticosus |
| ** Aster fruticosus | *** Calycanthus occidentalis |
| *** Brachysema lanceolatum | * Carpenteria californica |
| * Calycanthus floridus | ** Ceanothus cyaneus |
| ** Carpenteria californica | * Clematis lasiantha |
| *** Ceanothus microphyllus | ** " texensis |
| * Chiococca alba | * Cytisus canariensis |
| *** Clematis cirrhosa | *** Dendromecon rigida |
| * " texensis | * Genista monosperma |
| ** Cytisus canariensis | ** Helichrysum petiolatum |

164

| | |
|---|---|
| *** Dodonaea viscosa | * Heteromeles arbutifolia |
| * Hamelia erecta | ** Hibiscus diversifolius |
| ** Helichrysum petiolatum | ** Leucophyllum texanum |
| ** Hibiscus diversifolius | *** Loeselia mexicana |
| * Hypericum aureum | *** Lonicera etrusca |
| ** Leucophyllum texanum | ** " implexa |
| ** Lonicera chinensis | *** Lycium pallidum |
| ** Lycium carolinianum | ** " richi |
| *** Mahernia verticillata | *** Malvastrum coccineum |
| ** Malvastrum coccineum | *** Penstemon antirrhinoides |
| *** Pittosporum heterophyllum | * Pittosporum heterophyllum |
| * Poinciana gilliesi | ** Poinciana gilliesi |
| *** Polygala apopetala | " Polygala apopetala |
| * Prunus cistena | ** Prunus ilicifolius |
| *** Ribes viburnifolium | * Rhamnus crocea |
| * Rosa laevigata | ** Ribes viburnifolium |
| *** Salvia greggi | ** Salvia greggi |
| * Sollya heterophylla | * Sollya heterophylla |
| *** Spartium junceum | * Spartium junceum |
| * Teucrium fruticans | ** Tecomaria capensis |
| ** Yucca aloifolia | * Teucrium fruticans |
| *** Zamia floridana | *** Yucca tenuistylis |

## HERBACEOUS PLANTS

| -------EAST------ | ------WEST------ |
|---|---|
| * Abronia umbellata | * Abronia umbellata |
| ** Adiantum capillus veneris | *** Adiantum emarginatum |
| *** Anemone blanda | *** Anemone fulgens |
| ** Aphanostephus skirrobasis | ** Aphanostephus skirrobasis |
| * Asclepias currassavica | * Asclepias currassavica |
| *** Baileya multiradiata | * Baileya multiradiata |
| * Brodiaea (species) | * Brodiaea (species) |
| * Centaurea cyanus | *** Centaurea cyanus |
| *** Centaureum venustum | *** Centaureum venustum |
| * Chaerophyllum dasycarpum | ** Chaerophyllum dasycarpum |
| * Charieis heterophylla | ** Charieis heterophylla |
| ** Clarkia elegans | * Clarkia elegans |
| *** Clitoria ternatea | ** Collinsia (species) |
| *** Collinsia (species) | ** Cooperia drummondi |
| * Cooperia drummondi | *** Coreopsis (species) |
| * Coreopsis (species) | ** Corethrogyne californica |
| ** Crinum americanum | *** Dicentra chrysantha |
| *** Dimorphotheca annua | * Dimorphotheca (species) |
| ** Dodecatheon clevelandi | ** Dodecatheon clevelandi |
| *** Eriogonum tomentosum | * Eriogonum nudum |
| * Erythrina herbacea | ** Erythrina herbacea |
| * Euphorbia marginata | *** Euphorbia marginata |
| ** Gaillardia aristata | *** Gaillardia aristata |
| ** Gaura lindheimeri | ** Gaura lindheimeri |
| * Gilia tricolor | * Gilia capitata |
| ** Godetia grandiflora | * Godetia grandiflora |
| *** Habranthus robustus | *** Habranthus andersoni |
| *** Heliophila pilosa | *** Heliophila pilosa |
| ** Heliopsis helianthoides | * Hunnemannia fumariaefolia |
| * Lilium catesbaei | * Lathyrus splendens |
| ** Limonium sinuatum | * Limonium sinuatum |
| * Linaria maroccana | ** Linaria maroccana |
| ** Linum grandiflorum | ** Linum grandiflorum |
| *** Lonas inodora | *** Lonas inodora |
| * Machaeranthera tanacetifolia | ** Machaeranthera tanacetifolia |
| ** Malcomia maritima | ** Malcomia maritima |
| *** Mimulus luteus | ** Mimulus brevipes |
| ** Mirabilis jalapa | ** Mirabilis californica |
| * Onoethera acaulis | ** Oenothera tetraptera |
| ** Oxalis (species) | * Oxalis (species) |
| *** Papaver rhoeas | *** Papaver rupifragum |
| *** Penstemon australis | * Pellaea andromedaefolia |
| ** Phlox drummondi | *** Penstemon cordifolius |
| * Physostegia virginiana | *** Phlox drummondi |
| ** Sanvitalia procumbens | ** Salvia columbaria |

*** Scilla hispanica               *** Sanvitalia procumbens
 ** Sidalcea malvaeflora            ** Scilla hyacinthoides
  * Sisyrinchium bermudiana          * Sidalcea malvaeflora
*** Stachys floridana               ** Sisyrinchium bellum
 ** Stokesia laevis                *** Stanleya pinnata
  * Tricholaena rosea               ** Tricholaena rosea
*** Viola gracilis                 *** Viola pedunculata
*** Woodwardia virginiana          *** Woodwardia radicans
*** Zephyranthes (species)           * Zauschneria californica


THE SWEET-HERB PLOT---for discriminating tastes, will enlarge the realm of the housewife. The culinary herbs provide her with a rare opportunity to league beauty at the kitchen door with an added zest and smoothness in her cookery. These simple seasonings are things the ancients knew and are still in the process of being discovered. They appeal in the first place to taste and when it is realized to what extent smell enters into taste and the vital effect of both in digestion, their place in the garden will be assured. Herbal oils mix readily with the peptic juices for less disturbance in digestion and a resulting sounder health-tone of the body. When drying the herbage for future use, gather early in the morning in order that the maximum of the volatile oils be conserved, taking the younger tips in preference to the older wood. Certain vegetables of ornamental value are included for such uses as they may find.

Anise
  Pimpinella anisum
Artichoke
  Cynara scolymus
Balm
  Melissa officinalis
Borage
  Borago officinalis
Burnet
  Sanguisorba minor
Caperberry
  Capparis spinosa
Caraway
  Carum carvi
Chervil
  Anthriscus cerefolium
Chicory
  Cichorium intybus
Chives
  Allium schoenprasm
Coriander
  Coriandrum sativum
Costmary
  Chrysanthemum balsamita
Cress
  Lepidium sativum
Curry
  Cuminum cyminum
Dittany, Crete
  Origanum dictamnus
Endive
  Cichorium endiva
Fennel
  Foeniculum vulgare
Garlic
  Allium sativum
Ginger
  Zingiber officinale
Hyssop
  Hyssopus officinalis
Leek
  Allium porrum
Lovage
  Levististicum officinale
Marjorum
  Majorana hortensis

Miners Lettuce
  Montia perfoliata
Mint
  Mentha spicata
Orach
  Atriplex hortensis
Parsley
  Petroselinum crispum
Penny-royal
  Mentha pulegium
Pot-marigold
  Calendula officinalis
Red-pepper
  Capsicum frutescens
Rhubarb
  Rheum rhaponticum
Rosemary
  Rosmarinus officinalis
Runner Bean
  Phaseolus coccineus
Sage
  Salvia officinalis
Salsify
  Tragopogon porrifolius
Savory, Summer
  Satureja hortensis
Savory, Winter
  Satureja montana
Shallot
  Allium ascalonicum
Spinach, New Zealand
  Tetragonia expansa
Succory
  Cichorium intybus
Sweet Basil
  Ocimum basilicum
Tansy
  Tanacetum vulgare
Tarragon
  Artemisia dracunculus
Thyme, Mother of
  Thymus serpyllum
Water Cress
  Nasturtium officinale
Yerba Buena
  Micromeria chamissonis

OLD FASHIONED GARDENS---persist in the mind, a memory, and a beautiful one for some, since our mothers were prone to grace their gardens in the first person and play at cards in the evening. The names of many plants have come down to us associated with this thought and while the eternally changing order involves larger and possibly more colorful blooms, much of the fragrance and simplicity they knew in the beginning has been lost. Here and there one finds a species, a recalcitrant that has been left to us by the plant breeders....not too much improved. Many of them carry back to colonial times. Here they are, a page of names out of the past for those who are interested. Tradition will not be easily submerged and the haunting flavor of that which follows, will not be lost on those who were brought up in a garden.

Abelia
  Abelia grandiflora
Bachelor Button
  Centaurea cyanus
Bleeding Heart
  Dicentra spectabilis
Boston Ivy
  Parthenocissus tricuspidata
Boxwood
  Buxus microphylla
Bridal Wreath
  Spiraea cantoniensis
Canterbury bells
  Campanula medium
Cherokee Rose
  Rosa laevigata
Cockscomb
  Celosia cristata
Daffodil
  Narcissus pseudo-narcissus
Damask Rose
  Rosa damascena
Dusty Miller
  Centaurea cineraria
Flag or Fleur di Lis
  Iris germanica
Flowering Quince
  Chaenomeles japonica
Forget-me-not
  Myosotis alpestris
Gardenia
  Gardenia jasminoides
Goldenfeather
  Chrysanthemum aureum
Heliotrope
  Heliotropium arborescens
Hollyhock
  Althaea rosea
Honeysuckle
  Lonicera halliana
Hydrangea
  Hydrangea macrophylla
Japonica
  Camellia japonica
Jessamine
  Jasminum officinale
Jonquil
  Narcissus jonquilla
Larkspur
  Delphinium ajacis
Lavender
  Lavandula officinalis
Lavender Cotton
  Santolina chamaecyparissus
Lilac
  Syringa persica
Love-lies-bleeding
  Amaranthus caudatus

Magnolia
  Magnolia grandiflora
Marigold
  Tagetes erecta
Mignon Amaryllis
  Amaryllis rutila
Mimosa
  Albizzia julibrissin
Molucca Balm
  Molucella laevis
Moss Rose
  Rosa muscosa
Nasturtium
  Tropaeolum majus
Oleander
  Nerium oleander
Pansy
  Viola tricolor
Periwinkle
  Vinca major
Pinks
  Dianthus chinensis
Redbud
  Cercis occidentalis
Rose Moss
  Portulaca grandiflora
Rose of Castile
  Rosa gallica
Rose of Sharon
  Hibiscus syriacus
Rosemary
  Rosmarinus officinalis
Scarborough Lily
  Vallota speciosa
Snowball
  Viburnum opulus sterile
Stocks
  Mathiola incana
Sweet Alyssum
  Alyssum maritimum
Sweet Sultan
  Centaurea moschata
Tuberose
  Polianthes tuberosa
Poker Plant
  Kniphofia uvaria
Virginia Creeper
  Parthenocissus henryana
Virginia Stock
  Malcomia maritima
Weigela
  Weigela florida
Wistaria
  Wisteria floribunda
Woodbine
  Lonicera sempervirens
Yellow Daylily
  Hemerocallis aurantiaca

SPANISH PATIO PLANTS---for use in connection with mediterranean types of architecture....largely a reconstruction. They will be representative of the species known to have been used about the early habitations, together with more recent material of like character. They may help in reproducing that special atmosphere of repose and simplicity, that un-hurried pace so characteristic of the time. This, however, takes more than plants to attain.  In the main, these are subtropical in flavor, playing to warm walls with color and cool greenery. Sun-odors prevail. Water adds a sparkling touch. The floor may be left to dirt or imported decomposed granite. It is usually paved, and there is no grass in the strictly spanish patio. Planting beds will be depressed, rather than raised, to catch the surface water, while pots of flowering plants will be everywhere, to arrange, move about and re-arrange to suit any vagrant fancy that the place should produce.  Yellow through orange-red predominates and species with a mediterranean background of dryness....could be prelude and unpleasant taste of a future California garden.

## TREES

| | | | |
|---|---|---|---|
| ** | Acacia farnesiana | * | Olea europaea |
| ** | Brachychiton acerifolium | ** | Parkinsonia aculeata |
| * | Citrus (check species) | *** | Persea americana |
| ** | Cupressus sempervirens | * | Phoenix dactylifera |
| ** | Delonix regia | ** | Phytolacca dioica |
| *** | Diospyros kaki | * | Pinus pinea |
| * | Erythrina humeana | ** | Quercus agrifolia |
| ** | Ficus carica | * | "      ilex |
| ** | Grevillea robusta | *** | "      suber |
| *** | Ilex perado | * | "      virginiana |
| *** | Juniperus excelsa | * | Schinus molle |
| * | Melia azedarach | *** | Strelitzia nicholai |
| *** | Musa sapientum | *** | Tipuana tipu |
| *** | Mimusops elengi | ** | Virgilia capensis |

## SHRUBS

| | | | |
|---|---|---|---|
| *** | Acalypha californica | *** | Mimulus puniceus |
| *** | Anisacanthus wrighti | *** | Mirabilis californica |
| * | Arbutus unedo | *** | Mitriostigma axillare |
| * | Buxus microphylla | ** | Myrsine africana |
| ** | Calocephalis browni | * | Nerium oleander |
| * | Cestrum nocturnum | *** | Odontospermum sericeum |
| *** | Chorizema cordatum | * | Osmanthus fragrans |
| *** | Convolvulus cneorum | ** | Phlomis fruticosa |
| ** | Cuphea roezli | *** | Phygelius capensis |
| * | Cytisus canariensis | ** | Poinciana gilliesi |
| *** | Danaë racemosa | ** | Prunus ilicifolia |
| * | Datura suaveolens | * | Punica granatum |
| ** | Daubentonia (species) | *** | Ricinus communis |
| * | Erica melanthera | ** | Romneya coulteri |
| ** | Eriogonum giganteum | * | Rosa gallica |
| * | Erythrina crista-galli | * | Rosmarinus officinalis |
| * | Fortunella japonica | *** | Salvia sessei |
| *** | Fouquieria splendens | ** | Senecio petasitis |
| *** | Fremontia mexicana | ** | Solanum rantonneti |
| ** | Fuchsia triphylla | ** | Spartium junceum |
| ** | Genista monosperma | *** | Streptosolen jamesoni |
| ** | Heteromeles arbutifolia | ** | Tamarix africana |
| * | Laurus nobilis | ** | Teucrium fruticans |
| ** | Lavandula (species) | *** | Ungnadia speciosa |
| * | Lavatera assurgentiflora | * | Viburnum tinus |
| ** | Leonotis leonurus | *** | Visnea mocanera |
| * | Lippia citriodora | ** | Vitex agnus-castus |
| *** | Mahonia nevini | *** | Yucca (check species) |

## VINES

| | | | |
|---|---|---|---|
| *** | Allamanda hendersoni | ** | Cissus capensis |
| ** | Antigonon leptopus | *** | Clematis balearica |
| ** | Bauhinia galpini | * | Hedera canariensis |
| * | Bougainvillea (varieties) | * | Holmskioldia sanguinea |
| ** | Boussingaultia baselloides | *** | Hylocereus triangularis |

  *   Jasminum grandiflorum          *   Phaseolus coccineus
 ***  Kennedya rubicunda              *   Quamoclit lobata
 ***  Littonia modesta               **   Rosa laevigata
 ***  Manettia bicolor               **   Senecio confusus
  *   Momordica charantia            **   Solandra guttata
 **   Philadelphus mexicanus        ***  Vitis (check species)

## HERBACEOUS PLANTS

 **   Acanthus mollis                 *   Limonium (species)
 **   Agapanthus africanus            *   Liriope spicata
  *   Althaea rosea                 ***  Lotus formosissimus
  *   Alyssum maritimum             ***  Malvastrum coccineum
 **   Angelonia grandiflora           *   Mathiola incana
 **   Argemone mexicana               *   Mentha spicata
 **   Arum italicum                 ***  Mesembryanth. aurantiacum
 **   Asphodelus albus               **      "        speciosum
 ***  Beaucarnia recurvata          ***  Milla biflora
 **   Begonia sutherlandi             *   Mirabilis jalapa
 **   Bouvardia humboldti           ***  Morisia monantha
 ***  Bravoa geminiflora              *   Narcissus pseudo-narcissus
 **   Brunsvigia rosea              ***  Nepeta mussini
 ***  Canarina campanulata           **   Nicotiana alata
  *   Capsicum frutescens             *   Oliveranthus elegans
 ***  Cedronella canariensis        ***  Oxypetalum caeruleum
 **   Cheiranthus mutabilis         ***  Pancratium (species)
 ***  Chorizanthe staticoides        **   Papaver rhoeas
 ***  Cladanthus arabicus             *      "     rupifragum
 **   Clivia miniata                  *   Pelargonium (species)
 **   Cortaderia selloana            **   Pellaea  (species)
 ***  Cryptanthus beuckeri          ***  Petasitis fragrans
  *   Cyclamen indicum                *   Polianthes tuberosa
 **   Davallia canariensis            *   Portulaca grandiflora
  *   Delphinium ajacis             ***  Rochea coccinea
  *   Dianthus caryophyllus          **   Scilla hispanicum
 **   Echium fastuosum               **   Sisyrinchium bellum
 **   Epidendrum obrienianum        ***     "       bermudianum
 ***  Frankenia capitata laevis       *   Solanum pseudo-capsicum
  *   Gaillardia aristata           ***  Streptanthera cuprea
  *   Gazania splendens               *   Tagetes erecta
 ***  Gynura aurantiaca               *   Thymus (species)
 **   Helleborus lividus            ***  Tithonia rotundifolia
 ***  Heuchera sanguinea              *   Tritonia crocosmaeflora
 **   Iris unguicularis               *   Tropaeolum majus
  *      "   xiphium                 **   Tulipa clusiana
  *   Kalanchoë flammula             **   Venidium fastuosum
 **   Kniphofia uvaria               **   Vinca major
 ***  Lathyrus splendens            ***  Viola cornuta
 ***  Lavatera olbia                ***  Woodwardia (species)
 **      "     trimestris           **   Zantedeschia aethiopica
  *   Lilium candidum               ***  Zingiber officinale


     WALL GARDENING----where a dry or rubble retainer is convenient in
handling differences in elevation. Here is a place to use plants which
if not particularly wanting dryness, will reach  back where moisture
is  inevitably  conserved.  They should adapt easily to the plane of
the wall. It is a place too, for those that demand perfect and unqual-
ified drainage. Allow only small openings between the stones, with a
limited soil pack, in order that the plant may be forced immediately
into the business of getting back of the rock. Stones must be of adequate size and balanced in laying, with gravity pulling into the bank.

## WOODY PLANTS

 ***  Calocephalis browni             *   Helianthemum nummularium
 ***  Capparis spinosa               **   Hypericum reptans
  *   Cistus corbariensis             *   Hyssopus officinalis
 ***  Clematis lasiantha             **   Jasminum parkeri
  *   Cotoneaster microphylla         *   Juniperus conferta
 **   Eriogonum rubescens             *   Lantana montevidensis
 **   Halimium ocymoides             **   Lopezia albiflora

| | |
|---|---|
| ** Mahernia verticillata | ** Salvia officinalis |
| *** Malvastrum coccineum | ** Santolina chamaecyparissus |
| *** Micromeria piperella | *** Satureja intricata |
| ** Muehlenbeckia axillare | * Teucrium prostratum |
| *** Pimelea coarctica | ** Thymus vulgaris |
| *** Putoria calabrica | *** Thomasia purpurea |
| * Rosmarinus prostratus | ** Zauschneria californica |

## HERBACEOUS PLANTS

| -----FACE----- | -----TOP----- |
|---|---|
| *** Acantholimon venustum | ** Alyssum maritimum |
| *** Antirrhinum asarina | * Antirrhinum majus |
| ** Asplenium trichomanes | *** Campanula poscharskyana |
| * Campanula fragilis | *** Cheiranthus mutabilis |
| ** Cymbalaria aequitriloba | ** Cymbalaria muralis |
| * Dianthus caesius | *** Delphinium nudicaule |
| ** " deltoides | * Erigeron karvinskyanus |
| ** Erodium chamaedryoides | * Erodium chrysanthum |
| *** " corsica | ** Gazania splendens |
| * Gazania uniflora | ** Moraea catenulata |
| *** Lysimachia nummularia | * Nepeta mussini |
| *** Nolana prostrata | *** Nolana atriplicifolia |
| ** Oenothera tetraptera | ** Oxalis crassipes |
| * Oxalis hirta | * Pelargonium peltatum |
| *** Saxifraga sarmentosa | ** Pellaea andromedaefolia |
| ** Thymus broussoneti | *** Ursinia anthemoides |
| *** Veronica pectinata | * Tunica saxifraga |

## SUCCULENTS

| | |
|---|---|
| ** Aloe eru | *** Mesembryanth. lehmanni |
| * " variegata | ** " linguiforme |
| * Byrnesia weinbergi | * " roseum |
| ** Crassula monticola | * Oliveranthus elegans |
| *** " perfossa | * Othonna crassifolia |
| ** Cyanotis hirsuta | ** Sedum lineare |
| *** Echeveria pulverulenta | *** " morganianum |
| *** Mesembryanth. browni | * Sempervivum tectorum |
| * " cordifolium | *** Stylophyllum orcutti |
| * " deltoides | *** Umbilicus chrysanthus |

ROCK GARDENS----specialized developments that may consist only of a group of rocks appropriately planted or one that may take on the added significance of what may be termed the rockery. This garden is limited in plan and size only by the builders imagination and pocket book, but wherever possible, should take on some special meaning in design or materials. The rock is primarily for environment and normally to be submerged in importance to the planting, although full advantage must be taken of any particular character the stone has to offer. Local rock is usually to be preferred. Every possible exposure and combination of moisture, shade and soil reaction will be made available for plants. The list pre-supposes drainage and clear ways for deep-rooting....soils on the lean side. Adverse factors here in the south are low altitude and the long season. Remember that lichen grows in the sun, mosses in the shade, and know that marked success in this effort means....a gardener, grown up.

## SHRUBS
Scale should be emphasized here as it is of considerable importance that woody plants be reconciled in size to the project. Their large function is to accent the rock mass at the right point or help with contour where the terrain is too flat, to mould in profile a feeling for elevation. In general they are for character and form, and larger specimens may be required for that purpose, rather than the typical species which follow.

| | |
|---|---|
| ** Aeonium decorum | * Convolvulus cneorum |
| * Azalea obtusa | ** Correa alba |
| *** Berberis gracilis | * Cotoneaster microphylla |
| * Calocephalis browni | *** Cowania mexicana |
| *** Ceanothus impressus | ** Cuphea (check species) |

```
** Daphne odora                    *** Mahernia verticillata
 * Diosma ericoides                *** Mirabilis californica
*** Eriogonum arborescens          *** Muehlenbeckia complexa
 * Euonymus microphyllus            ** Nierembergia gracilis
 * Halimium ocymoides              *** Pinus mugo
 * Hebe (species)                    * Punica granatum nana
** Helianthemum nummularium          * Raphiolepis ovata
*** Hymenanthera crassifolia         * Rosmarinus officinalis
 * Juniperus conferta               ** Santolina chamaecyparissus
***     "      pfitzeriana          ** Satureja montana
 **     "      tamariscifolia      *** Sedum prealtum
*** Kleinia tomentosa              *** Serissa foetida
 * Lavandula (species)               * Teucrium chamaedrys
 * Ligustrum rotundifolium         *** Thomasia purpurea
*** Limonium perezi                 ** Thymus nitidus
*** Lonicera pileata                ** Turraea obtusifolia
 ** Lopezia albiflora               ** Zauschneria californica
```

## HERBACEOUS PLANTS

Spreading plants inclined toward rank herbage must be eliminated or watched closely in growth and restricted before lesser ones have been smothered out. Large annuals that reseed very heavily will be omitted altogether and others thinned out as found necessary. Bulbs and tubers must also be in scale and compatible in culture with cramped space, and where they may undergo division or reduction when this becomes necessary.

### ANNUALS

```
** Adonis aleppica                  * Lobelia erinus
 * Alyssum maritimum               ** Lonas inodora
** Anagallis arvensis             *** Malcomia maritima
 * Arctotis acaulis               *** Papaver nudicaule
*** Campanula erinus              *** Sanvitalia procumbens
** Dimorphotheca aurantiaca       *** Sedum caeruleum
 * Felicia bergeriana                * Tagetes signata pumila
 * Gilia dianthoides                 * Torenia (species)
** Gypsophila elegans               ** Ursinia anthemoides
            *** Zaluzianskya capensis
```

### PERENNIALS

```
** Abronia umbellata               ** Moraea glaucopis
 * Acaena microphylla              ** Morisia monantha
*** Acantholimon venustum         *** Nertera depressa
** Aethionema coridifolium          * Nierembergia rivularis
 * Ajuga reptans                  *** Nolana atriplicifolia
*** Anacyclus depressus             * Onosma tauricum
** Anagallis linifolia            *** Paronychia argentia
** Aphyllanthes monspeliensis       * Primula polyantha
** Arenaria balearica               * Pterocephalus parnassi
 * Armeria maritima               *** Ranunculus gramineus
** Campanula fragilis             *** Sagina subulata
***     "      mayi                 * Satureja intricata
*** Ceratostigma plumbaginoides    ** Saxifraga sarmentosa
*** Chironia linoides             *** Schizocentron elegans
 * Dianthus (check species)         * Sedum (species)
** Eriogonum nudum                *** Scutellaria indica-japonica
 * Erodium chamaedryoides         *** Silene schafta
 **     "     chrysanthum          ** Sisyrinchium macouni
***     "     corsica             *** Streptocarpus hybridus
*** Felicia petiolata              ** Thymus serpyllum
** Gypsophila cerastioides         ** Tunica saxifraga
 * Heuchera sanguinea             *** Verbena rigida
 * Iris unguicularis               ** Veronica nummularia
*** Linum salsaloides nanum       ***     "      pectinata
** Lysimachia nummularia            *       "      repens
** Mentha gatefossei              *** Wahlenbergia saxicola
```

### FERNS

```
** Adiantum capillus-veneris        * Cheilanthes gracillima
***     "      emarginatum         ** Pellaea (check species)
 * Asplenium trichomanes          *** Pilea microphylla
```

### BULBS-CORMS-TUBERS

*** Allium triquetrum          *** Muscari armeniacum
*** Anemone blanda               * Narcissus cyclamineus
 **    " fulgens   * Oxalis bowieana
 ** Babiana stricta             **    "    crassipes
*** Bessera elegans            ***    "    hirta
 ** Brodiaea uniflora            * Scilla hispanica
*** Chionodoxa luciliae          * Sparaxis tricolor
  * Cooperia drummondi           * Sternbergia lutea
 ** Dodecatheon clevelandi     *** Streptanthera cuprea
*** Galanthus byzantinus        ** Tigridia pavonia
*** Hesperantha stanfordiae    *** Tulipa kaufmanniana
  * Lapeirousia cruenta        *** Zantedeschia minor
 ** Lilium elegans               * Zephyranthes (species)

### SUCCULENTS

 ** Aeonium tabulaeforme        ** Kalanchoe fedtschenkoi
*** Aloe humilis               ***    "    flammea
  *   " variegata    ***    "    glaucescens
  * Byrnesia weinbergi           * Mesembryanth. aloides
*** Crassula argentea           **    "      aurantiacum
  *   " falcata       ***    "      bolusi
 **   " impressa        *    "      deltoides
 **   " monticola      **    "      glaucum
 **   " nana            *    "      lehmanni
***   " perfossa      ***    "      tuberosum
 ** Cyanotis hirsuta             * Oliveranthus elegans
*** Dyckia sulphurea           *** Rochea coccinea
  * Echeveria (species)          * Sempervivum tectorum
*** Euphorbia truncata         *** Stapelia divaricata
 ** Gasteria (species)          ** Stylophyllum orcutti
 ** Haworthia (species)        *** Umbillicus chrysanthus

BOG PLANTING---where one makes the best of an irrigation seepage,
a bit of marshy ground, or deliberately turns the overflow of a water
feature to account in the continuance of an aquatic effect. One of
the prime necessities is through-drainage, yet any flow should not be
strong enough to do any washing or influence the temperature unduly
downward. These plants want the acid reaction of a peaty compost, and
the size of the area involved will naturally relate to the source of
water supply. Keep this in balance, with growth as nearly static as
possible for plant as well as in animal life.

### WOODY PLANTS

  * Alnus (species)             * Liquidambar styraciflua
*** Amorpha fruticosa           * Magnolia virginiana
 ** Baccharis halimifolia     *** Melaleuca ericifolia
 ** Betula nigra                *    "      leucadendra
*** Calycanthus floridus       **    "      styphelioides
 **   " occidentalis  * Persea borbonia
*** Cliftonia monophylla      *** Populus fremonti
 ** Cyrilla racemiflora         * Salix (species)
 ** Eucalyptus robusta        *** Taxodium distichum
*** Ilex cassine              *** Zamia floridama

### HERBACEOUS PLANTS

  * Acorus gramineus           *** Ludwigia mulertti
 ** Alisma plantago-aquatica     * Mentha pulegium
 ** Anemopsis californica      *** Menyanthes trifoliata
  * Arundo donax                 * Oenothera hookeri
  * Cyperus alternifolius       ** Orontium aquaticum
 **   " papyrus       ** Peltandra virginica
***   " rotundus       * Pontederia cordata
*** Dipidax ciliata             ** Sagittaria lancifolia
*** Hydrocotyle rotundifolia    ** Saururus cernuus
*** Iris hexagona                * Scirpus cernuus
  *   " kaempferi     ** Thalia dealbata'
 **   " pseudacorus  *** Wachendorfia thyrsiflora

WATER GARDENING---works its charm in any development any place. It is not exactly indigenous to some portions of these regions, yet even there, no valid excuse can be given not to gratify the urge to at least sink a tub for lotus. If water is precious, make the most of it. The first cost is the heaviest, upkeep being comparatively low and the sum total an investment in pure joy. When a happy balance is reached in the pool between plant and animal life, there is little to add and the less disturbance one gets along with, the more successful it will be. If one must clean out, February is the time. Localities with slowly moving, warm waters will make the most of the exceedingly beautiful, but tender tropical water lilies.

## SUBMERGED PLANTS

These plants are distinctly valuable not only in keeping the water clear by absorption of impurities, they release oxygen within the water and in other ways serve to bring about a more natural and balanced status of plant and fish occupation.

| | |
|---|---|
| *** Aponogeton fenestralis | *** Ranunculus aquatilis |
| ** Cabomba caroliniana | * Trapa natans |
| *** Hydrocotyle rotundifolia | ** Utricularia vulgaris |
| ** Myriophyllum proserpinacoides | * Valisneria spiralis |

## STATIONARY PLANTS

Here are plants that remain anchored in the box of the pool or bottom of the pond. The foliage will be either floating on the surface of the water or held erect above, to aid materially in blending the two apposed elements that constitute the shore line. This is especially important where the line is of concrete, as of a pool.

| | |
|---|---|
| *** Acorus calamus | *** Marsilea quadrifolia |
| * Butomus umbellatus | *** Menyanthes trifoliata |
| ** Caltha palustris | * Nelumbium nelumbo |
| ** Crinum americanum | * Orontium aquaticum |
| * Cyperus (check species) | ** Peltandra virginica |
| *** Dipidax ciliata | ** Pontederia cordata |
| *** Eichornia azurea | *** Sagittaria (species) |
| * Hydrocleys nymphoides | * Saururus cernuus |
| *** Hymenocaulis caribaea | * Scirpus cernuus |
| * Iris pseudacorus | *** Thalia dealbata |
| ** Jussiaea longifolia | ** Typha latifolia |
| ** Limnocharis flava | ** Wachendorfia thyrsiflora |
| ** Ludwigia mulertti | *** Zantedeschia aethiopica |

## FLOATING PLANTS

The plane of the water may bear up certain plants of buoyant nature where they flower and live a normal existence, the roots suspended in the water for nourishment. An increase in herbage that encroaches unduly on the area of free water can easily be removed. Most of these plants will root wherever they come in contact with soil, on the bottom, in very shallow water or at the shore-line.

| | |
|---|---|
| * Azolla caroliniana | *** Myriophyllum proserpinacoides |
| *** Ceratopteris pteridoides | ** Nymphoides indicum |
| * Eichornia crassipes | ** Pistia stratiotes |
| ** Hottonia palustris | *** Salvinia auriculata |
| *** Lemna minor | * Trapa natans |

## MARGINAL PLANTS

The planting about the pool or small pond should furnish some definite connection culturally, by association or contribute something in the way of atmosphere of the aquatic. They should be of some refinement and the value of reflection in the water may not be overlooked. A lush, rank growth is natural in such a place while a sapless, thirsty aspect is entirely out of keeping. Give these plants an extra ration of water around a well sealed pool.

| | |
|---|---|
| ** Acorus gramineus | ** Azara microphylla |
| *** Adiantum emarginatum | *** Blechnum serrulatum |
| * Ajuga reptans | ** Browallia americana |
| *** Amorpha fruticosa | * Caltha palustris |
| ** Alpinia speciosa | *** Camassia leichtlini |

*** Colocasia antiquorum
  * Crinum (species)
  * Cyperus (check species)
*** Dianella intermedia
 ** Dierama pulcherrima
  * Duranta repens
*** Frankenia capitata laevis
  * Hedychium (species)
*** Helxine soleiroli
  * Hemerocallis aurantiaca
 ** Iochroma (species)
 ** Ilex cassine
  * Iris (check species)
 ** Kniphofia uvaria

*** Lobelia erinus
  * Nandina domestica
 ** Micromeria chamissonis
*** Primula (check species)
*** Ruellia devosiana
*** Schizostylis coccinea
  * Scirpus cernuus
 ** Senecio petasitis
*** Strelitzia reginae
 ** Streptosolen jamesoni
*** Thalictrum dipterocarpum
*** Wachendorfia thyrsiflora
  * Zantedeschia aethiopica
 ** Zephyranthes (species)

## WATER LILIES

And other forms with floating parts where the root system is firmly fixed on the bottom, may be used to relieve the flatness of the surface and embellish with greenery and gorgeous bloom. Specific kinds are listed, but check Compendium and local tradesmen.

  * Aponogeton distachyus
 ** Brasenia schreberi
 ** Nelumbium nelumbo

  * Nymphaea capensis
***      "      lotus
 **      "      zanzibariensis

ROSE GARDENS----depend almost as much on layout or design for interest in the landscape, as upon the plants themselves. The rose is in the nature of an exhibit, colorful, disconcerting in its select beauty; yet with-al, limited to the showing of the individual bush, a manufactory for bloom and not for foliage mass. Everything is important in their growing, initial preparation of the soil, choice of varieties to suit location and most careful and exacting attention to culture. They want very good drainage, a friable topsoil overlying one that is fairly heavy, cool and on the acid side of neutral. They must have the sun, especially that of early morning....a little shade over mid-day good. Crowd a little for mutually inter-shading of the stems. See that they get sufficient and uniform irrigation, good fertility and a mulch of manure, especially over the season of heat. Institute a spraying program that keeps them clean....healthy foliage of prime importance. Among the great number available, the varieties that follow have been found practical for general use in these areas and it is hoped the dispositions below may help in making selections. Check further with local plantsmen....locality important.

## OLD ROSES

This list of time honored names will be familiar to people with any extended interest in the subject. These oldsters have withstood the test of the years. A rose may come into a certain vogue or popularity through the efforts of a good press agent, but only merit will carry it through to a ripe old age. There will be something of love and romance here, with poignant and pleasant memories recalled, to the deep and the quick. This should make their planting well worth an effort to locate and special nurseries will be found growing such as are not regularly carried in the nurseries.

Marechal Niel (Lemon yellow)          Lulu (Coral-apricot)
Radiance (Red or Pink)                Mrs. John Laing (Pink)
K. A. Victoria (Pearly White)         Ulrick Brunner (Red-carmine)
Gruss an Teplitz (Dark red)           Ophelia (Salmon-pink)
Hoosier Beauty (Scarlet)              Lolita Armour (Coral-red)
Frau Karl Druschke (White)            Maman Cochet (White or Pink)
Duchess de Brabant (Pink to Rose) Louise Catherine Breslau (Pink)
Isabella Sprunt (Yellow)              Mrs. Charles P. Bell (Shell-pink
Mme Eduoard Herriot (Copper)          Rose Marie (Rose-pink)
Caroline Testout (Pink)               Mrs. Aaron Ward (Low-yellow)
Anna de Diesbach (Pink)               Killarney (White or Pink)
Safrano (Apricot-yellow)              General Jaqueminot (Crimson)
Louis Philippe (Dark Red)             Joanna Hill (Apricot-yellow)
Marie Van Houtte (White)              Paul Neyron (Dark Pink)

Duchess de Brabant (Satiny-pink)      Bridsmaid (White)
Souv. de la Malmaison (Pearly-pink)   Mme. Lombard (Pink)
La Reine Victoria (Rosy-pink)         Perle des Jardins (Yellow)
Devoniensis (Golden Yellow)           Claudius Pernet (Pale Yellow)
Gloire de Dijon (Salmon and Amber)    Angel Pernet (Orange)

## WEATHER-WISE

This involves climate, with heat and dryness and degree of moisture in the air as prime factors. Coast communities and other sections of high humidity, will have more difficulty with mildew and will want to use the more resistant varieties, together with those which open well in coolness. Some roses fade unduly in hot dry places and lose their leaves prematurely, or open too soon and fail before their time. This will be found especially true of singles and semi-doubles or those of only six to ten or twelve petals. Those with thick serve better in heat; the thin petals are more lasting in coolness.

### HEAT-HARDY

Mirandy (Dark Red)
E. G. Hill (Bright Crimson)
Caledonia (white)
Nocturne (Dark Red)
Christopher Stone (Crimson)
Night (Very dark red)
Autumn (Orange)
Hinrich Gaede (Copper-Orange)
Etoile de France (Crimson)
Lord Charlemont (Crimson)
Claudius Pernet (Light Yellow)
Mrs. E. P. Thom (Clear Yellow)
Lady Margaret Stewart (Amber)
Feu Joseph Looymans (Apricot)
Etoile de Holland (Rosy Red)
Juno (Bright Pink, Silvery)
President Hoover (Pink Yellow)
Crimson Glory (Bright Crimson)
Chrysler Imperial (Red)
Tallyho (Bi-color Rose Pink)
New Yorker (Red)
Show Girl (Deep Rose Pink)
Charlotte Armstrong (Cerise)
Lowell Thomas (Clear Yellow)
Helen Traubel (Bronzy Orange)
Sutters Gold (Yellow Orange)
Dame Edith Helen (Pink)
The Chief (Flame Copper)
Katherine T. Marshall (Pink)

### COOL-HUMID

Louise Catherine Breslau (Pink)
Mrs. Charles P. Bell (Shell Pink)
Rose Marie (Rose Pink)
Girona (Red and Yellow)
Angel Pernet (orange)
Lady Hillingdon (Apricot Yellow)
Madame Butterfly (Light Pink)
Fred Edmunds (Orange)
Mrs. Sam McGredy (Copper Orange)
Mme. Eduoard Herriot (Copper)
A. R. Waddell (Salmon Orange)
Duchess of Athol (Golden Yellow)
Golden Emblem (Clear Yellow)
Frederico Casas (Yellow Pink)
Chief Seattle (Apricot Gold)
Diamond Jubilee (Buff)
Saturnia (Copper Yellow)
California (Ruddy Gold)
Talisman (Gold Pink Carmine)
Hearts Desire (Luminous Red)
Shot Silk (Cerise Salmon)
Betty Uprichard (Salmon Pink)
Grand Duchess Charlotte (Coral)
Mark Sullivan (Cerise)
Ville de Paris (Yellow)
Lowell Thomas (Yellow)
Buccaneer (Yellow)
La Jolla (Pink to Cream-gold)
Rubaiyat (Crimson

## ROSES FOR SCENT

The elegance of this flower is universally associated with its delightful and winning fragrance, which is variously described as fruity, spicy or suggestive of honey. This extra capacity to enthrall, however, is restrained or does not appear at all in some varieties. This leaves one disappointed or actually disturbed with a glorious flower without its heritage of perfume. These varieties are among the more outstanding in this respect.

Crimson Glory (Bright Crimson)
McGredys Ivory (Off-white)
The Doctor (Very large pink)
Vesuvious (Dark Red)
Lady Hillingdon (Apricot Yellow)
Tallyho (Bi-color Rose Pink)
Sutters Gold (Yellow Orange)
San Fernando (Dark Crimson)
Hearts Desire (Luminous Red)
Etoile de Holland (Rose Red)
Mirandy (Dark Red)
The Chief (Coral Copper)

Radiance (Pink or Red)
President Hoover (Pink Yellow)
Kitchener (Velvety Scarlet)
Mme. Jules Bouchet (Blush White)
Mark Sullivan (Cerise)
Portadown Fragrance (Pink)
William F. Dreer (Pink Yellow)
Dame Edith Helen (Bright Pink)
Gen. Douglas MacArthur (Red)
Imperial Potentate (Carmine)
Mme. Albert Barbier (Pale Pink)
Duquessa de Penaranda (Orange)

Texas Centenial (Rose Red)         Sweet Sixteen (Light Pink)
Sonata (Deep Pink)                 Mrs. P. S. DuPont (Yellow)
Girona (Red Yellow)                Saturnia (Copper Yellow)
Applause (Changing Red)            Sutters Gold (orange)
Madame Butterfly (Pale Pink)       Taffeta (Carmine Rose)
Rev. Page-Roberts (Buff Salmon)    Debonair (Yellow)
Lamarque (White)                   Katherine T. Marshal (Clear Pink)
Christopher Stone (Plush Scarlet)  Hadley (Velvety Crimson)
Countess Vandal (Salmon Pink)      Rubaiyat (Crimson)
Tawny Gold (Modified Gold)         New Yorker (Red)

## CUT FLOWERS

Whether grown for cutting alone or in the rose garden, it is always desirable and convenient to have roses that do not open too rapidly. Keeping qualities and the tendency toward long stems suggest these varieties.  Those with the most petals will serve longest in water and those cut in cool weather the more dependable in point of time....split or macerate the butt-end of the stem before plunging.

Etoile de Holland (Rose Red)        Dame Edith Helen (Bright Pink)
Feu Joseph Looymans (Apricot)       Catherine Cordes (Cherry Red)
Grand Duchess Charlotte (Coral)     Talisman (Gold Pink Carmine)
Etoile de France (Crimson)          Cecil Brunner (Rose Salmon)
Hadley (Velvety Crimson)            Sunkist (Orange Yellow)
Hoosier Beauty (Scarlet)            Charlotte Armstrong (Cerise)
E. G. Hill (Dark Red)               Sweet Sixteen (Light Pink)
Joanna Hill (Apricot Yellow)        Peace (Creamy Yellow Pink)
Mrs. P. S. DuPont (Yellow)          First Love (Dark Pink)
Mme Chiang Kai Shek (Yellow)        Texas Centenial (Rose Red)
Heinrich Gaede (Copper Orange)      Signora(Scarlet Orange)
Golden Scepter (Golden Yellow)      Sonata (Deep Pink)
Radiance (Red or Pink)              Editor McFarland (Clear Pink)
Tawny Gold (Modified Gold)          Helen Traubel (Bronzy Orange)
Crimson Glory (Bright Crimson)      Fred Howard (Yellow)
Capistrano (Clear Pink)             Nocturne (Dark Red)
Los Angeles (Yellow Pink)           Applause (Cherry Red)
Countess Vandal (Salmon Pink)       Show Girl (Deep Rose Pink)
Golden Rapture (Golden Yellow)      Taffeta (Carmine Rose)

## ROSES IN SHADE

Nearly all roses will benefit with some shade in the far south. However, they will brook little competition from the roots of trees.  A cast shadow during the middle of the day is ideal, when the color in flower and the depth and substance in foliage is improved. The thin-flowered varieties, those with fewer petals will benefit in greater degree.  The following  may  be used in as much as half shadow with very satisfactory results.

Mme. Butterfly (Light Pink)         Eclipse (Yellow)
Safrano (Apricot-safron)            Heinrich Gaede (Copper Orange)
Will Rogers (Dark Red)              Lulu (Coral Apricot)
Ville de Paris (Yellow)             Mark Sullivan (Cerise)
Lady Hillingdon (Apricot Yellow)    Nocturne (Dark Red)
A. R. Waddell (Orange Salmon)       Mme Henry Guillot (Flame Pink)
William F. Dreer (Pink Yellow)      Mrs. P. S. DuPont (Yellow)
Etoile de Holland (Rose Red)        Shot Silk (Salmon Pink)
Cecil Brunner(Rose Salmon)          Golden Rapture ( Golden Yellow)
First Love (Dark Pink)              The Doctor (Very large pink)
Crimson Glory (Bright Crimson)      Taffeta (Carmine Rose)

## CONFORMATION

A great deal of the beauty of a rose lies in the shape or form of the flower.  This is not only true of the bud; the manner in which it opens and holds itself has a bearing on the satisfaction with which it will be used in the garden and the success with which it will be shown. Very double blooms will be more apt to ball and fail to open in a cold damp place while the other extreme, the thin tenuous textures, will hold to shape longer there.

Sunburst (Apricot Yellow)
Golden Emblem (Clear Yellow)
Lady Hillingdon (Apricot Yellow)
Mrs. Aaron Ward (Low Yellow)
Claudius Pernet (Pale Yellow)
Etoile de Holland (Rose Red)
Charlotte Armstrong (Cerise)
Debonair (Yellow)
Catherine Cordes (Cherry Red)
Mme Henry Guillot (Flame Pink)
Girona (Red Yellow)
Signora (Scarlet Orange)
Eclipse (Pale Yellow)
Saturnia (Copper Red)
Dame Edith Helen (Bright Pink)
Peace (Creamy Yellow Pink)
Hadley (Velvety Crimson)

Show Girl (Deep Rose Pink)
Feu Joseph Looymans (Apricot)
Neige Parfume (white)
Golden Rapture (Golden Yellow)
Mrs. Sam McGredy (Copper Orange)
Mme Butterfly (Light Pink)
Freiherr von Marshall (Red)
Mrs E. P. Thom (Yellow)
Mabel Morse (Golden Yellow)
Mme. Albert Barbier (Pale Pink)
Hoosier Beauty (Scarlet)
McGredys Yellow (Light Yellow)
Rapture (Light Pink)
Helen Traubel (Bronzy Orange)
Sutters Gold (Orange)
Forty-niner (Bi-color Red Chrome)
Mirandy (Dark Red)

## DISEASE RESISTING ROSES

Roses are subject to many ailments, insect pests and fungous infections which take much of the joy out of their growing, when not handled with firmness and in time. Keep ahead of the pests and know the satisfaction of rich green leaves and perfect blooms, or set out the following for a running start in the race. It is not enough to spray at stated periods, because there should at all times be a film of protection on the foliage, old as well as new. This is so important that growth periods should be given close attention....watch individual plants and see that new growth is not exposed long.

Grand Duchess Charlotte (Coral)
Rapture (Light Pink)
Safrano (Apricot Yellow)
Charlotte Armstrong (Cerise)
Lowell Thomas (Clear Yellow)
Lady Hillingdon (Apricot Yellow)
Rubaiyat (Rose Red)
Etoile de Feu (Orange)
Peace (Creamy Yellow Pink)
Mrs. Lovell Swisher (Copper)
Mission Bells (Salmon Pink)
Ville de Paris(Light Yellow)
First Love (Dark Pink)
Sutters Gold (Yellow Orange)
Eclipse (Pale Yellow)

Golden Emblem (Clear Yellow)
Condesa de Sastago (Orange Red)
Imperial Potentate (Carmine)
Duchessa de Penaranda (Orange)
Mark Sullivan (Cerise)
Radiance (Red or Pink)
Mrs. E. P. Thom (Yellow)
Angel Pernet (Orange)
Shot Silk (Salmon Pink)
Fred Edmonds (Orange)
Girona (Red Yellow)
Golden Sceptor (Golden Yellow)
Sweet Sixteen (Light Pink)
Mrs P. S. DuPont (Yellow)
Debonair (Yellow)

## FREE FLOWERING ROSES

Selected varieties in the matter of blooming habits. These may be profusely flowering at times or scattering out more or less over the year. The greater number will produce heavily in the spring with a lesser display in the fall. It is well in this connection to remember that a rose to be at its best, requires a rest period, and full advantage must be taken in the far south of any natural hesitations that may appear....surely in winter, sometimes in summer.

California (Ruddy Gold)
Fandago (Deep Scarlet)
Lady Hillingdon (Apricot Yellow)
Peace (Creamy Yellow Pink)
Radiance(Red or Pink)
Picture (Sparkling Pink)
Talisman (Gold Pink Carmine)
Texas Centennial (Rose Red)
Solfratare (Sulphur Yellow)
Etoile de France (Crimson)
Mrs. E. P. Thom (Yellow)
Hearts Desire (Luminous Red)
Mrs P. S. DuPont (Golden Yellow)
Ville de Paris (Light Yellow)

Mme. Jules Bouchet (Blush White)
E. G. Hill (Dark Red)
Lowell Thomas (Clear Yellow)
Padre (Coppery Red)
Mme. Eduoard Herriot (Copper)
Angel Pernet (Pink Yellow)
President Hoover (Pink Yellow)
Los Angeles (Pink Yellow)
Helen Traubel (Bronzy Orange)
Chrysler Imperial (Red)
Mission Bells (Salmon Pink)
Eclipse (Pale Yellow)
New Yorker (Red)
Snow Bird (White)

First Love (Dark Pink)              Buccaneer (Yellow)
Debonair (Yellow)                   Sutters Gold (Orange)
Diamond Jubilee(Pale yellow)

## ROSES FOR MASSING

In a class of bush roses notably lacking in material for combining into groups for an effect in the landscape, the following hybrids may be appropriated for the purposes designated. They are sometimes called shrub roses; require nominal pruning and compete more or less satisfactorily with other plants. The better bedding varieties will be low and spreading and colorful, the flowering stem shorter and weaker. The hedge wants a strong upright growth while the border rose will have either or both characters in combination.

### HEDGES

Gruss an Teplitz (Dark Red)             Cinnabar (Orange Scarlet)
General Douglas MacArthur (Red)         Talisman (Gold Pink Carmine)
Ragged Robin (Bright Crimson)           Grand Duchess Charlotte (Coral)
Cherokee (White or Pink)                Pinocchio(Salmon Pink)
Rosenelfe (Pink)                        Chatter (Velvety Crimson)
Louis Filippe (Red Carmine)             Valentine (Bright Red)
Mme Eugene Resol (Pink Orange           San Fernando(Scarlet Red)
Hearts Desire (Luminous Red)            Dainty Bess (Single Pink)

### BEDDING

Shot Silk (Cerise)                      Cuba (Orange Scarlet)
Marie Van Houtte (White)                Independence Day (Pale Yellow)
Crimson Glory (Bright Crimson)          Los Angeles (Yellow Pink)
Red Letter Day (Scarlet)                Pinkie (Pale Pink)
Lady Hillingdon (Apricot Yellow)        Goldielocks (Yellow)
Rev. Page-Roberts (Buff-Salmon)         China Doll (Rose Pink)
Fashion (Salmon Pink)                   Mme. Henry Guillot (Flame Pink)
The Fairy (Pale Pink)                   Fred Edmunds (Orange)
Mrs E. P. Thom (Yellow)                 Fiesta (Striped Yellow on Red)
Wellesley (Light Pink)                  Lilibet (Rose)
Hortulanus Budde (Gold Red)             Circus (Yellow,Pink and Red)

### THE BORDER

Vogue (Dark Coral Red)              J. Otto Thilow (Large Pink)
Ma Perkins (Pale Pink)              Floradora (Scarlet Orange)
Lilibet (Pink)                      Summer Snow (White)
Mission Bells (Salmon Pink)         Pink Bountiful (Salmon Pink)
Carousel (Red)                      Juno (Clear Pink)

## CLIMBING ROSES

The bending neck is something of an asset here since one looks upward into the face of the flower. Many of the best and most popular of the bush roses are available in climbing form, as will be found in any commercial catalogue. Those which follow are normally to be had only as climbers. Some of the oldest are still the most beautiful, frequently available in the nursery trade.

Pauls Scarlet (Scarlet)             Ednah Thomas (Salmon Pink)
High Noon (Golden Yellow)           Banksia (Pink, White or Yellow)
Blaze ( Scarlet)                    Reine Marie Henryette
City of York (White)                Captain Thomas (Creamy yellow)
Mme Gregoire Staechelin             Cecil Brunner (Salmon Rose Pink)
Bell of Portugal (Large Pink)       Gold of Ophir (Old Gold Apricot)
Perle des Jardins (Yellow)          Kitty Kinninmonth (Large Pink)
Reve d'Or (Apricot)                 Rose Anne (Orange Apricot)

## SINGLE ROSES

Simple blossoms, the virgin blooming of the species for an interpretation of the unstudied lovliness of the wild rose in the garden. They may be used in support of the rose garden or tucked away in odd spots, here and there at random in a naturalistic planting. As a group, they accept more shade; more satisfactory in coolness.

| | |
|---|---|
| Dainty Bess (Rose Pink) | Cecil (Light Yellow) |
| Mermaid (Creamy Yellow) | Vesuvious (Dark Red) |
| Killarney (Pink or White) | Austrian Copper (Bronzy Scarlet) |
| Kitchener (Velvety Scarlet) | Ragged Robin (Bright Crimson) |
| Irish Fireflame (Gold Apricot) | Cherokee (Pink or White) |
| Irish Elegance (Bronzy Pink) | Lulu (Coral Apricot) |
| Red Letter Day (Scarlet) | Piccanniny (Deep Red or Maroon) |

THE CUTFLOWER GARDEN---assumes a plot of ground set aside for the purpose of growing plants solely for crops of flowers....in quantity. The growing habits or the form of many plants leave much to be desired in their use for garden effect. Where they afford satisfactory flowers for cutting, they may be relegated to this place out of the ornamental scheme. Here they can be given the special attention necessary to the development of superior bloom, and taken without disorganizing the appearance of the border or the routine of garden management. A high content of potash in fertilizer brings about a better coloring and superior keeping qualities.  Almost always, a shock such as a boiling water dip of the lower three inches of stem will increase keeping time.  A few plants may be included here for greenery to take indoors with the flowers. Check with EVERLASTING FLOWERS and CUTFLOWERS for a more complete picture.

| | |
|---|---|
| *** Alonsoa warscewiczi | *** Heliophila pilosa |
| *** Anemone coronaria | *** Hunnemannia fumariaefolia |
| *** Antholyza aethiopica | * Iris xiphium |
| * Antirrhinum majus | ** Ixia maculata |
| *** Arctotis stoechadifolia | * Lathyrus odoratus |
| * Asparagus asparagoides | ** Lavatera trimestris |
| ** " plumosus | * Limonium sinuatum |
| *** " virgatus | * Mathiola incana |
| * Artemisia albula | * Narcissus pseudo-narcissus |
| *** Browallia americana | *** Nephrolepis exaltata |
| ** Calendula officinalis | *** Nicotiana alata |
| * Callistephus chinensis | *** Papaver rhoeas |
| * Chaerophyllum dasycarpum | *** Penstemon gloxinioides |
| * Chrysanthemum (species) | *** Phacelia whitlavia |
| ** Clarkia elegans | * Piqueria trinervia |
| *** Coreopsis (species) | *** Polypteris hookeriana |
| ** Cosmos bipinnatus | * Ranunculus asiaticus |
| *** Crocosmia aurea | ** Salpiglossis sinuata |
| * Dahlia pinnata | *** Salvia farinacea |
| ** Delphinium ajacis | ** Scabiosa caucasica |
| * Dianthus caryophyllus | ** Sparaxis tricolor |
| ** Eschscholtsia californica | ** Tagetes (species) |
| * Euphorbia pulcherrima | *** Tithonia rotundifolia |
| *** Freesia refracta | ** Tritonia (species) |
| ** Gaillardia aristata | *** Tropaeolum majus |
| * Gladiolus hortulanus | ** Venidium fastuosum |
| ** Godetia grandiflora | * Watsonia iridifolia |
| ** Gypsophila elegans | * Zinnia elegans |

THE BULB GARDEN---for bulbs, bulbous and near bulbous plants, with appropriate tubers and others that may be grouped with and handled as such, included for foliage this place will lack. Here one may indulge that deep-seated longing born of the charm in marvelous texture and coloring, together with the peculiar interest that attaches to their growing. They are comparatively easy to handle, with much divergence in size and concept as to use....some adapted to regimentation for beds or presented naturally in broken drifts or broad masses. The soil should be fertile in this place, light in texture and always sure in way of drainage. A wealth of material is at hand in subtropical regions, with much of it being overlooked year after year while we spend our time trying to educate the so-called dutch bulbs, in the ways of the south.  Set them at least twice in depth the thickness of bulb,

generally more shallow as taken south....deeper in a light soil. All
of the following will be found if one looks well for them.

### SPRING BULBS

These southern regions miss much of the early spontaniety
that has endeared this class of plants to so many generations of gardeners. Most of these bulbs will serve very well here and many of them
are more at home than they are in northern gardens.  These species are
always set out in the fall or early winter.

| | |
|---|---|
| *** Allium triquetrum | *** Moraea ramosa |
| ** Alstroemeria chilensis | *** Muscari armeniaca |
| ** Anemone coronaria | * Narcissus (species) |
| * Babiana stricta | ** Ornithogalum (species) |
| *** Bravoa geminiflora | * Oxalis bowieana |
| * Brodiaea (check species) | ** " cernua |
| *** Calochortus albus | *** Pasithea caerulea |
| *** Camassia leichtlini | * Ranunculus asiaticus |
| ** Crinum americanum | ** Scilla peruviana |
| ** Cyrtanthus (species) | ** Sisyrinchium bellum |
| * Freesia refracta | * Sparaxis bicolor |
| *** Hesperantha stanfordiae | ** Sprekelia formosissima |
| *** Homeria collina | *** Streptanthera cuprea |
| *** Hymenocallis caribaea | *** Tecophilaea cyanocrocus |
| * Iris xiphium | *** Tritonia hyalina |
| * Ixia maculata | ** Tulipa (botanical species) |
| ** Leucocoryne ixioides | * Zantedeschia aethiopica |

*** Zephyranthes atamasco

### BULBS FOR SUMMER

Here are a number of strong-growing bulbs and tuberous rooted plants flowering generally through the middle of the season or
over-lapping either extreme.  They are more truly perennial in character as regards the top and usually bloom over a longer period of
time.  They are especially serviceable in the foliage they bring to
this planting and the dependable touch of color mid-season.

| | |
|---|---|
| * Agapanthus africanus | ** Galtonia candicans |
| * Allium (species) | * Gladiolus (species) |
| ** Alstroemeria (species) | *** Gloriosa superba |
| ** Amarcrinum howardi | * Gloxinia speciosa |
| * Amaryllis (species) | *** Habranthus brachyandrus |
| * Begonia tuberhybrida | * Hemerocallis aurantiaca |
| *** Bessera elegans | ** Hymenocaulis calathina |
| ** Bletilla striata | * Kniphofia uvaria |
| ** Bloomeria crocea | ** Lapeirousia cruenta |
| '** Boussingaultia baselloides | * Lilium (species) |
| *** Bravoa geminiflora | *** Littonia modesta |
| * Brunsvigia rosea | *** Lycoris radiata |
| ** Brevoortia ida-maia | *** Milla biflora |
| ** Brodiaea coronaria | * Mirabilis jalapa |
| *** Calochortus kennedya | * Moraea (species) |
| *** Calostemma purpurea | ** Oxalis crassipes |
| *** Chlidanthus fragrans | *** " hererei |
| *** Commelina coelestis | *** Pancratium (species) |
| * Cooperia drummondi | * Polianthes tuberosa |
| * Crinum (species) | *** Scilla hyacinthoides |
| *** Crocosmia aurea | *** Sisyrinchium striatum |
| ** Cyrtanthus obliquus | * Tritonia crocosmaeflora |
| * Dahlia pinnata | ** Tropaeolum speciosum |
| *** Dianella (species) | ** Vallota speciosa |
| *** Dierama pulcherrima | ** Zephyranthes grandiflora |

### FALL AND WINTER BULBS

Many bulbs are distinctly and dependably fall-blooming.
Some carry over from late summer while others may be pointed for  that
time culturally. These dramatic gusts of color may be carried over in
our thinking of winter in these southern lands and certain color may
be planned for this bleaker time. Spring planting will be normal.

| | |
|---|---|
| ** Allium triquetrum | * Amarcrinum howardi |

| | |
|---|---|
| \*\*\* Amaryllis advena | \*\* Gladiolus hortulanus |
| \*\*\* Anemone blanda | \*\*\* Hymenocallis caribaea |
| \*\*  "  fulgens | \*\* Leucojum autumnale |
| \* Antholyza aethiopica | \*\* Ligularia kaempferi |
| \*\* Begonia multiflora | \*\* Moraea polystachya |
| \*\*\* Bravoa geminiflora | \* Narcissus (species) |
| \* Brodiaea uniflora | \*\*\* Oxalis hererei |
| \* Clivia miniata | \*\*  "  hirta |
| \* Colchicum autumnale | \* Ranunculus asiaticus |
| \*\* Crinum americanum | \*\*\* Scilla hispanica |
| \* Cyclamen indicum | \*\*\* Sternbergia lutea |
| \*\* Cyrtanthus mackeni | \*\*\* Tulipa kaufmanniana |
| \*\* Dahlia maxoni | \*\*\* Veltheimia viridifolia |
| \*\*\* Galanthus bizantinus | \*\* Zephyranthes candida |

## COMPANION PLANTS

Recourse to bulbs in any garden should include the use of other planting, termed as above. This will benefit the bulb off-season, conceal the curing leaves and act as a cover for the ground, with additional color. These plants must be studied in relation to the bulbs they are to accompany. They may be permanent or temporary, but should be shallow-rooted to accomodate themselves to extra demands for space in the soil. Sprinkle; do not soak deeply out of the bulb season. It is recommended that the flowering of these plants be planned either before or after that of the bulb to avoid color competition or clash, at the same time drawing an effect out over a longer period of time. Check further with CASUAL PERENNIALS.

| TEMPORARY | PERMANENT |
|---|---|
| \*\* Ageratum houstonianum | \* Abronia umbellata |
| \* Alyssum maritimum | \*\* Acaena microphylla |
| \*\* Anagallis linifolia | \*\*\* Arenaria balearica |
| \* Brachycome iberidifolia | \*\* Campanula fragilis |
| \*\*\* Campanula erinus | \*\*\* Centaureum massoni |
| \*\*\* Charieis heterophylla | \* Cerastium tomentosum |
| \*\*\* Dimorphotheca aurantiaca | \* Convolvulus mauretanicus |
| \*\*\* Emilia sagittata | \* Duchesnea indica |
| \* Eschscholtzia californica | \*\*\* Felicia petiolata |
| \*\*\* Gilia dianthoides | \* Lotus bertheloti |
| \*\*\* Heliophila pilosa | \*\* Nepeta mussini |
| \* Linaria maroccana | \*\*\* Mesembryanth. cordifolia |
| \*\* Lonas inodora | \*\*  "  filicaule |
| \* Malcomia maritima | \*\* Origanum dictamnus |
| \* Myosotis alpestris | \*\*\* Sagina subulata |
| \*\* Nemesia strumosa | \* Sedum album |
| \* Nemophila insignis | \*\*  "  altissimum |
| \*\*\* Nolana prostrata | \*\*\*  "  lineare |
| \* Phlox drummondi | \*\*  "  sieboldi |
| \*\* Sanvitalia procumbens | \*\*\*  "  stahli |
| \*\* Sedum caeruleum | \* Thymus serpyllum |
| \*\*\* Torenia flava | \* Verbena pulchella |
| \*\* Ursinia anthemoides | \*\* Veronica pectinata |
| \*\*\* Veronica tourneforti | \*\*\* Viola cornuta |

THE PAVED GARDEN---with water, or more simply conceived in the thought of a court or patio, has its special charm as well as plants. These gardenesque floors may approximate the harshly utilitarian purpose of concrete as flagging or blocks, to introduce a flexible feeling. This is a nice yielding to the amenities in eye comfort with broken lines to a pattern, so that the inconvenience underfoot is soon forgotten. An appropriate planting will give either a verduous carpeting as an in-between seal or set the flatness with tufts of foliage that heave with bloom in season. Use a preponderance of these raised plants to the side out of circulation, leaving the lower forms for walking areas. Guard against the necessity of having to hurdle tall plants or slipping on succulent herbage and see that the floor has sufficient slope for surface drainage away from the walking areas.

| PROSTRATE | RAISED |
|---|---|
| ** Acaena microphylla | *** Achillaea argentea |
| * Ajuga reptans | ** Aphyllanthes monspeliensis |
| * Arenaria balearica | ** Armeria maritima |
| *** Cotula squalida | * Brodiaea uniflora |
| ** Crassula nana | * Campanula fragilis |
| *** Cymbalaria aequitriloba | *** Centaureum massoni |
| * Dianthus deltoides | * Dianthus caesius |
| * Dichondra repens | * Erodium chrysanthum |
| *** Erodium chamaedryoides | ** Festuca glauca |
| *** Gypsophila cerastioides | ** Heuchera sanguinea |
| ** Haworthia tessellata | *** Iris graminea |
| *** Linum salsaloides nanum | ** Jasminum Parkeri |
| ** Mentha requieni | ** Lapeirousia cruenta |
| *** Mesembryanth. filicaule | * Lobelia erinus |
| *** Muehlenbeckia axillare | *** Mesembryanth. lehmanni |
| ** Nertera depressa | **        "        deltoides |
| * Nierembergia rivularis | *** Micromeria piperella |
| ** Oxalis bowieana | *** Muscari armeniacum |
| *** Sagina subulata | ** Oxalis crassipes |
| * Satureja intricata | ** Pellaea densa |
| ** Sedum brevifolium | * Primula malacoides |
| *     "     dasyphyllum | *** Pterocephalis parnassi |
| ***   "     hispanicum | *** Putoria calabrica |
| *** Stachys corsica | ** Scilla hispanica |
| * Thymus serpyllum | *** Scutellaria indica japonica |
| *** Umbilicus chrysanthus | ** Sedum lineare |
| ** Veronica nummularia | * Sisyrinchium macouni |
| *     "     repens | *** Thymus nitidus |
| *** Wahlenbergia saxicola | ** Tunica saxifraga |
| * Zoysia tenuifolia | *** Zephyranthes rosea |

BIRD SANCTUARY---as a part of the overall thought of a planting or as a unit in itself, introduces an element of activity or animation, and perhaps song. The vocal joy and lively presence of birds about a place is closely interwoven in this amiable and bewitching companion-ship one finds in nature. They may be encouraged to sojourn in a loc-ality if plants which supply them food in quantity are used. They take the wild species in preference to the more domesticated kinds. A fur-ther appeal is protection from cats and predatory hawks. A tangled brushy growth is sufficient for this purpose and may shield the spot where water is placed. Anything that is done for birds is repaid many times over in the insect pests consumed and given back to the soil.

| GARDEN | LANDSCAPE |
|---|---|
| * Aquilegia chrysantha | ** Alnus (species) |
| ** Aster (species) | ** Arbutus unedo |
| ** Berberis (species) | ** Ardisia paniculata |
| * Carissa grandiflora | ** Betula nigra |
| ** Centaurea (species) | *** Broussonetia papyrifera |
| * Cestrum (species) | * Cotoneaster (species) |
| * Coreopsis lanceolata | *** Cudrania tricuspidata |
| ** Delphinium ajacis | *** Ehretia elliptica |
| * Eschscholtzia californica | * Elaeagnus pungens |
| * Gailardia aristata | ** Fremontia californica |
| * Hypericum (species) | *** Ilex (species) |
| ** Lepidium sativum | *** Juniperus (species) |
| * Linaria maroccana | * Lonicera (species) |
| * Linum grandiflorum | * Lycium (species) |
| *** Mahonia (species) | *** Melia azedarach |
| ** Parthenocissus tricuspidata | * Morus (species) |
| *** Putoria calabrica | *** Myrica (species) |
| * Pyracantha (species) | *** Phoenix dactylifera |
| ** Scabiosa (species) | ** Platanus racemosa |
| ** Solanum seaforthianum | * Prunus (species) |
| *** Stokesia laevis | *** Rhamnus (species) |
| *** Tagetes (species) | ** Rhus (species) |
| *** Venidium fastuosum | ** Viburnum (species) |
| *** Zinnia elegans | * Vitis (check species) |

THE PLANT HOUSE---usually made of lath, batten or other material
that adapts to an open structure in the protection of growing plants.
This is the sure procedure in raising delicate plants, exotics that
require modified light and shelter from wind and frost. Some species
which normally show no objection to sun, will improve in color under
lath or cloth and we have the seeming paradox of both sun and shade
lovers growing together in some luxuriance. A portion of the house
with glass layed in, will frequently widen its usefulness as to range
of plant material served. The soil is ordinarily prepared by a generous admixture of leafmould and peat for the modified texture and the
general preference of these plants for humus and an acid reaction.
Check with ACID PLANTS, FERNS and FERN ALLIES.

## WOODY PLANTS

| | |
|---|---|
| ** Abutilon megapotamicum | *** Lapageria rosea |
| *** Acanthus montanus | *** Luculia gratissima |
| *** Allamanda hendersoni | ** Lygodium japonica |
| ** Alsophila australis | *** Macropiper excelsum |
| * Ardisia crispa | ** Magnolia stellata |
| * Azalea indica | ** Manettia bicolor |
| *** Bouvardia humboldti | * Monstera deliciosa |
| ** Brunfelsia calycina | ** Nephthytis afzeli |
| * Calceolaria integrifolia | ** Pachystachys coccinea |
| * Camellia (species) | *** Passiflora racemosa |
| *** Collinia elegans | *** Pavonia multiflora |
| *** Crossandra infundibuliformis | * Philodendron (species) |
| * Daphne odora | *** Pomaderris apetala |
| ** Eranthemum nervosum | *** Rhapis excelsa |
| ** Fatsia japonica | * Ruellia devosiana |
| * Fuchsia (varieties) | ** Scindapsis aureus |
| *** Graptophyllum pictum | * Stephanotis floribunda |
| * Heterocentron roseum | ** Strobilanthes dyerianus |
| * Hoya carnosa | *** Syagrus weddelliana |
| ** Illicium anisatum | ** Thea sinensis |
| *** Ixora chinensis | *** Tibouchina elegans |
| * Jacobinia carnea | ** Thunbergia erecta |
| *** Trevesia palmata | |

## HERBACEOUS PLANTS

| | |
|---|---|
| * Achimenes longiflora | *** Gynura aurantiaca |
| *** Aglaonema simplex | *** Haemanthus puniceus |
| * Alocasia macrorhiza | ** Helleborus lividus |
| * Alstroemeria (species) | * Helxine soleiroli |
| *** Anigozanthos flavida | *** Hidalgoa wercklei |
| *** Anthurium andreanum | ** Impatiens sultani |
| * Begonia (species) | *** Kleinia ficoides |
| *** Beloperone guttata | * Ligularia kaempferi |
| ** Billbergia (species) | *** Lilium (species) |
| ** Bletilla striata | ** Lobelia erinus |
| *** Bomaria carderi | ** Maranta leuconeura |
| ** Browallia americana | * Myosotis alpestris |
| * Caladium picturatum | ** Nemesia strumosa |
| * Calathea roseo-picta | ** Nertera depressa |
| ** Calceolaria herbeohybrida | * Oliveranthus elegans |
| *** Canarina campanuloides | *** Oplismenus hirtellus |
| * Cineraria cruenta | ** Platycerium bifurcatum |
| * Clivia (species) | *** Pelargonium alchemilloides |
| ** Coleus blumei | ** Pentas lanceolata |
| * Cymbalaria muralis | ** Peperomia sandersi |
| * Cyrtomium falcatum | ** Pilea microphylla |
| *** Dicentra spectabilis | * Primula (species) |
| * Dieffenbachia (varieties) | ** Rivina humilis |
| * Epidendrum obrienianum | *** Rohdea japonica |
| * Epiphyllum oxypetalon | *** Saintpaulia ionantha |
| *** Eucharis grandiflora | *** Sansevieria parva |
| ** Francoa ramosa | * Saxifraga sarmentosa |
| *** Fuchsia procumbens | *** Schizanthus wisetonensis |
| *** Gloriosa superba | * Schizocentron elegans |
| * Gloxinia speciosa | ** Sedum album |

| | |
|---|---|
| * Sedum brevifolium | *** Tropaeolum speciosum |
| ***   "    lineare | *** Veltheimia viridifolia |
| *   "    treleasi | *** Wedelia trilobata |
| * Selaginella denticulata | *** Zamia floridana |
| ** Strelitzia reginae | ** Zebrina pendula |
| ** Streptocarpus hybridus | ** Zoysia tenuifolia |
| *** Trichosporum pulchrum | * Zygocactus truncatus |

HUMID REGIONS---where the atmosphere may reach near the saturation point in moisture to become heavy with water, muggy at times....bayou country, as illustrative of extreme condition of air and ground. The lower extreme of this classification would be the fogbelt of the sea shores, especially the gulf coast and some little distance inland. The soil is very fertile and the water-table high. It will naturally be low country. This study contemplates such areas in a large way and smaller units within, or on the borderline....well enclosed units or a moist garden where the air is quiet and tends to hold a high transpiration of water. This category holds this as an essential factor in the ultimate and continued success of the following plants. Check with NATIVE PLANTS, FLORIDA and the GULF COASTS.

## TREES

| | |
|---|---|
| ** Acacia auriculaeformis | ** Eucalyptus (check species) |
| ***   "    macracantha | *** Harpullia arborea |
| ***   "    pravissima | *** Homalanthus populifolius |
| ** Acrocomia (species) | * Liquidambar styraciflua |
| ** Aleurites moluccana | ** Lyonothamnus asplenifolius |
| * Caryota (species) | ** Osmanthus americanus |
| *** Casimiroa edulis | * Magnolia grandiflora |
| * Casuarina cunninghamiana | * Melaleuca leucadendra |
| ** Coccolobis floridana | * Metrosideros tomentosa |
| * Crinodendron dependens | * Quercus virginiana |
| ** Cupressus guadalupensis | *** Sabal bermudana |
| ** Delonix regia | * Strelitzia nicholai |
| * Erythrina (Check species) | ** Terminalia catappa |
| *** Drimys winteri | *** Thespezia populnea |

*** Torreya taxifolia

## SHRUBS

| | |
|---|---|
| * Acalypha wilksiana | *** Ixora chinensis |
| ** Ardisia (species) | * Jacobinia carnea |
| * Azalea (species) | ** Leucothoe axillaris |
| ** Azara microphylla | *** Malpighia (species) |
| ** Berberis darwini | ** Michelia fuscata |
| *** Berberidopsis corallina | *** Mitriostigma axillare |
| ** Breynia nivosa | * Murraea exotica |
| * Brunfelsia (species) | *** Osmanthus ilicifolius |
| * Calceolaria integrifolia | ** Pentas lanceolata |
| ** Calliandra portoricensis | *** Pimelea ferruginea |
| ** Cestrum (species) | *** Pinckneya pubens |
| ** Cibotium schiederi | *** Rhamnus alaternus |
| ** Clethra arborea | *** Rondeletia cordata |
| * Coccolobis uvifera | *** Rhapidophyllum histrix |
| ** Codiaeum variegatum | * Senecio petasitis |
| *** Ervatamia coronaria | ** Serenoa repens |
| * Escallonia (species) | * Stenolobium stans |
| * Fuchsia (species) | * Streptosolen jamesoni |
| *** Galvesia speciosa | *** Strobilanthes dyerianus |
| * Hamelia erecta | *** Tecoma garrocha |
| * Hebe (species) | * Thevetia nereifolia |
| * Hibiscus rosa-sinensis | *** Tibouchina (species) |
| *** Ilex paraguariensis | ** Vaccinium virgatum |
| ** Illicium (species) | ** Zamia floridana |

## VINES

| | |
|---|---|
| ** Abrus precatorius | *** Cydista aequinoctialis |
| *** Adenocalymna alliaceum | *** Jaquemontia pentandra |
| ** Aristolochia elegans | ** Lapageria rosea |

** Mandevilla suaveolens
* Monstera deliciosa
* Solandra (species)
* Solanum wendlandi

* Stephanotis floribunda
*** Stizolobium deeringianum
* Thunbergia (species)
*** Urechites lutea

## HERBACEOUS PLANTS

** Achimenes longiflora
*** Adiantum capillus-veneris
* Aglaonema simplex
*** Agrostis maritima
** Alonsoa warscewiczi
* Alpinia speciosa
*** Aphanostephus skirrobasis
*** Arum italicum
** Befara racemosa
* Begonia (species)
* Bergenia (species)
** Blechnum serrulatum
* Caladium picturatum
* Crinum (species)
** Cyclamen indicum
** Dennstedtia cicutaria
* Dieffenbachia picta
** Erythrina herbacea
*** Francoa ramosa
** Gloxinia speciosa
*** Haemanthus (species)
* Helxine soleiroli
* Impatiens sultani
* Iris delta species
**    "   hexagona
***   "   kaempferi
*** Lycoris aurea

*** Micromeria chamissonis
* Mimulus luteus
*** Moraea ramosa
* Myosotis palustris
*** Nertera depressa
** Pasithea caerulea
*** Phormium colensoi
* Primula (species)
*** Psoralea pinnata
** Sabal minor
*** Sagittaria graminea
** Saxifraga sarmentosa
*** Schizostylis coccinea
*** Selaginella (species)
** Stokesia laevis
* Strelitzia reginae
*** Streptocarpus hybridus
** Thalictrum dipterocarpum
** Thunbergia cordata
** Tricholaena rosea
*** Trichosporum pulchrum
** Veronica (species)
*** Viola (check species)
* Woodwardia virginica
* Zantedeschia aethiopica
* Zebrina pendula
** Zephyranthes candida

ARID REGIONS----covering barren or near desert localities and hot interior valleys where plantings must make sudden adjustment for high temperatures, and sometimes frost. Other attributes in the plant that must be considered are fortitude in the face of exhausting winds, a minimum water requirement and a natural faculty for perseverance in baked out soils that are more than likely to show traces of alkali. With-hold moisture in the fall from tender things to ripen the wood. Herbaceous plants near the danger line may be given a little shade, while winter-spring may be stressed with plants that go down during summer. The wrong plant in this place may be sheltered, given plenty of water, a prayer, and survive, but it must take the heat or succumb. Check with NATIVE PLANTS, ARID SOUTHWEST and SOUTHERN CALIFORNIA.

## TREES

** Acacia (check species)
** Ailanthus altissima
** Arecastrum romanzoffianum
* Brachychiton (species)
* Casuarina equisetifolia
*** Celtis australis
* Ceratonia siliqua
** Citrus (species)
*** Cupressus (check species)
** Eriobotrya japonica
* Eucalyptus (check species)
* Fraxinus velutina
* Grevillea robusta
*** Koelreuteria paniculata
* Melia azedarach
** Morus (species)
* Olea europaea

* Parkinsonia aculeata
** Phoenix dactylifera
* Pinus halepensis
** Pittosporum phillyraeoides
*** Pistacia (species)
*** Populus fremonti
*** Prosopis (species)
*** Quercus (check (species)
*** Salix (check species)
** Schinus molle
** Sophora secundiflora
* Tamarix aphylla
** Tipuana tipu
*** Trachycarpus fortunei
*** Ulmus pumila
*** Washingtonia filifera
*** Yucca brevifolia

## SHRUBS

*** Abutilon palmeri
*** Acacia horrida

** Adenocarpus viscosus
** Arbutus unedo

** Atriplex lentiformis  
*** Baeckia virgata  
* Berberis gagnepaini  
** Buddleja (species)  
* Callistemon (species)  
* Calocephalis browni  
** Candollea cuneiformis  
*** Carissa grandiflora  
* Cassia artemisioides  
* Ceratostigma willmottianum  
*** Cercocarpus betuloides  
** Chamaelaucium ciliatum  
* Cistus (species)  
** Correa (species)  
*** Cowania mexicana  
* Cytisus canariensis  
*** Daubentonia (species)  
** Diosma (species)  
* Dodonaea viscosa  
* Elaeagnus pungens  
** Erica melanthera  
*** Erythrina crista-galli  
* Euonymus japonicus  
*** Fallugia paradoxa  
*** Forestiera neo-mexicana  
** Fouquieria splendens  
** Genista monosperma  
*** Grevillea rosmarinifolia  
*** Hakea (species)  
*** Halimium (species)  
*** Hibiscus syriacus  
** Jasmirm humile  

* Juniperus (species)  
* Lagerstroemia indica  
** Lantana (species)  
** Lavandula (species)  
*** Leonotis leonurus  
** Leptospermum laevigatum  
* Ligustrum (species)  
*** Lycium (species)  
** Mahonia (check species)  
*** Malvastrum (species)  
* Melaleuca (species)  
* Myrsine africana  
*** Myrtus communis  
* Nerium oleander  
* Photinia serrulata  
*** Pittosporum heterophyllum  
* Plumbago capensis  
** Poinciana gilliesi  
** Prunus ilicifolia  
***   "   lusitanica  
* Punica granatum  
* Pyracantha (species)  
*** Rhamnus alaternus  
*** Rhus ovata  
** Rosmarinus officinalis  
** Santolina chamaecyparissus  
* Spartium junceum  
** Syringa persica  
** Tecomaria capensis  
*** Thryallis glauca  
** Teucrium fruticans  
** Vitex agnus-castus  

* Xylosma senticosa

## VINES

* Antigonon leptopus  
* Bougainvillea (varieties)  
** Calonyction aculeatum  
* Campsis radicans  
* Clematis texensis  
** Clytostoma callistegioides  
*** Cryptostegia grandiflora  
* Dolichos lignosus  
** Ficus Pumila  
** Hedera canariensis  

*** Jaquemontia eastwoodiana  
* Jasminum officinalis  
* Lonicera halliana  
** Muehlenbeckia complexa  
*** Petrea volubilis  
*** Pithecoctenium cynanchoides  
** Pueraria thunbergiana  
*** Senecio confusus  
** Solanum jasminoides  
*** Thunbergia gibsoni  

## HERBACEOUS PLANTS

** Aethionema coridifolium  
** Ageratum houstonianum  
* Alyssum maritimum  
*** Anacyclus depressus  
*** Anemone blanda  
*   "   coronaria  
** Angelonia grandiflora  
** Aquilegia chrysantha  
* Arctotis (species)  
* Argemone mexicana  
** Arrhenatherum tuberosum  
* Babiana stricta  
* Brodiaea (species)  
* Brunsvigia rosea  
*** Calendula officinalis  
** Centaurea (species)  
* Ceratostigma plumbaginoides  
** Cheilanthes gracillima  
* Chrysanthemum carinatum  
* Cichorium intybus  
*** Cooperia drummondi  
* Cortaderia selloana  
* Cynoglossum amabile  

*** Delphinium cardinale  
* Dianthus (species)  
* Dimorphotheca (species)  
*** Encelia farinosa  
* Erigeron karvinskyanus  
** Erodium (species)  
* Euphorbia (check species)  
** Felicia amelloides  
** Festuca glauca  
** Freesia refracta  
* Gazania (species)  
*** Gladiolus hortulanus  
*** Godetia grandiflora  
** Hedychium (species)  
* Helianthemum nummularium  
*** Hesperantha stanfordiae  
** Hyssopus officinalis  
* Iris unguicularis  
**   "   xiphium  
** Ixia maculata  
* Limonium (species)  
*** Linum (species)  
*** Lupinus (check species)

*** Mathiola incana
 ** Mirabilia jalapa
  * Moraea iridioides
*** Muscari armeniacum
 ** Narcissus (species)
*** Nepeta mussini
*** Nicotiana alata
  * Oenothera (species)
 ** Ornithogalum arabicum
 ** Oxalis (species)
*** Papaver rupifragum
 ** Pellaea (species)
*** Penstemon (species)
 ** Petunia hybrida
*** Phygelius capensis
  * Portulaca grandiflora
  * Ranunculus asiaticus
 ** Salvia (species)

*** Sanvitalia procumbens
 ** Scilla hispanica
*** Sparaxis tricolor
*** Streptanthera cuprea
  * Thymus (species)
*** Tritonia (species)
  * Tropaeolum majus
*** Tulipa botanical species)
*** Ursinia anthemoides
  * Vallota speciosa
*** Veltheimia iridifolia
  * Venidium (species)
 ** Verbena (species)
  * Vinca rosea
*** Viola pedunculata
 ** Watsonia iridifolia
*** Xanthisma texanum
  * Zinnia elegans

## SUCCULENTS

*** Aeonium (species)
 ** Agave (species)
  * Crassula (species)
*** Doryanthes palmeri
 ** Euphorbia tirucalli
  * Mesembryanth. (species)
  * Opuntia (species)

 ** Othonna crassifolia
 ** Portulacaria afra
*** Rochea coccinea
*** Sedum(species)
  * Sempervivum tectorum
 ** Stapelia divaricata
  * Yucca (species)

MOUNTAINOUS REGIONS----plants which thrive in the rarified atmosphere of higher altitudes, withstand the lower temperatures and adapt
to the shorter growing periods experienced there.  Most plants from
warm temperate climates over the world have difficulty with the long
mild season of growth in the far south and react half-heartedly to
all stimuli.  They will flourish on these high mountain plateaus in
such a way as never to be expected at lower levels near the coasts.
The more natural forms will find a greater and more satisfactory use
in this environment.  Check with FROST PROOF and DECIDUOUS LISTS on
trees and shrubs. Consult BORDERLINE NORTH for further material.

## TREES

 ** Acer floridanum
  * Albizzia julibrissin
*** Alnus (species)
*** Arbutus menziesi
 ** Cedrus atlantica
*** Celtis australis
*** Citrus mitis
*** Cunninghamia lanceolata
  * Cupressus arizonica
***    "       forbsi
 **    "       sempervirens
*** Drimys winteri
*** Embothrium coccineum
  * Eriobotrya japonica
*** Eucalyptus erythronema
  *    "       polyanthemos
 **    "       viminalis
 ** Juniperus excelsa
*** Laurus nobilis

  * Libocedrus decurrens
*** Livistona australis
  * Magnolia grandiflora
 ** Maytenus boaria
  * Pinus coulteri
 **    "    pinea
***    "    sabiniana
*** Podocarpus elongata
 ** Prunus caroliniana
  *    "    persica
  * Pyrus calleryana
  * Quercus chrysolepis
 **    "       douglasi
 **    "       laurifolia
***    "       lobata
 ** Thuja orientalis
*** Torreya (species)
  * Trachycarpus fortunei
 ** Umbellularia californica

## SHRUBS

  * Abelia grandiflora
*** Arctostaphylos manzanita
*** Artemisia tridentata
 ** Aster fruticosus
  * Azalea indica
 ** Azara microphylla
 ** Bambusa multiplex
 ** Berberis (species)

*** Brickellia grandiflora
  * Buddleja magnifica
  * Buxus microphylla
  * Camellia japonica
*** Cassia corymbosa
 ** Ceanothus cyaneus
  * Ceratostigma willmottianum
 ** Cercocarpus betuloides

* Cistus (species)
* Cocculus laurifolius
** Cornus capitata
* Cotoneaster (species)
*** Cowania mexicana
** Daphne odora
** Dodonaea viscosa
* Elaeagnus pungens
*** Eurya japonica
*** Fallugia paradoxa
* Fatsia japonica
*** Fuchsia magellanica
* Gardenia jasminoides
** Hebe cupressoides
*** " traversi
* Hypericum (species)
* Ilex (species)
** Jasminum floridum
*** Illicium anisatum
* Lagerstroemia indica
* Ligustrum (species)
** Lonicera nitida
* Michelia fuscata
*** Myrica californica
* Myrtus communis

* Nandina domestica
** Osmanthus ilicifolius
*** Osteomeles anthyllidifolia
*** Philadelphus microphyllus
*** Phillyrea latifolia
*** Phlomis fruticosa
* Photinia serrulata
* Pittosporum tobira
*** Prunus lusitanica
* Pyracantha (species)
** Raphiolepis (species)
*** Rhamnus (species)
*** Rhus trilobata
*** Ribes glutinosum
** " malvaceum
* Rosa (species)
** Rosmarinus officinalis
*** Sambucus caerulea
** Sarcococca hookeriana
** Siphonosmanthus delavayi
** Sophora secundiflora
* Tamarix (species)
** Teucrium fruticans
* Viburnum (species)
*** Vitex agnus-castus

*** Xylosma senticosa

## VINES

* Ampelopsis brevipedunculata
*** Cissus striata
*** Clematis (species)
** Cobaea scandens
*** Doxantha unguis-cati
* Gelsemium sempervirens
** Hedera helix
* Jasminum officinale

** Lonicera halliana
*** Muehlenbeckia complexa
* Parthenocissus (species)
** Polygonum auberti
** Quamoclit (species)
* Trachelospermum jasminoides
*** Vitis girdiana
* Wisteria floribunda

## HERBACEOUS PLANTS

*** Adiantum emarginatum
*** Allium (species)
* Anemone (species)
** Althaea rosea
* Alyssum maritimum
* Aquilegia chrysantha
* Aster (species)
** Aubrieta deltoidea
** Bellis perennis
** Bergenia (species)
*** Bessera elegans
*** Brevoortia ida-maia
** Brodiaea (species)
* Calendula officinalis
** Calochortus albus
* Campanula (species)
* Centaurea (species)
** Cerastium tomentosum
* Ceratostigma plumbaginoides
*** Chlidanthus fragrans
* Chrysanthemum (species)
* Coreopsis lanceolata
* Delphinium ajacis
* Dianthus (species)
*** Dipidax ciliata
*** Elisena longipetala
*** Eremurus (species)
** Erodium (species)
*** Eryngium amethystinum
** Festuca glauca
* Gaillardia aristata

** Gaura lindheimeri
** Glaucium flavum
** Gypsophila (species)
* Hemerocallis aurantiaca
* Heuchera sanguinea
*** Iberis (species)
* Iris (species)
* Ixia maculata
** Jasminum parkeri
* Kniphofia uvaria
** Lathyrus splendens
* Lavandula officinalis
** Leucojum autumnale
* Lilium (species)
** Linum (species)
** Lupinus affinis
** Milla biflora
* Mimulus (species)
*** Moraea ramosa
*** Muehlenbeckia axillare
*** Muscari armeniacum
* Myosotis alpestris
* Narcissus (species)
** Nepeta mussini
*** Oxypetalum caeruleum
* Oxalis bowieana
* Papaver (species)
*** Pasithea caerulea
** Penstemon gloxinioides
* Petunia hybrida
** Phlox drummondi

*** Polianthes tuberosa
  * Portulaca grandiflora
 ** Primula (species)
*** Pteris (species)
*** Pterocephalis parnassi
  * Ranunculus (species)
 ** Romneya coulteri
 ** Saxifraga sarmentosa
*** Schizostylis coccinea
*** Scilla (species)
  * Sedum album
***     "  caeruleum
***     "  lineare

 ** Sedum sieboldi
 ** Sempervivum tectorum
*** Silene laciniata
*** Sternbergia lutea
  * Stokesia laevis
*** Tecophilaea cyanocrocus
  * Thymus (species)
  * Tropaeolum (species)
  * Tulipa (species)
*** Tunica saxifraga
*** Vallota speciosa
  * Viola (species)
*** Xeranthemum annuum

       ** Zephyranthes rosea


TRANSITIONAL AREAS---irregular bands of varying width that cross
the country east and west. This is significant locale in relation to
climate that becomes pertinent to any study or practice of the principle of localization in the use of plant materials.  Inclusion of a
plant in either of these borderline lists indicates the prime adaptation of the subject to either the warmer temperate regions to the
north or to the tropics on the south and not of first importance in
the subtropical regions lying between. Yet at the same time, and usually with qualifications, the same species may be used with more or
less satisfaction in other portions.....certainly in the so-called
borderline areas. Some of them may adapt far within, or indeed to the
entire area, as suggested by ratings. Favorable local conditions can
extend the use of a plant into unexpected spots.


## BORDERLINE SOUTH

         This is where one approaches the tropics, to find scant
literature and less instruction in an almost untouched field of ornamental horticulture.  Work now is coming along to bring it more in
line with that of the north and to effectively bring this extra brilliance and the seductive temperament of the place within the observation and understanding and, in some cases, within the practical use
of gardeners. There will be no deep cold here and metabolism goes on
with little change or marked influence from without. Much vegetation
rotting down makes for very rich soils unless they are loose and of a
leaching texture. These plants, as used northerly into subtropical
regions should not be hurried out of the un-accustomed winter chill.
Do not fertilize or otherwise stimulate them until late spring or
early summer....wait for some sign of interest.

### TREES

 ** Adenanthera pavonina
*** Anacardium occidentale
*** Andira inermis
 ** Barringtonia asiatica
  * Bixa orellana
 ** Brownea grandiceps
  * Bucida bucerus
 ** Butea frondosa
 ** Caesalpinia coriaria
 ** Cassia siamea
  * Cecropia palmata
  * Ceiba pentandra
  * Cocos nucifera
 ** Cordia sebestina
 ** Eugenia malaccensis
*** Faramea occidentalis
*** Garcia nutans
*** Gliricida sepium
*** Glycosmis pentaphylla

  * Gmelina arborea
 ** Haematoxylon campechianum
*** Hura crepitans
*** Hyophorbe verschaffelti
*** Kopsia fruticosa
*** Licania rigida
  * Melicocca bijuga
  * Pachira macrocarpa
  * Pandanus utilis
*** Polyalthia suberosa
 ** Posoqueria latifolia
*** Quassia amara
*** Radermachia pentandra
*** Randia dumetorum
 ** Ravenala madagascariensis
  * Roystonea regia
*** Schizolobium parahybum
  * Tamarindus indicum
*** Triplaris americana

### SHRUBS

*** Alyxia olivaeformis
 ** Ardisia oliveri
*** Banisteriopsis cornifolia

*** Baphia racemosa
 ** Byrsonima crassifolia
*** Calotropis procera

** Catesbaea spinosa
*** Centradenia floribunda
*** Cipadessa baccifera
 * Coffea arabica
 * Crossandra infundibuliformis
 * Dizygotheca elegans
 ** Ehretia microphylla
*** Excoecaria cochinchinensis
 ** Flacourtia indica
*** Gmelina elliptica
 ** Graptophyllum pictum
*** Heteropteris syringaefolia
 * Hibiscus schizopetalon
 * Hypoestis phyllostachys
 * Ixora chinensis
 ** Jacobinia ghiesbrechtiana
 ** Jaquinea keyensis
*** Jatropa curcus
*** Leea coccinea
*** Mascarenhasia elastica
 * Medinilla magnifica
 ** Malastoma malabaricum
 ** Montanoa bipinnatifidum
*** Mussaenda erythrophylla
 * Pavonia multiflora
 * Plumeria emarginata
 * Polyscias balfouriana
 * Pomaderris apetala
*** Portlandia platantha
 ** Randia aculeata

 * Robinsonella cordata
 ** Sanchezia nobilis
 ** Scaevola frutescens
*** Scutellaria ventenati
 ** Serjania glabrata
*** Stemmadenia galiottiana
 * Strobilanthes anisophilus
*** Synsepalum dulcificum
 * Tabernaemontana grandiflora
 ** Tephrosia candida
 * Thunbergia erecta
*** Tococa platyphylla
 ** Tournefortia heliotropinoides
*** Urera caracasana

## VINES

 * Combretum grandiflorum
 ** Congea tomentosa
 ** Derris scandens
*** Echites umbellata
 * Jasminum bahiense
*** Nyctocereus serpentinus
*** Paullinia thralictrifolia
*** Porana paniculata
 * Quisqualis indica
*** Syngonium podophyllum
*** Tetrastigma harmandi
 ** Vanilla fragrans

## HERBACEOUS PLANTS

 ** Aechmea mariae-reginae
 * Alocasia macrorhiza
 **     "      odora
 * Amomum cardamon
 ** Anthurium andreanum
*** Aphelandra squarrosa
 ** Asystasia gangetica
 ** Begonia heracleifolia
 ** Bertolonia marmorata
*** Bromelia pinguin
 * Calceolaria herbeohybrida
*** Chirita lavandulacea
 ** Columnea gloriosa
 ** Crinum zeylanicum
 * Fittonia verschaffelti
 ** Heliconia bihai
*** Hemigraphis colorata
 ** Hoffmannia refulgens
 * Hydrosme rivieri
 ** Hymenocallis keyensis

 ** Isoloma hirsutum
*** Kochleria lindeniana
 * Manfreda maculata
 * Maranta leuconeura .
*** Neoregelia marmorata
 ** Pellionia pulchra
 * Peperomia obtusifolia
 ** Phlogacanthus thyrsiflorus
*** Phoenomeria magnifica
 ** Pitcairnia xanthocalyx
 * Polypodium punctatum
*** Renealmia nutans
 * Rhoeo discolor
*** Smithiana hybrida
*** Sonerila margaritacea
*** Spathiphyllum clevelandi
*** Syngonium podophyllum
*** Talinum triangulare
 * Trimesa martinicensis
*** Xanthosoma bataviense

## BORDERLINE NORTH

Where the influence of season is the dominating factor and rainfall, while not always dependable in point of time, is more assured and higher generally....surely so in the west. Temperate climate plants are not ordinarily grown far into subtropical regions where the evergreen types are favored. The state or condition called dormancy in plants, is seldom complete in the so-called deciduous or leafdrop period. This reacts to prevent new growth during unseasonable warmth. It may be stressed here, that any growth labors under a kind of inhibition where there is no frost to force the plant into complete rest for a time. And that growth which may develop out of season, usually comes from low on the stem and will be inferior not only as to position, but in other ways having to do with quality.

## TREES

*** Abies venusta                    * Acer palmatum

** Acer macrophyllum            *** Maclura pomifera
 * Ailanthus altissima            * Magnolia soulangeana
 * Betula pendula              *** Metasequoia glyptostroboides
** Broussonetia papyrifera        * Paulownia tomentosa
** Carya pecan                  *** Populus trichocarpa
** Cedrus libani                 ** Prunus pissardi
 * Chamaecyparis lawsoniana    *** Pterocarya stenoptera
** Cryptomeria elegans           ** Quercus falcata
*** Crataegus carrierei          ** Robinia pseudacacia
** Cunninghamia lanceolata       ** Sequoia sempervirens
 * Ginkgo biloba               *** Sciadopitys verticillata
*** Liriodendron tulipifera       * Sophora japonica
** Lithocarpus densiflora       *** Taxus brevifolia

## SHRUBS

** Acanthopanax sieboldianum     ** Holodiscus discolor
*** Amorpha fruticosa             * Ilex aquifolium
 * Aucuba japonica              *** Ilex crenata (varieties)
*** Banksia nutans               ** Kolkwitzia amabilis
** Buddleja globosa              ** Loropetalum chinense
 * Buxus suffruticosa             * Magnolia stellata
*** Callicarpa americana        *** Mahonia aquifolium
** Calycanthus (species)         ** Meratia praecox
*** Caryopteris incana          *** Osmaronia cerasiformis
*** Cephalotaxus fortunei         * Philadelphus microphyllus
 * Corokia cotoneaster           ** Pinus mugo
 * Cotinus coggigria             ** Prunus cistena
 * Cotoneaster horizontalis       *    "    glandulosa
** Cytisus kewensis             ***    "    laurocerasus
***    "    scoparius           *** Rhus copallina
 * Daboëtia cantabrica          *** Rosa gallica
*** Daphniphyllum humile         **    "   muscosa
** Dasylirion glaucophyllum     *** Skimmia japonica
** Erica mediterranea hybrida     * Stranvaesia davidiana
** Exochorda racemosa            ** Thujopsis dolobrata
*** Forestiera neo-mexicana       * Ulex europaeus
*** Gaya lyalli                 *** Viburnun rhytidophyllum

## VINES

** Akebia quinata                 * Lonicera sempervirens
** Bignonia capreolata          *** Lycium barbarum
 * Campsis radicans             *** Lygodium japonicum
 * Clematis jackmanni            ** Rosa wichuriana
** Clematis paniculata          *** Stauntonia hexaphylla
*** Decumaria barbara            ** Vitis kaempferi
*** Kadsura japonica              * Wisteria frutescens

## HERBACEOUS PLANTS

 * Achillea (species)             * Briza maxima
*** Acorus gramineus             ** Brunnera myosotidiflora
*** Adenophora lilifolia         ** Butomus umbellatus
*** Adonis aleppica             *** Cabomba caroliniana
** Aethionema coridifolium       ** Calceolaria herbeohybrida
 * Agrimonia odorata             ** Callirhoë involucrata
*** Alisma plantago-aquatica      * Calochortus (species)
 * Althaea rosea                *** Caltha palustris
 * Amaranthus caudatus           ** Camassia leichtlini
** Ammobium alatum                * Catananche caerulea
*** Ammophila arenaria            * Centranthus ruber
** Amoracea rusticana             * Cerastium tomentosum
** Anaphalis margaritacea         * Cheiranthus cheiri
*** Androsace lanuginosa         ** Chrysanthemum tchihatchewi
 * Anthemis tinctoria           *** Chionodoxa luciliae
*** Aphyllanthes monspeliensis  *** Cirsium occidentale
*** Aponogeton (species)         ** Cleome spinosa
** Aubrieta deltoidea           *** Clitoria mariana
** Belamcanda chinensis          ** Colchicum autumnale
 * Bellis perennis              *** Commelina coelestis
*** Brasenia schweberi           ** Corydalis lutea

** Cotula squalida
* Delphinium grandiflorum
** Dicentra formosa
*    "       spectabilis
** Digitalis purpurea
*** Eremurus robustus
** Erianthus ravennae
** Eriophyllum caespitosum
** Erysimum (species)
** Eryngium amethystinum
*** Galanthus bizantinus
** Geranium (species)
* Glaucium flavum
* Gypsophila (species)
*** Hedysarum coronarium
** Helypterum (species)
*** Heliopsis helianthoides
*** Hottonia palustris
*** Hydrocotyle rotundifolia
** Iberis (species)
*** Ionopsidium acaule
** Iresine herbsti
* Iris (select species)
*** Kochia scoparia
** Lavandula stoechas
*** Lemna minor
** Lilium (select species)
*** Limnanthes douglasi
** Lycopodium clavatum
* Lysimachia nummularia

** Mazus pumilio
*** Muscari armeniacum
*** Nymphaea (select species)
*** Onosma tauricum
*** Orontium aquaticum
** Peltandra virginica
*** Pennisetum ruppeli
*** Phalaris arundinacea
*** Phoradendron flavescens
*** Physalis alkekengi
* Platycodon grandiflorum
** Pontederia cordata
* Potentilla cinerea
*** Proboscidia jussieuxi
*** Ranunculus gramineus
** Reseda odorata
*** Rudbeckia laciniata
*** Salvinia auriculata
*** Saururus cernuus
* Stanleya pinnata
*** Stipa pennata
*** Tolmiea menziesi
*** Trachymene caerulea
* Tradescantia virginiana
*** Trapa natans
* Tunica saxifraga
* Ulmaria filipendula
*** Utricularia vulgaris
*** Veronica lacinata
*** Valisneria spiralis

* Woodwardia (species)

# PLANTING CALENDAR

These monthly groupings for herbaceous material may be used as a general guide for planting. Their value lies in the fact that most plants have an area over the orbit of the year where performance is better; with another time best for digging or planting, if next seasons bloom is to be all that may be expected. Due to heat in California and beating rains in Florida, very early seeding in the open ground is hazardous late summer and autumn, yet does afford some opportunity for one to recover after losses, with established plants. Winter planting will take hold slowly, but will be satisfactory mild seasons. Seed sown midsummer should be placed deeper than normal, at least in part. This schedule will be subject to the usual limitations of local peculiarities and seasonal irregularities and allowances will be made when such are recognized. Latitude as an influence in moderation, is a more constant factor than longitude, the more successful southerly plantings tending to occur in the early months of an area in the spring; but reversed in the fall, with northerly plantings best executed during the early months. Check with the COMPENDIUM for further preferment in the matter of timing.

JANUARY

SOW IN OPEN GROUND---Abronia, Ageratum, Alyssum, Antirrhinum, Arctotis, Bellis, Calendula, Calliopsis, Callistephus, Carnation, Centaurea, Chrysanthemum, Clarkia, Cleome, Collinsia, Convolvulus, Coreopsis, Cosmos, Dahlia, Dimorphotheca, Eschscholtzia, Gilia, Godetia Gomphrena, Gypsophila, Larkspur, Linaria, Lupine, Mallow, Mimulus, Nasturtium, Petunia, Phacelia, Phlox, Pinks, Primula, Scabiosa, Stevia, Sweetpea, Verbena.

PLANTS---Alyssum, Antirrhinum, Arctotis, Bellis, Calendula, Canterburybells, Carnation, Centaurea, Coreopsis, Cynoglossum, Dimorphotheca, Heuchera, Iceland Poppy, Geum, Myosotis, Pansies, Petunia, Primula, Pinks, Scabiosa, Stocks, Verbena, Viola.

BULBS-CORMS-TUBERS---Alstrœmeria, Anemone, Babiana, Calochortus, Gladiolus, Hæmanthus, Ixia, Leucocoryne, Leucojum, Montbretia, Sparaxis, White-calla.

DIVISION OR CLUMPS---Acanthus, Agapanthus, Amaryllis, Aster, Dicentra, Gazania, Hemerocallis, Hollyhock, Japanese Iris, Sedum, Daisy, Shasta, Periwinkle, Thalictrum, Thyme, Torch-lily.


FEBRUARY

SOW IN OPEN GROUND---Abronia, Ageratum, Alonsoa, Alyssum, Amaranthus, Anagallis, Anemone, Antirrhinum, Aquilegia, Arctotis, Baileya, Bloomeria, Brachycome, Browallia, Calendula, Calliopsis, Callistephus, Carnation, Celosia, Centaurea, Charieis, Chrysanthemum, Clarkia, Cleome, Collinsia, Convolvulus, Coreopsis, Cosmos, Cynoglossum, Dahlberg Daisy, Dahlia, Diascia, Dimorphotheca, Emilia, Eschscholtzia, Exacum, Flax, Forget-me-not, Gaillardia, Gilia, Godetia, Gomphrena, Gypsophila, Helichrysum, Hunnemannia, Immortelle, Impatiens, Kochia, Larkspur, Linaria, Lobelia, Lonas, Lupine, Malcomia, Mallow, Marigold, Maurandia, Mentzelia, Mimulus, Nasturtium, Nemesia, Nemophila, Nicotiana, Periwinkle, Petunia, Phacelia, Phlox, Pink, Poppy, Primula, Quamoclit, Salpiglossis, Salvia, Scabiosa, Schizanthus, Thymophylla, Stevia, Stocks, Strawflower, Sweetpea, Verbena, Zinnia.

193

SEED IN FLATS---Ageratum, Alonsoa, Antirrhinum, Arctotis, Calendula, Callistephus, Centaurea, Coreopsis, Cosmos, Cynoglossum, Diascia, Exacum, Gaillardia, Geum, Gomphrena, Gypsophila, Iceland Poppy, Immortelle, Lobelia, Marigold, Mimulus, Nemesia, Nicotiana, Penstemon, Periwinkle, Petunia, Phlox, Rehmannia, Salpiglossis, Salvia, Schizanthus, Streptocarpus, Torenia, Trachelium, Verbena, Zinnia.

PLANTS---Ageratum, Antirrhinum, Arctotis, Bellis, Calendula, Canterburybells, Centaurea, Cynoglossum, Dimorphotheca, Exacum, Gaillardia, Geum, Heliotrope, Heuchera, Lobelia, Pansies, Petunia, Pinks, Scabiosa, Stocks, Verbena, Viola, Xanthisma.

BULBS-CORMS-TUBERS---Acidanthera, Alstrœmeria, Anemone, Anomatheca, Babiana, Bessera, Caladium, Canna, Colocasia, Crinum, Dahlia, Galtonia, Gladiolus, Gloriosa, Gloxinia, Hæmanthus, Ixia, Montbretia, Polianthes, Schizostylis, Sparaxis, Zephyranthes, White-calla.

DIVISION OR CLUMPS---Agapanthus, Ajuga, Antholyza, Armeria, Aster, Canna, Gerbera, Hedychium, Physostegia, Salvia, Sedum, Shasta Daisy, Thalictrum, Thyme, Torch-lily, Water-lily.


## MARCH

SOW IN OPEN GROUND---Abronia, Ageratum, Alonsoa, Amaranthus, Alyssum, Anagallis, Anemone, Antirrhinum, Aquilegia, Arctotis, Baileya, Brachycome, Browallia, Calendula, Callistephus, Calliopsis, Carnation, Charieis, Celosia, Centaurea, Chrysanthemum, Clarkia, Collinsia, Convolvulus, Coreopsis, Cosmos, Cynoglossum, Dahlberg Daisy, Dahlia, Diascia, Dimorphotheca, Emilia, Eschscholtzia, Exacum, Flax, Forget-me-not, Gaillardia, Gilia, Godetia, Gomphrena, Gypsophila, Hunnemannia, Immortelle, Impatiens, Kochia, Larkspur, Linaria, Lobelia, Lonas, Lupine, Madiera-vine, Malcomia, Mallow, Marigold, Moonflower, Morning-glory, Mimulus, Nasturtium, Nemesia, Nemophila, Nicotiana, Periwinkle, Petunia, Phlox, Pinks, Poppies, Primula, Pueraria, Quamoclit, Salpiglossis, Salvia, Scabiosa, Schizanthus, Stevia, Stocks, Strawflower, Thymophylla, Torenia, Verbena, Viola, Zinnia.

SEED IN FLATS---Agathæa, Ageratum, Alonsoa, Antirrhinum, Arctotis, Begonia, Browallia, Calendula, Callistephus, Canterburybells, Celosia, Centaurea, Coreopsis, Cosmos, Cynoglossum, Dahlia, Diascia, Exacum, Gaillardia, Gerberia, Geum, Gomphrena, Heliotrope, Immortelle, Impatiens, Lobelia, Lunaria, Malcomia, Mallow, Marigold, Mimulus, Nemesia, Nicotiana, Penstemon, Phlox, Petunia, Periwinkle, Rehmannia, Salvia, Schizanthus, Stokesia, Streptocarpus, Torenia, Zinnia.

PLANTS---Ageratum, Alyssum, Antirrhinum, Arctotis, Brachycome, Calendula, Calliopsis, Canterburybells, Centaurea, Coreopsis, Cynoglossum, Delphinium, Dimorphotheca, Exacum, Gaillardia, Gerberia, Geum, Heliotrope, Iceland Poppy, Lobelia, Marigold, Mimulus, Nemesia, Penstemon, Periwinkle, Petunia, Pinks, Salpiglossis, Salvia, Scabiosa, Stevia, Stocks, Verbena, Xanthisma.

BULBS-CORMS-TUBERS---Achimines, Acidanthera, Anomatheca, Caladium, Canna, Colocasia, Crinum, Dahlia, Galtonia, Gladiolus, Gloriosa, Gloxinia, Madiera-vine, Montbretia, Polianthes, Schizostylis, Tigridia, Tuberous Begonias, Zephyranthes.

DIVISION OR CLUMPS---Agapanthus, Ajuga, Antholyza, Antigonon, Billbergia, Canna, Gerberia, Hedychium, Physostegia, Plumbago, Romneya, Salvia, Sedum, Sisyrinchium, Stokesia, Torchlily, Tigridia, Water-lily, Zygocactus.


## APRIL

SOW IN OPEN GROUND---Ageratum, Amaranthus, Alonsoa, Alyssum, Anagallis, Anemone, Arctotis, Baileya, Bloomeria, Brachycome, Browallia, Calendula, Calliopsis, Canterburybells, Carnation, Celosia, Centaurea, Callistephus, Charieis, Clarkia, Collinsia, Coreopsis, Cosmos, Cynoglossum, Dahlberg Daisy, Dahlia, Diascia, Dimorphotheca, Emilia,

Eschscholtzia, Euphorbia, Exacum, Flax, Forget-me-not, Gaillardia, Gilia, Gomphrena, Gourds, Gypsophila, Hunnemannia, Immortelle, Impatiens, Kochia, Larkspur, Linaria, Lobelia, Lonas, Madiera-vine, Malcomia, Marigold, Morning-glory, Moonflower, Nasturtium, Nemesia, Nemophila, Nicotiana, Periwinkle, Petunia, Phlox, Pinks, Poppies, Portulaca, Pueraria, Quamoclit, Salpiglossis, Salvia, Scabiosa, Schizanthus, Stocks, Strawflower, Tithonia, Torenia, Verbena, Zinnia.

SEED IN FLATS---Ageratum, Antirrhinum, Begonia, Brawallia, Callistephus, Canterburybells, Celosia, Cineraria, Gaillardia, Gerbera, Geum, Lobelia, Nemesia, Nicotiana, Peppers, Petunia, Portulaca, Salvia, Torenia, Zinnia.

PLANTS---Alternanthera, Amaranthus, Begonia, Brachycome, Calendula, Calliopsis, Callistephus, Centaurea, Chrysanthemum, Coreopsis, Cosmos, Cynoglossum, Delphinium, Diascia, Exacum, Gerberia, Geum, Gypsophila, Heliotrope, Immortelle, Impatiens, Lobelia, Marigold, Mallow, Mimulus, Nemesia, Nicotiana, Oenothera, Periwinkle, Petunia, Phlox, Salvia, Schizanthus, Stevia, Stocks, Stokesia, Streptocarpus, Thalictrum, Trachelium, Verbena, Zinnia.

BULBS-CORMS-TUBERS---Achimenes, Acidanthera, Anomatheca, Caladium, Canna, Clivia, Colocasia, Crinum, Dahlia, Galtonia, Gladiolus, Gloriosa, Gloxinia, Madiera-vine, Polianthes, Tuberous Begonia, Schizostylis, Sisyrinchium, Tigridia, Watsonia, Water-lily, Zephranthes.

## MAY

SOW IN OPEN GROUND---Ageratum, Amaranthus, Alyssum, Anagallis, Arctotis, Baileya, Browallia, Calendula, Calliopsis, Celosia, Clarkia, Cosmos, Dahlia, Euphorbia, Flax, Gaillardia, Gilia, Gomphrena, Gourds, Gypsophila, Hunnemannia, Impatiens, Kochia, Larkspur, Linaria, Lobelia, Madiera-vine, Malcomia, Mallow, Marigold, Mirabilis, Nasturtium, Nemophila, Nicotiana, Petunia, Periwinkle, Phlox, Poppies, Portulaca, Pueraria, Quamoclit, Salpiglossis, Salvia, Scabiosa, Schizanthus, Strawflower, Tithonia, Torenia, Zinnia.

SEED IN FLATS---Ageratum, Anemone, Begonia, Cineraria, Gaillardia, Gerberia, Geum, Peppers, Petunia, Portulaca, Salvia, Torenia, Trachelium, Zinnia.

PLANTS---Acalypha, Ageratum, Alternanthera, Amaranthus, Calendula, Callistephus, Celosia, Centaurea, Chrysanthemum, Coleus, Coreopsis, Cosmos, Croton, Cynoglossum, Diascia, Exacum, Gaillardia, Gerberia, Geum, Immortelle, Impatiens, Lobelia, Mallow, Marigold, Mimulus, Nemesia, Nicotiana, Oenothera, Penstemon, Periwinkle, Petunia, Phlox-Pinks, Rehmannia, Salvia, Schizanthus, Stokesia, Streptocarpus, Thalictrum, Torenia, Trachelium, Verbena, Zinnia.

BULBS-CORMS-TUBERS---Achimenes, Amaryllis, Anomatheca, Brunsvigia, Caladium, Canna, Clivia, Dahlia, Gladiolus, Gloriosa, Gloxinia, Lycoris, Madiera-vine, Polianthes, Sternbergia, Tigridia, Watsonia, Water-lily, Zephyranthes.

## JUNE

SOW IN OPEN GROUND---Ageratum, Alyssum, Baileya, Calendula, Celosia, Centaurea, Cineraria, Cosmos, Dahlia, Gomphrena, Gypsophila, Impations, Kochia, Malcomia, Mallow, Marigold, Mirabilis, Nasturtium-Nemophila, Nicotiana, Periwinkle, Petunia, Poppies, Portulaca, Pueraria, Quamoclit, Salpiglossis, Tithonia, Torenia, Zinnia.

PLANTS---Acalypha, Ageratum, Alternanthera, Amaranthus, Callistephus, Celosia, Chrysanthemum, Coleus, Coreopsis, Cosmos, Croton, Cynoglossum, Gaillardia, Impatiens, Lobelia, Nicotiana, Marigold, Penstemon, Periwinkle, Petunia, Pinks, Portulaca, Salvia, Stokesia, Streptocarpus, Torenia, Verbena, Zinnia.

BULBS-CORMS-TUBERS---Acanthus, Brunsvigia, Iris, Leucojum, Lycoris-Nerine, Sternbergia, Tigridia, Zephyranthes.

## JULY
SOW IN OPEN GROUND---Alyssum, Baileya, Celosia, Centaurea, Cineraria, Cosmos, Impatiens, Mirabilis, Nasturtium, Nemophila, Periwinkle, Petunia, Poppies, Portulaca, Stocks, Venidium, Zinnia.

PLANTS---Acalypha, Ageratum, Alternanthera, Amaranthus, Callistephus, Celosia, Chrysanthemum, Coleus, Coreopsis, Cosmos, Croton, Gaillardia, Impatiens, Marigold, Nicotiana, Penstemon, Petunia, Portulaca, Pinks, Salvia, Stocks, Torenia, Zinnia.

BULBS-CORMS-TUBERS---Anomatheca, Brunsvigia, Iris, Leucojum, Lycoris, Nerine, Oxalis, Sternbergia, Tigridia, Zephyranthes.

## AUGUST
SOW IN OPEN GROUND---Alyssum, Baileya, Celosia, Centaurea, Cineraria, Cosmos, Flax, Impatiens, Malcomia, Mallow, Nasturtium, Nemophila, Pansies, Penstemon, Periwinkle, Petunia, Stevia, Stocks, Sweetpea, Venidium, Viola, Xanthisma, Zinnia.

SEED IN FLATS---Alonsoa, Antirrhinum, Canterburybells, Coreopsis, Cynoglossum, Delphinium, Gaillardia, Iceland Poppy, Impatiens, Forget-me-not, Iberis, Nemesia, Pansies, Penstemon, Periwinkle, Pinks, Phlox, Poppies, Primula, Trachelium, Verbena, Viola, Xanthisma, Zinnia.

PLANTS---Bergenia, Celosia, Centaurea, Coreopsis, Gaillardia, Petunia, Salpiglossis, Salvia, Stocks, Torenia, Zinnia.

BULBS-CORMS-TUBERS---Anomatheca, Dierama, Dipidax, Freesia, Gladiolus, Lilium, Nerine, Oxalis, Ranunculus, Sternbergia, Watsonia.

DIVISION OR CLUMPS---Arum, Bergenia, Dipidax, Nerine, Pasithia, Tritoma, Tritonia, Zephyranthes.

## SEPTEMBER
SOW IN OPEN GROUND---Abronia, Ageratum, Alonsoa, Alyssum, Antirrhinum, Arctotis, Baileya, Bellis, Brachycome, Calendula, Calliopsis, Canterburybells, Centaurea, Cineraria, Coreopsis, Delphinium, Dimorphotheca, Flax, Forget-me-not, Gypsophila, Impatiens, Linaria, Malcomia, Mallow, Nasturtium, Nemesia, Nemophila, Pansies, Penstemon, Petunia, Phlox, Pinks, Poppies, Primula, Schizanthus, Stevia, Stocks, Sweetpea, Venidium, Viola, Xanthisma.

SEED IN FLATS---Ageratum, Alonsoa, Antirrhinum, Arctotis, Calceolaria, Calendula, Canterburybells, Cineraria, Clarkia, Coreopsis, Cynoglossum, Delphinium, Dimorphotheca, Diascea, Exacum, Forget-me-not-Helianthemum, Heuchera, Iceland Poppy, Impatiens, Nemesia, Penstemon, Periwinkle, Petunia, Primula, Scabiosa, Stocks, Trachelium, Viola.

PLANTS---Aquilegia, Brachycome, Browallia, Calendula, Canterburybells, Cineraria, Coreopsis, Dimorphotheca, Gaillardia, Gazania, Lobelia, Stocks, Zinnia.

BULBS-CORMS-TUBERS---Acanthus, Allium, Alstroemeria, Anemone, Arum, Bergenia, Bloomeria, Brodiaea, Brunsvigia, Calla, Dierama, Dipidax, Elisena, Eremurus, Freesia, Gladiolus, Lachenalia, Narcissus, Nerine, Ornithogalum, Oxalis, Pancratium, Ranunculus, Sternbergia, Tritoma, Watsonia.

DIVISION OR CLUMPS---Agapanthus, Alstroemeria, Arum, Heuchera, Lilium, Nerine, Pasithea, Stokesia.

## OCTOBER
SOW IN OPEN GROUND---Abronia, Ageratum, Alonsoa, Alyssum, Anagallis, Antirrhinum, Arctotis, Baileya, Bellis, Brachycome, Calendula, Calliopsis, Canterburybells, Carnation, Centaurea, Cineraria, Clarkia, Cleome, Collinsia, Coreopsis, Cynoglossum, Delphinium, Dimorphotheca, Eschscholtzia, Flax, Forget-me-not, Gaillardia, Gilia, Godetia, Gypsophila, Larkspur, Linaria, Lunaria, Lupine, Malcomia, Mallow, Maur-

andia, Nasturtium, Nemesia, Nemophila, Nicotiana, Pansies,  Penstemon,
Petunia,  Pinks,  Poppies,  Primula,  Scabiosa, Schizanthus,  Stevia,
Stocks, Strawflower, Sweetpea, Verbena, Viola.

SEED IN FLATS---Ageratum, Antirrhinum, Arctotis, Bellis, Brachycome,
Calendula, Canterburybells, Carnation, Centaurea, Cineraria, Clarkia,
Coreopsis, Cynoglossum, Delphinium, Dimorphotheca, Exacum,   Forget-
me-not, Gaillardia, Geum, Godetia, Gypsophila, Iberis, Iceland Poppy,
Mallow, Mimulus,  Nemesia,  Pansies, Penstemon, Periwinkle, Petunia,
Primula, Scabiosa, Stocks, Trachelium, Verbena, Viola.

PLANTS---Alyssum, Antirrhinum, Arctotis, Bellis, Brachycome, Calendula,  Canterburybells,  Centaurea, Cineraria, Clarkia,  Coreopsis,
Delphinium, Dimorphotheca, Gaillardia, Gypsophila, Heuchera,  Iceland-
poppy, Iberis, Lobelia, Mallow, Pansies, Stocks, Viola.

BULBS CORMS TUBERS---Allium, Alstroemeria, Anemone, Antholyza, Babiana, Bessera, Brunsvigia, White-calla, Calochortus, Camassia, Clivia,
Commelina, Dierama, Dipidax, Elisena, Freesia, Gladiolus, Ixia, Lachenalia, Leucocoryne, Lycoris, Lilium, Moraea, Neomarica,  Montbretia,
Muscari, Narcissus, Ornithogalum, Oxalis, Pancratium, Ranunculus, Scilla, Bulbous Iris, Sparaxis, Tritoma.

DIVISION OR CLUMPS---Acanthus, Agapanthus, Alstroemeria, Amaryllis,
Anchusa, Arum, Billbergia, Bletilla, Crinum, Dahlia, Dierama, Eremu-
rus, Eryngium, Fall Asters, Gazania, Gerberia, Gloriosa,  Hedychium,
Hemerocallis, Heuchera, Japanese Iris, Lilium, Neo-marica,   Nerine,
Orchid Iris,  Oriental Poppy,  Oxalis,  Pancratium, Penstemon, Per-
iwinkle, Romneya, Physostegia, Shasta Daisy, Stokesia, Tigridia,
Tritoma, Veronica.

## NOVEMBER
SOW IN OPEN GROUND---Abronia, Ageratum,  Alyssum, Antirrhinum, Aq-
uilegia,  Arctotis,  Bellis, Calendula, Calliopsis, Canterburybells,
Carnation, Clarkia, Cleome, Collinsia, Coreopsis, Delphinium, Dimor-
photheca,  Eschscholtzia,  Flax, Forget-me-not, Gaillardia,  Gillia,
Godetia, Gypsophila, Iberis,  Larkspur,  Linaria, Lupine, Malcomia,
Mallow, Mentzelia, Nemophila, Nicotiana, Pansies, Petunia, Phacelia,
Pinks, Poppies, Primula, Scabiosa, Stevia, Strawflower, Sweetpea,
Veronica, Viola.

SEED IN FLATS---Agathaea, Antirrhinum, Brachycome, Calendula, Centaurea, Cynoglossum, Dimorphotheca, Godetia, Gypsophila, Iceland Poppy, Lobelia,  Mallow,  Mimulus, Pansies, Petunia, Primula, Scabiosa,
Stocks, Trachelium, Viola.

PLANTS---Alyssum, Antirrhinum, Arctotis, Bellis, Brachycome, Canterburybells, Carnation, Cineraria, Dicentra, Dimorphotheca, Forget-me-
not, Geum, Gypsophila, Heuchera, Iceland Poppy, Iberis, Mallow, Pansies, Penstemon, Petunia, Pinks, Primula, Stocks, Viola,

BULBS-CORMS-TUBERS---Alstroemeria,  Anemones, Anomatheca, Babiana,
Bessera, Brodiaea, White-calla, Calochortus, Camassia, Clivia, Freesia, Ixia, Leucocoryne, Leucojum, Lilium, Moraea, Montbretia, Narcissus, Neo-marica, Nerine, Muscari, Ornithogalum, Oxalis,  Pancratium,
Ranunculus, Scilla, Schizostylis, Sparaxis, Tigridia, Tulips.

DIVISION OR CLUMPS---Agapanthus, Alstroemeria, Amaryllis, Anchusa,
Armeria, Arum, Crinum, Dahlia, Dicentra, Eryngium, Fall Asters, Gaz-
ania, Gloriosa, Hemerocallis, Heuchera,  Hollyhock,   Japanese Iris,
Orchid Iris, Oriental Poppy, Pasithea, Penstemon, Periwinkle, Sedum,
Thalictrum, Thyme, Veronicas.

## DECEMBER
SOW IN OPEN GROUND---Abronia, Ageratum, Alyssum, Antirrhinum, Arc-
totis, Bellis, Calendula, Calliopsis, Clarkia, Cleome, Convolvulus,
Coreopsis, Dimorphotheca, Eschscholtzia, Flax, Forget-me-not, Gaillar-

dia, Gilia, Godetia, Gypsophila, Iberis, Linaria, Lupine, Mallow, Mentzelia, Nasturtium, Pansies, Petunia, Phacelia, Pinks, Poppies, Primula, Scabiosa, Stevia, Sweetpea, Verbena.

PLANTS---Alyssum, Arctotis, Calendula, Canterburybells, Carnation, Cineraria, Dicentra, Dimorphotheca, Forget-me-not, Heuchera, Iberis, Pansies, Penstemon, Petunia, Primula, Scabiosa, Stocks, Viola.

BULBS-CORMS-TUBERS---Alstroemeria, Anemone, Anomatheca, Babiana, Bessera, Calochortus, Haemanthus, Leucocoryne, Lilium, Montbretia, Muscari, Ornithogalum, Oxalis, Pancratium, Tulips, Watsonia.

DIVISION-OR-CLUMPS---Acanthus, Agapanthus, Amaryllis, Anchusa, Armeria, Fall Asters, Francoa, Gazania, Hemerocallis, Heuchera, Hollyhock, Japanese Iris, Pancratium, Penstemon, Peri-winkle, Sedum, Shasta Daisy, Thalictrum, Thyme,

# COMPENDIUM

The plants that have been used in the foregoing lists will be treated here with a brief description intended to bring out the salient features horticulturally and to establish the landscape point of view where that is pertinent. There are few plants that should be used in every garden, sworn statements of flower lovers notwithstanding. With complete and un-impeachable beauty, vigor and hardiness and other attributes favorable to acceptable performance, there will almost surely be the missing link that becomes the limiting factor under a given set of conditions. It is the thorough study and consideration of all these factors, along with good design, that makes for the successful garden of long utility for living, pleasure and wear. The material which follows should invariably be consulted as the lists are being used for it will offer the reader an opportunity to further evaluate the plant for himself. With this additional outlook or view and information, he will more clearly determine the possibilities of the individual, and the bearing it may have on the purpose or situation he has in mind. Moreover, it is not expected that this section be used to any great extent independently. Plants of obscure function or uncertain requirements will be found which may be translated into good use only with help as set forth in some list caption. Others will relate to some highly specialized condition or unusual effect not applicable to normal events in planting. Woody plants may be assumed to be evergreen unless stated as being deciduous, with a definitely recurring leaf drop.

ABELIA---small to medium-sized shrubs of bushy character which find many and varied uses in and about the garden. They are normally evergreen, but the foliage is sensitive to frost and may drop during severe winters north in these regions. They are highly ornamental for form and in leafage, very free-flowering in the sun or a little shade. They should be given reasonably good drainage and a fairly fertile soil kept open to the air. All are to be pruned in late winter or early spring.

*Abelia Floribunda*

-floribunda, "Mexican A." rather dense-spreading 3-4' or less, known to become as high as 6' south under exceptionally good circumstances, a prolific-blooming specimen for pot or tub, or in any place wanting an outstanding show of color; main crop of pendent, long-narrow-tubular, rosy red to light magenta flowers breaks in late spring, to trail out over summer and swell again in the fall;benefits with much peat or leaf mould in the soil and used as a mulch:water through drought This color is difficult to handle, but potent, the plant less vigorous than the following and not often seen.

*Abelia grandiflora*

-grandiflora, a general purpose plant of the first order, work-horse of the border, some 5-6' in height, the arching stems with abundant short-trumpet-shaped, flushed white or pinkish flowers June-August, while the reddish, starlike calyx-bracts persist into winter with color comparable to bloom:bright coppery green foliage enlivens as a hedge with frequent shearings during summer or

199

*Abronia maritima*

*Abronia umbellata*

grown as such in natural form and not pruned except to remove the
inevitable flash streamers....take old stems entirely, cutting to
a node or joint to prevent unsightly stubs:any soil or exposure.
     -schumanni, similar to above but more refined and not as big
3-4', the brighter rosy lavender flowers nicely shaded July-August:
leaves and flowers all in miniature:temperamental south, it is difficult to establish and hold, coming up in spring with much dead,
twiggy wood that is tedious to clear out.

*Abutilon hybrid*

## SAND VERBENA

   ABRONIA---western natives, loosely trailing perennials of some
importance in the desert or on the coast in holding sand or dry
soil in the wind. They may be grown as annuals in the garden,
but are firmly perennial and quite persistent when established.
They are extremely tolerant of salts in the soil, heat with extreme drought, blot out barren ground quickly and effectively.
The flowers are held in a verbena-like head of varying fullness
and are slightly fragrant. Sow seed in spring, widely spaced
and as deep as half an inch.
     -maritima, an excellent dark green foliage within reach of
salt spray, but not much color in bloom, the dark red flowers
set scantily along the far-rambling runners:native along the
coast in California.
     -umbellata, trailing or somewhat collected as to form,
best species to use in the garden for the greater refinement and superior color:large headed varieties available,
dark pink, May-July:boxes or beds or in the rock garden.
     -villosa, "Desert V." to be used under conditions of ex-
treme heat and in the sun:a flattish, tenacious mat of hairy
foliage surmounted by loose heads of white and rose to pink
flowers, summer and fall:too rarely seen.

*Abrus*

   ABRUS precatorius, "Rosary-pea" twining 8-10', or less when used
as a trailer over the ground where it becomes somewhat woody:an embrangle of hard scarlet seeds with a black eye, make this plant of
considerable note:flowers of white to red or purple in summer are
not important, but the seed by autumn in a rounding aggregation
of opening, twisting, persisting pods are securely attached
for arrangements:best in humid heat;deciduous in cold,may die.

## FLOWERING MAPLE

   ABUTILON---shrubs of open habit, seldom of pleasing form
but with handsome, hanging, bell-shaped flowers in white,
yellow or pink, markedly veined and nearly continuous.
They are hardy in more northerly regions along the coast
and are inclined to drop buds unopened in full sun in the
drier regions. They exhaust their strength early in life with
the prolific flowering....prune in late winter for desired
shape. They are adapted to protected places among other shrubs
in partial or nearly full shade, but will take some little exposure when acclimated.

*Abutilon megapotamicum*

     -hybridum, of the many crossed forms available, many of
them growing into tree-like, umbrageous heads from a low stem,
showing pleasing variegation in the maple-like leaves:charac-
terized by the generally larger flowers, well used individually or set in lower plantings.
     -megapotamicum, typically vining and to as much as 10', the
canes strung with the smaller bright red and lemon-yellow bells:a
single feature plant in youth for a basket, flowering at eight months
after which it will be planted out against a wall or with other
support. The hybrids are almost without exception slender-stemmed
and very erect shrubs....longer-lived.
     -palmeri, from the low desert in California, a small
shrub of open, stiff growth, the scanty, grey-blue foliage
very handsome when reduced to leaves, a loose open foil for
the small orange, erect cup-shaped flowers all summer:takes
desert heat but not full sun, wanting shade over mid-day:
wants comparative coolness, deep moisture in heat and
irrigation under domestication:tubs, tender in frost.

*Acacia farnesiana*

*Acacia melanoxylon*

## WATTLE

ACACIA---mostly trees, variously formed, frequently reaching maturity with as much breadth as height or only low, well-shaped bushes.
All have yellow or golden flowers, fluffy masses of tiny fuzzy balls
or tight little cylinders set precisely along the branches, characteristically pungent as to odor and in great profusion. The plant
is very rapid in growth and extremely short of life, an effective period of twenty or at most, thirty years being all that
may be expected....yet with certain picturesque qualities
developing in some species to carry on further. Some fertility of the soil is all they ask, along with drainage
and when established they will stand under considerable
or even total drought....but show it. Too much moisture
tends to hasten growth unduly to require frequent headings
back for shape or to withstand wind. This probably explains
their general preference in California over Florida, where
they fail to flower satisfactorily. They are practically
pest-free. The larger species should be held in drastically
where exposed to high winds. Seed may be broadcast under favorable conditions for larger effects in the landscape where a
few of them will naturalize.

-alata, a shrub, or vagrant-tree-like at 3-5', the green
foliage applied closely along the stem to form a decurrent flange
or side wing:the tiny flower balls appear in good crop April-May:
tubs or a casual insert for the shrubbery.

-armata, "Kangaroo-thorn" sprawling shrub 6-12' high and as
much or more across, the light green harsh, horny leaves warped
and sharply spined at the edge, mingling February-March with the
small yellow flower balls:must not be over-watered in a heavy
soil, shows dust badly and gangles in good ground to run down
slopes nicely as cover:one of the hardiest in frost.

-auriculaeformis, "Earleaf A." proven for Florida in rocky
sandy soils, a shade tree with a dense dark head of sickle-shaped leaves and spikes of pale yellow flowers, usually in two
bloomings:windbreaks if set closely together.

-baileyana, probably the most handsome of the lot, a
spreading tree to 30' with steel-blue, very nicely fashioned
doubly compound leaves running spirally the length of the stem:
massed, light yellow flowers January-March are often well open
and available for Christmas:better grown in moderate moisture
but will not flower in Florida. This is an unusually attractive tree, with more than ordinary refinement when
not forced, full of individuality in age, but going out
early in poorly drained heavy soils. It has a distinctly
purple-leaved form that is most acceptable for color.

-cultriformis, a medium-sized shrub, naturally
compact and dense as it grows under drouth or in poor
soil, more loosely formed as a small tree under better
circumstances:short, stubby, curiously knife-like leaves
are close-set and rigid, a further formalized accent:makes
a good hedge under ocean wind, grown informally or clipped:
flowers in March....heavily:comparatively long-lived.

-cyanophylla, " Orange W." shrub or small tree to some
30' or less, the branches drooping with the weight of almost
orange flowers March-April:body of the plant, whether shrub
or tree, is well built and filled out with the long, narrow,
light bluish leaves.

-decurrens, "Green W." slender tree with very attractive, finely divided, fern-like leaves:of very rapid and
rather substantial growth to 50', good shelter when closely planted, but shatters quickly when exposed to much in
the way of wind:a fascinating angled flanging of the smaller branches remains impressed as meandering lines on the
older wood:comparatively long-lived if handled carefully in
youth....do not force with water and fertilizer and head
back lightly from time to time.   var. dealbata, "Silver
W." with darker foliage of a frosted, bluish cast, the
pale yellow blooming March-April:survives in moist
clay soils and is rather widely planted:hardy in frost.

Acacia
verticillata

Acacia
armata

Acacia
pycnantha

Acacia
horrida

Acacia
longifolia

var. mollis, "Black W." has pale green foliage, with an
overall effect of symmetrical grace, the deeper yellow flowers
June-July:orange-red shows on the trunk and branches as the
bark fissures widen.

-farnesiana, "Huisache" "Popinac" a small, delicate grey-green,
spiny shrub or flat-topped tree of extremely open texture, native in
the Southwest, cultivated there and brought to California by the early
Padres:dark yellow flowers begin in January and reach their full glory
February-March:grows more slowly than most species, is very drought
and heat resistant and naturalizes a bit too readily in the wrong
places:flowers are laid away with linens for the fragrance:stands in as
much as twenty degrees of frost and does surprisingly well in Florida.

-greggi, "Texas-mimosa" shrubby, or frequently a small scrubby tree
to 20' for hot dry rocky places, where it makes practically impenetrable
thickets of thorny stems, the creamy-yellow flowers August-September:
hardy in frost in its native Southwest.

-horrida, "Karoo Thorn" shrubby or low tree-like with substantial,
but thinly appointed foliage and comparatively large orange flower
balls August-September:branches are set with inch-long, whitish,
needle-like thorns....good low barrier planting under severe salt
winds:deciduous.

-longifolia, "Sidney W." large shrub or tree-like with a rounded
head at 20', the flowers February-March, bright gold strung along the
branches as rigid points of color;best use is that of super-shrub instead of tree that must be cut to shape, the lower limbs sprawling
on the ground as they were meant to do:best screen in poor soils
under exposure to salt wind, sometimes clipped there as a large
wide hedge:survives in almost pure sand.

-macracantha, a bushy tree 20' with growth from a low trunk,
sometimes only a mound of fine feathery foliage, dark behind the
spring crop of yellow flowers:heavily armed when young and for
use then as a barrier, less spined when mature, but much more
substantial:use in Florida.

-melanoxylon, "Blackwood A." with reservations, an acceptable
tree, dense-round-headed in age, pyramidal in youth, growing in
any soil or situation to 40':makes an avenue tree, but suckers
badly and in lesser streets goes for moisture, taking curb and
sidewalk along....good break for wind and excellent to baffle
traffic noise:may require heading-in, to be done in early summer
to reduce the litter that follows the straw-colored flowers of
March-April:wants moisture, but adapts surprisingly to drouth.

-pendula, "Weeping Myal" an erect tree 25' with uplifting
limbs, the branches strictly hanging, streamers of bluish grey
leaves:uncertain in flowering and not early in life, but about
June-July:shows every indication of a longer life span, growing slowly to develop a fissured bark:massed plantings will
present considerable varietion in color and texture, sometimes
in form:deep rich soils with low moisture are indicated, the exposed and bending top tending otherwise to burn out in the sun:choice
for very special uses....a beautifully distinctive tree.

-podalyriaefolia, "Pearl A." an open-headed, rounding tree 25',
of very rapid growth, but short-lived even for this group when freely
watered:the short roundish leaves are of a soft light grey to match
the pale lemon-yellow flowering of November-January:brittle limbs
are best reduced from time to time if in wind....spring the best
time:self-sows rather freely and flowers in Florida.

-pravissima, from the twisted bean-pod, a tree, erect-drooping
and full in spread, growing 15-20' when given the moisture it can
use:bright green leaves are short-broad-triagular, the whole plant
gold tipped in winter, if and when the bronze flower buds hold:in
full effect February-March.

-prominens, "Goldenrain W." a tree 20-25', slender erect and
compact, darkly cast in precise outline with very narrow leaves,
the pale blooming February-March:notable for long, satisfactory
service and a minimum of litter.

-pruinosa, "Copper W." supple open-headed tree 30', of exceptionally rapid growth which consolidates well under exposure
to wind if not kept too moist....prune to keep head clear of fine
brush:foliage dark green, fernlike with the new growth appearing

over a long season in tones of copper and red, while the large trusses
of light yellow flowers spread out from February through summer. This
is a tree of many attractions, the variable and complicated shadings
giving a lively effect:very rapid growth for a windbreak.
    -pubescens, "Downy A." a very refined little tree 10-15', a
dapperling for the garden, the young branches covered with very fine
hair, the branches and at times, the entire plant bending under the
weight of the bright yellow blooming March-April:choice.
    -pycnantha, "Golden W." an erect tree to 25' or more, if pushed
upwards by surrounding growth; of very rapid growth which consolidates
satisfactorily in salt wind: quantities of flowers February-March in
large clusters of fluffy golden balls set against yellow twigs. This
is as handsome as any acacia and naturalizes in poor shallow soils.
    -retinodes floribunda, "Gossamer W." a round-headed tree 25',
normally quite variable in both shape and size, always, however, so
brittle-limbed; always breaking under small boys climbing:light yellow flowers are intermittent, more or less over the year, conspicuous March-May. This tree is very commonly used, is one of the best
species for moist ground, is subject to scale but easily controled.
    -verticillata, widely spreading as a shrub in the wind, slender
as a 15' tree as found against a building or high wall:dark, short
needle-like leaves are arranged in many repeating whorls about the
green stems....studded April-May with small, solitary rundles,
little cylinders of pale yellow flowers:shears is answer to a
shabby old age and the plant thrives best in soils of some
substance....yet, with time, establishing in sandy ground
under salt winds.
    -vestita, "Hairy W." shrubby, wide-spreading, the small
leaves wide-sickle-shaped, grey-green, soft to touch and feel,
and to the eye when the tiny flowers show in their rather different loose, lax clusters:better grown in heat, dryness and in
very poor soils....very useful there.

ACAENA---trailing evergreen perennials, eager mat-forming for a
cover, used as a sealer between rock or with flagging....but most
invasive. They take full sun, but do better in a little shade, as beneath trees, and always in fair moisture. A tendency to scatter widely about underground is marked and will reduce effectiveness materially....pinch out over-growths to hold in hand and to compress the mat.
    -fissistipula, a broad, furry mat of somewhat larger leaves than
the following which are decidedly bluish, the cover in depth 3" or more
and fairly dense:not well known and will not survive much dryness.
    -microphylla, a carpet of brisk, light green, tiny round leaves,
no flowers to mention; but proof  of their having been there in the
rosy-red burs summer and fall....survives light drought and is very
quick to fill in.  var. glaucophylla, a sheet less than an inch in
thickness, blue-green, quilted tightly to the earth, if held in.
var. inermis, has bronzy foliage in a 2-3" coverlet:crevices. These
plants become less dependable as used south in these regions.

ACALYPHA---soft-wood shrubby material, mostly vigorous foliage
plants with high color from the tropics for bedding out in warm
places or used small in a window or planter box. They may be grown
as shrubs in the garden south in Florida and out of frost in California. Generally they want good culture as regards soil, moisture
and feeding. They are subject to many pests, mealybug, scale, red
spider, with extended cold weather decidedly enervating from the
standpoint of chill and un-natural loss of leaves.
    -californica, "Tassel-spurge" a small native shrub, everbloom-
ing in the garden, with abundant typical, if very small spikes of
flowers that impart an overall lively or peppery aspect:tiny narrow leaves are edged with pink to match the rosy-red of the bloom-
ing:a low hedge with clipping and a practical plant in the garden,
although rarely seen....miniature qualities valuable there.
    -hispida, "Chenile-plant" the large tassel of flowers quite
showy in reds:foliage mostly green for massing in beds, but the plant
ultimately a large shrub that will succeed in a heavy wet soil.
    -wilksiana, "Copperleaf" variable, the typical bronzy green
leafage with orange or red and brown in various patterns:comes
along best in light shade, more intense by autumn and winter:re-

*Acantholimon venustum*

*Acanthus mollis*

*Acalypha californica*

*Acalypha wilksiana*

*Achimenes*

bounds quickly from cutting frost in straight, vigorous
stems.   var. godseffiana, more dwarf, 2-3' for small
restricted areas:dense bushy.   var. marginata, exceptionally robust, as high as 8', the leaf with a margin of
pink or darker, deepening to red by winter.   var. musaica, a
mosaic of color in the larger leaves, green, red, yellow, in
fiery red by fall to earn the venacular of "Firedragon", more
compact as a plant and will not survive even the mildest of
winters in California without help.

*Achras*

ACANTHOLIMON venustum, "Prickly-thrift" a low perennial of
sturdy, dense character, tufted and evergreen, a plant for the
rock garden or forepart of a dry border under the sun and with
sharp drainage:pink flowers repeat individually in a one-sided
head packed close with glumy buds that await their turn over May-
August:slow, tight growth to 6", persistent only in loose dry
soils that retain a modicum of moisture.

ACANTHUS mollis, "Bearsbreech" a bold-appearing perennial
of sturdy character, the effect of the huge, deeply cleft
leaves very striking, handsome:soil and fertility not so
important as surface drainage, while humidity and a little
shade in heat will help it over its most trying time in
the summer:erect narrow spikes 4' high carry the pale rosy
purple flowers over June-July, after which the failing leaf
is almost immediately replaced....logical time for division and
transplants:warm place in a deep, reasonably fertile soil. The
species  -montanus is shrub-like, with dark narrow and narrowly
lobed, heavily spined leaves:wants shade and warmth:pots and tubs.

ACER oblongum, "Evergreen Maple" dense, compact to 35' in height,
the lax, leathery leaves oblong, blunt-pointed, deep green, coppery
when young, infrequently lobed:a shade tree, but somewhat weak in
the wind:rare.   The species  -floridanum, is the preferred tree to
use as "White, Soft or Silver Maple" in these southern regions.

*Acanthu*
*montan*

ACHIMENES longiflora, tiny tubers, highly desirable for pots or
baskets in the house or outside in protective shade:afford continual profusion of bloom, white to lavender and blue to shades of
salmon to carmine in hybrids, June-October, the flowers long-
tubed, flat trumpets:light, loose soils well fertilized, with
much leafmould....water daily through heat, but sparingly in
the beginning:use 6 to 8 mature tubers to each 6" diameter of
container, starting February-April:should appear in from two to
six weeks, when pinch back as they begin to straggle:never allow to go dry until definitely going off in the fall....with-
hold water then:cut tops when ripened, shake out soil and
store dry over winter, or will serve in same container for
several years with considerable increase....take containing
soil with both large and smaller developing tubers for further
planting:partial to half  sunny windows as used in the house or will
serve as a ground crop in the lath house.

ACHRAS zapota, "Sapodilla" Stately round-headed tree 50',
slow in growth, compact, with horizontally extended limbs for
dense shade, the wood tough to resist wind:large fruits are
roundish with a rusty brown skin, the flesh yellowish, soft
and melting, as in a pear:not successful in California except in favored spots, cold nights being more of a drawback
than low humidity or extreme heat:withstands more dryness
in the soil than most tropicals.

ACIDANTHERA bicolor, bulb-like plants, the growth up to
18-24" high, very late starting in the spring:long-tubed,
cream-colored flowers are splotched at the base of the petal
with chocolate, August-October:set out February-April in fairly
substantial soil of good drainage....lift where water holds;
they rot easily:a faint aroma will be noticed indoors when
used as a cutflower or pot-grown:grown far north into
warm temperate regions, treated as gladiolas.

*Acokanth*

COMPENDIUM

ACOKANTHERA spectabilis, "African Wintersweet" slow-growing,
bulky, a hulking bush 5-8' high with an overall oppressive
feeling:interesting, however, in the dull red coloring of
berry, stem and leaf which will be found more marked in the
sun and during cold weather....all parts toxic or poisonous
when eaten:white to pinkish, daphne-like flowers of earliest
spring are very fragrant:best used in the lighter soils of the
coast where it submits to exposure:tender in frost.

ACROCOMIA---rare feather palms infrequently found in subtropical regions. They are highly ornamental, having drooping
spined fronds, with spines also on the trunk a hazard during
the early years....gradually weathering away. They are primarily
subjects for planting in Florida and along the Gulf Coast.
    -mexicana, remaining quite low or 10-20', the stem covered with
the hard petiole boots which ultimately drop, leaving deep rutty scars:
fronds are blue-green, the flowers yellow and very fragrant:does not
thrive under cold winds, but is frost hardy to Santa Barbara on the
west coast. Both want to be grown on the dry side.
    -totai, very tall, 50' or more with time, slender-stemmed,
similar to and substituting for royal palm in colder regions:of
rapid growth, the bole is sometimes swollen at the base as in
above and smooth except for spines and shallow scars.

ACTINOPHLOEUS macarthuri, "Cluster Palm" suckering to form
a tight clump of several to many slender 10', bamboo-like,
greenish-grey, ringed stems:a feather palm, the narrow leaflets
a light green, abruptly ended as if chewed ragged:round nuts hang
in clusters, green through yellow to red as they mature:wants a
little shade, is tender in frost and makes a tub plant:rare.

ADENOCALYMNA alliaceum, a bignonia-like plant, a climbing shrub
to be grown far south only, under sure protection from frost and
in good moisture:the elongated funnel-shaped flowers are full-
clustered, with a long terminal tendril, the leaves sometimes three-clustered as such, instead of being in twos:the
blooming is white to pale yellow and, at times, onion scent-
ed:may be grown as a shrub with pruning.

ADENOCARPUS viscosus, "African-broom" a shrub of open structure 3-5', untidy when forced, more presentable in dry sandy
soils in the sun....light pruning or terminal pinching advisable after blooming:slender branches are densely crowded with
the small three-parted leaves, while spikes of yellow, pea-
shaped flowers April-June, carry the feeling of lupine or more
like gorse:subject to the genista worm.

ADENOSTOMA fasciculatum, "Chamise" heath-like shrubs of the
California chaparral, varying in height and form according to
conditions, valuable for arid regions where no maintenance can
be given:dark foliage sets off the short, but beautiful blooming of May-June, white heads becoming unsightly all to soon:
hardy in frost and burns like tinder, but comes back quickly
when cut:not much more than cover in high wind and a cutflower of some merit when taken in bud.   The species  -sparsi-
folium, known as "Redshank" is interesting in silhouette and
for the shredding red bark:does well under summer irrigation.

MAIDENHAIR FERN
ADIANTUM---delicate, infinitely refined little plants, well
known for their fragile beauty. The dark purple or black stalks
and wedge-shaped leaves gathered together in flat sprays are
most effective in pots or out in the garden in cool, fairly
moist places in the shade. Good drainage and much leafmould
or rotted wood pulp bring about a condition for growth that
is ideal, a place where new fronds will develop all summer and
hold. Use spent plaster, limestone or cement chips, if the soil
is extremely acid:divide in February when crowded and give
very little, if any fertilizing.
    -capillus-veneris, "Southern M." for humid areas,
205

the running roots attaching to rocks or other objects in damp,
shaded places:slender, erect-spreading, as much as 18" high.
-caudatum, trailing, re-rooting to make a dense carpet 6" thru
and in fairly dry places:baskets.   -cuneatum, "Delta M." normally used in pots inside or for cool, shady corners on the terrace
or other frequented place for more or less temporary decoration or
other use:several well developed forms will be found.   -emargin-
atum, a little native of the Pacific Coast for a place among
rocks, better there as it is easily crowded out:wants dryish
conditions, but will go dormant without some moisture.

AEONIUM---woody stemmed and branching succulents that
have been given a considerable place in these regions.
They have much to offer the collection of succulents in
way of mass and flowers for some feeling for continuity in
planting design. The foliage is similar to the better known
sempervivum or house-leek, the rosettes usually flattened, the
leaf more nearly what may be termed conventional and frequently
with color. More moisture is required than with the average
succulent and they do not succeed in extreme heat:tender.
    -arboreum(atropurpureum)slender-stemmed, to 3' or less, spar-
ingly branched if at all, the rosette nodding and purplish, especially when winter comes along with the very effective yellow flowering in quite large heads:rather tolerant of hard going, as of soil
and scant moisture, but shows the suffering.
    -decorum, well-formed, a branchy little shrub of symmetry, some
12-18" high and as much across, the rosettes bluish green and shining, the flowers in the spring yellow to orange, may be flushed with
rose:precise and trim, exceptionally decorative and practical for a
pot:insists on a light, well drained soil with fair moisture.
    -spathulatum(tourneforti)a well branched woody plant 3-4'high,
rounding but not dense, working nicely into an appropriate place in
the shrubbery:rosettes are not flattened, the narrow, thickened
leaves splotched or streaked with red:dense heads of yellow flowers come in autumn or early winter, but are sometimes held over
until spring.
    -tabulaeforme, growing to 18", not so densely shrubby or
quite stemless, the light green, shining rosettes as much as
6" across, flattened and ultimately rising to something of a
point in the center:flowers are pale yellow and carried low.
This item is being overlooked as a motif in decoration.

AGAPANTHUS africanus, "Lily-of-the-Nile" variable, a tuberous-
rooted perennial 1-5' in height, widely and effectively used, the
pale to deep blue or pure white flowers in open globular heads a-
bove the lush leaves June-July....florets drop clean from the slender stalks which hold in an umbrageous form adapted to arrangements
:takes some shade, but blooms better in the sun, wanting good moisture while in flower and run-off for wet seasons:pots, tubs or the
open border where long life may be expected in fertile soils with
good body.   var. mooreanus is deciduous and very frost hardy.

AGATHIS robusta, "Dammar-pine" a towering tree with a straight
smooth bole that is interrupted only high up by the short, horizontal branches:the flattened leaf is wide and conspicuously veined,
tough and enduring:juvenile forms are used in tubs. This is a remarkable tree that has gone out of general use....would quickly be
revived, were the modernists to find it:shallow-rooting.

CENTURY PLANT
AGAVE---decorative plants of the desert and on the grand scale,
with great heavy rosettes of harsh, elongated, thick and spiny
leaves. From the center mass a tall flower stalk rises....after
a time, a striking object if not of any beauty and of no color
value. The original plant dies after this blooming, but the
offsets continue the process laterally until a jagged pile
results that will be very difficult to remove. They are for
wide open space, the smaller types only, in the garden. The
flower stalk appears in the course of a few years, seemingly
depending on moisture....century myth in bloom not tenable.

Aeonium
decoru

Agapan
thic

Agave

-americana, the rosette 3-5' in height and as broad, the
leaves blue or variously marked in white or yellow, the plant
stemless, resting upon the earth to build up the typical mass;
the great leaves, nicely and precisely marked in line and the
molded imprint of its neighbor by bud pressure, are much too large
and disorderly for general use.
    -attenuata, of refinement, but still over-size, the pale
green rosette of thinner leaves ultimately raised on a low stout
stem:the huge flowering stalk is crowded with persistent bracts
in the likeness of a catkin that bends back to the ground.
    -decipiens, the rosette comparatively small, not more than
18", the leaves dark, sharply keeled, set with black spines:the
inflorescence is greenish or yellow, November-December:pot and tub.
    -victoriae-reginae, in scale with the garden, low and without a
trunk, the narrow, sharply keeled leaves rigid, tightly clasping, 12"
long and broadly lined with a white band:pots or an accent plant.

AGDESTIS clematidea, quick-growing from a monstrous, exposed,
rock-like turnip-tuber, expanding cover for a waste place:nearly
white flowers of September-October are sweet-smelling:reddish,
branching streamers may be taken indoors after removal of the
strong-smelling foliage:rich moist soils, where there may be
an increase by means of offsets.

AGERATUM houstonianum, "Flossflower" an annual bedding plant
or low filler for the border, having full round masses of light
blue flowers in small fluffy heads:grows in any garden soil; it
likes it rich and not too cold or heavy:blooming is continuous
in frost-free areas, only temporarily set back cold spells or in
heat:sow preferably in spring or early summer, the later plants
being more likely to carry through cold weather:dwarfs for edging.

AGLAONEMA simplex, "Chinese Evergreen" long used for indoor decoration, a rugged stoloniferous tropical for line studies of the
unbranching 3' stems that are topped by the tufted oblong to lance-
shaped, durable 12" leaves:grows in moist soil or in water, used in
pots for deep shade:may produce a small calla-like green flower, if
or when the roots become sufficiently crowded.

AGONIS---woody plants that are pliable in structure, giving easily
to the wind which they are inclined to favor as a condition of existence....foliage with wearing qualities associated with dry climates.
Give them good drainage in soil that is not too fertile and not too
moist. They may be grown near the sea with a little protection. The
flowers come in close heads and are not very important except in the
matter of time. They resist drouth.
    -flexuosa, "Willow-myrtle" handsome tree 40', of drooping
habit, the scented white flowers born along the pendulous branchlets June-July....cut hard after blooming:crushed leaves give
off the odor of peppermint:hardy in some 10 degrees of frost.
    -linearifolia, "Juniper-myrtle" erect shrub 10-15' with line
value, the sharply upreaching stems lightly clothed with the short, rigid
needle-like leaves:winter-blooming in white, clover-like heads.

AGROSTIS---ornamental and lawn grasses, erect or creeping, wanting
fair to quite moist soil conditions as well as high humidity of the
atmosphere. Under these circumstances they will take close mowing
and thrive. The ornamental kinds are exceptionally handsome in
head, flower and seed.
    -maritima, "Seaside Bent" fine creeping grass for a velvety
lawn....only when well cared for in way of frequent watering
during heat, close cutting and regular fertilization:will not
endure mis-use in any way and give satisfaction:all operations
in management should be moderate and often as the plants are
shallow rooted and must have constant attention....golf greens.
    -nebulosa, "Cloud-grass" very ornamental, low-growing, with
distinctly airy effects in the garden and affording prime material for dry or winter boquets. This is not an immortelle,
but is used in that sense and relationship.
    -palustris, "Redtop" of very rapid growth and development,

Agdestis

Ageratum

Ajuga

Agrostis
nebulosa

to be used with blue-grass in new lawns as a nurse crop for
the early stages of growth:dies out gradually as the permanent
turf sets, or will take over some soils more efficiently than the
blue-grass, especially where drainage is poor.

AJUGA reptans, "Carpet-bugle" a creeping perennial with large,
lush leaves closely knit and hugging the earth as cover, the supporting narrow spikes of bright blue flowers from late winter
over spring into summer:uniform moisture is important, some
shade and a fairly good soil desirable but not essential:a
tendency to bronzy shading in the leafage culminates in purplish strains that are most attractive....all show effects
of cold weather:watch for crown rot during heat....reduce
water then and open up the mat to air.

ALBIZZIA---deciduous trees of rapid growth, having the refined airy character and general aspect of acacia. The leaves
are compound or frond-like, feathery and of a buoyant lightness in currents of air that affords an ever-changing mood in
the foliage mass:flowers of most extreme fineness in large,
near cylindrical heads or small and globular. They are used for
shade as well as for the color in flower and a wide range as to
hardiness in frost requires that care be exercised in selection
of species. All tend to re-seed and are littery, but the debris
in its fineness disappears readily into cover....even grass.
  -julibrissin, "Silktree" loosely known in the South as
mimosa, the hardiest but with difficulties in getting properly
established:form is spreading, even the first stems wanting to
go off angular, the branches later splaying out in overlapping
tiers of rather remarkable beauty....growing to 30', with light
green leafage and summer showing of pink flowers in silken bundles of frayed cording crowded to the extremeties:will not shape
up well in a container or in very much alkali:starts best as young
field grown plants, whipped up for head-room:take several stems when
offered and know the beauty they will support.
  -lebbek, "Womans-tongue-tree" a broad flat top at 40', the
limbs wide-spreading to make good light shade:defoliates in
late spring, the new leaves pushing off the old but dependable the balance of the year:greenish-yellow flowers in
tiny balls are tasseled like acacia, May-June, while tannish seed pods hang and rattle in the breeze with a strangely familiar chattering:as found in Southern Florida, the
roots are a nuisance in the garden, as are the seedlings.
  -lophantha, "Plume-acacia" growing to 25', more
densely foliated than either above, but quickly going
into a shabby old age, most valuable for quick shelter
against sea winds:silky yellowish-green flowers have no
color value, but do bring about a pleasing contrast with
the dark foliage:tender in frost until established and
generally a dolorous-looking specimen over winter, trying
to hold the leaves, frequently failing.

ALBUCA minor(crinifolia)large, tightly crowding bulbs that
throw an unusual and striking flowering effect....orange-tipped
stipules and a lumpish head of long, chartreuse, brown-marked
buds, the enameled segments bungling open in an awkward, heavy
handed manner, white and yellowish, May-June....a heavy scent
of almond, in warmth:more curious than beautiful and may
skip bloomings in the shade:set bulb one-third out of
the ground, in well drained soil that carries moisture:
frost-hardy and persistent, although the older bulbs will
break after a few years with resulting inferior flowers,
when the clump may be divided, using a sharp knife.

ALEURITES moluccana, "Candlenut" a spreading, semi-deciduous
tree 60', used for shade and for the striking contrast of a floury
smudging of the foliage at time of flowering:useful in poor dry
soils but stunting there, surface-rooting and constantly litter-
ing:larger use is in Florida where the species  -fordi is cultivated commercially, a small tree for shade and bloom.

# COMPENDIUM

ALLAMANDA hendersoni, "Golden-trumpet" a climbing shrub or
vining freely against a wall, on a roof or as forced high into
a tree, the clean shining leaves and large fragrant flowers of
substance, more or less over the year in warmth....going into
winter in full display:requires a rich soil and a protected
place, good drainage, good feeding, a low winter sun to draw
out the blooming, and to be as dry as possible through cold
weather....good run-off for rain in California.  The species
-neriifolia, "Yellowbell" is a much smaller plant, shrubby,
limber-sprawling 3-5', doing well in shade, more dwarf in sun.

ALLIUM---a large group of onion-like bulbs, most of them
with the typical pungent odor of bruised parts, but the more
highly ornamental kinds not offensive if left undisturbed.
They rapidly develop thrifty clumps or spread out as a pest if
allowed to seed. Use them in the border, appropriate sizes in
the rock garden, or with the culinary herbs....many are useful
in cookery, at the same time ornamental in foliage and flower.
They take any soil, in full sun or partial shade, flower well
over the year by species in loose rounded heads, white, yellow,
pink, rose, lavender and blue.
  -ascalonicum, "Shallot" culinary herb with lilac-colored
flowers:the bulb with a mild flavor of onion is harvested in the
summer and keeps well for winter flavorings:leaves are eaten in
the green state, in salads and soups or in stuffings.
  -caeruleum, clear blue flowers clustered in fairly tight,
spherical heads held two feet or more above the shorter three-
angled leaves:very handsome and desirable for cutting.
  -neapolitanum, "Daffodil-garlic" very decorative, purely an
ornamental plant as used, grown for the abundant, pure white flowers
May-June in the garden or may be held back for December-January in
the house for a sunny window:the splendid flowering heads are with no
trace or suggestion of onion when cut:naturalizes too easily in light
sandy soils, but an acceptable pest in poor ground.
  -porrum, the "Leek" with a rather rank growth to 18", or even
more, the flowers white to bluish:stem and leaf used like
asparagus or in stews is chief value:being for spring
salads primarily, it is available weeks before onion
tips are ready.
  -pulchellum, very choice for any grouping of garden
flowers and worthy thereof, slender stalks 15-18" of fat
pointed buds packed to bursting with rosy-lavender flowers
July-August, an uneven burst in fact, the blooming hangs
suspended like a rocket in the night....no pest, this:and
the increase is never enough to satisfy.
  -sativum, "Garlic" has very attractive purple flowers in
a roundish head:the bulb with strong seasoning powers, is gathered in when the foliage withers, braided together by the persisting
tops and stored hanging.
  -schoenprasm, "Chives" a free-flowering little plant that should
receive more consideration as an ornamental:the erect, compact habit
and attractive light purple flowers suit it well for edging in the
garden:foliage, with just the suggestion of onion may be used for
a delicate seasoning and may be cropped every two or three weaks
during growth.
  -senescens, lilac flowers in loose clusters June-July or later,
growing 10-15" in tight, well-held little clumps, united at the base:re-
seeds, but is easily kept in hand:probably best all-round garden allium.
  -triquetrum, suitable substitute for snowdrop in the far south, the
channeled leaves recurving, the nodding, ragged-fringed bells of white for
winter and early spring....last years seedlings will carry into summer:
spreads slowly and widely and tolerates considerable shade, easily kept
in hand:grows  8-12" high and is down all summer.

ALLOPHYTON mexicanum, "Mexican-foxglove" summer flowering perennial,
woody at the base and growing 12-15" high:purple, penstemon-like
nodding flowers in profusion early in the year
will repeat in the fall if not allowed to
go to seed....feed for this and liquid
manure will be found acceptable:sun.

209

### ALDER

ALNUS---deciduous trees or shrublike, but with height, haunting moist places or extremely wet soils along streams, usually
in the cooler areas such as drafty canyons. They are attract-
tive in the right locality, clean-cut and of high decorative
value. They are not showy except for a moment in the spring
as picked out in trailing catkins just before the new leaves
break. As indicated, they are for very special and occasional use and will almost of necessity be procured as saplings
from the wild, each of the following being for its own region.
They are of interest in subtropical regions largely as the hills
reach south with their modifying influence on climate. Grow them in
lawns, especially when irrigation is by flooding. There will be some
autumn coloration and the catkins will serve in arrangements.

-cordata, "Italian A." for general use and usually obtainable
in the nursery trade, a sturdy tree to 75', the leaves broad-
rounding, somewhat smaller than the natives and a lighter
green that takes on a burnished quality in heat.
-rhombifolia, "White A." a large shrub at lower levels, or a
pyramidal tree as it reaches into warm temperate climates:holds the
foliage late and leaves out early:native in California.   -rugosa,
"Smooth A." shrubby or a tree 25' in Northern Florida and in Texas:
leaves wedge-shaped, finely toothed:swampy ground.    -tenuifolia,
"Mountain A." growing 25', or less in the Southwest where the mountains spread out to merge with the plain, normally with several
clean trunks, but not suckering. These trees are very freshening
in extreme heat where water reaches near the surface for support.

ALOE---found at its best in lower Southern California where it
will grow freely under natural conditions of the climate, wanting
only a little water over summer to freshen and prepare for the raised, brilliantly colored candelabras which lift high, mostly to winter
suns. The heavy meaty leaves are arranged in such manner as to give
an irregular shape and texture to the individual plants as well as
in the mass....exotic in appeal, colorful and at once sprightly,
sodden, dull. They are invariably to be transplanted bare-root, with
no attempt made to salvage feeding roots, frequently allowed to lie
exposed for days before setting out. Large unrooted sections are
almost as satisfactory in planting and in some species, will be
flowering the first year....best supported in such manner that
the stem just touches the soil for rooting. They want a mild
winter and hot summer for best display.
-arborescens, thick, heavily notched, narrow recurving leaves in a sprightly, uniformly dense mass with many
erect heads of bright scarlet flowers midwinter:develops
a trunk of proportion to carry the weight of meat and a
very profuse blooming.
-candelabrum, large, sappy, triangular leaves and
unusually tall, typically three-forked flowering stems
which carry white-mouthed, bright orange-scarlet flowers
in the winter:trunk elongates ultimately to 20' for a
striking object and splendid display.
-ciliaris, widely scrambling, a succulent vine of note
and considerable use, becoming quite woody at the base and somewhat along the far-reaching stems:blooms in winter, the orange
and red flowers held erect in slender 8" laterals:set at the
base of a slope for coverage; and anywhere, see that the stem
lies on ground that does not carry free water....roots there
and can rot:very resistant to drought.
-distans, prostrate, with elongated, ultimately branched, massive traveling stems, as much as 6-8 through and
thickly set to thick and short, very stubby wide leaves
covered with white teeth:unmanageable, it is best used
as a kind of low filler in some out of the way place:
red flowers in summer, the segments tipped with green.
-eru, growing 18-24" in slender height, with a
branching stem, the dark green, shining, tapered leaf
lined at the edge with red teeth:flowers are red and
orange:precise in growth, both in line and mass, a
plant that may be used scale-wise in the garden

210

*Aloe plicati*

*Aloe eru*

*Aloe distan*

*Aloe salm-dyckii*

Aloe Variega...

Alpinia

Alonsoa

Alseuosmia

COMPENDIUM

-ferox, tall and branchless 6-8' with no basal growths
:handsome, very thick and wide leaves, blue-green or purplish, bronzy along the edges:flowers on three-forked
stems are greenish-yellow:natural standard, if clumsy.
    - humilis, low-massed clumps of tightly crowded ros-
ettes of comparatively broad leaves and red or yellow flowers
in the summer:may be used as a wide border of some formality if
little or no water can be given:an inch mulch of gravel at the
crown will be good insurance against wet periods and rot.    var.
echinata, low, the light green and very narrow, straight and
erect leaves with white teeth front and back:bright coral
flowers are raised in a single narrow spire, midwinter.
    -plicatilis, the perfect pot aloe, ultimately large
enough for a tub and very appropriate to a formal setting:
a sturdy, always visible little trunk and nicely branching
structure with its lyre-like rimple of narrow, tongue-like
leaves, add up to great individuality....an arresting specimen
anywhere:winter-blooming and rare.
    -salm-dyckiana, a very large plant and heavy, as high as 8'
with a 5-6' reach:great wide leaves are tapered to a point and
bowed, a yellowish-red-grey in color:red flowers in winter.
    -striatula, short-vining, rising on itself for a thick tangle
of a mat spread out on the ground or over rock:best use is that of
cover or filler for a hot slope:flowers yellow or orange in summer.
    -variegata, "Pheasant A." erect and stiff, a short-stemmed
little plant, measured in inches, both height and breadth:smooth,
primly triangular leaves are light green, three-ranked and closely packed together, marked transversely with broad white bands:the
small white flowers are penciled with green:pots or small rockery.
    -vera, forms a thick clump of erect, very narrow, definitely
channeled leaves as high as 24", a distinctive grey-green in
color:taller, unbranched stems carry yellow flowers over summer....later under extreme drouth.

    ALONSOA warscewiczi, "Maskflower" bushy annuals of good form,
usually carrying over in the south and developing a woody base
for even more uncharted time, on occasion:light red or scarlet,
fragile flowers are nearly continuous through warmth....cut back
in winter for further service or allow to reseed:sow in early spring
for color by midsummer....border, bedding or hanging baskets:may be
grown north into warm temperate regions, every advantage being taken
of heat and starting early:wants reasonable humidity.

    ALPINIA speciosa, "Shellflower" rank-growing but handsome tropical
masses of long-stemmed, spear-like leaves that have a spicy odor when
crushed:unopened flower buds in suspended clusters are tinged with a
pale pink, while the opened flowers are mottled orchid-like, yellow and
pink, strung along the string, shell-like, more or less over the year
in warmth:wants a rich soil that is moist and a humid atmosphere, while
any rest the plant seems to want should be encouraged by leaving it
alone:tuberous subject for a tub or a warm spot in the garden.

    ALSEUOSMIA macrophylla, "New Zealand-honeysuckle" a softwood shrub
under the shears, but vining when left on its own:large leaves are
rimpled, shining, light green, while the crimson flowers in erect
rigid clusters, late summer and fall, spread out more thinly the
balance of the year:thrives in moist, deep shade where much can
be done with the pruning shears to furnish such a place;the
foliage blackens under the heavier frosts.

    ALSOPHILA australis, a "Treefern" that develops a slender,
graceful stem, surmounted high in time by a light, umbrageous
head of long, light green fronds:does best in light shade of
trees with overhead spray....irrigate if in the sun, and well:
cold heavy soils slow down the comparatively rapid growth that
may be expected....do not force these plants:the fronds become
smaller with age; deteriorates in dry climates:tender in frost
when young....adapts:considered strongest of its kind:organic
fertilizer only, ground leafmould in the spring best....do not
use chemicals.

211

## LILY OF THE INCAS

ALSTROEMERIA---strong-growing but fragile tuberous perennials with two to three foot leafy stems and terminal clusters of white, yellow or red, shallow to deep bell-shaped flowers in early summer. They are grown in the open border out of
wind, in large pots to show, or kept for cutting. Characteristically prolific under ground, they soon fill deeply dug loamy
soils with tubers....raise and carefully divide at first indication of deterioration, August-October, removing the smaller
crowns and replacing the larger....avoid parting terminal bud,
old stem base and slender root, resetting at least 3-4" deep.
Keep moist in growth, but with-hold after flowering and never
allow to dry out completely. They want half or more shade in
heat, but mostly sun in coolness, always a rich soil heavily
mulched with well and surely rotted manure. These plants
have difficulty with alkaline salts in irrigation water or
in the soil and will not maintain serviceable foliage if not
leached out from time to time, manually or by rainfall. They
must have sharp under-drainage to a reasonably light soil.
   -aurantiaca, "Peruvian-lily" the yellow, wide-open flowers
are spotted with brown:grows 3-4' in height and will require some
staking and tying....a border plant.  -chilensis, "Chilean-lily"
pastel shades, red through pink to white:one of first to flower
and reaches up to 4', usually less:not always hardy in frost:pots.
-pelegrina, growing only to 2' with weak, flopping stems:large
open flowers are pure white or lilac spotted with red or purple,
dependable for bloom April-May:choice.   -pulchella, "Parrot-lily"
dark red closed flowers, the segments tipped with green and spotted with brown:grows 2-3' high, probably the hardiest and most
persistent for a bed and least shattering for a pot:stands in
less sun and is the first one to fail and go down in the fall.

ALTERNANTHERA amoena, brightly colored foliage plants for
low borders, edging or carpet bedding:narrow leaves in red
or yellow and green shear well for denseness although the
plant is naturally compact:set out in the spring in a warm
place and in warm and uniformly prepared soil:color is more
intense in sun, fails in degree as a border runs into the
shade....shearing helps to hold.

ALYSSUM (Lobularia) maritimum, a straggling annual with
white or lavender, very fragrant flowers six weeks from
sowing:grows in sand or clay with very little attention,
but prefers that the soil be sweet and not im-moderately
wet:lower forms are more compact for edging or may be sheared for form and to continue blooming:an old flower in gardening that naturalizes easily, and nicely for a softening effect.

AMARCRINUM howardi, bi-generic hybrid and rather a choice plant
for general use, large parts from an immense bulb, the flower being
that of amaryllis or brunsvigia, the foliage that of crinum. This is
notable for beauty as well size and is adaptable to a wide range of
conditions, great umbels of deep pink flowers August-October or on into
November:most striking for a large pot, a tub or out in the garden. It
is fragrant and quite hardy in frost.

AMARYLLIS---group of bulbs of absorbing interest for timing, varied
and vivid coloring and for a certain mental alacrity required of
the gardener to keep abreast of nomenclature. The flowering is
spectacular, tall and lily-like, huge blooms, as in some of
the hybrids, the generous mass of strap-shaped leaves substantial in season as a border occupant. They are largely
grown in pots and most species will be found rather far
north in warm temperate regions....set there below expected
frost penetration, but with not more than 6" soil cover. Use
a mulch in further protection. Field stock should be used in
the garden, generally set shallow, with the bulb covered. The
growth of foliage is very important, especially right after the
blooming and it should be fostered in service of next years
flowering....see that they have moisture then, especially if

competing with roots of trees or shrubs. The nakedlady amaryl-
lus will be found under Brunsvigia while the following species
are likely to be listed under Hippeastrum, just to complete the
line of confusion....may they last here for a time.

-advena, better grown in the garden in full sun and in soil
of good body:slender scapes rise 6-8" to carry narrow, clear red
flowers in summer....from which, the name "Oxblood-lily":the foliage comes with or following the bloom, flattening to the ground
and gone over summer:set new bulbs in the fall, but divide old
plantings in spring:prolific and very hardy in frost.

-aulica, "Lily of the Palace" stately plant 24", evergreen
foliage south, the scape always with two very gragrant flowers,
red with a bright green throat, winter:good humus.

-hybrids, under a common heading "Barbados-lily" mostly of
tropical origin, the large white to red flowers, two to several topping a stout, tall scape, with or before the leaves and
at any time of the year....even winter very far south, more
often in the fall, with sometimes a bulb coming up ever-blooming
and short-lived:form of the flower is generally trumpet-shaped,
sometimes very large and frequently quite flattened, solid with
color or broadly striped:tender. Many species that were known in
old gardens have disappeared in this welter of hybrids and now will
be seen more as sturdy strains as development goes on.

-immaculata, the long-tubed, fragrant, pure white flowers are
held to 30" high, summer-blooming:rare....and with rare beauty.

-rutila "Mignon A." variable, but usually smaller in size,
with short, inch-wide leaves and 3-4" red flowers in early summer:
stoloniferous for a wide spread in the garden, used also as a window plant in a pot.

AMELLUS lychnitis, an unstable herbaceous perennial 8-10" for the
garden, having daisy-blue flowers over summer and elongated, narrow
greyish leaves to erect stems for a neat pot plant:better used as
an annual, starting as early as possible in warmth.

AMPELOPSIS brevipedunculata, "Porcelainberry" a low woody
vine of considerable refinement, rapid in growth, climbing by
means of tendrils or used to clamber over rocks or a terrace
wall:foliage mass is light green and fairly dense, but not in
any sense heavy, serves nicely to accent the large clusters of
berries....pale greenish lilac at first, then bright blue and
sometimes at the last white, occuring over the span of Septem-
ber-October:pest resistant, and while not as vigorous as it
is known north, is still a very serviceable plant, enduring some drought when established:has exceptionally attractive leaf modifications in white and pink with the green;does
a good job as a filler for a planter.

AMPHICOME arguta, very short-stemmed, bignonia-like, a semi-
woody ground cover or very low vining, the clusters of rosy-lavender, trumpet-shaped flowers comparatively large:wants a fertile soil
and reasonable moisture:the crown, grown as cover, tends to remain
open, which calls for rather close planting, probably 2'.

ANACYCLUS depressus, a ground cover with perennial, prostrate or ascending stems well furnished with dull but handsome, remotely steel-blue leafage:the 2" flowers are like a
single chrysanthemum, the rays white or pink with a red reverse or the ray flower entirely red. This will be grown in
heat in the rock garden or adapted to a pot.

ANAGALLIS linifolia, "Pimpernel" a spready perennial of
some 12-18" height, becoming woody at the base with flowers in fall or winter, rose-colored, purple or clear blue:
wants a warm, fairly fertile soil in the sun:shear after the
flowering for more flowers next season and to reinforce the
perennial character which weakens considerably and soon, as it
is grown south in subtropical regions.

213

WINDFLOWER

ANEMONE---tuberous subjects of great and particular charm, or
attractive herbaceous perennials of strong growth, and permanency
for the border. Best results are obtained in deep rich soils that
have been lightened somewhat with a humusy material and where light
shade prevails. The foliage may not be depended upon for the entire
season, even with the perennials, but it is always good while it is
serving and in most cases is found a very real part of the value of
the plant. In the garden proper, the tuberous kinds are best lifted
after the foliage has ripened, dusted with sulphur and put away.
There are few pests of any importance, with an exception that
will follow.

-blanda, "Winter W." a low, transient little plant,
the foliage and flowers 4-6" high, coming from a hard, woody
rootstock that slowly spreads under the right conditions:blooms
in the winter in clear pinks or blues:may be transplanted at any
time, wanting a dry spot by itself where garden operations are
few and simple; naturalize.

-coronaria, "Poppy A." broad-petaled single flowers or
doubles in well developed strains, plants growing 6-8" in
height from a hard little tuber which is planted in the fall
for flowers in winter, but during winter for spring, or seed
may be sown in early spring in a warm light soil in the sun for
the following winter or spring:full range of color available,
the flowers pure white through shades of red and blue that cut
well and hold....always best in the south cold winters:keep a
planting moist while growing. Advice at variance with normal
is to procure first year or the smaller tubers, due to a
widespread and developing virus that reduces vitality.
Do not use the same ground successive years.

-fulgens, "Flame A." tuberous, for winter flowering,
reaching 12" in height, the flower with fiery scarlet petals around a mop of blue-black stamens:move only in late summer
after ripening; otherwise do not disturb, but leave it to the
seasons in a nook by itself:naturalize.

-japonica, "Japanese W." robust, long-lived perennial which
blooms in the fall, sometimes up until frost; otherwise, fails naturally and should be cut back:has excellent foliage but starting
late in spring, the leaf stalk directly from the ground from a
suckering, invading root system:flowering stems very straight
erect, bearing quantities of choice, pure white single to double
flowers, the pinks and purples of less quality:a border plant for
half shade in moisture....midsummer drought will show up in the
fall, yet roots rot in wet ground.   var. hupehensis, is similar,
dwarfed to 10-12" and restricted to rosy-lavender in color:use
in the fore part of the border or in the large rock garden.

ANEMOPOEGMA chamberlayni, good foliage masses with regular reduction, otherwise a little streaming and open:soft-grained,
sleek, pale yellow, short-tubed flowers, selfs or faintly striped with pink in the throat....good clusters over May-July:the
tendrils may be augmented by climbing roots on rough surfaces:
takes frost down to 20 degrees.

ANEMOPSIS  californica, "Yerba-mansa" native throughout the
arid Southwest, a coarse herb for wet places or a seepage that
is tainted with alkali:the dense cone of fertile flowers sur-
mounts a white, flower-like collar of bracts:collect seed from
the wild in damp places or along streams....spare the stock.

ANGELONIA grandiflora, the "Angelon", graceful perennial some
18-24" high, blooming through warmth, wanting a warm place in,
mostly sun:kills back under only slight frost, to flower the
following year....not long-lived in any event and may be used
only the one year:lilac to pale purple or blue, short-trumpet-
shaped flowers in loose heads:grown in the perennial border
or may be pinched back for more color as a kind of bedding.
This plant is generally at its height in blooming through
July and August.

214

COMPENDIUM

ANGOPHORA lanceolata, "Gum-myrtle" tall, slender, spreading in the top like eucalyptus, the white flowers, however, of
more value due to the true petals:the smooth, flaking bark of
this tree can also be compared, but the new growth in bright red
is more nearly like that of another myrtle, eugenia:a specimen,
shade or street tree for deep soils, wanting better conditions
on the whole than the gums.

ANIGOZANTHOS flavida, "Kangaroo-paw" an iris-like plant with 3-5'
widely branched stems of odd flowers June-July, which dry out on
the plant and stand for awhile with its strangeness:has decorative value when cut, but the foliage of more moment in the garden;
keep moist and cool over summer in half shade:pots, but the
leaves blacken quickly in drought.

ANISACANTHUS wrighti, "Texas-honeysuckle" native in the Southwest, a shrubby plant 3-5' with shining foliage and bearing two-
lipped, orange-red flowers in one-sided spikes July-September:
wants full sun in a dry bit of soil and will bear deep cutting
for decorating material or to the ground in February to renew
a moribund specimen:may be grown north into warm temperate
regions where the frost does the cutting.

ANNONA cherimola, "Custard-apple" an open-headed, semi-deciduous
tree 20', bearing large rough fruits with a pleasant pineapple
flavor that calls for no cultivation in the matter of taste:likes
a cool, comparatively dry climate as of the Southern California
foothills, with only light frosts:loamy soils best, but takes
either extreme in texture and tolerates a little limestone:re-
quires yearly, heavy and intelligent pruning which should not
be wasted on seedlings....budded stock only. A good tree will
provide an ideal desert when chilled, cut into halves to be eaten
with a spoon. This is one of the more practical of the so-called tropical fruits for cooler parts.

ANTHOLYZA aethiopica, "African Cornflag" as known in gardens is
very strong-growing, invasive, spreading out over much ground, a
bulbous plant with yellowish red flowers January-February:much
like the common montbretia, but more robust to the point of becoming a nuisance without compensating bloom....divide frequently and
keep seedlings out of the more refined areas. This is not attractive during the warmth of the year, but welcome for deep winter.
The species  -paniculata, is larger, earlier in flower,
grown for cutting.

ANTHRISCUS cerefolium, "Salad Chervil" the curled leaves
of this culinary annual have the delicate odor of anise and
may be used as a garnish, as in parsley:sow early in spring
and again May-June in a cool shady place for a lush cutting.

ANTHYLLIS barba-jovis, "Jupitersbeard" an erect tree-like
shrub 10-12', its strictly vertical lines only slightly veiled by the silky, light greyish leaflets:terminals are tipped
with clover heads of off-white March-April....brown and ab-
ject, spent by May:stands up to salt winds at the coast-line,
happy in heat, against sun drenched rocks, impatient of good
fare, preferring lean sandy soils with good drainage:well used
reaching up out of lower planting of like culture or formally in
repetition:small transplants will establish....make use of the
occasional seedlings:very distinctive in the right place.

ANTIGONON leptopus, "Rosa de Montana" "Loves Chain" "Corallita"
"Pink-vine" and others, widely loved throughout the lower South,
frequently and well named, now discovered for California where
it will do equally well making up in denseness for a shorter
blooming:a perennial vine, very high-climbing in rich soil,
but not flowering as satisfactorily as in poorer:turnip-
like tuberous roots ask for depth and warmth of its
ground, and moisture dry seasons, but surface get-
away for heavy rains....no tight soils:

215

the large, open sprays of rose-colored or pink flowers
end in a tendril and the vine is rampant over other plants
or support:blooms practically the entire year in Southern
Florida, further north coming back by mid-year after a cutting freeze, blooming normally only in the fall in Califor-
nia:best not set out until spring, well after the ground has
had a chance to warm up....takes then, three or four years
to collect strength in support of production possible:will
flower more freely in heat and survives as much as 15 degrees of frost when the crown has been mulched:much good cutting material, including occasional white breaks.

ANTIRRHINUM majus, "Snapdragon" perennial or biennial, but used
as an annual in bedding, highly developed strains, much planted for
the marvelous creations in color, shape and size of the head:soil
is best fairly heavy, nearly neutral and drained, firm and not too
rich but with strength:plants that are grown vigorously are more
resistant to rust:fertilize lightly when the flowers begin to come
and keep water off the tops as much as possible:sow in early spring
and transplant for summer, but in July-August for late fall and
winter bloom:pinch out the first tender growths for sturdy, branching plants....three types, large, medium and dwarf or tom thumb:
tolerates light shade, likes it in heat. The species  -asarina
is procumbent, rarely available, to be grown in baskets or in
certain types of bedding:the very attractive, heart-shaped,
notched soft leaves are slightly sticky to touch.

APHANOSTEPHUS skirrobasis, "Lazy Daisy" weak-growing, a
flopping annual with sharply glistening, pure white daisies
all summer:long narrow ray petals are tinted pink beneath,
but the color not showing through....close late afternoon
and nights:stake this or use among supporting growths, although it always falls flat with its face up:native in Florida
and along the Gulf Coast. This has something that gardeners are
over-looking, something quite worth the extra attention.

AQUILEGIA chrysantha, "Columbine" long-spurred flowers for a
lively and beautiful touch to the border, the color held high
above the substantial, active and handsome foliage:type is clear
yellow, but with tintings of lavender, pink and rose in the hybrids,
the best color in a little shade:vigorous in loamy soils that are
not too loose; will survive traces of lime and ordinarily are not
divided, being dependable from seed:sow early in spring or late
fall and allow to come along steadily.

ARAUCARIA---very erect conical trees of exceptional appearance
to be used occasionally on the larger places or in public areas
where contrast with the norm in planting is desirable in something of extravagance. Each species has its own distinct aspect
and peculiar appeal which is always to the unusual. All have
the characteristic harsh abrasive leafage and a uniqueness in
some respect and all may be grown first in a pot or tub before
being set out permanently. They will be reduced in size materially in poor soils and in dryness and will probably require
feeding as maturity is approached. Scrutinize new stock for
the white, cottony masses of the araucaria scale. They must
not be pruned since the branches growing to the ground
will minimize danger of the heavy falling cones.
    -bidwilli, "Bunya-pine" very wide-columnar, usually
less than 100' in height, coming to something of a peak
in early life, but flattening out with age:main branches
are drooping, the splayed branchlets set with the shining,
sharply pointed leaves in two rows:effect as a whole is quite
dense for a handsome specimen tree:the better one in dryness.
    -excelsa, "Norfolk Island-pine" pyramidal, 100' in height,
of precise regular growth, the whorled, thinly clad branches
set meticulously about the ship-mast trunk in layers:the
light green leaves are needle-like, short, comparatively soft and pliable, completely surround-

216

imbricata        Araucaria        excelsa        bid

ing and lying along the branchlets:while rigid in appearance, the
tree gives to the wind or lets it through. This is tender
and will be seen at its best only along lower coasts and
there only, in good size. It is used properly as a specimen
or at most grouped, never massed....or makes a low-sprawling
ground cover for large scale plantings if cuttings from the
side shoots are taken.

-imbricata, a wierd, un-lovely tree achieving the last word
in the grotesque and not at all to be desired for any general
planting problem:rope-like branches, clad in sharply pointed,
scale-like leaves are very long....curve and cavort in such a
manner as to fabricate twisting, tangled masses. This maze or
labyrinth of stems calls for the name "Monkey-puzzle" and with
reason:very hardy in frost and heavy soils.

ARAUJIA sericofera, a perennial "Climbing Milkweed", the foliage with an over-all whitish cast, the bell-shaped, fragrant white
flowers waxy-crisp, with suggestions of ivory, sometimes pinkish
from the faintly lined throat:twines closely about itself or a
support....with likely areas here for scale which must be kept
under control:very rapid growth under most difficult conditions
reseeding widely to become something of a nuisance....but useful where another vine will fail:any soil or exposure.

ARBUTUS unedo, "Strawberry-tree" an evergreen bush of high
quality and usefulness, ultimately an irregular-rounding tree
20-25':blooms October-January, tiny, hanging, white heatherbells
which give way almost immediately to large warty fruits, of the
size, color and texture of a strawberry:the dark brown of trunk
and branches breaks to reveal an inner red:any well drained soil
and any exposure:a general purpose plant of much merit. The species
-menziesi, is the "Madrone" of the Pacific Northwest and may be
grown south as the mountains work into Southern California or in
cool canyons at lower levels where the soil is acid and where moisture beneath carries reasonably well into summer.

ARCHONTOPHOENIX cunninghamiana(Seaforthia elegans)"King Palm" a
slender, smooth-stemmed tree 40-60' of exceeding grace in slim, tenuous line, to be used in localities nearly free of frost....takes
as much as ten degrees under favorable conditions and after having
become established:wants a moist rich soil to produce the light
purple, bole-studding flowers  of summer and the heavy clusters of
fruit that follow:trunk has been known to break in high wind.

MANZANITA
ARCTOSTAPHYLOS---slow-growing western shrubs of quality, to be
used there for permanent effects in and about the garden. Their
past, gardenwise, has been unimportant and obscure, due primarily to difficulties in propagation and procurement. Now, what
with hormones and other plant growth substances, the future, from
a domestic point of view should brighten. The foliage is leathery
rugged and frequently with color, the flaking bark with much of
red....pale at first, through green to red and finally dark brown
under summer suns. The flowers come in drooping clusters or
erect, tiny white to pale pink bells on the order of heather,
generally over winter into spring. They are clean-cut, require little or no pruning and want much humus in a well
drained, preferably gravelly soil. They do in sun or partial
shade and appeal to every sense but that of smell.

-diversifolia(Comarostaphylos)"Summer-holly" formless as a
shrub, infrequently tree-like 15', a California native to grow
in coolness with some summer water if possible:foliage is light
shining green, the flowers urn-shaped, pinkish white, followed
by dark red berries August-September:light soils are best although it does in one that is heavy, if drained:semi-shade.

-franciscana, for a cool exposure essentially, procumbent angular stems in a low re-rooting mat for banks
or grown as cover on more level ground.

-glauca, a coast species, dull and drab until
spring when it brightens with a revery of color,

217

the foliage taking on  faintly bluish tints which approach
that which is named peacock-blue:makes a small tree under
cultivation, and with help.
    -manzanita, the largest, sometimes tree-like 25', this
plant to be grown in heat, a mountain species with picturesque stems, twisting warm red in the sun or half-shade.

ARCTOTIS---annuals of a rather weedy growth of greyish foliage, the large daisy-like flowers of considerable beauty in
the precise form of the corolla and the delicate and infinitely
varied shades in coloring. They are easy to have in any light,well
drained soil in the sun where they are very resistant to drought.
They are said to germinate better if the seed be set on end.
    -acaulis, the plant stemless and with good body, 10-15"
high and as much across:color runs to yellows and orange to
purple, or white with a purplish reverse:practically everblooming and nearly perennial.
    -stoechadifolia, somewhat bushy, and 2-3' in height, the
flowers quite large and of a grey, pearly white or violet,the
disc bright blue....much wider range of color in the hybrids.

ARDISIA---leathery leaved evergreen shrubs, grown largely
in Florida for the exceptionally handsome berries. The flowers
are much less conspicuous than these long-stemmed, showy fruits
the heads being small and bouvardia-like. They should have
some shade and uniform moisture with fertility to produce
crops of berries in line with the possibilities. They are
difficult to transplant, and are subject to nematode and scale.
    -crispa, low and compact, a dark-hued plant, excellent for
a pot, the decorative value of the berry high for winter:takes
full shade but wants a little sun to deepen the red of the berry
which may fail to come out of the early yellowish stage....to
foil the birds and serve long into the new year.
    -paniculata, "Marlberry" dense bushy shrub, native in
parts of Florida or may be grown as a small tree 15-18'
under culture:fragrant pink or white flowers are bell-
shaped, more or less streaked with red and give way to purplish black fruits, mealy in substance, a meal, this, for
the birds:fall flowering, the crop of berries has ripened
for spring:transplants readily and may be moved into
gardens where it develops considerable value.

ARECASTRUM romanzoffianum(Cocos plumosa)"Queen Palm" smooth,
remotely ringed, shapely bole 50' with an active, open head,
a feather-duster top:a tree that is good for restricted root
areas, but wanting supplementary plantings to obscure the pole-
like later look of the stem, as of street plantings:set this barely below the old soil-line:coastal sections only in California and
as far north in Florida as Winterhaven....takes as much as 10 degrees
of frost with only foliage injury while hardy strains existing may
be grown in lower Arizona and in El Paso, New Mexico.

ARENARIA balearica, "Sandwort" very low and tufted, ultimately
carpeting, a dense mat of fine needle-like leaves less than an
inch long:may be used in places as a lawn substitute, but is very
difficult to establish and maintain as a turf area of any extent
unless in a sandy soil under good moisture dry seasons....more
dense, lower sods of lighter color in the poorer soils:does not
require shade, but benefits there in heat and will grow more
rapidly in cool places:use in a walk crevice, between flags,
or among rocks to seal and for the tiny white flowers that
pepper the surface July-August.

ARGEMONE mexicana, "Prickly-poppy" a sprawling ornamental herb
with bristly, silver-ribbed, thistle-like leaves and large orange
or yellow flowers in late summer:sow in a light soil in the sun and
allow to stand for they are very difficult to transplant at any
stage:remote or waste places best on account of reseeding too
freely at times  The species   -platycerus, with larger pink
flowers is more suitable for the garden proper.
218

COMPENDIUM

ARISTEA eckloni, "Bluebrilliant" a dense clump of iris-like
leaves, surmounted 12-15" by stiff flattish stalks of vivid, very
pure blue flowers December-January, scattering out over spring or
spring-summer in the north or cold seasons:tolerates some shade
and stiff soils, seeds and reseeds everywhere, but moderately and
easily controlled. A form  -major, is superior as to flower and
is less potent for seeding, March-April.

ARISTOLOCHIA elegans, "Calico Flower" a woody climber to 25',
with curious, yellow-green, inflated, pipe-like flowers during
warmth:wants a rich, moist soil in the sun or a little shade if
growing under dry heat:an escape, far south in Florida.  The
species  -californica, will be grown over a bank or climbs some
8-10':small greenish flowers are unimportant, but pipes.

ARMERIA maritima, "Seapink" a low, usually short-lived perennial,
growing in grassy mounds or clumps which draw together into a mat
two inches through:surmounted spring and summer by small, globular
heads of papery flowers in white, lilac or pink, mostly the latter
:wants a loose or very sandy soil in the sun and tolerates in high
degree the brine-laden winds along the coast:must have nearly
perfect drainage, otherwise not dependable.

ARRABIDAEA magnifica, high-climbing, a vine with ranging
stems, 30-40' or more, the dark foliage sparse unless held
in to consolidate:flowers are yellow-tubed, somewhat funnel
formed, flaring to rosy pink or light to dark purple in long,
loose clusters any time of the year....surely June-July on until
stopped by cool weather. This may be synonymus with the plant
known as Distictis riveri.

ARRHENATHERUM tuberosum, "Rattlesnake-grass" a low flattish mass of light green, white-striped leaves from a string
of little disc-like tubers, in line like rattlers buttons:
hardy in cold, rugged generally and drouth resistant for a
cover or an edging in the garden:foliage is down for a few
weeks over June-July, otherwise very decorative and dependable.

ARTABOTRYS uncinatus, "Tailgrape" shrubby or climbing, suspending by means of a little hook attached at the base of the leaf
stems:has oblong shining leaves and hard, grape-like, clustered yellow fruits, the insignificant yellow flowers intensely
fragrant, as of ripening fruit:branches will interweave into
a hedge-like barrier or suspend over a bank for an effect:
tender. The closely related species  -odoratissimus is the
cinnamon-jasmine of south Florida, to be grown in rich,
frost-free ground only.

WORMWOOD
ARTEMISIA---aromatic woody perennials or shrubs, grown
for the grey foliage, mainly in arid regions. They are
essentially drought resistant and very satisfactory in a
light, sterile rocky soil. When they become brushy as use-
ed in or near the garden, cut out the old wood in February,
at which time all previous years growth may be shortened or
the entire planting cut to the ground.
    -californica, a handsome native shrub with soft, very
finely divided foliage which is strongly aromatic and will be
found in two distinct shades, light grey and a kind of ground
green:not for the garden, but to be used in waste places and to
be kept down....sand dunes.
    -dracunculus "Taragon" for culinary uses, a loosely formed
perennial 18-24" high:both basal and stem leaves may be dried
in late summer and fall or used fresh in salads and in egg or
cheese dishes....scant ornamental value.
    -lactiflora, a woody herb, erect to 5' in the better
soils, purely ornamental with many creamy white flowers
in graceful panicles, to almost take the place of
astilbe in very mild climates July-September.
219

Aristolochia elegans

Aristea

Artabotrys

Arrhenatherum tuberosum

The form silver king is    --var. albula, of this species, of
extreme lightness in foliage and frosted as with silver, becoming lighter in drought or as the season advances:invalu-
able for cutting and decorative work with arrangements and
winter boquets:softly spreading in the garden 2-3' with running
roots that will be curbed, a rounded mound until cut up for material....renewed from the offshoots pulled out in control.
     -tridentata, "Sagebrush" a branchy shrub with quite grey
foliage, the leaves wedge-shaped with a pair of notches at the
tip:entirely immune to high heat with absolute drought and
makes good use of sterile rocky ground:a pleasing fragrance
reaches out from a naturalized patch, especially after rain:
a western native for near desert conditions.

     ARTHROPODIUM cirrhatum, "Rock-lily" vigorous tuberous-rooted
perennial, dependable, not spectacular, but very satisfying, a
choice plant for the discriminating gardener:a widely spreading
raceme carries many ivory teardrops hanging, buds that open to
pale lavender and gold against waxy, glistening white May-June
:hardy far into warm temperate regions, the foliage mass will
stand in absence of heavy frost while the unfurling leaves in
growth offer up an original study in the abstract:must have moisture
and takes as much as half shade, but the foliage there shot and disfigured by slugs and snails....control surely:a cutflower that does
not divide easily....use a knife when necessary.

     ARUM italicum, something of an oddity, a low tuberous-rooted peren-
nial 12-15" with highly ornamental, triangular arrow-shaped leaves that
are lined and marbled in chalk-white or yellow:a green, calla-like
flower in the spring is not as important as the yellow berries in
summer that finally stand red in the fall, and alone after the foliage has withered away....back by November:grow in some shade and
set low in  a fertile, moist soil:pots or will naturalize in the
right spot and stand through a light frost. The species  -palaes-
tinum, is the "Black-calla" , the inner surface of the flowering
spathe dark purple, or almost black in some lights.

     ARUNDINARIA japonica, "Metake" a running bamboo, but rather
slow-growing and comparatively easy to control and hold in rows
or clumps, the roots less competitive than most:wide corn-like
leaves at the top are active in the wind or droop in a
vain effort to conceal the untidy condition of the lower
cane:is equal to any unpleasantries or real hardship the
city or beach has to offer:screens, a windbreak or fence-
line....where there is willingness and time to keep it there.

     ARUNDO donax, "Giant-reed" a gross-growing, grassy plant,
a bamboo in appearance, growing at times 15-18' in season,
the stems standing all winter:used as a quick screen or in
a wet place that requires no refinement....never in or even
near the garden:to establish, lay mature canes horizontally
6" deep in a trench, October-November:reddish brown plumes
July-August will keep well if cut just before opening out:
old canes may be used for the Mexican type of woven fence.

     ASCLEPIAS currassavica, "Bloodbud" a milkweed for the
far south that won't take over:slender-erect, somewhat more
coarse than is desirable, but colorful and persistent:perennial
for poor soils and more or less waste ground, the flower a dark
red in bud, opening to buff, through gold to orange-scarlet June-
November from a late start:not for cutting, but if taken, boil the
stems in water to seal in the milky juices:may be grown in a pot
and taken indoors for bright color carried into winter:seed.

     ASPARAGUS---commonly called "Asparagus-fern" fern-like
vines, less often shrubby material to serve many decorative
and ornamental purposes in and about the house. Grow them in
pots or for porch or window boxes and baskets or in the soil
outside, where the incredibly competitive spirit can be held

in check. They are hardy out of doors in the absence of heavy
or killing frost; are vigorous in growth, but require feeding
to support the unusual demand for greenery. They stand under
deep drouth due to the thickly massed storage tubers beneath the
crown. The cut sprays have excellent keeping qualities and are
quite commonly used.

-asparagoides,"Smilax" low-growing, a slender twiner that can be
a prime nuisance in the garden, but easily checked, best in the early
seedling stage:the light, shining foliage is most always in good
condition....trailings for table decoration:tiny waxen flowers thru
February-March have a pleasant perfume and are responsible for the
blue berries of burden and woe.

-falcatus, "Sickle-thorn" a woody scrambling vine of a kind of
bamboo character with needle-pointed spines at the base of the leaf
by means of which it clambers 40' to form a loose stringy mass:a
good light shade cover for pergola shelter or open lath house, it
is fragrant spring and summer from tiny unseen flowers.

-plumosus, "Emeraldfeather" the foliage rather dense and
very dark in large triangular, lace-like, feathery sprays of
utmost fineness and held flat in a horizontal plane....a fine
debris drifts inside from near doors and windows:likes shade,
where the white autumn bloom will develop blue berries that are
less troublesome. --var. nanus, less robust and the more commonly seen:quite dense. --var. tenuissimus, shrubby, erect
wiry stems to a rounding outline, unavoidably and utterly sucker-
ing:tiny red berries lie throughout the structure in season:pots.

-sprengeri, seen more often indoors as a hanging house
fern, although tolerating much heat outside and grown in the
sun:foliage a very light shade to long, arched, branching
streamers, much less fine in texture than above:the pinkish
flowers are fragrant and turn out small red berries in time for
Christmas decorations.

-virgatus, a bushy, tenacious, stemmy mass, growing 3-5'or
more:may be held to restricted root space, as against a wall
where the dark, needle-like leaves can be developed enmasse
to lines as a kind of espalier.

ASPHODELUS albus, "Asphodel" an allium-like annual of merit
for naturalizing in dry ground where it spreads rapidly
from scattering seed:pinkish to flesh-colored or white,
star-like flowers late in winter or early spring are not
important:as used in the garden, the seedlings are thinned
out and a following companion plant planned to take over,
summer and autumn:rarely found, but useful for waste places.

ASPIDISTRA elatior(lurida) "Parlour-palm" for a very confined
atmosphere, a house plant with long, wide and shining, perfectly
smooth leaves from a common crown:may be used out of doors in pots
or in the ground in deep shade....any dry, dusty place:the variegated forms are brighter and much more attractive, but retain
their character only in sterile soil:prime for arrangements.

## SPLEENWORT
ASPLENIUM---a large, very diverse group of ferns with
cultural requirements almost as diverse as the plants
themselves are in size and form. In common, they enjoy
a plentiful supply of water at the root, and light shade,
while they also agree in a dislike for wet tops and an
extremely humid atmosphere. Study these wants and aversions well for the individual species before making selections....they are complicated.

-bulbiferum, "Mother Spleenwort" a beautiful specimen
with 18" fronds originating from a bulbous base, making a
rapid growth in warmth and sufficient moisture:loosen the
soil with leafmould and keep the tops as dry as may be, in
the winter especially....slight shade beneficial:may be
taken indoors with much satisfaction.

-felix-femina, "Lady F." somewhat bushy and 1-3' in
height with feathery, light green fronds serving from April
until November:likes a deep rich soil outside in the garden, with

221

with the roots in or near water....takes full sun in a
place that does not become too hot.

   -flaccidum, a basket fern, the broad, dark fronds
hanging to a depth of 2-3' or even more:wants slight or
broken shade, moisture and much leafmould in its mix:a
master basket plant or adapts to a rocky ledge with drainage
outwards:a variable species and not clearly defined.

   -maritimum, "Sea S." the exception that emphasizes the
rule, this plant bearing up under a modified salt wind and
serving well there, better with slight protection:rare.

   -nidus, "Birdsnest F." house or conservatory, having wide,
entire leaves 2-3' long in place of the usual type of frond, the
whole narrowing into a long stout petiole to a well defined crown:
becomes full grown and fully effective only in a moist atmosphere and
is long-lived there, serving in pot or tub:deep shade.

   -serratum, much as the preceeding plant, the edges of the
leaf notched and the stalk not as long. This is an out of door
subject, not generally available, native in Florida in deep
shade....growing there on down logs, a suggestion.

   -trichomanes, "Maidenhair S." a dainty little fern that
will not lose its foliage over winter, south, wanting shade
and the protection of the side of a rock:does with the minimum of soil, as of a dry rock wall.

### STARWORT

   ASTER---robust, usually late-flowering perennials for the less
refined places around the garden. They will show a strong preference
for the drier soils with drainage and good sunlight and require little
attention other than a normal breaking up of the thick woody crown in
some species. This may be done in the fall, but better in the spring,
reducing to single stems. Do not use seed or seedlings.

   -amellus, "Italian Starflower" wide-spreading, bushy 18-24", the
large handsome flowers in great profusion for cutting July-September, blue
to purple in many well fixed variety forms:does not tolerate a wet soil
for very long, nor will the most brilliant coloring develop in the
shade:divide this one infrequently, if at all:choice for the south.

   -fruticosus, a spreading, woody shrub 2-3', with a light branchy
structure and good back of foliage for a complete and full set of the
strong....really strong....purple flowers, April-June:wants little of
care, full hot sun and dryish, drained soil:a large showing of this
virile coloring will be difficult to place in the garden:may want a
careful weaning away from nursery moisture.

   -gracillimus, slender-erect, closely packed stems from a widely spreading base:the large rounded pyramidal head of white flowers
August-October, become decidedly tarnished in shade before their
time:better divided every year or two. This little plant, in form
and growth is very much like goldenrod, as useful with like treatment.

   ATRIPLEX---herbaceous plants and shrubs, not commonly grown and then
not in the garden, but in each instance invaluable for some special
condition of culture or place adverse to the general run of plants.
Much thought and some care should be given here in the selection
and comparing of species to do a job at hand, as these plants either
fail to establish altogether or assume undesirable proportion out of
character, defiant in the use of ground. They all have a talent for
handling various alkaline salts in the soil.

   -breweri, "Saltbush" loosely growing, a shrub that may be
forced high by surrounding conditions or wide-spreading, straggling with freedom, properly used in windswept places or easily
confined as a quick-growing clipped hedge....best in sandy soils
near the sea:the faintly silvered leaves are subject to the leafminer and source for further infestation:exists all year in California near the sea without irrigation or stands with wet feet.

   -hortensis, "Orach" an annual herb, the leaves of which are
used like spinach, requiring successive sowings to provide the fresh
herbage so desirable.   --var. atro-sanguinea, "Frosted Orach" a
crimson leaved variation growing as high as 4'. Neither plant
is particularly desirable ornamentally, the latter having uses
comparable to those of amaranth.

222

-lentiformis, "Quailbush" a low-spreading little shrub of
the desert, the foliage white rather than silvery, a chalk-grey
with a tint of rose in the bracts:sought in its haunts eagerly
for Christmas decoration....grown on hot, dry, sandy barrens
or not at all:no water whatever, going into summer:alkali.
    -semibaccata, "Australian Salt-grass" a prostrate herb-
aceous plant for an excellent mat of slate-green foliage:be-
comes impaired late season, ragged, unkempt, although the condition and season may be prolonged with a little water....a weed
in good moisture:covers large areas and fixes from seed in hard
dry banks to hang deep and dense where scarcely anything else
can establish and hold:seed.

*Azalea austrinum*

    AXONOPUS compressus, "Carpetgrass" creeping to make a dense
mat like bermudagrass, possibly less tenacious and more easily
eradicated:responds gratefully, sometimes too much so, to the
care and culture of a lawn almost to answer the quest for a
southern grass for turf....off color somewhat during
cold weather, but not hopelessly:sow seed January-May
for a stand the same season in a moist, sandy and particularly an acid soil:tolerates only moderate shading
and is rather unique in its freedom from pests....can
be a pest itself when the going is too good:not generally
to be found in the west.

    AZALEA---evergreen or partially deciduous, shrubs that
belong botanically to Rhododendron, but here following
horticultural usage in nomenclature....brilliantly and
profusely flowering in humid regions. The soil must be
moist and well drained, high in humus and attendant acidity.
They require but little attention after having become established, wanting a mulch rather than cultivation, with no pruning after
midseason. There are few pests, but one contact spraying in early
summer or late spring will be good insurance for mites. Be especially careful of irrigation water and fertilizers, that all
forms of lime introduced be leached out. They may be grown
well only northerly in these regions, best along the seaboard,
not at all in sharply arid areas, precariously in Southern California, where a high content to all peat is used in way of growing medium. They require increasingly more moisture and partial to full shade as attempted farther south. It is well
to remove any seed heads that tend to develop. Show them
against a good green background.

*Azalea indica*

    -austrina,"Florida A." growing 8-10' in height, with
yellow to orange flowers March-April:floret the shape of a
short funnel with far-protruding stamens and spicily scented.
    -indica, normally 3-5' high, the foliage rather glossy,
evergreen:large flowers are pink to rosy-purple or red, not
too seasonable but over the time of September-April:will take
some 10 degrees of frost or more, some varieties doing fairly
well in Southern California. When forced, greenhouse Christmas
plants are taken out into the garden, they should be watched
closely the first year while adapting to the out of doors.
    -obtusa, "Kurume A." single species with many varieties and
not a class or strain:branchy little plants, the slender meandering
stems with very small, single or double white, pink, salmon or red flowers December-April.   --var. amoena, low and compact, evergreen, but very
hardy in frost, the leaves small, and bronzy in winter, the flowers mostly purple to magenta.   --var. kaempferi, "Torch A." an upright or
spreading plant, a specimen thing, evergreen or nearly so, the comparatively large pink or red flowers abundant, fading in the sun.
    -serrulata, "Texas A." native in the gulf regions in high
humidity, a 6' shrub or ultimately a 20' tree where the
conditions are favorable:has shining leaves and white,very
fragrant flowers over June-August.

*Azalea obtusa*

    AZARA microphylla, "Oromo" medium-sized shrub of exceeding
grace, the slender branchings drooping at the ends in wide splays
of abnormal flatness and set in ordered rows of tiny dark leaves

*Azara*

that glitter with each shifting bit of light through open shade:will show best against a light back, as of a wall where the micro-flower so yellow and chocolate-scented may spread light and scent over late winter and early spring:later, orange-red berries pick out the shadows in quick points of color:wants fertility, good moisture, a humid atmosphere:tolerates dense shade and is generally a more satisfactory plant northerly, frost-hardy into warm temperate regions:use much leafmould in planting and cut into structure only to shape for use.

AZOLLA caroliniana, small floating aquatics, increasing rapidly to form wide mats and changing patterns of emerald green on still water or quiet eddies of a slow-moving stream....may be likened to odd chips and sprigs of arbor-vitae floating, fanciful in design, quixotic, and turning rosy-red or brownish in strong sunlight. Their coming is enchanting to the casual but understanding gardener and there is magic in the abrupt departure.

B

BABIANA stricta, "Baboon-flower" netted bulbs throwing a short angular stem of hairy, plaited leaves, topped at 8-10" with blue to deep purple flowers late in winter or very early spring....of uncertain performance:wants moisture in growth and dryness out of leaf,with drainage to insure....only tolerates light shade:spreads un-comfortably by seed and best management in this respect is to hold to clumps as nearly and as long as possible, removing the seedlings:frost hardy into warm temperate regions.

### CHAPARRAL BROOM
BACCHARIS---scrubby, weedy shrubs for utility rather than for beauty in the landscape, but serving their ungifted part well when used in the right place. The foliage is of a plain light green, sparse but effective as used, telling at some distance. The only strictly ornamental feature to be disclosed is the whitish, chaffy flower and the papery seed heads in autumn. They are rarely found in cultivation and to procure, they will be precariously dug in the wild or, better, seed collected. They will stand reasonably in salt spray.
  -emoryi, "Mulefat" native to the south pacific coast, but with forms extending well eastwards into the mountains, purely cover for distant ground or waste places:seed.  -halimifolia,"Groundselbush" will be found along the south atlantic and gulf coasts in wet soil or dry:growing 6-10' high, a full-rounding mass.  -pilularis, the "Coyote Bush" western native, of recent interest and availability, with much promise, shrubby or prostrate as a cover to 12" height and wide spread hugging the ground....drapes a declivity as a curtain, with soil to support sufficient growth:sand dunes.

BAECKEA virgata, "Heath-myrtle" a loose shrub with willowy pliable stems 8-10' high, scantily clothed with the narrow, nearly needle-shaped leaves:has small white to pink flowers mid-year for cutting:a good light, obscuring screen, easily thinned out to required density:no cultural difficulties.

BAILEYA multiradiata, "Desert Sunray" a white-woolly annual 12-15" from dry lands of the Southwest, good cover in an open situation under high heat, used in the dry garden:the several rows of bright yellow ray flowers have a ruffled effect and become parchment-like in a ground sheet that picks up the sun in its full blaze of light and holds it in a kind of haze of delayed reflection:blooms April-November from early sown seed and well through winter from late sowings on warm exposures.

BAMBUSA multiplex, clump "bamboos" in many forms and sizes, 6' to 35' or even more in rich, moist soils and atmospheric humidity:stems and leaves are variously striped and cut for luxurious and distinctive effects:new shoots do not open to foliage the stems until nearly mid-summer....a decidedly freshening influence for that time:hardy in frost and will do in the shade:withstands considerable wetness in a heavy soil.

BARKLYA syringifolia, "Goldblossom-tree" of regular form and structure, reaching 40' or more in height and well foliated, the medium green leaves those of the oldfashioned lilac, to 4" across, roughly heart-shaped:small golden flowers come together in large terminal heads in the summer:should have a fairly rich soil and uniform moisture:rare.

BARLERIA caerulea, growing 3-4', usually less, shrubby, spreading or nearly recumbent and fairly dense, but a bit stringy in shade:soft-woody stems are set with the short opposite leaves and closely packed bracts from among which the pale blue, funnel-formed flower appears....at any time or all the time in a warm place:grown with rock, in the perennial border dryish or makes a low garden hedge with some correction of growth:not common and not particularly good.

BAUHINIA---shrubs, trees, climbers, for a moment in the tropics....exotic in appeal to the eye, gorgeous color and curiously defining slit leaf. They should be given every advantage of warmth in exposure and in soil, but not high dry heat or drouth, when the leaves tend to burn at the edge. The soil should be only reasonably fertile for full flowering, but drained, especially in California....best sloped there for winter run-off when the foliage is either inactive or fallen. Pruning will be held to a minimum for the moderate growth desirable over a rank increase....remove brush for an open structure. They must be placed out of the wind and where cold air drains away quickly and easily. As grown from seed, they are variable so that one should be selective in choosing a plant and look for proven color. These are surely plants to gratify that urge toward the unusual.
  -acuminata, "Snowbush" a handsome, spready shrub 5-6' or larger as a crooked-stemmed little tree, a choice landscape subject:pure white flowers, never in abundance, but beginning early in life, dependable May-September, prime in their perfection, laid in among the light green leaves:chance seedlings from a planting is the surest source and they come true.
  -corymbosa, long-running, with thinly appointed, vinelike streamers 10-15', a natural arbor or other shelter cover, the small leaves giving a light shade:flowers also small, pale pink to purple late summer and fall:lianas will hang in rope-like lines to reduce a height or to pattern a wall.
  -galpini, woody climber or rambling shrub, 6-10', the striking orange-red flowers continuous from first warm days until early autumn chill, full-blooming against a warm wall as it stands in more heat than others:may require support and is easily guided, pinching out terminals any time in growth, but cutting into deep wood only after flowering, preferably spring.
  -grandiflora "White Orchid-tree" a sturdy trunk, but deviating from the perpendicular, sidling upwards to more erect-reaching branches of an open head 25-35', the foliage largely in the outer areas:large, pure white flowers are splendid at night, not as effective by day, midsummer through autumn. This tree is too seldom found....a prime garden subject.
  -tomentosa, "Saint Thomas-tree" shrubby, with rigid lateral branches or a slender little tree to 18' with yellow-grey bark that furrows in age and branchings that ultimately are drooping:foliage is a clear light green and drops quickly in cold or drought:the pale yellow petals of the October blooming hold together as a hanging chalice, scarcely opening to show the maroon blotch at the base, turn a queasy purple the second or third day and fall....but none-the-less with a certain attractiveness in the failing:espalier.
  -variegata(purpurea) "Orchid-tree" a spreading, round-topped tree,15-18', dense and twiggy from a

Barleria

Bauhinia
purpurea

Bauhinia
tomentosa

Bauhinia
galpini

Bauhinia
grandiflora

low sturdy trunk normally, the hardiest one in frost:blooms
in utter profusion January-March or as early as November, far
south in Florida, pale purple or pure white:foliage is substantial but impaired during the winter or completely deciduous, when the flowering is either more apparent or lost in
frost. Conjure up a vision here....a redbud gone mad,vaulting,
high-flown in fabulous size and extravagant abundance....port-
raiture of this thing in good bloom.

BEAUCARNEA recurvata, dracaena-like plant with a slender stem
that is marked at the base by a huge swelling bulbous growth:a
number of these stems may appear in support of a handsome canopy
of arching, sword-like leaves, to give the plant considerable distinction for pot and tub:becomes tree-like to 25' in the garden
and with time and in its native Southwest....south in Texas.

BEAUMONTIA grandiflora, "Heralds Trumpet" tropical vine with a
heavy growth of wood and herbage, lustrous leaves and great clusters of long-tubed, fragrant, white-trumpet-shaped flowers....an
Easter-lily with faint green veining:grows rapidly and blooms
abundantly in the sun, but where there is little or no frost,
March-May or continuous far south:much space will be required
for the sprawling growth, or braid into columnar form that will
stand of itself; or carry this 30-40' for distant use from spot
planted:prune immediately after flowering to develop laterals for
next years blooming....grafted stock or plants from cuttings taken
from flowering wood will flower sooner, more profusely and surely:
the root system wants a generous run while the top becomes a
tangle of great rangy stems when out of hand:rich, well drained
soils with moisture, but does not stand for long in wet ground
so that water may be with-held late in season to ripen wood:
evergreen, but foliage usually deteriorated over winter and
usually very slow coming back in spring:cutflower on grand
scale, the taking of which helps control.

BEFARIA racemosa, "Tarflower" native Florida shrub, variable in height 3-6' according largely to water content in
the soil:white, pink-tipped flowers are fairly large, in long
terminal spikes or racemes:blooms profusely, cuts satisfactorily and keeps for a week:better than name would indicate.

BEGONIA---low herbs with watery stems and succulent leaves,
grown for the vari-colored foliage as much as for the flowers.
In frostless places they may be left out over the year, although
essentially warm season producers, being extremely ornamental then,
used in many ways in southern gardens. Generally, they want good
shade and well-worked, porous, fibery soil....seemingly to fare
as well with stated stimulations with manure water or other
suitable feeding, as in natural or thoroughly enriched ground.
These plants are so infinitely variable that even the variety
generators must experience some difficulty keeping up with the
progression. Just know, that in the confusion, varieties and
forms entangle, clones and species may embrangle fiercely;
that races have been known to run backwards and that hybrids
are the order of the day. Use them as they are found. Forget
lineage and continue mentally sufficient. They are fibrous rooted, rhizomatous or tuberous.
    -foliosa, "Fern B." a neat, bushy plant, a little shrub or
climbing with the least help:stems in flat, fern-like sprays,
carry many tiny white flowers, a very distinctive plant for
a basket or with good body for the shady border, facing down
light shrubbery:takes much water, but must have drainage:this
one is fibrous.
    -gracilis, low and bushy with slender-erect, very
watery stems that are little branched and seldom more than
10-12" high:foliage is quite fragile and may be a pale green
or any shade through red, the flowers a pure, glistening
white, or luminous in tints of pink or rose into bronzy
shadings of red:the bulbils may be planted for increase
true to type or cuttings set;tuberous.

COMPENDIUM

*Begonia tuberhybrida*

-lloydi, "Basket B." long-drooping, floriferous in
many strong reds but entering very largely into the
breeding of basket hybrids:may be used as a ground
cover in prepared shaded beds:tuberous.

-multiflora, "Bedding B." low and bushy, with many
small single or double pink flowers in full clusters all
through warmth:bedding or pots in considerably more sun
than might be expected:fibrous.

-rex, striking plants for the foliage as bedding in
shade, or may be used in pots, the light rose flowers less
important than the leaves....much variety in etched patterns
of silver and grey or with purple worked in with the green:
foliage deteriorates under 40 degrees, but the root mat will
survive several degrees of frost under a light mulch:beds are
raised for better results:rhizomatous.

-ricinifolia, very strong-growing, a large plant for
use out in the open landscape with reasonable protection:the
large, deeply cleft leaves are 12-15" across, rounding, of a
bronzy cast over the green:flowers rosy-pink in many loose
heads held high above the foliage in winter:rhizomatous.

-rubellina, a large leaved type with shallow-lobed
leaves that are dull green with brown spots, ascending
from a strong root-stock:pale pink flowers weave about
on long weak stems:best use hanging baskets:rhizomatous.

-scharffi(haageana)a bedding type for cool places or for
pots to move around out of heat:spreading, comparatively strong
bushy habit and very good foliage color....large leaves red-vein-
ed, entire and waving, the long-stemmed flowers pink with rosy
shadings:fibrous.

*Beloperone tomentosa*

-semperflorens, "Waxflower B." low plants with many erect stems
that are close-set for good bedding, flowering continually in profusion, pink, rose and deeper shadings:does alright in the sun but with a
harsher coloring in both leaf and flower....real beauty comes out in
just a little shade the heat of the day:fibrous.

-sutherlandi, strong-growing, a large plant 18-24" in height
and as much across, very dependable with rather thin pale
leaves and sparse, small orange flowers all summer:
tuberous and will be subject to mildew.

-tuberhybrida, "Tuberous B." large single or double
flowers, fantastic in their modifications, moods and
tenses, marvels of color and form and texture all thru
summer:sprout the tuber by the first of April or earlier
south, using peatmoss in a flat or directly in the pot
where they will stand....tuber laid with concave side up
and flush or slightly under the soil, tilted for run-off of
surplus water, but kept moist:grow in pots, baskets, planters or
in beds beneath open-headed trees in a mix of peatmoss, leafmould,
spent manure and sandy loam....always moist but not wet....do
not feed until established:ailments include mildew and rot besides snails and slugs....remove failing leaves and flowers,
but leave stems to drop off naturally and allow to go into night
dry:lift when through, shake out soil and dry out as tops are dying back,dust with sulphur and store neither dry nor too damp.
All this they are worth....if they can be grown well.

*Begonia ricinifolia*

-verschaffeltiana, an immense plant for a tub, growing to 3'
and to as much as 8' across in warmth, a lush, vigorous, close-
held body of large green, lobed leaves from stout stalks:small,
rosy-pink flowers, raised high on strong branching scapes afford
a spectacle March-May in a fibrous enriched soil:rhizomatous.

*Beloperone californica*

BELOPERONE---attractive soft wooded plants with good filling
service in and about the garden. The full herbage rises from a
close crown, but restricted in the sun or as grown too dryish,
spreading-invasive when grown too lush. The over-lapping, terminal bracts are colorful and interesting, somewhat unique, taken for
cutting. They want warmth, a friable soil and the sun, although they will
take fairly deep shade if necessary....everything in moderation.

-californica, "Chuparosa" spreading low, only 2-3'
in height, shrubby, the interlacing grey-green
branches hard and bare all summer and fall,

227

*Beloperone guttata*

coming to life after rains with foliage and red flowers:season
may be drawn out by late irrigation, under domestication, but the
natural life habits will be reasonably observed for good results.
This is a showy plant if rested at the proper time.

-guttata, "Shrimp-plant" has reddish brown bracts all through
the warmth of the year, purplish and more pronounced as a feature in
shadow. There is a chartreuse form,   --var. longispicua purpurea, a
dwarf that stands neatly for a pot.

-tomentosa(comosa), widely sprawling,  or rising on support,the
growth as much as 5-6' with rosy-copper bracts, the flower with an
orange lower lip to a yellow tube:blooms late fall and winter in a
warm place, surviving considerable neglect....banks or used as a
ground cover. Unfortunately this plant is seldom found in the nursery
trade where it needs a friend to promote bright color for winter.

BERBERIDOPSIS corallina, "Chile Coraldrops" a climbing
shrub of distinction and rarity with dark leathery leaves,
heart-shaped, irregularly toothed and spined that hold in the
absence of frost:small round crimson flowers in handsome sprays
in the way of a fuchsia, drip like blood July-September:wants a
warm exposure, but in coolness of climate, humidity and some protective shade:likes acidity, but will reach out of prepared soil
into alkalinity and gradually adapt.

### BARBERRY

BERBERIS---spiny, very ornamental, small or medium-sized shrubs,
deciduous or evergreen, valued primarily for the foliage, but with
small, drooping yellow flowers and variously colored berries of note.
Soils should be well dug and not necessarily rich, but light in
texture to facilitate drainage and surely moist, for these plants
really suffer in drought. Small sizes are preferable in planting
and may be set deeper than usual in some species so that lower branches
may root, an aid in overcoming a natural aversion to mild climates. All
withstand considerable shade, but are shy there in flower, and more in the
fruit that sets. They are not strictly at home in subtropical regions,
but the following are used successfully under good handling.

-darwini, erect-spreading 3-5' and evergreen with small, very handsome hollylike leaves that are dark and glossy, bronzy in winter, the bush
flecked with crimson of the falling leaves:most of the flowers come
in early spring, scattering out over the rest of the year and concurrently with the dusted blue berries:give an extra cool
place with moisture and shade. The species   -gracilis is
similar, used in small scale projects and under essentially
the same treatment and conditions.

-gagnepaini, erect-arching, bushy, with a close crown,
5-6' in height, evergreen, the elongated leaves conspicuously clustered....light colored and morbid in the poorer
soils:stands in a warmer exposure than above and where it
may become a little dry. This is rather showy in flower
and may be used in considerable heat, if moisture is kept up.

-wilsoni, deciduous, a low-spreading twiggy little shrub,
almost prostrate at times, the yellow flowers not conspicuous
but late-dropping leaves will reveal an inner glow of coral-
colored berries:foliage bronzes as it fails or may be nearly
evergreen far south:one yellow blooming in the spring.

BERGENIA cordifolia, perennials for fairly deep shade or fleeting sun....full sun in coolness:has a low woody crown and generous clump of round leaves to 6" across, dark and shiny with wavy
margins, evergreen:flowers in spring clear rose on nodding stems
12-15", usually less:light soils rich in humus and well drained
are desirable, best for longivity....watch for thrips:divide when
the clump appears to be too woody, each growing point set again
as a cutting, best done August-September. The species   -crassi-
folia, is similar and winter-flowering, while the species
ligulata, likewise similar, is summer flowering and white. There
is an over-all chartreuse coloring here due to green center.

BERGEROCACTUS emoryi, yellow-brown cylindrically jointed cactus,
a prostrate ascending mass, violence and ordered massacre for inter-

228

lopers, cover besides, for dry rocky ground with no moisture
other than scant rainfall or ocean fog:too strong and invasive
for the garden or succulent collection, possibly outside as a protective measure:has good color, of carrying power to effectively cover distant ground:a pest in the wrong place and must be reserved for
hillsides....no low ground, where it soon rots out.

BESSERA elegans, "Coraldrops" transitory little bulbous plant, pin-
point of color for the while....and a special place:dainty over-all
with a drooping, one-sided cluster of bright red or scarlet, bell-
shaped flowers with contrasting blue anthers July-September:allow
this a dry spot in the garden where the collecting bulbs can rest
after growth....should not be encouraged to start before its time
since scapes are thrown in succession, depleting and exhausting the
very willing bulb unduly:hardy into warm temperate regions in open
woodland spots:naturalize.

BETULA nigra, "Red or River Birch" a slender graceful tree to
a round head at some 50' or less, more in low wet places:the early
years are frivolous with the shaggy, glowing, flaking sheets of
shining cinnamon-red bark, wistful peelings which continue several
years before giving way to more dignified apparel. This is the preferred birch for subtropical regions although the type species of
the European white birch, result of graft failure in the cutleaf
variety, will be infrequently seen in fair size and condition:two
clean, pestfree trees for the lawn, the good green leaf sometimes
silvered beneath to break over in the wind for a lighting effect.

BILLBERGIA---stemless plants, having hard, horny, spiny-edged
leaves arranged in an elongated rosette, deep and tube-like to catch
and hold water for use. They are best grown in a mixture of sand and
any fibrous material such as peat, leafmould or osmunda....may
be attached to such support as rustic wood, detatched bark or the
trunks of trees. Perfect drainage as above is required and watering from overhead except when in flower. They want sun, to filtered
sunlight, to half shade and may object seriously to any bungling attempts at feeding. The original rosette deteriorates and dies after
flowering, when offsets take over, or are detached for increase:pots
for patio or house or grown under lath. The flower is in the form of
a spike, erect or drooping, the stem enclosed partially by a red or
pink bract. They are not of much value between bloomings.
    -nutans, may be grown in the ground in ordinary garden soil,
spreading by means of elongating stolons to make a sizable clump:
flowers are slender and hanging, blue, yellow and bright green,
February almost by the calendar.
    -pyramidalis(thyrsoides), a much larger plant with erect-
dense, club-like spikes of red, violet-touched flowers, a real
sight in bloom in late summer or early autumn:should be divided each year for new plants.
    -saundersi, the foliage reddish as seen from beneath and
mottled in cream from above with reddish spines set along edges
of the leaf:flowers are lemon-yellow, edged with blue, the blue
of a gention:baskets.

BLECHNUM---coarse ferns with wide, stiff and deeply cut fronds,
more particularly successful in a selected atmosphere than is usual with plants. They want good moisture at the roots, but not necessarily over the tops and will survive fairly dry air indoors.
Their likes and aversions  differ markedly as follows and they will
spread out into wide patches by means of root-like stolons.
    -moorei, growing 12-15" in well prepared ground, sometimes more
outside:has a well defined crown that may become trunk-like 6-8":
the more refined species to use in a pot in half shade.
    -occidentale, growing to 18" in well prepared ground, normal-
ly 8-12" in a pot or in poorer soil:wants water at the root, but
never over the tops when they tend to blacken:does in a fibery
mossy medium or grows in gravelly or sandy soils:fronds last
rather well when cut and will find effective use in
arrangements:the plant is free of pests and disease
and  will be used in California and Southwest.

229

Bessera elegans

Billbergia thyrsiflora

Billbergia nutans

Blechnum occidentale

-serrulatum, "Sawfern" growing in mucky ground or around the edge
of a swamp, the fronds rather finely toothed, 18-24" long and as much
as 10" across, a rugged plant with strong traveling roots to carry
it on for large and dense foliage masses:native in Florida.

BLETILLA striata, one of the ground orchids, a plant for strong
color, and foliage that stands out in the border, but for individuality, rather than for mass or form:sun or half shade in ordinary or
the better garden soils, persisting there with little attention,
a loose clump of plaited leaves and sharp, rosy-purple flowers,
April-August:wait for more complete decline before dividing the
hard knotty crown, usually September-October, building up the de-
pleted soil in replanting:pots, allowed to crowd or the open bor-
der:a cutflower that may be grown indoors, winter hardy in frost.

BLIGHIA sapida, "Akee" curious and useful tree from the tropics,
30' or more in deep rich soils that are medium heavy and where the
climate is moist:rigid, erect, with an open head of dark, glossy,
compound or "walnut" leaves....may be pruned to compact:unimportant
flowers are fragrant, any time in warmth, but the fruit is very decorative, yellow to red as exposed in degree to the sun....splits
open for a look at black seeds bedded down in a white pulp,edible;
established trees withstand some light frost, but are extremely
tender while young....semi-deciduous then.

BLOOMERIA crocea, "Goldenstars" blooming in early summer, a
small bulb with grassy leaves and open heads of golden yellow
flowers held 12-18" high:for naturalizing in the open in loose
soils in the sun and with drainage:starts readily from seed
sown in early spring, or bulbs when obtainable:pots or other
container for casual color:native in California.

BOCCONIA frutescens, a rare and none too handsome tree 25',
with one to several stems to a canopied top of long, deeply
cleft leaves:to be used only in a fertile soil under good protection and culture and particularly, care in watering....other-
wise a poor thing:primary use is for the juvenile foliage as it
is grown in a planter box, ultimately removed out of doors to a tree
or other planting as a filler:decorative value is the only valid and
lasting interest to the average planter:tender.

BOLUSANTHUS speciosus, a slender erect, open-headed tree 25' with
an exceptional flowering, an over-all of bright blue, pea-shaped
flowers spring-summer, but only with a warm exposure....flower
buds may kill in cold weather. This is a choice tree for a restricted domestic area:semi-deciduous, the tree itself is hardy
in as much as ten degrees of frost, if prepared.

BOMARIA---herbaceous twining vines for at least half shade. In
effect, they are climbing alstroemerias, with much the same form in
the flower and in coloring....pendulous, deep-hanging heads. They want
a rich soil with leafmould, plenty of moisture during growth in early
spring into summer. They may be cut to the ground, when the roots
with attached tubers may be divided for increase. They are pestfree.
    caldasiana, very strong-growing 15-20' with full-hanging umbels
of flowers that break from the blunt ends of the streamers, each a
veritable fizgig or pyrotechnic of flaming red-orange at any time
of the year, but mostly in warmth....then the entire growth dies
back, recedes into the perfectly round tubers.
    -carderi, smaller, precise and lovely hanging flowers in
loose, elongated clusters, rosy pink or spotted purple at the
tips of the enclosing petals:large pods split open later for a
showing of the orange seed:hanging baskets, up and down.

BORAGO officinalis, "Borage" an annual pot-herb with handsome heads of starry blue flowers held to 2', late summer
and fall:leafage used to flavor beverages, as a garnish,
in salads to impart a cucumber flavor:withal, it becomes a distinct and pleasing addition to the
border in poor soils.      230

Bletilla striata

Blighia

Bomaria caldasi

Bomaria carde

BORONIA elatior, heath-like shrubs 3-4', grown for the remarkable fragrance, blooming quickly from seed, short-lived unless
with perfect drainage, yet must be kept in some water if there
is none below to tap....large pots for quick performance, fav-
orite of the florists, and excellent from their point of view;
abundant dull, rosy-red, half-open bells suspend from erect
sprays through spring....cut back sharply when through:very
hot or very cold winds may be fatal....very choice, very difficult, not a landscape subject. The species  -megastima, is smaller,
and with bright scarlet to maroon flowers.

### PAPERFLOWER

BOUGAINVILLEA---long ranging tropical vines or creepers of very
rapid growth in heavy wood, the top very undecided but ultimately
settling down and filling out to the ravishing, glowing spread of
color associated with the name. These plants will take any amount
of water with drainage and stand in serious drouth as well, probably in better color there....withhold moisture as a plant goes into
flowering. Soil is really important only as it affects hardiness,as
poor ground helps to control and ripen wood in climatic border
areas frostwise. The color of the bract deepens in cold weather
and in drought, with the very height of color coming out of heat
and the sunniest places....may be pegged down on flat ground as a
cover or spread over wide banks and allowed its way.
Pruning these plants, what with large thorns and heavy
wood, is a man-sized operation and should not be put off
with misgiving....it can become impossible. New hybrids
appear from time to time, some of them in rare and unusual
coloring, not always robust....these are known and dependable.
    --Barbara Karst, bright red with a more restrained char-
acter in growth, more refined and very free-flowering:best
cane type to develop in a tub.   --Crimson Lake, an old variety and still startling from the standpoint of color, mostly
late summer into winter.   -lateritia, an old species in use and
still choice, along with the new, a splendid shade of pale brick-
red or terra-cotta....comparatively quiet.   --Praetorius, the
yellow of the first tones changing to golden salmon, summer or
winter or any time....which is more or less true of all.
--Sanderiana, a hardy, comparatively rugged plant, the purple
to magenta acceptable alone for its strength or with white
or pale blue....clashes elsewhere.   --San Diego Red, rampant
and nearly continuous in flowering, with very large bracts,
easily handled and fairly hardy in cold.   --Temple Fire, shrubby,
and dense-growing, requiring only a little pinching in for a good
round figure and form for a tub.

BOUSSINGAULTIA baselloides, "Madiera-vine" perennial, twining,
the slender, winding stems regularly spaced with the very light,
shining leaves which mingle evenly with the fragrant white flowers
of August-November:tuber develops to great size in rich, sandy
soils for a long-lived and permanent plant....tiny tubercles from
along the stem  may be planted at any time or seed may be sown in
the spring for flowering the same year:grows quickly when established to as much as 20' in one year and goes wild in moist soils.

BOUVARDIA humboldti, loosely spreading shrubby material with weak
stems straggling 2-3', grown largely for cutting material:flaring
clusters of red to white or pink, long-trumpet-shaped flowers are
born continuously or any time in warmth....white form intensely
fragrant, but the red with better shape and use as a bush:
pinch back early to strengthen stems, later taking flowering
shoots which will encourage further blooming....cut the entire
plant to the ground before spring:fertile moist soils on the
light side are best and one that is on the alkaline side for top
condition in production:some shade middle of the day good, but
too much or any other real adversity or pressure reduces down
to....mealybug:tender. The species  -alexanderiae, a low,
brittle-stemmed, semi-woody plant with strange but attractive
off-white flowers is native in Lower California.

231

BOWKERIA gerrardiana, strong-growing shrub 6-8' with dark, roughened leaves, a substantial foliage set with white, satiny, slipper-
shaped flowers, yellowish in bud, occasional rather than freely
carried, coming into quiet play July-August:a general purpose
shrub of merit were it more often obtainable:a plant for the deep
border or out of genteel company, as it is ill-smelling at times:
hardy into warm temperate regions.

### BOTTLE TREE
BRACHYCHITON---trees from foreign deserts for use as shade and
in the planting of streets where heat is high, flowering much
more freely there and generally more satisfactory. They are
mussy and carry  ugly seed pods too long for the little ornamental value they have, but that faculty of storing water against
deep drouth confirms them for hot places. Use them only in deep
soils since the heavy tap root has difficulty with rock or hardpan
near the surface. Deterioration or die-back of terminal growth may
indicate too much water or root trouble of a physical nature,
nutritional difficulty or possibly mild frost damage. This is a
frequent manifestation and the immediate answer is to encourage
a lower, more vigorous stem to take over while the cause is determined and remedied. The term Sterculia is synonymus.
   -acerifolium, "Flame-tree" erect to 60' with large, deeply
lobed light green leaves similar to maple, drop for the flowering period:scarlet-red flowers in erect trusses all over the tree
July-August, shatter to lay a ruby-red patch beneath, a certain
kind of beauty....messy only when trampled:does not flower every
year, wants protection from wind and is quite tender in frost.
The species   -discolor, with pink flowers and possibly better
form is somewhat similar, but seldom obtainable.
   -populneum, "Kurrajong" dense, erect and rigid-conical, a
tree 50' high, the smaller, very light green leaves variously
cut and shaped, but mostly like poplar and acutely pointed:the
small, greenish white, bell-shaped flowers hang like lily of
the valley, sometimes splattered with crimson within, May-June,
unimportant:the bole or trunk is conspicuously swollen at the
base and smooth, while the seed pods are gathered to tint for
indoor decoration....good riddance in the landscape:a prime
and excellent tree for extremely arid regions.

   BRACHYCOME iberidifolia, "Swanriver Daisy" a winsome, rather
delicate but compact little annual 10-15" for filling or part
time border service:best during cool of the year, spring and
autumn or even pointed for winter, south:successional sowings,
allowing 6-10 weeks....lasts only some six weeks:the comparatively large heads come in white, rose and in shades of blue, with
the clear coloring of cineraria....and in other ways similar,
but with the finely divided leaves.

   BRACHYSEMA lanceolatum, "Scimiter Flower" erect, ultimately neat-spreading, loosely formed, a shrub 3-4' with deep
crimson flowers, clustered or solitary, studding the stems
sparingly....but a good display in tilth:leaves elongated,
dark blue-green above, silk-silvery beneath:considered difficult to handle, but so , mainly when coddled....successful
in drained sandy soils in the sun and under considerable exposure....always with flowers:be careful of fertilizers and
study closely the moisture requirement related to soil.

   BRASSAIA actinophylla,"Octopus-tree" grown in pots and tubs
indoors in good light to full sun in the garden where it will
make a slender, easily branching, erect-growing tree 25-35'
the very large palmate leaves shining, light green, leathery,
while the upright branches are terminated by a large, whorled inflorescence of red flowers in late spring or summer,
not often or soon in California where it is having
difficulty deciding whether or not it likes the
climate. The fruit is a round purple berry
which stains a pavement.
   232

Brachychi
popul

Brachy

Brachycome

Brev

Bravoa
geminiflora

# COMPENDIUM

BRASSICA nigra, "Mustard" from the wild, a tall, rank-growing annual for covering distant ground with the very effective light yellow of the blooming in early spring:young leaves are used in salads, winter and spring, the seed planted thickly in early fall:a weed when it comes to seed in the wrong place.

BRAVOA geminiflora, "Mexican Twinflower" bulbous, growing to as much as 2' in rather uncertain height:has very long, narrow and at times almost grass-like leaves and slender scapes bearing rich, coral-red flowers in the likeness of a tuberose for form, late winter and spring:insistent on good drainage and may be grown into warm temperate regions.

BREVOORTIA ida-maia, "Floral Firecracker" native western bulb with grassy foliage and loose clusters of bright scarlet flowers tipped with green, June-July:the blooming quite unusual, striking, the head held 2-3' high, rather stiff, long-lasting with a little shade, satisfied in deep, loose, well drained soil enriched with leafmould:hardy well into warm temperate regions.

BREYNIA nivosa, "Snowbush" grown far south in Florida and precariously in frost-free areas of California for the colorful foliage of such pale beauty:loose-growing shrub 3-4', the leaves 1-2" long and nearly as wide, variegated as below:used in a hedge or in a pot for a sunny winter window:shearing or pinching out is indicated under most conditions, either bringing out the new growth in pale pink or a fairly pure white in the shade. --var. atropurpurea, strong-growing, the foliage dark purple. --var. roseo-picta, "Calico-plant" the leaf splattered and mottled with white, pink or red.

BRICKELLIA grandiflora, "Tasselflower" a sprawling shrubby plant for moist shady places, tucked away inconspicuously, used largely for the unmatched and pervading fragrance summer evenings:useful in warm temperate regions, a western native from high cool canyons.

BRODIAEA---bulbous plants, mostly western natives throwing stems of slender swaying grace to naturalize in the less worked parts of the garden, or grown for cutting, the flower being very long-keeping. They are best planted out early, either spring or in the fall and almost surely in the sun, generally in light, gritty or gravelly soil that is fertile and drained. Some species will be found in clays that do not get much water. They should be massed closely for an effect and left alone until unquestionably crowded. This seldom happens....remove then, when enough bulbils or offsets will remain to carry on. Seed sown immediately after ripening will produce blooming corms in 3 to 4 years. They want little to do with active manures.
    -bridgesi, "Cluster-lily" the flowers large and wide-opening, reddish violet in loose umbels of up to fifty florets when well established:blooms in May and can be grown in light shade:one of the more attractive and not too common.
    -capitata, "Bluedicks" very common, with narrow, linear leaves and weak, slender stems as tall as 2' carrying close heads of white, lilac, violet, but mostly blue flowers March-April:wants a dry slope and takes a heavy soil without hurt.
    -coronaria(grandiflora), "Harvest B." the latest to flower, clusters of bright lavender or violet blue tipping 12-18" stems June-July:rather more insistent on a light soil:sun.
    -lactea, "Wild-hyacinth" large clusters of white April-May, the mid-vein of the petal marked green:tolerates a wetter, heavier soil, and one that is poorer than the foregoing.
    -laxa, "Grassnut or Ithurials-spear" sends up a 2' stem with a large, full cluster of pale to fairly dark flowers or white, very finely textured, washed over with lilac:one of the more choice and showy species, naturalizing in cold wet ground.
    -uniflora(Triteleia)"Spring Starflower" low, leafy little plant with short-stemmed pale blue flowers late winter-spring, solitary from a lush mat of ribbony leaves....fades in sun to white, holds in shade:increase is rapid to become a nuisance: stands in a dry soil, the flower tending to close dull days.

233

BROWALLIA americana, "Amethyst Flower" an annual with flattened, fluted little trumpets in very desirable shades of blue,
fading out in full or a very hot sun, continuous through warm
weather into autumn....at its best the later months and may be
flowered in enough warmth, through winter:not exacting in the
matter of soil, but must have constant moisture....and that
warmth:sow early, in flats and bring along, again in warmth, and
set out as soon as the ground seems to have warmed up:pots, bedding or used as a filler beneath open-headed trees.

BRUNFELSIA---attractive shrubs from the near tropics, very
sensitive to cold weather which will delay normal flowering
or ruin the flower in bud. The wood is soft and so slow to
ripen in the fall that every effort should be made in late
summer to halt growth....with-hold moisture and fertilize hab-
itually only in the spring. They tolerate rather wet ground,
with drainage and flower much more freely when the root-mat is allowed to bind, as in a tub. They want acidity, some shade and moisture.
     -americana, "Lady of the Night" with slender stems to 8',
only obscured by the soft, light green twill of the leafage, the
color entering into the base of the single, long-tubed flowers
that start out greenish, open to white, changing through creamy-
yellow to dull ochre as they fail....intermittent and at least three
weeks in flower some time during warmth:the partially closed calyx
cup is a likely spot for ant-deposited mealy-bug....watch for it;
an unusual fragrance is intensified warm nights.
     -calycina, has dull, dark foliage, in places with a suggest-
ion of purple, the flowers lavender-purple or blue, white-eyed and
crumpled, short-tubed, starting to fade out the second day, and in the
end, nearly white:practically everblooming, starting in January, south,
with the heaviest showing during a warm spring, spreading out over
summer with a singularity of both blue and white flowers in-
termingling:takes but little frost and then only when well
prepared for it.     --var. eximia, a smaller plant, usually
only 2-3', rather more dense-growing, with more bloom, and
that concentrated in spring.     --var. floribunda, the one
more commonly found, a rich purple with a pronounced area
of white at the center. This is sometimes referred to as
"Yesterday, today and tomorrow"     --var. macrantha, extra
choice, the flower paler over-all, grading deeper outward
to the edge from the center.

BRUNSVIGIA rosea, "Belladonna or Naked-lady" long known as
plain, ordinary amaryllis, bulbous, in strong-growing packed
masses for a flash-flowering, drama in the garden, a spectacular effort sometime over July-September in satiny rose-red
or pink lily-like trumpets in crowded umbels that come bare
from from the papery sheathed bulbs....no benefit of foliage
then, unless provided extra by the gardener:set new bulbs any
time out of growth, probably May-June with neck just showing,
in well-dug enriched ground....heavy feeders, but no green
manures....divide September-October. These plants must be
kept dry as possible over summer, watered, however, thru
periods of drought over winter in Florida and along the
gulf coast. They may be used into warm temperate regions,
but only so far and in places where winter foliage can survive and function to prepare for blooming....ultimate flower
failure is end result otherwise. They don't do in a container.

BUDDLEJA---rank-growing, soft-woody shrubs with rather
handsome heads of whitish, yellow or purple flowers that
scatter out over the year by species. They succeed best
with sun and in the heavier soils that are retentive
of moisture or damp places where drainage is good.
There is little object in encouraging growth since
they are very rapid to develop and vigorous to require hard pruning if one is to have the blooming,
and even the bush, where and when wanted. This is done
in each case after flowering, with tip-pinching later
as they come along to develop strong laterals, or the

234

*Buddleja lindleyana*

plant completely rejuvenated by cutting to the ground.  These
plants may be grown far south into the tropics and at the same
time serving north in warm temperate climates as kill-back shrubs
and treated somewhat as herbaceous perennials.

   -asiatica, very erect slender lines 10-15', the cane-like
stems of very rapid growth and thinly clad, scarcely covered
below by the light greyish green foliage, topped by narrow
spikes of white to yellowish flowers in winter:one of the best
of the quick-growing screens for temporary use.

   -davidi magnifica, "Summer-lilac" with tall, angular, more
or less arching stems of very rapid growth 5-8', coarse foliage in
abundance and handsome large, cone-shaped heads of deep purple-
blue flowers June-October, the florets with a conspicuous eye of
orange. This is profusely flowering and with a certain fragrance.
It is the more commonly found, with improved varieties available.

   -lindleyana, erect-spreading, arching 3-5', a shrub of comparative refinement producing long, narrow-tapering heads of a
soft purplish violet July-September....unusual and very attractive, given good culture, wanting the better soils and moisture to
develop the quality potential. This can be a brushy, scraggly
little thing of no import, but with attention to pruning, a superior subject for the low planting area....cut deep, with form
and structure in mind, reducing fine twiggy growth from time to
time for the vigor it lacks.

   -madagascariensis, lusty growth, overpowering, straggling
out 15-20' or more, reclining, piling up on itself as high as
8-10', submerging every lesser thing about:gross in every way,
the yellow winter flowers are ill-smelling, but not carrying to
far....restrict to very special uses, such as cover....on the
grand scale....a cheap material that does a lot of work.

   -nivea, medium-sized shrub 6-8', rather free at the base, the
extremities clothed with a dense white-wooly tomentum or fuzz,
a velvety covering that is telling to the eye:lilac or purple
flowers in late summer are not conspicuous:rare.

   -salvifolia, decidedly more evergreen than the foregoing,
of more compact habit, spreading in growth 3-5', the relatively
large spikes of pale yellow or lilac flowers delicately scented
in winter:grows in rather heavy soils with either generous or
scant moisture....another rare species deserving of more attention far south:tender.

   BURSARIA spinosa, "Sweet B." small spined relative of the common
pittosporum, shrubby and weak-growing when young, or a small tree
of style and grace, with a leafy flow of drooping lines in movement:
fleeting white flowers in pyramidal clusters touch the lag-end of
summer and carry on as red berries:attend to staking and pruning to
get the young plant up:spines as weak as the plant itself, only
threaten:rare

   BUTIA capitata(Cocos australis) "Pindo Palm" very slow growth, ultimately 25', bare of the leaf-boots at the base only:fronds a dusty
grey-blue and sharply arched:a rugged, precise plant in heat and
very indifferent soils, one that will service several pots a tub
and go into the ground for still further utility of long duration;
don't risk too near the sea as it deteriorates under cool exposure
to salt bearing winds:frost hardy, just into warm temperate
regions, a bold spot for the eye....compelling attention.

   BUXUS microphylla japonica, "Boxwood" a common shrub 3-5', slow
of growth to make a dense definite form and outline with just the
least shearing, otherwise somewhat loose in structure:the yellow
green foliage which burns in heat with full sun, is flecked with
vermilion during cool or cold weather, drops in deep frost:ground
should be open, deeply dug for a good start, fertile and never
allowed to dry out completely:hedges, tubs or in the landscape,
growing naturally as any other shrub....don't disturb the shallow
feeding roots by digging. The species  -harlandi, is less understood but with promise, erect-narrow-dense for a low hedge 18-24",
better used in heat, but with overhead shade and sufficient moisture....burns:good little shrub in the right place.

Buddleja asiatica

Buddleja madagascariensis

Buddleja magnifica

Buxus

BYRNESIA weinbergi, "Mother of Pearl Plant" low succulent
with beautiful grey-green-violet, thickened leaves which take
on bronzy tints in the sun and show traces of pink in the new
growth, the green dominant in shadow....does not stand up
under much exposure:rock work or bedding of parterre
nature, in which case the white flowers may be snipped
in bud:a house plant or cover for a planter....takes
some neglect outside, the sun-wind combination the weak
link.  Graptopetalum paraguayense is synonymous.

C

CALADIUM picturatum, soft climate plants with large arrow-
headed leaves for pots or select spots in the garden:has
striking aspects in coloring, white, silver, yellow, red
and even blue in candid markings together with a kind of
translucence that is effective in changing light:wants are
constant....warmth, shade, fertility, drainage, moisture and just
plain good handling:predominately green in the leaf will indicate
those best fitted to grow outdoors....set tubers inch-deep March-
May, but February in pots, protected, using soil prepared with bone
meal, sand and leafmould with slight moisture at first, increasing
with growth, later feedings with manure water:when foliage begins
to dull out, with-hold moisture, lift when completely faded, dry
out in a dark place and store over winter in a sack with naptha-
line flakes or equal. Superior forms may be be increased by cutting rhizome or tuber into segments early spring, dusting cuts
with sulphur and placing in flats of leafmould or sand or peat,
kept barely moist. These should never be crowded, tops or tuber.

CALATHEA roseo-picta, a tropical herb for use indoors or in a
shaded planter box, grown for the foliage, the wide, stalked leaf
12-15" long from a close crown, dark green above with red along
the midrib and in  areas of the margin, dark purple beneath:wants
a loose loamy soil with' leafmould and sand....above all warmth:it
will deteriorate out of doors in cold weather and may pass out.

CALCEOLARIA integrifolia, "Bush Slipperwort" with showy, tiny,
pouch-like flowers in large indeterminate heads of pure yellow or
reddish brown, shrubby and low to the ground, sometimes only 12
inches through the mass and spreading generally 2-3':can be
stiffened up in woody growth to 2-3' or even 4-5' when
crowded:takes heat with the help of shade, wants good
humidity with drainage in a rich soil that is fibrous
with leafmould:blooms more or less continuously thru
spring and summer and will survive as much as ten degrees
of frost:coasts for coolness and prolonged flowering, it
is short lived, when forced to hard.

CALENDULA officinalis, "Potmarigold" low-growing garden
annuals with golden yellow or orange flowers with minor modifications, the precise head varying considerably in degree
of doubling:nearly indestructible as a garden flower, blooming in poor soils under drought....naturalizes in sandy soils
beside the sea:pots and bedding, sometimes grown for cutting:
leaves of the new growth and the petalage are of value, used
to flavor soups, or substitutes for spinach:sow seed in August
or September for winter bloom or any time excepting
in extreme heat or high humidity.

CALLIANDRA---tropical and subtropical shrubs for
frost-free areas, essentially exotic and about
the last word in fineness of parts throughout
the plant. the foliage is decorative, in the
likeness of the ferny types of acacia and is

carried well by the long slender stems for cutting. The flower is
a pom pom, more or less balled into a spherical head of tenuous
filaments and stamens which will suffer in rain and heavy dew.
The more protected gardens should make much of these outstanding plants. They should have a good garden soil in the sun,
and while they generally have high moisture requirements, they
recover from a fairly deep wilt without difficulty.

-californica, known in California and used there, native
farther south in Mexico, an open lacy shrub 3-4' with rather thin
purple flowers in the typical arrangement:stems are armed with sharp
spines. The species  -eriophylla, is similar, less in height,
native in the arid Southwest, used there.

-inequilatera, "Powderpuff" substantial and wide-spreading
to 15' across, 6-8' in height, having comparatively rugged and
leathery leaves, medium green with bronzy new growth:flower heads
are 2-3" in diameter, full-round and dark pink, autumn through
winter into spring:place against a warm wall for sure winter color
or espalier for an outstanding effect....for any shade involved.

-portoricensis, not persisting for long in California except
under the most favorable circumstances, spreading there as a low
shrub, becoming tree-like to 20' in the south of Florida:filmy
white flowers in small, tufted heads are notably fragrant in the
evening....bedraggled by morning by the dew, ruined at any time in
rain, with no insurance against total destruction.

-tweedi, distinctly upright in growth 6-8', the slender
stems visible through the haze of the foliage, the finest of
fabrics in the garden:scarlet to purple, half-round heads come
in late spring and summer, frequently again toward winter....the
hardiest in frost, as much as 10-15 degrees.

## BOTTLEBRUSH
CALLISTEMON---rugged, exceedingly serviceable shrubs, most
valuable in heat and aridity, although performing very well
under humidity. The flowers are set around the terminal twigs
in close cylinders, it being the long, out-thrust styles
and filaments  that make up the visible inflorescence and
its spectacular appearance. The head will be larger in a
loose or sandy soil, as will the entire plant....restricted
in heavy rock-bound ground. These are loosely built plants and
sparsely foliated so that a general overhaul with the pruning
shears in late summer not only corrects this, new flowering
wood develops. They are notably resistant to drought, somewhat
to frost, do well in limestone soils, are tolerant of alkali.

-brachyandrus,"Mallee B." a slender shrub of very open
structure, the leaves reduced to near needle proportions, a
dusty soot-grey, grimy-looking, not pleasing, but forgiven
in new growth, and in flower:brushes of red filaments that
carry yellow anthers, a yellow filigree over-all in July,
backed by the orchid tones of the silky new shoots:an old
plant, almost lost to the nursery trade.

-lanceolatus, the one most commonly seen and almost
always as a large rounded shrub 8-12', reduced in age to a
single stem, tree-like 25' in Florida....as large in California
in humidity and in sun;largest heads are found in this species, a
bright crimson and gorgeous display in the improved forms sometime a-
long February-July....mediocre or quite worthless in most seedlings.

-rigidus, all parts steady, fixed from the first growth, stiff
stems and rigid-held brushes which are smaller and less colorfull,
less attractive that the preceding, but can be held in place over
a much longer time than any of the others.

-viminalis, large shrub or tree-like 25' with hanging branchlets
the flowers dull purple, smaller, blooming well over the year with
only occasional interruptions:prune for strong limbs that reach up
straight and hold....do not force:hardiest one in cold.

CALLISTEPHUS chinensis, "China-aster" well-known late summer
and autumn flowering annuals, white and tinted pink, violet,
purple and blue:wants a well dug loam prepared with manure
and with enough moisture to keep the young plant coming along
without any pushing:sun and heat make sturdy plants....steady

237

*Calliandra porto-ricensis*

*Callistemon lanceo-latus*

*Callistephus (single)*

*Calo-cepha-lis*

growth a prime requisite in disease control:don't set out
too soon as plants lift better in later stages of growth,
with less check or hold-up....cultivate shallow, the roots
being at the surface. These plants are subject to many ailments, root-aphis and a virus of the leaf known as yellows or
wilt for which use tobacco dust or fumigant....burn all wilted
plants. A new place for planting these each year is good insurance and best management. They are scarcely worth the effort as
required south in these regions and each year they are less often
found. The single varieties are more practicable to handle.

CALLITRIS robusta, "Cypress-pine" a rare tree of indeterminate size but comparatively rapid growth, the very erect branches
starting from very near the ground to follow upward in a compact,
tight formation:does much better in sandy soils than in heavy
ground where it is ill at ease, scrawny in growth, eventually a
dilapidated specimen....otherwise satisfactory under varying conditions of dryness and fertility....do not force, when it tends
to break away and weep, the tip growth becoming lax, hanging.

CALOCEPHALIS browni, "Cushionbush" solid, dense, a dome 2-3',
somewhat woody, building up into a series of mounds of a metalic
silvery sheen....chalk-white with too much water or in age, somewhat so merely out of growth:flowers June-July come as roundish
buttons, silver fretted over with the gold of stamens....fail, persist and bedraggle in late summer if not sheared:relieve of wood
and foliage from time to time, cutting deep for brush to be used
indoors in a vase or dry boquets....keeps as long as a year if
taken reasonably dormant:resents moisture and probably should not
be·grown in heavy ground unless drained....short-lived at best:
shows dust and grime:cut out dead patches as they develop, in
order that side growth may fill in.

CALODENDRUM capense, "Cape-chestnut" symmetrical tree to as
much as 60' in deep, fertile soils, a dome in outline, at times
seen covered with color, the leaves barely breaking through the
completeness:rose-lilac flowers develop in loose but prim heads
like a large powder-puff, the tree itself a master "puff" in
full bloom:performance is erratic, flowering usually after too
many years sulking, generally May-June, known to repeat in
autumn, after growth. No catalogue will outdo the actuality
of this tree in good flower, but budded stock must be used to
guarantee early flowering and highest quality in coloring:the
foliage may drop in cold weather, but breaks new soon:wants a
light substantial soil with less than average irrigation and
that laid deeply:tender when young, surviving 15 degrees frost
after having been established:choice.

CALONYCTION aculeatum, "Moonflower" perennial vine, climbing
to 15', or much more in rich moist ground, the purple or white,
satiny flowers like morning-glories....open suddenly at dusk,nor-
mally closed by the middle of the following day unless over-cast:
blooms July-September, or much later far south:may be held to a
pot in furnishing a blank wall quickly:sun and moisture....soak
the seed well before planting.

CALOPHYLLUM inophyllum, a smooth, grey-barked tree to 60',
having clustered, very fragrant, pure white flowers erect in
the axils of the dark, leathery leaves February-March, repeating August-September:use along the coasts southerly in wind and
wind-blown spray, the rigid branchings twisting about there in a
picturesque manner of growth:tender in frost.

CALOSTEMMA purpurea, rare bulb with winter growth of narrow, strap-
shaped leaves and sturdy 18-24" stalks of rosy purple flowers in the
narcissus reminder, appearing bare of leaves June-August:wants a
well drained loamy, leafy soil and full sun:pots.

CALOTHAMNUS quadrifidus, "Brittlebrush" straggly shrub 6-8' or
much less, more contained under garden culture and of an
238

ornate, decorative quality when kept under control:prune hard
after flowering or reduce to a rough-cut hedge which recovers
quickly after cutting to bloom again....an espalier, adapting
in design as thin crimson lines:flowers in a brushy shag of
brilliant color more or less over the year when not disturb-
ed:thrives under exposure, in dryness and in poorish soils.

## ROSE OF JAPAN
CAMELLIA---woodland shrubs for the deeps of the year and
all the year:deliberate in growth for long-extended service;
very select, with many choice varieties, improving year by year
to a wider utility in planting. The back-drop of excellent foliage of varying greens and pattern is durable, serviceable the
entire year and sets off to advantage these floral creations
that rival the rose in form and color....but counter-season.
They want a fertile, well drained soil high in humus, with constant moisture and warmth over summer when flower buds are in
the making....high humidity then. Give them moderate shade in
heat and north or east exposures, although they benefit with
more sun as affecting bloom than is generally realized. Feed
every six weeks, March through August, but advisedly and related to growth, using an acid fertilizer with light mulchings
of leafmould continually rotting away beneath. Don't cultivate
and don't prune these plants except very lightly in spring to
correct the structure. The blasting of buds may be traced to too
low setting as planted, a too dry or too moist soil or atmosphere, especially a serious drying out the previous year; poor
drainage; a variety character or an abnormally heavy crop. Dis-
bud early when obviously over-bearing, mid-summer at the latest.
Transplanting is best done winter-spring when plants are dormant
and still blooming. When buying, select plants in flower to be
surely pleased and take few blooms in interest of form and future crops, twisting off the flower for floating or cutting
back only a few buds into current seasons growth.
-japonica, long known and respected, loved throughout the
South as japonica, the flower plain, of simple cast, direct to
us from the hearts of generations of gardeners....now in many
choice forms, distinctive singles to full-pouting doubles,white
and all the way through red:a large modeled shrub, compact and
twiggy, blooming by variety October-January, some as late as in
April:subject to scale and aphis, buds and new growth.
-reticulata, gorgeous bloom, an upstanding but sparsely
branched shrub, an addition to the list that is rare as yet,
having a dull, dark foliage and large, wide-flaring flowers:
the brush of yellow stamens is backed by undulating, buckling,
rosy red petals of a radiant sheen that seems to scatter a purplish light:slow-growing at first, with only one flush to be
expected, more rapid later and probably a tree 35' in the end.
There is much for the future here.
-sasanqua, a loose, straggling shrub, low-vining, or erect-
rigid forms for open situations.... most variable, with kinds that
may be used almost as a vine, pegged down as a ground cover or as
an espalier attached to a wall in easy flowing lines:pure white to
deep pink, single to doubling flowers are less precise, wild roses
September-December, not long-lasting, shattering all too quickly:
may be used in the poorer soils and more difficult situations.

## BELLFLOWER
CAMPANULA---popular group of herbaceous perennials, some of which
adapt well in subtropical regions and supply there several free-
flowering species of much charm and grace for color in the border
and in the rock garden. They are not so particular as to fertility, but demand ground be well drained and like it with
a gritty, grainy or gravelly texture. A little lime brings
about a more vibrant coloring with white of exceptional
purity or lustrous tints all the way through pink, rose,
lavender, violet-purple and blue to be had. They thrive
best in the upper parts of these regions and should be
given the advantage of half shade in heat, but the sun

in coolness. Many species will adapt south, the following
having been proven, are usually available, if one persists.
    -erinus, an annual for bedding, edging and in the rock
garden:small heart-shaped leaves are glossy and the pale blue
stemless flowers are with a lighter center:may run out after a
time in near tropical regions of excessive humidity, so that new
seed may be required to continue a planting.
    -fragilis, perennial, a spreading prostrate mass of dark fol-
iage with an abundance of wide-open, lavender-blue bells July-
October:likes a warm place, but not in too much sun:use in a
rock wall, in the corner of a paved court or patio as a cover,
in a pot, hanging basket or window box.
    -isophylla, "Italian B." prostrate perennial with handsome
glossy leaves and white saucer-shaped flowers of substance, close
to and intermingling the foliage July-November:light, fairly dryish soils with a little shade as used in pots, baskets and in a dry
rock wall:pinch back for mass and to check streamers that are getting
out of hand.    --var. mayi, naturally a little more compact, with soft
pale blue flowers and grey-wooly leaves  as above:less vigorous, choice.
    -medium, "Canterburybells" biennial,or available in strains with
the annual character bred in, any or all invaluable for color in
a fixed scheme:outline of the plant is broad-pyramidal with a
stout stalk 1-3' high, crowded with the wide, full bells in
many brilliant hues:grown well, it may be necessary to stake
and it must not be forgotten to have new plants coming along
for replacement, if desired to continue.
    -poscharskyana, "Dalmation or Serbian B." vigorous and
far-reaching, invasive, too aggressive to use among the others
or more refined plants, but valuable none-the-less in many
other garden situations:foliage mass rather close-knit, to 6"
through, supports 15" flowering stems that are strong, but slanting, ultimately bedding down the blue blooming: a cover plant
that spreads underground, occupying the ground completely.

    CAMPSIDIUM valdivianum, "Chile Trumpetcreeper" burly vine
that develops a thick woody stem as it climbs, short and stout
and massive as held in for cover:good fabric of clean, shining
foliage, particularly immune to disease and pests:small yellow
flowers make up in numbers for what they lack in brilliance in
May-June. This plant will climb high or may be retained low in
bulking rolls over a bank or other declivity....a stout fellow
with plenty of heart for what it takes in adversity.

    CANARINA campanulata, "Canary Bellflower" rare tuberous per-
ennial 3-5' that may be carried along for years in successive
containers, if the deciduous character of foliage and stem can be
grasped and the plant managed correctly....with-hold water when the
yellowing leaves indicate a desire for rest:may be flowered any or
most of the time from October to March....large bells, yellowish,
with purple veining, washed faintly over-all with a dull red:plant
is watery, fleshy in character throughout and very delicate, calling for a refined and generous mix of good loam, leafmould and some
coarse sand:may be divided while dormant....cuttings difficult.

    CANDOLLEA cuneiformis, a slumping shrub 3-4', erect at first and
rather prim, eventually lapsing, subsiding in mass, semi-sprawling, but with a certain character in the slouch:rich, clear
yellow flowers February-June in the pattern of a wild rose
with the petals rolled in:thrives in heat and in considerable dryness, when the large, lumpish red sepals deepen for
an effect:of good garden constitution, but only with perfect
drainage to handle surplus water, otherwise of short useful-
ness:choice shrub when well handled.

    CANELLA winterana,  "Wild-cinnamon" a slender tree, south
in Florida, or lower, shrubby from frost more northerly and
in California, having stiff lateral branchings, dense with the
shining, durable, aromatic leaves:good tub plant for display of
the many attractive qualities....foliage, the cinnamon-scented

grey bark, the flowers of lavender to purple with the yellow stamens
standing stark against the petals and at last, the red berries in the
concept of holly:growth is very slow for a compact plant to stand
long in very heavy soil, in dryness or in moisture that is slow
to clear up....abiding, a plant for the ages.

CANNA generalis, the common "Garden Canna" variable in height
and coloring in both foliage and flowers, highly tropical in looks
as well as in culture, companion plants of the ornamental grasses in
large scale bedding:wants a good garden soil enriched, the sun and all
its warmth held, together with an abundance of moisture:may be had in
flower April-November, left in the ground indefinitely, thinning in
February-March by removing spent stalks for higher quality. The extremely exotic nature of these plants permits little place in the
spontaneous feeling of the average garden. Reserve them rather, for
the formalized bed of a public place where they will be in better
scale and where the blare of primitive colors may be submerged in
cold concrete and the uncertain approval of crowds....subdued color
only in the garden. The species, -iridiflora, growing to 10'high
with green stalks and leaves to 4' long and with handsome rose-
colored drooping flowers is sometimes available, the better one
to use in the landscape or garden.

CANTUA buxifolia, "Miracle Bush" half-climbing shrub of rather
weak growth except under adequate conditions of soil and moisture,
with a sufficiency of these things desirable, and also modera-
tion:flowers hang as long, glistening trumpets, orange shaded
with rose to brittle stems that will bear protection in wind
or tying to secure....normally March-May, but subject to variation depending largely on moisture:likes half shade. This is
an untidy shrub....prune to guide growth and correct the natural dishevelment, removing old wood at the base and pinching the
laterals:survives into warm-temperate regions in warm places.

CAPPARIS spinosa, "Caperbush" trailing 2-3' or the stems
somewhat longer and raised in a more bush-like conventional
manner, growing best in very loose dryish soils:rather large,
solitary flowers, loosely put together are delicate and shatter
easily, the purple filaments etched sharply against the crinkled white petals:bud and berry are used in pickles or condi-
ments, the plant in the landscape over walls, banks or in
the rock garden or other well drained place.

CAPSICUM frutescens, "Redpepper" an annual for the herb
plot or cutflower garden, or the smaller varieties grown in a
pot for a showing of the brilliant crimson pods:larger pods
are strung to hang indoors or outside in the Mexican fashion,
as in a patio for color and atmosphere;the many varieties are
based on shape, size or coloring of the pod.

CARDIOSPERMUM halicacabum, "Balloon-vine" rapid-growing annual
or a perennial vine to 10', having curiously inflated seed vessels
which may be used as festoons or otherwise in decoration:fruits continuously far south in loose warm soils, a garden plant there and
becoming perennial:climbs by means of tendrils. The species -hirsu-
tum, perennial vine in the south, growing 20-30' affording good overhead cover, the green of parchment-like lanterns tannish as
they mature in thick clusters, may be tinted for color and
have been wired for tiny bulbs in miniature lighting effects.

CARICA papaya, "Papaya" herbaceous tree to 25', extremely
tropical, the sturdy stems tapering upwards, forking into erect
branches which in turn are topped by the very large bright
green leaves:melon-like fruits hanging from the base of this
structure are sweet, but sometimes distasteful due to a musky flavor:
rich, loamy, drained soils important since the plant rots at the
soil line in excess moisture and requires to be forced in growth
to mature fruit in border regions. They grow and produce south
in Florida, but are limited in California by frost to only the

241

most favored spots and there the cold nights impair the
flavor of such fruits as may mature. Every artifice known
and available must be applied to foster and conserve heat,
even to wrapping the trunk and covering the top in time of
frost. A hardier species, -candamarcensis, has golden yellow fruits of poorer quality and a more umbrageous head.

CARISSA---spiny, strong-growing shrubs of branchy habit and
rapid growth, attractive in foliage, flower and fruit; highly
ornamental over-all, but to be used in the garden with discretion.
Due to thorns, it is urgent that extra thought in selection be giv-
en here in the matter of size, form, and especially in placement,
for....the less one works with these, the happier the day. Primary
use as a barrier is suggested, hedges, a screen on the boundary or
impassable thickets to curb trespass. There the grievously cruel
thorn becomes an asset and not a liability and hazard. The thick,
durable and glossy foliage serves year-round, the large flowers,
pure white or tinted and rigid-starlike are more or less continuous, while the conspicuous red fruits may be used literally as cranberry sauce. They may be set out in any good
soil in the sun, with little attention necessary when
properly used....excepting only a thorough spray spring-
summer for thrips and red spider. They are tender in frost.
    -arduina, "Hedge-thorn" small-leaved, naturally a
dense plant, double-spined, the better one to use as a
clipped hedge, growing to 10', but easily kept low:smaller
white flowers are profuse, the fruits small, dark red, clustered. This is the hardiest species in frost.
    -carandas, "Christ-thorn" very erect, a rigid shrub with
stout slender stems to 20' in time:leaves short and blunt at
the tip, while the clustered, long-narrow-tubed pink flowers
are set in the axils of the leaves....red fruits turn black:
This makes a very effective screen.
    -edulis, straggling, spreading and thickly branching, the
purple flowers in full heads so that the clusters of small fruits
in a good set are cherry-like, the size of a small marble:tender.
    -grandiflora, "Natal-plum" the most commonly used, a general
purpose shrub of rounding habit, dense rather than open in structure, bright green set with those large fragrant white stars, the
flowers:these are occasional rather than ample as to set, carrying on through warmth, eventually overlapping and mingling with
the large ruby-red, elongated fruits. Superior forms of this are
selected and propagated in the nurseries.    --var. compacta, less
vigorous, with smaller leaves, a low dense mound of refinement.
--prostrata, is low and flat-growing, sometimes with too frequent,
erect-surging stems that must be kept down if the plant is to serve
its distinct purpose....ground cover, banks, facing. The variety
--minima, is in miniature as a whole and in all its parts.

CARNEGIEA gigantea, "Suwarro" a large tree-like cactus, the
immense ribbed branches closely paralleling the erect trunk:a
striking object, but of some difficulty in growing under domestication....certainly as of humidity when it stem-rots:near deserts.

CARPENTERIA californica, "Tree-anemone" beautiful western
native shrub having terminal clusters of large, waxy-white
flowers April-July;should be protected from wind on a slope,
making sure in any event there is no standing water:wants some
moisture and slight shade....north slope good in excessive heat
or far south:lends an air of refinement scarcely to be expected of a plant so brushy in nature....suckers and in other
ways wants direction with a knife to fit for the garden:con-
trol aphis which causes the naturally revolute leaf to go
into a disfiguring roll inward:hardy into warm temperate
regions. This rather unusual and seldom used shrub should
make a satisfactory substitute for the oldfashioned mock
orange or what is known widely in the east as syringa, a misnomer
that persists even into these horticulturally foreign lands. This
likeness extends to the cane-like character of the stems.

242

COMPENDIUM

CARUM carvi, "Caraway" the seed used with bread or in the
flavoring of pastries, the root dug and eaten as a vegetable
and the top adapted to salads:for culinary purposes, this herb
with its small white or pinkish flowers in loose heads, will be
sown in the fall and preferably in a heavy soil.

## FISHTAIL PALM
CARYOTA---distinctive smooth-stemmed trees with a modified frond,
the leaflets triangular, jagged at the ends. They are rapid in growth
in fertile warm soils with drainage, but are mostly used in tubs or
under other root restrictive situation. After release into open soil
they quickly reach maturity when a hanging inflorescence repeats a
downward stepping on the trunk until the tree dies in completion
and in exhaustion. They like atmospheric humidity, want moisture
in abundance when in growth and are at their best in shade. They
have difficulty with wet feet California winters.
     -mitis, attaining 25-35' after it gets into the ground,
grown first for use in the tub, suckering there and afterward
to make continuing clumps with a close crown:established plants
will take only five degrees of frost:choice.
     -urens, "Toddy P." the trunk tapering from a slight bulge at
the base, light-colored, with conspicuous rings:very large,
graceful fronds are cut into segments in the effect of many
fish-tails. This is one of the most striking of the palms to be
seen in Southern Florida, infrequently in the warmer spots of
California:yields a beverage that is wholesome and tasty.

CASIMIROA edulis, "White-sapota" tropical fruit tree 50' for
ornament and shade in favored localities:does where citrus is
grown, the fruit clustered in bunches, large greenish yellow
plums spring and summer:pulp melting, with a recognizable peach
flavor, and with the added suggestion of honey in the better var-
ieties:likes a humid atmosphere with warmth and does in a heavy
clay, but no lime:litters badly and should not be placed
near a walk on account of dropping fruit:survives 10 degrees
of frost, but may be badly hurt.

## SENNA
CASSIA---a mixed group of shrubs and trees from far tropical places or near temperate lands, wanting in common the sun
with its heat and light, a soil verging on dryness or at least
well drained....otherwise with varying wants. The foliage is
reasonably refined, very finely divided or a little coarse,
not in size but as to texture and always light toned. The
abundant flowering  is in gold or yellow, rarely pink and
always extremely showy. They are short-lived, but rapid-growing
to quickly come into service inter-filling the lower elements
of a permanent planting. All are sensitive to cold and require
to be pruned regularly for best flowering....trees want attention to structure the first years, the shrubs to be thinned out
and opened to light. They all tend to exhaustive seed bearing,
so that any pods which can be removed early, and especially with
the young trees, will conserve strength for further growth and
flowering. At the same time this removal will correct an untidy
period which is one of the great faults of the group.
     -artemisioides, "Wormwood S." an attractive, shapely shrub 3'
high or somewhat more, easily pushed too high in excessive moisture
with resulting bare base. There is much refinement in foliage and
flowers, the leaves reduced to a needle-like structure of pleasing texture, a light greyish green with sulphur-yellow flowers to
carry from late winter through spring into summer, when pods are
removed:will not survive much frost,but takes high heat and dry-
ness:the best one for dry, warm, arid climates.
     -corymbosa, shrubby, very often tree-like and umbrageous at
10', a bright canopy of green above splayed supporting stems
beneath:light golden flowers are dependable September-October,
or earlier south:wants moisture with drainage and something to
be planned to come up beneath or from behind to supplement the
bareness. This plant is hardy into warm temperate regions,
returning from the crown after a killing freeze.

243

*C. artemisioides*

*Cassia fistula*

*Cassia splendens*

*Casimiroa edulis*

-fistula, "Goldenshower" an erect tree 30' with a light open head, the extremities of the branches tending to droop:pale gold flowers suspend airily in long clusters, mainly beneath the foliage on the previous seasons growth....prune in summer for this, to accent the flowering:frost-free areas only:choice
-grandis, "Pinkshower" a fair sized tree in Southern Florida, with up-reaching limbs, well branched, the lavender buds opening to rosy pink February-March....lay a warm spread on the ground as they fall:tender and wants protection from the wind, growing best in a medium-heavy loam:semi-deciduous.
-nairobensis, a coarse, widely spreading shrub, the stout branches sometimes stretching out on the ground:larger leaves are clear green, but with an unpleasant odor when brushed against or crushed:the very large, erect heads of yellow flowers, November-March, may be continuous in very warm areas:growth is flashy and rank, the bush overgrown and seedy-looking without regular pruning and some irrigation:very tender in frost.
-splendida, a low, wide-spreading, branchy shrub 5-8', a dense tangled, brushy mass, as much or more across as high:spectacular and timely show for autumn and for winter, if the foliage holds; golden yellow flowers October-March are large, abundant, colorfull.
-tomentosa, straggling shrub of less merit, erect slender stems sparsely branched at 6-8', having light yellowish green leaves and scattering yellow flowers now and then, concentrating late winter and spring:thin and disorderly after a few years, especially in heavy soils or in the absence of sufficient moisture.

CASTANOSPERMUM australe, "Moreton Bay-chestnut" sturdy tree 40' or to 60' in good going:has exceptionally fine, light green foliage, the individual leaf rather glossy, thickish, compound, very serviceable and free of pests:the 6" spikes of the inflorescence will have yellow flowers that run into orange and red and appear directly on mature wood, even the trunk, July-August and lightly scattering: not spectacular, but considered a flowering tree southerly:wants full sun in youth, gets it in age by default when grown in heat, as of the interior in deep soil of some fertility and with underlying water for thrift....can be disappointing elsewhere:hardy in 10 degrees frost.

## SOUTHSEA IRONWOOD

CASUARINA---queer trees of the near tropics, frequently mistaken for pines, but only in semblance there-of....almost facsimile. They are out of a past age to intrigue observing gardeners and serve in places where little else will survive. They are slender trees with whip-like branches that give to the wind, the leaves in mystic, feathery tufts, needle-like, jointed and pulling apart like the horsetail. All are extremely rapid in growth in all soils, sand or clay or coarse gravel, wet or dry and with any soil reaction, adapting particularly to and much used in brackish places. They yield willingly to the first push of the wind; may be used in reclaiming sand or for any other purpose along the shore, protective of other planting or as a hard-shorn hedge....frost the principal and about the only limiting factor. They tend to root-sprout in wet Florida soils and quickly exhaust ground anywhere in detriment to neighboring growth, especially in California where the root-mat tends to the surface. They are essentially utilitarian.
-cunninghamiana, "Australian-pine" as high as 70' with a strong, regular, rather dense, broad-pyramidal form of fine branches that are well provided with dark green foliage:the hardiest in frost except when very young, less resistant to driven spray with salt, but probably the best one in wet ground.
-equisetifolia, "Beefwood" from the red of the heartwood, growing 60-80', the largest one of the group in the end, the hanging branches with lighter green foliage:tender in frost, but utterly rugged and unshaken in all other adversity, unfaltering and uncomplaining in salt spray, wind, black alkali, drought or wet feet:a hard tree, wood as well as physique.
-lepidophloia, normally a tree 40', frequently multiple stemmed with an up-curling of limbs and branches to a good foliage cover:

grown as a windbreak in wet soils or dry rocky ground....roots
in deeply to hold in wind:suckers too badly for any domestic use.
    -stricta, "She-oak" very slender to 30', of exceptionally
rapid growth, a fairly good tree for streets, but not in the
wind since the long pliant branches of very long leaves seem unable to fix in the face of continual breeze and whip to windward
for a one-sided specimen:the better one to use inland:may sucker.

    CATHA edulis, "Khat" an arabian shrub 10', or tree-like to as
high as 35' when encouraged upward, rarely grown for the edible fruit
or white flowers:the shining leaves and twigs are used in beverages,
while the winter aspect of the foliage is marked in dull tones of purple and red, which character tends to reduce as a specimen ages:foliage
hangs quite late in the absence of frost of any degree....evergreen in
warmth:takes care of itself, wanting only nominal attention.

    CEANOTHUS---brushy evergreen shrubs, mostly of the west, merit-
ing much wider attention as experience in culture and hybridization lead to firmer ground in the garden. The following are natural species, to be used largely in wild plantings, some few adapting to domestic use. The flowering is splendid, if erratic under
culture, the play of light through delicate trusses lambent, almost etherial, a unique fabric of irradiation apparent to all who
will look. These plants are vigorous and rapid in growth in warm
light soils in the sun. Avoid heavy ground generally and by all
means one that is tight. Survival there will be short since
drainage is probably the controlling factor. They resent pruning.
Pinch out tips in time to shape the young plant for its place
in the garden and to reduce weakening seed production....go
deep into wood late fall or early winter and then, only if quite
necessary to open up structure to light or flatten prostrate
forms. The summer leaf drop has a bearing on location and
management in the garden....no fertilizer except leafmould
as a mulch at any time, or well rotted manure or compost
very lightly in the winter. Planting is best done in the fall
using young, well established container plants only, and in
prepared pits. Watch irrigation closely as to time and amount
the first season, with little if any summer watering afterward.
Keep them as close to nature as possible.
    -arboreus, "Catalina C." a large shrub, or more often
tree-like 20', with comparatively large, slate-green leaves,
the main crop of pale to deeper blue flowers, lavender in the
bud, February-March, or January, south....a lesser repeat of
bloom in summer:takes more water without hurt than most and is
one of the more persistent species in a heavy soil:may be
flowered in a little shade.
    -cyaneus, "Lakeside-lilac" always shrubby with angular
open growth 6-8', as high as wide, the thick stems green-warty:
foliage dark, shining, the flowers in large compound trusses like
oldfashioned lilac, deep blue or sometimes a very pure white, light
lavender and rose in the bud May-June, or later in moisture:hard to
establish, more difficult to hold....young plants only, to start
out in gravelly soil, with high heat and nearly absolute dryness. Its glory, as of the garden is mostly posthumous and a
memory. It hybridizes so readily that it is seldom found in
in the nurseries in a pure state....handsome crosses there.
    -foliosus, "Wavyleaf-lilac" a spreading plant 2-3' high
and to 10' across, good cover for dryish ground, the shining
foliage of high quality, the light blue flowers March-May:is
difficult to establish, better used northerly in these regions
and into warm temperate climates.
    -gloriosus, "Point Reyes Creeper" low-spreading, the pros-
trate stems rooting, a choice foliage cover for ground, having
lavender-blue, fragrant flowers March-April:to be grown in coolness with a little moisture and shade inland:good garden plant,
but keep alkaline irrigation water off foliage and going through
the ground to prevent concentration....leaves are shining and
distinctly holly-like:frost hardy. This is a most attractive little
plant and can be grown widely in coolness and with sweet water.

-grizeus, growing 2-4' in height with much more width, a ranging, stemmy individual 10-15' across, the horizontal character brought out in other ways....large, deeply marked, semi-glossy leaves are silvery beneath....dark blue flowers for March-April followed by jet black seed pods:vigorous, aggressive, withstanding considerable alkalinity and out of season moisture. This is probably the better one to use south under domestication, but too large for the garden proper....don't crowd anywhere.

-impressus, "Santa Barbara C." rather dense-growing, mounded 3-4' for full sun surely, having blue flowers in various intensities February-April:small round leaves are deep-marked and somewhat rolled under in too much heat:growth rapid in sandy soils, where it is quite persistent....short-lived in heavy ground. A distinctly ornamental kind to be used rather freely in and around the garden.

-microphyllus, "Sandflat C." native east, prostrate, a mat only 6" high, or to 2' as a straggling bush from a woody crown:white flowers in February-May in tiny loose panicles:very small, nearly round or elliptic leaves are thickened:semi-deciduous and seldom obtainable.

-papillosus, with extremely darkened foliage of a viscid, glandular roughened character, spreading in form 3-5' with dark blue flowers that are carried loosely on long stiff stalks March-April.   --var. roweanus, only 18" high, an attractive variant, low-spreading as a ground cover or used with large installations....among natural rock.

-purpureus, "Hollyleaf C." select species for rather general use 2-4' high, having stiff, erect stems of dark and shining leaves and deep blue to purple flowers February-April:wants a little shade and careful irrigation, otherwise short-lived:temperamental, even for these, but highly satisfactory in the right place;tends to get out of control unless headed back from time to time.

-verrucosus, "Coast C." dense rounded 3-7' as found exposed along the Southern California coast, more straggling under cultivation:small round heads of white flowers in late winter carry on into spring:juvenile leaves are holly-like, later notched at the tip and more rounded, a dark, dull green. This is a comparatively practical plant to have in more common use and is being overlooked.

CEDRONELLA canariensis(triphylla) "Canarybalm" shrubby, 2-3' in height, the white or purple flowers arranged in rigid rings about the stems:both foliage and flowers smell of camphor and lemon, an exciting sensation, at the same time soothing and envigorating:rare

## CEDAR
CEDRUS---trees for grandeur, stately specimens expressing majesty in nature, towering to 100' or more, the very effective foliage in small bundles of short needles, dark green or bluish. They are known as the true cedars and may be counted upon for any substantial or dignified functional part to play in the landscape and should be allowed the maximum of space in which to develop the characteristic form and to display a very real beauty. There are no known diseases nor insect pests and they are clean and tidy. They are difficult to transplant except as established in containers, should be root-pruned in the nursery row for balling out and will be used almost anywhere, avoiding wet ground. Heavier, drained soils are to be preferred.

-atlantica, "Atlas C." broad-pyramidal, the growing top erect, the needles rigid, dark green:limbs may break down with the over weight of water in a lush, well irrigated garden....withstands drier conditions.   --var. glauca, intensely glaucous, blue-green, more irregular, the ideal Christmas tree, lower limbs curving, a cross-ruff of stems upwards, dangles, festoons.

-deodara,"Deodor" literally Gate of God, finger-point towards Diety, embracing inner urges and predilections of man, the tree narrow-pyramidal, the growing tip and branchlets drooping, bluish-grey-green, leaves more soft and pliable:a cranky tree always, with either too much or not enough moisture:see to drainage.

CELTIS australis, "Nettle-tree" off-symmetry, oval, 60', elm-like, especially the leaves, dull grey-green:adapted to hot arid countries for shade, wanting water to establish:good in wind, for streets, but roots at the surface a problem:not a garden tree, deciduous.

## CORNFLOWER

CENTAUREA---oldfashioned garden flowers, most of them with decidedly good coloring for the border, well fitted for and much used for cutting. The seed may be sown directly in the bed or plants obtained, in which case only young stock is acceptable. Overgrown flat material almost never comes along satisfactorily. These plants will reseed and come true. They are all satisfied in a marl or limestone soil.

-cineraria(candidissima)"Dusty Miller" a robust perennial 18-24" or to 3' in the better garden soils, better lower and in poorer ground: thistle-like, purple or yellow flowers may be allowed to develop or the plant may be sheared low in bedding for the light grey foliage.

-cyanus, "Bachelorbutton" an annual, slender-erect and erect branching, 18-24" blooming from early spring until fall, the white, pink, purple, but mostly blue button-like flowers on long naked stems:the rather scant foliage takes on a slightly silvery cast from fine whitish hair when young.

-dealbata, "Persian C." perennial in the likeness of the sweet sultan, a neat, compact plant 18-24" high, the pale green leaves silvered beneath, the large rosy-lilac flower heads with the typical fringe, summer:garden border, but dry, not wet.

-moschata, "Sweet Sultan" slender, fragrant annuals for filling in spots in the border or grown in the cutflower garden for the white, yellow or light purple flowers in summer:common garden plant.

CENTAUREUM(ERYTHRAEA)---low herbs for very special uses in and about the garden where they are sheltered from the wind and find a warm sandy soil that is not overly fertile, and free from lime. They will be well used in the rock garden or naturalized in the near environs of the home, according to species. They claim distinction for exceptional purity in the coloring of the flower.

-massoni, "Rose-gentian" a tufted perennial 3-4" high, to be used in rock work or on the floor of a paved court where it will reduce in height to as little as an inch in traffic:lush foliage is bright green and at times almost concealed beneath the sheet of waxy pink flowers June-August:uniform moisture is indicated, at least a quarter shade and a neutral to acid soil:rare and better north.

-venustum, "Conchalagua" an erect and erect-branched Californian 8-12" with good body and symmetrical outline, unexpected for an annual:rosy pink, erect flowers are touched with white in early spring,with moisture....a drier place in the garden:taken with its full root system, the plant, with or without water, keeps.

CEPHALOCEREUS senilis, "Oldman Cactus" a sturdy ribbed column of indeterminate height, spined, wooly with long white hair at the top or following down; a striking object, stand-in of note against a dark background:lives to great age, becoming quite large when it finds its place and survives:cannot be expected to flower for a number of years from planting:nocturnal.

CERATONIA siliqua, "Carob or Saint John'sbread" a dense, full rounded tree 50', admirably suited to arid lands....only well drained soils in Florida and not often used there:deep-rooted and very resistant to drought in sandy soils, slow and stunted in clay, tolerating some alkali....irrigate deeply and frequently there:an historic tree, the bean has been used as food for centuries:streets, although sometimes difficult to bring up in uniform sizes:October blooming, the flower in tiny red clusters studding the hard woody branches and even large primary limbs:difficult to transplant, a ball of earth should be taken, if not obtainable in a container:shows but little dust beside a dirt road.  --var.bolser is a selection based on fruiting, used when grown for the bean.

CERATOPTERIS pteridoides, "Water Fern" floating, or grown in a pot submerged in a pool:large, deeply lobed leaves lie flat on the surface of the water, while more finely divided seed leaves will emerge more or less erect:young plants are produced at the edge of the matured leaf and detach in time for increase:acts like water-hyacinth, but much less of a nuisance for smaller surfaces:native in Florida. This is more of a novelty than having any practical application.

SUBTROPICAL REGIONS

LEADWORT

CERATOSTIGMA---low, bushy, wiry-stemmed little plants with
very pure blue, phlox-like flowers in some abundance. The foliage
is dark, with reddish tints submerged, coming easily to the surface with any check in growth. They are notably serviceable under
stress of weather or any unusual wear, dry to touch, with an unpleas-
ing glandular harshness. They want the sun, but tolerate some shade
and make a valiant attempt at thrift in sterile soils that are hot and
dry....either light in texture or heavy. They are deciduous for a time.

-griffithi, "Burma L." with a vigorous, shrubby growth 3-4', held
to a close crown or the stems streaming out vine-like, lying on the
earth as cover or draping a bank 6-10':light blue flowers August thru
November are scattering rather than profuse while the foliage takes on
ruddy hues in a poor soil, crimson as it falls:definitely deciduous.

-plumbaginoides, classed as a perennial, a delightfully spreading mass with underground stem-roots spreading out farther in a ring
of many sparingly branched stems 6-10" high and 10' or more across:
remove old crowns at deterioration and replace with the scanty rooted material that will be found:especially valuable on the ocean.

-willmottianum, finely branched, thinly foliated shrub 2-4', grown
with perennials or with shrubs for the refining influence:blooms brilliantly and continually, June-November:fails in frost and flinches in
extended cold, the foliage gradually draining to earth, starting back
the first warm days of spring....use flowering stems in bowls before
cold weather arrives. An excellent little plant when well used.

CERATOTHECA triloba, "African-foxglove" biennial, tending to become
perennial south, stout slender stems 5-6', scantily clad with
leaves and with no basal clump:the lilac-purple flowers
with extended lower lip finely lined....mount gradually
for a mild showing of color September-October:height and
stringiness and an unpleasant odor suggest the back of the
border:starts late, but will be grown for the clean spiring
height in line and the tough growing qualities.

CERCIDIUM torreyanum, "Palo Verde" a stemmy, round headed tree
25' or only a brushy shrub of the desert:bright green thorny
branches are bare most of the year, releafing with rainfall or
other moisture....overall effect, in or out of leaf, a light,
bluish green:immune to heat and drought and does in any soil that
is not too tight. This is frequently confused with another and
larger tree, the Jerusalem-thorn, an introduced species.

REDBUD      JUDAS TREE

CERCIS---small deciduous trees, sometimes shrublike, very freely
and very early flowering in the spring. Stems and branches are studded
directly and throughout with wine-red flowers which are so unruly with
other reds as to require a lone place in the flowering scheme. They are
well along before the heart-shaped leaves make an appearance. Give them
a deep porous soil with rather good moisture for best results or will
do in thin, drier ground for less. Do not prune except when shaping
the tree in youth, or in opening up the head to light in later life;
but reducing, sometimes in arid regions, in anticipation of a peculiar dieback. They like some shade and should be so indulged in
heat whenever feasible. They are difficult to establish when
planted bare-root....early spring, the better timing.

-occidentalis, a western species, shrubby to some 12', dense
and rounded, or a slender-stemmed little tree with a rounded top and
open structure:root system goes deeply for water.

-siliquastrum, growing to as much as 40' in height, but usually
progressively less as taken south, the rosy-purple flowers notable for
size rather than for abundance:pods seen in rifts through the matured
foliage are bright red before turning brown, the two phases lasting for
several weeks:a large scale espalier, where a tendency to crooked
limbs may be intensified for character:better one in heat.

CERCOCARPUS betuloides, "Mountain-mahogany" western native,
a shrub at 12' of slender, open growth or a gnarled little
tree to 25' in the better soils:has a neat, clear-cut, soft

248

greyish leaves and an interesting seed appendage that is strangely curled and twisted for an unreal lighting effect in a slanting
light:thrives under varying conditions of moisture and soil, loam,
gravel or in heavier ground:takes light shade or full, blistering
sun which silvers the stems through the thin furnishing of leaves.
This neat, attractive native domesticates very satisfactorily.

CEROPEGIA woodi, an interesting little plant, long-trailing in
habit, the roundish succulent leaves with at times considerable
color:long-tubular, waxy flowers are pink and go in pairs to
decorate the stems....as from a basket:has some value and
greater possibilities with the development of the pure decor
idea, growing indoors as well as outside, in the lath house
or as cover over gravel with succulents:wants a period of
rest in dryness, good moisture otherwise.

## CLUSTERFLOWER
CESTRUM---tropical shrubs for practically frost-free areas and
warmer. As used northerly, they lose their habit of spontaneous,
more or less continuous flowering, to become erratic or intermittent, as affected by moisture, temperature or physical operations in
the garden. Experience, however, points to some apparent preference
in season, and species will be found best encouraged for that time, with-
holding water after flowering and trimming then. They tend to become weak
and viney in maturity and should be kept reduced to strong wood. Cropping
is prodigious, the berries white, black or red-purple and stems taken at
that time may be taken indoors. Soil preference is for the lighter
textures, but fertile to support the rank growth and enormous flowering, yet heavy enough to maintain uniformity in moisture.  They
will want the sun, but take shade and are subject to mealybug.
   -aurantiacum, "Yellow-lilac" vaguely orange-colored, an erect
bushy shrub 6-8', rather open but with foliage evenly distributed:
crops of flowers appear spring-summer, sometimes again in the winter,
almost continuous south:prune down to two or three primary stems.
   -diurnum, "Day-jessamine" growing 10-15' with comparatively dark
and shining foliage with creamy-white flowers that are fragrant by day,
intermittent....known as "Inkberry" in parts, due to black fruits that
are eaten by birds:the better one to use by the sea on account of the
resistant leaf:winter-blooming far south.
   -nocturnum, "Night-jessamine" an erect, stiff-stemmed shrub 8-10'
with a thin, light green leaf and two summer crops of intensely night
fragrant greenish flowers:consider prevailing air currents about the
house and use in a place where the overpowering scent will not be objectionable, yet available in reduced waves:prune lightly after first
summer flowering to check the formidable growth and to provide
new wood for the next blooming toward autumn:abundant white fruits.
The species  -parqui, with narrower leaves and black berries,
growing 4-6' in height, is similar, hardier in frost.
   -purpureum(elegans)medium sized and erect, with terminal
parts weighted over by the red-purple flowers the cool of the year,
mainly winter:requires occasional cutting back, the herbage working to the extremities of the willowy stems:covering, nights of
expected frost or a fine spray early next morning may save a
blooming, yet the plant is probably the most cold resistant
of the group and the most popular.

CHAENOMELES japonica, "Flowering Quince" a deciduous shrub
3-4', nearly evergreen south, the angular, picturesque branches
studded with the pure white, rosy-red or orange, appleblossom flowers
before the new leaves unfold January-February:buds are formed by the
middle of November for stems to be cut and taken indors to open in
water:prune laterals to spurs to encourage flower buds, otherwise
to shape the bush and reduce brush that accumulates inside....done
immediately after flowering:spray in winter to control scale and
other pests that take advantage of temperate climate plants in a
frostless land....look close, they may come in with the new
plant:brilliant varieties for special uses....espalier.

CHAENOSTOMA---sub-shrubs for sunny places, quietly
colorful, erect in growth and bushy for hedging. They

should have a reasonably friable, warm soil that is not wet over any extended period and are constituted for heat and drought in considerable amount. They are very attractive little plants when found in the right environment.

-grandiflorum(Sutera)growing 2-3' in height and somewhat spreading, the light, smoky-blue flowers August-November:good for cutting material and makes an excellent flowering hedge.

-hispidum, low-spreading 12-15", compound-mounding with plenty of space, densely formed and practically continually sprinkeled with a fine white bloom, concentrating May-July:grow dryish in warmth, when it shears readily as a box border.

CHAEROPHYLLUM dasycarpum, an annual of easy culture, reseeding to become an enchanting pest wherever allowed to take hold....easily eradicated:forking stems 3-5' spring from stout support to offer an area of wide flat heads of pure white filigree, peppered over-all with contrasting white dots, summer into autumn, according to the time of sowing and germination:may be considered a refinement of "Queen Anns-lace" for large cutting material or the entire plant may be removed, the roots washed out and placed in water for a period of service....an immortelle of sorts.

CHAMAELAUCIUM ciliatum, "Geraldton Waxflower" a loosely formed shrub, erect 10-12' with staking, usually losing its way in youth and deviating laterally, or the stems warping downward to sprawl out flat or down over a bank:foliage with a faint scent of lemon is thinly appointed, needle-like, scant support for the mildly fragrant flowers, white through rose or deeper January-April:particularly long-lasting as a cutflower, wanting a well drained soil in the sun:clip back after flowering to develop wood for next years flowering:no fertilizer, ordinarily.

CHAMAEROPS humilis, "Hair Palm" a slender fan palm to 25' in rich moist soils, less in sterile, dry ground, but a good tree either place:may be grown many years in a low clump of many stems or suckering seedlings, or may be cleaned up to 3-7 formalized trunks, when it makes its maximum height:straw-yellow flowers appear in a close mass about the crown, the yellowish berry mass ripening and rotting there:somewhat tender when young, but has been grown into warm temperate regions in protected spots....at least 10 degrees of frost.

CHARIEIS heterophylla, "Kingfisher Daisy" choice annual 8-12" for bedding or filling in the border, producing brilliant blue, solitary daisies, the ray petals rolled under:any good garden soil in sure sun, with moisture during growth, later persisting through considerable dryness and going into summer.

CHEILANTHES gracillima "Lace Fern" for very dry, hot and well drained soils, among rocks or in close fissures:tufted, spreading little fronds 3-5" long, the tiny brittle leaves rolled back and in....don't ever wet down in the sun. This little fellow should be starved of everything but sunlight.

CHEIRANTHUS mutabilis, "Wallflower" a woody perennial 18-24" with the typical foliage of the wallflower, a little bush:the cream-colored or yellowish flowers change through purplish tones to dull shades of reddish brown:sun to half shade with drainage and dryness:the better one for southern gardens.

CHILOPSIS linearis, "Desert-willow" straggly shrub or a slender tree 25', of delicate character in the tracery of branch and stem, almost weeping, brushy in the wild: lavender, trumpet-shaped flowers are striped with yellow and appear all summer in the face of everything the arid southwest has to offer....above ground:water beneath there, or garden moisture applied will make this a presentable tree, serviceable for light shade where few others will do:adapts surprisingly to Florida where it gets its fill of water.

250

COMPENDIUM

CHIOCOCCA alba, "Tropical Snowberry" native in Florida,
scrambling, a trailing shrub or somewhat erect 6-8' with
rugged, leathery leaves and yellow, honey-scented, bell-
shaped flowers in summer:white berries to cut all winter.

CHIRANTHODENDRON platanoides, "Devils Handflower-tree" as
broad as high, probably 35', with large 8" soft leaves more
like paulownia than sycamore, yellowish and buff:summer
blooming, the bizarre, dull red flower is striking, not
handsome, but taken and wired for decorative purposes:a
museum piece, hardy in 10 degrees of frost. This is an
unusually beautiful tree from the standpoint of the interior as one looks up into the developing structure....an
illusion there, a vague golden light as of a sudden burst
of sunset through clouds....dispelled by the glower of the
down-reaching hands.

CHIRONIA linoides, "Starpink" for a warm, loose, well drained soil in the sun, an herbaceous plant 18-24", woody at the
base, a mound of pink, starry flowers over late summer:shear
back before winter to clear up spent wood, to compact the new
plant and to insure the generous flowering of next year:pots.

CHLIDANTHUS fragrans, bulb with yellow, shallow-trumpet-
shaped flowers spiced with the scent of lemon, with the
foliage, May-July....if at all....difficult to bring
into flower:set deep in Florida, shallow in California
and take in over winter for dry rest:if no bloom, set
in inconspicuous place, abandon, wait....with hope
only deferred, not dashed. General and accepted way
to handle is to set closely together in a fertile,
sandy loam in sun, with humous added, kept moist while
growing:don't divide:rock garden, border or pot.

CHLOROPHYTUM elatum, herbaceous, with primary use as a
ground cover in deep shade, baskets or pots....particularly
effective elevated, new plants developing weight on the stem
to depress the herbage in a cascading manner:flowers ivory-
white, the long channeled leaves either light or dark and plain,
or striped with white or yellow.   --var. picturatum, is dwarf,
with yellow at the midrib in a rough stripe.

CHOISYA ternata, "Mexican-orange" clear-cut, compact shrub
4-6' with bright green, three-parted leaves and pure white,
very fragrant flowers springtime and intermittant:rapid
growth when satisfied, wanting occasional reduction of
wood which may be taken in bloom as cutting material, or
the plant may be clipped as a flowering hedge:moisture is
important in the production of flowers, but best grown on
the dry side for longivity....drainage even more vital,
as a strong plant may go out suddenly in moist, heavy
ground:frost hardy to Washington state and Virginia.

CHORISIA speciosa, "Silkfloss-tree" an erect shapely plant
50-100', with a stout, grey-green, spine-set trunk, handsome
rather than beautiful,unless in flower:not a tree for the gard-
en, but one that fixes the attention in the landscape:variable
in degree of spine-set, size and shading of the flowers, blooming October-December, or later south and at times in the spring:
the large flower, suffused with brown at the base of the petal, creamy to pink and deeper, is a spectacle....the tree
rather bizarre without this diverting color:palmate leaves
thin out over winter, the fallen flower debris messy:some-
what drought resisting, tender in frost until it reaches above.

CHORIZANTHE staticoides,"Turkish Rugging" a wiry, finely formed
mass of delicate reddish stems and tiny flowers in the carpeting of
dry California soils:a nap of only a few inches or 10-15", material
for winter boquets:an annual with seed available only in nature:
shake out ripened head over earth to be covered:very special uses.

251

CHORIZEMA cordatum, "Flowering-oak" low-spreading shrub or
climbing 5-6', the pale, spiny-edged leaves a generous back
for the orange and red, pea-shaped flowers February-June, all
tending to lighten or actually fade out in the sun....partial
shade, or at least a north exposure:chief difficulty with this
is over abundant moisture in the summer when it should be resting
after the long flowering....a slack time,then, in appearance:bank
plantings,or well used among low shrubs as a filler:prune rather
sharply in early summer:short-lived

CHRYSALIDOCARPUS lutescens, "Goldfeather Palm" slender, ringed
stems to 25', in a circular clump, grown out of doors only in the
south of Florida, used in tubs elsewhere:the plume is most gracefully
arching, the entire plant luxuriant in a very special way for terrace
or patio, the feather of the yellow petioled fronds persistent nearly
to the base....a clean, fresh effect....and also the floor beneath:
withstands no drought, demanding uniform moisture and should
have some shade:suckering mildly.

CHRYSANTHEMUM---mostly late-flowering perennials for cutflower or rock garden, the herbaceous border taking any or
all of them for good value and service. They want the sun
although heavy shade thrown early morning or late afternoon
will lessen their light day for a natural advantage in these
southern regions. They are heavy feeders of the first table,
strong-growing to require extra and frequent attention to
division, also irrigation as related to the shallow rooting,
no overhead spraying. They move easily and plants will be kept
available in the well managed garden for late or unexpected
changes. A yellowing of the leaves usually indicates a lack of
balance in feeding, either too much or not enough available
food. Cultivation must be very shallow....manure mulch better.
    -balsamita, "Costmary" for culinary purposes, a perennial
2-3' in height, having tiny, rayless flowers and herbage with a
mint or lemon fragrance that is beguiling in cookery:notably sweet-
smelling in the sun and choice in its class:no color for the garden.
    -carinatum, "Painted Daisy" an annual of vigorous, if rather un-
tidy, frowzy growth and virile summer color, the large flowers with a
purple center, dark behind the usually white base, the zoning red or
yellow with many variations:grows 2-3' high, the flower tending to close
in too much shade:an old plant in gardens that should be planted early
in the spring for full results.
    -frutescens, "Marguerite or Paris Daisy" large white or yellow
daisies of rank growth and coarse herbage, becoming woody at the base,
bulking to 3' height and spread, flowering spring, summer and on into
winter:a better plant in poor soils, but with drainage, calling for but
little attention beyond occasional pinching in of terminals. This will
be subject to nematode which it resists easily enough, but in the process impregnates the ground about. The cautious gardener will bring into
his soil nothing but cuttings of this plant which take readily.
    -mawi, "Moroccan Daisy" a dense woody base for the rounding, fine-
ly massed foliage 5-6", the flowering stems to 15" and very slender with
comparatively large, dark-eyed white to pinkish flowers over summer:is
adapted to fairly dryish soils having drainage and wants but little at-
tention:good long-stemmed cutting.
    -maximum, "Shasta Daisy" robust perennial with quantities of very
large white-rayed flowers June-September:long-lived, hardy in all ways,
with no pests, asking little and giving so much:divide every few years
discarding the hard central portion:excellent cutting. This may be
had in several distinct varieties which extend the flowering, if fed.
    -morifolium, the florists "Mum" and related varieties, which in
garden practice should be renewed frequently from northern grown
stock, for results that may be expected....deterioration is rapid
in the south and disease organisms active:want a rich, deeply dug
soil that is retentive of moisture and never to be permitted to
dry out:set rooted cuttings April-May and pinch back in about six
weeks:top-sprinkle mornings until buds open, then irrigate at the
ground:if new stock is not used, divide clumps each year, but not
before April, since new plants will make too much wood at the

expense of flowers:late varieties will be caught by rains
in California, but this will be more likely of the early
ones in Florida.
 -parthenium(Matricaria)"Feverfew" robust, persistent, self-
sowing, an over-looked old time perennial that likes the south:erect
loose heads on rather stiff stems 18-24", with prim little daisies,
gold and white buttons, an excellent plant to face down leggy shrubs:
a tendency to flatten out at the base is marked in the following.
--var. aureum, "Goldfeather" carpeting, with yellow, buttony little
daisies and golden foliage that may be retained indefinitely if it
is sheared occasionally....close, fine mat fitted to the earth.

 CHRYSOBALANUS icaco, "Coco-plum" a spreading shrub, normally 3 5',
occasionally dense tree-like, far south to 25', with tough, leathery
leaves that glisten in sunlight, making good foliage along the coast
under salt spray:white flowers are not important and the white pulpy
fruit which turns black by July is collected in the wild where it is
native, south in Florida:hedges,standing in poor soils,sand or clay.

 CHRYSOPHYLLUM caineto, "Star-apple" handsome woody foliage plants,
the slender branches set with broad leaves that are a milky green on
top, a rich golden-russet-brown beneath....beauty with a radiant,
sparkling quality:grown only along the coast, protected in Southern
California, a tree in Southern Florida, fruiting there....sapota-
like, spherical, star-wise in section, the sweet white pulp with
large embedded seeds:survives frost down to 26 degrees in sandy,
well drained soils....keep up fertility and take into winter with
dry feet. The species  -oliviforme, "Satinleaf" is similar, but
with smaller purple fruits:more dependable in cold.

 CHUSQUEA tessellata, a low, grassy bamboo, to be used as a
ground cover, climbing a few feet with likely support, or into
shrubbery:persistent under garden conditions, invasive:the flower,
born in terminal spikelets, may be used in dried arrangements.

 CIBOTIUM schiederi, "Mexican Treefern" immense, rectangular
fronds, ultimately crowning a stout 10-15' stem, then gracefully
drooping:heat resisting and tender, found in Florida and along
the Gulf Coast, northerly and in California only protected.

 CICHORIUM---herbs grown for culinary purposes and for the
handsome blue flowers which come in a kind of purity and a
clarity that the gardener always appreciates and values. They
want above all, that the ground be well prepared and deeply, to
accomodate the long-tapping root....otherwise rugged and
exceptionally persevering under difficulties.
 -endiva, "Endive" with purple or pale blue flowers and very
ornamental foliage which is used in late summer salads:sow seed in
early spring indoors and set the plants out by midsummer, or sow
outdoors April-May, the one ready to crop by late summer, the other
in the fall when greens are scarce:the slightly bitter taste may
be eliminated by tying the outer leaves together at the top, to
bleach out the heart....done when the center shows a trace of
white. Gardeners could use this more....for health.
 -intybus, "Succory or Chicory" slender perennial 2-3', the
creased, rigid stems set with wide, pale blue flowers June-October:
will stand close planting in the border to concentrate the color
and to minimize the stemmy character:the pulverized root mixed
with coffee, modifies the flavor or may be used alone as a
substitute:limestone or alkaline soils favor blue in this
flower, an acid tends to change over to pink.

 CIENFUEGOSIA(Alyogyne)hakeaefolia, an hibiscus-like shrub of
very open structure and thin foliage, the leaves finely cut into
linear segments, better used than hibiscus in dry ground:the large
single flowers are pale purple, deeper in the throat, blooming in
the summer:prune to prevent too much straggling and allow no
standing water at the crown:a filler. This is a valuable
material in landscape work of a temporary nature.
253

CINERARIA cruenta, highly developed herbs that are extremely showy when well grown, having almost incredible coloring,
soft tones of depth and purity, memorable experience in white, red
and especially blues in combination and infinite gradation:pots for
this color in the house or outside in bedding in coolness and shade
as beneath pine or oak or on a north exposure:practicable only in
the cool of the year, late fall and early spring....winter in the
absence of frost, always in a porous, acid soil that has been enriched and well worked:better obtained from the nursery as sturdy
going plants, but seed may be sown midsummer for bloom February on:
no feeding until shortly before the buds open, using blood meal, manure water or other strong organic to boost:keep tops dry in flower, although it may be noted that a fine spray in early morning of frost may
save the planting:reseeds in a favorable spot, the new blooming of
surprisingly good colors. The species  -stellata, is taller and
less compact, the flower smaller, less colorful. Both wilt quickly in drought and are disfigured by leaf-eating insects, snails,
slugs, and especially the leafminer....burn affected leaves.

CINNAMOMUM camphora, "Camphor-tree"  open-headed and wide-
spreading 40', the foliage a light shining green gathered at the
ends of the branches in a dense, rounding dome. This is most attractive when new, in its pristine cover, the tender bud-pink
lingering on into the early coat which means spring in the south,
dull yellow green or a queasy bronze by winter:unimportant yellow
flowers are followed by beady black berries that are important as
litter only:stout tree this, standing ravenous in the soil, with
large primary roots working to the top, releasing the oil everywhere....has no place in the garden:does not tolerate a wet soil,
takes traces of alkali:prune early for head room, but little cutting required in the mature tree:no diseases and no wind damage.

CISSUS---tendril-climbing vines of importance, foliage plants,
a diverse group and mostly robust, with stout woody stems;others
not so large, with a certain refinement calling for good culture
and a quiet exposure. They have been gathered together here as
segregates from other well known genera on botanical characters not always obvious to gardeners, so that a descriptive
portrait may profitably include an allusion in each case to its
better known past. These are comparatively clean plants overhead
and those with tubers at the crown will take drought without
much hurt. They react variously to frost as will be noted.
    -adenopodus, an herbaceous trailer for half shade, young
leaves carmine, then bronzy green, red beneath:flowers are
of some value, pale yellow in 4" clusters that may be used
indoors:very rapid growth and very tender.
    -antarctica, "Kangaroo Treebine" high climbing, with
handsome, shining leaves that will carry over several years
in good condition, making for clean cover overhead....the
pergola or other open structure:hardy in some frost.
    -capensis, "Cape-grape" the plant with very large leaves
the lobes broadly rounded, evergreen down to the frost line,
dropping and tender from there on:a great vine, very high climbing from ultimately a 6" base and sinuous woody stem of thick corrugated bark....dense canopy for shade within reach of sea winds:
foliage will take on tones of bronze and crimson in winter, but does
not necessarily drop:clustered, reddish to pale blue grapes may be
eaten, but have no value:tubers at the crown.
    -hypoglauca, the thick, long-wearing leaves are a modification
and similar to virginia creeper, pale and shining for an especially pleasing study in texture:an admirable plant for pillar, a
dense overhead or lays an interesting net over a bank, superb
as a low filler beneath tree trunks about a swimming pool:is
hardy in light frosts:choice plant with many adaptations, slow
to develop body, finally vigorous, strong and long-lived: new
growth rusty-colored, sears in a hot sun, but hardens up
very soon....half shade in extreme heat.
    -incisa, "Marine-ivy" high climbing, 30' or more,
with fleshy, warty stems and root-like tendrils, the
pale green leaves three-parted:stands in ocean wind

Cissus hypoglauca

C. discolor

C. antarct

C. thom

Cissus capen

and may be adapted as a bank cover:native in Florida:hardy.

   -rhombifolia,"Japanese or grape-ivy" with the smaller
leaves of boston ivy, shining, dark, exceptionally attractive
in way of foliage, eventually with clustered dark blue berries:
low banks, curb covering, low walls, high climbing in coolness,
it likes a little shade, tolerates deep shade:requires good soil
and  some attention to bring out full capability to please:
boxes, hanging baskets, subject to mealybug:tender.

   -striata(Ampelopsis sempervirens)"Grape-ivy" very much refined as of slender climbing lines and virginia creeper leaves
in dark miniature:climbs rough surfaces by means of aerial
rootlets:quite hardy in frost, usually holding foliage.

*Cistus maculatus*

### ROCKROSE

CISTUS---low and spreading, very freely flowering little shrubs,
blanketed throughout summer with single flowers formed like the
wild rose, crepe-like and only of a single days duration....in full
perfection, mornings. The plant is short-lived at best; will not
tolerate a heavy clay soil for long, nor excessive moisture, de-
lighting in a loose, dry, gravelly place....wanting and standing
in any degree of heat....very much at home in the sandy soils of
the ocean. Start with small, pot-grown plants as these plants
are notoriously difficult when an even tenor of growth is disturbed....will not transplant after establishing and brook but
little pruning, only shallow pinching of terminals or shearing,
late season. They must have all the sun possible, which means
a southerly exposure. Available material is mostly hybrid in
origin, and are at their best in California.

*Cistus purpureus*

   -corbariensis, hybrid, a low expanding mound in sufficient
space, to cover more ground than its normal 2-3' height, unusually
attractive and floriferous, both white flowers and foliage fresh-
appearing under rather deep drouth, leaf much roughened.

   -crispus, for a hot, dry place in the large rock garden; more
contained as a shrub and with more normal uses as such:has thick,
soft, crinkly grey leaves and large deep rose or purple flowers.

   -ladaniferous maculatus, a large erect-growing bush to as much
as 5', a sticky mass of dull dark foliage and large crimpled white
flowers marked with dark purple at the base of the petal:starts
blooming in April and carries on frugally through summer, with
not much color at any time:tolerates slight shade.

   -purpureus, a hybrid, growing 3-4'high, bushy to 6' across
in maturity:flowers as much as 3-4" across, lilac-purple with a
typical maroon blotch....very good color for a group with so much
maverick coloring, strong, but acceptable in most places.

   -salvifolius, procumbent and widely spreading, fitting closely to dry gravelly slopes or rocky ground:small white flowers
are quite abundant:use as cover or in the rock garden.

*Myer Lemon*

CITHAREXYLUM spinosum, "Fiddlewood" an upright, graceful, open-
headed tree 50' or less, with slender branchings of glossy leaves
and fragrant white or yellowish flowers in long narrow racemes:the
berries change through red to black....a tree for the far south in
the reminder of wild cherry of the north:dry, exposed places.

CITRUS---orange, lemon, grapefruit with many lesser and smaller
members of a genus of woody plants so well known in the economy
and in personal use as to call for little comment....strangely,
too seldom considered from an ornamental viewpoint. The form of
the individual species; the super-effective fragrance of the
flowers; the very substantial appeal and sight of the fruit,
together with a compelling attitude that amounts almost to romance with people who have not seen or who are about to contact
the tree for the first time, place it in the first rank for formal planting....with only less value in a naturalistic scheme.
Culture is of basic importance and this varies with soil and the
local climate. It is advisable to consult and be advised by the
local nurseryman in the management of these  highly bred and
demanding trees. Retain this contact. Generally, they should
have the warmest spot available, with good drainage, air as well
as soil, shelter from wind, shallow cultivation, uniform irrigation,

*Rangpur Lime*

but gauged to season and only moderate, but scientific feeding.

-aurantifolia, "Lime" a small branchy tree bearing the under-sized round fruits similar to a lemon:juices have very fine and a distinct quality in flavoring certain beverages, while the smaller size seems to relate to the container used in making up soft drinks:wants light, but regular pruning to keep the natural-ly brushy head open to the sun and air:rather more tender in frost.

-aurantium, "Seville O." with sour fruits, the tree heavily spined, rugged and more persevering under trying conditions of soil and exposure, probably the least temperamental of the lot: affords comparatively rapid growth as a landscape material or may be used for quite awhile in a tub.   --var. myrtifolia, a smaller plant, shrubby, with handsome dark narrow leaves, along with a more contained and refined structure:espalier.

-deliciosa, "Tangerine" an undersized orange tree in effect, having small flattened fruits that are ordinarily eaten out of hand, at least one for any home planting:meat somewhat dry, comes out clean and unbroken, piquant in flavor, very desirable:hardier than the orange in frost and starts bearing earlier.

-limetta, "Sweet Lime" with large, dark green shining fruits the shape and size of a lemon, the pulp full-meated, very juicy and quite fragile....usually considered the more desirable for home use since it can be eaten out of hand, the flavor not as strong as common lime.

-limonia, "Meyer or Chinese L." a large bush against a wall or a slender, multiple-stemmed tree 15', with lighter green foliage and more pinkish flowers, the fruit large, of superior quality although mild and developing color on the tree comparable to that of an orange:suitable in size and quality for the home orchard over the other lemon variet-ies, bears heavily and early to produce fruit for several families. This is hardy in frost, but plagued by various diseases and suspected of being a carrier of a menacing viris.

-mitis, "Calamondin" the hardiest of all in frost, compact, a neat little tree 10-15', exceedingly ornamental, the small, pale reddish fruits displayed at ends of the branches, while the meas-ureably larger flowers are the sweetest of all to smell, of all the species:marmalades.

-sinensis, "Orange" the tree medium sized, very ornamental in every way, to be used only in cultivated ground for good and con-tinued development:more than ordinary care required in the matter of pruning, and especially spraying in control of the many pests:varieties of high quality fruit available, summer and winter. Don't try to grow oranges unless prepared to care for them and don't expect to pick any cheap fruit.

-taitensis, "Otaheite O." very small, a bush, or tree-like in marked miniature for a small tub, or grown in an average pot of some size for a time, seldom in the ground:tiny white flowers are pinkish outside and the leaf crenulate or indented along the edge:espalier. This is most ornamental and in telling ways as a well grown specimen will show....difficult to find.

CLADANTHUS arabicus, "Gold of Araby" an annual for sun and heat, an open line growth that is unique in structure and relation of the parts, each large daisy moulded or stamped as in gold, clasped and firmly held the way of a precious stone in a mount....this in a developing whirl of ferny growth....a kind of triangulation, repeated in breadth and in height until some 3' or more is attained....dark maroon buds lying ever above to take over in turn:dryness for low growth, in order that the pattern may be appreciated from above....a major wilt in drouth, however, will ruin and stop the performance;May-June.

CLARKIA elegans, "Mountain Garland" a colorful annual for the flower garden or grown with the wild flowers, at times used for the color in window, porch or planter box; wants a light warm soil in the sun, but in coolness with rather low fertility when the blooming comes quickly from seed and is over all to soon:sow in November and again successively March-May or beginning somewhat earl-ier south....does not mind crowding which helps support and correct straggling, weak growth:flowers comparatively

large, very double, the petals more or less fringed, rose colored or
purple, sometimes white:suitable for the center of a large bulb bed
or gives unusually long service cut. Here will be found a marked
grace in the tip-winding stems and long fuchsia-like buds not often
seen. The species -pulchella, native in the west, is more dwarf and
slender with a maximum growth of 12-15", single, the long petals lobed,
streaming, appealing in simplicity, liveliness in air; lilac and white.

### VIRGINS BOWER
CLEMATIS---vines and loose, flopping perennials, many of them
native in parts of these regions, others largely from the Mediter
ranean area. They are characterized by brittle stems from a woody
base to considerable refinement in the top, but undisciplined so
that they must be kept close to the pruning shears for appearance
as well as for air circulation. They want a fertile, fairly light,
drained soil with shade, certainly low at the crown....and lime. The
full gamut of color will be found here, yellow, red, purple, blue and
pure white, even greenish, while the fruiting effects are a distinct asset, with expectancy in lustrous silken tangles. They are
especially susceptible to nematodes and object seriously to any
disturbance at the roots. Some will be difficult to find.
    -armandi, quite vigorous, a definitely evergreen vine of
high quality, climbing 20' or more and with a wide spread of
cover....dark and substantial:white flowers in considerable
abundance appear March-April, bringing the scent of almond:must
be kept in hand.        -baldwini, "Pipe-hyacinth" an herbaceous perennial with 12-18" stems of pinkish or purple flowers March-April,
native in Florida.        -balearica, flowering in the winter, the bell-
shaped, greenish yellow flowers spotted with color within.
-cirrhosa,the foliage a dark bronzy green with the leaves variable in shape, climbing to as much as 10', the creamy-white flowers sweet-scented, late winter or very early spring.    -crispa,
"Leatherflower" climbing 10', the urn-shaped fragrant flowers a
deep blue or dark purple, May-August.        -indivisa, with heavy
woody stem, climbing to as much as 40' at its energetic best:a
very large, milky-white flower that begins in winter and spills
over into spring in California:foliage dark and durable, massing
in weight to require strong support.        -lasiantha, "Pipestem
C."native in California, scrambling over rocks and shrubs in
dryish soils:the large, glistening whitish flowers, April-May,
make way for the more important fruiting bodies which carry into the dusty end of the season....keep away from open roads.
-texensis, "Scarlet C." climbing only 5-6', the leathery urn-
shaped flowers almost closed, a brilliant reddish rose or scarlet,
buff to pink within, June-November, the silvery seed ravelings
ultimately mingling with the color:native in the Southwest, but
hardy far north and rather more common in the nursery trade.

### GLORYBOWER
CLERODENDRUM---coarse, rapid-growing, with soft wood to indicate
a general weakness in frost:vining or shrubby, the terminal flowering heads outstanding individually and in the mass, with some
perspective and if tipped back occasionally for flowering wood.
They will take some light, sheltering shade and are vigorous in a
moist heavy soil to a degree that prevents use with other plants
with less resolve. The shrubby species dominate; are inclined
to escape; are suckering for good or for bad according to
placement and use. Leaves are large and handsome, but distasteful as to odor, on too close aquaintance. They are
striking plants for special purposes, but must be used
with discretion....in a tub, if proper space or place is
not available.
    -bungei(foetidum)a spreading, loose growth 5-6' with a
strong pungent odor, suckering to make a broad mass when the
stems are headed in to make more flowering wood:the rosy red
flower heads are large, compact, to 8" across:suckers freely
and at long distances:subject to scale....none know why. The
variety Cashmere Bouquet has an extra full head of flowers, the
later following buds deep-set within the pink spread of florets.

-fragrans, the flowers double, white or pale rose in a
dense head, the leaf very large, sometimes 12" long, the
bush itself 6-8' high:suckers in repletion, always an over-
measure, with forms that run wild in Florida....watch this one.
    -myricoides, an open-spreading bush 4-6' with a thin foli-
iage of rather thin glossy leaves that are comparatively small:
flowers are blue, vagrant heads off and on , May-November in the
sun or partial shade:a good filler, non-suckering, not in any way
pungent, surviving light frost and comparatively choice.
    -siphonanthus, "Tubeflower" erect unbranching growth and
variable height, 2-8', grown as a kind of herbaceous perennial in frost, has large clusters of white, long-tubed flowers that are open at night, while the long-lasting berries
are red, held within brown-red bracts:striking plant and
easily handled, but rarely seen.
    -speciosissimum, an erect shrub 3-4' or sometimes more
in rich, moist soils, having quite large dark glossy, heart-shaped
leaves and dull red or scarlet flowers continually throughout warm
weather:few if any suckering shoots and is very tender in cold.
    -thompsonae, "Bagflower" remarkable study in color contrast, a
twining woody vine, blooming all summer in warmth, starting late in
California, August-October or a little later:the bright scarlet flower is partially inclosed in a white, sac-like calyx in a singular
arrangement that spots the plant at once:not vigorous and better
used as a climbing shrub or held to shrub-like proportions.

    CLETHRA arborea, "Lily of the Valley-tree" erect and bushy,
with many stems, or a slender line of a tree to 20' at the other
extreme, the elongated leaves of high quality, rolling under
in disfigurement in dry heat;long in bud, June-July, long in
untidy seed, October-November and in between, generous spikes
of white flowers:wants a sheltered place in a moist soil
that is drained, neutral to acid, with much leafmould
worked in....and best in humidity:very choice, hardy in
10 degrees of frost. When the terminal cluster of flowering
spikes is cut with a backing of leaves, a ready-made, one-piece
lily of the valley corsage results.

    CLIANTHUS puniceus, "Parrotsbill" a half-trailing woody perennial,
or climbing 6-8' with help, the intensely brilliant crimson flower
in the likeness of a lobsters claw, winter or any time:infrequent-
ly used as a climber, mainly in bedding of unusual coloring and
pointed for season....plant seeds in pots and set the resulting
plants out in a sunny place. The species   -dampieri, is more
spectacular, very rare, and most difficult to handle, but hardy
in as much as 15 degrees of frost.

    CLITORIA ternatea,   "Butterfly  Pea" perennial, somewhat
twining, climbing 3-4':the back petal, or standard is very large,
a vivid and uncommon blue, wavy-rimmed with lighter markings and
white at the base....wings comparatively small:flowering scatters
out over summer, hesitates in drouth, ceases in absence of relief:
has a tendency to doubling and pure white comes up at times;choice.

## KAFIRLILY
    CLIVIA---of permanence and good body, tuberous-rooted, of excellent fol-
iage when well grown and very noticeable in decline when neglected. The
bloom is held erect on stout stiff stems to 18", orange to bright red,
the many-flowered clusters full and pre-dominant, a full-red head of
seed almost as much so. They should have a moist rich soil and a
considerable shade factor....only a stippling of light, else the
flower falls short of perfection and foliage tends to burn.
They must never dry out, nor will they do their best in a
cold spot, going into winter best with reduced moisture.
Protect from excessive winter rain in any way possible.
The foliage is particularly indicative of condition, dark
and rich-looking in thrift, yellowish when doing poorly. Use
bonemeal or liquid manure in feeding and only in growth. Let
them crowd in pot or bed, transplanting with roots any time out
of flower, June-July or earlier. They always resent disturbance

258

and are best grown in containers.....will take 10 degrees frost.
   -miniata, the leaves sword-shaped, pointed, flowers open,
erect on the stalk, January-April, or the hybrids at anytime,
pale to reddish burnt-orange to scarlet or almost yellow: the
hardiest and the least exacting in culture.
   -nobilis, very wide, close-ranked, strap-shaped leaves that
are blunt-pointed, the flowers more closed, tube-like, curved
downward or drooping, red, with a tip of green on the petal March-
June. There appear to be strains of this that are nearly everblooming in the south.

   CLUSIA rosea, "Monkey-apple" for use far south against the
ocean, tree-like, erect or spreading slowly in the wind, flattening and shrubby there with stout, crawling branches from a
stubby trunk, or only a damaged crown left after frost....maybe
a strangler on other small trees:leaves are heavy, wavy, 3-4" a-
cross, the flowers thick-petaled, transient, white to delicate
pink:does with very little soil and affords a solid feeling in
a tub against a wall....splendid in its great leafage.

   CLYTOSTOMA callistegioides, "Painted Trumpet" a tendril-climb-
ing vine with short-tubed, throat-lined, lilac to violet-blue
flowers March-May:tends to fade in the sun, better used with a
little overhead shade midday and in a good garden soil with
moisture. This may not be as vigorous as other well-known segregates from Bignonia, which will be found under Anemopoegma,
Doxantha and Phaedranthus.

   CNEORIDIUM dumosum, "Spicebush or Berryrue" native twiggy
Californian of neat growth and habit under cultivation, a
little brushy in the wild where it manages in the driest
of sterile soils....orange-gold as it goes into winter:
white, faintly flushed flowers February-March are not of
too much importance nor are the dull, brownish red fruits
that follow, but the bush has much merit for economy in its
maintenance:takes irrigation with drainage, growing 2-5' in
height, erect-rounding and of medium fine texture:keep this
pinched in for desired form or use to fill out a native
planting that abuts on the home grounds....refinement.

   CNEORUM tricoccon, "Spurge-olive" a soft-shrubby plant
18-24" with erect-flaking stems, eventually an inert, livid
green mass, studded in turn by the tiny yellow flowers and dull
red berries that are held closely together in threes:not striking
but of value facing down low shrubs or in the perennial border for
substance....a blunt dingy little plant that points up the lustre
of its neighbors....but with a modest allure of its own.

   COCCOLOBIS---small trees for frost-free coastal areas where they
take salt wind and adapt to all soils, clay or sand or fertile
loams, wet or dry:size of a particular plant will depend on
the ground largely and the dependably varying shapes on the
exposure. They are vancouriers of domestic gardening in the
south of Florida and are still as usefull in the protection
of other plantings as in the early days.
   -floridana, "Pigeon-plum" erect tree, frequently multiple
stemmed 15-35', the foliage dense to a rounded top, pear-shaped
fruit greenish, edible:screens under wind and in drouth.
   -uvifera,"Sea or Shore-grape" low, stout, sprawling in wind:
close-set, round, leathery leaves are shining, red-ribbed, coppery
when young, coloring again before spring before dropping:creamy
flowers in March bring on strings of purple fruit by October....the
bush a filler, picturesque of stem:fruit for a kind of wine.

   COCCULUS laurifolius, "Himalayan-laurel" erect and gracefully spreading, an arching shrub 10-15', or even more, to
be used in places of importance, for the high quality and
in soils of good tilth:leaves are leathery, very characteristic, laurel-like and very dark to bring out the strong
venation:likes shade and a moist loamy soil, but will

*Cneorum*

*Cneoridium*

*Clusia*

*Cocculus*

*Coccolobis floridana*

*Coccolobis uvifera*

tolerate some dryness when established, growing slowly, but
very surely into a handsome individual of picturesque quality
in stem:hesitates in the beginning and tends to lag the first
year or two....plant only well established material:prune to
accent the arch in stem for individuality in a specimen:long-
lived and hardy into warm-temperate regions.

COCHLOSPERMUM vitifolium, "Buttercup-tree" for frost-free
areas only, but well worth testing and adapting on the fringe
of climate south in these regions, when the reward will be great
in success:of rapid growth, open-headed, sometimes as high as 40'
in total warmth, soft wooded to require protection against heavy
wind:spectacular bloom, the 3-4", close-clustered, brilliant,
shining yellow flowers come at a time when the large, grape-
like leaves are wanting....spring:most choice.

CODIAEUM variagatum, "Leafcroton" shrubby foliage plants
that are infinitely variable in the leaf, the form or shape
or in the lobing as well as in the coloring and its pattern:
color ranges through yellow, orange, pink, rose, red and in
crimson, along with various greens in usually distinct and
pleasing patterns and combinations:used for pots and in tubs
out of doors or inside, but in no frost....withstanding a
few degrees when hardened off in advance:want rich porous
soils in the sun or a little shade with constant attention
in control of red spider and mealybug. They are gaudy, parti-
colored man-made creations largely, the beauty of some of the
hybrids eye-arresting for a flourish in plant composition and
are largely used in the floral trade, highly developed and well
fitted all-round for Florida, grown only in containers in California.

COLEUS blumei, "Flame-nettle" foliage for shaded places, the attractive leaves with many interesting combinations in color, red, purple,
yellow and green in soft shadings:wants a warm, moist, fibrous and
fertile soil for complete satisfaction:pick out the flower heads as
they appear and shear the plant back at first sign of legginess; or
vigorous varieties, in absence of frost, have been grown to second
story windows with support:bedding, window or planter boxes, pots.

COLLETIA cruciata, "Crucifixtion Thorn" "Anchor-plant" curiously
formed, shrubby plant with large, thorn-like bodies serving in way
of foliage:the tiny white or colorless flowers of mid-winter are
laid closely against the pallid green or white-grey, frequently
flattened stems:an oddity, with few uses in garden or landscape,
blooming at any time in recurring moisture.

COLLINIA elegans, a dwarf, very graceful little palm for a pot,
normally seen at 3-5' in slender height, the stems clustered or
solitary:narrow thin leaflets are soft-silky in appearance, a
clear green:tolerates and indeed, requires some shade in heat,
surviving scarcely any frost, deteriorating when young in
merely cold weather:indifferent to drainage, reaches 8-10'
when set out of doors....the lath house.

COLLINSIA---western natives, free-flowering annuals with
delicate coloring through mid-summer, in the flower garden or
with the wildflowers. They are easily grown from seed sown in
spring or in the fall in a fertile leafy soil that is well
drained, and in low sun or partial shade....found in the wild
best satisfied on slopes leading away from the sun.
    -bicolor, "Innocence" with weak, bending stems 12-24", the
flowers rising in repeated whorls, white and purple or lavender,
becoming more intense in the shade, the purple inclining to
change to rose in high sun:better grown in rather good moisture
since they carry into the dry time of summer.
    -grandiflora, "Bluelips" a smaller plant, less than 12" in
height in the poorer soils:the lower lip of the flower will be
found ordinarily in blue or thereabouts while the upper one
will be white:the better plants in the wild will be found
in warm, granite soils with a good leaf mulch.

260

Cochlosperm
Vitifoliun

Codiaeum

Collinsia

Colletia

# COMPENDIUM

COLOCASIA antiquorum, "Elephantear" tuberous plants from
the far tropics with a rank growth of immense, bright green
leaves to as much as 3' long and nearly as wide, the odd, lily
like flowers hidden:used in large scale bedding in public
places or to distress and discourage small, always chewing and
raiding boys:rich, very moist, preferably sandy soils in heat
with slight shade....cover very lightly at the crown.

COLVILLEA racemosa, for frost free ground, growing to 50' there
with a stout straight trunk of reddish bark and an open spreading
top of lateral branchings, a dome of fine, feathery, somewhat
ferny foliage:extremely showy October-November, the orange-
scarlet flowers closely packed in 15 18" arching racemes,
while the tingent yellow extending stamens give an overall
wash of buff....then an orange spread beneath as the flower
remains drop. This is a tree with a future, subject to more
study and experience in culture, and degree of hardiness it
can attain in cold:limestone soils.

CONVOLVULUS---plants from hot, dry countries and intense
sun, adapted to most of the far south, particularly in the
regions of the Southwest where more favorable all-round conditions prevail naturally. The first cultural refinement will
be drainage, that of light, and preferably gravelly soils....then
heat, dry or moist, but preferably the first, to bring the buds
out. These flowers are little morning-glories for form, with
uses far removed from those suggested by the name.
   -cneorum, an erect-spreading little shrub, 2-3' in height
and 6-8' across in heat with moisture, the elongated leaves a
silvery grey, tapering inversely toward the base:white flowers
are tinted with pink on the reverse side and last all the way
through May-September, nearly continuous where warmth holds,
and profusely:a pot plant, with further service in the
ground, if not previously abused, compact in dryish, poor
soils, rather sprawling elsewhere and not flowering nearly as well:choice when grown right.
   -lineatus, flat-growing, building up a 2" mat of the
typical, but narrower and pointed leaf of above, silky-silvery
over-all and spreading laterally through the soil with deep-
tapping, thick roots....thoroughly occupying the ground in depth
and vigorously to the side:bedding down there are many small,
typically morning-glory flowers less than half an inch across,
white, but appearing pink from the strong backing color:cover in
a restricted area of soil or between flagstones as it is inclined
to scatter far....and rapidly.
   -mauretanicus, "Ground Morning-glory" a prostrate perennial
to use over low walls, slopes in the garden or as cover, for the
flowers which are of a pale, very pure blue, an inch across June-
November:makes a vigorous growth of some 3' across in good moisture,
less dry, but still thrifty:dwarf forms available are more tufted.
   -tricolor, a garden annual, to be used in drouth and heat,
bedding loosely, better in the border or mixed bed:plant
is erect 12" or semi-prostrate, always branching, somtimes
with red flowers, but mostly blue with yellow deep in the
throat, surrounded by white which merges with the dominant outer color...generally over late summer:sow seed early where the
plants are to stand, in loose, fairly fertile soil.

COOPERIA drummondi, "Rainlily" native bulbs of the Southwest,
summer-flowering, the solitary, up-facing, star-like blooming
erect on naked stems 6-10", sweetly scented at night, waxy and
pure white, tinged with red outside....fully expanded only in
the evening, lasting two to three days:dryish, well drained,
cool places, but under the sun. They appear with the rains or
rise under irrigation after rest....will be seen springing into flower in the lawns of Austin, Texas at such times:naturalize.

COPROSMA baueri, "Varnish-tree" shrubby ordinarily, but may
be grown as a small tree, or with forms that are completely
prostrate:adapts to shade, but prefers the sun, except in high

Coprosma

Cordia
boissieri

Colvillea
racemosa

Convolvulus
cneorum

Cooperia

261

heat:has difficulty with extremely heavy soils, liking and
thriving in, to make a characteristic growth in sand at the
high tide level along the ocean:white berries come on the matured wood among the roundish, leathery, very light green leaves
that appear as highly polished or glazed:becomes unsightly in
its woodiness at the base unless pruned out to the few required stems early in life.  --var. variegata, the leaves are
blotched white or marbled in yellow, cream, or with yellow-
green on a darker background....probably better in heat than
the type-form. There are at least two obscure species of this that
can be used as ground cover.  -kirki(microphylla)procumbent, a
loose, coarse mat to 12" through, the inch-long, very narrow leaf
a dull olive-green, is not very dependable while the species,
-petriei, is prostrate, only to 6" high with white or greenish
flowers and bluish or purple fruits:rock gardens....probably the
hardiest in frost. All these are subject to nematodes, and while
they are successfully resistant....become carriers.

CORDIA boissieri, "Texas-olive" a bushy plant or small many-
stemmed tree 25' with dark, velvety-wavy leaves and large, white,
short-trumpet-shaped flowers with yellow centers, clustered ter-
minally, spring-summer....ivory-white fruits by August:wants fair
moisture and withstands some frost.

COREOPSIS---herbaceous plants, mostly garden flowers for summer
and autumn, exceptionally free-flowering, but usually lacking in an
effective foliage cover. They thrive in any soil, put up with much
drought, but pay back in pure gold any water spent in their interest
and for any other attention given their culture. They must have full
sun to be at their willing best and respond with more enthusiasm in
the lighter soils.
    -lanceolata, a common perennial 18-24"with lightly fluted,
golden-yellow ray-flowers all summer and into autumn for very good
cutting:vigorous under average garden conditions, they may be
tied loosely while still young to restrict later sprawling
and general untidiness. There is a tight-prostrate form.
    -maritima, "Sea-dahlia" erect perennial 2-3', ultimately
bushy, with a low woody crown, the finely divided foliage scant,
very light green and glistening....glorying in salt wind:abundant
canary yellow daisies July-August:native in California, but not
often seen in gardens:seed for naturalization.
    -tinctoria, "Calliopsis" an almost leafless annual growing 1-3'
in height, the slender stems topped by smaller daisies, the rays a
dull yellow, touched at the base with purple in a kind of zoning:has
a bad habit of seeding early if the flower is not taken....or make
successive sowings if continued flowering is desired:dwarfs for edging.

CORETHROGYNE californica, "Coast Daisy" perennial herb for sand plantings, a dune or beach development:has harsh, dry growth to 18", usually
less and spreading out, prostrate, grey-white-cottony....marked when
young and again in age, but more dull:flowers have the typically gold
center, with lilac-purple rays:makes dry material for boquets:seed.

CORIANDRUM sativum,"Coriander" culinary herb with small, white or
delicate purple flowers, both of a misty-grey over-wash and foliage
very finely cut, shredded, aromatic:seed used in confections and in
pastries for the pungent taste:lightens a heavy spot in the border.

CORNUS capitata, of all the "Dogwoods" this is probably the best
under subtropical conditions, certainly at lower levels:large shrub
or bushy tree 20' or more, of somewhat droopy character:best in a
cool place for the creamy-white flower-bract June-July and following red fruiting head October-November, also in sun with neutral to
acid soil:typical greyish or slate-green foliage holds.

CORONILLA glauca, small shapely shrub, unless
forced into brushy growth, normally 3-5' high,
erect, with bright yellow flowers of some fragrance in winter:partial to a light soil, failing
altogether in a sticky clay....give full sun and add

a little lime for thrift:recovers slowly from a heavy pruning,
with a generally poor appearance to be expected over summer:a
good plant to carry in mind for terminal pinching.

CORREA---low, scurfy shrubs, stem and foliage, coming from the
dry sandy plains of Australia and sometimes called "Australian-fuchsia"
probably because of total opposition in kind, fact and culture. This
is significant and points the way in American gardens. First a dry,
well drained site; next the sun, and finally, resist the urge to fertilize these plants and know what can result from temperance as apposed to indulgence in the growth of some plants....low, proper, tight
mounds to the earth or a hugging brush of splaying dry herbage. Drainage is very important and they resent green manures which can be fatal,
in excess. Blooming generally can be expected over the period October
to March. They should get along with the very minimum of irrigation
after having become established.
    -alba, has thick, round, box-like leaves that are almost
white with a wooly tomentum, wanting very sandy soil....resents
salt spray:a flowering hedge 2-3' in height, but only where
all conditions are met:small white flowers midwinter.
    -speciosa, variable, usually around 3-4' in height, the
flowers largely of the green called chartreuse and running
into pink through deeper shades to red.    --var. magnifica,
and truly so, if grown as above; a 5' mound to as much as 8' ac-
cross with foliage to the ground, the leaf dark green above,
bronzy beneath, carrying into the green of the flowering....can
be easily and successfully grown by the rules.   --var. neglecta,
with rather pure scarlet flowers, somewhat more close-knit at 18-
24" height. --var pulchella, the one most commonly seen, low and
spreading, 18-24" high and as much as 10' across in thrift, quite
stringy in shade:flowers are long-tubed, greenish, tipped in rosy
pink November-April.   --var. ventricosa, with dark red flowers.

CORTADERIA selloana, "Pampas-grass" a large, belligerent clump
6-8' in height, a tight, swaying mass of saw-edged leaf blades,
surmounted quite suddenly in the fall by the large, unusually
handsome white plumes:rapacious in any soil, this plant takes
and holds its place against all comers:in anticipation of rain,
the heads should be cut and taken in. This is too dangerous and
aggressive to have in the garden....seal it off anywhere with a
low, protective planting that will fight for survival.

CORYNOCARPUS laevigata, "New Zealand-laurel" for deep shade,
grown shrubby there or lined high in several straight stems
under high headed trees:large leaves are dark, glossy, substantial, revealing the stems, easily compacted with the shears:wants
a fertile, moist soil of depth and will grow well under some exposure;the large, clustered, plum-like fruits change through orange
to blue-black, toxic when eaten out of hand from the bush, but
edible when steamed or steeped in salt water. This is doubtless
responsible for the lack of interest in a beautiful tub plant.

COSMOS bipinnatus, common annual with tall leafy stems 3-5', the
foliage feathery and rather scant, scarcely obscuring the stems:will
flower in the fall or earlier, large, daisy-like heads in yellow or
pink in many shades, to red purple or crimson:better results in a
sterile sandy soil and when the growing tips are pinched out:sow
early for a longer flowering:stake if necessary and bring along as
uniformly as possible:no fertilizer.

COTONEASTER---evergreen shrubs, some species becoming deciduous
northerly or under frost. They are rapid-growing, erect or procumbent,
gracefully arching or angular-lined, the mass characterized by lack
of substance in foliage, so that line becomes important in their
appreciation and use. The wythe-like stems are decorated first with
the primly clustered white or rosy flowers, then with the brilliant
berries, late fall through winter. They thrive in heavy clay soils,
if drained and will want a little lime where the ground is very acid.
They resent any degree of shade, but are tolerant and fairly revel

under exposure to wind. No pruning is necessary other than an occas
ional thinning....reduce long growths in winter, with natural habit
of growth in mind, because errors will show up here quickly....use the
berry-laden stems indoors. They transplant with extreme difficulty except from a container and have few serious pests or diseases. Consider
them well from the standpoint of use, for these are among the best of
the general purpose shrubs, with some one suitable for nearly
any demand in or about the garden.

   -decora, very spreading, a low, prostrate, rather close
mat of short ascending stems, eventually 12-15" high and
6-8' across:the white flowers April-June are appreciable,
the plant alive and glowing by late summer with the large
red berries:does not  shade the ground sufficiently to discourage stoloniferous grasses which grow up through, unless
kept down:good ground cover, free of weeds.

   -francheti, spreading and gracefully fixed at 6-8', thick
leaves noticeably creased, dull green, tending to drop in winter
for a thorough showing of the berries:flesh-colored flowers to
nearly pink are regularly set along the stems in clusters, the
unusually persistent berries orange, tinged with red.

   -harroviana, more or less pendulous, 5-6', the dark, glossy
leaves more leathery and at their best in a little shade:flesh-
colored flowers are followed by bright red berries. This is one
of the more attractive of the larger species, but seldom seen.

   -microphylla, "Rockspray" low and branchy, a tangled effect of intermingling stems for banks or rock work:the very
dull and equally scant foliage is relieved by the tiny off-white
flowers that precede the rosy-carmine berries:must be flourishing
to be acceptable and is much used south....work in much humous before planting.   --var. thymifolia, very small and clumpy, compact
for the company it keeps:rock garden and facing down other shrubs.

   -pannosa, one of the more handsome, 10-15' beautifully arching
stems of greyish foliage, set to white or pinkish flowers in season,
weighted down with the orange-red berries:prune only to remove entire
stems in retaining the inherent grace of the shrub. This means allowing space when planting, for height as well as ultimate spread horizontally, since it outlives any mass value, developing thick crooked
stems to a canopy, finally taking over as almost pure line.....an
excellent screen where ornament is also a consideration, such as a
setback of dwelling from street or highway.   --var. nana, a dwarf
form of most distinctive value in clever hands, the long-twisting,
sturdy stems, set like fishbone fans that are filled out with lighter
leaves, traveling....asking for a wall to lie against, a corner to
turn, and splay again....ornate there, an arabesque in silhouette;has
time for all this in the slow growth....can happen naturally.

   -parneyi(lactea) spreading at first, then erect and more contained at 5-8', compacted more easily without destroying the intrinsic beauty of the plant:has larger, greener leaves for a more dense
coverage, clothing itself well to the ground:brilliant red berries.

   -simonsi, a bushy form of greyish foliage 3-4' with rather more
attractive white flowers June-July, and orange-red berries:good as a
facer for the shrubbery or may be clipped as a hedge.

COWANIA mexicana, "Cliff-rose" low branchy shrub with small dark,
lobed leathery leaves, good back to show off the creamy to sulphur-
yellow, single rose-like flowers May-October:bark is shreddy and the
plumes of the feather-tailed fruits ornamental:grows in dry, rocky
ground and in scale with the rock garden, but a much larger plant
in thrift and growth of fertile ground; to 6-8':native Southwest.

CRASSULA---succulent plants of extremely fleshy character in stem
and in leaf, but with more normal uses in the garden than the description would imply. They have wide tolerances for plants of this
nature, full hot sun to deep shade, moist ground to one that bakes out
and becomes excessively dry. They are weak at the crown and rot during a
long wet spell or in poorly drained ground, so that porous soils and good
run-off are good insurance. They find good use as massing material in a
cactus collection where the individual plant is stressed, a place that
will want a certain coherence for unity.

   -argentea(portulacea)"Jade Plant" shrubby, with meaty, opulent

trunk and stubby branchings, growing 18-24" in a container, 6-8' in
the ground, blooming mid-winter, many sharp little flowers with pink
overlying white:an excellent natural hedge in dry ground, a plant with
many practical qualifications.
   -falcata, the thick, oblong leaves lying against each other
on a bias, with a sturdy stem emerging for a showing of the spectacular crimson flowering of August:absolute drainage:pots.
   -impressa(schmidti)very low, matting, to carpet the ground,
a brightly colored red in the winter from the leaf mass, light
red flowers in summer:bedding or in the rock garden.
   -lycopodioides, "Princess-pine" an erect, spreading mass
of green, leaf-sheathed stems:exceptional resistance to drought
and useful as a filler in other succulent plantings.
   -monticola(rupestris)weak slender stems to 12" in length
set with small, very thick, light grey leaves, the attractive pink and white flowers in winter....fair color then.
   -perfossa, "Necklace-vine" trailing, with the long stems
drawn through the disc-like leaves like buttons:dry walls.
   -tetragona, stems rigid-erect, set with light green,
curved, meaty leaves in four ranks, 18-24" high:flowers are
terminal, white or crimson. The species  -quadrifida or
multicava, with wide comparatively thin, dotted leaves, offset in pairs will grow in shade;small white flowers are nearly continuous and used for a kind of cutting.

   CRINODENDRON dependens, "Lily-tree" round-headed at 25' with
dull, dark, live-oak-like leaves that need help of a bright-
ening nature:small white hanging'lilies'throughout the body
of the tree are brisk against the moping, brooding foliage,
a mis-match May-June or on thru July, but helpful:following
orange capsules open to show black seed in a bittersweet re-
minder:shallow-rooting and essentially moisture-loving, good
lawn tree if kept in water, otherwise littering with an un-
natural leaf-drop besides the flower and capsule fall....better with
a deep cover beneath:roots work out of the soil, lower branches will
depend too far and the interior brush must be kept clear in interest
of the blooming. Withal, this is an interesting and useful tree. Its
sister species,  -patagua, has crimson flowers, not so vigorous.

## CAPELILY
   CRINUM---goodly sized summer-blooming bulbs which may be used for
bold and permanent masses in places where the root mass will not be
disturbed and where they in turn cannot over-run lesser neighbors.
When transplanting, save all possible roots in service of earlier
blooming, and set shallow, as much as half the neck out of the soil.
Water generously from beginning growth until first sign of failure,
when with-hold....flush tops during hot weather. They like rich
soils that are kept fertile....hearty feeders. The clustered, very
large, lily-like flowers, or the segments narrow-linear, all held
well above the foliage. Snails mark the leaves of choice hybrids.
   -americanum, "Swamp C." native in Florida and along the Gulf
Coast in low wet ground, the white flowers raised 18-24" , petals
or segments ribbon-like, either before or after the foliage January
until March. This is intensely fragrant.
   -erubescens, "Carib C." a low mass of sharply tapering leaves,
throwing stalks of white flowers tinged outside with purple, June-
July:foliage wilts to the ground in insufficient moisture.....even
the flower stalk will sag with its weight:deciduous.
   -giganteum, a large 5-6' plant, the bulb itself to 12" through,
the leaves 3-4" wide and 2-3' long, the fragrant, pure white flowers
very large, as many as 6-8 in a ringed cluster, pendent:wants half
shade for best performance, in a cool place where it will bloom
from time to time depending on moisture and length of season.
   -longifolium(capense)very hardy in frost and grown far
north with mulch, together with superior forms, both pink
and white and listed as C. powelli and C. moorei.
   -sanderianum, the leaves with wavy edges, the white
flowers washed with bright red outside and only a few to
the cluster:very tender in frost, used in subtropical
regions only on sufferance.

265

*Crinodendron dependens*

*Crinum giganteum*

*C. amabile*

*Crinum americanu.*

CROCOSMIA aurea, "Coppertip" bulbous, with narrow, iris-like leaves and copper-tipped orange to yellow, trumpet-shaped flowers on branched stems July-August:light loamy soils of more than average fertility will serve for a longer than average persistence. These are divided every few years and renewed or lifted, as grown north into temperate regions.

CROTALARIA agatiflora, "Rattlebox" an open-branched shrub 6-8' with greenish flowers October-January, the blooming extending at either end on very slight stimulus:is coarse at best, gangling, the foliage thin and not very attractive, a light bluish green....poor dry soils will tend to hold growth in check for more refinement:cut back hard for flowering wood and to straighten out the disorder....wait until depth of kill-back, if any, shows clearly....withstands only 5-6 degrees of frost.

CRYPTANTHUS beuckeri, crowded rosettes of harsh spiny foliage, the long horny leaf brownish green or bronze, striped with rose or spotted with lighter tones of green:a pineapple like plant, requiring moisture in summer, dry as may be the balance of the year and little attention otherwise:white flowers are born low among the leaves, late winter-spring: use in a pot or out in the rockgarden with drainage.

CRYPTOSTEGIA grandiflora, "Rubber-vine" burly bignonia-like plant that climbs or sprawls semi-shrub-like, distinguished as against bignonia by the milky sap:leaves are dark and glossy, the flower short-tubed, light purple held erect in a three-forked cluster July-October:may be grown in Southern Florida, elsewhere in favored spots, Imperial Valley....alkaline soils there, the color fading out in full sun or extreme dryness.

CUCUMIS dipsaceus, "Teasel Gourd" with bristly stems and kidney-shaped leaves, a running annual vine with a hard bur roughened and bristly:used with the gourds for ornament.

CUCURBITA pepo ovifera, a grand running annual, producing, usually pear-shaped gourds that are used ornamentally in ways known only to the gourd phalanx, known also by the yellow flowers.

CUDRANIA tricuspidata, "Silkworm-tree" spiny deciduous shrub or tree 25', sometimes used as a hedge, clipped or free-form, and again, planted for bird food:pale green bark notable and bright red fruits edible but of little account, as large as a hulled walnut and very messy underfoot:rare.

CUMINUM cyminum, "Curry" a low, untidy culinary herb with rose-colored, red or purple flowers of note:seeds are used for flavoring pickles, in pastries and in soups:ornamental points are few....isolate or use the color over a dry, faltering spot outside the garden.

CUPANIA anacardioides, "Carrotwood" wide-spreading, well-moulded, round topped tree 40', affording dense shade, the leaflets dark and leathery for unusually good wear in the wind:unimportant white flowers winter and spring and leather-tough, splitting fruits that are a nuisance underfoot:tree of good trim, moderately slow in growth for metropolitan conditions and for use there or in other difficult spots:streets.

CUPHEA---shrubby little plants with the basic stems woody, semi-herbaceous in at least part, with all extremes as to form from low neat bushlings to larger, sprawling, slouching, only half-woody herbs with an unpleasant clamminess to touch. All are tender and will appreciate a warm exposure out of doors and to be kept in good moisture....reduce this in fall to harden off.
     -hissopifolia, "Elfin'erb" low and woody, with nice natural form and trim outline, grown largely as a curb for boxing in the herbage of a bed in a formal layout:tiny lilac to lavender flowers are not conspicuous, but serve to enliven the foliage for a

sparkling aspect in bloom, all through warmth, tender in frost,
dropping the leaves, dull and uninteresting all winter:may reach
to 2' in height, but normally much less:resents shade.

    -llavea, "Red-white and blue Flower" shrubby, colorful, for a
rather general use in bedding, for baskets or the bright color to
be used as a low filler in a planter box, but in the sun.

    -platycentra(ignea)"Cigarplant" a low branchy little thing 12-15"
used in the garden or in pots indoors:the tiny, elongated, tubular flowers are scarlet in the semblance of a lighted cigar, quite profuse
at times, lighting up more or less over the warmth of the year:pinch
out the growing tips for a compact form:pots safer, with slight shade.

    -roezli, procumbent, semi-erect 2-3' either herbaceous or becom-
ing woody, according to handling....usually very straggling and not a
subject for the well ordered garden....does bring to it a vivid spot
of color when most needed.

## CYPRESS

CUPRESSUS---important coniferous trees for the far south,of considerable ornamental significance, of striking habit in many distinct
forms, with foliage nicely refined, always pleasing, of an unusually
tight texture and frequently showing considerable color. They may be
stressed for the definite role in detail they play in this southern
landscape, whether free and flowing, with more or less drooping lines
or a strict, sharply erect, emphatic, exclamatory figure that stands
out in any company. This emphasis on form is a sublimation of lean
living, light soils with drainage and without excess fertility and with
scant moisture. The wood does not recover readily from a cut, so that
they are best set out from a container and in small sizes. For the same
reason, any deep shearing or the pruning of heavy stems should be done
in early summer to allow for healing and recovery. Bring these trees
along slowly in order that the root system may keep up with
the top for bracing strength in the wind. Most of them are frost
hardy just well into warm temperate regions.

    -arizonica, loosely pyramidal 40', sometimes columnar
the early years, the foliage a light grey-blue, dense for good
contrast with other forms:tolerates heat and some cold, but owns
to one fault that bulks large under cultivation....topples in the
wind, wet weather, due to a scanty rooting. Moreover, it is not
easily moved on its own roots which are slow to take hold. In
the wind-pass city of El Paso, the nurserymen grow these handsome trees on a stronger stock which will hold in the wind.

    -forbsi, "Tecate C." offered as a substitute for monterey
cypress, in its decline, but not for the immediate coastline,
wanting heat above all else for ease:grows to 30', with the typical
red cherry-wood bark of the young tree and greyish foliage so fitting
for dry hills....from whence it comes:immune to the cypress fungous.

    -funebris, "Mourning C." spreading-pyramidal 50', becoming less
regular with age:light green foliage hangs with the flattened branches
in a melancholy feeling and expression, the general effect being that
of spanish moss:a distinctive tree, lively in movement in a breeze,
as against heavy construction or concrete mass.

    -goveniana, native in California, low and brushy or a tree
40', erect and compact-conical when young, spreading out later,
leaning at odd, un-natural angles:noteworthy for the abundant
cones for contrast, as for texture against the bright green of
the foliage which holds so well in heat and drought:picturesque.

    -guadalupensis, a most beautiful tree, broadly oval at 50
with a short, heavy trunk, mahogany-colored, dividing sharply
into many slender, erect, smoother and redder stems that weave
in and out beneath the tighter, outer cover of dark bluish foliage;
tender. This tree is styled in age with an arresting, theatrical or
dramatic quality and would be much in demand if better known. It
is an aristocrat of the very upper crust, wanting only to be
propagated and promoted....for the good of the industry.

    -lusitanica,"Portugal C." spreading, broadly pyramidal
at 40', of comparatively rapid growth, the branches pliable,
flexible and with a tendency to droop at the tips....accented
in some specimens to extend into the branching:blue of the
foliage is light and rather vivid as color, the dominant impression as a whole that of elegance:dry or

267

rocky soils or better....seems immaterial.  --var. benthami,
a stately tree of rapid growth to 70' pyramidal in structure
with short horizontal branches to a cone roughly:quite tender in
frost and will be restricted to the south.   --var. knightiana,
with a broader base and upturned branches, the branchlets regularly spaced in flattish sprays, fern-like and drooping..
    -macrocarpa, "Monterey C." wide-pyramidal 50' with rigid,
spreading limbs from a short, heavy trunk, the dense foliage dark:
an excellent break against the wind, it subsists under almost any
condition of the soil or exposure, enduring when lashed by salt spray,
happier there than when brought to town and civilization where the
story is sad....a rugged tree going out under effete living before
its time:limit its use to unfavorable conditions not to be found in
the garden and consider its use as a hedge only temporary:subject
to the so-called cypress canker or fungous:can be picturesque.
    -sempervirens, "Italian C." very slender, columnar to 60', as
normally and almost exclusively grown, a narrow shaft of dense, dark
green, rather somber, tight-textured foliage:with-hold water for the
better tree; avoid a rich soil and never fertilize, since the erect
side growths will lean and break away from the perpendicular with
an over-weight of foliage....cut away at any time or tie back temporarily while the ration is being reduced:dead twigs indicate the
twig borer and should be removed and burned....even this an indication of too good living:tends to lose lower branches south in
Florida. Seedlings as and if found in the nursery rows are quite
variable and trees may be found among the rogues which display a
marked character and individuality. The nurseryman who does not
see this and fails to mark and preserve individuals, overlooks a
valuable asset for himself and destroys material that should be a-
vailable to customers of understanding and appreciation.

CURCULIGO capitulata, stemless plants with broad, plaited, tapering
leaves directly from the soil in the likeness of seedling palms, arched, tremulous, uneasy in only the slightest movement of air, quiver-
ing:tuberous roots favor proximity of water or good irrigation:pots
inside, a planter or in the ground out of doors in deep shade or in the
open:leaf 3-4' long and 6" wide at the middle, somewhat boat-shaped.

CYANELLA orchidiformis, platonic, flowering without passion, a quiet
little thing, but with grace and polish, a bulb with an erect, widely
branching stem of small, orchid-like, pale lilac to bluish flowers in
March:wants a light, fertile soil in good sun, but no heat, good moisture while up and in growth:may be grown in a pot for typical uses or
plunged as such in the garden....but close since the color does not
carry:stands with poor drainage or in water for awhile, but must be
lifted for the rest period. This is a little pallid, but a choice
bit and something to treasure. The species   -lutea, is much in
miniature, a sparkling touch of yellow that is easily over-looked.

CYANOTIS hirsuta, trailing, somewhat succulent, a plant for a
hanging basket in difficulty or used in rock work:leaves are a
bright, shining green above, but covered beneath and lined at the
edges with long hairs that give it a certain coarseness....pur-
plish in the shade:survives hot sun and drought, when the hair
changes color to impart a brownish cast.

### CYCAD
CYCAS---curious, stubby, palm-like plants for tubs or to be used
outside in comparatively frost-free areas. They are very slow growing, the sturdy trunk clothed with the old leaf base, ultimately
smooth with exterior growth rings showing. This is topped by a
rounding rosette of glossy, wax-like, rigid-ferny leaves. They
do best in partial shade with good air circulation. Soil and care
or any special culture seems of only passing importance so that
they survive considerable neglect. The leaves or the plant, itself, are most decorative indoors. The first species below will
be recognized by the flattened leaflets, while those of the other
are curved and rolled over. They are picturesque in age and as
to branch in swirling, angular, upreaching stems.
    -circinalis, "Fernpalm" growing 10-15' in two or more stems
268

from the base or branching at some point of injury or other:the
more rapid in growth, but tender....may recover after foliage
loss in frost to become hardier:fronds with a spread of 6-8' in
a full, well developed head:leaflets flat.
     -revoluta, "Sagopalm" somewhat lower, 8-10' and not as often
found branched, the leaflets rolled under:hardier in frost, but is
subject to a peculiar blight that is little understood.

CYCLAMEN indicum, the florists "Cyclamen" with improved strains for
winter flowering, almost exclusively indoors:plants are usually obtained new each approaching season, but may be held over with correct and
careful handling....keep in pot balance of winter and over summer, held
in a cool place just moist enough to prevent shriveling leaves, curing
gradually with diminishing moisture as long as the leaf holds....no quick
wilting:when new growths appear in autumn, shake out old soil and re-
pot in a new, rich, composted soil and feed with strong manure
water or liquid fertilizer:blooms longer in moderate temperatures and flourishes only in a moist atmosphere:warm places
out of doors in a little shade and no cold water....use from a
sunny hose, or can-warm in the sun:subject to thrip, red spider.

CYDISTA aequinoctialis, "Garlic-vine" bignonia segregate,
the white, pink or lavender, purple veined, tubular flowers
and dark foliage in good body, blooming off and on, but concentrating at time of aequinox:tender and best used south in
Florida and favored spots along the Gulf Coast in poor sandy
soils:bruised leaves give off scent of onion, but not strong nor
penetrating....should not operate against its use.

CYMBALARIA---creeping herbs, perennials for the rock garden and
other special places such as partially shaded ground in moisture as a
fine cover or trailing from a low elevation in coolness. They are not
exactly fragile, yet will not prosper with rough handling, nor as well
in the sun and not in very dark shadow. They should have much humus in
an open soil with continual moisture. They re-seed, but moderately.
     -aequitriloba, a close-growing mat less than half an inch
through, tiny round, overlapping leaves, the flowers emerging
on thread-like stems during warmth:flagging or a crevice or
rock wall in coolness when it seals quickly and thoroughly,
as behind the stones, appearing again at a distance and repeating. Notice that all these suggested uses tend to insure
uniform moisture, the controlling factor. It is easily lost,
but can come back from self-sown seed:delightful, if held.
     -muralis, "Kenilworth-ivy" similar to above in many respects
but much more rugged and persistent, trailing, with much larger leaves
that are very nicely and finely lobed, the flowers similar and more
abundant. This requires little or no attention in moisture and will be
found ideal under darkened indoor conditions or outside, hanging in
gentle growths to soften harsh lines or covering the flat:reseeds freely.

CYMBOPOGON citratus, "Lemon-grass" forming large loose clumps of dominating blue-green leaves, growing to 3' or more in height, strong in an
essential oil that smells of lemon:has ornamental uses, but must be held in.

CYNARA scolymus, "Globe Artichoke" large coarse perennial to
back up the herb garden for an extra bold effort or anywhere
that calls for an active spot of foliage:the sharply cut, grey-
green leaves are highly ornamental for a time, become equally unsightly after the flowering head develops....presentable again by
fall or early winter:white, violet or blue, thistle-like flowers
and the edible base that develops, make this plant a striking
object and utilitarian....just remember distressing off-period.

CYNODON dactylon, "Bermuda-grass" a creeping, very sinewy plant, to
be used in areas of very hard wear for summer green....color off badly
in winter....for which feed well in October or supplement with dichondra or other winter lawn substitute:seed only in late spring or summer,
sowing separately in a spreader, such as in a pail of sand:thrives in
sand or clay, but fertility must be kept up for color. This does not
invade blue-grass or other lawns as a weed by seed developed under

269

normal lawn conditions. The almost exclusive source of infestation
is green barnyard manure....compost same thoroughly or use a
commercial fertilizer. The bermuda-grass, as of a mixed planting, will dominate in the sun, but the reverse is true in shade.

CYNOGLOSSUM amabile, "Chinese Forget-me-not" annual or biennial, loosely pyramidal in structure, the open panicles of flowers white or light pink, but mostly blue, normally spring and
summer....may be brought into flower at most any time:seedwhere
they are to stand, blooming in 7-8 weeks in a light, sandy,
preferably poor soil:as a cutflower, take as the lower branches
of bloom are at peak:burs objectionable near a path:reseeds.

CYNOSURUS cristatus, "Crested Dogstail" a lawn grass for moist
or shaded places, the better growth in late summer and autumn:not
persistent to become well established, but will effectively nurse
slower, more permanent grasses along, especially when planted
late:lawn mix or grown in the garden for dry boquets.

CYPELLA herberti, one of the more uncommon "Shellflowers" a
tapering 12" plaited leaf, somewhat like iris, nearly evergreen south, more often down over winter:erect 18-24" stems
carry dull chrome-yellow flowers in the general area of July
August:wants sun, a warm, light, sandy soil of good fertility
and moisture at all times:individual flower lasts but a day.

GALINGALE
CYPERUS---sedge-like plants of the south. They are not affected by
any ordinary cold weather or even frost and reach fairly far north for
hardiness. Smooth slender stems are topped by grassy heads of foliage
or the leaves flattened and narrow in the nature of bamboo, the inflorescence a handsome brownish spike in seed, greenish in flower. They are
strong-growing in wet places where the soil is rich, submerged in a pot
or grown at the bottom of water. They are singularly ornamental, with
a true significance brought out only in connection with water and they
never rise to their full artistic proportions without it.
     -alternifolius, "Umbrellaplant" the slightly arching stems
3-4', surmounted by flat fans of narrow extended leaves which droop
at the tips:tops may die down completely in extended drought and renew luxuriantly in moisture.    --var. gracilis, duplicating the type
but only 12-15" high, sized for a pot or in scale with a small garden
pool. Sometimes known as"McCoy-grass", this and the type reseeds badly.
     -brevifolius, "Kyllinga-grass" sedge-like mat for cover in open
or waste places, or turf of sorts in poor soils:horizontally creeping runners spread out, flowering stems rising 6-8" with heads at
any or most of the time, the 4-6" leaves clustered round:mow for a
rough turf under some moisture:not persistent northerly.
     -esculentus, "Chufa" grown for the edible tubers, but ornamen-
tal, 2-3' with grassy heads of fantastic effect. This is an attractive thing but liable to spread as a weed.
     -papyrus, "Paper-reed" dark three-cornered stems 4-8' or as much
as 10', gently curving and tapering progressively upwards to a nearly
globular head of long wire-like leaves to as much as 12" through:hold
to a box in a pool as it is invasive.
     -rotundus, "Nut-grass" sometimes useful in covering large areas of
periodically wet waste, growing 6-12" or 20" under conditions:a pest in
any other situation, even moist fields, almost impossible to eradicate....tending to run out in patches when closely grazed or frequently mowed:start with seed or nutlets or not at all.

CYPHOMANDRA betacea, "Tree-tomato" shrubby, of tropical
aspect in the lush, large soft leaves and highly colored
fruits, growing quickly to 10' high:pinkish flowers have a
slight fragrance, but the foliage unpleasantly scented:the
smooth fruits change in color through green to purple and
dull red and may be eaten out of hand, the flavor being
slightly acid and tomato-like:purchase young plants
only, to be set out finally at about 18-24" height
with a good set of roots developed.

CYRILLA racemiflora, "Black Titi or Leatherwood" native in
Florida and along the Gulf Coast, an evergreen shrub of some ornamental value, but not well known: has long, narrow, shining leaves
and hanging white flowers June-July: grows in moist peaty soils, in
swamps or along streamsides, dwarfed and more dense in drier soils:
wants slight shade and must be pruned for shape; is reliably hardy
throughout these regions and far north, when it becomes deciduous.
A low tree of similar character and nearly related, to be used in
like manner, is Cliftonia monophylla, known locally as"Titi, Ironwood or Buckwheatbrush" . Neither plant is significant in gardens
and will be found only in their locale, as taken from the wild.

### IFAFA LILY
CYRTANTHUS---bulbous plants with long, funnel-shaped hanging flowers
in a full rounding head. The leaves are small, narrow, strap-shaped, a tiny
amaryllis, even to the close-packed bulbs and sudden stout scape of bloom.
These South Africans will take water throughout the year in reasonable
amounts with no apparent harm and as a point in culture, the bulb should
never be dried out very completely. They want the sun.
        -mackeni, pure white flowers January-March, to be used in a pot or
outside in the garden: evergreen.   -obliquus, "Fire-lily" the bright red
flowers May-June, the sickle-shaped leaves appearing after the flowers:
to be used where a low spring annual will cover the bare mass
of bulbs which will be on the surface.

CYRTOMIUM falcatum, "Holly Fern" a light green, glossy-leaved
plant of value for foliage contrast with other ferns, a good
subject for a planter: rugged, but characteristically contained
out of doors or inside, tolerating drier air and ground, growing low into warm temperate regions: a spreading symmetrical clump
to as much as 3' across and as much in height....dwarf forms: watch
for brown scale and hose away dust out of the cupped leaves.

CYTISUS canariensis, one of the "Brooms" an erect spreading
shrub 5-8' with light green, refined foliage and showy masses of
bright yellow flowers in the spring, a lesser crop in the fall:
essentially for arid climates in dry, gravelly, sterile, rocky
soils....grow them there and only there, where they may develop slowly and hard. This is mainly because of the genista worm, a
pest very difficult to control, defoliating at any time, spring,
summer, fall....at its worst when the plant is grown lush and soft,
as in a garden. The snail considers it a choice item also....bait
beneath effective. Prune regularly after flowering, not cutting in
to old wood, from which new growth fails to break satisfactorily.
When grown as above, they may be started from seed to advantage,
otherwise request plants grown from cuttings for the more select
in form and color. They must have full sun for flowers.

### D

DACTYLIS glomerata, "Orchard-grass" coarse, but suitable for a
lawn mix designed for excessive wear in shaded places, drouth and
low fertility: should have good drainage and frequently applied lime
in highly acid soils.   --var. variegata, compactly tufted plant,
allowed its full 12" height, the light green blades marked longi-
tudinally with silver: ornamental as a grass, useful as a border.

DAHLIA---common tuberous-rooted plants, perennial in the south,
but still lifted and stored over winter. Soil is not as important as the sun, regulated moisture and periodic fertilizing as growth comes along. For cutting, the lower leaves are
stripped and the bare stems plunged into hot water and left a
few hours in darkness. Remove spent blooms when they turn brown
at the back. Strains of dwarf forms represented by the names
Coltness and Unwin are invaluable for a kind of coarse bedding

and are available as tubers or well established flat material or may be grown from seed quickly and cheaply.

-maxoni, "Tree Dahlia" semi-woody perennial on the grand scale, the great cluster of flowers gawking down from a 12-18' height, several knotty stems to a canopy of single rosy pink flowers in the fall. This spectacular and altogether satisfactory plant in its place, is practically unknown to the planting public, being so unwieldy to handle in the ordinary nursery channels. However, lower sections of the stem take readily in moist soil....placed where they are to stand, set at an angle in a depression which is gradually filled in:use within or behind shrub masses and out of the wind.

-pinnata, the garden "Dahlia", multiple in form and color, may be set out as early as April, but a late blooming in the south is to be preferred, with May-June a better time and still later far south in Florida:make a generous hole, preparing the soil a month ahead of planting with rotted dairy manure and a balanced organic fertilizer:lay tuber slanting on its side and cover, leaving a basin which gradually fills from watering and cultivation....don't irrigate heavily at first and don't feed again until buds are formed....stake high and strong to carry the heavy flower:lives on for years in the garden, blooming as early as April....usually lifted when the top fails and stored with the stem end downward:do not divide until planting time, splitting the stem to separate eyes:avoid extremely heavy soils, a dry one, and by all means a place that is open to the wind:they are heavy feeders, with both sun and drainage quite essential.

DAIS cotinifolia, a broad shrub 8-10' or a narrow, round headed little tree 25', of symmetrical, orderly growth, requiring but little attention to pruning, unless cut lightly for blooming wood:the rosy-pink flowers in neat full heads in summer....dry up on the tree, retained late as brown masses and disturbing element:foliage is crowded to the ends of the branches to form an open dome:has all the character and appearance of a broadleaf evergreen,but drops its leaves.

DAMNACANTHUS indicus, rigid, branchy shrub, 3-5', very dense in growth, the thick, short-stemmed leaves dark and shining, lighter beneath:always in service of a garden and its people, flower or berry, the fragrant white blooming overlapping the coral red berries of the previous season:choice and rare.

DANAE racemosa, "Alexandrian-laurel" for very special uses; dense, rigid, shrubby, growing 2-3' all around, where it thrives, the branches somewhat arching,the stems leaf-like, glossy with a high shine, medium green:the less important flowers are white and terminal for an effective showing of the large, soft, coral-red berries that wrinkle and dry up on the stem:tubs and planter boxes in some shade.

DAPHNE odora, "Sweet D." open-shrubby, rigid, 2-3' high and as much across when in thrift:dark leathery leaves and waxy white flowers or light purple, hug the thick branchings late winter and early spring for a remarkable fragrance:wants a well prepared soil in a cool place with partial shade, the soil leafy and drained: don't prune; don't cultivate; don't fertilize unless decidedly lacking in thrift, using then a complete acid food....keep a light mulch of leafmould continually rotting:difficult at best, this is better grown northerly.

DATURA---tree-like shrubs with a rank growth of soft wood and a velvety, coarse, strong-smelling herbage that is universally unattractive. The flowers hang singly, great trumpets swaying in the breeze, and heavily, artifacts of some dissimulation of interest, but not of great beauty....never-the-less planted from time to time. They are naturally adapted to use as standards, doing best in a moist, rather heavy soil, or stand in some dryness. They require reasonable fertility and may want pruning, according to place and use.

-sanguinea, will make a slender tree 15' high, with the

272

flowers architecturally moulded, orange and red, with penciled
lines of deeper color, all with the quality of an engraving.
This is the hardier in cold.
    -suaveolens, "Angels-trumpet" growing to 10', but usually
less and with more mass broadside, bushier:the nearly white flowers are lined with green and faintly touched with lilac May-June,
single or double, tube in tube.

## EMBER FLOWER
  DAUBENTONIA---rapid-growing shrubs for exciting color and quick
effects. They will grow 4-6' in height or more, are stemmy and
not very dependable in pattern of development....desultory,
fitfully irregular, slender lines to a spreading top. They are
not long-lived and should be used with more permanent plantings designed to take over. They may be flowered all through
the heat of the year if seed pods are removed as they form.
Cut back in late summer for flowering wood. The first below
will generally be found in Florida, the other in California
and the Southwest. They are reasonably frost-hardy.
    -punicea, with red-purple flowers in locust-like racemes, it
should have good drainage:probably the hardiest.   -tripeti, flame-
colored, dropping foliage very easily in cold.

  DAVALLIA canariensis, "Rabbitfoot Fern" creeping by means of a
hairy rhizome which is aerial and part of the ornamental scheme:
wants good light, a very leafy soil and moisture,where it will be
used as fern cover or climbs rough surfaces after a manner:fronds
may be as much as 18" in height, shedding in winter:baskets.

  DEERINGIA amaranthoides, wide-spreading as a shrub or climbing 15',
the foliage a light green or variegated most pleasingly in white:re-
fined in a way that reaches for grace in a manner all its own....an
old plant with many decorative ways for today, shamefully abandoned
to its past:insignificant greenish flowers and red berries, but both
intriguing:broad masses over a bank or piling high against an ob-
struction or only a filler among the more modern, if you will:choice.

  DELONIX regia, "Flamboyant or Royal-poinciana" a wide-spreading tree at
40', of rapid but substantial growth in frost-free areas, spectacular
in bloom, orange-scarlet May-June or later, a glorious spread of
color beneath:without foliage for a time in early spring when the
fluted bole and gnarled branches are most apparent....transplant
just after this period or November-December far south. There is
considerable color variation, in quality of the tree and in its
habit of growth:aggressive roots work at the surface, the tree
tending to stunt under restriction:not successfully grown in
California, probably due to winter wetness or cold nights.

  DELOSTOMA roseum, a large bush from a single crown or low bole,
tree-like, the body round-topped and fairly dense, wanting moisture with reasonable drainage:bignonia-like, rosy-pink flowers in
summer and scattering, followed by long purple fruiting pods, although seed seldom sets and matures....prune in early fall to
increase the flowering:rare, due to difficulty in the propagation of new stock.

## LARKSPUR
  DELPHINIUM---as known and grown in northern lands, is
not likely to be duplicated in the south of these regions.
The handsome hybrids are seldom seen, then grown by spec-
ialists under special conditions...fresh, home-grown seed
if possible, sown immediately offers best chance for success. Vitality even then, soon runs out to require a fresh
infusion from the north. In their stead will be found the annual below and such natives as may be grown under conditions
that are favorable. They want full sun.
    -ajacis, "Rocket L." an erect, slender, very thinly
foliated annual 18" with violet or blue flowers in the
spring if sown in the fall and in summer when sown in early
spring or will seed itself to come up in late winter:any good

273

soil, but not too rich and light in texture, friable:escapes.
    -cardinale, "Scarlet L." slender stems 2-3' with bril-
liant, helmet-shaped flowers in the spring or delayed into
summer, grown under domestication:haunts dry gravelly washes
of Southern California, in nature, places where it gets deep
moisture late season: a perennial for the dry border, long-lasting
when cut:slow fron seed.
    -nudicaule, native in California, perennial 12-15", with a
loosely swung, scattering of flowers, scarlet and yellow June-August, the
leaves mottled and of a glossy sheen:wants a cool place in loose, grainy
or gravelly soil and slight shade....large rock crevice. The handsome
Ruysi hybrids of Europe are developed in part from this species and may
be grown precariously in subtropical regions.

    DENDROMECON rigida, "Bush-poppy" native shrub in California, having
slender, graceful stems of light green, leathery leaves, straggling
in nature, but from a rather close crown under domestication, bushy;
the small lemon-yellow "poppies" are attractive and in goodly numbers, scattering out over the year, concentrating April-May:always
difficult to establish, more easily held, wanting loose, gravelly
ground that is not too fertile:some little pruning to clear out the
brush for new wood, and irrigation over late spring and early summer will extend the flowering materially and present a better looking plant:espalier against a hot wall.

    DENNSTAEDTIA cicutaria, "Cup Fern" a large plant of rapid growth for
quantities of splendid fronds for cutting all summer:takes shade or sun,
but wants moisture in a porous, friable soil and fertile for the cuttings
that will be taken....fronds 3-5' long and 2-3' wide;wants humid air.

## BLUEBERRY LILY
    DIANELLA---wiry-rooted perennials for the open border or in a container
for awhile. They are vigorous in growth, wanting better than average moisture, taking some shade with benefit southerly or in heat, spreading widely by means of strong, suckering stolons. The narrow, sword-like, partially channeled leaves are tinted purple at the base, enclose the slender
branched flowering stem with its load of overlapping flowers and the
berries, spring-summer. These are choice materials and very rugged,
but the bringing into flower sometimes a mystery, always a challenge. They want no alkali, not even passing aquaintance with
the ubiquitous nematode.
    -intermedia, more spreading underground, 2-3' high, the
flowers purplish-blue:pots, but better with straight sides, the
strong roots tending to push the ball up and out:more dependable.
    - tasmanica, with a more distinct crown, growing 4-5', easily
mistaken for New Zealand Flax, the flowers light blue, the berry a
turquoise, cut and polished like porcelain....on such slender ped-
icels as to appear suspended in air:tubs.

## PINKS
    DIANTHUS---herbaceous plants with typically grassy leaves, frequent-
ly clump-forming, in many instances coalescing to form a mat. They are
of easiest culture, growing in dryish, sterile, fairly stiff or even a
baked out top-soil when drained, yet holding moisture below. Rock chips
are to their liking, particularly if limestone. They should be given
full sun and are at their best in a dry rock wall with moisture to
tap behind the stone. They improve with shearing after bloom.
    -caesius, "Cheddar P." spreading perennial with up-raised white
or pink to rose-colored, fringed flowers May-July, a loose mat 3-4"
through:welcomes lime, but not dependent upon it.
    -caryophyllus, the border "Carnation" a large sprawling
plant, perennial but wanting renewal  each spring from cuttings,
or layer lower stems of the old plant September-October for a
better spring start:has the original fragrance of clove and stands
out for pure, intense coloring from white to lightest pink to
the deeper reds and maroon, practically continuous over the
year:wants a fairly rich soil with humous and moisture for
good size....disbud, especially during heat....mulch for a
cool soil. Superior flowers will be possible only with good
drainage and periodic deep waterings in dry weather.

-chinensis, the typical "Pinks", old garden favourites
that are particularly appealing in retrospect, annuals, blooming May-October, or sometimes carrying over until next spring,
to die aflowering:grown from seed and available in well-fixed
strains, singles and doubles, with miniature forms: a cutflower.
     deltoides, "Maiden P." perennial, becoming dense, invading,
a dark green sod with the tiny pinks on relatively long stems,
April-June:tenacious and long-lived in dryish soils, sand, gravel or clay, just so long as they get uniform, if little moisture
and not too much:must not be used next to a grass turf for obvious
reasons. There are many named varieties.

     DIASCIA barberae, perennial, or treated as an annual, the odd rose, pink
or salmon flowers touched with gold in the shallow throat, somewhat like a
nemesia, but blooming June-August:becomes drought resistant when established, neat in habit for a pot or out of doors in the ground of warm, sunny
places:set April-May from an earlier spring sowing:too rarely used.

     DICENTRA chrysantha, known as "Golden Eardrops", a woody peren-
nial with plentiful rue-like foliage of a pale, glaucous-blue cast
and full clusters of sulphur or golden yellow flowers, sometimes
an old gold.....inverted hearts, hanging over spring-summer:grows
2-3' in height or, at times and places 5', very erect, to be used
in dry, hot and sharply drained ground only and with total sun:a
splendid plant in full flower and foliage display....draw out the
combined effect into a longer season by careful irrigation, moderation as important as depth:native in California:seed.

     DICHONDRA repens "Lawnleaf" a grass substitute, close-mat-
ting stolons with tightly over-lapping, small round leaves:re-
quires little or no mowing in a pure stand, if handled correctly....ration water and fertilizer to hold nearly static:stands
still in a packed soil and wears down under traffic, returning
quickly, with rest, from the abundant seed, is nearly always at
hand;sods are better in starting a small area, but seed should be
used in established lawns or larger plots....may appear as an
unwanted weed anywhere....will be the weed of future gardens:
sow in bermuda lawns for color in winter:stains white shoes and
clothing, slugs defoliate unless controlled and stoloniferous
weeds must be eradicated when they first appear. This is so important that advantage should be taken of dewy mornings or times of
misty rain, when foreign leaves stand out to be seen:fertilize in the
spring, and lightly for a low, compact mat....no green manures at any
time. In the beginning, prepare and level the ground, re-leveling
after watering in for a uniform stand and color, best planted in
May-June or in September-October, as indicated by yellowing
leaves....stolons, sod-plugs or seed.

     DICRANOSTIGMA franchetianum, "Chinese-poppy" perennial, a
rounding form of loose structure 12-15" from a strong woody root
system:foliage a light, glaucous blue, finely cut, largely basal,
and marbled in white, a pleasing pattern to go with the fragile
lemon-yellow to orange, poppy-like, inch-wide flowers over spring
and summer:grows in any garden soil, but not exposed to the wind
in any amount:open border or rock garden.

     DIEFFENBACHIA picta, "Dumb-cane" foliage plants with handsome,
leafy tops, stem and wide leaf suggestive of canna, but only as to
form since the leaves are variously colored in stripes, spots or
splashed in yellow, a contrasting green, in white or ivory:bedding as
young plants, later in planters, pots or other in rich, moist soils
that have been well prepared with a compost for humous....type form
will stand in free water for a time and may be cut to the ground when
too much stem shows:most varieties resent direct sunlight.

     DIERAMA pulcherrima, "Grassybells or Wandflower" bulbous
perennial 3-5' high, the narrow, sword-shaped leaves
forming a more or less bushy clump to support the
wand-like flowering stems:flowers, blood-red or
only tinted, bell-shaped, suspend from the tips

275

to test the slightest breeze May-June:an ixia-like plant making a permanent
clump with moisture and drainage, never being allowed to become hard dry:
wants warmth in the sun....transplant late summer or early fall.

### CAPE MARIGOLD

DIMORPHOTHECA---colorful garden flowers, good material out in the
open, waste ground,where they make a valiant attempt at service. The daisy-
like flowers are available as early as six weeks from seed, reseeding to
carry on indefinitely in loose, sandy soils or those well drained. They must
have full sun, open imperfectly cloudy days and close at night. They will be
found in some degree of flower almost any time of the year.
    -annua, slender sprawling plants 15-18", the white rays ting-
ed purple or blue from the reverse of the petal....generally most
available over spring-summer:controlled by time of seeding:escapes.
    -aurantiaca, one of the most dependable flowers for winter,
perennial, actually annual as used, the older plants being replaced
by the more desirable seedlings that spring up thickly:a thick and
spreading body of foliage 12-15" high, smothered in full flower by
the smaller white, orange or salmon daisies, rays burnished for full
effect in the sun, zoned with black at the center for contrast.
    -ecklonis, "Star of the Veldt" an erect, bushy, robust perennial
becoming woody at the base, a very rugged plant , adapted to heat and
dry places in a hot reflected sun and in utterly nondescript soils that
will support no ordinary vegetation:large white daisies have a bright blue
disc or button at the center, the ray flowers showing blue from the back,
but only when partially closed or when rolled in from deep drought. This
is more susceptible to seasonal influence, but still erratic in flower.

DION edule, a curious, stubby cycad, the coarse, fern-like fronds originating in a circle to form a horizontal plane around the top of an over
sized and clumsy trunk:normally seen at about 3' in height, but ultimately 5-6':may be grown in the open or in a damp plant house and will be
known from Cycas by the notched leaflets and flattened rosette:rare.

DIOSMA---fine-textured, heath-like shrubs, bushy and well-formed from a
close crown, nicely suited for many garden uses. The foliage is finely cut, comparatively light in tone, the more or less elongated,
beady leaves intermingling with the tiny starry flowers of March-
April on into summer. Use and culture have some in common with
heath, but better garden plants in adapting to soil and moisture. They are widely used in California.
    -ericoides, "Breath of Heaven" growing 3-4', with white
bloom, drought resisting or takes ordinary irrigation:good flowering hedge that submits to consistent but not deep shearing:
foliage gives of its delightful fragrance when brushed against
or when dampened.   --var. reevesi, more spreading and
not so high, generally 2-3' with fewer and larger flowers.
    -pulchra(Coleonema)not as branchy, the leaves longer
and appressed to willowy branchlets:light red flowers are
not as abundant, starting earlier:pinch out the long
growth in spring and do not feed heavily.

DIOSPYROS kaki, "Persimmon" deciduous, but with a distinctly subtropic flavor and overtones, low, open and spreading as
a shrub, or a fair-sized tree bearing the large orange or scarlet fruits on past seasons wood....good color for the autumn
landscape:wants a deep, rich, loamy soil with good drainage and
uniform irrigation up to fruiting....fruit drop can usually be
traced back to insufficient moisture some time during growth:as
fruitful in California as in Florida, a low frosty place being important in health and performance, with implications in quality of
fruit:prune for new wood, to open up the head and to hold back
extending branches for strength to carry the crop and exhibit
same....hold fruit by bringing along without checks.

DIPIDAX ciliata, bulbous, with two-parted, very erect,
dark and very smooth rush-like leaves for line and to form
a clump:the tight cone of flower buds, purple with hints
of lavender, emerge from the fold of the leaf December-
February, and open as a spike of fading purple, finally

colorless excepting the deeper purple center....down over
summer and fall:set deep, August-October and keep quite
wet while  active:bogs,seepages, ponds or a pool.

DISTICTIS lactiflora, strong-growing vine, bignonia
segregate, the dark leathery leaves ample for all ordinary purposes, but not abundant:large trumpet-shaped
flowers, however, in generous clusters of purple that
shades into lavender March-October, and rather consistently in flower all that time, or longer far south:slow to begin,
best in coolness, climbing rough surfaces:choice.  The related
plant  known generally as D. riversi has a long flowering tube
of yellow and usually with a flare of royal purple.

DODECATHEON clevelandi, "Shootingstar"  an early flowering
little herb of transient nature, native in California:the 6-8"wiry
stems rise from a tufted clump of leaves at the ground to carry tiny,
active, dart-like flowers reminiscent of cyclamen, of slight fragrance
and color, white or lilac touched with yellow:the dry, ripened roots
may be planted 1-2" in depth in the rock or wildflower gardens or the
species naturalized by seed:likes a heavy soil, but not required.

DODONAEA viscosa, "Rock-willow" an erect, rigid shrub 8-12'in
height with light green, winged leaves, of little ornamental
interest:adapts, however, to almost any adverse condition of heat,
alkali, wind or drought and driven salt-spray, invaluable when circumstances such as these, concentrate:serves well to bring a kind
of refinement to rough places and will shear up into a good hedge:
native in the Southwest.   --var. purpurea, has dark purple foliage, a fast color in hot sun and attractive.

DOLICHOS lignosus, "Australian Pea" a low perennial vine which will
rapidly cover a low wall or fence with a loose blanket of persistent
foliage, the leaves, however, dropping in substantial frost:abundant
flowers are purple and rose or white over a long period:may be
easily grown from seed, ultimately spreading out as cover.

DOMBEYA---winter-flowering woody plants, of extremely rapid development, shrubby or  a small tree with soft wood of unsubstantial
quality. The flowers come in a modified spherical head, hydrangea-
like, held erect or hanging free on long stringy petioles, almost
hidden by the rough leafage....dry up and turn brown in place for a
long period of untidiness. They will tolerate excess moisture, want
the sun for good flowering, are very tender in frost:deep fertile soil.
     -calantha, wide-spreading as a shrub 10-12' or will reach to 20'
as a tree, the arching branches tipped January-May by the rosy-pink
heads which are held above the soft leaves:rare and probably the best.
     -natalensis, "Cape Weddingflower" shrubby or grown tree-like of
several erect stems from a low trunk, the vertical lines rather thinly
appointed with scented, poplar-like leaves:pure white flowers in
straggling heads of small balls are fragrant.
     -wallichi, "Pinkball" a tree except in cold places, but the top
still stemmy in the way of the shrubby kinds:of good foliage, the
leaf large and rough, partially hiding the lavender-pink flowers
that hang in large balls. A hybrid  --cayeuxi, only 5-10', with
a hanging head is to be used in a shrubbery for winter color.

DORYANTHES palmeri, "Spear-lily" large desert succulent with a
wide, sword-like leaf to form a compact rosette at the ground:the
long, pointed heads of red flowers are whitish within and tower to
15':years pass before coming into flower, but provides a bold plant
for a tub or other use early, to be set out ultimately in the gard-
den or with cactus to await the event....moisture will hasten.

DOVYALIS(ABERIA)caffra, "Kei-apple" vigorous, rangy, long-
thorned and cruel, a coarse shrub for rough protective purposes, hedges or thickets on a large scale:bright green foliage
stands under wear and wind and large, golden yellow fruits are
edible, used in preserves, slightly acid to
taste:tolerats salt in the ground or

*Distictis lactiflora*

*Dodonaea*

*Dolichos*

*Dombeya calantha*

*Dovyalis*

277

air and established plants will take as much as 15 degrees
of frost without particular harm:a burly plant that will
stand in absolute drought, the foliage unaffected. Keep as
dry as possible for good crops.

DOXANTHA unguis-cati, "Catsclaw" very high-climbing on a
wall, clinging vine with short-tubular flowers March-May:a
scant foliage gives value to an interesting net-work of stems
and backs with a certain freshness the soft yellow blooming:
one of best for arid conditions, wanting the sunny side of the
building anywhere:deciduous. A tendency for all activity to concentrate at the extremities must be discouraged early and from
time to time....cut near the base to keep new growth coming on at
the ground....repeat as required to have new flushes following
upward for a more complete cover. This vine was known as
Bignonia tweediana....very hardy in frost.

DRACAENA---ornamental woody plants, a variable lot of tender
shrubby or tree-like material for planter boxes or pots to use
indoors or outside for patio or terrace. Here they are useful
only in the juvenile stages of growth, being removed in their
time and set in the ground for maturity....some only far south.
Foliage is mostly adaptation of the sword motif or modified
along ribbony lines, frequently with color, stripes, spots or
blotching, the flower seldom of note. They will do satisfactorily under average conditions of soil and exposure. The
genus Cordyline is similar, included here as noted.
    -australis(Cordyline)slender stems and narrow leaves will
mark this as one of the most common in cultivation, the matured
tree with large panicles of white flowers spring-summer or any
time....not material, dry up and hang too long for eye comfort.
These trees are usually brought up with one stem, stout and
devoid of interest, where several such from a stubby base, or
a branching habit started earlier for individuality is much to be
desired. Large specimens may be moved, care being taken to preserve
undamaged, the heavy-pointed tap root which will be found approxim-
ately a fifth the height of the specimen....sometimes adapting flat
to hardpan. Color in the red leaved form is not fixed, may go.
    -draco, "Dragon-tree" a low, solid rosette in the planter box,
lat r a corpulant and grotesque tree form as high as 30', fat and
stoggy trunk to a few stout, opulant, bud-like branches, repeating the stiff rosettes of leaves at the ends:wants very
little moisture and grows anywhere:not ornamentally desirable....a large piece for the succulent collector:hardy.
    -fragrans, "Cornplant" very slender stemmed, 6-8' even-
tually, but as used in decoration much smaller, the wide undulating leaves curving gracefully downwards in the lax semblance of a stalk of corn:pots for table decoration, an inside
box or for any purpose wanting a fine display of leaf color
and line interest:many varieties based on white, yellow and
cream in the leaf as longitudinal stripes:red spider.
    -godseffiana, very small, as used in a pot or box,
branching freely, tender, but reaching 6-8' outside far
south in warmth, adapting to considerable shade:greenish
yellow flowers in neat tufts, winter in warmth, suffer in
comparison with the foliage which is dotted and blotched in
silvery white;choice.
    -stricta(Cordyline)slender woody stems 10-12' shrubby
and weak, requiring support in maturity unless pruned hard
for strength early:very narrow leaves collect about the ter
minal growth like a feather duster, green with suggestions
of purple....ends in a handsome panicle of dark lavender flowers
over summer:grow in a pot to tub to ground for a very choice
and desirable garden plant:scale infests and is difficult to
reach:sun or full shade, with indirect light.
    -terminalis(Cordyline), "Ti-plant" generally low-growing
3-4', but much higher far south in warmth, the short broad
leaves elliptical, strongly veined, colored through white,
creamy to rose and various shades of red:use this indoors
or in a pot outside that may be moved in frost.

DRIMYS winteri, a particularly handsome, openheaded tree 50'
or less, of fairly rapid growth in moist soils:magnolia-like,
dark, leathery leaves are aromatic, good in moderate wind of a
cool climate:flowers are milky white, an inch across, solitary or
clustered and any time January-July:could be mistaken for madrone,
due mostly to the smooth reddish branches and twigs....and a substitute for in coastal areas:hardy into warm temperate regions:rare.

DUCHESNEA indica, "Mock Strawberry" perennial, trailing, rooting
again and again to make a loose mat that tightens in the sun, under
moderate trampling:flowers are clear yellow instead of white of the
strawberry; and the fruit, the dry inedible fruit a mere trumpery,
a jest thimble-rigged for the birds....crimson jewels, however, to
the eye, bedded down among the typical strawberry leaves:a cover for
the ground, where it will adapt to considerable shade and dryness.

DURANTA---tender tropical shrubs, very generally used in these
regions. They are vigorous in growth in moist heavy soils, but
very susceptible to frost, the slightest touch searing the thin
leaves which also droop  at first sign of drought. The naturally
brushy character and rapid growth call for considerable and
regular pruning as used in the garden. Head in these plants
and thin out each spring, although timing here, is not so important since they  seem always in flower or fruiting, the two
functions overlapping in constant color. The foliage turns to
shades of dark purple during cold weather, black in areas.
    -repens(plumieri) "Pigeonberry" erect-spreading 15', nor-
mally quite thorny, the needle-pointed spines at the base of the
light green leaves:lilac-blue flowers come along all spring and
summer, with occasional motes later among the berries which are
abundant, close-massed, beaked, pale yellow, lasting over winter:
must have uniform moisture to be at its best:probably the hardiest.
    -stenostachya, "Golden Dewdrop" as above, but much superior for
garden use, the plant darker, more compact, rounding, with more character in stem, ultimately a canopy at 8-10' supported by several thick angular or twisting stems:flowers are of a deeper shade and the thorn is
reduced to a spur or entirely absent.

DYCKIA sulphurea, a low stemless succulent with hard, harsh and horny
leaves that are spined or toothed along the edges:forms a clump, to base
the slender lines of the blooming, rather showy spikes midsummer or
later:rock garden or succulent collection in an exposed, dry spot.

DYSCHORISTE linearis, perennial 18-24", actually more shrub-like
and usually serving as such with dull, dark purple flowers that
are obscurely spotted with purple:native in the Southwest, but
not to be grown typically....attractive and short-lived.  The
species  -oblongifolia, a rare native of coastal Florida
has blue flowers and should be grown dryish, as of there.

E

EBENOPSIS flexicaulis, "Texas-ebony" a shade tree 50' or
only some 20' with several stems, of rapid growth in rich soil
and moisture, drained:half-inch thorns base the dark leaves
which contrast the white in the matured bark:short spikes of
yellow flowers are not conspicuous, but with some fragrance
appear after rains, or any time under irrigation:native.

ECCREMOCARPUS scaber, "Glory Flower" an herb-like bignonia,
ultimately woody at the base, 8-10' as a climber, but the soft
growth killing back in frost:blooms the first year from seed in
terminal racemes of yellow to orange and scarlet:hanging basket
plants if pinched in, window boxes to fill and depend or they
may be grown on mesh wire as a quick screen for a sitting out
area:free-flowering in warmth, July-September:short-lived.

ECHEVERIA---low stemless plants, the meaty leaves either thick, rotund, spiny-tipped in a close rosette or the leaf broad, thin and wavy. In either case the stout flowering stem will emerge from among the leaves to hold a drooping, quietly colorful cluster of short-tubed bloom. They are planted for the rare metalic tintings in some of the wider, more typical leaves or for the flattish masses of crowding rosettes of others, all to be used effectively among rock....bedding of sorts, where they are worthy year-round. Little is required in way of sustenance and they will thrive in any rooting medium that supplies little more than moisture. Two very distinct and fixed aversions are high heat and nematodes. They want good light and drainage.

-amoena, in miniature, small rosettes to half an inch across and flattened, the mat seldom more than an inch through, but the flowering may rise to 8" for a coral showing:a green cover in cool places, better used with rock or between flagstones.

-clavifolia, a hybrid with small sappy rosettes piled in crowding masses on the ground or growing among the dead boots of a palm trunk:rock work or bedding, a border to line a walk or path.

-derenbergi, very low, a cover of sometimes little more than an inch in thickness:leaves are greyish white with red margins, to crowd the flat with small rosettes or fill in a large crevice;the flowers are held 2-3" high, the heavy petals sharply pointed, reddish yellow:an interesting, irregular mat.

-harmsi, a shrubby, branching succulent 10-15" high with bright color shortly in the summer, the five-angled, short-tubular scarlet flowers nearly closed, tipped with yellow when opened:loose soils of especially good drainage, some fertility, and warmth for good blooming....otherwise frost-hardy:pots, planters for the vivid coloring and with rocks. This is synonymus with Oliveranthes elegans, or may be a larger plant.

-metalica, the comparatively large leaves watery but thin and soft, beautifully shaded with blue tones and pink, nicely blending under a wash of lavender:the thick-stemmed flowers are yellowish with red tips, summer.

-pulverulenta(Dudleya)"Chalk-lettuce" native Californian in the south along the coast, thriving best where it gets the fog: the medium thin leaves are powdered with white so that the large rosette stands out against a dark rock or effective on a cliff, high in the wind:coral or orange-red flowers in the spring, best in light shade:pots.

-setosa, the small leaves rounded in a very precise rosette which is flattish at first, later rounded, furry overall due to a fine hair:red flowers are tipped yellow:wants excellent drainage, best with a collar of rock chips:choice.

ECHINOCACTUS---globular, deeply ribbed forms of cactus, sometimes effectively used with aridity in the landscape or, prime for the collection of succulents. They are highly individualized, developing few or no offsets, the spines strong and many. The flowers appear alone or in groups on the upper portion of the body, sometimes on the tip of a tubercle. They want heat, dryness in summer, drainage in moisture.

-cylindraceus(Ferocactus)"Barrel C." round, ribbed, native to western deserts, growing almost anywhere to 3' in height and a diameter of 12" or less:short-stalked, pale yellow flowers in the winter are attractive, colorful.

-grusoni, almost spherical when young, later as much as 4' high and 2' through, the body flattened at the top:bright golden spines are set so closely overall as to give the appearance of solid gold....spectacle for the landscape, near or far: red and yellow flowers come on as anti-climax.

ECHINOCEREUS rigidissimus,"Rainbow C." low-growing, with several ascending cylindrical stems or joints, banded alternately in white, yellow, red or brown....hold comparatively large pink or purple flowers:native in the Southwest and is well used in considerable mass and over large areas of dry rocky hillside where the haze of color may be seen and appreciated:spreads from seed from only a few joints.

Echium
wildpreti

ECHINOCYSTUS macrocarpa, "Chilicothe" perennial vine, transient as to
herbage, but very permanent otherwise....for the ages in the immense rugged tuber....liability in the garden:foliage appears with the California
rains for an almost instant coverage to 20' across....good for as many
days....dries up in summer heat:mediocre white flowers and a spiny, gourd-
like seed vessel are of some moment in interest, the tuber and its littering issue, to be accepted as on site or seed can be found by the undaunted.

## VIPERS BUGLOSS

ECHIUM---coarse herbs, the flowering stems few from a base, or many from
a low crown, becoming woody below and developing a furrowed bark. They are
splendid for broad effects in rough, unkempt places, poor rocky land that
requires quick if not too permanent covering. Sterile soils will bring
out a more completely developed and colorful spike of flowers, with less
intrusion of undesirable bristles and bracts. They can be quite spectacular with good color. It is well to remove spent spikes down to foliage.
    -fastuosum, "Pride of Madiera" cast in a rough mold, a shrubby
plant with a low woody stem and many erect-curving branches, a many-
moted candelabra 5-8' high and the whole as much or more across:will
adapt to the most impossible places and soils, surviving utter drouth,
the 12-18" spikes of blue flowers May-June. The color is variable to include shades of purple, the best of which may be marked and continued by
means of cuttings.    --var. Alfred Hottes, is an exceptionally pure blue
in many slender heads for an effect in line:choice.
    -wildpreti, "Honeyplant" biennial or nearly so and not dependable
beyond the second or, at most the third year, so that replace- Echium
ment must be made if conditions are not favorable for reseed- fastuosum
ing....does so sparingly:a single stem is normal, 3-4' high, the
flowering head generous, to 6" through, crowded with florets of a
most pleasing shade of rose:greyish leaves of size, a clump at the
ground, reducing in size following the stem upward:a good thing to
get started in out of the way places, or a garden plant, in scale.

EHRETIA elliptica, known as "Anaqua", south in Texas where it is
native and very much at home, either shrubby 15-20' under difficulties or a shade tree 50' in cultivation and as domesticated for
a garden:has attractive and fragrant yellow flowers, probably in
two bloomings, while the small orange fruits are taken by the
birds:not important, but with much meaning in the right place.

EICHORNIA---aquatic herbs, very rank-growing and a little coarse
but of extra value for conditions involving extremely moist soil
or mud in its worst aspect in control....and open water.  And
control is the first factor in their consideration since growth
is such that other plants are invariably choked out unless they
are in some way or other protected.
    -azurea, "Water-orchid" Stationary and well anchored in mud of
shallow waters or with lilies at greater depths:rather free in habit
of flowering, the pale blue or purple flowers beautifully fashioned, the bright yellow center vaguely enclosed with white. Try it
in a low, wet, undrained place in the garden.
    -crassipes, "Water-hyacinth" the entire plant free of any
anchorage, floating by means of swollen, bladder-like leaf petiole
or stem, or rooting in mud if within reach:when used in an artificial pool with no soil or other growth, a pinch of fertilizer from
time to time will nourish and satisfy a natural greediness....does
not tolerate alkaline waters and fails in a concentration:flowers
are pale violet, blue and yellow on short, stubby stems, erect
or curved upwards from among the bladders:has become naturalized in streams and lakes of Florida....a menace there.

Echinocystus

ELAEAGNUS pungens, "Silverberry" a rigid spreading shrub 4-6'
or much more, the stems spurred with a kind of spine, the entire
plant frosted with a unique metalic scaling that glistens and
glitters in the sun....dreary subject in shadow:flowers inconspicuous, but the fragrance identifies the blooming in autumn:the
berries are silvered brown, while variations in the foliage will
include blotchings of white yellowish or pink and other markings:
stands salt in the air and in the soil, but must have drainage as
of sandy soils:head back for compact body or prune for streaming

Eichornia
azurea

growth to 15' or more as desired.    --var. fruitlandi,hybrid
form, tree-like 10-15', the silvery character intensified,the
slender, graceful stems weighted with the crowding berries:
prune only to retain grace, pinching out terminals for sturdi-
ness necessary to carry the prodigious crops.    --var. reflexa,
rampant, climbing into trees in Florida by means of hooked
spines:fragrance spreads in a moist atmosphere.

ELAEODENDRON orientale, "False-olive" dense growth from
a stout trunk, a pyramidal tree 45' with dark and
glossy, leathery leaves that hold until covered by
the new ones from above....nice contrast:unimportant
greenish or white flowers and yellowish fruits; to be
used in tubs, later in the ground, a street tree under
exposure. The juvenile foliage is very fine in texture
with segments long and narrow, tenuous, having a red
midrib(Aralia chabrieri)which gradually change and pass
into the the above description for adult form. These latter stages  usually result from  the earlier use of the
juvenile in indoor decoration so that a dual purpose
exists for those who know and find the first.

ELISENA longipetala, large vigorous bulb, in effect and in
form a "White Spiderlily" down over winter, up 2-3' high by
April, blooming May-June, pure white with little or no suggestion of green, 4-7 long-lobed flowers to each sturdy scape, opening in succession:satisfactory in as much as half shade and in a
heavy soil:not commonly seen and may be grown into warm temperate regions with a mulch:set in early fall for first years bloom.

ELYMUS arenarious, "Dune or Sea-lyme Grass" coarse perennial
with a strong, creeping root system, suitable for and much
used in holding drifting sand.   The species   -glaucus,
is a blue-leaved, garden subject with uses in decoration
and arranging:grows 3-5' high, sometimes available.

EMBOTHRIUM coccineum, "Firebush" subject interest....brilliant
color:large shrub or a tree 40' if staked carefully and held,
suckering at the crown when allowed its way:surface-rooting
and wants moisture with drainage in an acid soil with much
humus worked in and as a mulch....little or no fertilizer and
then only organic:prune for use, as of place and to develop
flowering wood:fall planting indicated as best, with a little
shade beneficial the first years. Distinction in coloring of
bloom is outstanding in consideration of this plant, where
certain nuances of the vivid orange-vermilion in a subdued or
late light are exceptionally striking and beautiful. It is hardy
far north into warm temperate regions, with difficulty in propagation and precarious youth doubtless responsible for rarity.

EMILIA(Cacalia)sagittata, "Tasselflower" an annual 15-18" from
the tropics with rather brilliant orange and scarlet or yellow
flowers for a striking show of color in the garden:sow seed where
it is to stand February-April for blooming June onwards:may be
cut at height of flower and dried out as an immortelle.

EMMENANTHE penduliflora, "Whispering Bells" an annual, native to
California, producing many creamy-yellow flowers that are suggestive of lily-of-the-valley for form, better adapted to dry sunny
slopes in the landscape than to gardens:flowers dry on the stem
in way of an everlasting....a desert plant wanting heat.

### BRITTLEBRUSH
ENCELIA---coarse straggling subshrubs for dry, rocky, arid ground
in heat, the plant rough, harsh to feel, always unkempt in appearance, but very practical and useful in waste places of intense
heat and dryness as cover. The brush may be cut to the ground
after bloom to induce a neater showing.
    -californica, "Bush-sunflower" straggling native 3-4' in

height, having large, daisy-like flowers, fresh to the face of
a cliff in April, haggard and spent by August:the broad base
is stout and woody, the branches dry but herb-like, making
much dead wood that is easily kept out:likes and takes exposure along the coast, dwindling inland as it encounters more
extreme heat.
    -farinosa, "Encienso" a low, dome-shaped bush 2-3'over-
all, the stems whitish with the silvery tones spread out over
the foliage at any time, but particularly winter-spring:masses
of golden-yellow flowers after rain a spectacle, diorama of the
desert....reduces in off-season moisture along with silvering.

    DNTDLDA arborescens, "Corkwood" broadly rounding shrub, or tree-
like 20' with large, light green leaves and flattish clusters of the
inch-wide, white daisy-like flowers any time....subject to situation
and culture:adapts to a tub for wide mass and arching line when developed, but foliage is the outstanding asset:coastal subject:rare

    EPIDENDRUM obrienianum, one of the "Ground Orchids", to be grown
in a pot or outside in a warm place in the sun or partial shade in
heat:long stems are weak and flopping, to become almost climbing
with adding, air-rooted growth....either reduce or support:cutting
material midwinter or almost any time when established to its
liking, the bright, coral-red flower long-lasting out of
water....boutonniere:use much leafmould in the soil and as
a mulch:only a few degrees of frost. The species  -coch-
leatum, "Cockleshell Orchid" from the tropics is hardy in
a few degrees of frost, everblooming in warmth as above,
pots and baskets.

    EPIPHYLLUM oxypetalum, "Queen or Orchid-cactus" in the
nature of a cactus, actually one, with woody stems and succulent flange-like leaves with sizable cereus-like flowers of
gorgeous color and rich texture:many hybrids bring out the long
line of coloring from pure white to yellow and all steps through
red, blooming at night, or the flower at least in better condition
then:usually requires some slight support or absolute, out alone;
calling for little care culturally, growing low in the crotch of a
tree or on palms in the leaf-stubs:wants are moisture, a little feeding over summer....nothing in winter, to foster rest:start
with a water-retentive growing medium that holds fertility.

    EPISCIA species, trailing, master basket plants with
attractive foliage of a delightful downiness, bronzy, maybe with hints of blue, edged or with the venation stencil-
ed in a precise pattern of emerald green:forms are close-
cascading, up-lifting or prostrate, a mass cover from which
the normally velvet-textured flowers pear severally or in
single blessedness:want a fibery, porous soil mix, kept
moist but not wet and warmth, but coolness as of shade.
They thrive best in a humid atmosphere as of Southern Florida or a well enclosed California patio and may not be grown
in any frost or even extended cold weather....take indoors or
shelter:use liquid fertilizer freely, but in good dilution.

    ERANTHEMUM nervosum, "Winter-blue" tender shrub 3-4' with
dark, embossed leaves and little phlox-like flowers coming from
behind green bracts that make a tight head:blooming a clear blue
but infrequently rose-colored January-April:requires shade in a
rich, light, fairly moist soil and may be pruned severely after
flowering, or practically cut to the ground to renew:grow this
in the plant house, or tolerates deep shade with good air
drainage out:foliage deteriates in full sun.

    ERCILLA spicata, a woody creeper, or climbing by means of
aerial rootlets, self-clinging on rough walls with a little assistance...northern exposures only:foliage substantial, leather
like, the flowers pale purple in long racemes, the berries dark
purple the way of a pokeberry:prune to control herbage:rare.

283

EREMOCHLOA ophiuroides, "Centipede-grass" for lawns in
dryness, but growing in all soils, sand, muck or drained
clay and in full sun or the least shade....no lime:creeping
runners are most vigorous, an interminable pest in wrong
places:color of turf bluish or yellowish, according to
the soil, its content and reaction:mats close to the
earth and should not be heavily fed unless a power mower
is available....green over winter if moist. This may be
pictured as a finer textured St. Augustine-grass and probably should be limited in use to the Southwest.

*Erica melanthera*

ERICA melanthera, "Blackeyed Heath" erect growth 5-6', nicely
rounded, a twiggy mass of fine, beady to needle-like leaves in
whorls for an exceptional refinement of foliage:set all winter in
a profusion of delicate, urn-shaped, rosy-pink bells, peppered
over-all with the pronounced black spots of the anthers:an effectual shrub in the garden in sun or shade, having no special requirements in soil or of culture....may be pinched in for form
in a pot or used for the winter color indoors. The wider known
species of heath may be grown northerly in these regions, but
south, successfully, only under special conditions that are
impractical to maintain for long.

*Erigeron*

ERIGERON karvinskyanus, "Mexican Daisy" a small stringy perennial
with white daisies that quickly take on tints of pink....shearing
may extend an already long blooming period:rugged and persistent,
rooting and re-rooting to spread solidly over a large area and re-
seeding to just miss being a nuisance:takes drought, heat, frost
and makes a creditable showing in very poor soils:will bloom first
year from seed and eventually makes a loose structure 8-12" thick.

ERIOBOTRYA japonica, "Loquat" an erect round-headed tree 20',
decidedly ornamental, with large, very attractive, rusty-green
leaves, bark of the older tree pleasantly mottled brown:white
flowers November-January are slightly fragrant while closely
bunched, oval or slightly pear-shaped yellow fruits follow by
February, maturing under average conditions with a slightly
acid flavor:wants a heavy loam, takes limestone or a marl
concentrate, hardy under deep frost, but not fruiting well
under more than a few degrees:use budded stock for fruit,
but a seedling may do better for shade and ornament:sub-
ject to both scale and fireblight:seaside. The species
-demissa, is superior for foliage which changes through
a remarkable coppery series in coloring, bright green
to crimson as the leaf fails....a blotch disfigures:spring
flowering (around April), low among last years leaves.

*Eriodictyon*

ERIOCEPHALUS africanus, a finely built shrub 18-24" in
height and spreading, having white-silky, slightly scented beady leaves and tiny starry white flowers, touched
with purple at the mouth, midwinter:withstands second
degree exposure to salt wind, wants sun and good drainage, tender in frost. This is a little grey greasewood, to be
used in somewhat the same way, but treasured in the way of
all miniature things that touch the garden with fine feeling.

ERIODICTYON crassifolium, "Yerba Santa" a straggling
shrub that is native in the south of California, infrequently used to cover dry, exposed soils of extremely poor
quality:handsome, thick-furry, grey-blue leaves are aromatic, in harmony with the one-sided cluster of blue
flowers February-May:fails to close in satisfactorily,
so must be pruned to thicken in summer:blooms longer
near the ocean and the foliage holds its appearance
better there:collect rooted plants for a start and
establish first in a container, sow seed or take root
cuttings in January and set where the plant is to stand.
This is a difficult plant to get started and to maintain,
but is well worth an effort for the native charm and
beauty and unusual interest.

*Eriobotrya*

*Eriocephalis africanus*

COMPENDIUM

### WILD BUCKWHEAT

ERIOGONUM---woody material, sub-shrubs of the Pacific slope,
adapted to hot, dry places, baked out soils in the sun where they
flower through the heat of the year. The foliage is usually grey
to silvery, a felt over green, delicately shaded and the leaves
nicely arranged. This, together with other subtle modulations
in coloring and inter-textured habit of growth, place them
within the ken and appreciation of the arranger. They cut well
when fresh and at the last, when the seasons heat has had its
sway, they may be taken and classed with the immortelles. Some
may be used in the garden in light soils having good drainage and where moisture and fertility does not stimulate a
plant out of all character.

-arborescens, spreading, bushy, 2-3' or more, a good
close mat of green-grey surmounted by broad, flat heads of
rosy pink flowers June-August:grows under salt spray and
should be pinched out early for any form to be had.

-fasciculatum, growing 1-3' high and as wide, or even
prostrate, the work-horse of the group, the leaves almost
needle-like, greenish; the white heads of flowers, carried
closely, turn russet by the end of summer:seed may be sown
on new fills of poor soil with satisfying results....winnow
directly over the ground by beating the cut brush together
late in summer. Be sure seed is matured.

-giganteum, "St. Catherines Lace" is an erect shrub
6-7' with wide, flat, silvery grey leaves and umbrella-like,
lifted, flat heads of creamy or soft pink heads of flowers
all summer. This plant develops an architectural, free aspect
of branching for unique structure, normally....becomes leggy
unless in the wind or pinched back:does well under cultivation.

-nudum, rather more herb-like than above, a perennial with
very dark green, handsome heads and spoon-shaped basal leaves,
and 2' stems, branching to carry the knobby clusters of white
or cream-colored flowers until late summer:rock garden.

-rubescens, low-spreading, good cover, a mat of white-wooly
green, the latter just apparent beneath the rose-colored to red
flowers in distinct, button-like heads:suspends over a low
bank or will prosper in a heat-soaked planter where little
else can be expected to survive.

-tomentosum, "Dog-tongue" perennial, straggling 2-3'
from a woody base, the flowers white to pinkish with many
intermingling bracts:leaves are elliptic, green above and
whitish beneath. This one is native in Florida.

### STORKSBILL

ERODIUM---low herbaceous plants, much on the order of the
wild or specific forms of geranium, of particular value for
hot, dry or sterile places in the sunny border or anywhere in
the rock garden. There they lend mild color under trying situations from early summer on. They are among the longest,
most steadily blooming, hardy plants available in their
class and among the most persistent.

-chamaedryoides, stemless rounding tufts that tend
to flatten out in a dark mat of small scalloped leaves
that are somewhat glossy to back the white, pink-veined
flowers, May-November. This may be used with flagging.

-chrysanthum, a loosely tufted plant 6-8" high with
pale, silvery, very finely cut foliage and chaffy, straw-
colored flowers some time in summer:give this a well drained place, rock garden or dry wall.

-cicutarium, "Alfilaria, Filaree or Pin-clover" entirely different from the others, an annual that is low-spreading or somewhat tufted in covering dry, barren ground over
winter, a bright mantle of green:widely naturalized through
out inhabited arid regions, useful there, but a weed
elsewhere:will seed and can be mowed as a winter
lawn that dries up over summer:fruiting heads can
be a nuisance....but of intense interest.

-corsicum, a little rock plant that

285

*Eriogonum tomentosum*

*Eriogonum fasciculatum*

*Erodium trvinum*

*Erodium chrysanthum*

E. chamaedryoides

makes a mat some 3-4" through, supported by a tap root of
burrowing capacity, going deeply around rock for moisture:
small, roundish leaves are greyish, hugging the ground in
a tight mat, the comparatively large flowers a soft pink.
    -gruinum, an annual with violet-blue flowers to three-
quarters of an inch across in early summer and scattering;
the foliage will carry traces of red, fails quickly and becomes trashy:late sown seed may carry over until the following year, biennially:not important.

    ERVATAMIA coronaria, "Crape-jasmine" an orderly, well
formed, very neat shrub, grown in warmer parts only if
flowers are expected, usually 3-5' high, but as much as
8' in Southern Florida, easily grown there:trim, three-
forked stems carry an open cover of very attractive light,
shining green leaves which blacken in the mere suggestion
of frost....survives when covered:single or double, pure
white flowers may be likened to gardenia, solitary or
in stiff branched clusters, sweet-scented or not:will
twist open full in warmth all summer, or continually far
south, later progressively northerly until they will not
open at all:holds back in California due to night chill so
that first crop buds carry into winter unopened....force on a
warm wall, but not in direct sun:choice for a tub that can be
moved about for suitable warmth.

    ERYTHEA---robust palms, outstanding in their deliberate way of
living, so slow in growth as to tax the patience of the most tolerant gardener. Recompense is the remarkably clear-cut over-all
effect from the clean-ringed 40' rigid trunk to the broad handsome
fans which hold their color unimpaired until they drop....again it
is clean. They are among the most satisfactory of the palms in
the cooler coastal climates, but not so good in hot, interior
parts. It is almost obligatory to fertilize for growth and to
irrigate generously in dry soils, although they are most resistant to drouth. They make no debris that is not quickly
and easily removed, have no petty points of annoyance and
require minimum care culturally. They move readily in large
sizes and are surprisingly hardy in frost.
    -armata, "Blue Palm" very apparent beauty revealed here
in the clean trunk to the compact top of silvery blue fans,
while the feathery-tressed inflorescence, angling 12-18' toward the ground is something one remembers until the next time
it happens, July-September....shows best in the open as a specimen tree:best one to use in heat and is hardy in Texas to
Austin....a remarkably beautiful tree.
    -brandegeei, very slender, with a natty spherical head at
around 100', the smaller fans dark green above, paler beneath to
persist, but peeling loose after a time if allowed to collect in
a natural hang....the thin, appressed boots remain tight against
the stem when the fan is cut green, for a nice pattern following
up the trunk:rare, but not for long if palm admirers could see it.
    -edulis, "Guadalupe Palm" the fans a clear bright green all
the year, the petiole breaking easily to leave a clean trunk:the
round fruits are edible, with a flavor of apricot, of little use.

## CORAL TREE
    ERYTHRINA---summer-flowering herbs, strange thorny shrubs,
or spreading, irregular trees with growth and performance
during the warmth of the year, thin and gnome-like over
winter or bare....but still showing color in some species. They
require a rich soil and constant, if little moisture with drainage to produce the rank herbage and crowded masses of keeled
coral-colored flowers. This flowering will be more
complete if each years wood has been ripened thoroughly for the following seasons bloom....with-hold
moisture and fertilizer as summer advances. They
want warmth, insist on sunlight and like fair air
humidity, but apparently not too much fog, as of

the immediate coastline. There is considerable confusion as
to nomenclature in some of the species which follow.

-bidwilli, a hybrid that may be grown as a kind of
cover, interpolated in high ground cover such as honeysuckle....normally with a stubby trunk up to 5-8' and short
laterals with long, loose spikes of bright crimson flowers:
considered the hardiest in frost.

-corallodendron, always low, 15-20' and with as much
spread, the crimson flowers after the leaves in loose clust-
ers:keel of the flower usually fails to open....tree-like.

-crista-galli, "Cockspurthorn" a wierd-looking shrubby
plant for occasional use in the shrubbery for a flash of color
late summer and autumn:consists of a low woody stub, becoming tree-
like with a fantastic branching that is particularly noticeable,
dormant over winter-spring:throws 5-6' branchlets by summer, which
are spiny and only half woody....drop when blooming is over or
after the leaf-drop;plant is just as well obscured over the
winter period:good moisture for good performance.

-herbacea, "Coralbean" herbaceous, with prickly stems
2-3' long from a thick, heavy root or crown, flowering May-
July....not unlike the poker plant in conformation and in
effect:native to the Gulf Coast regions and may best be
cut to the ground from time to time.

-humeana(caffra, constantina)"Kaffirboom" a tree,
or tree-like to 30' or more, with erect heads of drooping flowers that are a brilliant orange-red, flowering
through as much as eight months of the year, over the
leaf-drop of October into winter and continuing into
spring....leaves out again late spring, or may hold a
few leaves all year. The erratic performance may explain
the plethora of names found here.

-poeppigiana, "Bucare" a tree 35-50' of loose spreading,
angular structure:dark red in close tight clusters over winter
and spring....like redbirds roosting in the nearly leafless
branches:of rapid, rather uncontrolled growth.

ESCALLONIA---strong-growing shrubs of considerable value in
the landscape, used in every day gardening. They are adapted
to open spaces rather more than to the garden and are of special
service in connection with the wind problem and tainted soils of
ocean communities....much used in California. They are freely
flowering, not spectacular and with an unfortunate habit of
holding the dead and drying flower head for a disconcerting
messiness between bloomings. Nor are they always regular in flowering, some being intermittent and not dependable for time,
others just plain erratic. They resent dryness yet may not be
watered too much because of the excessive growth that results
and hard pruning required....may be reduced at any time, best
in between flowerings. Many hybrids appear that are usually
better suited to the garden, leaving the natural forms for the
open landscape. They are not at their best in Florida and the
hardier species may be grown north into warm temperate regions.

-franciscana,random flopping stems or restricted, and streamers led 8-10' on support, good pillar plant with enough correction to keep in line, the deep rosy-pink flowers spring-summer, of
rather dependable timing....an odor of apple a distinguishing
feature:hold to one or only a few stems for vigor;banks.

-glasniviensis, a hybrid, growing 3-5', a trim, rather open
specimen, even sprawling discretely when left on its own:of
considerable refinement, considering its relatives, the pink
flowers being described as appleblossoms, and justly so
for color if not in form:choice but temperamental.

-langleyensis, another hybrid, a general purpose
shrub 10-12' high with erect, not ungraceful stems that
are finally spreading to an umbrageous top, a sturdy plant,
ultimately with stout trunks:light pink flowers and glistening, rather light green foliage beneath at least two bloomings
spring and fall:no discrimination in the matter of soil, but
must have moisture and probably considerable pruning since
it usually finds itself in a spot too small to accomodate.

*E. crista-galli*

*Escallonia organensis*

*Escallonia rubra*

*Escallonia langleyensis*

        -montevidensis, erect shrub or round-headed tree
at 20', a massive dome and heads of pure white flowers
late in winter, again in summer....stand out over the top like
snowballs:very large plant, highly satisfactory, long-lived.
        -organensis, erect, reddish brown stems 8-10', the
spreading branches densely foliated with smooth leaves that
shine, the new growth with the suggestion of color:pink to
rosy red buds open white in broad terminal clusters in the
summer:tender in frost, to become heavy-stemmed, a canopied
shrub....trunks ultimately as much as 6" through at the base.
        -rosea, more bushy and less tree-like in maturity, erect-
spreading 5-6', or more if forced:smaller clusters of attractive rosy flowers:foliage is clammy, sticky to touch, a rough,
dark green, with an odor that is slight but objectionable at
close hand:strong-growing hybrid that is best used away in
the wind seaside, where it is quite resistant to salt.
        -rubra, another closely related hybrid, but much
less vigorous, more contained in growth, amenable to
garden requirements. This is a smaller shrub than above
with red flowers in summer, to be given care for results.

    ESCHSCHOLTZIA californica, "California-poppy" a low tran-
sient of sappy character, with the well-known orange, cupped flowers, now available in creamy whites and fairly well
fixed forms shading into red:treat them as annuals in the gard-
en, in light, rather dry soils....drainage important:cut, they
will last in water if the bud is taken early as it opens.

## AUSTRALIAN GUM
    EUCALYPTUS---trees of character, for good or for evil. Typical-
ly Californian, they stayed, these trees, and now they are every
where in the older plantings; large, huge, of indifferent girth
and height, littering, wide-wasting, but with smaller species,
some merely shrubs. With-al, they find places in the landscape, with suitable kinds for the garden, and while they
have been widely disseminated, they find reality and greater
usefulness in arid lands. This is so marked that every effort
must be made in Florida and other warm-humid places to find
adaptable species....if used at all. Those found best suited
to the California coastline, or those known inhabitants of
wet ground or swamps, will presumably be preferred. Certain
smaller species may be used in the garden, but the larger
ones have no possible place about houses or with other
cultivated plants. This is due to invading, filching roots
and toxic oils that taint both air and soil....above all,
is an almost certain liability for removal and the great expense involved. Large limbs are brittle and split or twist off
in the wind or merely drop with an over-burden of water, usually in early morning. Pinch out soft growth in youth and prune
later to correct structure, heading back occasionally to build
up caliper or thickness for strength. They are littering all
the time, leaf, flower, fruit and deciduous bark. With notable
exceptions each way, they will stand under 10-12 degrees of
frost. They have no pests or complaints....how could they.
        -blackeleyi, a handsome 40' spreading tree to use in damp
and water-logged soils; fine in bud, better still in flower,
the leaves, however, quite large, heavy and with a well defined midrib:rare, but valuable in just the right place.
        -botryoides, "Mahogany G" stately tree for humid lands, 100'
plus, the foliage a good dark green, the deeply furrowed bark per-
sistent:windbreaks and shade, where straying will permit.
        -caesia, slender growth to 20' with only a 10' spread, the
brittle hanging branches carrying brilliant rosy pink flowers July-
October, again January-March or intermittently:silvery grey foliage,
whitish branchlets and mealy-white capsules merge into the
light brown of the heavier wood to serve as decorative material of quality to take indoors....bark of trunk scales
off to show dull red:requires good drainage and resists moderate frost and drought:garden subject of
appeal, a clean tree blooming early in life.

*Eschscholtzia*

*E. crucis*

*Eucalyptus caesia*

*E. erythronema*

*E. lehmanni*

COMPENDIUM

-calophylla, dense, well-formed, umbrageous tree 35',
for shade or street planting along the California coast:the
white, pink or creamy flowers appear in great trusses fall
or spring....winter, warm years:growth comparatively slow and
the corky bark is persistent:wants good moisture, but to go into winter dry....tender.
    -cinerea, "Argyle-apple" decorative, a medium-sized tree,
the light-toned bark marked at the branch base in pale red,
which appears again in the small mealy-white and roundish leaf.
    -cladocalyx, "Sugar G." very slender, single or multiple-
stemmed, the light, mottled trunk standing sharply against a
dark background:erect splayed branches follow sparsely to the
top which is scantily furnished with foliage, but tuft-like
on the grand scale, etched against the sky....the motif in
the artistry of the eucalypt most often pictured:exception-
ally resistant to drought, heat and does in the most impossible soils:tender. A dwarf form is difficult to find.
    -cornuta, "Yate-tree" broadly round-headed at 45', to be
used for shade or, in some cases, for roadside or highway de-
velopment:will stand extreme heat under irrigation or in soils
that may be tapped deeply for water....but best along coasts.
    -crucis, "Silver Mallee" shrubby 10-15', of outstanding
decorative value indoors as well as outside:rotund buds
are red and burst into creamy flowers November-December:
prune frequently for an over-all silvery effect.
    -eremophila "Sand Mallee" shrubby, or a small gar-
den tree with erect slender stems, the foliage holding
pretty well to the ground, dark, the leaf elongated and
thickened:reddish capsules open to white or yellowish flowers
June-September, maybe again in late winter. This will grow in
almost pure sand under drought and some frost:sand dunes.
    -erythrocorys, "Redcap E." a small garden tree with weak
stems 15-20', whitish, with contrasting red branches:brilliant
crimson bud-caps remove to present golden-yellow filaments in a
most remarkable floral display, a catch-the-eye appearance any
time during warmth....remaining bright green cups retain the
color after having been dried out:does in heavy soils that are
well drained and likes lime, but kills out in as much as 10
degrees of frost:pinch out terminals early to promote body in
the stem and additional glorious color.
    -erythronema, "Redthread", generally a nicely form-
ed, rounded, much refined tree at 15', branchy and compact but not dense:clustered, brightly stimulating red
flowers of late-winter-spring, together with the elegance in form and texture, lend unusual distinction:will
survive utter drought in poorest soils and some frost;choice
    -ficifolia, "Flame Eucalypt" substantial round-headed
tree to 45', a warm, brownish, heavy trunk and large, dark,
leathery leaves, extremely showy in bloom:with odd trusses
of flowers at any time, it concentrates usually January and
February, probably again with a lesser display in September-
October....masses all the way through white, pink, rose and
scarlet to the most startling crimson:temperamental, its best
culture calls for coolness and reasonable moisture in a light
fertile soil with drainage....or stands in complete drouth in
adobe when matured. There may be some relation between early
flowering in the individual and a tendency to stunt, so that a
removal of flowers before forming seed may be beneficial....as
long as they may be reasonably reached. In any event, unless
setting out proven colors, more specimens than expected to mature
should be used, thus allowing for removal of stunts and poor color.
This tree develops a very sturdy trunk without help, goes into a multiple-stem easily and is one of best for color along
the shore in high salt wind:very choice, well grown.
    -forrestiana, "Forrest Marlock" shrubby-tree-like
8-10'with over-sized shining leaves for such a small
plant:solitary, long-hanging, quadrangular red buds
open to yellow filaments in flowering:in scale for
the garden, very decorative, pinch in for a showy
specimen:tubs.

E. erythrocorys

E. ficifolia

E. globulus

Eucalyptus forrestiana

-globulus, "Blue G." very large tree in deep moist soils
to 200' or more, the wood especially brittle, dangerous,
dropping of its own weight of water without wind:bark shreds
to litter insufferably while the roots sap out a large area:
light blue buds show in contrast against the dark mass of the
foliage, as do the white flowers November-January....may continue until April:growth very rapid for windbreaks, especially with
water beneath....do not use elsewhere and know that the ultimate problem is eradication of the great buttressed tree:will
not survive for long in shallow, dry soils.   --var. compacta, retains for a considerable time the blue of the
juvenile leaves of the parent, bushy and symmetrically
round at 15-25':low windbreak or screen and a safer
tree for the years.

-grossa, shrubby 6-8' or more, for a moist soil:
large leaves are thick and shining, bright green:red
buds with bronzy shadings open September-December to
the yellow filaments of the flowering.

-lehmanni, "Fingerstall G." much rounded at 25',
the foliage mass normally retained low, used for the
definite form in situations of drouth, heat and shallow
soils:develops bronzy tints in the foliage, the old leaf
turning bright red the second summer....imprinting on the
consciousness, imparting to the tree a delightfull inner
glow through the new leafage:structure of the stem of interest
in  the many-horned seed capsules in cluster, persist and imbed in
the developing wood....curious but not ornamental:tender.

-leucoxylon, "White Ironbark" slender tree 35-50 or 100' in a
fertile deep soil....must be deep, with wind:the white bark will
be smooth generally, but yellowish in certain roughened areas,
deciduous:secondary aspect is that of hanging branches of grey
blue foliage, the flowers white, purplish or rosy in close,
furry clusters November-February:hardy in frost, persistent in
alkali ground, under smog, only reasonably drouth resistant.

-macrocarpa "Desert Mallee" a heavy-stemmed, sprawling
shrub or may be trained into a gangling tree of character 15',
the mealy-white leaves thick and rigid in ranks along the newer
wood:a spectacle in bloom, the 3" flowers scarlet to crimson,
but only striking and not particularly handsome:takes heat
and drought and must have perfect drainage....no heavy
or wet soils nor a well kept garden.

-maculata, "Spotted G." rapid growth 60-100', the
bark deciduous in large spotty patches:leaves are long,
to 12" at times and narrow, the inconsequential flowers
in summer:a general purpose tree for average requirements.   --var. citriodora, "Lemon G." exceptionally
ornamental, an attractive tree 75' with the deciduous
bark peeling clean, the new layer smooth, white with
a suggestion of green showing through from beneath, a
polished appearance....striking accent with contrast
in trunk and slender, up-raised limbs:light green,
lemon-scented leaves are revigorating to smell, flowers
white, sometime July-October:takes but little frost, not
any when young, loses symmetry by breakage in the wind:is
generally used in the more respectable places for the refinement....but litters the bark as long as six weeks. It
is most picturesque as the top shows against the sky.

-nutans, "Nodding G."  may be 6-15' high, bush or a
small, irregular tree, either one most colorful in bloom,
the crimson filament of the flowers tipped with white anthers, October-November:roundish leaves are greyish, with
clear glandular dots having a transparency, distinguished.

-polyanthemos, "Australian-beech" open-headed tree
100', usually much less, the handsome, round, grey-blue
leaves of the early years tending to become more narrow
and green:bark persistent and the white flowers of January-
March are tiny in bud, frothy and cloudy as they break open
and an inversion as they fail and droop:hardy in as much
as 15 degrees of frost and very resistant to drought. An

290

E.
leucoxy

E. polyanthemor

E. preissiana

E. pulver-
ulenta

irregular habit of growth suggests early attention to
pruning with structure in mind and the placement of the
crotches for strength in the wind.

-preissiana, "Bellfruit Mallee" stout shrub, straggling and struggling to make a loose mound 10' high and as
much and more across....do not attempt a tree form out
of this:blooms August-December-February, large flowers
in rippling shaggy masses of rather striking greenish
yellow:persistent and forming low in ocean winds.

-pulverulenta, "Silver Mountain G." a scrawny, gangling, twisting tree or expanding shrub as cut back for the
foliage....mealy-blue or silvery, the rounding leaves in
pairs clasping the stem:chief value and use is for material
in decoration....moist soils for quantity, but dry at time
of cutting for heightened silvered aspect. This is a pinched and spindling tree, poor or picturesque, as guided and
developed by the inevitable heavy cutting.

-pyriformis, a slender rigid tree 15', marked by the
drooping branchlets and clustered crimson or golden flowers:
leaves leathery and thick through:use is in the garden for a
specimen accent in a dryish spot:tender in frost.

-robusta, "Swamp-mahogany" an old species in use that
still finds a place in planting, proven for Florida:growing 50'
or more, it is rugged and full of character, with well-wearing,
leathery leaves for wind, and dark brown, persistent bark, deeply
furrowed:brittle in the wind and untidy, it is rapid in growth in
wet places, low or swampy ground:takes alkali, but not much dryness, adapting in some measure....no point in this with so many
drought resisting species.

-rostrata(camaldulensis)"Red G." handsome tree of regular,
symmetrical growth to as much as 200' in deep soils, to be used
in high heat, drought, heavy soils, frost and alkali of considerable concentration. This is a great, handsome tree, but
must be used with discretion and some grasp of implications
for the future involved.

-rudis, "Desert G." for high heat and deep cold, a 75'
tree that will be well used where the thermometer gyrates suddenly and to extremes:slender controlled growth with a pleasant
drooping quality of the lower branching:windbreaks or street
plantings, especially where it finds a little moisture below.

-sepulcralis, a "Weeping G." and a variable specifically,
usually slender erect 35' with hanging, plum-colored branches
and pale green or white flowers in small clusters during fall
or winter:possibly less littering than most and frost hardy.

-sideroxylon rosea, "Red Ironbark" very slender erect,
then spreading, open-headed at 50' with a slendid crop of
rosy pink flowers midwinter onwards into spring:the tight
bark breaks open to show fissures steeped in blood-red or
coral, sooty over-all. This is one of the best of the larger
eucalypts to plant near habitations, clean, decorative, deserving of wider use, hardy in considerable frost. The type
form, with pale grey bark is as satisfying as the more
florid variety above, and much quieter.

-stricklandi, growing 20-40' in rather uncertain height,
of rapid but sturdy growth and consolidation for generally
adverse conditions:leaves are thick and durable, the masses
of flowers held close, greenish or yellowish....nondescript
creation, but somewhat scented December-January:streets.

-tereticornis, "Grey G." the pale grey bark unusually
smooth after scaling off, a large tree of quite rapid growth
to 150', essentially for unfavorable conditions of soil and
climate, one of the best of the larger gums in maturity,
but difficult to handle the early years in making a tree
in the ordinary mold....stake and prune to correct.

-torquata, "Goldfield G." highly ornamental, with
slender reddish stems 12-15', of fairly rapid growth,
shapely, the foliage of a greyish cast:comes into flower
at from two to three years, or possibly in bloom in the
container when set out:distinctive buds, bronzy to

291

E. stricklandi

E. sepulcralis

E. pyriformis

E. torquata

bright vermilion,spot the open head for weeks, then open
to rosy tints any time October-June or continually:resists
drought and dwarfs easily and long to a tub:choice.
     -viminalis, "Manna or Ribbon G." from the long-shredding
bark that collects and hangs interminably in a crotch....more
acceptable as litter beneath where it can be gathered for re-
moval:a very large tree that may be expected to do 300' in a
good bottomland soil:leaves are quite narrow on hanging branchlets, the flowering an indifferent white at any time or all
the time. This is for heat and cold and the higher altitudes
in a place where it may stand forever....be careful.....be
careful with all of them and be happy.

     EUCHARIS grandiflora, "Amazon-lily" tropical bulbs for the
lower Gulf Coast and Southern Florida, California only when
supplied with night warmth....wanting besides, fertility,
humidity and protection from summer sun at its height:the
fragrant, pure white sparkling flowers with the texture
of fine-grained alabaster, have the appearance of the
short-trumpet daffodil and succeed through warmth and
moisture primarily:bloom may be expected only of plants
that are established and have had a minimum of recent disturbance at the root....best in a pot or tub. Such a select
item is bound to require a special culture and the challenge
is largely in adapting available knowledge to locale. Set them
any time, and better crowded in a coarse fibrous medium soil
with drainage, the low neck just showing:bring along in partial
shade, but shift into more sun for blooming....return to shade,
with-holding water to force a short period of dormancy, when the
leaves should hold if handling is correct:repeat by starting water
and fertilizer....repeat from time to time for flowering.  It is
a matter of jerking this plant into bloom, it would seem, with
something of patience, but more of belligerency.

     EUCOMIS undulata, "Pineapple-lily" bulbous, the large furl-
ed, dark and dull leaves from a rosette, clasp and hold the
tight-cylindrical, spike-like raceme of liliaceous flowers,
crowned with a tuft of small leafy bracts July-August....the
following seed capsules embed in a mass of leafy bracts. This
is distinctive in bloom, the white flowers turning through a
chartreuse to dark green with purple button....light up like
a torch in a lowering light:wants moisture, but must be allowed to dry out reasonably when dormant:sagging of the flowering
scape will be first from too much shade and second from drouth,
when sun, or at least more light will bring it erect again:it
wants a rich, gritty loam and is easy to handle in sun to less
than half shade:set shallow, in late fall, but deeper to 6"
as grown northerly in frost....solidly joined bulbs may be
cut apart with a knife:pots, or in the garden.

     EUGENIA---well-known and attractive shrubs and trees of
a soft, refined nature that suggests and requires protection from wind and frost. They are notable for the generous
fruiting, both from an ornamental approach and that of the
culinary art....can in fact be a nuisance and should be
kept clear of surfaces that stain. The foliage in all these
plants probably carry the major aesthetic burden, either in
distinction of leaf or texture of mass. A combination of shallow rooting and large moisture requirement indicate the
heavier soils, where the necessary water can be provided
and held. Do not grow them too lush because of the over
production of litter and pests. They are subject to scale.
     -edulis(Myrciaria) slender willowy shrub or small
limber-limbed tree, the greyish foliage downy with a
fine rusty pubescence:fruit orange to yellow, comparatively large, edible but of little value, the tree of
more value ornamentally for the contrasting grey that
is not often found in plants for moist places. This is
not exactly rare, but is too seldom found in the trade.

292

-jambos, "Rose-apple" a small, spreading, open-headed
tree to 25 ', less under hardship, the limbs and branches
supple, whip-like:fruit orange to yellow, comparatively large
and fragrant, eaten out of hand or used in jams or confec-
tions:flowers very large, greenish to white massed filaments;
the large narrow and blunt-pointed leaves stand out and will
have difficulty submerging as foliage; most handsome as taken
indoors under an artificial light.

-paniculata(hookeri)an erect slender tree 35', the patchy,
more durable foliage masses opening to reveal the slim verticals
of the stems:heavy bunches of dark purple to magenta fruit are
stripped before their time in the wind:light green leaves are
shining, with coppery undertones. --var. myrtifolia, the
"Brush-cherry", wide-columnar, a tree 50', the glossy, rich
green leaves with strong traces of red in the new growth,
very sensitive to wind carrying salt....sears in the most ordinary blows, dropping entirely in drouth, renewing in moisture:
submits to any amount of shearing in shaping the tree or as
a hedge:so universally used under the shears, few gardens
know the beauty of the full columnar form as a tree:fails
to fruit in florida:do not force, account of pests.

-smithi, "Lilli-pilli-tree" an erect shrub or narrow-
columnar tree 20' with bronzy green, leathery leaves that will
shine and an unusual shade of pale lavender berries:has uses in
the garden that are being overlooked while the strings of fruit
are particularly favored for decoration and arrangements:does
best in a little thrown shade and with a little peat or leafmould worked into the soil:lacks vigor unless well supplied,
and will be found somewhat tender in frost.

-supraaxillaris, an escape in the south of Florida and
probably the best one in adversity....wind, poor soil and
dryness:shrubby or a tree 25' with very large dark leaves
that are pale beneath....turn over in the wind for a show,
good in developing lively masses of foliage.

-uniflora, "Surinum-cherry" normally a shrub, 6-8',
wide-spreading with light, faintly coppery green foliage
of good winter color in reds and dull purple....always
attractive and presentable in good thrift:may be pruned
and stands long in a tub where the deeply ribbed, glistening crimson fruits are unique as a display, spicy in flav-
or, eaten out of hand or used in cookery....deserts, salads,
pies, puddings, as a juice or relish combined with celery and
orange:bears after four or five years, with a long yearly
season:good hedge, but should be knife-cut, not sheared and in
this instance, fragrance is the only area of competition between
white flower and red berry:better in a moist climate, as of Florida
and the Gulf Coast:choice and useful item anywhere in these regions.

EUONYMUS japonicus, substantial arching shrub 5-8', or may
be pushed to 15':thick, leathery leaves adapt to extremes in
heat, frost, smog or exposure on the ocean....and with fertility and some care, develops a soft, dulcet tone-quality
that might be described as timbre along with this toughness:
established plants will bear brilliant crimson berries when
unpruned, but the plant will be more often found shaped for a
tub or sheared as a hedge. Coming as it does, in dull tones of
somber green, the varieties are bright and cheerful as follows.
--var. albo-marginatus, the leaves with a narrow margin of white,
becoming silvery, the stems rather more stiff upright, moderately slow in growth.   --var. erecta, somewhat as the type, but
more erect-dense, the foliage a brighter green, a strong point
in the shrubbery.   --var. aureo-marginatus, the leaves a gold-
en yellow at the center, an irregular pattern laid against the
dull, dark green of the margin.   --var microphyllus, dwarf, a
compact and substantial massing of slender erect stems 12-15",
the foliage a bright, shining green, with depths in
tone, soft, too lush in good thrift when it is subject to scale and mildew:low hedge and worthy garden
plant, but not in shade unless grown very dry.

293

EUPATORIUM sordidum, weak-stemmed bush 3-5',
sprawling, the stems and large leaves covered with
a dense reddish hair or scurf:a giant ageratum in
flower, with an illusive fragrance  that is gently
penetrating, haunting; the reddish purple heads 4"
across, densely packed with both closed and open
florets over March-May....red, budding head colorfull most of the winter:moisture the main determining
factor in growth, with mealybug a serious pest.

## SPURGE

EUPHORBIA---bizarre, fantastic, but matter of fact in the
garden and sometimes useful in the landscape, these shrub-like
plants are of a large, diverse group, many of them succulent,
others woody or herbaceous in character. All will have the milky
sap and colorful bracts that are so conspicuous in some species
and so highly colored as to function in place of the flower
for display. They come from far-flung parts of the world
and thrive under varying conditions of  soil and moisture.
They are all tender in frost and generally want moisture
during growth if they are to hold the foliage.

-grandicornis, a striking plant, either shrubby or tree-
like, the pale green, oddly formed stems set with large
brown spines or thorns:curiosity even in a cactus planting,
to be used to center the attention.

-heterophylla, "Mexican Fire-plant" an annual shrubby
plant of herbaceous nature with weak stems 18-24", the
dark leaves marked with brilliant scarlet, usually at
the stem end, but not determinant in pattern or degree
of coloring:pinch out early for low color in mass:no
rich soils in interest of high color:reseeds.

-lathyrus, "Caper S." "Mole-plant" a trim, sleek,
well-groomed plant with exactly ordered, well mannered
leaves in four lines of the erect stem, seemingly waiting
for an order....parade rest or other:said to be so objectionable to burrowing rodents as to keep a vicinity clear:the
white markings set the leaves up for rather a handsome plant
that is not obtrusive as tucked away for service.

-marginata, "Ghostweed" an annual for bedding in poor soils,
dry or moist, the leaves entirely white, mottled or only edged:sow
seed thickly April-May, effective July-October and later....keep this
pinched in for a compact functioning mass:indoor decoration or may be
prepared and used effectively in dry boquets.

-neriifolia, shrubby or tree-like, a large succulent grown as
an oddity or as a hedge in connection with cactus or other
succulents:leaves are out only in winter, this function
being carried on through the balance of the year by
green corrugated stems:irrigate only when in leaf.

-pulcherrima, "Poinsettia" the shrubby, widely
branching manufactory for the popular Christmas decoration, better grown with the cutflowers or behind
lower shrubs, as used in the landscape:the great flat
cluster of crimson bracts terminate the brittle stems
November-January, so that a hard pruning in March will
increase the set of bearing wood for the following
year and almost any culture will bring the crop along.
Best practice seems to be good moisture through the summer,
with-holding toward the end so that they go into winter dry. Feed
only to keep the plant steady....potassium high for color:reduce
entire stems for size in the head, but tip the terminals at intervals of about two months for a good mass of foliage and resulting smaller heads....latter treatment, without spring cutback
develops a striking landscape subject for color in place
and in only a few years:set cuttings for new stock at
time of heavy cut, March-April, where they are to
stand, leaving them exposed to the air a day or two
to set sap....water very sparingly until rooted:when
harvesting crop, immediately thrust bleeding end into
moist earth to stop flow, sear later in flame, boiling
water or melted wax:full doubles and yellows available.

294

-splendens, "Crown of Thorns" a low-sprawling or climbing shrubby plant with woody arched stems and cruel, sharply pointed thorns:blooms profusely late in the year and scattering out into summer, or at any time in warmth; the peculiar flower is two-parted, as of bracts, a soft, light red on slender, stiff little stalks:used in a pot, over a low bank, any place out of the way. This is protective on a small scale and without enough body to give warning against the thorns.

-tirucalli, "Milkbush" a large, bulky plant with good mass in the cylindrical stems and green, pencil-like branchlets or joints, all from a thick, woody trunk:a strong spot in the open landscape or good body and background for the succulent collection, tips reddish over winter for the only color the plant has to offer:grows in any soil, irrigated or not, requiring no attention whatever, keeping well within bounds without cutting....well mannered, civil, restrained.

-truncata, low, sod-forming, spineless, flat-cushioned masses, adapting to dry country life:tiny berry-like bodies of note, myriad and unending when growing in thrift that spread out to fill in between rocks, or may be used for covering a restricted flat area in the sun:sharp drainage and proper exposure seem to be controlling factors.

EURYA---very select, nicely foliated shrubs, generally three to seven feet in height, erect, well defined as to line, to be used occasionally in partially shaded places in soil that is always uniformly moist, drained and high in humus for the slightly acid reaction. They are grown first for the handsome, clearly defined leaves as foliage and last for the very ordinary flowers which have some little fragrance with which to pay their way. The long-lasting berries are of more consequence, but will depend on male-female principle of plants together, for a set. There are no serious pests or diseases, but alkalinity in water or soil will inhibit noticeably. They are cold-hardy.

-emarginata, the small leaves thick and leathery, notched at the tip, primly spaced flat-wise along regular, precisely set, lateral branchings in a fan-like arrangement....effective in silhouette against a white wall. This will sicken in more than a trace of alkali and take a long time in decline before it finally dies.

-japonica, may be grown as high as 20', tree-like, of the woodland fringe character, the thickened glossy leaves toothed and having a red mid-rib:greenish white flowers are of some fragrance and red berries appear by late summer or autumn: many variety forms may be grown in containers, being mottled or blotched, adapting to dryness in moderation:hardy in frost.

-ochnacea(Cleyera)with pale, glossy leaves, reddish at first, the color finally retained along the mid-rib:creamy-white flowers are more attractive than above and with some fragrance June-July, while red berries may last out the entire winter; not as hardy as the others above and wants a degree of shade, depending on humidity of the atmosphere.

EURYOPS---shrubby plants, with large, yellow, daisy-like flowers on long stems all fall and into winter, frequently on into the following spring...good for cutting. The leaves are very finely cut into thread-like segments that fail to make much of a show and become very scant low on the stem. They should be cut back after flowering, retaining only a few of the leaves along the stems; and in any event, the summer is definitely off-season for an appearance. They want full sun and drainage with good run-off for heavy precipitation, better dryish over summer. They are short-lived and succumb in frost.

-athanasiae, slender, erect stems 3-4' in height with very large, clear yellow flowers.

-pectinatus, more compact than above, growing only 2-3' high, the smaller flowers on the golden side:silvered over-all by a soft white pubescence.

295

EXACUM affine, herbaceous bedding material, or the little
plant sometimes used in a low pot that complements the select color of the bloom, compact growing without pinching in,
with small five-pointed, soft blue flowers that are touched
at the center with yellow May-July:blooms within six weeks of
spring-sown seed, or lay in flats in September or February for
plants to set out about April:grows 12-15" high in cool places
with at least half shade, and in well prepared soil.

## F

FABIANA imbricata, "Chile-heath" a spreading shrub 3-5' with long-
tubular flowers March-June, set thickly and at random along the stem
of fine heathery foliage....the flower whitish and never pure:this
resents extremes in soil, exposure or micro-climate and requires
attention to form in pruning:grown in California in a little overhead shade in heat, but in full sun in coolness....substitute
there for species of erica:drainage important.

FALLUGIA paradoxa, "Apache Plume" a rare shrub in culture, having slender, divergent stems in a spreading structure 2-3' over
all, a tangled, twisting mass in time, but with points of some
quality:small white flowers April-May like a wild rose, to be
followed by a tawny, long-tailed fruiting appendage of considerable interest, overlapping the bloom and later, greenish, then pale pink, deepening:warm exposures in the sun in
sandy or gravelly, dryish sterile soils....likes lime. This
is native in The Southwest, a dry country plant that will take
some water and has a future in the landscape when better known.

FATSIA japonica(sieboldi)half-woody shrub of character and tropical aspect, bold in appearance, the several naked stems weak and
gangling, topped by the large, palm-like, deeply lobed leaves in
the making of a canopy....low and bushy at first and kept so
for awhile by pinching out the terminals:foliage lustrous in
deep shade, a light green that yellows out in sun:flowers are
white in winter, the structure of the pyramidal inflorescence
of more note than the color....berries a good blue:will want a
little shade and takes some salt wind, generally rugged and well
able to compete:one of the most common of the tropical accents,
but hardy in frost far north:prefers a fertile, sandy soil.

FATSHEDERA lizei, high-climbing in the likeness of English ivy,
but with the larger leaves of Fatsia, a strong-growing cross between the two genera, dark against walls, or into trees, trying
to climb jokingly with the rudimentary aerial rootlets:a rugged
plant under most conditions of soil, exposure and wear.....new
growth tender, subject to aphis and damage in wind:cut hard to
keep in hand....first promise dimming out in a lack-luster of
disappointment:so much better while young....cut hard from
time to time in renewal of wood.

FEIJOA sellowiana, "Pineapple Guava" an open-growing shrub
6-8' with high ornamental character, but grown almost more
for the fruit:leaves glossy-green above, chalk-silvery beneath, the contrast most apparent in the wind although the
leaf is held rather rigidly:flowers most attractive spring
and summer, an ensemble in crimson and white, a full button
of stiff filaments....and basic petals that are used in
making tea:better satisfied in the dry air of the Southwest
and in California than in the more humid areas for fruiting,
but does not like the extreme heat:grows in any good garden
soil and will not object to a little lime or marl as it
may occur:stands in as much as 15 degrees of frost.

COMPENDIUM

## CHINA MARGUERITE

FELICIA---low herbaceous plants, eventually with a semi-
woody base, rather rank-growing in too much moisture and
not at all happy there. They are sensitive to cold weather and
will look badly over winter and in the shade. The plant may
be sheared back in the fall or removed altogether, starting
again in the spring, or foster the growth of seedlings that
will be found. These plants develop rapidly with warmweather
and take over good space before summer:drier soils always.

   -amelloides, "Blue-marguerite" a spreading herbaceous mass
of rough, glandular leaves built close to the ground, the daisies
light blue and gold held high above on slender dry stems, normally
heaviest spring-summer, but almost at any time of the year depending
on conditions:the recurved rays open more fully in sun warmth, are
waxy with the lustre of enamel or painted china.

   -bergeriana, "Kingfisher Daisy" an annual for spring-
summer, a transient little thing only 8" high or even less,
with many solitary daisies, ultra-indigo of exceeding purity
held high for the sun....closing, almost under a cloud, the tiny
narrow rays curling back into a tight crown-like roll:sow seed
early for a delight, repeating again and again....finally
finding its own nook, establishing there to reseed and return of its own each spring:rock gardens.

   -petiolata, "Pink-marguerite" trailing, prostrate, an
interlacing, flattened mat of soft green, lower, rosy pink
daisies:use over a bank in the garden, in a basket or box
or as bedding, sheared. This is more in the nature of the
typical perennial and may be grown far north into warm
temperate regions:choice cover.

   -echinata, shrubby, a rounding mound 15-18", building
up from spreading, semi-woody branches, blooming spring-sum-
mer-fall:value is form and more permanence, but with the color
leaving something to be desired....purplish, in heads to 2"
across:clearer strains may be produced by selection, and cutting grown for dissemination:hardy in frost.

   -tenella, "Basket-marguerite" narrow leaves to a sprawling
mass of brittle erect stems for something of form:flowers a pale
blue of purity in flurries over summer....shear when it begins
to hesitate in blooming....will repeat:master plant for a pot
or basket in the sun or a border plant:tends to short life and
blooms itself out in year or two....early spring cuttings will
take over and flower same season.

## FESCUE

FESTUCA---annual or perennial lawn and ornamental grasses,
those used for turf normally included in a general mix for
sowing under special conditions such as for drought and soil
or shade, with high cutting beneficial and over-irrigation
detrimental. The leaves are tough and bristly to provide
extra good wearing quality.

   -glauca, "Blue F." a fine-leaved ornamental tuft grass
that ultimately pulls together in a solid thick turf,used
in the garden as a border plant or for an edging....occasion-
al clipping desirable:grows 6-10" in height, the type being
green, but ordinarily seen in the blue form:will not survive
in a wet, undrained place and will be increased by division.

   -elatior(pratensis)"Meadow F." very coarse, a grass
for exposed lawns that are to get but little attention,
or places where clipping is a chance and adventure:in-
cluded in a lawn mix for excessive wear....roots bur-
row in thoroughly to hold soils in a run-off over a
slope or steeper ground that must be held against
wind or water.

   -rubra,"Red F." creeping, traveling far underground, rooting at the joints or nodes:withstands
drought and considerable shading, making a very good
turf with close mowing....poor acid soils should be
limed. Chewings Fescue is a finer leaved form of this
that grows in tufts instead of running:sow plentifully.

FICUS---tough woody plants, mostly trees with thick, rubbery, leathery leaves, coarse and gross in every way, sapping the soil, ever demanding and taking their share and more of the best the garden has to give. There they are desirably conspicuous by absence, yet do find places and uses where a blunt sensitivity and hardened character may serve. They prosper in any soil any place from the poorest and most dry to brackish muck of sorts, when drained out....smaller leaved species take saline winds in better shape. The foliage thins out under drought to a semi-naked condition and they may suffer in attack of thrips. They seldom require deep pruning. Use them advisedly and well and they are a source of some satisfaction....otherwise a prime garden irritant.

-benjamina, "Weeping-laurel" spreading, a dense top of comparatively small leaves, while drooping branches bestow some grace to a tree that stays within reasonable bounds, one that may be set in turf, although small red figs, the fruit, drop there as a fine litter:best of the smaller rubber trees in drought:frost-tender.

-carica, the domestic "Fig" an edible fruit of commerce, deciduous tree of 20' height, essentially of the door yard:chief ornamental exhibit a showing of the massive bare limbs, ash-white and most picturesque for shape, accent over winter:fruits well in poor soils and in loamy gravel, with light irrigation up to crop maturity, very little afterward....does not crop well in poorly drained ground and less well in a humid atmosphere:the very large, handsome leaves of great lobes were useful in the long past of the human race, serve now as over-head cover for the heat of summer:set high above a water table in Florida.

-elastica, "Rubber Plant" large tree as used in tropical countries for shade, reserved here for tubs to be used indoors or as a pot plant for special decorative purposes:the rosy leaf-sheath is an added attraction, with newer forms and varieties available as desired:tender in frost.

-lyrata(pandurata)"Fiddle-leaf Fig" with very large, rumpled and leathery leaves shaped in the likeness of a violin, the plant grown indoors or outside, first in a tub, ultimately in the ground, where it will do 25', one or more slender stems from a low trunk....a garden tree, if you will, of unusual interest and appearance:is of more appreciation of desirable soil and location and likes a mulch against hot sun:round-headed shade tree in Florida, but in California, grown only southerly along the coast.

-macrophylla, "Moretonbay Fig" tall and extremely widespreading, a tree for shade over bare ground or surfacing material such as gravel where the massive trunk abutments can push out and where the roots themselves may work out of the soil as they will....never in lawn or solidly covered areas:takes moisture or none, frost and exposure seaside.

-pumila, "Climbing Fig" robust vine, making much wood and supplying dense cover, tight-fitting for masonry:fairly rapid in growth from a very slow start, holding in heat and wind and drouth:to space closely is in error since one plant will cover the side of a building of considerable size, and of all the several plants in the garden, this is the most predatory....best use probably as a kind of ground cover or to be set at the base of a cliff or great rock.   --var. minima, the above in miniature and easily mistaken for it in the juvenile form, to be used in smaller areas, base of a large sun dial or a wall where it will retain the early refinement....if the true dwarf is procured:cool exposures only.

-religiosa, "Bo or Sacred Tree of India" small tree of very slow growth in California, not dependable there, more rapid in Florida where it becomes of a size suitable for shade, specimen or street plantings:the dark poplar-like leaves are smooth and slick, with a long-drawn appendage, tail-like....rustle in the wind:no aerial roots.

-retusa, "Indian-laurel" dense, round-headed, 40' with small leaves, shining and dark, contrast for the small yellow figs of summer....litter. This is a small rubber, but still out of scale for residential work, ideal in mass for large formal work:consider placement carefully.

298

COMPENDIUM

FIRMIANA simplex(Sterculia platanifolia)"Phoenix-
tree", known also as "Parasol-tree" from the broad
top in age, and also as "Varnish-tree" from the wet
drenching of brownish fluid the opening pods afford
the unwary:erect-spreading 40' for streets, in lawns,
for shade, with unimpressive cream-colored flowers in
early summer:bark notable....a smooth, greyish green
that extends into the twig structure:complicated pod-like
fruits with attached pea-like seeds are taken dry and open,
tinted for decoration:tree moves in larger sizes and is hardy
well into warm temperate regions.

FOENICULUM vulgare, Fennel" is somewhat ornamental as a light
filler, cultivated as an annual for the yellow summer flowers:
sow successively for the young thread-like leaves which can be
used for soups or in place of spinach....seeds in dressings
for fish:best grown in out of the way places due to escap-
ing seedlings, or covers waste ground efficiently.

FORTUNELLA japonica, "Kumquat" , small, very handsome
as a tree 6-8' with round edible fruits....tiny oranges
in miniature:naturally dense in growth and foliage, it has
the general culture of citrus:hardier, however and more ver-
satile all-round, standing in the ground, but very generally used in a tub because of size and adaptability:bears the
fruit very early in life, more freely in heat. The species
--margarita, with longer and more narrow leaves, has oval
fruits, is more vigorous to 10-12', used in the garden.

FOUQUIERIA splendens, "Ocotillo" large, most unusual
shrub from western deserts, adapting in dry subtropical
areas:erect, rigid, beautifully wrought canes, normally 10'
in height, set thickly with hooked spines:brilliant scarlet, tip-
set flowers in irregular clusters in late winter....spectacular
then, leafless and with only the moulded stems the balance of the
year:being unlawful to dig plants from the wild, place a portion
of cane in pure sand and keep wet, when leaves shortly appear,
followed by rudimentary roots....with-hold water then and allow
to go dormant before transplanting:succeeds permanently only in
high heat, used there as a living, hedge-like, armed fence.

FRAGARIA chiloensis, "Strawberry" low perennial herb, increasing
rapidly to mat proportions by means of runners:used as a lawn substitute or other cover, the dark, glossy foliage backing countless
white flowers:requires little attention other than irrigation as
found necessary:set in October or in March, using vigorous young
plants and feeding immediately with a balanced fertilizer:cut back
late in winter or early spring with the base plate of the mower
set high, remembering that a very thick mat discourages flowers
and fruiting....if such is desired:dunes northerly, salt dunes any
where. The species  -californica, "Wood S." is smaller in all the
parts, the foliage paler, to be grown in more shade.

FRANCOA ramosa, "Snow Wreath" a sturdy, tufted perennial 18-24"
for half shade or more in moist, sandy, neutral to acid ground
where it will spread out into a sizable colony:slender flowering
stems rise from the tumbled rosettes of undulating, pallid leaves
to bear narrow spikes of white flowers held 3-4' high May-July for
excellent cutting:will not succeed in heat, with thrips the controlling factor in its culture....control with spring spray.

FRANKENIA capitata laevis, "Sea-heath" adapts to
dryness when deeply rooted, wanting moisture or wet
ground, a cover, creeping far, a flat rooting mat of
fine wiry stems:small, rosy pink flowers June-September
fleck the fine coverlet, then coalesce....colorful and
delicate patches against the beady, blue-green of the
foliage:grows in the shade, but flowers satisfactorily
only in the sun, good cover against the sea:very choice
and rare, but not for long....surely.
299

## ASH

FRAXINUS---deciduous trees of open structure and rounding
outline, generally of rather light foliage, compound leaves that
drop so easily in dryness or frost. There are variants, however,
that tend to be evergreen, or that are such under certain cultures
and exposures. They want a deep fertile soil with moisture beneath,
as found in bottomlands or northerly....a north slope with sub-drain-
age down from above. Pruning with these trees is very important, especially as the young specimen spreads out above head-room.

-dipetala, "Foothill A." slender erect 15' or to 35' under the
most favorable circumstances of culture or in nature, otherwise in
the form of a bush 8-10' or less, dropping leaves in the heat of the
season, or can be held over practically evergreen with deep irrigation and in coolness:spring flowers with the new leaves in a kind
of spring-break effect that is refreshing, splendid for these
regions of eternal summer....two large creamy-white, fluttering
petals:must have a cool, protected spot for results, north exposure or an over-hang as of tall trees, a soil of good humus and
to be kept cool with a mulch....leafmould:rare in nurseries.

-uhdei, "Shamel A." an evergreen form of very rapid growth
to use under both extremes of heat and cold:foliage a deep dark
green above a smoothed trunk of grey:young trees are subject to some
spider damage and tend to branch low....whip to a stem and head the
plant at 8-10' or wherever desired:prune for strength in the wind.

-velutina "Arizona A." open-headed and very graceful, 50' or
more, pyramidal when young, but soon going into a high umbrageous
form with drooping branches in maturity:appreciates a deep fertile
soil, but grows most anywhere, poor ground in heat, in alkali, with
salt in the air, just so long as sufficient moisture is available:
native in the Southwest, to be seen generously shading the streets
of Phoenix and elsewhere in Arizona and all through the great valley in California.    --var. coriacea, "Montebello A." has leathery
leaves that are much roughened, while    --var. glabra, "Modesto A."
has smooth leaves, both being refinements of the type.

FREESIA refracta, popular little bulbs for late winter and
spring, very prolific of foliage in season, of flowers that are
super-scented and of the bulblets that will be thinned out as
required:superior cutflowers in the original yellow and with
pink, lilac, rose and purple in hybrids, the latter not as
sweetly scented:move September-October, remembering the larger corms will bloom first....cool soil and not very much
moisture. These are prime garden escapes, scattering every
where, flotsam and jetsam of the garden, amiable estrays
that may be held somewhat in hand by removing seed.

## FLANNELBUSH

FREMONTIA---native in California, tree-like shrubs from
10-12 to 20' high, glorious March-June, the large, flat-
cupped yellow or orange and gold flowers with the bronzy brown back,
stunning in a full blooming. Excessive moisture, or any water during
summer dormancy is the important "do not" point to remember as
well as drainage, full sun and heat....hillsides with the maximum of all these, best insurance for these regal plants. Individuals seem to vary as to water tolerance out of season, while
alkali, as in irrigation water is abhorrent, if not ruinous.
They are short-lived in gardens, uproot in wind, wet seasons,
but come on rapidly as young plants, or even from fall-sown
seed. Fall planting best in order not to require excessive
irrigation next summer....large problem is a studied weaning of new plant from water:wood reduction in late summer
helpful. The flower keeps several days when cut, at least
one bud opening pale yellow-green with a green veining
to go with the mahogany of the withering flower:watch scale.

-californica, more spreading in growth, with clear yellow flowers in early spring:the hardier in frost.

-mexicana,more erect, with larger leaves and flowers,
tawny orange, later spring scattering into summer:more
rapid in growth and is probably on the whole, the better
plant to grow under domestication.

300

COMPENDIUM

FUCHSIA---climbing shrubs, pliable, tractable in the hands of
the gardener, mostly requiring support, usually of a soft, succulent or sappy-rampant growth. They are so variable as found in
nurseries and in so many hybrid forms, that few of the original
species are ever seen. Bloom is marked by its abundance, richness
and variety in combination of coloring and with the persistency
with which good culture and care are rewarded spring-summer-fall,
or even year round. All do best in a humid atmosphere with more or
less shade and constant moisture, in a cool fertile soil that holds
none of the excess moisture they are sure to experience. Mulch them
rather thickly with leafmould and force-spray with water during hot
weather....no wind and little frost. When it is found necessary to
prune by way of a major operation, it may be known that one has failed in the early shaping for use or place. Cut out undesirable growth
regularly as it originates; pinch out and keep pinching until flower
buds are formed, knowing the flowers come on new wood. The endless
variety forms may be referred in part to the following.
    -arborescens, distinctive, a shrub, or the growth of medium
soft wood piling up until a neat little tree 15' results, but
brushy within unless pruned out:foliage will take more sun than
most:open heads of narrow-tubular flowers range through darker
shades of pink to a bright winey-red or purple January-April,
or with occasional heads at any time:choice.
    -corymbiflora, an old plant, the long canes scrambling
or climbing on suitable support:tube of the flower, in few-
flowered clusters is long and grades from being almost colorless at the base to light and fairly deep reds:sun or shade
on pillars or elsewhere as a landscape subject:may be used
north into the Carolinas along the coast.
    -fulgens, the type with shorter tube, broader flare and
larger flowers generally, 3-4' or less in combinations of red,
white, purple and blue....more showy varieties hereabouts.
    -magellanica, the very small flowering types usually, some-
times shrubby in variety forms, but more often vining at considerable lengths, all parts small and quite refined, but becoming
brushy in a large way if unattended:takes more frost than others.
    -procumbens, sometimes known as "Trailing Queen" a low viny
little thing with short, weak stems, to be used under typical
conditions in hanging baskets, in boxes or may find a place
in the rock garden:the tiny flowers, almost without color,
almost worthless aside from a generic interest....a short
tube with blunt, returned orange petals and blue stamens;will
defoliate in any sudden check, but returns soon:ground cover
in deep shade or with ferns.
    -triphylla, a more or less conventional shrubby figure
at 3-5', the best for color in the open landscape as an in-
tegral part of the shrubbery:dense clusters of average narrow tubular flowers in a single, fixed shade of light coral or
rose, almost everblooming in warmth:does not like heat, but
takes considerable sun, and suckers mildly in time.

FURCRAEA gigantea, "Mauritious Hemp" succulent, a hard-leaved
plant with wide, sword-like leaves in a great, pale green rosette:
flowering may be likened to a colossal chandelier, not predictable as to time, and happens only once, when the plant dies:
reproduction is by means of bulbils which drop, dart-like
from the 20', imposing flower stem, to fix in moist earth and
grow:a spot plant for difficult places like sand against the
ocean, or will remain small as graduated from pots to tubs.

G

GAILLARDIA aristata, "Blanketflower" a sprawling perennial 18-24" in height and spread, to be used in the border
in full sun, a prodigious bloomer for lasting material to
cut, autumn reds and smoky yellows banded at the center

301

Fuchsia arborescens

Fuchsia fulgens

Fuchsia (types)

Fuchsia procumbens

with contrasting color May-November:avoid heavy soils or a
spot that is wet over any length of time and do not overfeed:
use low stakes and tie early if desirable to restrict spread
and renew yearly from cuttings in case of a superior strain:
very resistant to drought. There are annual forms, but the
above may give better service, used as an annual.

GALTONIA candicans, "Summer-hyacinth" succession of 2-3'
spikes from a prolific ground cluster of bulbs, each head of
scores of pure white, hanging bells late summer-autumn:grows
luxuriantly in fertile soils in the sun, staked for neatness,
but most effective as a casual, unruly mass against a dark background....best left alone as long as possible:start from seed,
flowering bulbs sometimes developing the first year.

GALVESIA speciosa, "Bush-snapdragon" sprawling shrub, much
branched, arching stems to a mound 3-5', more across:foliage
of good wearing quality, light green, the flowers a clear red
March-June and later, or practically everblooming in the right
place....a little shade if grown in heat, subject thereto the
caterpillars of several insects....better grown in coolness, in
substantial soils and a little water when called for:native in
California and does surprisingly well as a cutflower.

GARBERIA fruticosa, scrubby little shrub in nature, but with
ornamental points to be found under cultivation, growing normally 3-5' with dense heads of pink to rosy purple flowers:a
native of Florida in waste sandy soils....dunes, hammocks.

GARDENIA---notables; of the blood, shrubs of more than simple
elegance, being of very essential worth and distinction, with
flower and foliage of substance and beauty when well grown.
The leaf is normally dark and shining, a contrasting back for
the waxy white flowers that have few equals for fragrance.
They are not easily handled. Give them warmth concentrated, as
of the sun primarily, plus its reflected or stored heat from a
wall or even that from surrounding concrete when growing in
even mild coolness:likes some open shade in extreme heat and
uniform moisture with drainage. The soil should be slightly
acid, fertile, high in humus, both from peat and leafmould,
with always the good mulch. Transplant, if possible, just as
activity begins in the buds, with any exposure except direct
south, unless with shade over noon. They are rarely pruned,
but new growth may be stopped at 3-4" by pinching out tips.
Take flowers in early morning for purest scent and remove the
spent blooms to cancil out the offensive odor that develops.
They are subject to nematodes, but resist....become carriers.
   -jasminoides, known in the beginning as "Cape-jasmine" usually 3-5' in good thrift, better grown in tubs in nearly pure
peat and leafmould, plunged as is, if set out in the ground:will
flower through May-September profusely, scattering at either end:
use complete acid fertilizer lightly each month spring-summer to
hold color of foliage....humic content of the soil especially
important here. They are grown all along the California coast
and inland, in the lower South and along the seabord north to
Virginia.   --var. florida, the leaves larger and extremely
glossy, flowers larger and not so abundant but over a
longer period, easier grown in the open ground,
reaching 3-4' in height.   --var prostrata, low
and ultimately spreading, 6-10"high and 2-3'wide:
much leafmould in the soil and a frequently replen-
ished mulch, along with heat, the secret of success
with this....tiny gardenia for bouttonier.   --var.
veitchi, smaller edition of the type, growing 2-3' high,
with more and somewhat smaller flowers.
   -thunbergia, an amiable plant, this, of little temperament, except possibly in the matter of blooming, vigorous to
8-10' and as broad....reported far south in Florida to as
much as 25' across:stout, rigid, light grey branches and
contrasting black-green leaves, a self-supporting pattern
302

of delight against a hot white wall....standing espalier
unique. The single white flower flares in overlapping petals,
round starlike, a swirl of sometimes 3-4" wide ending a long
curved tube that protrudes from an interesting greenish calyx:
blooms in summer and freely only in heat....only the foliage
otherwise....very fragrant at night, the purity tarnished the
second day in the sun, then brown. Said to resist the nematode
quite successfully....practical and easily grown:rare.

GARRYA elliptica, shrubby to 8', native northerly in Cali-
fornia:wants a light, well-drained soil that is fairly rich,
a place in the sun, but out of direct and strong wind, hardy
in 15 degrees of frost.long slender catkins of most unusual
character, greenish or yellow, stand out against the dark
foliage in winter....memorable art-object that could well
be adapted in decoration:purple fruits hang late and the
bush is tenacious when started young in gravelly ground
or on rocky slopes:seaside. The variety  --thuretti, is
a hybrid with glossy leaves that are whitish beneath,
tender in cold and better used south, east or west.

GASTERIA---low succulents, stemless plants with ornamental value as grown in pots, but extensively used in the
rock garden where the body of the plant may be expected to
remain within the area of the rock. They are particularly
suited to the smaller gardens. The short-ranked pattern of
growth works out with thick tongue-shaped leaves which are
roughened with raised dots. Culture is essentially the same
as in Aloe with the matter of drainage stressed, plus shade.
    -pulchra, the leaves as long as 10", dull dark green,
originating in a spiral placement, covered with elongated,
white raised dots:rose-colored flowers are pendent from the
10-15" stems.   -verrucosa, the leaves to 6" long, a dull
grey-green with white crowded tubercles or worts:flowers are
red or rose-colored.

GAZANIA---herbaceous plants for permanent bedding or used as an
edging for the garden border. They make a more or less close mat
of foliage with colorful daisy-like flowers, the base of each narrow ray set with a precise spot like the eye of a peacock feather.
They grow thriftily in any well drained soil, but in the sun since
the flower remains closed in shadow, even dull overcast days.
    -coccinea, a mound or fairly loose clump of broadly cut
leaves, the bronzy-red flowers on long stems: a border plant
to be used in the fore-part or in a kind of bedding:reseeds
rather freely in places, the seedlings probably hybrids in
many colors and much wider time coverage.
    -splendens, flat-growing and quite compact at the ground,
useful as a ground cover in light or very sandy soils where
few plants will hold:literally a sheet of orange March-May.
    -uniflora, more loosely growing than foregoing, with a
light lemon-yellow flower late in spring, scattering out
into summer or more or less recurring over the year:the
leaves curl over in poor light or at night to show the
white reverse.

GELSEMIUM sempervirens, "Carolina-jessamine" a climbing
twiner from southern woods where it sheets trees with
its gold in spring and fills the air with the near scent
of wallflower:flower is bell-shaped, light gold with a
deeper throat, while the light, yellow-green foliage is
better with a little shade, but flowering better in good
light....stems more stocky there:sparse at best in California, all growth tending to crowd to the top....shorten the
shoots after flowering to reduce tangle:survives 15 degrees
of frost and will be found in warm temperate regions to
Virginia and into Oregon along the coasts:blooms in the
winter in the far south. There are no pests. Hold this
in sufficiently to keep new wood coming up from
the base.

Gardenia jasminoides

Garrya

Gaura lindheimeri

Gazania

Gelsemium

GENISTA monosperma, "Bridalveil" shrubby and spreading,
as usually found, ultimately erect and tree-like 10-12',
probably multi-stemmed with branches gracefully hanging:the
fleeting foliage is for only a short time in winter, the fine
mass of stringy green branchlets carrying on in place of the
leaves....faintly silvered, very thin, filamentous, melting into
the air almost as a part:the translucent, practically colorless
flowers appear white at times and in certain lights, spring and
again in the fall:grow them hard, in drought and impoverished soils,
nearly pure sand, where they will be poor food for the genista worm
which works on the herbage of this and others.

GERBERIA jamesoni, "Transvaal Daisy" blooming at any time of the
year far south, but generally May-November, the original coloring
very strong, a rich vermilion, the hybrids, however, subdued in
quieter shades of pink, yellow and orange:set plant with the
crown level with the earth, neither higher nor lower and allowing for settlement, but higher if there is any question
of water run-off:full sun and heat of primary importance
along with a light, enriched soil....only organic fertilizers....everblooming with regular and heavy feedings
in absence of frost:keep moist during growth by flooding and as infrequently as possible, doing a thorough
job that sprinkling cannot duplicate, getting water
away from the crown quickly....allow time to dry
out well on top before repeating:divide after
three years or so, February or October:cutflower of
excellence that may be grown into warm temperate
regions if given a rough mulch and gravel at the crown.

GEUM hybrids, "Avens" herbaceous perennials of merit in the far
south for the border, having a clean,persistent, rather finely
divided foliage and well defined color in the flowers through
summer:want a deep, rich, well drained soil with good moisture
through heat and appreciate a little shade in hot places:longer
lived in the lighter soils, but do very well for a time in the
heavier types. All representatives of this group available to
gardeners are hybrids.
    -Bradshaw, with a notably good body of leaves and
quite double, rich scarlet flowers on long stems for cut-
ting:use in the border in fairly deep shade.
    -Stratheden, more weak and straggling, with com-
paratively scant foliage, the golden yellow flowers with
fewer petals:not robust, short-lived....but with that
vague attraction of the insubstantial.

GILIA---mostly small western annuals, some known in
gardens, all of them easily grown in sandy soils in the
sun. The foliage is always sparse, the leaves narrow,
sometimes thread-like, with no body, the flowers freely produced and brightly colored, formed generally in
a phlox reminder....fact noted by gardeners and used in
popular names. They will be used in a rather casual manner, sowing seed where they are to stand, in the border,
the rock garden or broadcast with the wildflowers.
    -californica, "Prickly-phlox" low and straggling
or procumbent, a plant that may be shrubby and variously branching, the flowers with toothed petals,
rose-colored, blooming in spring:poor dry soils only, in
the rock garden or naturalized:a woody perennial.
    -capitata, "Queen Anns Thimble" an annual 2-3'with
light blue flowers dried for winter boquets.
    -densiflora, "California-phlox" erect slender stems
with thickly clustered white or lavender flowers in the
spring:filler in the border or grown with the cutflowers.
    -dianthoides, "Ground-pink" low-spreading tufts, a
precise little annual, usually less than 6" high when it
is used in the right place:flowers comparatively large
and flattened, looking up to the sun....and you, lilac
or purple with a yellow center, a true miniature:a

304

*Gilia dianthoides*

*Genista monosperma*

*Gilia rub*

*Gerberia*

*Gilia californica*

very personable little thing, but transient:rock garden, where
it will return year after year if situation is right.
    -dichotoma(Linanthus)"Evening Snow" reaching 12" in height, in
full flower only in the evening or at night, the long-tubed flowers
loosely clustered, white with purplish throat....lasts well in point
of time, becoming larger day by day, but going at the last into a
period of unpleasant odor:must have heat and drainage.
    -lutea(Leptosiphon)sparkling little annual 6", heathery, loose
mounds set to tiny stars very early season and later, if seed has
been saved and sown late....rosy pink, lilac, lemon-yellow, and
all with a pale yellow center:lasts for years in the right garden.
    -rubra, "Standing-cypress" a strong-growing, rather spectacular
plant, having brilliant scarlet spikes 3-5' high in marked verticals
from last years rosette of ground leaves:native in Florida, biennial.
    -tricolor, "Birds-eye G." erect spreading, 18-24", foliage
in the usual scantiness but with a nice laciness, better adapted to and long used in gardens:larger, nearly bell-shaped
flowers are grouped in threes with blended tones of lavender,
purple and yellow:border as a filler and cutflower garden.

GLADIOLUS---iris-like plants for the garden or border for spot
color there or to take as cutting material, probably best grown
with the cutflowers, considering the uncertain nature of the top
and disturbing bulblets left to clutter the ground. They would like
a rather stiff loamy soil, well and deeply worked with manure that
is surely rotted. Poor results come of a cold wet place, where heat
should be assured and coarse gravel worked in to pick up and carry
warmth through cool nights. They should have full sun. Thrips, red
spider and sometimes a wireworm cause trouble and should be controlled. Soil reaction may be neutral to slightly acid, and the
ground will not be allowed to dry out completely in growth.
    -blandus, "Painted Lady" for the garden, growing 18-24" high,
with wide open flowers, white to light red and carmine in the early
summer, June or before.
    -colvillei, an old strain of hybrids, again for the garden, the
flowers small and very early in the spring, white and pink to deeper reds....of fair decorative value....pots. There are many such
hybrid groups derived from the smaller, little known species,
few of which equal the type species in charm and satisfaction with which they will be grown in the garden.
    -hortulanus, the garden "Glads" , highly developed
forms, always a cutflower and preferably grown only as
such and with the cutflowers:time of blooming relates directly to  when the bulb is set....start January-March at about ten
day intervals and again August-October far south for bloom going
into winter, the later plantings being more subject to thrips;
force with fertilizers high in phosphates. These plants have no
place in the border, largely because of form; mainly, however, it is root competition and cultural complications
that drag on highest performance:take crop in late afternoon in bud and allow time in a cool shady place before
going into water:lift bulbs and store in sacks with napth-
aline flakes or other, in a cool dry place.
    -tristis, the smaller growing species, 15-18", the
flowers off-white, with hints of yellow June-July, very
fragrant at night:makes a permanent clump that is down late
summer and fall:preferred species for the border:free of thrips.

GLORIOSA superba, a "Climbing Lily" with forked, tuberous roots
and slender top rising 8-10' with support, grown in a tub or in
the ground beneath an open shrub....mark the spot:set February
or March or as late as May, the earlier best, the tuber on
side in half shade or sun:wants warmth and abundant moisture
spring-summer, dryness or excellent drainage over winter
when down....safer lifted in California....left in Florida:
very sandy loams required, of good fertility, but no man-
ures:flower lily-like with recurved segments July-September, yellow turning scarlet, the flame spreading from the
tip:exotic corsage:stem is brittle, it and tuber easily
lost, but flowering is feasible grown as above:rare.

*Gilia capitata*

*G. blandus*

*G. tristis*

*Gloriosa*

GLOXINIA(SINNINGIA)speciosa, as known in gardens, a tuberous root-stock with a low, stemless mop of velvety leaves
which deteriorate under overhead watering:bell-shaped flowers,
selfs or combinations of rather sober reds and blues,or white
with variations available summer and autumn:usually started
in pots or flats and shifted either to permanent pots or
into a moist shady location in the garden that has been
well prepared with leafmould:dry out gradually in the fall
and store cool-humid or leave in the pot to cure and shake
out in spring for a new start:responds to fishmeal quickly
in growth and color:choice, comparatively easy to bring along.

GODETIA grandiflora, "Satinflower" erect, rather rugged annuals for  rather poor, sandy or loamy ground either in the gard-
en or outside in the open landscape for bright seasonal color,
easily and quickly attained. They are sturdy in growth, if a
little floppy, very free flowering and particularly valuable
for bridging over that period between spring and early summer
heat:flower large, single or semi-double, rose-red with deeper center, the light clusters making up nicely as cutflowers:
some little shade is beneficial and late-sown seed a failure.
The species   -bottae, is native in California, a single
flower in the lighter reds.

GOMPHRENA globosa, "Globe-amaranth" an annual with clover-
like heads which may be classed with the everlastings, having rather lurid coloring, white through yellow, pink, red,
violet and purple July-September:thrives in any garden soil,
but with sun and heat required for best results.

GOSSYPIUM sturti, "Desert-rose" shrub for heat and extreme
dryness, growing in any exposure 3-6' high, best in a light,
gravelly soil:the single flowers are mallow-like, pale lavender
with a dark purple center, August on into winter:tender in frost.

GREVILLEA---flowering shrubs and trees in quite general use for
the good foliage and for the floral contribution, which is not an
ordinary thing. They are very rapid in growth and resistant to
drouth, in fact wanting dryness in rest to survive. This they
are too seldom allowed in the garden,with resulting short life
and questioned reputation....or is it the intelligence of humans
in question. Heavy wet soils are anathema, and fatal, with no
quarter given....only extension....like the gravediggers daugh-
ter, they like it for a time. Deep pruning is not advisable,as
the wood fails to heal properly and in good time, leaving weak
links in a very active chain of growth. The lighter, sandy or
exceptionally well drained loams that are not too rich are not
only desirable; they are mandatory. Avoid all kinds of root
disturbance and all forms of lime.
    -banksi, "Crimson Coneflower" large shrub with an open
body of dull, dark green, deeply divided leaves, the lobes long
and narrow, a loose foil for the erect heads of dark crimson
flowers January-May and from time to time:must have a light,or
sandy and very thoroughly drained soil in the sun. This is a
striking plant in flower, but so uncertain in trust with the average gardener, as to suggest only odd specimen use.
    -obtusifolia, growing only 6-10" high, spreading out over
the ground in a dense furry mat 10-15' across, or even more
in warm granite soils....marked all the warmth of the year
by clusters of the typical red flowers, massed low among
the pale green leaves:must have the sun and will grow in
very difficult soils that are short of most things that
other plants consider necessary:planting stock should
be well established, but not rooted through the container....watch water particularly....the getting
through the soil more important than the water itself.
This is another case where the weaning away from the
saturation of watering a plant is subject to in its
youth, and as it grows up in the nursery, and as it
comes along in the can yard, is significant.
306

-paniculata, wanting the ground as dry as dry may be after
a sufficiency for an almost continual, massed, frothy-white
blooming:cut out the few erect shoots as they appear and a
splendid ground cover results:ignore the plant and a raised,
conforming bank cover, a tangle that fits closely and stays
if water gets away:rare and choice, most demanding of site.
    -robusta, "Silky-oak" with not a thing to suggest an
oak, but an ornamental of the first order if handled sens-
ibly:a tree, developing rapidly to 75' in moisture, slower in
drought:leaves much refined, fern-like and dark, littering at
all seasons:a subject for informed pruning as the brittle branches are weak in the wind when grown rapidly....head back for more
strength, starting early and continuing in order to obviate any
heavy cutting:takes heavy irrigation or excessive natural moisture, but the better trees are always found in dry ground:large
trusses of golden flowers extend out on a flat plane to lend
an oriental effect April-May:any soil will satisfy and the tree
is reliable where optimum water requirements hold.
    -rosmarinifolia, attractive spreading shrub 3-5', bushy,
low to the ground and more or less compact-running, a fine
mass of durable foliage with pink and white bloomings at any
time:hardy in frost and fairly trustworthy.
    -sulphurea(juniperina)a low shrub 2-3', of rather dense
character, inclining to roundish form and rather neat:leaves
are short, stiff and rolling over at the sides, whitish under-
neath:flowers pale yellow, sometimes touched with red:rare.
    -thelemanniana, "Spidernet" of medium, furry growth 5-8',
rather dense, if not growing too rapidly, the velvety floss of
the bright green foliage set to sparkles of ruby-red flowers in
varying amounts over the year:drier situations again,if the
plant is to be held permanently....surplus water only stimu-
lates to shorten life and force growth that has to be cut out,
weakening the plant until it will not stand of itself....goes
out in the wind, due to shallow roots that never had to forage
about for sustenance and moisture.

  GREWIA occidentalis, a large spreading shrub with small leaves
of the linden, easily grown in a plane, flat against a wall or
the flexible stems carried far....naturally built for pleach-
ing:erratic as to bloom, but more or less over the year in
the south, heaviest February-May, the rosy red flowers
profusely set in among the leaves like many-pointed stars:
neat, clean, clearcut plant, but unruly and of rapid development 8-12' or with lianas, long-reaching for service
farther away....excellent flowering hedge grown on support,
as of a fence or the streamers inter-woven and strength-
ened, pinching out and pruning so that it stands alone,a
great sprawling entangled mound when left to its own devices. The species  -caffra, has larger, more full and
light purple flowers....continuous in a warm, sunny place.

  GREYA sutherlandi, growing as a low shrub of irregular form
and structure or a small tree:very large, vivid green leaves
are few but effective and show dark against a white patio
wall or reveal the ramification of stem beneath:flowers of
brilliant scarlet in spikes with the extended stamens of a
bottlebrush....starting quite young:does in some shade, but
sun is required for good blooming and drainage of the soil for
thrift. Rest this plant after a period of growth is completed for better results in flowering,at which time dryness is indicated to fix and consolidate wood:rare.

  GRINDELIA robusta, "Gum-plant" western native, a perennial for alkali soil, suitable for and worth little
else, but with yellow daisies as something of a show in
winter:short-lived, but reseeds to keep badlands covered as well as may be. A prostrate species -arenicola,
may be used as low cover in trying situations, spreading
2-3' across:seed, or collect where available.

307

GRISELINIA littoralis, a number one plant against the
sea, grown well only in coolness and moisture, a shrub
as normally found and used, 6-8' or more, or tree-like
in time, out of the wind:main attraction the medium sized leaves, clear light green and shining....very durable in salt wind:hardy into warm temperate regions.
The species  -lucida, has been grown in California as a
decorative plant in shade, used for the tannish stems in
the open or as espalier....also a tree, in the end.

GUZMANIA cardinalis, "Burning-heart", sometimes called "Panama
B. H.", also "Heart of Flame", doubtless synonymus with Bromelia
balansae, low to the ground with harsh, horny and sharply toothed
saber-like leaves....over-all effect of a pineapple:leaf is dull
red at the tip in winter, turning to most violent crimson in the
sun in summer, lower down at the base...literally a burning heart:
spectacular in a reasonably moist soil,where the mother plant is
replaced at the tips of short, stout stolons, ultimately to be
crowded into a fiery, impenetrable, lacerating mass that may
be renovated from time to time in interest of co-habitation,
or the gardener must indeed be tough:inflorescence a short
club-like affair, heavy and purplish blue.

GUAIACUM officinale, "Lignum Vitae" very slow-growing for
a tub, with ultimate use as a slender, dense-topped tree to
25', suitable for a small garden or patio:the brisk, twiggy
head can easily be kept at standard or eye height where the inch-
wide blue flowers appear nicely all around the circumference,
uniformly, without having to be turned for light March-May:
light green, leathery leaves are glossy....drop in cold

GYNURA aurantiaca, "Velvet-plant" shrubby, but soft-built,
quite tropical, a strong note for color, the stems and leaves
covered with a fine hair, a purple pile that glows in the sun,
the color diminishing as it enters shade:pinch out the tip to
branch low and continue for compactness:warmth the controlling factor....full sun for best color:best grown in a pot
and taken indoors as a window plant over winter:mealybug.

GYPSOPHILA elegans, "Babysbreath" filling material
for boquets, an annual with which to fill a vacant
spot in the border or grown with the cutflowers for
this primary use:small white flowers come at any time
and easily point for either side of winter:any garden
soil that is not too acid, light in texture for good
drainage, and dry preferably:lime.

H

HABRANTHUS---low bulbous plants, closely related to the
better known zephyr flowers, to be used in the same way, and
grown substantially under the same conditions. The leaves are
long and narrow, usually under 12", loose, rather than
with any compact feeling at the base, the up-reaching,
comparatively large star-like flower deep pink or a
yellow with pink shadings. They do not require a rich
soil nor as much moisture as above relatives.
-andersoni(texana)"Copper-lily" growing to 8" in
height, the smaller, flattened flower yellow with a
coppery suffusion, showing red veining outside:Texas.
-brachyandrus, "Parana-lily" flower more like an
amaryllis, smaller, funnelform, pink above, red-purple below April-July, blooming in response to moisture.
-robustus, "Argentine-lily" strong-growing, with a
large pink flower, profuse and blooming before the foliage is full.

## BLOODLILY

HAEMANTHUS---striking bulbous material with tropical
accent in leaf and coloring, varied in habit of growth
and performance for nearly frost-free areas. They are
rare in cultivation and probably will be better grown in
pots without, or until more experience in handling them
in the garden is available. It is known they want good air
humidity, although the developed flower head will last
longer in comparative dryness. Give them a sandy soil in
good humus content, half to three-quarters shade and never
allow them to completely dry out unless to be lifted and
stored....and no shriveling then. Fertilize with a liquid and
disturb as little as possible. Let them burst a pot. They are
expensive and subject to frost damage....mulch lightly in cold.
      -albiflos, rather thick, succulent leaves and pure white
flowers in heads 2" across and held 12" high in the fall:set
this bulb shallow and keep a light mulch of leafmould.
      -coccineus, two large leaves per bulb that may be
prostrate or semi-erect and up over winter:see that this
one remains dry over summer when the dark red flowers appear in August or September, well before the new growth:
takes more sun than the others.
      -katherinae, the "Great Bloodlily" with large, pale
leaves, erect and paddle-shaped, the 6" spherical head held
as much as 2' high, pink to dark red ball of a thousand florets May-July....lasting several weeks, down by November, beginning growth again February or March:follows on from pot to
tub to ground where it will be easily lost wet winters in Cal-
ifornia:not too difficult to handle and not too much trouble,
considering the reward:select bulbs for color, when the individual florets may be detached and made up into a corsage: an
altogether spectacular plant, in a choice shade.
      -puniceus, essentially for a pot, having dark wavy leaves
on long petioles that are spotted with purple, failing only a
short time in summer, the new growth starting so quickly
that the change may not be noticed....practically evergreen:
the August flowering is not conspicuous, orange of a kind,
hardly lifting out of the calyx cup, but the large crimson
berries in tight, erect heads are; last for months:deep shade.

HAKEA---tough and rugged shrubs of more than passing
interest and usefulness in the landscape, but to be had
in the garden only advisedly and with caution. Their chief
worth lies in the practical, being of value mainly for extremes in drought, heat cold, saline and sterile ground,
the flowers of interest, but with no appreciable show.
The foliage carries the aesthetic load, with character that
is sharply divided into two main groups, a needle type and
one that is broad and long like the phyllodia leaf of certain
acacias. Both wear well under natural stresses and stand
against salt wind as hedge or screen or in belt plantings
for protection. They must have good drainage or quick run-
off in a heavy soil, not too much moisture generally and a
minimum of fertility. They are difficult to plant and have
no pests or diseases.
      -elliptica, a large shrub, erect and very shapely or may
be grown as a small and very handsome tree, the leaves wavy
edged, a rich, yellowish bronze when new, holding in the
mature leaf several months:quite the most attractive
of a utilitarian lot, seldom obtainable:not so good
in high wind or extreme drought....the better garden
subject, particularly in tree form.
      -laurina, "Sea-urchin" erect and broad as a shrub
or a rigid, dense, rounding tree 25' for very hard wear,
undergoing all adverse conditions at the shore....but requiring a season usually, to adapt to the worst:flower is
a crimson and gold ball close-held to primary wood, larg-
ly concealed beneath the foliage, most interesting mid-
winter or sometimes in flower by autumn:adapts to clays.

309

-pugioniformis, "Daggerleaf" a shrub, widely spreading, a broad mound and perfect dome as grown without interference, 10-15' across but not as high:the rigid leaf serves as
a cruel and uncompromising, needle-pointed dagger. This is
not a handsome plant, but highly protective, has unimportant flowers that are scented; adapts to heavy soils.
    -saligna, "Foleywood" naturally dense, a shrub 8-10'
from a low base or trunk, a tight-growing and excellent
wide hedge, sheared or not:pale green, willow-like leaves
take the wind without hurt, the new growth reddish for a
change in its even pace, while white nubbins, the flowers,
April-May, lie within the foliage and may be missed....but
par for arrangements:light soils for long life:frost-hardy.
    -suaveolens, "Needlebush" erect at first, 8-10', but later
spreading out in some symmetry, dense, with a light green prickly foliage that is gently coersive to intruders; an unclipped or
lightly pruned hedge of merit in the lighter, drier soils, even
pure sand, but goes out in the wind if grown too lush, due to
shallow rooting:fluffy white flowers in small, thimble-like
heads show in fall and/or winter.

HALIMIUM---low shrubby materials in greys for sunny spots
in soils that are most inhospitable; gratifying shrubs for
the frugal gardener; good furnishing for meagre ground, a
bank or other unproductive space where plants find themselves
very much on their own. They may be considered in a class
with the better known sun and rock-roses, with like culture,
but the flowers yellow. Moisture wants are difficult to fath-
om, something to study in light of local climate and in relation to the soil in which they are to stand. Too much or too
little water can be the measure of success and satisfaction with
which they will be grown....but always the sun and sharp drainage.
Shear back after flowering and feed only on sure demand.
    -halimifolium, erect growth 3-4', ultimately sprawling, the
comparatively large leaves chalk-white, with no vestige of
green, durable, case-hardened under the sun for exposure,
drop in dryness when unprepared:large, pure yellow flowers
June-July may be sheared for a probable second blooming.
    -libanotis, spreading bushy shrub 18-24" or less, with
foliage in the semblance of rosemary, but much more orderly,
prim, not sprawling:white, half-inch flowers may be suffused
with yellow or not, spring:must have some moisture in heat,
and will tolerate light shade if required.
    - ocymoides, growing 18-24" or very low, procumbent, or
may be pushed up to 3' or more against support:small, bright
yellow flowers, purple-splotched, are profusely born over
spring-summer or scattering:rock garden or the face of a
dry wall. This little thing is a glorified sun-rose that
just fails the arrogance of a rock-rose and may substitute for either....medium moisture with dry periods in
between for consolidation and settling down, best.

HAMELIA erecta, "Scarletbush" native Florida shrub that
is vigorous of growth in warm places....tender, but recovers quickly after a freeze:wavy leaves are bronzy purple at times, with a red mid-rib, the smaller branches
and leaf-stalks also in color:orange-scarlet flowers in
erect clusters, summer-autumn are followed by bluish or black
berries as large as peas....almost always in fruit or flower:
partial shade in a moist, rich soil of reasonable drainage is
desirable: grows 5-10' high in Florida, only 2-4 in California,
dwarfed there in dry heat in the sun and only a tight mound.

HARDENBERGIA---vines, twining closely to some 10-15' in the
sun, if not in too much heat, best in slightly shaded places
of good soil and air drainage. The flowers are especially
attractive, with that inborn appeal to be found in the
diminutive and where simplicity in form and purity in color
is marked. Here are nicely formed clusters of tiny, pea-shaped
flowers of very clear shades, winter into the edge of spring,

*Hamelia erecta*

*Halimium ocymoides*

*Hardenbergia comptoniana*

*Harpullia*

and in profusion. The plants are vigorous in growth, with an
unusual elegance, always refined and conditioned for appearance
unless in high heat over summer. They adapt to a dry atmosphere
where peat and leafmould have been used generously and are hardy
in some frost when established.

  -comptoniana, affording a light, lacy cover of attractive, five-parted leaves, as usually grown....plants from the
seed of this form in three short broad leaflets:flowers are
always dark blue, only infrequently rose February-March:a
pillar or porch plant or may be pegged down as a ground
cover:the cooler exposures are best.

  -monophylla, heavier over-all, more vigorous, hardier, the
single leaves larger, leathery, more durable:shrubby in absence
of support or twining upon itself, the flowers January-February
in delicate pastel shades of rose, lavender, lilac or white, but
seldom blue:use as a vine or bank cover or as a temporary filler
among shrubs....low and controlled:stands in the poorer, heavier
soils, submitting to more heat and dryness, in 15 degrees frost.

HARPEPHYLLUM caffrum, "Kafir-plum" an open-headed, spreading,
rather rigid tree of very rapid growth to 35' in good ground, the
leaves thick, dark and shining, tufted near the ends of stubby
branchlets....copper-red of the new growth contrasting:fruits
are edible, dark red, the size of an olive and somewhat the same
shape, slightly acid to taste:tender in frost, but usually recovering without too much damage, frequently multiple stemmed.
This tree develops a quaint or picturesque aspect in age that
should not be overlooked when appraising species.

HARPULLIA arborea,"Tulipwood" a tropical tree to 40', dense,
round-headed, a broad dome of light, glossy green:summer flowers
are not conspicuous, but provide the two-parted, cherry-like seed
pods that are so lavishly displayed over winter....coloring up well
by September, full-red by Christmas:wants a warm place, surviving
as much as 10 degrees of frost if hardened off, best within coast
influence in a deep, fertile soil:rare, but available from time
to time in both Florida and California.

HAWORTHIA---low leaf succulents, the plant either stemless or
the small, thick, warty leaves crowding along the erect stem
which does not show. Many offsets will develop around the base.
Uses are confined to small scale gardening and more appropriately with rock, suiting the plant itself. Shade them in extreme
heat and use more sand that soil in ground preparation....some
peat moss good to hold the slight moisture they require.

  -attenuata, the three-inch, long-tongue-like leaves are
roughened by coarse, raised dots, green above, whitish beneath:
rose-colored, tubular flowers are lifted 15-20" on slender stems.

  -reinwardti, the plant close-knit, rigid-erect, the body of
stubby, curving, tongue-like leaves spirally packed about the
stem in alternating rows:flowers are white or greenish, lined
with rose:pots or in the rock garden.

  -tessellata, succulent, flattened, molded to fit the earth,
the watery, close-clustered bodies serving as leaves, bulbous in
appearance, limpid and almost translucent, lined with a lighter
green:flowers white with green markings:use to seal narrow fissures or to close rock:an interesting, useful succulent.

HAZARDIA cana, California shrub for dry rocky ground in
coolness:adapts to gardens where it will be grown for the
handsome 8" grey, leathery leaves....flower inferior, a
yellow, turning purple as it falls:rarely found.

### BUSH VERONICA

HEBE---nicely branching shrubs or dense, pleasing little art-
icles for the border or rock gardens of the Pacific Coast, within reasonable reach of fog....elsewhere more or less of an experiment, probably possible in shade and moisture. They are rather
showy in flower, with some very pure blues, although a more
lasting impression will be that of form, exceedingly free

and graceful, or fixed and regular. They will be better
grown in soils of body and average fertility, but well
conditioned with organic material. They should have fair
drainage and constant, if only slight moisture. Few of them
ever attain size or proportions generally ascribed. At best
some are a little uncertain and their alpine nature must
be recognized if successfully grown. They take full sun,
but favor some shade in heat and glory in the coolness of
sea breezes. The old flower heads will be snipped off in
presenting their best appearance, but shears with-held in
further cutting....resentment there and little need. There
is confusion as to specific and horticultural forms.

-andersoni, rounding, fairly dense little bush of regular outline, the clear, dark blue flowers set against the
bright green of the leaves most of the summer:the species
most commonly found.   --var. imperialis, probably the
hardiest and most easily grown, but the brilliant purple-
crimson flowers difficult to placate in combination:stands
more sun and heat than most.

-buxifolia, very dwarf, as found south and naturally very dense with rigid, light green, box-like leaves:
good low, curb-hedge and not too difficult to handle in
the right place....goes out quickly in poor drainage:the
white flowers seldom set, then grudgingly, spring-summer.

-carnea, more open in growth, due to thinner foliage,
the outline still regular, but blurred, 3-4' high with rosy
pink flowers, heavy May-August, but in good flower all the year
in the right place:no problems culturally, good in the sun and
hard by the ocean....one of most practical for general use, but
can be pinched in methodically for improved appearance.

-chathamica, very low, prostrate in the more adult stages,
of exquisite daintiness and superb contrariness, 6" or 10-12"
in the beginning and in continued thrift:leaves in flattish,
almost fern-like sprays, at their best lying against or upon
a rock:the bark breaks into chunky rings about the stems
which show considerable bareness below....set closely
in order that the spray of one overlaps the bare crown
of the next:lilac to lavender flowers:choice.

-cupressoides, spreading, massive, and very close-
knit, a shrub with dark, scale-like leaves to a very
tight covering and pale lavender flowers in early summer:
grows 3-4', but in sterile, drained ground with good humus conditioning....more satisfactory northerly and better used in a
formal relationship:difficult to hold....looks like cypress.

-glaucophylla, erect and rather dense-rounding, less fixed
in outline, usually 18-24" high, seldom more than three feet, irregularly mounding:most attractive grey-blue foliage and white
flowers in summer, when it can be persuaded:handsome and rather
practical plant, more relaxed than most, adapting to considerable heat and shade:should be better known.

-hulkeana, total departure from normal, one of the most
beautiful and distinctive; open, rather than dense, 2-3' high,
the arching stems set precisely to coarsely toothed, thick
leaves and terminal clusters of lilac to lavender flowers
April-May....duplicates an oldfashioned lilac in color and
in form, even to the subsidiary nubbin of bloom, and in size
when well grown:rarely seen....too rarely. This makes good
cutting material and in any event, flower heads should be
removed before seed, a drain it may not survive for long.

-menziesi, superior plant for blooming, spreading,
12-15" high, very finely textured for the spreading of
reflected light:flowering an invitation to sweets, massed
lacy heads of pure white over spring-summer. This is
rather easily grown:choice, but with drainage.

-traversi, a rounding little plant of only medium denseness, quickly thickened under shearing:grows naturally some
18-24" in height, with sturdy, dark brown stems with most durable off-green foliage, white flowers scattering out over the
summer....when they choose to scatter. This is one of the best
for general use, however, one of the hardiest:good hedge.

312

*Hebe imperialis*

*Hebe chathamica*

*Hebe traversi*

*Hebe andersoni*

## IVY

HEDERA---woody vines, close-climbing on masonry walls....halls
of time, or more mundane, ground covering in sun or deeply shaded
places. The stout leathery leaves are durable, wearing well under
most tests. These plants will make good use of a fertile soil and
also get the most out of one that is not so rich. They take heat
and drought, by-passing a natural aversion to both. Any cutting
that may seem necessary is best done February-March, including
the heading away from windows. Don't starve these plants and do
not over-feed....over-watering builds a likely daylight harbor and
refuge for snails and slugs and other pests that run around nights.
Use the Algerian species in heat, the English forms in coolness.

    -canariensis, "Algerian I." particularly adapted to the far
south, a vigorous and over-running type, high-climbing with very
large, shallow-lobed leaves that are bright green and comparatively widely spaced on the runners:wants sun, takes heat and
dryness, better in California:white variegation most used.

    -colchica, heart-shaped leaves, not definitely lobed,
closely spaced for efficient covering, yellowish in appearance from a pale golden pubescence:climbs high, with time,
or runs over the ground where it is easily kept tight.

    -helix, "English I." the dark leaves are more or less
deeply lobed to give unusual character and variation in
texture, used in normal manner as cover or may be grown as a
low, formal hedge on support. There are many varieties based
on shape, size and other refinements in the leaf, on variegation;
in degree and placement of markings....lines, blotches or marbl-
ing; on the form which the lobes take or on color....usually the
winter reaction in purples:one is an erect shrub in miniature with
no thought in climbing....a line study and pattern of leaves set
in echelon. The foliage of this species will burn in dry heat.

## GINGERLILY

HEDYCHIUM---vigorous tropical herbs of erect sturdy growth 3-5',
the canna-like stems and leaves ornamental in line, the flowers
colorful in terminal clusters. They are in bloom generally thru
summer-autumn, want plenty of light, warmth and air, good moisture early season while in growth, doing with much less later:will
stand in wet ground, if necessary. Treat them like canna, dividing each year, or allow to remain as a bushy clump. They have a
fragrance that becomes more penetrating toward evening and will
take some shade, but with poorer bloom. They have something of
grace lacking in canna, together with a more decorative aspect
used as cutting material. Cool, heavy, rich soils are best.

    -coronarium, "Garlandflower" sometimes to 6' in rich soil,
the very large, tubular flowers a pure white, touched with
green at the edge of the lip, exceptionally fragrant:stands
more sun without hurt, yet a protected spot is indicated:
produces in considerable shade....the most practical.

    -flavum, "Butterfly-lily" comparatively weak-growing
3-4', the flowers red and yellow or orange, having wider
uses in large scale bedding, pleasantly fragrant when
fresh, a little rank as they fail.

    -gardnerianum, an 8-12" flower spike above the fol-
iage, bright yellow with red filaments in a feathery cyl-
inder about the stem:the more easily flowered under average circumstances and the hardiest in cold.

HEIMIA myrtifolia, a rugged and fine-textured shrub 3-4'
that is rounding and fairly compact, the strong, wiry stems
erect-recurving from a closely held crown at the ground and
suited essentially for hedging....seedlings come along rapidly to keep cost within reason:a toughy that manages well in
situations of tight sterile soils and hard exposure:should be
given full sun for best blooming, the flowers opening successively upwards in whorls of three, close about and toward
the tip of new wood in the summer:seed clusters persist on
the old wood to present an untidy aspect for awhile....may
be removed in the fall, as with a sickle....should not be
pruned hard in interest of good form.

313

HELIANTHEMUM nummularium, "Sun-rose" in allusion to the
flower, its shape and sun-loving disposition, prostrate and
evergreen, woody, the foliage glossy or hoary grey....the latter
much the more successful south:sheets of bloom April-June may be
red or yellow or anything in between, single or full double in
many named varieties:takes hot, dry and sterile soils and excessive moisture in good drainage:benefits with lime....do not
disturb root system:the flower lasts but a day, always at its
best in the morning, some varieties continuing through early
summer....shear back for more:rock garden, low slopes, cover.

HELICHRYSUM---everlasting flowers, herbaceous or woody and climbing, but in all forms retaining the immortelle character of
chaffiness in the flower. They will grow in any garden soil
in the sun, with reasonable moisture or dryish. The heads
are cut and hung away to dry in a well ventilated place to
dry out slowly, the flower hanging downward. These are all
sturdy, persevering, plodding plants that will take for
themselves a place in the sun....and an unkept garden.
     -bracteatum, "Strawflower" stout, branching annual 2-3'
high, one of the better known of the everlastings, having a
large flower in white, red or yellow and combinations:any good
light soil in the garden; but for reasons, better grown with
the cutflowers:crop should be taken before the flower is
fully expanded:sow seed early in spring.
     -diosmaefolium(Ozothamnus)"Snowy Everlasting" an erect,
woody plant 3-5', or climbing 10-15', the dark leaves that are
so like rosemary, almost hidden May-July beneath the clustered heads of white flowers....almost lost to the nursery trade.
     -petiolatum(Gnaphalium lanatum)a kind of "Cudflower"
semi-woody, a reclining, piling mass of dry stems, climbing
high on support, relaxing lower on itself....rampant in growth
to submerge a stout but unwary neighbor if not held in:late summer shearing does this and at the same time clears up the failing flowers which detract:white-wooly, plushy foliage is very
presentable, efficient covering for a bank:may be used directly under salt wind and spray, burning in storms, but recovering almost immediately:renew from time to time....used north
into warm temperate regions as summer bedding.

HELIOPHILA pilosa, "Cape-stock" a delicate little annual,
quite variable as to form and height, usually 6-10", the flowers in long sprays, normally a clear, light blue although
white, lilac or yellow frequently comes up:light, warm
soils in the sun suits this, with moisture surely in the
early stages of growth:cuts well and some forms may be
used in bedding or as an edging....sow seed early where
they are to stand:attractive, but not well known.

HELIOTROPIUM arborescens, "Heliotrope" an erect or
spreading perennial, an old plant in gardens, the fragrant
lavender to purple, sometimes very dark flowers tending to
fade out in the sun....yet requires a warm place in a rich,
open soil with good drainage:makes an attractive garden
cover if branches are hooked down with wire loops....do this
on a mild slope facing north, away from high sun.

HELLEBORUS lividus, "Hellebore" a christmas-rose suited
to the south, distinctive and substantial as a perennial
18-24", a mound of sprightly, leathery, three-parted leaves
and clusters of greenish "strawberry" flowers from late
winter on into spring:grow in part shade in a well drained
soil on the acid side of neutral....but lightly:will do
in a pot for a season or so, then to be moved into the
right spot in the garden....prepared with much leafmould:
Do not wait too long for this change, since mealybug attacks immediately vitality is reduced.
This is a very choice and worthy item for a
long term in the garden and may be
classified almost as a shrub.

314

COMPENDIUM

HELXINE soleiroli, "Angeltears" a light green mossy
fluff, a mat in the shade and in good moisture, becoming more sod-like with increasing sun unless in marked coolness....retreats and advances with shade over
the year:fertilize if necessary by working in finely
sifted leafmould:lath house or with ferns. This may
become a weed in lawns or a lawn substitute in shade.

HEMEROCALLIS aurantiaca, "Yellow Daylily" robust herbaceous
perennial with an excellent foliage structure of lax, sword-
shaped, channeled leaves and large, funnelform, soft yellow
flowers:last only a day, but several to the stem carry blooming erratically over summer....intermittant or found with some
flowers any day in the year, far south, where evergreen types
are favored:border plants for sunny places in any reasonable soil, wanting moisture but taking dryness, flowering
less in shade, reduced with crowding....divide any time out
of flower, building the soil up again with manure:no pests.
The smaller species  -thunbergi, may be used for fragrance
at night, while the red and copper hybrids will be found.

HESPERALOE parviflora, "Red-yucca" native in the Southwest, a low clumpy plant with long, harsh, narrow leaves
for an irregular mass reminiscent of aloe, the curving
flower stalk 3-4' high:flowers nodding, green and rosy-
red, with white filaments August-September:dry, and
rather poor soils will do, where they will be hardy
well into warm temperate regions.

HESPERANTHA stanfordiae, "Evening Flower" very small
bulbs for a sunny spot against a rock or other marker,
as and if held through the early stages of development:has a
fragile, 4" iris-like drift of leaves and a membranous, enclosing structure containing the satiny, lemon-yellow flowers that
are open only in the evening....only an incident as spring is
coming in....something to anticipate and capture for a moment:
wants to be dry over summer, when it will persist and gradually
grow in stature as the bulb strengthens, and with other
changes, attains some 10-15" in height:rare.

HESPEROCAULIS undulata, "Desert-lily" a typical plant
of the Southwest, deeply seated bulbs throwing a leafy
rosette of leaves after winter rains, the leaf blue-green,
ruffled and edged in white:flowers waxy-white with a green
band down the  back of each petal, few to the cluster, but
with more wet seasons and a better over-all performance then,
or with understanding management in the garden....a great show
then:collect bulbs if eager and in earnest, digging as deeply as
18" for the small white corm, setting again as deep if in a dry,
well drained place, if not use seed and wait for an extended
patch to develop....note the number of "if's" here and decide on
collected seed as being the more practicable and sure.

HETEROCENTRON roseum, a tender, soft-woody shrub 2-3' in height
in moist, loamy soils of substance:the deep rose flowers are
erratic in appearance and may be expected any time in warmth
or in response to stimuli such as moisture or fertilizer
applied suddenly after being with-held for awhile....nearly
everblooming far south under continuous good culture:shade.

HETEROMELES arbutifolia, "Toyon" a large, rather heavy
shrub or tree-like 25' with splendid dark foliage for the
year, white flowers for June and full-cropping red
berries that are held for winter....and the birds:re-
sists drought and may be grown in heat, but wants
coolness and takes reasonable summer irrigation in
good drainage:do not force, when the pleasant bushiness is lost in legginess and a disfiguring leaf-
blotch:native in California, grows but will not berry
in Florida:prime Christmas decoration if berries hold.

315

*Hesperantha stanfordiae*

*Hesperocallis*

*Hetero-
centron*

*Heteromeles arbutifolia*

HEUCHERA sanguinea, "Coralbells" tufted herbaceous perennial for the garden border or edging:slender flowering
stems for good cutting emerge from an unusually attractive
clump of broad, shallow-toothed leaves to carry the small
white or pink, rose or crimson bells, spring into summer, or
longer in light shade:wants a fertile soil with a sand or
gravel content....decidedly intolerant of a heavy clay:trans-
plant after a wet period if possible, and set with the crown
high since it tends to rot there in dampness....old crowns may
be divided in October, but new plants are more satisfactory in
immediate performance:subject to mealybug.

HIBBERTIA volubilis, "Guinea Gold" trailing, but better
used as a climber, vigorous in good tilth, the medium dark
foliage a likely setting for the large, single, rose-like
flowers of pure gold, rather profusely born through the
warmth of the season:growth is usually fulfilled at a
height of 8-12' when it may go into decline without
good treatment....reduce to lower wood and start over:
very much subject to thrips and red spider which must
be controlled by spring spraying....probably best in
three-quarters to half sun to help in control:choice.

### ROSE MALLOW
HIBISCUS---semi-shrubs, shrubs and tree-like shrubs of
tropical character and simple distinction, showy in the
extreme in flower. Cultural requirements are not complicated, demanding only moisture and a rich soil or applied fertility for the herbage they must have to develop and exhibit
effectively the sometimes gorgeous blooming. They are without exception so tender in frost and so slow to resume their
growth in spring, and especially after hurt, that the
normal flowering season will be delayed until late,
after a cold winter. There are no serious diseases
or notable pests, but alkalinity in the soil or
irrigation water will hold back growth.
    -arnottianus, a spreading shrub or small tree
20' far south, the single fragile flowers pure white
with a prominent, extended red pistil, very fragrant all
summer and autumn....winter south, mild seasons:rare.
    -diversifolius, a woody perennial 2-3', a low-
spreading and rather thin unkempt mass of ragged
foliage most of the year, probably killing back to
hard wood in winter:all parts are hairy, prickly
to include the 2" primrose-yellow flower that is
marked deep in the center with dark purple, normally June-November....continual through a warm
winter:short-lived, but re-seeds for a long-time
occupation of an area:some care is appreciated.
    -huegeli, "Skyblue H." flowers with more than a sug-
gestion of blue, faintly tinged with red, bell-shaped and
only partially open, continued through cold weather, but
grow in a tub to move in out of frost or deep cold. A
large shrub, 7-8' in rich soils that are high above the
frost line, to be grown dry, late summer and fall to hard-
en off for winter:rare and difficult to hold.
    -mutabilis, "Cotton-rose" shrubby plant with a few al-
most leafless stems, or tree-like 6-9', hardy enough at the
crown, but killing back to there in only light frost:large red
flowers open up bright in the morning, first white then pink,
deepening in tone through the day, normally July-October.
    -rosa-sinensis, strictly tropical, a heavy-wooded shrub,
enduring scarcely any frost, better without, damaged deeply for a very slow recovery:wants much moisture for a
good appearance, but gets along with surprisingly
little at times in California when established:the
great urn-shaped, single or double flowers come in
all shades of pink, red, rose and yellow, along
with pure whites of great beauty in the design of
the flower:blooms all through warmth and a mild
316

Hibiscus diversifolius

Hibiscus tiliaceus

H. rosa-sinensis

H. sabdariffa

Hibbertia

winter, the individual flower lasting but a day, rolling
up and dropping as considerable litter by weeks end: a
shrub 6-10' in Southern California, but a small tree, south
in Florida with pruning....the knife will do many good things
to this plant in fitting the form to situation, opening the
body to light....done late spring to catch and remove winter
injury:fertilizer pays dividends, should not be over-done.
    -sabdariffa, "Roselle" reddish-tinted biennial, growing
3-5', the fleshy parts of the red or yellow flowers edible, a
substitute for cranberry sauce, used also in jams and jellies or
as an infusion for beverages:quick-growing hedge, densely foliated
to the base, sparkling in autumn with the bright red calyces:deep-
rooted, better with minimum moisture, wanting a light, loamy soil
in good heat:fertilizers low in nitrogen are indicated.
    -tiliaceus, "Mahoe" straggling shrub or tree-like 20', the
sinuous branches interlacing to make a kind of bower with a
little help or will practically creep as a cover in the wind:the
yellow flowers turn to red by night as they fail:resists drought
and salt winds, cut to the ground by frost;the tense round leaf
varies as to size, leathery and smooth above, white beneath.

   HIDALGOA wercklei, "Climbing-dahlia" rare plant, in effect
a single dahlia or giant cosmos, a striking subject for a
cool place with morning sun, shaded over noon and until
the light is low:ray flowers orange-scarlet, the disc being
yellow:hardy under a little frost, returning from a woody
crown when frozen back:the lighter soils:novelty.

   HOLMSKIOLDIA sanguinea, "Mandarin-hat" from the shape of
the calyx, a round hat-like affair, a kind of bract which
cups the tiny flower and carries the color, many of them that
crowd into a loose head, grading from orange to red, a glowing
thing in the sun:blooming irregular, but always with some color
in just the right place, dependably summer-autumn:wants a little
shade in high heat, but will flower satisfactorily only on the
stem reaching light:climbing shrub for warm rich soils, having
long liana-like, scrambling stems when pushed culturally, loose
shrub-like when held in.

   HOMALANTHUS populifolius, "Queensland-poplar" for frost-free
areas, a small tree, rounded at 15' or with an open shrub-like
structure:triangular leaves drop at any sudden check in its
growth, the old leaves flecking crimson as they fail, the
new ones coppery as they come on....almost immediately:not
important, but with a distinctly tropical after-flavor in
these regions:to be used only near the coast in California, far south in Florida:short-lived.

   HOMERIA collina, bulb-like plants forming an unruly
mass of twisting two-foot, grassy leaves, but sparkling
March-April with the bright red to orange or yellow
flowers:wants drainage and prefers dryness in late summer:pos-
sibly the most persistently scattering from seed of all the
South Africans....as delightfully weedy as a spreading bed of
cowslip or dark patch of forget-me-not.

   HOUSTONIA floridana, native Florida perennial growing to 18" in
height and fullness, spreading widely in good moisture and preferably a little shade:foliage very finely divided, thread-like, the
small, crossed flowers purple, in delicate leafy heads:top may
kill back in a late frost....otherwise hardy.

## KENTIA PALM
   HOWEA---handsome palms, quite wide-spread by long use
indoors as a tub plant for hotels and other building
lobbies....not so much in the home. These same plants
will be found growing out of doors in these regions
in sun or shade and under considerable wind, if
hardened under protection....no high heat or
deep frost. They are slow to take hold, but are

317

worth a considerable wait for the extremely attractive character in stem and head. They are comparatively clean trees and may be grown with interest in line
and when young, can be crowded together for unusual
effects in mass that carry over into the maturing
trees as they come along.
      -belmoreana, "Curly P."not as tall, but more grace-
ful than the following, the fronds arching, even the leaflets in a bending, semi-horizontal plane:not commonly to
be found out of doors and probably not as hardy.
      -forsteriana, "Thatchleaf P." has an angular look, placed
beside the above, a tree eventually to 60' with a green, ringed
bole, usually irregular with slight distortions from the symmet-
trical, if only in the pattern of the rings:fronds reach erect
angular, the leaflets hanging:stands in severe salt wind, but
does burn in a storm. These trees can be trained from youth
into adult-hood to nearly duplicate the cocoanut palm, with
feather-duster top and gently winding line leading upward in
a kind of irresolution from the typically swollen base.

      HOYA carnosa, "Pink Wax-vine" tropical climber with precise
rounding clusters of geometrically perfected, waxy-white flowers, each touched at the center with a wash of pink:is fragrant, warm nights, continuous under tropical conditions, but
normally only in summer in these regions:do not remove flowering parts, since the same stub repeats over several years:
thick, meaty leaves burn and scorch in the sun, so that shade
is required, but along with warmth to bring out the bloom:sup-
port on trellis or train on wire, from free soil or pot, the
root system demanding little space....attempts to root-climb on
rough surfaces, does climb a rough trunk into over-head shade,
with help:holds back stubbornly in a poor soil and is subject
to mealybug and nematodes....no drouth, when the leaf shrivels,
shrinks and wrinkles out of shape and recognition....a too low
light intensity aids in this deformity.

      HUNNEMANNIA fumariaefolia, "Tulip-poppy" perennial, be-
coming woody at the base by  second or third year, finely
formed leaves are deeply cut, succulent on a juicy note
and consistency, bluish, to make an elegant foil for the
glowing, lemon-yellow of the bloom....seemingly luminous of
itself rather than of the light of day....come along freely summer-autumn, short-lived individually:shear back
in winter for more bloom next year, but not to deeply:
wants a warm spot, where seed may be sown with better
over-all results than from sets from cuttings....will
not be kept in a container for long.

      HYDRANGEA macrophylla, gross-growing, soft-wood shrub
3-5' round-topped, with sharp outline, but with less vigorous forms that are loose and spreading:canes end in interesting and colorful heads of flowers of specimen quality;
immense and full round in case of the sterile type, smaller and
flattened for a much more delicate and artistic feeling in the
fertile flowering heads:should have deep, rich, loose ground in
shade, with good moisture in summer and quickly available fertilizer just as the heads begin to set:prune when necessary to
open the mass, removing old canes toward the center, heading
in others, done before new growth starts. The tendency for
color to alternate between greenish, pink and blue may be
controlled or intensified by incorporating alum in the soil
for blue, suphate of potash or gypsum for pink with, theor-
etically, a neutral soil for the greenish white. The old
French hybrids are highly colored, the petal fringed or
frilled, the heads cutting successfully to keep, after the
true flower has opened:tubs.

      HYDROCLEYS nymphoides, "Waterpoppy" aquatic with small oval
or heart-shaped leaves, floating or lifted:flowers simply cupped, golden yellow, raised and continual in warmth, but not in
the shade:tender.

Hunnemannia

Hydrocleys
nymphoides

Hylocereus

Hymenanthera
crassifolia

COMPENDIUM

HYLOCEREUS triangularis, a "Nightblooming Cereus" that
is rampant, half-woody, succulent, climbing on masonry or
into trees:only warm locations, but will burn against a full
south wall:responds to moisture and a fertile soil, flowering
through warmth, periodically, tapering off at either extreme:a
moist atmosphere is beneficial, but not necessarily moisture in
in the ground for best results....flowers, not wood the aim. The
great white flower against the blackness of night becomes a neighborhood event, with parties held in its honor....and in appreciation for the wonder of it.

HYMENANTHERA crassifolia, a low-spreading shrub, the recurving just short of recumbency in the matter of stems,
ultimately building up 2-3' or more in height, a mound that
is fixed, rigid and brushy, with white furrowed bark and
tiny, thickened leaves, durable in the wind; deciduous, the
plant spreading wider than its height:flowers March-April,
are not important, but white to purple berries are notable
and persistent:rock gardens on a large scale or does in almost pure sand near the sea:frost-hardy into warm temperate
regions, as is the species   -traversi, low and tree-like.

### WHITE SPIDERLILY
HYMENOCALLIS---bulbous plants with curious but beautiful
and fragrant flowers, the long, narrow segments, together with
the webbed filaments, bringing the whole into a spidery feeling
and appearance. They require no special treatment other than
ordinary garden fertility, the sun, and moisture during growth.
This should be enough to insure flowers which sometimes fail
to develop according to schedule....may skip a year. Don't be too
disappointed for the unusual blooming is quite worth a short span
of time. Set to bury the bulb full length and when dividing, retain all the roots possible.
     -calathina(Ismene)"Basketflower" the white of the cup is
more pronounced by reason of a clear green striping June-July:
flower is held well above the lush 2' clump of strap-shaped
leaves, a cutflower that is grown north into warm temperate
regions, either lifted or mulched over winter:temperamental,
but the one for California.   --var sulphurea, has pale yellow flowers, while the hybrid   --festalis, with a pure
white flower is superior, uncommon and expensive. It is
somewhat taller and later blooming.
     -caribaea, a lower plant for wet places, a good damp spot
in the garden or will stand in warm, shallow water:ever-
green south, the pure white flowers in winter or early in
the spring:better grown in Florida or along the Gulf Coast.

HYMENOSPORUM flavum, "Sweetshade" an erect, open-headed
tree to 40' with pale, yellowish green foliage, the bloom
April-June, honey-scented and honey-colored....honey of
a tree when grown well....color of flower deepens to
ochre, dwindles with the shedding pollen and adds to
the litter:a garden tree essentially, useful for a
very narrow street, a tree of unseemly extremes, either
narrow, thinly tapering upward or scarcely getting up off
the ground....a broad bush:guidance and correction with the
shears most important, watching for outside influence,
recognizing the whorled character of the branching and cutting out the weaker limbs in time to strengthen those left:
do not force with water or fertilizer, allowing slow, consolidating growth that is so desirable and so seldom attained.
This is a very select and useful garden tree and well worth the
thinking and physical effort to bring it along for service.

### SAINT JOHNS WORT
HYPERICUM---mostly low, fragile shrubs or procumbent and
only semi-woody, all with a great deal of beauty, both in
foliage and in flower....brilliant spots of gold over the year
They favor fairly moist, heavy ground, even soils that are on
the wet side, making the best of those that have become im-

319

poverished or go dry. They take the shade of over-topping
trees or that which is thrown, when the blooming period is
lengthened and quality of the flower improved. They may be
pruned lightly in the fall for increase in flowering the next
summer. Be careful with green manures since they are very sensitive and may die under a heavy application. Some plants for
the rock garden will be found here.

-aureum, an erect woody shrub 3-4' blooming June-August in
rocky soils in nature, meaning warmth, but enduring more shade
than others:native in the south and more likely to be found in
the east of these regions:quite reliable.

-calycinum, "Aarons-beard" low, half-woody plants, single
stems rising from a spreading root system, each tipped with a
single large yellow flower June-October:likes a good, moist
soil in shade, but gets along, and with fair service in stiff
dry ground in the sun:shear back each spring to renew the mat.

-floribundum, quick growth 5-8' with very light green foliage
and loose, indeterminate clusters of small droopy flowers, a light
golden yellow all summer, concentrating April-June....keep them
coming by breaking out the spent heads....a draggle-tail affair
unless cleaned up from time to time with the shears:a filler.

-henryi, another raveling that shows little of form or conformation, a little messy as a twiggy bush 3-4', but good for the
massed effect of pale yellow flowers running together without
shape or order, themselves of little cast, but taking the
sun literally for a unique, mellow lighting that affects
surroundings:a presentable plant if reduced and held to a
few stems....means much pruning.

-moserianum, "Goldflower" of good form, low-mound-
ing 18-24" or more and very free with the large, golden,
well set flowers, the massive button of filaments tipped with red anthers....a long summer season:altogether a
tidy little bush for general use, but a little tender.

-reptans, procumbent stems, re-rooting to build up a
beautiful bright green mat of considerable depth, bronzy in
autumn:soft golden flowers, small and clustered, only partially opened, are reddish in bud:messy by the time flowering
is over, but may be tiddied up with the shears which
will start new growth:ground cover or use with rock.

HYSSOPUS officinalis, "Hyssop" a handsome, rather
neat shrublet for the herb garden or flower border, as
much as 15-18" high, the greater part of the wood soft
and herb-like:the dark foliage is used in salads and
the bright blue flowers, all the way through June and
September, are dried out for later use in soups:thrives
in rather hot, dry and barren places, even dry walls:let
it have all the sun and a little lime for good measure.

I

## HOLLY

ILEX---evergreen shrubs, valued largely and universally used for the
great ornamental possibilities of foliage and berry. English holly may
be grown northerly in these regions and along the coasts in coolness with shade, but is more subject to scale and becomes indifferently disposed progressively as taken south. The following species
may be substituted there, or taken on their own intrinsic values with no apologies offered or called for. All are difficult
to transplant without the help of some plant growth substance
and have definite demands culturally, generally wanting moist,
fairly rich soils that are drained, but with species for a
wet place. Some or all of the leaves should be stripped if
and when dug bare-root....done in October or November.
These plants are polygamous or partially so and will

320

berry of themselves, but they, and the gardener, will be
comforted if there is a male plant somewhere in the background. Set more plants than required and cut out the
excess males for a high proportion of berrying wood.

-cassine, "Dahoon" the light green spineless leaves
widely spaced for teeth, a shrub or small tree of character
in stem, set with dense clusters of small, bright red berries
all fall and winter:native east in the South, in or at the edge
of wet ground, but may be used in California in moisture.

-cornuta, "Chinese or Horned H." an erect, eventually wide-
spreading shrub of rigid, bushy growth, the leaves very dark and
shining....rectangular adaptation of the typical holly pattern,
hard and horny, with a half-twist accenting the four or five
great spines:berries comparatively large but not very freely
produced:does poorly in cold or very heavy soils....best one for
the drier, hotter localities.   --var. Burfordi, spineless, very
deep green rounded leaves, of medium height and branching low,
growing in considerable shade:an age variant that berries very
easily and without benefit of sex.   --var. nana, dwarf and
rounding, only 18-24" in height:not a common plant.

-paraguariensis, "Yerba de Mate" found south in Florida,
shrubby or tree-like to 20' with a low, irregular trunk and
horizontal branchings of dark, very glossy, wavy-toothed
leaves:reddish brown berries are used to brew a tea. This
is sub-tropical and stands in wind,some little drouth.

-perado, Canary Island H." symmetrical, conical bush or a
tree to 35' with flat pale green, spiny-toothed leaves, elliptic
and very evenly spaced on the branch, as in English holly:certain
plants will bear the very dark red, nearly black berries without
cross pollinization:adapts to the drier atmospheres.

-vomitoria, "Yaupon" large shrub or slender tree-like, evergreen south, deciduous under frost, and either form as high as 25' in
rich ground that does not go too dry:rigid, grey-white branches
are densely set with small light green leaves and glistening
red berries, thick-clustered around growth and reach of the
branches of the previous years growth, September-April.

ILLICIUM---aromatic evergreen shrubs, closely related to
magnolia, the flowers, however, more in the likeness of
michelia or banana shrub, solitary or grouped in the axils
of the leaves which are very short-petioled. They belong in
the border area between temperate  and subtropical regions
and their modified climates, wanting primarily shade, moisture and an acid soil built up with the mould of leaves.

-anisatum, "Anise-tree" shrub or narrow-tree-like 10-15',
the flowers greenish yellow, to an inch across, little magnol-
ias set in among the leaves May-June:the attractive and familiar foliage is light in tone, with an odor of anise and must
have rather substantial shade in dry heat.

-floridanum, shrubby 8-10', with purple to dark red flowers
to two inches across and nodding, the many petals very narrow, weak in
the sense of thinness, July:native in Florida and back from the
Gulf Coast in humidity.

IMPATIENS sultani, "Touch-me-not" an erect bushy herb, with
wood at the base and having sappy stems and watery leaves:grows
2-3' high and as much across in good thrift:flowers white
or tinted rose or pink to pale scarlet....bleach in the
sun, pass out in heat or dryness:grown far south, they
are perpetually flowering, abundantly in winter if the
seed pods are cut:straggling can be shaped agreeably by
tipping and cutting out weak growth. This old plant is
being over-looked south for winter color.

IOCHROMA--- rather soft of wood, bushy, shrubs in the
6-8' range for height, rapid in a notably loose growth,
rank in foliage, the clustered, long-tubular flowers not
profuse, but persistently carried, scattering out over
the warmer part of the year. They do with considerable
shade, but want sun; thrive in cold heavy soils, but

321

Ilex
paraguariensis

Illicium
floridanum

Impatiens

Iochroma
lanceolatum

will take them light and warmer in preference. They require continuous moisture and wilt easily during dry weather, if not watched and given help.

-fuchsioides, of extremely willowy habit with orange-scarlet round-tubular flowers in hanging clusters or at times found with the flowers scarcely gathered together:tender in cold.

-lanceolatum,"Purple-tobacco" the bush gracefully formed, the roughly arching stems supplied with a cheerless green but otherwise good foliage:flowers of a strange shade of dull, livid blue, squarish-tubular with a short flare, the full clusters few and scattered: thrifty and serviceable shrub in good culture, too seldom used.

IPOMOEA---annual and perennial climbers or trailing to great distances over the ground, some becoming quite woody, surely so at the base. They are scarcely equaled in rapidity of growth, luxurious in screening and for cover, known for ease in culture, popular in appreciation. While they prosper in poor ground, they handle one that is rich without the usual over-reach. They prefer good moisture. Give them every advantage of the sun since the flowers tend to close in its absence....yet clearer coloring will be noticed in broken shade that is on the sunny side. They take well to a container in the quick furnishing of terrace, patio wall or pillar. There is some confusion in the botany of these plants, but to the gardener, these are all morning-glories.

-horsfalliae, long streamers that are well supplied with foliage, set generously all summer with pale purple to rosy red flowers:leaf is divided into five to seven leaflets, oval and tapering to the common base:cover for a steep bank:perennial.

-leari, "Blue Dawnflower" outstanding in the group for size of the flower and splendid purity in coloring, semi-woody and long-scrambling, constantly repeating the deep blue flowers throughout summer....changes to pink as they go off:the lighter soils are always best:perennial.

-pes-caprae, "Beach M. G." creeping, running out to great lengths, streamers to 60' long: somewhat more bell-shaped, the flowers are blue or purple:cover for sandy ground or to invade a little used beach, rerooting at the joints down to the high water line. This is the most robust of all and can get out of hand, unless with moisture control:perennial.

-purpurea, the common "Morning Glory" the plant trailing without support to carpet waste places or unsightly dumps with greenery and color; white thru red to purple and blue in the summer, normally open only in the morning:may be held to a pot:annual.

-setosa, "Brazilian M. G. " twining stems covered with stiff, purplish hairs, the large, grape-like leaves heart-shaped at the base, deeply lobed:rosy purple flowers are pink at the center August-September:an especially good quick screen on account of the foliage....leaves to 6" across:perennial.

## FLEUR DE LIS

IRIS---a large group of strictly perennial plants, tuberous-rooted or bulbous and so widely varying in culture as to have but little in common....as between species. The flag, as a class, leaves something to be desired in performance, far south, but the following will be grown through most of these regions with much satisfaction. In the main, soil is not as important as the sun and the timing of moisture, for they have an almost universal desire for a dry rest after flowering. They react unfavorably to green manures, so that active material should not be used....only such as has been exceptionally well rotted or none at all....yet fertility for root growth is very important in relation to next years flowering. Most of them are effective as cutflowers, some lasting as long as three days if only tight buds of beginning color are taken at dusk. The native types are better used in Florida.

322

-alata, bulbous, with nearly stemless flowers, white
and blue, vanilla-scented December-January:should go where
there will be no disturbance, a place that will allow the dormant tuber a good baking out in the summer sun....no water then:
salvage all roots  in transplanting:rock garden:rare.
-delta species, the "Louisiana I." a group of beardless,
very slender and graceful forms from the lower Mississippi valley, of varying height and of great variation in color from tan
to yellow, wine-red through to coppers and lavender-blue:many of
them are difficult in combinations, all essentially water-loving
for at least damp soils in the garden:want good humus in a rich
soil....do well in California with the moisture necessary.
foetidissima, "Gladwin I." livid blue and lilac flowers of
low quality, but opulent seed pods break over the scented leaves
to make a showing of seed....bubbling up out of the break, a
frothing mass of bright red spoondrift to be taken for dry
bouquets or arrangements:a persistent plant, a colonizer,
even in California, long-lived in the border from seed.
-germanica, the common garden flag, bearded, rugged,tol-
erating  all extremes of soil, with drainage....even to the
latests improvements, marvelous creations in form and color
and in size scarcely recognizable, but all within the
name:likes lime and will find acidity in concentration
objectionable:transplant any time after blooming up until
July or somewhat later, hardly covering the rhizome, best
done in October in very hot climates, while August-September
is good for new stock from the north:do well in beds, alone or
in a mixed border where they are very resistant to drought, in-
sisting on moisture only in growth and in bloom....taller varieties bruise in the wind....don't be afraid of a little shade
southerly and in high heat. Many varieties are less satisfactory as taken south and from the multitude of names, the
average gardener may better choose those which have held
their place in the local lists.
-hexagona, native in southern swamps and environs,
the full flowers lilac or white, a little pallid, but invaluable near water or a wet spot in gardens of its region:will
grow to 3' in height, erect-leafy, the flower large.
-japonica(fimbriata)"Orchid I." a delicate flower,
both in form and in coloring, beautifully marked in white,
pale blue and yellow....orchid-like, used as such in a
corsage, although short-lived:freely produced in wide-
branching panicles, late winter and early spring, in a
moist comfortable soil with a little shade for hot places. The
type form may prove to be a little temperamental, but hybrids
in common use are so vigorous as to require renovation every
year or so:choice and very practical.
-kaempferi, "Japanese I." moisture loving, better grown
near the coast in California:very large, flattened flower thin
and translucent, white, violet and blue with yellow May-July:
well used for the masses of rigid, straight leaves which tend to
burn in a hot sun:wants a rich, warm, acid soil, wet deeply, a
want that suggests flooding....a high water table within reach of
roots ideal:do not permit crowding:divide October-April.
-unguicularis, "Winter I." erect slender leaves, 10-12" and
slightly fragrant, short-stalked flowers, lavender-blue any
time in the winter, November-April:wants a warm, light soil,
with lime in any acidity, takes and likes extreme heat and
dryness over summer, although it does not go down:foliage
is dense and holds in a tight clump, never invasive. These
clumps are difficult to divide and hold in the new planting
so that extra care must be exercised in choosing time and
following attention....note start of activity in late summer
or fall, dig then and reduce foliage.
-xiphium, "Spanish I." large, sleek flowers of formalized
charm, blue, violet and yellow in well marked varieties, excellent
for cutting March-May:bulbs may be lifted after bloom and ripened
or left in place where the stand can dry out some over summer:a
drained place is essential and the foliage must be allowed to go
brown:begin setting as early in the fall as possible:choice.

323

Iris Xiphion

Iris
kaempferi

Iris
germanica

Iris
unguicularis

SUBTROPICAL REGIONS

ITEA ilicifolia, an attractive foliage shrub 3-5' or
as much as 10' under conditions of coolness and deep soil:
a plant of symmetry and much grace in the slender stems:the
roundish leaves are dark and shining, meticulously toothed
and uniformly:small greenish-white flowers droop in long
tail-like clusters or catkins August-September:will benefit with shade, suited to exposure and locality; is in
slight degree drouth resistant and hardy in any frost that
will be experienced in these regions:choice.

IXIA maculata, "African Cornlily" bulbs for early spring,
or late flowering into the early part of summer in rich,
sandy loams:yellow, orange, pink, crimson or purple flowers come on long stems for cutting:set bulbs in fall for
late winter and spring, but in early spring for summer:per-
mit the foliage to ripen and wither completely before disturbing the bulb....a mulch in hot spots or shade cast by
other herbs over the resting period beneficial....only a
minimum of baking, but must have the sun in growth when it
will build up quickly from seed:hardy into warm temperate
regions, but does not persist....set deeply and mulch.

J

JACARANDA acutifolia, sometimes known as "Green-
ebony", an irregular tree to 50' in deep, rich soils
that have good drainage; there with a handsome, full-
round head....with some little attention to early corrective pruning:heads of lavender blue flowers are
loosely formed, erect May-June, but through July or
later after a cold winter....litter the ground beneath
as a colorful carpet.....of better quality if the tree
is grown dryish, winter-spring:rapid growth throughout
these regions, limited only by frost, when it recovers
from shallow killback. This tree is actually deciduous
for a short time in February-March, the ferny leaves
being pushed off by the swelling buds of new growth. It
flowers better in California along the coast.

JACOBINIA---tender sub-shrubby plants for lath house or cool
moist places of broken shade in the garden. Young plants that
have been pinched in for form are sometimes grown on in pots
for areas where close attention can be given. They want a rich
soil with much peatmoss or other fibery material worked in.
Use them as fern allies for the lush feeling for foliage they
impart to a planting or in any place with that special combination of moisture and shade and good open humusy soil.
    -carnea(Justicia)"Kings Crown" an erect strict growth of
almost herbaceous stems 3-4' with terminal heads of rose colored flowers, grading into deeper reds:a yearly heading in is
desirable or the entire removal of selected stems, to keep
the plant in shape....done in the spring, it is ready for
bloom by early fall or winter....feed generously for extra
bloom, done also in the spring:large roughened leaves are
veined in purple; are left in rather bad shape by winter in
any but a very warm, protected spot.
    -pauciflora(Libonia), bushy, rounding, 18-24", sappy in
the new growth, the smaller leaves yellowish green:tubular
flowers of scarlet, tipped with yellow for an overall orange
effect, winter-spring:a little stringy in too much shade.

JAQUEMONTIA---tender herbaceous vines that ultimately
become somewhat woody, spreading-low-bushy, sending
slender streamers aloft on support, fence or
shrubs or draping a hot rock. They are blue-

flowered, the bud opening precisely, as of folds in
paper, retaining the creases in the matured flower in
the semblance of inch-wide morning-glories. These plants
are not only drouth resistant, they like it and resent the
coolness of the coast and summer irrigation very decidedly.
Sharp drainage is a necessity and when grown in the right
place, make an outstanding show.

   -eastwoodiana, the greyish foliage a low bed for the
salver-shaped, sky-blue flowers, everblooming in heat and a
warm dry soil....grow only in sun concentration, with a wall
or rock or a floor to hold and dispense the warmth through
night:rocky hillsides, planters, baskets, native to islands
off Lower California:choice.

   -pentantha, rather more dwarf, with darker foliage and
reddish stems:the white-centered flowers are generally for the
spring, open mornings, closed by late afternoon. This one is a
native of Florida and is more tolerant of people and gardens.

## JASMINE

JASMINUM---shrubby or scrambling, but mostly climbing, woody
vines very commonly grown in gardens, located where the refining influence may be put to work and where the fragrance will
do the most for people....near a porch or lanai, over the pergola, otherwise on a down wind for carry and dispersal. They
want the sun, tolerate but little shade and survive the heaviest
soils only with good drainage....avoid if possible. Otherwise,
they are easy to grow, only the very tender species going out
or damaged in frost, some being quite hardy. A common fault
with the climbers is the bareness that develops at the base,
but this can be remedied by growing to several stems and from
time to time cutting one all the way back so that it may break
with a new supply of low foliage....done in winter.

   -azoricum, "Canary J." shrubby in poorer soils or dry,
vining under better circumstances, as of the garden, a densely
foliated plant of deep, shining green, touched with grey when in
drouth, the pure white flower of substance, like stephanotis or
bouvardia and of the same excellence in bloom....the flower to
as much as an inch across, clustered.   --var. bahiense, very
choice but tender, to be grown far south in Florida or in the
warm foothills of Southern California.

   -dichotomum, "Goldcoast J." climbing, but with no heavy wood,
much refined, with thick glossy leafage, pink-lined buds to very fragrant white flowers that are set off by red calyces....effective in the
evening:continually flowering far south:tender in frost.

   -floridum, a bush with a dense, stemmy crown to a 3-4' height,
close-packed low, but loosely spreading at the top for an unclipped
hedge or to face down shrubbery with legs:the one to use where space
is restricted....foundations:very small yellow flowers in warmth and
scattering:pruning a problem, in getting to the cut....use hook.

   -gracillimum, "Pinwheel J." scrambling as a brushy shrub or
high-climbing, with soft, dark greyish foliage and fragrant white
flowers, dependable for winter in absence of frost:a natural tendency for leafy laterals to originate from old wood, keeps the leafage low....but prune out surplus stems for air circulation.

   -humile, "Italian J." shrubby under the shears, but otherwise
with far-flung stems, or tree-like 15-18' with an umbrella cover
of light yellow-green leaves that shine in the sun:pale yellow
flowers summer-fall and into winter, some years as late as
Christmas:may be grown as a standard to one or several twisted
stems to a formalized top:tubs.

   -mesneyi(primulinum)"Primrose J." a shrub, short-sprawling
vine or high-climbing on support....less naturally climbing:soli-
tary, semi-double, hose in hose flowers appear in January, pale
yellow, richly toned, fading in full sun:thrives in poor soil
and very hard frost:don't prune until through blooming in the
spring, reducing new wood for laterals to bloom the following spring....a cutflower, the color outlasting the leaf.

   -officinale, "Poets J." tall, slender, arching
stems as a kind of shrub or weak-vining, clambering every
where in Florida:the fragrant pinkish flowers of summer

Jasminum grandiflorum

Jasminum humile

J. gracillimum

Jasminum primulinum

extend into winter or scatter out over the seasons in warmth:
tolerates considerable heat and drought.   --var. grandiflorum,
"Spanish or Catalonian J." with larger flowers and more rigid
stems, but much less fragrance.
    -parkeri, a shrublet, seldom as much as 12" height, more in the
nature of a cover, spreading laterally 18-24"....shear top to spread:
tiny yellow flowers, half-inch tubes, the thickness of the lead in a
pencil May-June:survives deep frost and adapts to salt wind.
    -pubescens, "Downy J." easily kept in hand as a shrub, but will
climb, if allowed to run:stems covered with rusty-yellow hair and
white, especially star-like flowers show as rigid points against
the dark foliage:scentless and everblooming:tender.
    -rigidum, an erect shrub 8-10', only the tips of the new
growth showing any inclination to wander:white or yellow flowers go with a slick, light green foliage which carries just
the suggestion of yellow:no call to prune this plant unless
too tall for situation, and topping disfigures:naturally a
dense plant and neat....use correctly in beginning.
    -sambac, "Arabian J. shrub, loosely growing to 5', but
with climbing tendencies:large whitish flowers blacken in
water, as of irrigation spray, are very fragrant, turn purplish as they fail:perpetually blooming in warmth and must
not be planted elsewhere....and warm exposures anywhere:a
little shade best and better used with other growth to support the scant foliage:not too satisfactory generally, but
tried for the exceeding fragrance:represented in gardens by
--var. Grand Duc, semi-reclining, with full double flowers
that are pure white and   --var. Maid of Orleans, semi-
double white flowers, tending to climb. Both are tender and
subject to scale insects and will be used with discretion.

## WALNUT

JUGLANS---deciduous dual purpose trees, infrequently used in
these regions for the landscape and about habitations for the light
open head and its agreeable shade....and for the nuts. The leaves
come out rather late in the spring, but well before summer heat, so
that maximum sun may be enjoyed without the extreme. They want a
light, deep, fertile soil and will be set bare root....no containers, only nursery transplants on account of tap roots. The natives have local significance in park and highway plantings.
    -californica, a black walnut, shrubby in nature or a fair
sized tree in rich soils with water below:nut is nearly round
and deeply grouved....planted in place will make the better tree.
    -regia, "English W." round-headed and widely spreading, as
high as 75', but usually much less, grown commercially for the
thin shelled nut of high quality:the thrown shade is dense and
may require thinning for domestic purposes.
    -rupestris, another black walnut native in the great south-
west:a slender stem to 30' in height, to be used locally:and do
not overlook the advantages of placing nuts in place for better
trees:protect from rodents and grazing animals.

## JUNIPER

JUNIPERUS---hardy ornamentals, standard for all parts of these
regions, a diversified group of coniferous shrubs and trees with
scale-like leaves and a splendid will to survive. The erect
forms are of value in formalized plantings and as used to spike
a natural setting. The prostrate and shrubby kinds make good
ground cover or find a place against heavy foundations, excellent free forms in contempory layout.  They do best in loamy,
sandy or gravelly soils of fair moisture or dry, while most
will develop better form and color in poorer ground. As a
rule they take poorly to fertilizers and very heavy soils,
do not tolerate much shade and are comfortable generally
at the seashore under exposure. Blue enters largely, with
grey, in the coloring of the foliage, but always subdued
and dominated by the green. There are no pests of note.
    -barbadensis, "Bermuda or Florida-cedar" a tree
with much the form of the better known red-cedar, growing to 40', with  stouter  branches and pale bluish

326

COMPENDIUM

green foliage, a dense-spreading, round-headed tree in age:
used south in Florida and along the Gulf Coast on the sea.
-californica, small pyramidal tree or spreading, irregular
shrub with dark foliage, but newer growth silvery:native in the
driest sandy or gravelly places or rock crevices....adapted to
such places only, in a man-made landscape....see to drainage.
-chinensis, the type seldom found in the south, but with
many varieties in wide use. --var. argentea, dwarf, dense and
broad at the base, coming into a rough cone, greyish green with
scattered tufts of white or yellowish sprays that lighten the
over-all effect materially:not as rugged as the following, but a
desirable variegation. --var. pfitzeriana, well clothed, dark
vivid green, an angular, shrubby plant, ultimately to some 5-6'
in height and probably more across, the branches spreading
out horizontally upward in a flat vase form:a tendency to
grow one-sided early fits it for an angle :stout, superior
plant that may be depended on for long service nearly any-
where:give it space for the future by using fillers.
-conferta, "Shore J." prostrate and wide-spreading, the
attractive bluish green foliage distinctive, soft to feel
and eye, plushy next the earth, later more angular as heavy
wood is developed:un-affected by driven salt spray where
drainage is good....number one cover or draping a slope
against the sea:hugs the ground but with arching branchlets
to 12" high, a flat mat only a few inches through with early
shearing:fails in extreme heat and dryness:dunes.
-excelsa, "Greek J." compact, cone-shaped, broad at the base,
very dense, the blue-grey-green foliage an outstanding shade to
use for distance:grows very slowly, counted on for 5-8' service
in height, eventually much more:transplants comparatively easy,
is long-lived and subject especially to red spider:takes salt
in soil and air, but not driven spray nor does it thrive in
dry heat. --var. stricta, is more columnar, the foliage a
marked grey and the plant hardier to range into warm temperate
regions:too rarely seen south.
-pachyphlaea, "Alligator J." native in the Southwest, a
tree 50', the bark breaking deeply into squarish sections,
for identification and name:foliage bluish....no heavy frost.
-silicicola(leucayana)"Southern Red-cedar" broadly pyramidal and very dense, 50' when well grown, but in age, rounding
and open, picturesque:native south in Florida and along the Gulf
Coast into Texas, a better plant in these regions than red-cedar.
-torulosa, "Hollywood J." probably to 25' in height ultimately,
so outstanding and with such dramatic effect as now to be over-planted, and in poor places for the form....oriental in feeling, with a
tufted foliage of bright green:naturally develops into several erect
and twisting, tortuous stems, devious in a way that is unique and
most handsome, in thrift....see that a tree comes to project in
good color and other evidence of health....has difficulty coming
out of a serious setback in growth or conditioning. Watch also for
a tree that has not been cut in too heavily for cuttings, showing
usually at the base. Don't ever stake this, even in the wind. Here
is character that must come of itself and environment.

JUSSIAEA---strong-growing aquatic plants that may be used out
of doors in or near water or in very moist soils that are dependable for moisture all season. They are erect or prostrate, perennial in a sufficiently and surely warm climate, rooting well to
hold moist earth or mud, where water movement is not too swift.
They are coarse and grasping for space. Use carefully.
-longifolia, "Primrose-willow" the three to five angled
stems are erect, sometimes becoming woody, again only an annual
with total herbaceous stems:bright yellow flowers are carried in
the axils of the leaves during summer:use this in pots submerged
or directly in the soil.
-repens, "Primrose Creeper" prostrate, branching and rooting
at the nodes to make an evergreen mat for the large yellow flowers:
the stems and leaves are floating or partially submerged:will not
flower well in water that is very deep and more freely when it is
crowding itself, as in a pot or sunken box.

Junip-erus pachyphlaea

Jussiaea repens

Kaempferia

Kalanchoe tubiflora

327

K

KAEMPFERIA involucrata, low herbaceous plants with thickened tuberous root-stocks, grown mostly for indoor uses,
but precariously out of doors protected from hot sun:the
purple and green leaves are ridged in sympathy with the
lay of color....deciduous and down all winter....lilac
flower in summer:irrigate and feed well during growth,dry
as may be over winter:slugs will mar the leaf.

KALANCHOE---an unstable group of rank-growing succulents
with opposite-placed, soft fleshy leaves and bright yellow,
scarlet or purple flowers, erect or drooping in an unusually
effective inflorescence. The flowers appear mostly in the winter
on into spring, are colorful and long-lasting. These plants will
renew themselves by the rooting in of fallen leaves or by seed
to such an extent as to make a nuisance of a handsome plant and
interesting group, at least in the well-kept garden....pots:grow
them somewhat dryish for better form and coloring, best where the
sun is modified over noon. They are all quick fillers for color
in the planter box, to be removed when they overflow the side
out of hand. Bryophyllum and Kitchingia are found here.
     -aliciae, tall and straggling, soft-hairy, with compari-
tively large green leaves, suffused along the edges with dull
red:has orange-red flowers, pendent tubes over fall and into
winter:better in a slightly moist soil that is not rich.
     -beharensis, tree-like on a small scale, due to quick-
shedding of the leaves which are quite large, plush-like, grey
rust-colored:striking forms to be used casually and as occasion-
als in the garden, but for a very definite eye-catching purpose.
     -blossfeldiana, an erect, strong-growing plant with heads
of up-looking scarlet or orange flowers, sometimes beginning in
December, carrying through into spring....at least the buds
show early:good garden specimen for the border or used in the
larger containers:does not become leggy.
     -fedtschenkoi, erect and fairly strong-growing, sometimes
rather fragile, a plant for partially shaded places in moist-
ure:delicate-shaded leaves in bluish tones and yellow to orange flowers late winter-spring:structure is branching-pyr-
amidal for a comparatively neat, precise note in a darkened
place....even there renewing too freely from the falling
leaves:one of the older forms, still choice for gardens.
     -flammea, good rounding structure and growth, a tight
mass of off-green for the border or large pot:a master plant
for a basket in sun:flowers yellow to orange-scarlet.
     -glaucescens, smooth little succulent, the dollar-wide,
thin meaty leaves of a metalic bluish green, the flowers a
dark red or yellow:bushy, with a more substantial body.
     -marmorata, a large plant for this group with wide thin
leaves, but of typical succulent character, spotted or marbled in dark purple:more striking than handsome and tends to
straggle rather badly in old age....renew early.
     -orgyalis, very much simplified structurally, essentially
a foliage plant with clean-cut, thickened leaves more in the
ordinary conception of a leaf, colored and toned in rich
shades of brown, touched with gold in the new growth: will
reach 2-3' in height and has yellow flowers with the brown.
     -tubiflora, typical semi-succulent in many repeated
vertical lines of slender stems set with yellowish brown
pencil-lined leaves, topped by the erect, long-tubular red
or yellow flowers:reseeds everywhere, a prime nuisance, but
with uses few others will duplicate in this type of thing.
     -uniflora, the stems hanging from a basket in partial or
rather close shade, or prostrate, rooting at the joints for a
bright green cover in specialized plantings, lath house or other:
the single red flowers are more abundant in average moisture
and half-shade. This lacks the dash, splash and splurge of
the others, but has sound, practical uses.

KENNEDYA rubicunda, "Coralpea" a vine, twining 10-20' with
rather sparse foliage and dark red, pea-shaped flowers May-July
the grey, deeply furrowed stem of maturity gives a definite,

Kalanchoe
marmorata

Kalanchoe
uniflora

Kalanchoe
fedtschenkoi

Kalanchoe
orgyalis

interesting and sophisticated line about post or pillar or
across the face of a contemporary wall or panel:wants good
moisture in growth and a reasonably fertile soil:prune after
the blooming has passed, taking new shoots back to within
two or three inches of the woody structure....excepting ex-
tensions desired in further growth:endures dryness, which
will restrict growth materially and is frost-hardy.

KLEINIA---meaty, thick-succulent plants with white or yellow,
thistle-like flowers and other outstanding characters that may
place them in the collectors category....but each, as suggested
here, serving some practical landscape or garden function. They
must have the sun in full and a gravelly, well drained, preferably sterile soil.....may lose foliage in extreme drought.
Loose or detached stems will be allowed to lie exposed for
a period before being set for rooting.
    -articulata, "Candle-cactus" a queer, rather tall,
dry-succulent with bright green leaves under some moisture:
used for the gracefully moulded, lined joints, a series of
them that go to make up the stems:articulated in such a way
that they fall apart very easily in a natural way of propagation....messy after a high wind or passage of a small boy.
    -ficoides, with rather a thick growth of stems and a kind
of powdery white or bluish leaves, sharply pointed and somewhat
flattened at the edges, flange-like:may be used in some shade,
but does not flower there:pots for the precise form and
texture:close-clustered, whitish flowers.
    -radicans, trailing, adapted to the rock garden or dry
wall, or used hanging from a pot or basket:leaves are green,
quite swollen, round and thick, hooking slightly into a sharp
point at the end:the white of the dead flower persists.
    -repens, low, very meaty, a plant with spreading, fleshy,
cylindrical leaves that are distinctly blue....not bluish:it
is erect at first, working out eventually as a ground cover,
a little coarse, size of the leaf depending largely on soil.
    -tomentosa, becomes a woody bush to 18" high, decorative
by way of contrast where cultural conditions are right, cylindrically flattened, blunt-pointed leaves are covered with a
white felt:takes some water in the summer, but wants as little
in the winter as can be arranged....see to run-off and sub-
drainage:of great interest and beauty in a large pot.

KNIPHOFIA uvaria, "Torch-lily or Redhot Poker" a perennial
of many hybrids, itself of uncertain origin, a border plant
with large clumpy masses of grassy leaves and 2-4' stems with
orange and scarlet or yellow flowers, the hanging tubes closely packed in an oval, erect-pointed head:blooms in late summer, northerly, going into autumn; but more or less continuously over June-October in the south when stimulated:strong-
growing and very showy, they appear best against dark shrubbery where the brilliant color has a back:takes a very moist
soil, but goes to foliage in too-rich ground....drained gravelly ground best:transplant in spring, leaving the crown high,
even to mounding slightly:full sun for good spikes.

KOELREUTERIA paniculata, "Goldenrain-tree" deciduous, to 40'in a
good, deep soil, ordinarily found in colder regions, included here
for its bearing on arid conditions:broad masses of bright green
foliage are at first dull red as the leaves unfold, while the
flowers in large panicles May-June are bright yellow and take
a considerable place for themselves in the landscape as spring
merges with summer:bladder-like fruit capsules likewise dominate, changing from a whitish aspect through pink to brown
by October with the falling leaves....then the crooked character of the stem and branches, to lend a picturesque air.
This is a tree for sad affliction and disaster, suffering in
turn the unhappy trials of heat, deep drought, frost and
alkali, the sweeping, desiccating wind of barrens and
smog of cities. The species  -formosana, "Chinese
Lantern-tree" is nearly evergreen, a better tree, but
rarely found:tender.

Kniphofia uvaria

Kleinia articulata

Kleinia repens

Kleinia radicans

CAPE COWSLIP
LACHENALIA---low bulbous plants that bloom very early in the spring or by midwinter far south. Set closely together, they present a lush, succulent mat of small, strap-shaped leaves from which the naked flower stem rises with its string of erect or hanging flowers. They are fascinating if not showy, used in pots, baskets or other container more often than in the ground where summer water is hard to keep down. Set out August-October, in a sandy soil for drainage and with added leaf mould or peat moss....minimum irrigation until growth has started....then uniform and constant:fertilize with a weak liquid; control slugs and snails....move at will, in flower if the need is urgent. They are not commonly grown.
    -aurea, a strong-growing hybrid with wide, lance-shaped leaves that are faintly mottled and yellow flowers that go purplish as they fail.  -pendula, the flowering stems to 12" high, with flowers both erect and hanging, red touched with yellow December-January.  -tricolor, foliage frequently spotted with purple, the long flowers pendent, yellow tipped with red.

LAGENARIA leucantha, "Calabash Gourd" rampant annual vine for a ground cover or quick screening purposes;a hard-shelled fruit is variously shaped and designated in accordance with form the individual takes, a dipper, the hercules-club, serpentine, bottle, spoon, sugar-trough and others:unimportant flowers are white, culture simple:seed.

LAGERSTROEMIA indica, "Crape-myrtle" a well-formed shrub, rounded and tree-like, rarely a slender tree 35', sometimes with several stems of warm red, sinewy gripping bark and more or less columnar if the feather is held into the top:bears quantities of showy, crinkled flowers July to September in a wide range of colors from pure white through pink, rose, lavender red and bluish, the latter not too definite and pleasing....be careful of color and procure proven colors if possible:common along the Gulf Coast and in Florida, grown sparingly in California where it will mildew....spray in winter with lime-sulphur or equal and in summer, dust with sulphur. In any event, it is grown there satisfactorily only away from the coast in dry air and seldom will be seen closer to the shore than eight or ten miles, in maturity. They are difficult to establish and if not taken from a container, should be moved with balls of earth....best as activity begins in the spring. Prune for symmetry, that being inherent in the plant, and to produce more bloom in an individual that is lagging....cut back 10-15" all round in winter before growth starts and irregularly deeper for larger heads. Leaves turn gold and red before they drop. The species  -speciosa, "Queen C.M." a tree to 50' with a dark, spreading head, has a remarkable flowering that weights the branches downward, pink, deepening to lavender and purple May-July:tender.

LAGUNARIA patersoni, "Whitewood" a shapely tree of regular growth 35', a plant for wide use in ocean communities for the exceptional wearing quality of the leaf in salt wind:foliage a dark, olive-green set with the fleshy pink flowers May-July, scattering into September:prune immediately after bloom for structure and to clear out the drab fruit vessels which hang late and detract seriously:does poorly in shallow, heavy or very sterile ground and will show it soon in a thinning out of a normally very satisfactory leafage:a pyramidal tree of considerable merit for streets with a draft of wind.

LAGURUS ovatus, "Harestail-grass" tufted annual 8" high, the soft, plushy, rounded heads held high above the foliage, nicely turned, egg-shaped, an everlasting for winter boquets:an escape.
330

COMPENDIUM

LAMARKIA aurea, "Goldentop" an annual ornamental grass with
elongated, narrow heads of feathery flowers in various shades
of yellow and gold:may be used in the garden, better grown as
an immortelle or with the cutflowers and....cut to keep
from spreading seed or....naturalize in dry ground.

LANTANA---half-hardy shrubs, trailing and bushy, perpetually flowering, when kept active and in absence of frost.
They do not require a fertile soil nor one that is moist, and
bloom more profusely without fertilizing....a minimum of each
for strong, vigorous performance. Prune in early fall, for wood
to flower over winter. This can be a yearly renovation of plants
that loose their youth early. Grow them almost anywhere, but always in full sun. They endure maximum heat and drought, may
kill back completely to the crown and,in the end, return.
     -camara, a wide-spreading, brushy shrub 3-5' or dwarfed,
compact and scarcely 2-3', the dense little flower heads buff,
yellow, pink, orange and red or white:use in the border as a
facer, allow to straggle over a bank or drop down the face
of a retaining wall:bushy varieties are obtained from selected cuttings, while seedlings, spread by the birds range far,
making much wood at the expense of bloom, gradually becoming
a serious annoyance. The churlish foliage of this plant is
violently pungent and irritating to touch, with a principle
that amounts to an allergy with some people.
     -montevidensis(sellowiana)trailing, prostrate, a tangled
woody mass producing the purple flowers freely all the warmth of
the year....very susceptible to cold, when it holds back:window
or porch boxes, planters, over slopes or serves as a ground
cover, sheared back from time to time. There are two forms, a
self and one with a lighter center, both of some difficulty in
color combinations:survives utter drought at the crown, but
must have some moisture to show well.

LAPAGERIA rosea, "Chilebells" a slender twining vine with dark
leathery leaves and narrow, waxy, bell-shaped flowers, rosy or
pink to crimson, a blooming of considerable substance, generally late winter into spring:bells are strung singly along last
years wood for the first blooming, but tend to cluster on the
current seasons growth late summer or fall, good years....wrong
micro-climate or an off-season may throw it off so that it, just
blooms or fails altogether:must have shade and moisture in growth,
a loose, grainy soil of fair fertility, one that does not become
too highly acid and remains cool....always:better not attempted
where temperature goes very deep below the frost line:very
choice and very difficult....snails and slugs:rare.

LAPEIROUSIA cruenta, "Anomatheca" bulbs for spring-summer,
sometimes up again for late fall and carrying over into the
winter....down in late summer:flowers are positive-starlike,
in line, bright red with a blotch of carmine at the base of
the three larger petals....all on a very small scale:reseeds
freely in a light soil, avoid clays:cutflower in miniature.

LATHYRUS---annual and perennial plants, scrambling or climbing, as a class so well known as to require little description.
Strangely, they are in greater danger from cold than far north,
since the plant is more susceptible to frost when in flower.
The far south will best have their blooming over with early by
using early varieties. The specific forms are grown in rough
tangles over a bank, quick-hanging down the face of a wall,
between shrubs for early temporary effects, or climbing on
support....with cultural wants and points as follows.
     -littoralis, Beachpea" for very sandy or gravelly soils,
the flowers purple with white wings May-August:a sprawling
plant without tendrils:native west in coastal regions:seed.
     -odoratus, "Sweetpea" deserving the best in way of seed
and care, an annual:prepare the ground deep and wide for the
ranging roots, pulverizing and mixing grass clippings or strawy
manure, anything of like nature that will decompose quickly to
hold moisture:introduce at the same time a little spent lime

331

or old plaster and firm well, any fertilizer used at this time
being kept beneath the seed:sow early flowering strains September-
November, to flower in April-June, mulching the tender shoots
as they come through....light shade in heat prolongs flower-
ing:irrigate, do not spray in watering, and that as infrequently as may be, conserving moisture by the shallow cultivation of
a dust mulch:liquid fertilize from time to time after the first
flower buds set, applied after rain or irrigation:pinch out
terminal shoots at six weeks and nip the earliest buds for
strong plants:heavy soils best:use trench method in sandy soils:sow
thickly and thin out to about 6" in the row....protect from birds and
snails....allow maximum sun and good moving air:cut the flowers frequently, preferably before dew dissipates....remove early seed
pods to draw out flowering.
    -splendens, "Pride of California" a native plant for dry
arid regions, to be used as a garden subject, a strong plant
there with much vegetation:comes ultimately many stems from a
woody base in a great verduous entanglement, with large rock
or over a bank:very large flowers, pure white or rose-
violet April-June:seed can be found.

    LAURUS nobilis, "Sweetbay" the classic laurel, to name all
laurel-like plants of all time, used almost exclusively in
tubs indoors or outside, an erect, slow-growing shrub, or tree-
like, with an aromatic, dull yellow-green foliage of leathery,
durable quality and inconspicuous, small yellow flowers March or
April:rugged plant under ordinarily difficult conditions of soil
or exposure, growing 25-35' in height, multi-stemmed, with an architectural feeling for both detail and mass:shape up in summer, using
a knife in order not to mutilate the leaves, or shear when the new
growth is half complete....stimulates a second concealing crop of
leaves:not reliably hardy in deep frost.

    LAVANDULA---low brushy shrubby material on the herbaceous order,
used as either, grown in the garden, better adapted for longer life
in dryish, sterile or rocky soils outside and they take more exposure than is generally known. Any severe pruning should be done
around March, the best procedure being, however, to take wood with
the flowers as they are cut over summer....take to allow light deep
within the bush. They want all the sun and good drainage.
    -multifida, "French L." erect bushy 2-3' with handsome, finely
cut, medium green leaves and lilac-blue flowers in rather precise
terminal heads:pots into a tub if it holds up well or into the gard-
in for quick service, better suited there than the following:neutral
to acid soils, a biennial or short-lived perennial depending somewhat on handling:tender in frost.
    -officinalis, "English L." more woody, 2-3' and gradually
spreading out wide, perennial and long-lived:foliage grey,
the slender heads of blue flowers held high above on rigid,
wiry stems:heads are cut and dried when half opened in flower, used to scent linens....used for this, a plant may soon
become a family institution, good for many years when located right, becoming stronger with the years....but only
when the going is rough:greatest fragrance in the garden
will be in hot sun, but tolerates coolness near the sea,
including an occasional drenching when established:lime.

    LAVATERA---mallow-like plants of somewhat weedy appearance,
grown for rather special purposes out in the open landscape
or about the garden where refinement is of no particular
object and where rapid growth is desired for screening or
inter-filling. They all tend to lose the lower leaves in
drouth and flower generally over summer. There is no place
for them in the immaculate garden.
    -assurgentiflora, "Mission Mallow" in nature, a scrubby
shrubby growth, sometimes 3-5' the first year from seed,
tree-like, frequently found whipped up and defined as such
10-15', thin of structure to match the rapid growth:the
foliage light, with a greyish cast, the single pink mallows lined with deeper red April-September:naturalized

332

*Laurus*

*Lavandula officinalis*

*Lavandula multifida*

*Lavatera assurgentiflora*

in thickets along the California coast in sandy soils and
there, quick protection against the wind.

-olbia, bushy perennial, semi-woody at the base or
almost entirely so far south, growing 3-5' in good soils and
with moisture over summer:stemless, reddish-purple flowers
stud the softer wood beneath the dull green foliage.

-trimestris, "Mallow" an annual 2-3' to be used in the
flower garden as a filler or in the border for the silvery
white, rose-pink or red flowers: likes a deep, fertile soil in
the sun:seed is placed where the plants are to stand March-
April, the seedlings thinned to 12-18", or planted some time
in June for fall flowering.

LAWSONIA inermis, "Mignonette-tree" erect shrubby growth
or a slender tree 20', the pendulous branches clothed airily
of the thin, light green foliage, nearly or quite evergreen:
flowers creamy-white to rosy-red in terminal heads are not
conspicuous, but very fragrant....of mignonette or that
of a tea rose:may be grown dryish and stands in very mild
alkali:prune lightly to stimulate flowering, when the plant
becomes more compact:narrow hedge in the sun.

LAYIA elegans, "Tidytips" a low spreading annual 12",
having daisy-like, light yellow flowers, the rays tipped
with white to appear as a kind of zoning, February-March:give
a light sandy soil in the sun:native in California, but will
do for a time in Florida sands.

LEONOTIS leonurus, "Lionstail" a rough weedy shrub of
flashy growth and flashing, flaunting color, a tawny
orange arranged in close whorls about the erect stems in
late spring and again in the fall:good filler in the shrubbery, but watch for mealybug and prune lightly between flowerings,
heavier in early winter....cut to the ground every few years to
completely renovate:a better plant in the drier soils where irrigation can be used to accent periods of bloom:re-seeds in the
garden to become a nuisance:does not flower in the shade....a low
traveling mat there, reaching out for sun:may be used into
warm temperate regions as a tender perennial.

LEPIDIUM sativum, "Cress or Pepper-grass" an annual salad plant,
unimportant as to bloom, but with ornamental foliage, the leaves
variable from bluish to yellowish, curled nicely or much divided like parsley:eaten by birds and grown with that in view as
much as for the mild peppery flavor imparted in cookery....too
strong in the summer for salads, but excellent fall and winter.

LEPTOSPERMUM---rugged shrubs of character or rangy tree-like
20-30', for high heat inland, punishing wind seaside, dry and
sterile soils anywhere. They may not be grown for any length
of time in heavy ground and are most demanding of drainage.
Being so essentially of the wild , the matter of taming must
be in mind always if domestication is to be complete and enduring....wants, culturally, are known, positive, absolute.

-citratum, an uncommonly beautiful plant that is not
commonly seen or available, even the naming somewhat uncertain, growing 6-8' or more, slender-erect, willowy and very
pliable of stem, the branchlets weeping, finely clothed with
pale leaves that are very aromatic of lemon....pinch:choice.

-laevigatum, "Australian Tea-tree" a large shrub, well
composed, if hulking, usually with several tortuous, angular stems that become thick and limb-like to a low heavy
trunk....distorted and twisting in age to aquire an exceedingly picturesque quality:the lightish, slate-green foliage
is tough and glories under full exposure to salt-laden
wind, while one supreme shawing of durable white flowers,
serves April-May:do not prune except early, to get the
structure into the air and, possibly, to accentuate the
non-conforming habit. This plant is commonly grown, but seldom with the full possibilities in form and character under-

Lawsonia
inermis

Leonotis

L. laevigatum

Leptospermum
scoparium

stood and actually realized.    --var. compactum, dwarf
form, dense, naturally compact, growing some 6-8' high
a dark, blue-green and not flowering as freely as the
type. This must be grown from cuttings taken from
selected individuals, less than fifty percent
coming true from seed.

   -scoparium, more bushy than the preceding species,
slender erect, of open structure, the leaves needle-like,
usually reflecting in some degree the color that is so dominant in the flower, pink, rose, crimson or maroon and a
white of sorts, near singles to full doubles, very profuse
November-May. Most available stock is of hybrid origin, confusing in variety and in sizes of from 2-3' upwards to 25':wants
good moisture in drainage when young, tapering off into dryness
in maturity:pots and tubs.

   LEUCADENDRON argenteum, "Silver-tree" a rare and beautiful tree
to high-pressure the imagination of all true gardeners, 25-35',
of characteristically loose and gangling limb structure, yet
with some symmetry as grown on slowly in a lawn with constant,
if meager moisture; a branchy thing in pure silver, the leaves
tufted in the outer perimeter, an aura....bait for the unwary.
There will be silver and gold cones at the ends of the
stout shoots, but not until after 15-20 years, very uncertain years, since usually these trees pass out before
their time. Much moisture and perfect drainage is indicated,
probably best supplied from below, as by periodic deep irrigation with capillary return:probably little or no fertilizer and that doubtless organic....start with a young plant,
humility and supplication....matured specimens all along lower
coastal California prove they can be grown:very choice.

   LEUCOCORYNE ixioides, "Glory of the Sun" small bulbs with the
appearance of a wide-open brodiaea in flower and somewhat the culture of an ixia:light, well drained soils are desirable, sloped so
that excess rain will be shed.....otherwise use in a pot, allowing
to dry out for a rest after flowering:narrow leaves at the ground
support the 12" stem and umbel of flowers, lavender-blue, grading
back towards the center through white to yellowish green February-
March....very fragrant in some strains, not at all in others:
set deeply August-September and keep moist in absence of rain:
cutflower for a sunny place in coolness:sometimes difficult.

   LEUCOJUM autumnale, "Snowflake" for the south, a long-lived
bulb to naturalize or to be grown in the garden:white, nodding flowers come any time from late fall to early spring in
accordance with handling:makes a large thick clump in almost
any soil, better in the lighter textures:down all summer.

   LEUCOPHYLLUM texanum, "Ceniza or Senisa" an erect, bushy
shrub 3-5' with ash-grey foliage and light violet or lavender
to purple flowers which are almost barometric in reaction to
summer rain along its native Rio Grande....blooms in anticipation of rain, always after:very ordinary soil, minimum moisture and just enough winter pruning to curb a tendency to straggle under domestication....full sun important:dwarfs available.

   LEUCOTHOE axillaris, "Bush-lily-of-the-valley" handsome spreading shrub 3-5' with dark lustrous leaves to set off the pink buds
of winter and following tiny white bells strung so precisely
along end shoots in spring:moist, acid soils in shade, the
clear green with red in sun, bronzy in the fall....good
for decoration and arrangements:native in upper Florida in
damp and wet woods, blooming there March-April:no lime.

   LEVISTICUM officinale, "Lovage" perennial 3-5' for
celery-like stalks and aromatic seed used in confec-
tions:large dark leaves are decorative, the plant long-
lived in rich moist soils with part shade:should be
divided in the fall:ornate.

COMPENDIUM

LIBERTIA grandiflora, an herbaceous perennial with sharply pointed, stiffly erect, sword-like leaves in a close clump 18-24" high
and long, weak and bending scapes of clustered, pure white flowers April-May:ordinary garden conditions and culture, but with
sun and with drainage:border plant for definite form.

LIBOCEDRUS decurrens, "Incense-cedar" columnar tree 100', usually less with a thick low trunk, dark cinnamon-red bark and
short lateral branches:thuja-like aromatic foliage is retained almost to the ground in the open and brings to places of few trees a
pungent, woodsy fragrance:wants a well drained soil of medium texture
and is normally slow in growth, but responds quickly to moisture for
as much as 2' in growth a year:an excellent, upstanding ornamental, much used in the west below its native mountains:an accent
plant on the grand scale, either inland or in coolness along
the coast....but not in strong wind, in smog or industry dust.

LIGULARIA kaempferi, "Leopard-plant" tuberous-rooted perennial to 18", a rounded mass, the leaves 6-10" across,
spotted with white or yellow, infrequently with rose or
pink:throws tall, nearly bare stems of unexciting yellow flowers September-October, blurry heads that are not
as important in the ornamental scheme as the leaves:pots
indoors or outside in good soil or poor and up to deep shade.
The size of the leaf regulates to pot area and fertility of
the soil:frost-hardy into warm temperate regions.

PRIVET

LIGUSTRUM---practical and very useful shrubby material, evergreen
south or dropping foliage late, or only thinning out over winter.
They are well able to care for themselves in almost any soil, under
nearly any exposure, in more than ordinary drought, dry ground beneath trees or seaside. Their use as hedging is perhaps over emphasized, as the matted, greedy roots are quite un-merciful and take eager
toll from nearby lawn, flower bed or other planting. Natural form of
the plant is pleasing as used in the shrubbery or out alone, the
white heads of flowers and close-clustered blue berries being more
than worth so little effort. Prune any time after the berries have
passed, but in case of the hedge shear late in summer to induce
foliage growth which will be more likely to carry through the
winter. They have no pests and succeed surprisingly far south
into the tropics.
    -henryi, a spreading bushy growth 8-12', trim as to form
and nicely suited for specimen use or as a natural flowering hedge, with only nominal clipping or none at all:dark
leaves are substantial, large and sharply pointed:tubs.
    -japonicum, "Japanese P." Large shrub or small tree 20'
round-headed, with large, durable leaves and fragrant
flowers July-September, the new growth reddish:excellent
large clipped hedge in a very hot situation or will endure
considerable cold, when it becomes deciduous:the best one to
grow under arid conditions.   --var. rotundifolium(coriaceum), a low
shrub of extremely slow growth, much smaller, with leathery round
leaves curled over and very dark when matured:low garden hedge
controlled with a knife, rather than sheared, desirable anywhere restricted growth is a consideration:milky-white flowers May-June in tight little heads:deep shade in a tub or
in the ground....burns out in a hot sun.
    -lucidum, "Wax-tree" very large shrub or a tree to as
much as 30', suitable for a narrow parking in the street or screening....excellent tall, sheared hedge or grown free:large dark leaf
and a waxy-white, sweet-smelling head of flowers April-May complete
a portrait of a most valuable plant for the south:salt winds.
    -ovalifolium, "California P." large erect shrub of especial-
ly rapid growth, having thick glossy leaves and large panicles
of white flowers, much used as a clipped hedge or in the
lower element of a windbreak:withstands salt spray, wind,
smoke and dust in almost any degree, survives a considerable freeze:grows in the shade, but will not retain foliage
as well as out in the sun:garden forms which follow will be

335

Libertia

Ligularia

japonicum

Ligustrum

Ligustrum
rotundifolium

vigorous, healthy and pest-free.   --var. aureum, very
erect with the typical white flowers above the yellow
foliage:use to lighten up the drier, darker spots in
the garden or to vary a dull border planting:some-
times seen mixed with the original green in a
hedge, a piebald effect that is not unpleasant,if
a little tricky.   --var. variegatum, with white or
yellow markings in the leaves, sparkling touch for contrast in the border, less erect and not so stiff as in the
type form and other varieties.
     -quihoui, very different from all the rest, quite ornamen-
tal and will be grown as a flowering shrub of neat erect habit in
the garden, a dense, well rounded voluptuary of ease and felicity
at 5-6', branched from the ground, or a small tree of note when
desired:trusses of white flowers to 12" long August-September, together with berries of an unusual shade of purple-lilac....fall into
this over-all sense of eye comfort:too rarely seen.

## LILY

LILIUM---to well known for any futile attempt at evaluation, the important thing being first, which to grow far
south and only second, how they may be ingratiated and made
comfortable. Generalization in this attempt will name
first, drainage; it must be sharp, then soil; it must
be cool and shaded, the bulb; should be firm, fertilizers; should be organic, but no manures, transplanting;
as soon as possible after bulb has ripened....a pocket
of sand beneath is good:cut the flower in late afternoon
with stems as short as will do and leave in a cool, shady
place one-half hour before placing in water. In planting,
line the pit with wire netting or hardware cloth against rodents, if any and remembering they will travel distances to reach
this feast. They are not easy to grow and hold, but hybrid
strains developing hold much promise for the future.
     -candidum, "Madonna L." the most fragrant and probably
the most important garden lily, pure white, growing 3-5' in
height:especially susceptible to disease and should be dusted with sulphur before planting....set out of the way of
other plants and shallow:prefers a fairly heavy soil in
the sun and will tolerate a dryish, sterile limestone
soil:blooms fairly early, May-July:an old lily in gardens.
     -catesbaei, "Southern Redlily" slender stems 2-3' in
height with up-raised flowers, orange-red, July-September,
native in the south and a good lily in these regions.
     -henryi, one of the most resistant to disease, growing
a good 4-6' in height, the very large, bright, orange-yellow
flowers with reddish spots, August-September:heavy loams and
in half-shade in a limy soil and set very deep.
     -longiflorum, "Easter L." strong clumps with many stems
bearing clusters of waxy-white flowers, the long tube frequently greenish at the base, April-May:very fragrant and one of the
most satisfactory in southern gardens....tolerates a fairly
heavy soil. Harden off the potted plant from Easter for use
in the garden and treat as above for long service.
     -parryi, stems 3-5', the flowers lemon-yellow with
conspicuous brown anthers and slightly spotted, June-
August:has a strange, illusive fragrance as grown under
more or less arid conditions:weak growth calls for a
sheltered spot:native in the Southwest.
     -regale, "Royal L." indeed princely, and a rugged
fellow, seemingly little disturbed in heat and drought, in
lime, in the wind or freezing weather:a first class cutflower that should be deeply set....disease resistant:has
tough, flexible stems 3-5', with pure white trumpets that
have a pleasing fragrance July evenings.

LIMNOCHARIS flava, "Marshflower" perennial aquatic, grown
in shallow water or in a pot plunged in a pool:the light green
lance-shaped leaves stand out of the water 12-18" as do the
yellow flowers, the petals bordered in white:no frost.

COMPENDIUM

### SEA LAVENDER
LIMONIUM(STATICE)---herbaceous perennials, normally developing a hard, knotty crown, with the dark, usually bluish,
very leathery leaves at the ground. They are of most value
as cutflowers, being used as filler material in all manner of bouquets or treated frankly as immortelle....which
they are. Outside, they belong in the rock garden, the border and with the cutflowers by species, or anywhere that the
light airy heads show to advantage and suffer the least interference in development. Give them a light, dry, sandy, sterile soil
and leave them alone....they persevere in hot sun. Take the flower for drying when the head is prime.

   -bellidifolium(Statice caspia)perennial,low-lying leaves,
round and clasping the stem, arranged upward in reducing size;
feathery heads of light blue and white, very minute flowers
are raised 12-18" with good tough stems for cutting late summer and fall:aristocrat of utmost fineness with a place in the
sun literally and figuratively:down over winter,back late spring.

   -perezi, shrubby plant, or at least with the hard, woody
structure at the base, long-stemmed leaves raise the mass to
18-24" and more across:large heads of blue and white flowers
are raised higher on wiry stems practically all year:hybrids
are most in use and reseed very freely for new plants.

   -sinuatum, an annual in pastel shades of white, yellow
pink and blue, available any day of the year, a slender
plant that will naturalize in poor sandy soils.

### TOADFLAX
Linaria---annual and perennial herbaceous plants, tender in frost,
but re-seeding to carry on. They are rugged in other respects,some
being tenacious almost to the point of annoyance, in places an actual nuisance. All are desirable in the garden or its near environs,
when used in reasonably moist, fertile soils in the sun.

   -dalmatica, a "Butter and Eggs" for the far south, an erect
perennial 2-3', a large clump above ground, massed, strong-running
roots below:bright yellow flowers May-June may be removed by a
shearing so that the plant produces again in late summer:renov-
ate when signs of exhaustion show, renewing with root portions
after building up the soil:robust, aggressive, invading.

   -maroccana, slender annual, 12-15" for bedding, cutting
or to be grown with the wild flowers:foliage is nearly grassy,
the flowers in pastel shades violet, purple and yellow:sow thick
in the spring, again in  late summer-autumn:oldtime garden flower.

### ORNAMENTAL FLAX
LINUM---annual and perennial plants with exceptionally clear
coloring in flower, the blooming fragile, the flower opening only
in the sun, short-lived but coming along in quick succession.
They want a sandy, drained soil that is not too rich, in a spot
that is not heavily irrigated and where the roots can sink deeply for moisture to see them through the dryness that is part of
their background. While they are short-lived in the garden, re-
seeding is comparatively free and the youngsters are more eager
in any event....and more effective. These are in no sense subtropical, but must be included for heat, dryness and sterility.

   -grandiflorum, "Flowering-flax" an erect, slender annual
in varying shades of red, a plant for the garden, thriving in
the better moisture and fertility there than the following:the
flower will not cut, will appear and re-appear for a long and
satisfying blooming from late winter into the heat of summer:
may be necessary to weed out seedlings....there may be none.

   -narbonnense, an excellent perennial in the right spot
where it can spread, bushy, 18-24", becoming woody below:
the glistening flowers are large, to 2" across, more often
less, light blue with white at the center, all summer:keeps
fairly well when cut, but of longer duration on the plant,
remaining open all day....take just before buds open.

   -salsaloides nanum, a low mat, or to 3" with pearly
white flowers over midsummer, the white varying, reacting to
light:carpeting, rock work, wide between flags:sharp drainage.

337

LIPPIA---forgotten shrubs, plants of yesterday,
ground covers, new to horticulture or out of style
for the moment, just as useful as ever, when used right,
simply waiting for fashion to turn the corner in return.
Generally, they are better in the lighter, poorer soils,
fertilized discreetly only when they show signs of lagging.
Learn to leave them to their own devices until need for help
is shown. All are at their best in a dry climate.
     -canescens(repens)"Lippia-grass" lawn substitute for
almost any soil or exposure that is not too cold....best in
heat:coarse, thick runners have ammple grey-green leaves in
thrift and hug the earth closely in a tight carpet....an uneven stand probably will relate back to careless or irregular
soil preparation:all summer the pale lilac flower buttons
come along, a feast for the bees, hazard for small children
and bare feet:a yearly top-dressing of rich, sandy loam mixed with sifted or ground leafmould is about all that will be
necessary, along with an occasional drink.
     -citriodora, "Lemon-verbena a straggling garden shrub 2-3'
or more, if forced:notable and loved for the cool scent of the
foliage, described as lemon, the leaves being dried out, placed
in sachets:use sparingly, pinch out tips and cut back from time
to time to hold in:flowers minute and inconspicuous, purple or
lavender and white in loose terminal heads:a small standard of
interest which has a tie-in with the taking of foliage for pot-
pourri and cooling drinks....actually suited more for special purposes than for an effect in the garden....one or two plants.
     -ligustrina, "Beebush" native in the Southwest, growing 8-12'
in height, the pale, brittle branches tipped with spikes of white
flowers which are sometimes tinted with violet....fragrant, as of
mignonette, attracting bees....and people:wants lime to be completely at home and in nature, is found on low ground.
     -nodiflora, "Mat-grass" a verbena-like perennial, tenacious-
ly rooting in holding exposed slopes in the wind or sandy soil
against water:foliage is greyish and the white to pale purple
flowers are attractive, but secondary to above use.

## SWEET GUM

LIQUIDAMBAR---trees of distinction, deciduous, stately in or
out of leaf, symmetrical with pleasant and interesting qualities in texture and coloring that go far in forgetting the
short leafless period in winter. They want a deep soil of
some fertility, but thrive in poorer ground if moist, and
while never very rapid in growth, they are quite slow, stunted in dry places. They favor acid soils. Nursery-grown, at
least twice transplanted trees are much the easiest to
establish, and at time of planting should be liberally
pruned....take from a container whenever available. They
stand in salt air but not much wind, may be used in street
plantings and in rather narrow parkings in deep soils that
are permeable. They are clean trees with no pests.
     -formosana, "Feng-tree" from the orient and reputed to
become a large specimen, broad-spreading, without the warty
bark of the following and with smaller, three-lobed
leaves, rounded instead of pointed....crimson alone, in
fall coloring, lasting later into winter, more persistent,
almost evergreen, excepting for the coloring.
     -styraciflua, erect tree to 100', probably not as tall in
subtropical regions, narrow-pyramidal, the leaf a regular five-
pointed star:the truly marvelous autumn coloring in gold and
reds is the outstanding exhibit and lasts as long as six weeks,
even in California....then the characteristically warty
branches and deeply furrowed bark beset with unique corky
ridges....was there all the time:very early and inconspicuous flowers set the hanging bur-balls of winged seed.

LIRIOPE spicata, "Turflily" a plant of lily-like
properties, but not in apparent character, the foliage
grassy and at the ground, the violet flowers June-September in short spikes, blue-black berries then, until

spring:a ground cover far south in the sun, but used mostly
in the shade, in deep shadow where little else survives:
very drought resistant in gravelly soils or clay, performing well in the tropics or under frost....cosmopolite in
the plant world:foliage body to 12-15", dense, lush, with the
leaf erect or with a slight curve:variegated forms common.

LITCHI chinensis, "Leechee-nut" slender tree 25', ultimately spreading with a broad-rounding top:bears clusters of
edible nuts, grown essentially for the crop....strawber-
ries in form and texture and somewhat in color:wants a
deep, very rich, preferably acid soil that has been well
prepared with manure dug in and used as a mulch, to be kept very
moist, but with drainage:an excessively warm climate is not favorable nor is a cold exposure, although it will adjust to very
mild frost:granite soils are good....difficult to establish at best
and more difficult to crop....but an accomplishment.

LITTONIA modesta, bulbous, with 3-4'running stems or
climbing by means of bright green, curling leaves, narrowing to a long tip in the semblance of a tendril:open-
bell-shaped orange flowers are pendent all summer, if
not allowed to go to seed:set among well-spaced shrubs
or use in a pot, providing support:wants to be dry as
possible over winter....lift and store in California,
or turn a pot on side:seed pods ornamental:rare.

### CHINESE FRINGE PALM
LIVISTONA---rare and hardy palms with high decorative value in the landscape as well as indoors. The
sturdy stems are ringed remotely at the ground, but tend to
hold the boots above if not removed. Fans are round or kidney
shaped and split back various depths from a few inches to midway
or better. The free segments remain rigid to more or less carry
out the plane of the fan or break at, or break near the outer
end of the cut, the tips then hanging as a drop fringe.
    -australis, "Corypha P." growing to 50' or more and one
of the hardiest of the palms, the dull dark fans almost exactly round, the segments free nearly to the base.
    -chinensis, "Fountain P." the head a dense globe atop
the heavy trunk, the rounded fans wider than long, with
shallow cuts, the nibs hanging:used in tubs, later planted out in the garden where they will grow to 25' in slow
height:the inflorescence of late winter-spring consists of
many rigid stalks of strawy-yellow plumes.
    -humilis, with a stubby stem as thick through as 12" and
only 6-8' in height normally, or as much as 15' exceptionally
and ultimately:used formally in a tub.

LOBELIA erinus, low, spreading annual, compact for bedding or
edging, the flowers pale or dark blue, carried profusely all summer into winter in warmth....shear if it attempts to quit too soon:
does best in fertility and coolness, not too shaded:compact forms
may be used in carpet bedding.   --var speciosa, much as the type
with larger flowers, and white eye:boxes, baskets....trailing.

LOESELIA mexicana, a bushy shrub 2-3' with bright red, tubular
flowers late winter, native Southwest and sometimes seen in Southern
California:drought and heat, rarely available but found in old
gardens:good garden shrub of much restraint.

LOLIUM multiflorum, "Italian Rye" a coarse lawn grass
to be used thickly planted alone or in a mix designed for
very hard wear....even here, it must be spread thickly in
order to put off the inevitable patchy day it begins to die
out:a handsome, bright green cover or forage plant, naturalized in poor, rocky ground, re-seeding to return each year in
delightful  sheets of motion in the wind:one of the best of
quick covers in holding new slopes or steep banks against erosion in wind or water....a problem, however, in removal.

Littonia
modesta

Litchi

Lobelia

Lonas

SUBTROPICAL REGIONS

LONAS inodora, "African Daisy" growing low in 6" mats of the
finely divided foliage, somewhat ferny, something of alyssum,but
the flowers golden and formed in the likeness of ageratum:an annual
for a long season in the garden, beginning from early spring-sown seed;
pots, bedding, edging, a filler between rocks, the foliage delightfully aromatic:an immortelle of sorts.

HONEYSUCKLE

LONICERA---deciduous and evergreen vines and shrubs, cherished
by gardeners over the years, grown for the translucent berries,
but more especially for the subtle fragrance of the delicately
tinted flowers, so marked early morning and evenings of dew.
They are not showy in flower, but own to an un-named sprightliness
in all these subjective things that have endeared them to the generations....until now, when new and more striking forms do
nothing more....than bring back these implanted impressions
of the irrecoverable past. They are that and at the same
time general purpose plants of great usefulness, transplanting in leaf if handled carefully....best from a container, better in a cool soil, but taking heat and wanting
sun, and tolerating shade. The moist quiet of the woodland is to their liking, but they flower more freely in
the open and respond to the breezes off the sea back of
the salt-line. Very little dead wood develops so that
little pruning is required, the climbers restricted and
thinned out, shrubs shaped or opened up for air. Most of
these species are frost-hardy.
    -confusa, low evergreen vine or pinches in nicely
for a sprawly shrub for slopes that do not go absolutely
dry:has superior foliage, blue-green and leathery for wear,
holding in cold:massed flowers are showy and abundant, each
widely expanded, light yellow May-June, with a lesser blooming in September:a superior plant that should be better known.
    -etrusca, "Italian Woodbine" evergreen climber or used
sprawling over banks, bluish green foliage and clusters of very
handsome flowers May-August, yellow with reddish tints, finally a deeper yellow:best one for heat and dry air;rare.
    -hildebrandtiana, "Great Burma H." in the nature of a pro-
digy, bulking large among the tranquil honeysuckles, but well-
grown for size and reach....high-climbing with leathery leaves
that take a lot of salt wind without hurt:flowers immense,
as long as 6-8" and slender, yellow at first, later with a
hint of red, finally dull ochre as they fail, tender in
cold, and best in some broken shade in heat.
    -hispidula, "California H." a native shrubby plant
but throwing long streamers in a garden, set sparsely
with small leathery leaves and unimportant whitish yellow flowers April-May:flings about in nature, clambering
over rocks and shrubs....pinch in to build body.
    -implexa, a low branchy plant, somewhat shrub-like but
scarcely climbing, the short, pinkish flowers July-August,turn
creamy-white as they age:takes heat, hot sun and drought.
    -japonica halliana, "Japanese H." vining to 15' ultimate-
ly a weighty mass requiring sturdy support, better used
with heavy construction, evergreen south, but dropping leaves quickly in frost:very fragrant white
flowers change to yellow as the season advances:will
grow in any soil, in heat and drought and some shade:
prune in winter to lighten mass.   --var. aureo-reticulata,
not vigorous, the lighter green leaves netted and marbled
in yellow:wants shade and a better soil....unique and
pleasing in boxes or baskets:does poorly cold weather.
--var. chinensis, streaming, the new wood reddish, the
foliage with ruddy tones, the lips of the yellow flowers red.
    -nitida, "Box H." a dwarf shrub, the arching stems a pattern
of dark beady leaves in sprays that come out distinctly against a
white wall or can be made to grow downward for the same effect:
requires winter pruning to bring out the true grace in
the sprays....anarchy and confusion without direction;
low box hedge, hardy in frost, salt wind and shade.
340

-pileata, "Prim H." an evergreen shrub having the general
appearance of privet, low and spreading, prostrate at times,
the glossy foliage very persistent:creamy flowers are fragrant
April-May, hidden in among the leaves and of no particular
note except as preceding the purple fruits:frost-hardy.

LOPEZIA albiflora, "Mosquito-plant" delicate, airy, flopping, a half-woody perennial of vigorous winter activity,
down over walls, blanketing banks, even used as a ground cov-
er:clouds of minutely fashioned, gay little flowers done in white
and pink, hover and settle down on the bushy structure January and
through March....for all the world like a swarm of mosquitos waiting interminably to strike....happy thought.has poor appearance in
summer and should be sheared lightly for then....companion plant
for summer bulbs:short lived.

LOTUS---sub-shrubby material, prostrate plants to be used
primarily as ground cover or grown in a planter, infrequently
in a basket. They want the sun and are quite intolerant of
shade. They will be longer lived in loose, lightish soils
that have good, deep drainage and tend to hold the sunheat
such as sand and rock chips. They cover over very rapidly
and can not be counted upon for very long.
  -bertheloti, "Pidgeons-beak" trailing very rapidly,
splaying out over the ground as a very flat cover or draping
a bank, the bluish-grey foliage very finely divided into thread
like segments for much refinement:scarlet to dark crimson flowers May-July, tend to fade out in hot sun:watch this closely for
mealybug and pinch out growing tips to thicken.
  -corniculatus, "Birdsfoot Trefoil" variable perennial, trailing, procumbent or a plant 18-24" high as a forage crop:most common
use is that of a ground cover, with forms that are absolutely flat
and carpeting....less than half an inch through, a lawn substitute
then, propagated a-sexually for uniformity:a clear, bright green.
  -formosissimus, "Sand Trefoil" brushy, thinly foliated arching
stems 12-18" carrying tiny yellow flowers touched with red in late
winter-spring, and well into summer in coolness, as of coast land:
very light, dry and sterile soils or nearly pure sand under exposure to salt wind:native in California where a related annual kind
is found, prostrate and running, lying flat to the ground.  This
complements the thin character of the perennial above.
  -mascaensis, bushy, mounding, eventually and soon,
a spreading mat of silver in the sun, the white of the
foliage blanketed with yellow, pea-shaped flowers, closely
massed for color, April-May:sharp drainage.

LUCULIA gratissima, a very select and most perverse shrub,
bushy-rounded at 5-8', more or less, compact from the inevitable
cutting of the rosy-pink flowers of December-January....a marvel
in delicate coloring and wonderment of overwhelming fragrance, a
perfume that lingers on in the dying flower:grown only in coolness
and in shade, at least half, with uniform and constant moisture in
a rich, well conditioned mix of loam, leaf-mould and peat or other.
In all this, there is still not the final clue to happiness and
complete success, so that this plant will be grown or attempted
only by the hardy in spirit or those of inflexible resolution
and staying power....a challenge.

LUDWIGIA mulertti, aquatic with small yellow flowers of little
consequence, but the purple in the leaf both above and beneath
water striking in sun:may want slight shade in heat, but the sun
warmth held over night in deep water or cement is the answer.

### LUPINE
LUPINUS---herbaceous materials, annuals and perennial, the
latter becoming woody at the base and eventually brushy. They
are extremely showy massed in the border or scattering out with
the wildflowers, the white yellow or blue flowers in erect
brittle spikes which are only fair to cut, but effective
and not long-lasting. They like an open position in well

dug, light or sandy drained ground that has just reasonable
nourishment or will do in rather poor soil. They seem in the
main to resent lime, at least in concentration, and the
presence or absence of certain beneficial soil bacteria,
doubtless has to do with success and failure. Either extreme
in soil reaction will be detrimental. Too little is known a-
bout this conditioning of the ground, but wherever possible, a
little soil known to be suitable can be used by way of inocula-
tion or impregnated seed used. Seed sown where the plant is to
stand is always better, even with the woody kinds, more rapid
development and longer life resulting....not advisable to try
transplanting at any stage. They are short-lived at best
and an area should not be cleaned until the pods have
released seed for the following year.

-affinis, a low annual 10-15" or less, producing
tiny, very light blue flowers very freely in the spring:
native in California....broadcast in low ground.

-arboreus, "Tree Lupin" a ragged woody shrub with a
soft, uncertain top, growing 3-8' in coolness as of its native Pacific coast, bearing quantities of pale yellow flowers
May-August:found in sandy soils near the sea where it is hardy
in wind and such heat and dryness as will be found there.

-hartwegi, tall, hairy annual, as much as 2-3', but
usually much less:large uneven spikes of purple flowers
June-August:naturalizes readily in barren soils.

-longifolius, shrubby perennial 3-5' with handsome spikes of
blue flowers over greyish foliage:found in nature on the floor of
dry rocky canyons of Southern California, to be grown under like
conditions although it may do for a time in the garden for late
winter and early spring bloom:rather choice.

-paynei, from California, a splendid shrub to as much as 8'
under average conditions, spreading accordingly, the foliage a
masterly construction in silvery-green, at its best....somewhat the
worse for summer wear:flowers fragrant, white, pink, blue in spring.

-texensis, "Bluebonnet" an annual 12", silvery hairs over-all
giving a lightish cast to the green, setting for the white and blue
flowers:dryish or gravelly soils that are not very rich....natural
rainfall best:sow July-September in full sun, soaking seed over
night and do not irrigate, unless late in California....early
sowing for longer flowering:naturalize.

## BOXTHORN

LYCIUM---spiny shrubs with a smooth, light green, rather
succulent leafage and showy berries, the flowers not significant, but for the berries. To the gardener they are of import
for hedging in out of the way places, but clear of worked
ground since they re-seed badly and sucker when the root is
disturbed. The bushy, thorny scrub of half-vining stems and
meaty leaves offer good protection and excellent food for the
birds. All are drought resistant in loose, sterile soils or
make more of a show in better ground.

-carolinianum, native in the South, a shrub of some 5' in
height, with very thick leaves and the usual, but larger, round
red berries. This and the following will be used in humid areas.

-chilense, a large brushy shrub with very light green foliage
and abundant orange berries, especially attractive to birds for the
protection available within the interlacing branches and weighty,
frosted foliage which they eat:stands in California without irrigation after having been established.

-pallidum, "Bush-matrimony" erect shrub 3-5',native
in the Southwest in high heat and punishing sun, the
flowering of some value in the landscape, a greenish,
irridescent white, with berries July-August:no suckers.

-richi, "Box-matrimony" a California native for rugged service near the sea, procumbent, building up on itself or semi-erect, with tiny round red berries and pale
leaves that may be reduced to bead-like proportions in
heat and dryness:exposed banks or pruned and headed
in as a low hedge or may be grown as a ground cover
by cutting out erect leaders in early stages:splays.

342

# COMPENDIUM

LYCORIS---spectacular bulbous plants for casual use in the garden where they are for a moment theatric, dramatic as they flash into flower late summer, subsiding as quickly and completely. They are winter-growing and want shallow-planting in the sun or very slight, broken shade. Give them a light soil with considerable leafmould worked in and leave them alone to build up a good muster of bulbs. The fragrant lily-like, opalescent flowers with segments crisped and curled, attach in wide umbels at the head of naked scapes. This is all without benefit of foliage, so that neighboring plants or low-spreading cover should be planned to reduce the bare period. They are inclined to temperament, but are worth a considerable effort in finding just the right place....amiable there and most pleasing for many years. Soak the ground deeply just before expected bloom to break out a full flowering.

-aurea, "Hurricane-lily" with golden yellow flowers or a kind of orange, the segments twisting and twirling, but the bulb quite uncertain in bringing forth:wants to rest during the wet season, blooming during the dry time of the year....much better used in Florida and along the Gulf Coast.

-radiata, "Red Spider-lily" a brilliant coral-red that is more effective without companion color, alone August and September:increase is usually good, but the bulb mass should not be disturbed for division until the ground is clearly running out....two likely times, May-June after the foliage has died down and October when the flowering has been completed.

LYONOTHAMNUS asplenifolius, "Catalina Ironwood" a slender tree to 30' with a splendid and unusual foil of foliage, of much more than ordinary interest in the ferny leaf and large, open truss of flowers, white May-June....the eye lowering then to the red bark, loosely hanging, gradually shredding:must have sure drainage, run-off for the surface in way of a slope, and a gravelly or other surely permeable soil beneath; and deep for a little extra insurance:wants but little water, but a cool, humid atmosphere is favorable, along with good nutrition for the luxuriance that is there to be had:considered difficult to grow, but above will cover essentials....late summer irrigation can be suddenly fatal:foliage may be taken indoors for the unusual pattern in decoration, having a quality of inlaid wood or frostwork.

LYSILOMA latisiliqua, a slender tree 50' with fine, airy, ferny foliage of the fine-leaved acacias and like them, should be grown dryish for a better tree and fuller crop of the white-green flowers:loses foliage easily in winter for a good shade sun combination with season....summer-winter.

## M

MACADAMIA ternifolia, "Queensland-nut" an erect, ultimately rounded tree 35' with a slender trunk and thin branchings of dark foliage, bronzy when new, the mature leaf hard-leathery, long and narrow, irregularly spined or without:deep light, rich soils, moist in early season, dryish afterward:is of slow growth and pretty well does its own pruning after a good limb structure has been attained, but hold in for limb-strength under exposure....takes wind, but with poorly placed limbs splitting out, and recovery slow:small, white-tasseled flowers not important but do produce round nuts with rich white meat, coming into bearing late:combination of utility and beauty, but branching low for the garden:tender

MACHAERANTHERA tanacetifolia, "Tahoka Daisy" a bristle-topped 18-24" free-flowering annual for rather wide and effective use in the rougher environs of the garden:strong-

343

growing, finely presented, the foliage as well as the clear
lavender flowers June-November:has a pungent odor and will be
easily grown, re-seeding or sown in the fall or very early
spring:can be used as a cutflower, but closes at night.

MACKAYA bella, an erect, straight-stemmed, flimsy-wooded
shrub 3-4' with bright green foliage which blackens under the
least frost, the whole plant suffering a setback over winter
to leave the pale lavender blooming for whatever warmth the
latter part of the summer has to offer:moist, rich soils are
indicated, those tending to acidity....but not demanding:prune
sometime in winter, removing surplus canes or checking the top to
force out lower, weaker growth to spread as a flat cover in shade.

*Mackaya*

MACROPIPER excelsum, semi-woody, angling, weak-growing, serving
low in a pot at first, later in the ground or climbing from a larger
pot:large rounding leaves, yellow green, like a shallow-lobed ivy,
tough, dull and light-absorbing but shining beneath:indirect or
filtered light only, taking deep shade in moisture after having
outgrown pot or basket:a lifter that may extend upward 8-15'
in the end:a green flower spike in March develops into a
tight 3" head of yellow berries:aromatic.

*Mahern*

MAGNOLIA grandiflora, "Southern Magnolia" erect stately
tree 75' or not so high, some forms wide-spreading, all parts
large, the whole with a heavy substantial feeling, the leaves
glossy above, rusty beneath:flowers a pure waxy-white April-
July or later some years, the petals falling away to reveal an
erect, cone-shaped body that will carry the crimson berries:takes
much abuse, with generous root-room but shows it, growing slowly
the first years, more rapidly when established.   --var. lance-
olata(exoniensis)much smaller tree, slender erect with distinguishing narrow leaves, to be used in a restricted place. These trees
do best in rich, well drained soils and particularly resent any
cutting of the roots, with transplanting a very real hazard:
best period for this is spring, as the buds swell and the
growth starts, a less reliable time being September:the
container plant is safe for all sizes:prune only to
direct structure, March-April, painting after each
cut. They belong primarily in the upper rim of these
regions and grow very slowly far south.

MAHERNIA verticillata, "Honeybells" prostrate and very
twiggy, with many pale yellow flowers of delicate fragrance in
February-June:use where drainage is good and where moisture is a
minimum for reasonable permanence....low slopes and banks in the
larger rock garden or a planter:a low branchy mass in the nature
of a shrub, the rough-rusty stems and light green, deeply cut
leaves building up 12-18" and out 5-9' as a close cover:usually
short-lived, due to the moisture factor:full sun best.

*Mahonia nevini*

*M. fritolrard*

### HOLLYGRAPE

MAHONIA---very decorative shrubs that are valued for the
hard-horny-spined leaves which take so easily to color if
faced with the abnormal. The tiny golden flowers appear in
late winter or early spring, followed by blue berries which last
late into summer and constitute the chief orniture. All are native forms that come to the garden or landscape with a certain
lack of sophistication, a singleness of purpose that points quickly to their place in design. They come to us accustomed to the
pressure of adversity and may be grown in dry, gravelly or sterile
soils. They will endure a heavy clay, but will straggle, are not
so desirable in humidity, as of garden or climate; adapting.
They have much in common with the evergreen barberries and make
free-standing hedges of merit, subject only to terminal pinching
or infrequent mild reduction of older wood.
    -lomariifolia, striking and beautiful, a plant with erect,
6-8' caney stems that are well set to flat sprays of quite dark
and long, deeply cut leaves, the green holding rather well in
the sun:flowers clear yellow, terminal in broad spikes that

*Mahonia lomariifolia*

show and carry remarkably, autumn into winter....the following berries large:an extra choice plant of refinement for a
prominent place in the garden.

   -nevini, wide-spreading shrub 6-8', of rather stringy
growth that eventually closes in for a good, if stemmy mass of
light, blue-grey foliage set in turn with bright yellow flowers
January-April and orange-scarlet berries for the birds....in a
literal sense:only tolerates shade and moisture, full sun and
heat required to bring out true character:hedge in dry gravelly
ground that will want but little attention:native in California.

   -pinnata, better used in the south than the Oregon-grape
which it favors in the holly-like leaves, spined and shining, burnished, rich in ruddy coloring over winter:yellowflowers and blue
berries:should have a little shade for the foliage and may be used
in dry soils beneath exhausting trees:native in California.

   -trifoliata, "Agarita" with handsome bluish grey foliage, the
leaves in threes, narrow and sharply pointed, remotely spined
along the sides:native in the Southwest where the berries
are gathered for jellies:grown in dry, rocky ground and
transplanted from the wild for hedges, November-December.

   MAJORANA hortensis, "Sweet Marjorum" an erect, branching perennial, but cultivated as an annual for the aromatic
grey-green leaves and small white flowers:green parts are
used to flavor meats or meat pies, soups and stews, usually
combined with sage:a border plant of some value.

   MALACOTHRIX californica, "Wild-marigold" native California
annual 6-12" high with shades of blended yellow April-May, the
flower much flattened, precise and regular:appears best mornings
and should be grown in loose soils for repeat performances.

   MALCOMIA maritima, "Virginian-stock" small spreading annual for
garden beds or used as a quick filler in the forepart of the border
to 6-8" in height:bloom appears as if enameled, white, rose, pink,
lilac and crimson, the colors mixed together in casual and happy
confusion:the loose heads come on steadily throughout spring and
summer....sown late summer or fall for an attempt at winter:rock
gardens, where it carries on indefinitely as desired.

   MALPIGHIA---shrubby material for the warmer parts of these
regions, better where humidity is high, the coastal strip in
California, low in Florida and along the Gulf Coast into the
state of Texas. Their uses are specific and varied, with not
too much difficulty in the growing, although not commonly
found in any of these regions.

   -coccigera, "Singapore-holly" bushy, 18-24" or more,
with very small leaves like holly, but oval in outline:fring-
ed flowers are slightly fragrant, white or a delicate pink
over summer....fruits red:likes leafmould in a moist, substantial soil, with some shade in a very hot situation:
a rigid, restrained growth fits this for a kind of loose
hedge and for pots which can be taken in, cold weather.

   -glabra, "Barbados-cherry" glossy-leaved, with axillary pink flowers which are followed by small red fruits
that are acid to taste, used in jams and jellies:desir-
able hedge in the 6-8' range of height, but plants are
quite variable as grown from seed....use cutting-grown.

### FALSE MALLOW

   MALVASTRUM---straggling shrubs or more or less bushy,
having wythe-like stems that are pliable and whip-like. These
are specific forms direct from nature, but with enough refinement for or near the garden, in places where living is more
than a matter of graceful acceptance. They are accustomed to
heat and stark drought, while the typical, ranging, ever quest-
ing roots rummage deep in dry, gravelly ground for sustenance
and better plants for having to do so:just
a little help for continued good appearance
into and over summer.

345

-capense, symmetrically bushy, a shrub 3-5' of handsome outline for the drier areas of the garden, adapting
to considerable moisture:slender, arched stems carry small
reddish purple mallows that are only half an inch across,
early summer and scattering along at any time.
    -coccineum,"Prairie-mallow" a spreading woody perennial for
dry, well drained ground in the sun; the half-inch, dark brick-red
mallows do not open wide, begin flowering in the spring, nearly continuous over summer with a little moisture:grows in long running stems
from a definite crown, nice ground cover, rampant over a bank or hanging down the face of a wall....surprisingly handsome foliage as grown
under domestication, never a nuisance from rooting in:rather choice.
    -fasciculatum, native of the greater Southwest, found in dry washes
and other poor ground, a pallid, greyish thing, very irregular, or of no
form whatever, sparingly stemmed and scantily set with the finely hairy,
lobed leaves:not for the garden, invaluable holding fresh fills:seed.

MALVAVISCUS arboreus, "Turkscap" straggling as a shrub 3-5'or struggling upwards with support to 35', a formless fabric of very
slender stems and light green, velvety leaves that may be
guided high into trees, as a screen or splayed low and wide
over a bank as cover:solitary, nearly closed dark red hanging
flowers are followed by white berries which soon turn red:will
want uniform moisture, but adapts to dryish ground, where it
stunts:not as desirable as the following, but more persistent and dependable.   The species,  -grandiflorus, is normally larger, as grown shrubby, more contained, but spread-
ing:good medium green body of foliage, a plant making better
use of rich, moist soils, but very tender to cold and very slow
to come back out of frost....if it does.

MANDEVILLA suaveolens, "Chile-jasmine" deciduous, twining
15-20', a vine of rapid growth, but with scant coverage until
it settles down to produce....large pure white flowers that are
incredibly fragrant, June-August:narrow, heart-shaped leaves are
effective against a pillar or in drifting wisps from above....wants
light, climbs for the sun, becomes bare below if lower growth is not
encouraged:frost-hardy into warm temperate regions.

MANETTIA bicolor, a slender twiner 3-4' for the lath house
or outside in a protected spot, where it will flower more
freely in more light....eastern exposure usually right:will
bloom continuously through warmth, the velvety, dazzling
scarlet tubes tipped with a small yellow star:wants a
light soil with much material worked in for humus:pots
with low support or pinch in for dense-rounding form.

MANGIFERA indica, "Mango" tropical trees for shade and perhaps fruit, used for such in Southern Florida, growing there
very tall in deep rich soils, an oval in outline or tending to
flatten out in a wide spread....retaining the roundish top:in-
differently disposed to serve in California, now partially prov-
en for mild coast sections and warmer foothills, but becoming
fully grown only as tropical parts are reached, with humid conditions....drier season to ripen fruit:growth erratic, coming
in flushes as indicated by reddish or coppery tints in foliage:
matured trees stand in some wind, but no frost while in growth:
select varieties only, for fruiting.

MARKHAMIA lutea, erect tree 25', colorful in flower and
bignonia-like, yellow, purple-lined in erect clusters:
foliage handsome, the red of the new growth persisting
in maturity, clinging to the veining of the nicely
crimpled leaflets....dropping in cold or drouth:garden
subject of great merit, but seldom found:lighter soils.

MARSILEA quadrifolia, "Water-clover" with four identical leaves raised on slender 10" stems, a trailing
aquatic with strong, lush growth in water or in a
pot submerged, or rooting in outside, the top

Marsilea

Malvavisc

Manettia

Mandevilla

breaking over into water, or at least interupting the line
of the pool:start with rooted pieces of the runner. This is
an interesting and diverting thing, but overwhelming if not
kept in check....easily held.

### GILLYFLOWER

MATHIOLA---grown largely for the florist trade, yet well
known and long used in gardens. Much work with these plants
has developed strains that pretty well support the season with
cutflowers. Give them a rich, mellow, well worked soil that is
well drained. Do not save seed for next year because reversion
is quick and sure, usually to very unpleasant purples. They are
cool weather subjects for flowering and must have their growth
before heat. They are standard for the flower garden.

-bicornis, "Evening Stock" straggling annual with lilac or
purplish flowers, with no attraction as such, but highly scented at night or after rain:the closing flowers through daylight
make of this plant a sorry sight....something to smell and
not to see....tucked away out of view or at least obscured.

-incana, "Common Stock" actually a woody perennial, but
used as biennial exclusively, developing quickly erect stalks
to 18" in good height and fullness, the greyish foliage clean,
dependable for free mass and movement:flower heads of various
density, of singles or doubles in white, rose, yellow and purple or deeper and having a distinctive fragrance. The type or
perennial form is best pointed for winter, the same used as an
annual for spring or early summer while other strains, such as
Brampton or other will be used to carry on later:pinch back for
more flowers or allow to come along naturally for a good garden
display. They are not worth having unless well grown.

MAURANDIA erubescens, growing 6-8' in height, a slender vine
of herbaceous growth, the base definitely woody:white-throat-
ed lavender flowers open partially like a snapdragon summer
and fall into winter, the whole plant of tropical luxuriance in places warm enough to allow complete development:
climbs by means of the twisted leaf or flower stalk and since
the young plants require minimum root space, they adapt nicely
to baskets and boxes for refinement brought to special places·
sow September-March, or earlier indoors to insure longest
possible season....set deep and shade:rich soil, drainage.

MAYTENUS boaria, "Mayten" an erect, gracefully drooping
tree that may actually weep, in good thrift:very select
for an unworked garden, but suckering when roots are cut,
for a copse type growth:tiny interpolations, the flowers, are
yellow, of little note, clustered along the long willowy stems:
foliage is real attraction, very light, fairly dense when doing
well, making up readily into festoons and lasting when taken in-
doors:the pliable branches act splendidly in the wind and the narrow leaves take some salt without hurt:likes moisture, but will
stand fairly dry:good tall clipped hedge in considerable frost.

MEDICAGO arborea, "Tree-alfalfa" rather coarse, a reedy, half
woody ornamental of shrubby structure 6-8', but mostly spreading at 3-4', not beautiful, but serviceable seaside in sand and
wind:has clover-like leaves as very sparse and uninteresting foliage, doing little more than delineating the stems, with orange-
yellow flowers in the same analogy:blooms any time of the year,
with scattering flowers at any time, dependably in winter, even
through a light frost. The species  -denticulata, "Bur-clover"
is also of value, seaside in more or less saline ground that has
some drainage:an annual to use as a nurse crop, but advisedly on
account of the burs....a stick-tight nuisance.

### BOTTLEBRUSH

MELALEUCA---a large group of shrubs and smallish trees, somewhat showy in some of the flowers, the foliage of unusual wear
ing qualities, the entire plant and all of them utterly hardy
under some condition or combination of salt water, wind,
mud under foot or deep drought....fire on occasion.

Few of them bring much, or any refining influence to the garden, but
on the other hand, none are so coarse and undesirable as not to have
some obscure value there or in the near vicinity. They find their place
and large usefulness in broad foliage masses where near intolerable
growing conditions hold, places where ornature will be foregone in
service of another kind. They grow rapidly, are long-lived, with
strong, exploiting roots that must be kept from less contentious
plantings. The knotty fruiting clusters that remain about the stem
at yearly stages, add nothing but a slight interest in kind....a
distinction of doubtful comfort. Prune in late summer and know that
these plants will almost always become larger than anticipated.

   -armillaris, "Honey-myrtle" an upright or spreading shrub, the
drooping branchlets covered with short, pliable, needle-like leaves,
the cylindrical head of white flowers surrounding the stem May-June:
a large garden shrub, very large in time, in a most unusual and picturesque way, thick-tortuous or winding, trunk-like stems to an umbrageous top at 12-15' and as much spread....a spot for light shade
under-planting, if drainage is good.

   -decussata, handsome shrub of some refinement, bulking too large
for the ordinary garden, erect 15-20' or urn-shaped and spreading 8'
high and much more across, over-growing itself in good soils and with
moisture:good appearance year-round with bluish foliage and small
lilac to lavender thimbles of bloom, June-July:excellent and very
practical landscape plant for exposure.

   -ericifolia, "Swamp Paperbark" large supple-stemmed shrub or a
small tree with longer, pliable branches, to be used with impunity
in wet places, seepages in California and the Southwest, swamps in
Florida and along the Gulf Coast:survives considerable alkali water,
stands up and gives to heaviest salt wind:suckering.

   -huegeli, "Chenile" an erect, rigid shrub 10-12' or the outer
stems gracefully arching when standing free, clothed densely around
the branches with bright green scale-like leaves:pure white flower
heads are dense-narrow, unusually handsome June-July with a primitive
quality that admits of no tincture:garden-worthy except for size:do
not over-irrigate without drainage:very ornamental, the clothed stem
used for arrangements; one of best in salt wind; not easily found.

   -hyperiscifolia, "Hillockbush" spreading 8-10', gross-growing,
but with a dependable off-green foliage and very large crimson flower brushes May-July:makes rapid and substantial growth in poor, dry
soils, but the knotty fruit knobs are especially marked there and
detract:does not flower well in Florida.

   -lateritia, erect-spreading, a shrub with graceful lines and
loose texture for thin screening, a plant of some extra refinement;
scarlet flowers in a large brush are much subdued for color, somewhat the shade of a robins breast....sometimes named in that re-
lationship:suitable for the garden if well placed.

   -leucadendra, "Cajeput-tree" a slender, not unattractive
tree 35' for service in very wet ground, or dryish with irrigation, standing in either place with alkali or salt, wind or
weather and liking all:distinguished by thick, punky layers
of white bark, of interest and some beauty as picked out in a
subdued light....the slant of early morning or the lowering of
evening:survives light frost which will touch the foliage with
vague tones of purple....vague and indescribable fusion with the
white bark:withstands high wind and tends to re-seed.

   -nesophila, "Tea-myrtle" an erect-spreading shrub 8-10' or a
slender tree 25' when kept to a single stem:bright green foliage is
stoutly made and maintained against hard and continual usage, each
twig tipped some time during summer with a rosy-lavender or pink cone
of flowers:equal to almost any adverse condition, including especially
salt winds, dry and sterile soils:supreme on the ocean.

   -styphelioides, "Black Tea-tree" with a white bark, striking and
rare, a tree growing to 40' or more in a deep rich soil, rigid and twiggy in appearance, the white, spongy bark becoming black below:small,
creamy or off-white flowers appear at the tips of the twigs, while the
myrtle-like leaves are light toned, harsh and horny, sharply pointed:
thrives under a wide range of conditions, wet, brackish ground, under
some drouth:a lawn tree, the litter of leaf and flower disappearing quickly into the turf. A nearly related species,
-genistifolia, the white "Fleece-tree" is marked by a

348

M.
hype
iscif

Melale
decussat

M. nesoph

picturesque, twisting of the upper branches:bark is less
papery and there is a heavy flowering in June. This seems to be
extra tough and has been used for streets.

    -thymifolia, dwarf, a shrub only 2-3' and of considerable re-
finement, not only because of size, but of parts and resulting tex-
ture:has a red to strong purple flower in the summer that is acceptable in itself, but difficult in combinations.....too rarely found and
more rarely in good color harmony....a garden shrub in the right place.

    MELIA azedarach, "Chinaberry" deciduous, erect tree, open-headed
at 40', of very rapid growth, tenacious in heat, drought and frost,
but comparatively short-lived and not to be used where a cleaner and
more ornamental can be grown:pale lavender purple flowers March-May
are followed by yellowish berries that are eaten by the birds and
strung as beads in ornature:a shade tree where shade is most needed, but a grand source of litter and seedlings, inappropriate in
any place of pretension to cleanliness or finish. There are forms
which are nearly evergreen, south in Florida.   --var. umbraculiformis, "Umbrella-tree" the branches radiating at an acute
angle upward from the top of a short trunk as the ribs of an
umbrella, lower growing than the type for a very dense shadow
which is of great comfort and much used in hot regions.

    MELIANTHUS major,"Honeybush" a spreading, stemmy, woody
mass 8-10', used largely for tropical effects and against
the planes of contemporary architecture in places the exacting system of roots can be accomodated:the restless,
uneasy foliage mass is a clear, grey-blue, finely cut
on a large scale, unique in textural value:dark reddish
or chocolate-colored flowers on long spikes late winter
or spring are only incidental to the general appreciation
of the luxurious leafage:becomes very untidy if not groomed,
the rough, gangling stems cleaned and removed as required. The
foliage soots badly in shade, less in sun, the result of aphis,
with white fly a nuisance. The species   -minor, is sometimes
available, similar, but only half-size....lower to the ground.

    MELISSA officinalis, "Lemon or Beebalm" one of the culinary herbs,
a perennial 2-3' in height, becoming woody and somewhat invasive, too
widely spreading in the flower garden:white or yellowish flowers
keep well when cut, although of little importance:the spicy,
lemon-scented leaves are used to flavor beverages or substitute for tea, either fresh or dried.

## MINT

MENTHA---rather well known herbs, with some that are comparatively new, the foliage very strongly scented; some with ornamental implications, but mostly they are grown and devoted to the culinary
art. They are very strong-growing generally, too aggressive for the
garden, no comfort to the neighbors and will of necessity be curbed
in moist, fertile soils. Renew frequently and only from the
rooted runners since the younger plants contain the active in-
gredients in larger proportion. Require constant moisture.

    -gatefossei, prostrate, trailing, strongly scented, vigorous
and invasive:suspends in flowing lines around a rock, a running, almost liquid stream of white-green, the coursing leafy stems splaying out delta-like on the flat:a cover in wet places or use in the
damp rock garden:an appreciable white flowering in sharp, narrow,
pagoda-like heads in early summer.

    -pulegium, "Pennyroyal" perennial, prostrate, well used in
a heavy wet soil where it cannot encroach into other ground:the
rough leaves have an agreeable odor and are used for seasoning,
while the small lilac or bluish flowers appear in dense whorls at
intervals along the squarish stems:greedy plant that takes every
thing within a wide reach.

    -requieni, creeping, minute in all its parts, the tiny, light
purple or violet flowers July-August:makes a thin, flat, cushiony
mat in moist places about stepping stones, releasing a marked and
pervading odor of peppermint when crushed under foot:must have
a certain light shade for good color, yet seems eventually

to require considerable light, if not direct sun early and
later in the day, if it is to last for long:difficult to hold
at best and should have a moisture retentive soil, lightened
and mixed thoroughly with ground leafmould:very choice.
  -spicata, erect stems 18-24", the very prolific herbage
with many uses in jelly-making and other forms of seasoning
as with lamb cuts:roots spread to become a major menace so
that a planting should be headed off by a curb or walk.
One small piece will start the descent and eventual downfall.

  MENTZELIA lindleyi, "Blazingstar" an annual of rather straggling character, quite trashy as the blooming goes off, redeem-
ed by the brilliant yellow flowers of summer:wants to be kept
out of the wind, and the failing should be cleared up as soon
as convenient after flowering, the debris possibly set aside
in order that matured seed may be shaken out later....over the
same ground or into a container to store:the gorgeous bloom
opens and is fragrant in the evening....border, or better with
the wildflowers:native in California.

  MERYTA sinclairi, foliage plant on the grand scale, immense
pale, leathery leaves on long petioles, veined to a strong
pattern:a large, loosely constructed shrub or small, broad
tree 20' for partial shade and uniform moisture:fruit black.

### FIGMARIGOLD

  MESEMBRYANTHEMUM---low succulents, with the body of
sappy, watery leaves lying close to the ground or raised and branching, with more or less dry wood. Essentially arid country plants, they demand full sun and heat,
adapting readily to drought and sterile soils. They
take moisture, as of the garden, without harm to themselves
and present a good appearance over the year, but must have
drainage. They find many common uses as cover for dry barren
ground, with many species of some refinement, and less blatant
color for drier spots in the garden. Nearly all can be used
in the larger rock garden. The leaves are flat in the likeness of a conventional leaf or cylindrical, short or
elongated and triangular in cross-section, frequently
set with a crystalline dotting, blisters or with some
coarse hairs. The flowers are daisy-like, full-petal-
ed, in many sizes and in all colors except blue, some
species bearing so profusely and with such intense color
as  to be disturbing to the senses under close scrutiny. It
is a large, uncertain group botanically, still being re-
aligned. The original generic name will be used here, with
the segregate or newer designation used in parenthesis.
They are set new as cuttings, rooted or not.
  -aequilaterale, native along the California coast,
trailing, closing in for good body, the solid leaves medium
long-triangular:foliage tough and the wiry stems mat down
to hold drifting sand effectually and permanently:few large
purple or clear yellow flowers spring-summer.
  -aloides(Nananthus)very low, the long-narrow-pointed
leaves set with many minute dots, a rhomboid in section,
rich, dark green:grows in a tuft like a little aloe, eventually closing in to form a mat covered with out-sized yellow flowers in the summer:a dry garden subject.
  -amoenum, low, bushy, erect or somewhat spreading, with
most brilliant, dark purple-red flowers spring-summer:a prodigy
of color that is not for the garden but to be shown distantly in
the landscape as cover or over low banks.
  -anemoniflorum(Cephalophyllum)an open, running, rooting
mat that is extra neat in growth, a possible distant lawn
substitute:pale pink to salmon, rather large flowers over
at least six weeks in spring:choice.
  -aurantiacum(Lampranthus)a dwarf, semi-woody little bush
with a good body:narrow, round, rather soft-succulent leaves,
the plant erect and partially procumbent:large brilliant colored orange flowers May-June in such profusion as to conceal
the greenery of the foliage:good pot plant for a hot spot.

-bolusi(Pleiospilos)"Livingrock" an odd 3-4" hard-succulent
body lying at the ground in exact mimicry of worn grey rocks
among which they should not be planted, for obvious reasons:
has a relatively large yellow flower in late summer or fall.

-browni(Lampranthus)dense mound of slender woody stems and
small, hoary, cylindrical leaves:color of the flower is change-
able, with crimson, rose and copper in evidence, dominating at different times as the lighting shifts or all colors may show at once:so
brightly spectacular in the spring that it must be used with discretion
in the garden or the area will be submerged by the color....and by the
spreading herbage:hybrids are available with remarkable colorings.

-cordifolium(Aptenia)trailing, with dark and glistening, heart-
shaped flat leaves, nicked around the edges....blankets the ground or
hangs from an urn or box:tiny bright red flowers are few and not effective, considering the company....one to grow in shade:has been in
use many years, out of fashion and out-shown....but still good in the
sense of cool freshness that is rare in this group.

-croceum(Hymenocyclus)rank-growing in a low, fairly tight
mass or trailing out in a stringy growth in poorer ground,
the bluish-grey leaves triangular, blunt at the tip, in good
color over the year:blood-red flowers of medium size, turn to
mahogany shades in the sun or as they fail:nearly everblooming
and not too much color at any time:some refinement here.

-crystallinum(Cryophytum)the oldtime "Iceplant" of grand-
mothers window in the winter, transient, an annual for cover,
winter-spring or sometimes allowed to remain in a planter when
a seedling turns up in the soil....exciting against a contemporary backdrop:the large, flat mass of heavy, undulating, extremely watery leaves are coated literally with glistening
blisters that are filled with fluid....throw the light back
tumultuously....redden under the sun and disappear:seed.

-deltoides, a low, close-growing mound of comparatively
delicate, deftly fashioned, short-triangular leaves with a tooled
quality in being, as if taken fresh from a mold, pale bluish-
grey:tightly massed; light-lavender-pink flowers, gathered together in a kind of coagulation over the plant May-June, completes
a picture of a very choice little plant that moves in on one:for
the garden, most interesting in a pot for a sunny spot.

-echinatum(Delosperma)trailing, ultimately building up a pile of
wiry stems set scantily with short, pickle-like leaves covered with
stiff hairs or prickles:the 12-18" mound is decorated with small, grouped flowers in the spring, light yellow or buff, continuing off and on.

-edule(Carpobrotus)"Hottentot-fig" vigorously spreading and
never piling, a very coarse-growing plant, probably the best of
all for dry barren ground where all the elements must be met without help:has typical triangular leaf with point, but only occasional flowers, a kind of yellow that turns to light purple before they
curl and drop:ground cover for large areas against erosion or to
hold dirt fills with both surface and deeply penetrating
roots:never an ornamental, a robber under irrigation.

-filicaule(Lampranthus)long, reddish, thread-like or
stringy stems and very small, cylindrical tapering,
curved leaves, a thin veneer cover or may be grown between
stepping stones:in late winter or early spring, rosy-magenta
flowers rise on slender stems in irregular patches of color.

-floribundum(Drosanthemum)"Dewflower" prostrate and closely carpeting with greyish, glittering, tightly pressed foliage
and tightly packed, light, rosy-pink or magenta flowers May-June:
fibrous, penetrating woody roots are efficient in holding fresh
dirt fills while the top will pass all the run-off without wash:is
possible to walk over, but inconvenient underfoot:the color is very
attractive alone, but difficult in some combinations:common.

-glaucum(Lampranthus), makes a dense little bush of good
quality, as against its fellows, growing 18-24" high, a slight
out-spreading of woody stems set with up-lifting, short-rigid,
slender-triangular leaves....base for the sheeting light yellow flowers in spring:for drier spots in the garden, pots.

-laeve(Malephora)flat plushy carpet of small, tongue-
shaped leaves in bright green, rather dense growth, surmounted in spring by light yellow flowers having a red-

351

dish reverse that becomes more apparent as they close:a
ground cover and of nearly sufficient restraint to use
in the garden....does not thrive under extreme drouth.

     -lehmanni(Corpuscularia)low-mounding, with a close-
packed body of curiously shaped, stubby leaves and straw-
colored or yellow flowers:better used in the rock garden or
in a pot, where it develops very slowly.

     -linguiforme(Glottiphyllum)an oddity, fabricating a thick
intricate mat of pale but vivid green, somewhat curled, large
leaves that are two-ranked, quite fleshy, flattened, tongue-
like and as long as 6", half an inch through. There are light
yellow flowers, at times white and again, bronzy, mainly in the
winter:watch closely here for snails and slugs.

     -maximum(Astridia)a succulent 12-15" shrub, erect, rigid,
with firm-textured, three-angled, unevenly flattened, short-curved
leaves that are greyish or bluish or both and remotely dotted:the
few flowers are comparatively small, very short-stemmed, terminal
from among the closely packed leaves, light pink, fall-winter:pots.

     -odoratum(Conophytum)"Coneplant" a night-flowering species
with yellow, sweet-scented flowers....unusual for these plants that
so want the sun and which show such distaste for darkness as to not
open dull days:collectors item or to tuck away in an intimate spot
to open and serve thoughts engendered by the moon.

     -puterilli, spreading and somewhat bushy, with small but bril-
liant purple-magenta flowers that are not showy in mass:good woody
plant for form in the rock garden of size:more mannerly and restrained in growth than most of these plants.

     -roseum(Lampranthus)a low brush of erect or spreading stems and
very bright, rather large and very handsome flowers in many delicate
shades of pink to rose to deeper, sometimes in two tones in a kind
of zoning. Here are some of the most attractive and some of the
best coloring in the series, a distinct release from the dominating almost stunning action in close aquaintance with the others.
These plants soon lose their identity and merge in a thick mass to
12" through, breaking in spots to show deep shadow.

     -speciosum(Drosanthemum)a woody plant, tangle of wiry stems
forming a gently undulating mound or mounds 18-24" high, the foliage somewhat crystalline, the whole covered in spring early, with
bright scarlet, green-centered flowers of some size and in utter
profusion...a spectacle in full color.

     -tuberosum, very low, tufted little plants which soon coalesce
in a dense mat, the leaves very tiny, beady, set with minute spines
for an over-all fuzzy aspect:minikin flowers of summer are large
enough to show magenta....not objectionable because of scale and
its lowly place against the earth:rock work and flagging:choice.

     -uncinatum(Ruschia)bushy, with erect stems somewhat woody
and substantial, a dull green, but brightened late spring and
summer by the lavender pink flowers:may be used in the garden
or as a border plant in dryness.

     -verruculatum, low and widely spreading, with medium long,
half-round, short-tapering leaves, ultimately covering a wide area
and building up to 8-12" height unevenly:small, light yellow flowers are set closely in a clustered effect like cut stones:dry banks
fade out beneath this excellent species....a quiet homely little
cover with an aptitude for living with a garden.

METROSIDEROS tomentosa,"New Zealand Christmas-tree" usually shrub
like from a marked tendency to sprout at the crown or a tree with
great interest in winding curving stems; or can be brought up
to a single simple trunk by staking and rubbing out all the
sprouts as they appear at the ground....nurserymen can
plumb this by crowding liners both ways and cutting apart
after the stems have grown rectiliner to a head....a good
street tree then:of signal importance near the sea, the
greyish body of the foliage is set May-July with tight
clusters of dark red flowers, the mass flattish as in
flame-eucalypt....a color that carries far:grows not so
well and slowly in heavy soils, more rapid in sandy loams,
with good moisture or actually wet, or will adapt back to
drouth and exposure of its original native condition:

contrary to general rules, set this out in the wind only
in good size or after the grey, adult foliage has developed, the thin, shiny juvenile leaf being too tender. This is
a prime subject for salt-burdened wind, in its maturity and
makes a durable hedge against the sea:not hardy in frost.

MICHAUXIA campanuloides, an unusual herb, a flat purplish rosette of crinkled, long, deeply cut leaves 12", at the ground in a
kind of rotation:second or third year sees an erect stem emerge
with bristly leaves in reducing size following up from the
crown, 3-4' in height, but as much as 8' in exceptional
thrift....white, wheel-shaped flowers June-July, the narrow
petals turning sharply back as they mature:rich sandy soils
or slopes that will protect the vulnerable crown over wet
spells, especially winter. The massed blooming is a most striking thing and beautiful, and the plant must be treated as biennial from seed; best spotted in the border as a novelty.

MICHELIA fuscata, "Banana-shrub" bushy, erect to as much
as 15', but not often that high south and of medium slow growth,
the foliage yellow-green and in good shape all year:petals of
the brownish-yellow flowers, edged with purple or carmine,
April-June, give off the odor of banana that is more intense
in the sun....wanting shade in heat:light, fertile soils in
good humus and uniform moisture where it may be sheared in
formal shapes, as for tubs:hardy under 15 degrees of frost and
will be used into warm temperate regions. The species
-champaca, rarely seen, has light green, larger, leathery,
glossy leaves and creamy flowers with sachet value, used in
the garden for the sweet, musky scent.

MICROMERIA---prostrate, more or less herbaceous, or the
plant a small bushling for the rock garden. The foliage is
highly aromatic and sometimes used in cookery for meat seasoning. They are rather neatly put together for this type of thing
which is notoriously casual and heedless of neighbors.
    -chamissonis, "Yerba Buena" a creeping perennial with
a minty fragrance in the foliage and small purple flowers,
a ground cover that spreads vigorously in loose, leafy and
moist soils in the shade....roots and re-roots at the tips:
native in California in cool, humid canyons and may be used
in a garden near a path for full measure of pleasure.
    -piperella, bushy, sub-shrubby, a trim little spreader to
use with rock or to cover sloping ground that requires to be
contained....woody stems root down thoroughly:has small,
bluish-grey leaves and round, buttony heads of flowers, pale
pink, May-June:warm, dryish soils in the sun where it may
be mistaken for thyme....even to the scent.

MILLA biflora, "Estrellita"or "Mexicanstar" bulbous, with
lax, scant and elongated grassy leaves and pure white, waxy,
salver-shaped flowers held face up-lifted, flat to the sun;
exceedingly fragrant at first but gradually depleting, the edge
of the failing petals becoming translucent and colorless for an
additional transient effect....masterpiece of direct and artless
simplicity:good results in rich soils, in a pot or for fleeting
service in the dry border, June or July:choice.

### MONKEYFLOWER

MIMULUS---wildlings for moist places in semi-shade, some quite
at home in the garden, all developing in good form and color in
the right spot there or outside in a somewhat protected place.
They have the open-mouthed flower of the better known snapdragon,
the tube more or less fluted, the mouth widely flaring, usually
ruffled....altogether nicely fashioned, winsome, manna from the
wilderness. The coloring is acceptable, if not always clear, very
quiet, running through yellow and red, nicely spotted
or splashed. They are native in the west.
    -brevipes, an annual with short-trumpet-shaped,
clear yellow flowers, sometimes tannish, April-July:the

353

form of the plant is loose, the stems weak, semi-sprawling
or hanging from a rock crevice:does not require so much moisture, takes more heat through bloom, wants more sun.
     -cardinalis, perennial, with weak slender stems rath-
er scantily provided with foliage, but having attractive
bright red flowers with yellow throat:fragile plant for a
shady border or wet spot in the wildflower garden.
     -luteus, the "Garden Mimulus" highly developed strains for
garden beds in half-shade:large flowers, mostly in shades of yellow, are spotted or splotched with brown or brick red:sow early in
the year indoors and set out about May....seed that is broadcast
should be shaded....late plantings will attempt to come back the
following year, without too much success. At best these plants
have difficulty keeping up the pace in the average garden, but
are deserving of a trial and some study in placing.
     -puniceus(Diplacus)"Sticky M.F."native shrub in the
south of California, varying in height from 15" on poor,
dry ground exposed to the wind to 3-5' in deep, rich soils
at the bottom of sheltered canyons:leaves are disagreeably
sticky, a very dull green, the flowers red; sometimes they
come in tarnished gold, either tending to mahogany shades in
the end. Hybrids available will be used in the garden where
a natural untidiness may be reduced each spring with the
pruning shears....don't cut into deep wood, remove entirely.

     MIMUSOPS elengi, "Spanish-cherry" neatly built tree 30'
with uniform, slender branches to an open head:half-inch
white flowers appear in the axils of the dark, rigid, oval,
sharply pointed and shining leaves while the inch-sized
yellow fruits are edible:recovers quickly from frost or a
serious burning from salt wind.

     MIRABILIS jalapa, "Four-O'clock" a rugged, persistent
perennial, a brittle top from a large, roundish tuber, to
2-3' in height, erect-spreading for good body in the border
or as a garden hedge:flowers come white or in rather intense
reds and yellows, frequently striped in any of these, opening in late afternoon and during cloudy days:may be moved
about, but seedlings are quicker and the normal method
of beginning....seedlings out of place a nuisance, and
to be removed before becoming established:poor soils,
drouth resistant, an excellent subject for hard use.
A relic species  -californica, is shrubby, low spreading 2-3', with dark rosy-purple flowers spring-summer; is a select
little plant, but seldom available; a landscape material that gardeners might help conserve by using.

     MITRIOSTIGMA axillare(Gardenia citriodora)a low spready plant
that is shrubby, but with much soft green wood, supple, yielding stems and mellow, deeply furrowed yellow-green leaves,
almost as difficult to keep in tone as a gardenia:the white
flowers, like citrus are pink in the bud, in full axillary
clusters March-April; are fragrant and tarnish to an ochre
as they fail....tenacious, holding long in full, failing
yellow, to impart an inner glow to the structure, the new green
surrounding:warmth required for proper nutrition, a good, live,
fertile soil that is fairly moist, shade in extreme heat....wilts
in drouth and in hot sun, but recovers when relieved.

     MOLUCELLA laevis, "Molucca Balm" "Bells of Ireland" an annual,
grown for the shell-shaped green bracts that surround the flower;
excellent and much used in arrangements, the straight or curved
stem lines almost fixing themselves:any garden situation where
it will be ready to use by mid-summer from fall or early spring
sown seed....usually reseeds to carry on indefinitely.

     MOMORDICA charantia, "Balsam-pear" annual vine, luxuriant in
festoons of yellow flowers and strangely warted fruits
that split open to reveal the sculptured seed in
bright crimson, August-October:the leaves

Mimulus puniceus

Mirabilis jalapa

Mitriostigma

Monstera

wilt easily with lack of moisture and should be removed
for a fresh crop to set:sow in spring after the ground
has warmed....comes quickly, among last to go in autumn.

MONARDELLA lanceolata, "Poleo" a branchy annual for sandy
ground or sea dunes, having generous heads of violet-purple flowers June-July:grows 18-24" in poor soils that become quite dry over summer:native in the west.

MONSTERA deliciosa, "Ceriman" striking climbing plant with
immense, perforated dark leaves that bring immediate response
to the status tropical:fruit a wierd club-like body that may be
likened to a short ear of corn, edible where it matures, with the
blended flavor of banana and pineapple....ripe when the shell of hex-
agonal scales is ready to pull off:grows inside or out of doors in a
warm rich soil that stays moist....wash leaves from time to time:
spray with a hose during extreme heat:free of insect pests or
disease and recovers from light frost....slowly:tubs on support or well-grown on a tree trunk. See Philodendron.

MONTIA perfoliata, "Miners-lettuce" a native pot-herb of the
west, with actual uses in salads:the stem passes through the
thickened, meaty rounded leaf, the whole plant to be used:grow
on a cool slope, where it will be available as long as moisture
lasts...turns reddish in sun:rock garden casual, but anywhere
else in the garden, an early spring weed.

MORAEA---iris-like plants for sunny places. They have the
typical flattened flower and the sword-shaped but narrower
leaf, the stem carrying the flower, however, long and weak,
flopping, bearing flowers from time to time. These stems
must not be removed as long as they show traces of green,
since all following bloom will be lost and the plant forced
to produce another before flowering again....leave at least
one node, if taken. These plants in general surmount adverse growing conditions, but respond to good culture in a
dryish, hot soil, flowering more freely there. They resent any
degree of shade. There are no pests and they will survive many
hard knocks otherwise and produce generously.
    -bicolor, erect growth 18-24", leaf and flower stem, the
creamy-yellow flowers dark at the base of each petal for an over-
all modification:makes a strong, well contained clump from a
tight crown, doing in the better, moist soils in the garden.
    -catenulata, vigorous and low-spreading, the leaf-mass in
fans, only 12" high, the 2-3' flowering stalk lying on the ground
if not staked:flowers are small, white with a large yellow signal
blotch and blue stamens of note, any time during summer:well used
in a basket for the hanging flowers or at the top of a dry wall:
re-seeds too freely....cut pods before they open.
    -glaucopis, of medium height and growing strength, for a more
refined area of the garden, the flower white with a blue-black, circular signal blotch:give it a sandy soil or drainage:rock garden.
    -iridioides, "Fortnight-lily" very strong-growing, for the more
rugged parts of the garden or outside....stands under calamity and
ruin:leaves gathered together in subsidiary fans, the flower white,
with light yellow bands and touched with blue at the crest:blooms
at regular intervals of two weeks throughout summer and from time
to time the balance of the season:stout-hearted plant again
for dry, baked soils, or near muck under a burning sun or
will do and flower in light shade:the more common species.
    -pavonia, "Peacock-iris" the leaves much narrowed as
compared with the ordinary iris and the flower large, orange-red with a dark greenish or blue-black spot at the
base of the petals:not too vigorous in a heavy soil.
    -polystachya, a large plant, growing to 3' in height and
very floriferous in rather well defined bloomings, spring and fall,
into winter with warmth of a protected spot:flowers a bright lilac-
blue with yellow:hardy, used north into warm temperate regions.
    -ramosa, a small plant, but very busy at the crown and trembly
in a breeze, down after flowering for a short rest in summer, beginning growth again September-October....mark the spot and divide

Momordica
charantia

Monardella
lanceolata

Moraea
glaucopis

M.
bicolor

in August:the small, delicate flowers are held erect in an
open structure, light yellow with a darker zoning June-July:
a garden plant, wanting moisture and fertility, not typical
of the group in appearance or culture and too seldom seen.

MORISIA monantha, "Mediterranean-cress" rare little plant for
full sun in a sharply drained place among rocks:spreads underground with small flat rosettes of tiny dandelion leaves a-
bove, close mat and rest for the half-inch flowers....golden
yellow, April into summer:the mat becomes too thick when in
thrift and should be divided in early fall. This is not for
the better garden soils where it flourishes in degree and
manner out of character....poor ground and dryness holds
down to mat proportions where it is best and longer-lived.

### MULBERRY
MORUS---small, deciduous, fruit-bearing trees, of little ornamental value, grown for shade and to provide food for birds. They
find their greatest usefulness in heat and under drought or in hard
frost. They will do in loose, gravelly soils where but few other
trees find it possible to thrive. They are quite littering under
foot, but serve up most welcome shade with these same leaves that
are so curiously variable.
      -nigra, "Persian or Black M." the very large leaves deep-
ly toothed but scarcely lobed, dull green and affording an extra dense shade:black fruits are large, sub-acid; the better
one for human use:round top is inclined to flatten out in age:
normally reaches 15-20' for height, not so tall south.
      -rubra, "American or Red M." a native tree farther north,
growing in these regions to some 40' or less, the generally
heart-shaped leaves roughened above and downy beneath:dark purple fruit May-June, smaller than above, used for birds and domestic fowl. There are fruitless forms that may be grown for shade,
and the     --var. kingan, has superior fruit.

MUEHLENBECKIA complexa, "Wire-vine" an odd vining plant for
utility of a high order, covering rocks, walls or a rickety fence
thoroughly, if not quickly:the tumbling, tangled wiry stems will
carry tiny rounded leaves and small flecks of fleshy, colorless
flowers, all in a rounding, dense mass:stands in wind and heat
and some salt in the soil, considerable cold and can be held
in some dryness by adapting. The species   -axillare, is a
low-matting duplication of the above, a tight, close, inch-through
cover, carpeting ground that does not become too dry....rock work and
crevices. Another curious and obscure species   -platyclada(Homalocladium)"Centipede-plant" is clambering in long, jointed, glistening
stems, leaf-like and ribbony, set to tiny flowers, the beady seed
vessels red against the pale green.

MURRAEA exotica, "Orange-jessamine" a rounded shrub 3-5' or
very slender and erect, easily made dense under the shears to
suit the formal, either in the ground or to a tub....broad as
a hedge:exquisite in foliage and all the way through flowering
and berry, the fragrant, pure white bloom over April-July; will
scatter out further, so that the earlier large red fruits overlap:
regarded very highly for the garden, the culture that of citrus,
resenting especially wind; wanting warmth, good fertility, drainage and a little shade in high heat. A form known as -paniculata,
is more treelike, or amenable to suggestion, may grow to be
25' high in warm humid climates, flowering there several
times a year or continuously far south, berrying profusely....exciting and excellent cutting for Christmas.

### BANANA
MUSA---tree-like herbaceous plants with heavy watery
trunk-like stems. The great broad leaf is most fragile
in the wind, becoming torn and tattered, a condition of
dilapidation that is unending under exposure. They
are highly tropical in appearance and in fact. Give
them sunlight in a place where warmth can be held,

356

a rich soil with continued attention to fertility, copious
water at all stages of growth for the rank herbage and the
fruit....if any. Air drainage, as of a hillside or ground
opening out of a patio will have a bearing on frost damage.
    -cavendishi(nana)a dwarf species, only 4-6' in height
over-all, with slender, narrow stems and leaves in a close
clump:may be used in a tub, fruiting in more cold than
others....protect further by taking in cold nights.
    -ensete, "Abyssinian B." purely ornamental, the
single stem as high as 25', usually much less, thick and
swollen at the base:has wide, oval-shaped leaves, the stalk
continuing into the blade as a purple midrib, the inflorescence, likewise purple:no suckering here.
    -sapientum, the "Edible B." growing in shabby, un-
combed clumps of untidy, shredding stems, each one dying
and rotting away after having fruited....remove:quite
tender in frost and must have every aid in protection
if it is to fruit....not particularly good then.

MYOPORUM laetum, a large, uncouth shrub of dense,
sullen growth or a small sturdy tree in the wind:es-
sential value and use is at the shore within reach of
the spray; scarcely excelled there for the punishment
it will endure....not to be used elsewhere:substantial
dark foliage of supreme wearing quality and very small
whitish flowers with purple markings, of note only in
that they survive along with the leaves:nematodes.

MYOSOTIS alpestris, "Forget-me-not" reminds us of old gardens and times that were good, long used in amity and mutual
good will by gardeners; tiny flowers for humility, very blue
and fragrant of an evening when fancy prompts and one looks
backwards:must have shade in the south, moisture in the ground
and much leafmould:get started as soon as possible, sowing in
the fall or very early spring:self-sows and flowers any or
all the time, spring-summer in coolness.

MYRIOPHYLLUM proserpinacoides, "Parrotfeather" an
aquatic, the long slender stems regularly whorled in
light green feathery foliage:roots at the edge of a
pool or in very shallow water, filling ditches, the
stems reclining and partially submerged or floating
for a time when broken loose:aquariums.

MYRSINE africana, "African-box" for rather general use
in sun or partial shade in light or heavy soils, in poor
or fertile, but always with drainage and good run-off:a
bushy shrub 3-4', or single stems shooting suddenly out
of the body of the plant to 10' or more, tree-like:the
small leaves are roundish, dull yellowing green with bronzy
under-tones, durable for wear....pinch out terminals for a
compact plant. This should not be sheared as a hedge, the
quick-shoots breaking from the top plane too suddenly and
too often for reasonable control:slow to start:lime.

### MYRTLE
MYRTUS---bushy shrubs, valued highly in subtropical
regions and much used there for the clear-cut pattern of
fruit and foliage and flowers. They are compact or very
easily made so by shearing....the white, flushed, fuzzy
flowers still showing back of vent and leaf. The foliage is
aromatic and the bloomy blue berries are set with regularity
among the leaves. They want the sun, stand in some drought, but
not so well in extreme heat; do poorly in very moist ground and
in deep shade where they are more susceptible to thrips and red
spider. They are used a great deal in hedging and may be grown
satisfactorily in lower warm temperate regions.
    -communis, the "Classic M." a shrub that is
quite variable, yet reduced to and available in
well fixed forms so that the varieties are best

357

considered in planting for defining character. --var. italica,
much taller than the type and naturally more compact,
almost columnar to 15', an oval in outline. --var.
microphylla, more refined from the smaller leaves, lower
and more spreading, with darker foliage, the overlapping
leaves narrow and sharply pointed:may be used for a hedge
that does not run into the shade. --var. minima, dwarf, only
10-15" high, with all parts in scale, a natural curb hedge.
--var romana, "Roman M." the leaf so wide as to be nearly
round, a very light green. --var. variegata, covering a
number of very pleasing variegations which may be used without
too much concern or stint for light contrast in the border or any
place where brightness is a consideration and asset.

-ralphi, erect, slender and willowy stems to as much as 10', of
high decorative value, the leaves a dull bronzy green and nearly
round, the flowers pure white and the fruit dark red:may be
grown tree-like by using a knife.

-ugni, "Chilean-guava" small shrub of very open structure, the tiny hard leaves light, almost yellowish, rolled
back along the edges:attractive white or slightly flushed
flowers of early summer are followed by fragrant, light
purple berries that are sometimes edible, having a flavor
of wild strawberry, used as a desert when well grown:wants
an open, fertile and loamy soil with good drainage....give
it a little shade in heat, as of deciduous trees.

## N

NANDINA domestica, "Celestial-bamboo" an erect, precise
and very neatly set shrub of distinction and of marked
decorative value against architecture, eventually 6-8'
in height and featuring strictly vertical lines in the
cane-like stems:flowers in large terminal heads, summer,
to carry through winter as red berries:foliage is most refined and elegant, bronzy as it breaks, crimson with cold
or as it drops:some shade is desirable in heat, but better
flowers and fruit develop in sun:moisture a necessity for
thrift, yet an established plant will adapt to dryness in
a surprising way, but showing distress and making almost no
growth:start with field-grown stock if possible or cut the
smaller plants to the ground after a year for an increase
of shoots:fruiting heads will be more full if plants are
grouped for cross-pollination. --var alba, with an
attractive ivory-colored berry is seldom seen.

NARCISSUS pseudo-narcissus, the common "Trumpet
Daffodil" , a spring-flowering bulb of popular address
and easily handled under very ordinary conditions. A
loamy soil on the heavy side is to be preferred, but
should be deeply dug, well drained and of good fertil-
ity:takes a little shade and the bulb should not be disturbed until clearly running out....dry as may be over
summer:set in early autumn, placing depth not more than twice
the diameter of the bulb or slightly more in sandy soils. They
want coolness and moisture in growth and do not succeed far south
in Florida. The dwarf species -cyclamineus, has very special
uses based on scale of plant, while the species -tazetta, the
"Polyanthus or Paperwhite N." with large clusters of smaller flowers
may be grown in a pot or naturalized, blooming in winter.

NELUMBIUM nelumbo, "East India Lotus" a bold, conspicuous
aquatic for comparatively shallow water, strong-rooting,
predatory to an extent requiring that they be grown alone:
large round leaves, along with the flower, work up out of
the water and show in high relief....if only against the
sky, low:grows in a small pool, or even in a tub for awhile,

but for real and permanent satisfaction must have a large
body of water with plenty of mud and complete freedom for
the roots:fragrant white, pink or deeper colored flowers are
particularly handsome as they come out of bud. This is not the true
Egyptian lotus, but is known and accepted as such in common usage.

NEMESIA strumosa, annuals, gay little plants for bedding, growing
12-15", but with more dwarf and compact forms, riotously colorful in tintings of pink, rose, orange, scarlet and yellow,
mingling:wanting essentially coolness, they are better pointed for the general area of winter, far south, spring and fall
more northerly:they are sun-lovers and must have expert handling as seedlings, with constant, if light moisture to keep
them moving along:any checks, such as drying out or leggy
growth from forcing, or premature flowering is to be avoided:
refuse flat material indicating any of these:ready for bloom
six weeks from sowing, January-February and again August-
September....in shade:set out as closely together as 6",
pinching out the tips....takes a little dryness when established, but too much hastens maturity and decline. This is
not easy to handle, but very choice when well grown.

NEMOPHILA menziesi(insignis) "Baby-blue-eyes" a low
straggling annual with blue, white-eyed flowers of singular beauty in purity all spring and summer:sow August-
September for spring flowering and April-June for summer:
good filler for the border or the more compact forms may
be used in bedding or edging in cool, moist soils in the
sun, but with shade in heat:the lighter soils best.

NEOMARICA(MARICA) gracilis, "Walking-iris" a tropical iris
in effect, a full stout clump 2-3' with an arched outline, an
accent for the border, wanting long shade over noon:the flattish flower with white, yellow and blue, April-May, extends
downward on a long leaf-like scape, lowers then to the earth
of its weight and takes root:divide in autumn and re-set very
shallow....also the small new plant which may be propped or
staked just touching the ground if taken before the roots have
formed:pots and baskets indoors or outside in good moisture.

NEPETA mussini, "Mussinsmint" perennial, for a dense blanket of
greyish foliage 12" through, aromatic in the sun, with usually two
distinct pale blue bloomings at either end of summer, either with a
shearing after the first or not:good filler for the border or the more
compact-growing suitable for bedding:transplant only in the spring to
cover dry ground, effective over a sterile bank or slope where it will
maintain itself with a minimum of care:odor of the foliage so attractive to cats they bed down with it....in the exuberance of spring.

NEPHROLEPIS exalata, "Sword Fern" erect, with straight or slightly
curving fronds, useful in circumstances of heat, dryness, total shade
or poor soils....speaking of the type form:the many varieties
require better conditions, are attractive and commonly used
house plants, with gas fumes the limiting factor in growth:
tone them up with some time out of doors when the foliage
can be thoroughly flushed.   --var. bostoniensis, "Boston F."
with long, very gracefully arching, sweeping fronds:a standard
plant indoors.   --var. plumosus, as rugged and hardy as the
type, the leaflets again divided.   --var. whitmani, the wider
fronds short, less arching and more feathery, irregular, cut and
recut as in fine lace.

NEPHTHYTIS afzeli, tropical creepers or climbing with support on
trees far south, indoor planters or a damp, roughened wall outside
in deep shade:known for and largely used as a pot plant for the
juvenile leaves which are arrow-shaped, dark green or with lighter
markings over the green:ultimately, and much later, the matured plant
has lance-shaped leaves in a palmate arrangement as a kind of loose
cover in the shade of lath, and mistaken for Christmas-rose:very moist
soil or will grow for a time in water, indoors or out.

359

NERIUM oleander, "Rose-bay" large, bushy, bulking
shrub or tree-like to 20' with shaping, either form
useful in warm localities or cool, but primarily
suited to heat:blooms profusely in summer, purest white
through pink, rose, scarlet and a kind of buff for yellow,
single salver-shaped or full double, all in large generous
clusters:some will begin as early as April, far south, others
lasting as late as October, particularly the reds....comes into flowering earlier and lasts longer away from the coast, where it
is less subject to scale....a menace:thrives best in the sun or takes
light shade, the soil damp or dry, better moist until flower buds set,
then dry....drainage important:good in humidity, but best in heat
which ripens and hardens seasons growth properly for
next seasons crop bearing:root-prune to hold down a
plant that too often gets out of hand....grows in a tub
or makes a standard of merit. The "Sweet-scented Oleander"
-indicum, growing 6-8', with extra large clusters of
often double white, rosy-pink or red, fringed flowers
2" across is musk scented, rarely seen:the narrower leaf
is rolled back along the margins:choice.

NERINE---extra select and most interesting bulbous plants
with strap-shaped leaves and funnel-form, flaring flowers
with singularly subtle and brilliant color in late summer. They want the sun and are not too difficult to
flower if given a long rest, beginning at time the leaf
goes back. If this is not practicable in the garden, they
will be better grown in a pot. Use a fertile, sandy soil
with leafmould to feed and peatmoss to keep it on a slightly
acid basis....very hard water to be avoided. Generally transplant over summer and the clumps allowed to crowd with the least
interference possible:feed with a liquid fertilizer as growth begins and avoid heavy soils....or modify.
    -bowdeni, one of the easiest to flower, the head held to
15" high, the flowers dark rosy pink in a large umbel through
autumn:does not always go dormant, or in most cases for only
a short period....probably the best one for garden or border.
    -curvifolia fothergilli, flowering stems to 18" high,
with larger red or scarlet flowers late summer or early in
the fall:must be kept dry over early season for.....one of
the most beautiful of the bulb flowers.
    -filifolia, in miniature and holding foliage over, the
nearly prostrate leaves, thread-like while the light red flowers August-September, are full clustered, held 10" high on
wiry stems for cutting:transplant any time, better October.
    -sarniensis, "Guernsey-lily" raised 12-18", the stout,
solid scape carrying ten to twenty flowers in a cluster, white,
pink, rose to fiery crimson, each with the narrow, ribbony segments or petals and long, out-thrust filaments:color is especially pure, with a scintillating quality that glitters and sparkles
in sunlight, September-October:set deeply for flowers, as much as
3" of soil covering.   --var. coruscans, distinguished by a heavy
coruscation, luminous in bursts of reflected light as it moves
in a breeze....a glittering as if dusted with a sand of gold
and silver, 8 to 12 flowers in a cluster:rich soils, crowd and
do not disturb:start in the fall by watering with a liquid
fertilizer and see that it gets its dry rest.

NERTERA depressa, "Coralbead" perennial, making a close
mat of slender, fragile stems and mossy foliage, but only
in coolness:small, translucent orange-red berries lie embedded on the surface....matchless in way of mossy coverings in damp, sandy soils in some shade....wants light, but not
direct sun and wants never to be dried out completely:humid air
beneficial, but not most important and light dressings of ground
leafmould in autumn will feed. Any popularity this little gem
has had in the past has been lost, so that now it is scarcely known. This is due to failure in berrying, with rational
and intelligent irrigation the probable answer....spraying or
sprinkling at time of bloom prevents pollination and set of

360

*Nephthytis afzeli*

*Nerium*

*Nerine bowdeni*

*Nerine filifolia*

*Nertera*

berries....answer....allow water to filter in from the side, not over the top. Look for the minute flowers about May, handle correctly and the reward will be great and goodly.

NICOTIANA alata, "Sweetscented Tobacco" an annual of rather wobbly structure, 2-3' in height, blooming late summer and fall, used in a pot and staked or as bedding on a large scale, with or against shrubs....always in a warm place in rich ground out of the wind:long, narrow-tubular flowers flare at the mouth, star-like, white, crimson or yellowish, closed through the day but open at night with a peculiar, penetrating odor:better in a dry atmosphere, set out not earlier than May and not in the same ground consecutive years....account of fungous dis-eases that carry over in the soil:heat important.

## CUPFLOWER
NIEREMBERGIA---striking color for the garden, low plants on the order of ornamental flax, but with more body, little known and meriting much wider attention. They are herbaceous or semi-woody, some prostrate, all endowed with a direct and simple appeal that is matter-of-fact and colorful. They are not sturdy, and not very persistent unless working under favorable conditions of soil and moisture....best in the rock garden where they will not be elbowed aside. The flower tends to fade in full and direct sun and the shrubby kinds may be cut to the ground in autumn to renew.
   -caerulea(hippomanica)a low, bushy-erect mass 12", that will be covered much of the year with lavender-blue flowers: may be treated as an annual, renewing each year or sheared back in the winter for superb color the following summer: good color can be retained by means of cuttings:bedding, low dividing hedges or grown in the fore-part of the border.
   -frutescens, shrubby, growing 2-3', the flowers at the extremities of the willowy but erect stems, white, suffused with lilac and blue or dark purple July-October:a border plant in dryish or damp places, or used in a large pot for nicely rounded form beneath the color:broken shade will reduce fading.
   -gracilis, the very slender stems weak, sagging or drooping beneath the blooming, growing not to exceed 12", but spready:white flowers veined with purple are deeper in the throat and touched therewith yellow:window boxes, rock work or baskets.
   -rivularis, "White-cup" prostrate perennial forming a mat of closely packed, spoon-shaped leaves only an inch through, sprinkled, and sometimes almost covered with the white finely crinkled, flat-cupped flowers, the throat with yellow:full sun to slight shade in a moist soil that is drained, but always with moisture....a cool slope ideal where moisture follows down a hard structure beneath:top-dress in spring with sifted leafmould and bonemeal:slugs will defoliate unless controlled.

NOLANA atriplicifolia, "Chile-bellflower" perennial herb, usually treated as an annual, more or less erect 10-15", with un-attractive spoon-shaped leaves that are meaty,dull green, from angular purplish stems:flat, bell-shaped flowers from summer on into early winter are white, violet or livid blue with a lighter throat and close at dusk or fold dark days:pots, baskets or quickly fills a shallow planter: sandy, rather sterile soils in the rock garden.   --var. prostrata, streaming out wide, less than 6" high and several feet across.....runs beneath neighboring plants to light:dull blue flower has purple lines in the throat.

NOLINA parryi, sometimes known as "Bear-grass" rosettes at the ground, yucca-like, of harsh slender leaves in broad clumps:rigid-rounded panicles of greenish white flowers will emerge, large and fairly tight, coming to a sharp point from a full-dense body. These are striking plants, native throughout the greater Southwest, to be used only occasionally and casually to point up a dry hillside planting, always in good drainage....no wet winters on the level.

Nierembergia Frutescens

Nierembergia rivularis

Nicotiana

Nolina

Nolana prostrata

NOLTEA africana, "Soapbush" an erect irregular shrubby
plant with the dull, off-green, lead-colored foliage of a
buckthorn....in the end a multiple-stemmed little tree to
20' with an open, rounding top:naturally rather dense-growing
when young, can be kept so as a hedge....good in salt wind:small
white flowers of May-June serve only to brighten the dreary foliage. This is interesting and for a tough job along the coast.

NOTHOPANAX arboreum, "Ginwood" shrubby, in repeated dark
vertical lines of soft, greenish stems or may be held to one
trunk at 25':grows rapidly in light shade and will tolerate a
deep shadow in moist fertile soils. This is a very choice plant with
high decorative value....but not in much heat.

NUXIA floribunda, "African-green" spreading, bushy, very much like
an elderberry in structure, or may be tree-like 15' with long, evenly draped leaves for effective screening at close quarters:the
creamy-white flowers of January-March are collected together
in large heads:requires much space for natural growth, will
take drought or some moisture, resents wetness under foot and
to much shade....a good plant when intelligently handled.

NYCTANTHES arbor-tristis, "Tree of Sadness" shrubby under only
light frost, a tree 30' in near tropical places:fragrant white
flowers are salver-shaped from an orange tube and appear only at
night, dropping the following morning:very sensitive to cold weather
and goes into chill very quickly:wants good fertility, a little lime.

NYMPHAEA capensis, representing "Water-lily" plants for the plane
of water. Species from the tropics may be grown in these regions,
along with standard varieties found over the rest of the country
and all from lowlands for horizontal planes, the flat leaves
floating or crowding out of the water, with flowers likewise
raised or resting. They want a very rich medium, a heavy mud
in which to grow, with full sun, and will achieve better bloom,
and more, in still water that is not too fresh:transplant them
in February and do any cleaning out at that time, but only and
if absolutely demanded, to save disturbing the balance of life
there which insures clear water. Full advantage should be taken
in subtropical regions of the gorgeous tropical kinds that
may be grown there, the white lotus as well as the blue
above and its spectacular variety zanzibariensis, together
with the red India hybrids.

NYMPHOIDES(LIMNANTHEMUM)indicum, "Water Snowflake" small
floating aquatic with a heart-shaped leaf and tiny, raised,
flower with a yellow spot of down:produces these flowers in
considerable abundance and reproduces rapidly in warmth:a
typical and appropriate little plant for tub culture.

O

OCHNA multiflora, an erect-spreading shrub 3-4' with
rather crowded, finely toothed, long narrow leaves of a
bronzy cast when new:fragrant, dark yellow flowers are
short-lived May-June, followed by capsular fruits, the
seeds on the exposed bright crimson receptacle, at first
green, then black....most unusual for a close-at-hand inspect-
ion:wants a well drained soil, a cool slope away from the sun
or somewhat less than half shade:use only well established
plants of this to save loss:tender.

OCHROSIA elliptica, "Wedge-apple" a handsome shrub of
erect lines or an open-headed, limber-limbed tree 20' the
whorled blunt leaves at the ends of the branches.....with

dense corymbs of strawy flowers produce obscurely nut-like
fruits that are like those of carissa in the early stages,
easily mistaken then, last all winter and drop....crushed,
release the odor of violets:resists salt wind:tender.

OCIMUM basilicum, "Sweetbasil" tight little bushlet with aromatic leaves that may be used for a delicate clove flavoring in
cookery:perennial in rich soils, becoming somewhat woody in time
or may be pulled up in entirety while still in flower and hung a-
way to dry for later use....in any event, take before flowering
is completed:bloom tinged bluish or light purple:edging in sun.

ODONTOSPERMUM sericeum, a rigid shrub, naturally dense and
rounding, a lively thing in the sun, a busy and tense-grained
mass 4-5' high, with as much spread to the ground:undulant,
silvery-silken leaves turn high-lighting lines to the sun for
an exceptional brilliance and enclose each yellow daisy for an
acceptable corsage....for daylight:blooms spring-summer-autumn,
and very freely:dead leaves persist on the stems beneath the rather
tight foliage cover....may be rubbed off when objectionable thru a
vent:essentially for the sun in spirit, most useful under exposure
and in dryish, barren soils:tubs....highly decorative....and rare.

SUNDROP          EVENING PRIMROSE
OENOTHERA---confused botanically, but very clear as to loveli-
ness in the daytime, in particular at night; sun-loving herbaceous material for dry sandy soils out in the open landscape, some
very questionably used in the garden. The foliage is coarse, with
undiscliplined, flopping stems, but persistently flowering in
season, suitable for semi-arid places, valley sands or those of
the seacoast. The large flowers of the evening primrose are open
and usually scented at night, while the buds, if taken in the afternoon with just a little color showing, will open in water as dusk
approaches....a timing and virtu for freshening the dinner table.
The sundrops bloom generally by day. Take rooted off-sets
in the fall for propagation, but divide in the spring.
    -acaulis, a "Sundrop" biennial, or a short-lived per-
ennial, the gleaming, fragrant white flowers by day and
as much as 4" across full-open, resting lightly on the
tangled litter of stems and tattered leaves:waste places
or remote borders where they can dig in for increase.
    -caespitosa, another "Sundrop", in spreading tufts
of growth, to form large colonies in out of the way
places, on warm sunny slopes or among rocks....probably
the most self-contained species for the large rock gard-
en:huge, pure white, fragrant flowers of a day turn to
pink as they go off, June-July.
    -cheiranthifolia, "Beach-primrose" covers sand or dry
gravelly banks with its silvered leaves and white-yellow
flowers:has that glistening, sun-lively quality of a
buttercup, the flower by day:native west.
    -hookeri, an "Evening-primrose" , also native in Califor-
nia, biennial, with light yellow flowers which open in the evening:
plant is quite large, the coarse stems erect to somewhat spreading, sometimes quite loosely growing, always weedy:found in nature in very wet places or a cup in quite dry ground that will
collect winter rains....suggests use in domestication.
    -tetraptera, "Mexican-primrose", the type a straggling
pink-flowering cover for hard, dry ground with nothing to
offer a more fastidious plant:spreads fiercely by means of
underground runners to become a pest of the first order,
safe to use in a restricted spot....an impossible bit of
ground between curb or walk and building foundation or
other....absolutely waste ground:hybrids available are
easier found, less furious in demands, pale pink, white.

OLEA europaea, "Olive" a round-headed tree 25' with
an exceptionally handsome and distinctly grey-green
foliage, the leaf silvered beneath:purple fruits are
ornamental in a sense, but also a source of squashing,
363

staining litter. The characteristic beauty of this tree develops
only in heat and dry, meager soils as found in arid places and is
quickly lost under a sufficiency of moisture and nutrients. The
large, matured tree is easily moved in autumn and early spring,
the period of bloom and slipping bark being the least desirable time....use hormones and do not box unless to be carried
a great distance. The species -chrysophylla, is of tropical origin, a better tree in Florida and along the Gulf
Coast, or even in California in warmth and moisture:slender,
stems in a bushy overall, the branches densely clothed with
dark, leathery leaves that are yellowish beneath in the beginning, later a lighter green than the surface above:takes some
exposure in soils that are only dryish.

OLMEDIELLA betschleriana, "Guatamala-holly" shrubby, with
several erect-meandering stems or a slender tree 25' having unusually attractive foliage, the leaf holly-like within an oval
outline....a light milk-green, the new growth verdant progressively through a harmony of ruddy pastels to apple-green:the
natural growth is open in character, dense under some compulsion, seemingly without cultural complications:screening
and large hedges or grown for awhile in a tub:choice.

ONCOBA routledgei, a large, spreading shrub or ultimately
a small tree 15-20' with glistening, bright green, wavy and
sharply toothed leaves:the 2" fragrant white flowers are
centered with a fluff of yellow stamens May-June:may be
grown in rather stiff heavy soils, and dryish after having
been established:tender and will drop leaves in frost in
interest of survival....go into winter dry:rare.

ONYCHIUM japonicum, "Japanese Parsley Fern" with fronds of
medium length, very lacy and delicate, irregular in growing:
the claw-like lobes are somewhat twisted or contorted, but are
as graceful and as finely set as maidenhair:wants a partially
shaded place with a loose, friable soil.

### LILY TURF
OPHIOPOGON---another class of grassy plants of the
lily family, making a more or less dense mat of growth
in the nature of turf as grown out of doors or may be used
as individual plants in pots, window boxes or planters. They
have thick under-ground root-stocks with fibrous roots that
are almost tuberous, the clumps easily broken up and reset.
They will grow in full shade or out in the sun.
    -jaburan, "Snakebeard" strong clumps of lush dark
leaves 18-24", narrow sword-like but more gathered, as in a
hattock, sometimes with the inevitable stripings of yellow
or white:flowers June-July, white, lilac or blue, completed
in time by dark violet berries set precisely along stiff
straight stalks:pots, boxes or a place in the border.
    -japonicus, "Japan-grass" not as full as the preceding
and much more commonly used, the dark green leaves very narrow
and grassy in the turf sense, 4-10" in height unless kept cut:a
cover beneath trees out in the open or lining a path as a border
or low curb:whitish or violet-purple flowers are not conspicuous
and may be overlooked, but not the tight heads of blue berries:
aim to cut back before the flower-fruiting time or afterward, or
possibly only once a year in the spring....a sickle job. These
plants are found mostly in Florida where they thrive as turf in
sandy soils where grasses will not survive for very long. They
are used in California, ornamentally in pots and in the border.

OPLISMENUS hirtellus, "Basket or Awn-grass" a frail plant,
branching, creeping, the leaf blades comparatively thin, with
broad, long stripes of pink and white:use in some shade as a
ground cover in some restriction or other such as a plant
house bed:set out new plants 12-15" on center, but closer
as an edging when it will have to be held in:may be used
in a basket lined with moss:tender.

COMPENDIUM

## PRICKLY PEAR

OPUNTIA---spined succulents, generally referred to as
cactus....the true cactus, grown largely by fanciers in
collections, also with obscure uses in the landscape.
They have little place even near the garden except to produce an atmosphere or setting for a very special project, at
times used for protective purposes against intrusion. The effect
as a whole, away from a natural environment, is fantastic and amus-
ing rather than pleasing, with beauty only in the flowers. The matter
of soil is not material, but they must have sun, and they will stand
for any amount of water where drainage is sharp. They prefer to come
along in a normal way as of absolute summer drouth.
      -basilaris, "Beavertail" low and spreading with reddish
bristles over the flattened joints and dark purple flowers
of great beauty.   -biglovi, "Juniper Cholla" erect stems
with cylindrical joints that are roughened and pale green
covered with long, white spines.   -leucotricha, has a
large flattened circular joint and yellow flowers of some
note.   -linguiformis, reclining, spiny mass of long and
tongue-like joints that covers a large area of ground in
time, fitting nicely to a bank.   -microdasys, "Teddy-
bear C." erect and wide-spreading, a plant with joints
tightly packed, soft golden bristles and many lemon-
yellow flowers:the minute spines are more dangerous than
the larger, in that entry is not realized and little pre-
caution exercised in handling....yet probably likliest one
for the garden, based on interest and refinement. -monacantha,
large and erect, branching from near the ground, the terminal
joints much thinner, bright green:yellow flowers. A variegated
form is popular, having much thinner joints that are marbled in
lighter green and yellow....an over-all whitish cast:weak growing, sick-looking, only a novelty.   -santa rita, a low, rather
compact aggregation of reddish joints and unusually beautiful yellow flowers.   -tuna, "Indian-fig" a tall sturdy plant, woody and
somewhat tree-like, the dark, flattened, elongated joints with
few or no spines and yellow flowers that turn reddish:the
handsome, very ornamental fruits in considerable quantity,
come in shades of yellow and orange with red and are eaten.
In preparing the tuna, cut a slice from either end of the
body of the fruit after rubbing away all bristles. A longitudinal cut will permit the laying back of the outer jacket to
expose and make available the pulp which is ready to eat....no
flavor to mention with any enthusiasm.

ORIGANUM dictamnus, "Crete Dittany" the prostrate stems
rooting in to make a more or less tight carpet of dull
grey, wooly leaves:loose, purplish flowering heads ascend
6-8" June-July, if allowed to come into flower:running
growth may be pinched in to thicken the mat of less than an inch
through:good cover for hard, dry ground. A culinary herb.

ORNITHOGALUM---spring and summer flowering bulbs for various and
rather well defined purposes in the garden or border, to be used
also in pots, but probably best plunged out in the garden by reason
of the disorder and dishevelment of the leaf mass. They may be naturalized in out of the way places, as of the wildflowers. All will
do in any well drained soil where bulb increase will be rapid. They
are not hardy in deep frost and must be protected north.
      -arabicum, a low-lying mass of long leaves from which
twisted stalks rise to carry a head of creamy-white flowers
centered with a large, gleaming, jet-black bead April-June:
fails to flower some years and is the better one to use
in a pot....and in high heat.
      -thyrsoides, "Chinkerinchee" with dense pyramidal
heads of straw-colored, creamy or deeper buds that will
open to pure white with a brown eye, the earliest one to
bloom in the spring.   --var. aureum, in various shades of
yellow and gold over a longer flowering period. This is an
unusually good cutflower. It should be well fed in the
garden to provide bulbs to grow with the cutflowers.

ORTHOCARPUS purpurascens, "Owls-clover" native in California, an annual featuring lurid color in the bract, clover-like
heads, rosy-pink or purple touched with white or yellow....stim-
ulated and made possible in nature by late rains:may be used in
the flower garden, but will be found more at home in out of the
way places,waste or barren ground, depressions that catch and
hold the fall of rain....water must not stand too long....makes
a great show of color there....when the rains come.

ORTHROSANTHUS multiflorus, a "Morningflower" and for only a day,
but the plant and its blooming dependable for many weeks in the gard-
en or may be grown in a pot as a grassy clump 12-18" high, or sometimes running underground to make something of a colony:spikes of
small, deep blue flowers, tiny iris forms over summer:the flowers
open successively over short periods.

OLIVEWOOD

OSMANTHUS---shrubs of considerable quality and substance,
of exceptional interest to the plantsman, used by him in garden
or landscape, being somewhat temperamental and not always satisfactory with others. They are important for the foliage
rather than for bloom; the flowers, however, more than a
gesture, give of themselves in perfume where they fail
in an appeal to the eye. All take a little shade and all
are hardy in frost, some growing well north into warm temperate
regions, becoming dwarfed and less vigorous as taken south in
these regions. They may easily be mistaken on foliage characters
for various species of holly, but the blue berries, in their
time and strange exotic fragrance will distinguish.
     -americanus, "Florida-olive" native, a brushy
shrub or a tree form to 40' having whitish bark, large,
lustrous, olive-like leaves and a mildly fragrant blooming in
January or February:hardy along east coast to Virginia.
     -armatus, a large, spreading bush, ultimately 10-15' having
very large, oval, pale green, spiny-toothed leaves that will be
a spot of brightness in deep shade....well used against dark
walls:flowers September-October with an unusual and penetrating fragrance that spreads throughout the garden.
     -fortunei, a hybrid with very erect slender stems 5-6'
or more for good line value, only slightly modified low in
the woody stem area by dull, dark, elongated leaves:the
fragrance comes in June:choice.
     -fragrans, "Sweet-olive" shrubby, with willowy, pliable
stems that may reach out in a vining way to 30' in length;
and again, take on a tree-like shape as it goes into age:
has considerable potential for the picturesque:tiny yellowish flowers May-June afford an exquisite and very
strong fragrance....cut wood may be taken indoors to scent
a room;an old plant in gardens, the more commonly known.
     -ilicifolius, "False-holly" large erect shrub or in-
frequently a small tree with dark, almost black-green foliage of irregularly spined leaves of leathery texture and, at
times, in almost exact duplication of English or Chinese holly:
fragrant white flowering in fall or very early spring, with a
following crop of blue berries on plants of some maturity.
--var. argenteo-marginatus, leaves edged in white, not as large
as the type.   --var. atro-purpureus, leaves and twigs purplish,
later green and only tinged with the color.   --var. aureo-marginatus, leaves edged yellow or somewhat variegated in same.

OSTEOMELES anthyllidifolia, a slender-stemmed shrub of filmy
delicate texture, evergreen or dropping the leaves in frost:
grows 3-5' high, with greyish foliage, the scant set of tiny
leaves of superlative daintiness, as are the diminutive plum
blossoms in April....all too short, the time, but followed
by blue fruits for an extension:wants a fairly loose, dryish drained soil in the sun or takes the normal irrigation
of a lawn:good narrow hedge and all the more attractive
when showing stems....seen through a misty haze of leaves
for a last word in refinement.

OTHONNA crassifolia, "Pickle-plant" a trailing succulent, or
becoming somewhat woody at the crown, the light green leaves
shaped like little sausages and massed closely as cover for
selected ground:small yellow flowers are produced liberally
in the sun and most any time in warmth:dryish places in the
rock garden or baskets, or stems root-in to hold a slope.

## WOOD SORREL
OXALIS---tiny bulbs, or with bulb-like root-stocks, growing in the shade in loose soils well supplied with humus, or
out in the sun in poorer ground; disappearing when their
time is up, as suddenly returning, and by the calendar,
also on time. The clover-like leaves are typical and they,
as well as the flowers, tend to close or fold together dull
days, and sleep at night. Drainage is important and some effort
should be made to leave the easily traveling kernels undisturbed and in place....can be obnoxious when spread around into the
wrong places. August-September is a good time to get into the
bulb mass for division or transplants....use in pots, in thin
edge of grass or naturalize.
   -bowieana, "Cape-shamrock" to spot here and there between
flags or out in the lawn where it quickly takes advantage of any
thin places in the turf:has the large green leaf of the shamrock
but its nativity is wrong, to let it out in the race to carry on
the green:flowers are large, variously colored, a pearly white to
yellow and orange or pink, the whole plant carried close against
the earth, any time November-February, sometimes October.
   -cernua, "Bermuda Buttercup" small lemon-yellow flowers raised high on quick-appearing stems, the flowers by early spring:the
dissemination has been largely by means of other plants....hitch-
hiking, the tiny kernels tucked away among the other roots for a
ride:naturalize out in the open where they will return year in
and out as waving patches of color....handsome weed in the gard-
en that invades a lawn to no purpose and difficult to eradicate.
   -crassipes, loosely mounding clump 10-12", almost evergreen
south and nearly everblooming, the high point spring-summer, the
small pink flowers sometimes turn up white in rather close
clusters:does not seed to become too much of a pest....tuber-
ous:takes some shade, but requires the sun to bring out full
brilliance:pots or in the garden.
   -hererei, fibrous-rooting, for a pot or basket, the elongated, slender stems woody, straggling, erect-hanging to face the
container with the light-green of the strange watery petiole and
leaf combination:tiny yellow flowers in winter, but mostly during
warmth. There may be some confusion in nomenclature here.
   -hirta, bulbous, the finely divided foliage full, effective,
abundant in its time, usually falling enmass of its own weight, to
rest upon the ground....more erect in full sun:bright rosy pink
to red flowers over winter-spring....not too accountable in
blooming....sometimes in the fall.

OXERA pulchella, a little known, lusty strapping shrubby
plant, bulking very large against anything with which it is
placed; a climber with broad-throated, trumpet-like flowers
that could be continual in sufficiently uniform warmth, generally autumn from late summer, sometimes through winter into
spring....flower buds are tender and kill easily in frost
where the plant is hardy:grows in the sun, best in a little
shade in high heat, where the pearly buds bubble and dribble open,
hanging suspended like unfurling parashutes:may be held, shrubby
at the base, with the streamers carried high, far and away for an
unusual service.

OXYPETALUM caeruleum, "Southern-star", but claimed by Texas as
their special little one, a greyish, flopping perennial or twining a few feet if given some support, hard-herbaceous stems from
a woody base:the up-facing, five-pointed stars are of a most
beautiful, pale, silver-dusted blue, tinged mauve in the bud,
accented when open by the deeper center:annual or short-lived
perennial, re-seeding but no nuisance:pots.

P

PACHYPHYTUM bracteosum, a shrubby succulent, nearly woody
at the base, heavy-stemmed and with grossly thick and large
roundish leaves of a dusty, pale bluish grey:nodding tubular
flowers gather together in a loose head like "Dancing Ladies"
in a breeze....opening with a pop to dominate July with their
brilliant orange-red coloring:quite resistant to drought and
loves heat, tenacious in all soils.

PACHYSTACHYS coccinea, "Cardinals-guard" tropical shrubs
for warm places, where they make bold clumps that weigh down
their neighbors with the pressure of color....scarlet to crimson in summer:leaves are comparatively large and shining, at
their best in shadow, the plant becoming quite dense in the sun,
but with poorer color:grows normally 5-7' in height and responds
quickly to moisture and fertility:may be treated as an herbaceous perennial in the north and mulched over winter.

PANCRATIUM---summer-flowering bulbs with strap-shaped
leaves and solid scapes bearing loose heads of transparent
papery white flowers that are very fragrant. They refuse
to bloom in summer moisture of any great amount, but call
for moisture during growth, in absence of rain....much more
successfully grown where this can be kept under control and may
flower without benefit of foliage. They must have full sun and
a generally dry , sandy or gravelly soil. Culture of these must
not be confused with that of the white spider-lily....they are
similar only in appearence.
　　-illyricum, "Spirit-lily" the greyish leaves usually with the
flowers June-July, but quailing, ready to sag and depart....prob-
ably takes more moisture at this time without affecting bloom. This
is the hardiest  in frost and the more commonly grown.
　　-maritimum, "Sea-daffodil" the staminal cup giving this one
the appearance of a daffodil, but from a shorter stalk and in July
or August:the narrow, sharp-pointed, blue-green leaves show a
decided twist in their length and tend to hold evergreen, but
the blooming sometimes naked:withstands some alkali.

PANDOREA---stout, far-reaching climbers with fairly heavy
wood, aloft and beneath, rooting deeply and too widely thru
a small or intensely cultivated garden. They are attractive and useful when handled properly, but develop none
of their best points if not understood. They must have
all the sun possible and plenty of root-room, with
regular winter pruning, else the foliage thins out and
blooming suffers, with that scattered and ineffective. A
naturally rich soil is to be preferred over fertilizing, but
in any case, much available food is required....heavy soils
best, with adequate moisture but not over-done. These are
clean for vines that make so much wood.
　　-jasminoides, "Bower-vine" scant foliage and plenty of
wood, the white flowers in open clusters usually have a purple
splotch in the throat, may be a beautiful, pure white, a rose or
pink self, scattering out over summer-autumn.
　　-pandorana(Tecoma australis)"Wonga-vine" the foliage bright green
and shining, the trumpets small but abundant, creamy-white obscurely
spotted with purple or the spots wanting, February-April. This is
excellent for overhead cover or may be used on the ground.

POPPY
PAPAVER---annual and perennial plants, gallant, flaunting color for garden or border, the fragile crumpled flowers short-lived individually, but coming along in quick
succession. They want a light soil in the sun, one that
is not overly rich, to be fed but little if any, and
that laid deeply as the ground is prepared. The best
results are always from seed sown where the plants are
to stand with no attempt to cover the fine seed. Merely
firm the soil lightly and melt further with a fine spray.

Oxera

Pancra

Pandorea

jasmin-
oides

368

Pachystachys

The seed pods are considered ornamental, taken for
tinting and used indoors.
   -nudicaule, "Iceland P." perennial, the slightly greyish foliage at the ground, with wiry stems carrying nodding
buds that open to the  delicate white, reddish or yellow flowers  of satiny texture spring-summer, or pointed for winter in
the south:rock garden or cutting, with a certain value used as
bedding....cut only in early morning and as the bud opens:short-
lived and must be grown as an annual for good results.
   -rhoeas, "Corn P." annuals, including the Shirley and other
strains, showing great variation in form and coloring, blooming
from April to September from seed sown successively November-July
and thinned to 6":cut buds that have only the suggestion of color
and char ends of stems before placing into water.
   -rupifragum, "Spanish P." good perennial for the south,
widely spreading from seed, a strong growth at the ground:
magnificant flowers May-July are as much as 5-6" across,
splendid in the morning but shattered by noon of a hot day
or soon thereafter, light red or apricot:poor dry soils for
best results, clumps moving when small, doing in light shade.

*Papaver Rhoeas*

   PARKINSONIA aculeata, known as "Bigota in Texas, Ratama in
Arizona, Paloverde" in California eroniously, "Jerusalem Thorn"
elsewhere and probably with more authority; a spreading, bushy
tree 25', as wide as high, a wildling that has never really been
tamed, but with as wide a tolerance in culture as is its distrib-
ution over the world:sparse, light green  rudimentary leaves drop
in cold or utter drought to let the green stems carry on while
the pale yellow, henna-touched flowers along the thorny branches
summer and fall, may continue far south:thin and scrawny in a
shallow, poor soil, it thickens and swells to goodly proportions
in deeper ground to make a full, handsome body, if tenuous and
showing other benefits in blooming:tolerates maximum heat and
drought or takes some coolness and moisture and frost.

*Parkinsonia*

   PAROCHETUS communis, "Shamrock Pea" a tangled growth of long
running stems set very sparsely to little clover leaves that
have a brown crescent at the base of each leaflet:miniature
sweetpeas on long slender stems in summer are rich in cobalt
blue to tiny pink wings:hanging baskets, pots or with rock in
a light sandy soil that does not dry out:a perennial, normally
from seed since it is difficult to hold to a container:sun.

   PARONYCHIA argentea, "Whitlow-wort" prostrate, a bright,
lightsome little thing, creeping, a perennial that builds a
thin fabric of beaming, spangled herbage to an inch through
in dryish places in the sun:flowering comes May-June, minute
fluffs of yellow, tiny jewelled tittles in a setting of silvery bracts that glisten and throw back to the sun....not
tolerant nor serviceable in shade:rock gardens in heat.

   PARTHENOCISSUS---deciduous, high-climbing vines of vigorous growth and good name. The clustered, bright blue
berries are ornamental and serve in the south midwinter.
The foliage covers completely or less so, according to
species, but with all affording brilliant autumnal
display, coloring in scarlet to crimson. All cling
to masonry, either closely or precariously, easily
to the bark of trees or other more roughened surfaces.
Cut stems back to 6" when setting out since the new
shoots are more efficient in taking hold. Rich, moist
soils are best and any exposure will do except in heat.

*Parthenocissus lowi*

   -henryana, "Silvervein Creeper" unusually ornamental, a half-
cling species, the five to seven parted leaves light green with the
veins picked out above in white, a flat wash of purple beneath:a
little shade required to bring out coloration fully:grows vigorously, but not as dense cover as the following:a ground cover.
   -tricuspidata, "Boston-ivy" sometimes known as "Japanese-
ivy", very tightly clinging to the smoothest surfaces and
getting started earlier in the spring:the three-parted

369

*Parochetus*

leaves eventually stand out from the wall on long petioles
to roll and billow in a breeze, losing a rather fine moulding in age and drop, leaving the outworn stalks, which
loosen later.     --var. lowi, the leaves similar but smaller and twisting on the petiole, revolving in low-relief, out-
sculptured medalions that are spaced sufficiently, although with
some frugality, along a unique pattern of lines; stems meandering across the heavy, flat face of masonry; running, rather than
close-covering.   --var. veitchi, more like the type form above,
but less active and more contained, more slowly closing as cover, but eventually quite dense:a medium sized leaf....north
and east exposures are best.

PASITHEA caerulea, herbaceous perennial, a grassy clump of
leaves....up in early winter from a tight mass of small, watery
mass of translucent bulb-bodies tied together with minute root-
like strings....down completely over summer and may be dried out
or not:this rest period should not be disturbed, it being so
easy to slice into the root-mass....mark the spot....setback
is serious:blooms March-May, the enlarged stamens showing
high-yellow against the dark beauty of the starry blue flow-
ers:bearing stems are 18-24" high, but soon flopping, the leaf
breaking over so that the foliage is straggling, if not actually
slatternly, until down for rest. This untidiness is less pronounced as light intensity in increased and moisture decreas-
ed when a slight irridescence is brought out:must not be allowed to dry out during growth and flowering.

## PASSION FLOWER
PASSIFLORA---tendril-climbing, more or less herbaceous,
vines that are grown primarily for the striking flower which
is of exceeding interest, intricate in design and rich in
coloring, of legendary religious significance. These flowers
hang in a kind of festoon or cluster to depend from trees or
an overhead, planted in the garden in a strategic place
to take advantage of this character. They are subject
to periodic swarms of army worms and others, and species
must be chosen from among those known to be the least
susceptible, if satisfaction in having them is to be enjoyed. Give them a rich, moist soil where the atmosphere
is not too dry and don't allow the foliage to become very
dense....thin out leaves from time to time.
    -alato-caerulea(pfordti)hardy hybrid for very quick
coverage:stems are slightly winged, the plant very free in
flowering, nearly always with some bloom far south, white,
pink, purple or blue, any or all colors with the same plant;
has a slight fragrance and the heavy growth should be checked.
    -caerulea, a rather good foliage of five-lobed leaves,
almost free of caterpillars:flowers may come in pale shades of
pink to purple, but mostly they will be blue, sometimes a pure
white. This is the hardiest in cold.
    -edulis,"Passion Fruit" a burly vine that is grown commer-
cially for the edible fruit which is eaten directly with sugar,
or used in confections and in the preparation of drinks:becomes
woody at the base and requires strong support for the leafage.
    -manicata, the leaf three-lobed, the flat flower a strong
scarlet with a blue crown:may be in flower at Christmas, surely February-April and intermittently.
    -mollissima, the leaves three-lobed, deeply
toothed, the smaller flowers long-tubed, pink or
rose:rather more resistant to drought than others.
    -quadrangularis, "Granadilla" with strong, four-
cornered stems carrying large yellow fruits which are
used to prepare drinks or cooked green as a vegetable:
more tropical in its requirements:use far south.
    -racemosa(princeps)slender growth, high climb-
ing or carrying nicely from place to place dribbling
its color freely when satisfied with conditions:rather
thinly foliated, the leaf is more leathery and three-
lobed, the most immune to pests of the lot:will go

out suddenly in poor drainage or where free water fails
to get away quickly and reacts quickly and unfavorably to
cold weather:smaller, up-turned flowers in elongating
clusters are a soft red with purplish nuances to a white
crown, the whole suspending 15-18":slow to establish and
later coming into flower, but choice....very select.

PEDILANTHUS tithymaloides, "Redbird-cactus" an erect
succulent, growing to 6' in height, the branchings usually leafless at which time the red or purple flowers, the
shape of a shoe or pointing bird, poise on the tips of the
branches....winter in warmth:dryness in winter is preferred,
but moisture the balance of the year:tubs.

STORKSBILL

PELARGONIUM---perennials, popular and well-known, universally used for a pot indoors or out, in bedding where the
virile coloring will fit into a scheme. The foliage is so
very strong-smelling as to be objectionable to some. This
is quite typical of all species and will be used for the
aroma....where it is aroma, and not smell. Leafage is
quite durable for wear in difficult places and the plant
may be headed back for increased bushiness....selective
pinching out through growth. Soil is best on the lighter
side, not too rich and may well go dry. They really will
grow most anywhere and give an account of themselves.
    -crispum, "Lemon-geranium" tall and woody with fancy,
curled, highly scented leaves, the small violet flowers of
little account for color:withstands considerable drought and
thrives especially in a poor soil....a pleasant odor.
    -domesticum, "Martha Washington-geranium" broad
woody plants with good foliage, rich and varied color
in the flowers, reds and pinks and purples, very good
color as spring merges with summer....a later blooming is less important:prune in October, but not cutting
deeply into hard wood, just shaping for next year and
then, pinching out first growth for bushiness. These
are practical and most useful plants, with color comparable to that of azaleas, overlapping and following
them. They take much exposure seaside.
    -alchemilloides, widely spreading, a plant with
sprawling, sappy stems from a woody base, the large and
attractive leaves velvety, light green, covered with a
soft pile that affects a whitish cast in certain light:
fits nicely over a low slope, grows in shadow and will
adapt to drought:small white to pink to purplish flowers are of little consequence.
    -echinatum, "Sweetheart-geranium" tuberous-rooted
with short, stubby stems and a kind of rudimentary thorn
or prickle, the heart-shaped leaves wavy, covered with a
whitish tomentum:small white flowers with a purple center
may turn completely purple or the white may gradually go
deep pink:growth is slow:deciduous.
    -hortorum, the common "Geranium", sturdy, rugged, much
maligned individual that carries such a large burden in pots
and boxes....nothing is superior for wear:almost always in
some color, coping effectually with heat and reflected light,
poor soil and any exposure, these plants are for the masses to
grow into shrubs in the open ground. There are many varieties,
of which one, --var.Salleroi is distinct, low-rounding, 6-8"
in height, the leaf very pale green, edged in white.
    -peltatum, "Ivy-leaf Geranium" relatively weak-growing
for form, but a sturdy plant, sprawling, suspending from
a window box or basket, covering impossible ground effectively, or draping a low bank for color and erosion control:
the flowers are possibly more attractive than the preceding
in shades of pink or rose and red with variations as stripes
and mottlings....one very good lavender is common:this will
appreciate more care and concern as to its activities, soil,
moisture and exposure....no total shade.

371

*Pelargonium domesticum*

*pelargonium alchemilloides*

*pelargonium crispum*

*Pelargonium peltatum*

SUBTROPICAL REGIONS

PELLAEA andromedaefolia, "Coffee Fern" a wiry-stemmed, rock-
loving little plant growing freely in limestone soils or other,
under full exposure to sun and wind, heat and drought, in fact
everything an arid climate has to offer:the 10-15" fronds are
tufted in thrift, loose in nature and more or less spreading,
the hard little leaves brownish, almost crimson at times, in
the sun. The species  -densa, is dwarf and very compact,
less rugged than above:rock gardens. The species  -falcata,
growing 15-18" with larger, once pinnate fronds, the leaflet
very leathery, the frond 4-6" across:the better one to use
in the garden....lime:pots.

PELTOPHORUM inerme, "Yellow-poinciana" rapid-growing,
shallow-rooted, a vigorous tree 50', erect-spreading for shade:
the flowering in large trusses, erect and terminal, grape-scent-
ed, yellow with deeper under-tones June-September or any time,
the bloom intense-luminous, especially as it is shaded. This
is evergreen where moisture holds, the new leaves russet over
the old:resists steady wind, but breaks in a storm or goes
out in soggy ground, due to scanty rootage....better all-
round in dryish soils:seed pods a deep rich red, turn black
and hang all next season.

BEARD TONGUE
PENSTEMON---coarse western herbs, mostly with a tendency
toward woody bases; or are actually shrubby. They are to
be adapted to the garden of flowers, the border outside,
the rock garden or fall in naturally with the wild flowers. The display of rich color begins in the summer when the
average plant is letting up, but heat seems only to spur these
plants on to further effort. They accept a wide range of soils
in the sun and like the quick drainage of gravelly ground. A
clay or adobe is tolerable if moisture gets away or through.
Drought comes to them as a matter of course, but the blooming
will extend if this is tempered. They should not be fed often,
if at all, the bloom suffering in the excessive wood and foliage
stimulation. On account of the weedy aftermath of flowering, plants
may be cut back immediately after bloom, certainly by autumn.
-antirrhinoides, "Bush-snapdragon" a graceful shrub, as found
in the garden, less so in nature, scraggly but colorful there in
arid soils, where it breaks into growth with the winter rains:
takes irrigation within reason and is highly qualified to be
grown under domestication with intelligent care, the season
lengthened....dormant by mid-summer, unkempt then and better
not watered:remove old stems entirely as they begin to straggle or cut to the ground in the fall for a neat new plant next
year:russet buds barely suggest the flare of gapping, pure yellow flowers March-June. This plant is native in Southern California; is choice but difficult to find in nurseries:seed.
-australis, native east, erect 20-30" with veined,
bright reddish-purple flowers to an inch in length, grows
in loose, rather acid ground and should have a little shelter from the sun....not so comparatively rugged.
-centranthifolius, "Scarlet Bugler" harsh-stemmed, loud-
mouthed, blaring, a coarse perennial 3-6' to naturalize in
low out of the way ground and heat:brazen spectacle in crimson
and grey blue to go with the hot sun it craves.
-cordifolius, shrubby, with long slender stems and leafy;
almost climbing in a kind of exuberance in the spring, but
failing and only flinging about over rocks and shrubs or any
thing a gardener may put in the way, much in the way of a
honeysuckle showing off....its scarlet bloom:goes quite
dormant in the summer, resenting water then:remote spot
in a gravelly soil, easy from seed as a ground cover,
pinched in to consolidate.
-gloxinioides, a garden"Penstemon" large and showy,
now represented in gardens by beautiful hybrids, a race with
very large flowers, mostly in red and white and combinations;
in flower at any time or always, better renewed yearly to have
the more choice kinds. Do this by means of cuttings.
372

COMPENDIUM

Sever slips of selected plants partially September-October,
allowing to remain on the plant for a few days or until the
cut begins to heal or callus over. This facilitates rooting
when the cutting is placed in sand, or may mean that it can
go directly into a container. These plants tolerate a heavy
soil and some fertilizer, should be cut to the ground in the fall
if not re-newed. A few good varieties of this species will furnish
some very real sustenance over the color-hungry time of the year.
    -heterophyllus, very attractive and an acknowledged border
plant for fairly dryish places, woody at the base, a stemmy mass
12-18" or more:covered with intensely blue flowers all summer and
occasionally a touch for winter, warm years....pink, purple or
lavender shadings according to light:wants a sandy loam or
well-filled gravel, fails in wet clay ground....but wants
always a modicum of moisture:bedding and filler:short-lived.
    -palmeri, with greyish-green foliage and creamy-white
flowers that are tinged with pink, native in the Southwest:for
high heat in the garden or environs....better with a little
moisture, but in very well drained soil.
    -spectabilis, very coarse as a plant 2-3' high, open and
spreading wide, with light, grey-green foliage and many flowers, rose, blue and dark purple:native in California on dry
hillsides, to be seen from a distance....the color carries.

PENTAS lanceolata, "Egyptian Starcluster" sub-shrubby material for pots or large bedding uses out in the sun or with
partial shade in well drained, fertile soils that do not dry
out excessively:tender, but comes back after a killing frost,
to be given every aid in warmth for a very distinctive and
handsome blooming:light pink to purple flowers, bouvardia-
like in dense clusters, almost continuous far south:may
be sheared for continued activity:no diseases.

PEPEROMIA sandersi, "Watermelon-plant" a stemless herb for
a pot or bedding down with ferns in light shade, but not
in very much moisture:small, leathery, oval-shaped dark
green leaves have longitudinal bands of white, or may be
vaguely spotted or mottled.

PERESKIA aculeata, "Lemon-vine" cactus-like but leaf-bear-
ing, shrubby at first, then clambering to as much as 30', the
interesting link between the succulents and woody plants:many
creamy-white flowers are tinged with green and are born periodically for the juicy, lemon-colored fruits, the shape of a gooseberry, the size of an olive and edible:foliage drops easily in the
cold or any other sudden shock....an espalier, if held in. The species
-bleo, is more in the nature of a small tree to be used somewhat as the
above, but more strong for color....rose to light red.

PERSEA---ornamental, generally evergreen trees, grown besides
for fruit and shade in tropical or near tropical parts. They
want a fertile moist soil with humus to provide generously
toward the lush, handsome leafage or to supply the where-
withall for the manufacture of the exceedingly fatty
fruits, large or small. They have no important pests.
    -americana, "Avocado or Alligator-pear" a dual purpose
tree, most variable in size, irregular as to shape, suitable
for shade, standing in a lawn....so frequently the seedling
making the better tree for this purpose....but littering excessively at wrong time of the year:grown almost entirely,
however, for the fruit which is widely used in salads and
extensively cultivated in these regions commercially:adapt-
able in the matter of soil, they want one deep and thoroughly
drained:locate out of the wind or plant closely together for
mutual protection:advise with local nurseryman for variety.
    -borbonia, "Redbay" native in the woodlands of the
lower South in very moist or wet ground, a tree there
40' with dark, smooth, heavily scented leaves that turn
orange-crimson late winter-spring:blue berries have an
ornamental value, the size of a large olive and not
373

so littering, but the tree a little coarse for the average garden. The species    -indica, brings more refinement to a domestic project, is of like character, but a
great deal smaller and grows in drier soil:laurel-like.

PETASITIS fragrans, "Winter-heliotrope" a perennial for
waste or uncultivated ground remotely located, having very
large, dark, coarse leaves that are covered with a furry tomen-
tum:grows 8-10", spreading vigorously underground as cover or in
holding banks of dry clay soil:blooms in January, the whitish,
purple or lilac flowers scented of vanilla:runs wild, ber-
serk in good garden soils....to be used advisedly.

PETREA volubilis, "Purple Wreath" "Sandpaper-vine" a
twining woody plant for southern parts only, blooming
profusely June-August, or as early as March, south in
Florida and periodically:flowers are small, five-pointed
stars in long-stemmed racemes, the outer portions, the
sepals, lighter, greyish-blue or purplish; the central
parts, the petals, opening later, darker, dropping earlier:
performance at best is uncertain, wanting a fertile soil, high
heat and possibly a little shade over noon:may be grown as a
broad bush to the ground, but high-climbing in warmth or
with direction, the sand-papery leaves with an infusion,
lavender-black over winter, going greysh over-all as they
drop in spring....striking material for the arranger:may
not be grown in frost to flower early since the flower
buds, carried over on last years wood, are killed.

PETROSELINUM crispum(hortense)"Parsley" low plant to
be grown handily at the kitchen door where it supplies
herbage for the place as much as for garnishing dishes
for the table:greenish flowers may be cut out to prolong
the life and service of the foliage....doubtfully carried
beyond first year:wants a deep, mellow soil and to be
sown as early in spring as practicable....slow to come.

PETUNIA hybrida, the common garden annual, with different strains and forms adapted to special purposes
such as bedding, boxes or hanging baskets. They are positive for effects, reliable always, single or double, ruffled, fringed or fluted velvety flowers in white, pink,
rose, blue or purple all through warmth:safe plants
in an over-fertilized soil or does in a poor one,
sacrificing size and herbage only, dependable for flowers the
entire season, and to the very end:sow seed fall or spring
or get fresh young plants in preference to holding over. Some
forms of above may be fragrant at night, the parent species
-axillaris, certainly so and heavily laden with the perfume.

PHACELIA whitlavia, "California-bluebell" a 12-18" annual
for any garden in the sun, used as a filler in the border
or most appropriate in among the wildflowers:coarse and
hairy, frequently sticky-viscid, although not too objectionable, the flowers a very deep, pure blue, sometimes purplish:being wildlings, they are content in a
light, sandy or gravelly soil that is drained, where they
will bloom in six weeks from spring sown seed, or may be
planted in the fall. There is much trash left from the show.

PHAEDRANTHUS buccinatorius,(Bignonia cherere)the "Bloodred
Trumpet" a popular vine, very strong-growing for excellent cover, the foliage dark, evenly distributed:large flowers, red trumpets with an orange tube spread out over the warmer seasons
or cover the entire year with rather brilliant and
dependable color:pruning is of considerable importance in a continued and maximum display....cut out
weak wood and reduce terminals just before the first
flush of growth in the spring. This is a general purpose
plant of the very first consideration.

374

PHASEOLUS---ornamental beans, twining for quick service in
screening or for general garden purposes. They have no particular soil preferences, but want certainly to have all the
sun available. The flowers approach the form and general
character of the sweetpea. They will be started from seed.
      -caracalla, "Snail-vine" perennial, high-climbing or trailing
far along the ground in absence of support....can be something of a
pest, but is attractive under control:flower light purple, coiled as
the shell of a snail, slightly fragrant, everblooming in warmth.
      -coccineus, "Scarlet Runnerbean" an annual pole bean that also
ran....hopefully upwards with its clusters of white or scarlet flowers in summer, along with an edible bean that will damage on the
ground....dual role:sow where the plants are to stand at about
12" apart, in the spring, taking the bean while still soft
and before the thick markings invade the whitish shell:dry-
ness at the roots affects the plant adversely and the
flowers may not set for a crop.

PHILADELPHUS mexicanus, "Jasmin-del-Monte" from far
south, but high up, a sprawling shrub or vining 15',the
long cord-like stems suspending in many repeated vertical
lines for a simple homespun curtain for the garden:flowers
in late winter or spring and sometimes again in late summer are creamy-white and very fragrant:requires good moisture and at least fair soil for growth and production that may
be expected:prune in summer to keep in hand,snipping out the weak
growth to encourage the vigorous shoots that will flower next year:
grows in considerable shade and is quite hardy in frost....but dropping foliage. This is a southern relative of the oldfashioned "Syringa" of the North and East and will bring back nostolgic memories to many gardeners who have gone south.

PHILLYREA latifolia, "Mock-privet" nicely moulded shrub
or a small tree 25', the top spreading rather stiffly:has
substantial leathery leaves that are very dark and somewhat shining:grows under conditions of drought and heat
and frost, in light or very close clay soils and in very
deep shade:the body of the plant will set with many dull
blue berries by the middle of the summer and may carry over
into winter....a rugged plant and very handsome, giving of
good measure and usually running over.    -var. media,
lower and rather wide-spreading, rigid, growing 6-8'.

PHILODENDRON---foliage plants of bold appearance,
conspicuous, dramatic in relief and especially in the
shadow they will throw; of substance and dependability;useful
indoors;decorative for the patio or protected terrace. Divided into two types; one is climbing while the other is arborescent, self-sustaining, tree-like, the leaves originally at
a crown at the ground, following a trunk upward in growth.
They adapt to a wide range of light intensity from full sun
in coolness to deep, dark shade; are free of all disease
and pests, tenacious, obstinate when fixed in place, persevering. They are not reliable under frost; require a
syringing or wash from time to time in dust or smog;
want uniform, but not excessive moisture and to be fertilized only to maintain color....liquid forms probably
better. Great emphasis is now placed upon them for use
against the ample surfaces of contemporary architecture.
      -erubescens, the large leaves abundant, roughly
triangular with great swings at the corners, or elongated heart-shaped, tinged reddish, a greyish wash over-all:
climbing.    -evansi, very handsome, a hybrid with dark and
shining arrow-shaped leaves, the edges of the black, leathery
plane undulating in sympathy with the arching petiole:compar-
atively rugged in sun wind and frost.....a superior plant:
arborescent.    -hastatum, very large, heart-shaped leaves of
particularly heavy texture and rich, dark off-green coloring:
climbing.    -imbe, the medium-sized leaves green
above, rusty-red beneath:short internodes give this

*Phaseolus coccineus*

*Phaseolus caracalla*

*Phillyrea latifolia*

*philo-dendron imbe*

*Philadelphus mexicanus*

species a compactness in growth that is distinctive:pots
indoors:climbing.   -oxycardium(cordatum)down to earth
species, the comparatively very small leaves heart-shaped
and sharply pointed:long-trailing stems indoors are useful
as line in decoration:climbing.   -wendlandi, with long,
narrow, stout-ribbed leaves that form a tight rosette of re-
finement:arborescent, since it does not climb, yet without
stem, so to speak:a little difficult....dark shade, moisture.

PHLOMIS fruticosa, "Jerusalem-sage" straggling shrub 3-4' with
very thick, deeply creased, furry-grey leaves and dusky yellow
flowers in whorls along the stems that are erect, all summer and into winter:hardy in heat and drought, standing
hard under salt wind, but seemingly unable to counter the
attack of mealybug....make sure in setting out new stock,
that it is not infested....dip bodily for a time in the
insecticide....treat soil. The plant may not be worth all
the trouble of constant watch, but it does have very definite value in places and gives no trouble in clean ground.

PHLOX drummondi, spreading annual 8-10" for summer bedding
or blooming indifferently at other times far south:blooms in
some profusion with full sun and in attractive shades of pink,
lavender and crimson....tries at yellow and turns up a kind of
buff:does in poor soils, but will use better....heavy clays
not suitable....lime beneficial:sow seed early in the spring
and bring along without checks in growth such as drouth or
the drag of weeds; or set plants April-May:pinch out the
tips at least once, and again later to prolong the effective season. They do not transplant successfully in
the garden after establishing....selfs are considered the
more desirable colorwise and can be stressed by thinning out.

## DATE PALM

PHOENIX--handsome trees, ruthlessly domineering, over-bearing,
vigorous and easily handled, as of themselves, used for ornament, for the shade or grown for the fruit. They are held to
a single stem; or such as will sucker, will be grown in clumps
of several stems which will accent the bristle of the great
mop of fronds. This group includes those from the most massive
of gross-growing trees to probably one of the smallest and most
refined; an embodiment here of coarse, harsh growth to that of
exceeding delicacy and grace in organization. They are essentially dry climate plants, but grow anywhere in the absence of
killing frost; wanting and thriving in heat with good moisture
or wanting in water, good fertility or none. They are particularly tolerant of brackish water at the root and salt winds
through the top. Being attractive to the outlander eye, they
are also entangling and deceptive, so that some have come to
exert an over-riding influence in the sub-tropical landscape
that seems scarcely warranted in view of splendid and distinctive trees literally begging for attention.
    -canariensis, "Canary Island D. P." the most bulky one of the
lot, growing to 75' in height, and probably more in California; in
good proportion otherwise....great massive trunk and dense, wide-
spreading feather for an impenetrable head, the huge strap and
whopping batch of berries a veritable Pleiades of orange against
the unbroken green in the fall:stands under all adverse circumstances except wet feet in a cold, undrained soil:smothering
shade cast by this tree together with a ravenous rooting about
in the soil suggests discretion in the thinking of small lot
owners....not even near a garden is too close for comfort in
other plantings:hardy in frost.   --var. tenuis,  has the
same top but in reduced size, the stem nicely slender:makes
a good close-set clump in large scale planting.
    -dactylifera, "Date P." the fruiting palm of desert
countries, coarse, ungainly although not as bulky as above,
suckering at the ground or as an out-sized witches-broom at
odd spots on the stem, in no way attractive in strict appraisal, yet with a certain dignity in its place....birds

and people do seek out the softening fruit:requires a
hot dry atmosphere and warm nights to mature a crop of
dates and gardeners have long since found out the worthless-
ness of chance seedlings....should not be used in a cool area:
takes considerable alkali in the soil.

   -reclinata, "Senegal D.P." one of the most beautiful of the
palms,having a comparatively refined head above slender arching
stems that rise with a winding twist, frequently 25':a natural
tendency to sucker at the crown may be encouraged and controlled,
resulting in plumy clump of much character:one of the best,and
surely the most practical among the commonly known palms to use
in bringing out the south-sea motif in marginal areas of cold:
somewhat tender, taking only about 5-6 degrees of frost.

   -roebelini, "Pigmy Date" a delicate, dainty, dapper little
tree only 3-6' in height, with the typical and usually nicely
blending, gently arching fronds, the stem with a slight bend:
the foliage mass holds in place for longer service and a less
dense head without thatch:used in a pot for table or other decor
indoors, moved on into a tub for long service there, finally into
the garden where it will be the very personification of grace.

   -rupicola, "Cliff D." an extremely narrow bole of persistent
boots of the spent and cut fronds, growing to 40' in a deep, rich
soil with some moisture:the mop or head is smaller and softer in
eye appeal than the other larger species, the lower fronds hanging, the leaflets lying flat with the central rib, limp:there
is considerable refinement here, wanting protection from wind.

   -sylvestris, "Wild Date" an uncommon form, of rather
rapid growth to 50', the sturdy bole retaining the frond boot
for a long period of time:the head is crowded, irregularly
rounded, and greyish over-all.

### FLAXLILY

PHORMIUM---austere, dominating, perennial clumps of harsh,
basal leaves, sword-shaped, erect or bowed, accent plants
that are formalizing and very affirmative. They take exposure well and any reasonable soil, reaching full size in one
of good body and fertility with moisture. The leaves will
clatter in the wind, a drum roll for the ear, an anchor for
the eye. The flowering stalks are stout, held high above.

   -colensoi, the leaves channeled, arching 3-5' long, the
flowers in a 10-15" head:requires moisture to be at its very
best....good anyway:use indoors or out.   --var. metalica,
the leaves a dull, brownish red....rather more refined.

   -tenax, "New Zealand-flax" a full body of rigid, tense,
strictly erect flat leaves 6-8', the 24" flowering head high
above June-July....dries sapless on the plant, taken for decoration in dull mahogany shades. This plant is of little value except for form or as used in line but takes any amount of exposure
seaside.   --var. Veitchianum, light green, striped yellowish.

PHOTINIA serrulata, exceptionally ornamental, an evergreen
shrub of parts, a beautiful plant with interest year round:
dark glossy leaves are tinted in spring with rosy suffusions,
bronzy later....picked out fall and winter or at any time with
occasional crimson leaves preparing to drop:broad flat clusters of flowers in full pink bud by March, out May-July, are
as much as 6" across, turn to scarlet berries as the season
advances, lasting until December or later....seldom a proper setting:tolerates shade and should have some far south:
wants a heavy soil with drainage and all the frost that
can be managed....takes extreme heat, but a better plant
northerly and in coolness:prune in winter just enough to
encourage new growth in direction desired....inclined to
stagnate after a time south:spray with a fungicide early
summer for a leaf blotch, the only blemish in a very rewarding plant. The   --var. nova, is a more compact and
spreading form, lower....may be the species   -glabra.

PHYGELIUS capensis, "Cape-fuchsia" a fragile, brittle-
stemmed, brushy shrub of no disclipline, the weak stems
requiring much cutting and early tip-pinching for a

sturdy specimen around 2-3' height:best grown somewhat
dryish in heat to mature wood for winter that will carry
over winter for flowers next year....used north into warm
temperate regions, mulched, blooming late, if at
all:tawny, scarlet, pendent-curving tubes are
precision-set in wide panicles August-September in
upper regions, nearly continuous far south:use in a tub
or against a warm wall, where it will carry along for a
considerable length in time and with help:planters.

PHYLLANTHUS acidus, "Otaheite-gooseberry" grown far south
in Florida where it goes wild, or precariously in Southern
California in frost-free areas:interesting slender tree to
20' or shrubby, of tropical origin and aspect, but not so very
ornamental:sharply acid, white or greenish fruits hang from
mature wood in long racemes like currants, used in jams and in
jellies:drops leaves easily, certainly with cold or drouth.

PHYLLOSTACHYS aurea, "Golden Bamboo" of considerable
refinement with many stems, easily persuaded for a compact clump that may be held:a billowing, weaving growth
of slender, yellow canes, flattened markedly on one side,
clear below of leaf and messy sheaths:grows 10-15' in a
good soil near water or when irrigated. Related species give
black stems or only the nodes colored:not hardy in frost.

PHYSOSTEGIA virginiana, "False Dragonhead" sturdy, strong-
growing perennial 2-3' high with rose or light purple flowers
in slender, clear-cut spikes of squarrish form:grown in the border where it will take fairly rough treatment and furnish good
color July-September:plant is dense and bushy, as of erect
lines, with parts sharply moulded:any fertile soil in the
sun, but cool and moist, or damp ground within reach of the
energetic roots:must be divided frequently and rigidly controled....a weed for spreading underground and runs out shortly, to be started over again with rooted sections of the
division....build up the soil.

PHYTOLACCA dioica, "Umbu or La Bella Sombre" round-
headed, densely foliated, a chunky tree to 60' with e-
nough soil to support....should be deep and drained:the
large, leathery leaves and hanging racemes of white flowers are like a wild cherry....actually a pokeberry:the
rapidity of growth amazing in the right soils; with
huge abutments to the short, thick trunk....disappoint-
ing in shallow ground, the typical solid structure of
the tree breaking up into many distorted slender or
stringy leaders from the stumpy base:extremely drouth
resistant, but very tender in frost, dropping foliage
in cold. This is a tree of distinctly spanish flavor in
history and atmosphere, useful in rough places for shade in
high heat, but not in the vicinity of construction or very
near habitations.

PICKERINGIA montana, "Chaparral Pea" spiny, tenacious shrub
3-5' in ground that is loose for drainage and in the sun for heat,
somewhat suckering:arching stems hold the foliage well, carry the
lupin-like flowers May-June, rosy-pink to crimson or magenta:more
floriferous if moisture is drawn out with blooming:California.

PILEA microphylla, "Artillery-plant" low, with succulent, sappy
stems; prostrate, arching or raised to 12" and set with the tiny,
light green leaves in a lacy, fern-like composition that sways with
grace in air movement:use in a pot, in the dry fern bed, as an edging there or in like spots:use with rocks in sun or shade, the latter a little to be preferred....better irrigated at the crown than
with an overhead spray. The species  -nummulariaefolia, also
known as "Creeping Charley" has larger leaves of
pleasing pattern, used as a cover far south in
warm, humid places....indoors northerly.

378

PIMELEA ferruginea, "Riceflower" a compact, rounding
shrub 2-3', box-like in form and texture, dark green:
rosy-pink, more or less over warmth, concentrate spring
and summer:wants humidity, an open, slightly acid soil
and uniform moisture....must never be allowed a deep-wilt:is
short-lived, at its best the first two or three years, vitality
in the end reduced by incessant flowering:look for red spider and
make sure of drainage....standing water at any time dangerous: the
plant better grown northerly as is the species  -coarctica, growing prostrate, trailing, 2" through the open mat, to be used with
rock or over sandy slopes under moisture and away from hot
sun....or at least quarter shade:flowers whitish and
abundant. These plants are normally difficult to handle,
but quite satisfactory in the right spot.

PIMPINELLA anisum, "Anise" a tall herb with yellow-
white bloom midsummer, full, branched, feathery heads that
are quite ornamental in a wild exuberance of growth:very
easily seeding to become a pest, if allowed to establish;
do not allow to set and mature seed or the crop surely collected for culinary or other purpose.

PINCKNEYA pubens, "Fever-tree" shrubby or tree-like to
25', growing in the sandy areas of Florida swamps or along
streamsides where it can reach out for water....very difficult to bring along elsewhere:wants a rich soil and good
shade, at least until well established:the 3-4" clusters of
whitish flowers are of little account, but the bright pink leaf-
like sepals are quite showy:only occasionally grown in its area.

## PINE
PINUS---coniferous evergreen trees for ornamental planting, essentially practical in character, symmetrical and of
a soft tenuous beauty when young, normally taking on a picturesque quality in age, They are inexorably tap-rooted for
dry, sandy or gravelly soils and have been fitted by nature
to ground scantily provided with plant food. So true is their
being in this latter respect, that they may be thrown seriously out of step by heavy feeding, with elongated, gawky growth
resulting. They are not tolerant of shade and reach typical
form only when not crowded. Transplanting after having been
established is inadvisable, not always possible, best done
in early autumn. They are more common in California.
    -attenuata, "Knobcone P." a straggling, broad-crowned
bushy or sprawling little tree, sometimes reaching to 25' in
height:has greyish foliage, not always ornamental in a sense of
finish, but invaluable for extremely hot, dry and sterile hillsides of the Southwest and California:always a picturesque item
under the right influence, wind and chance and soil.
    -canariensis, "Canary Island P." slender-erect, and symmetrical,
a tree of regular growth to 75', densely pyramidal when unhurried,
the long, clustered needles blue when new, a lively green when it
settles down:of very rapid growth with some irrigation, only less
in the absence of moisture:probably the best large pine for a
small place:will not tolerate much salinity.
    -caribaea, "Slash P." makes a very rapid growth in low,
wet ground that is not too heavy:native in Florida and difficult to handle as a landscape material, not often found under
cultivation, useful as above....a picture, however, with high
splayed head breaking against a light sky.
    -coulteri, "Bigcone P." western native, a mountain tree 75',
of pleasing proportions, the lower branches drooping while the
upper ones ascend to a narrow rounding head:a good specimen
pine with dark bluish foliage, the form rather compact, of
comparatively slow growth at lower levels, better in altitude.
    -edulis(cembroides)"Pinyon" small brushy tree at 20' and
later, becoming more scrubby, with light green leaves in tufts
or alone in a single, stout needle:limber growth in youth easily points out laterally with a prevailing wind and fixes:dry or
rocky hillsides but slow-starting:native in the Southwest.

-halepensis, "Aleppo P." a small, normally symmetrical
tree at 40',of very rapid growth in poor soils and under most
adverse conditions, especially seaside and in alkali ground, but
short-lived anywhere:branches are pliable and slender, the foliage
thin, a light grey-green:not so ornamental, a second class tree,
but useful when used as above.

-patula, "Jelecote P." of much refinement, growing to 75',
with pale or yellowish green, very long, drooping needles that
are fine and silky:a pine to use on home grounds, of extremely
rapid growth, but consolidating well:tender.

-pinea, "Italian Stone P." a rounded bushy thing in early
life, becoming massive, open-headed and picturesque in age, gradually
losing lower limbs....those remaining reaching upward to support a
dense top or dome as the ribs of an umbrella:very slow in growth
and takes a fairly heavy soil:watch for cottony signs of the
juniper mite and control it.

-radiata, "Monterey P." growing to 60' with irregular and
wide-spreading limbs that are well-covered with the clear,
vivid green of the foliage:too easily forced for growth
under cultivation and liable to go out early in very dry
or very wet soils without drainage:very susceptible to the
double-spotted mite:one of best against the sea.

-sabiniana, "Digger P." the trunk usually divided, further
divided into erect, very pliable limbs....branches can be knot-
ted at the ends:silvery-grey-blue foliage throughout the open,
rounded head:one of best in heat, but so open in texture as to
cast little shade....throws in with the hard light of the desert,
tinsel in the shimmer of a hot land.

-torreyana, "Soledad P." in nature a small, greyish, open-
headed tree of outstanding scenic quality for dry exposed places:has
less value as grown under domestication where it will develop much
too rapidly, becoming thin and gangling, seldom to aquire the beauty
and special interest that normally attaches....taking the
space and province of a better tree:suitable, but not
recommended for gardens in dryness.

PIQUERIA trinervia, "Stevia" a large bedding plant with
many small white flowers which are also much used as a
filler in making up boquets....comparatively indifferent
to sun, shade or general treatment:keep cutting to extend
blooming:ordinarily used as an annual, is perennial south,
but not effective as such....seed or cuttings taken in
late winter or very early spring:pots.

## PISTACHE
PISTACIA---humid and dry climate plants of comparatively
slow growth, very drouth resistant in deep soils. They are
adapted, ready-made for high heat or cold, are seldom bother-
ed by insect pests or disease, but will require some attention
to pruning in the matter of structure, especially in the beginning. This is a cosmopolitan group of trees with many origins
and diverse character, not commonly to be found in these
regions, but with much to offer the landscape.

-chinensis, deciduous, 50' or less with a broad rounding head
of heavy branches that spread, wide above a short trunk:grown mostly for shade in hot countries, there and elsewhere for the brilliantly colored leaves that hold late in autumn....brief glory
in crimson:male tree the more heavily foliated, very hardy
in frost and stands in alkali of considerable concentration.

-simaruba, "West Indian-birch" with distinctive
flaking bark, a tree to 70' of rapid growth to a leafy,
spreading head:will manage in rather poor rocky soils, but
requires considerable humidity to prosper:deciduous.

-texana, native in the Southwest, a tree 30', evergreen
south or the foliage holding late, northerly, warm winters.

-vera, "Pistachio-nut" deciduous spreading tree usually under 30', grown for the edible nut:deep fertile
soils with moisture to produce proper crops, although
growing under drought....likes heat:trees budded to superior strains best:male-female for pollination.

# COMPENDIUM

PITHECOCTENIUM cynanchoides, a white bignonia, so to speak,
evergreen and fairly hardy in cold, known by the color of the
flower and by the yellow spines covering the fruits:rare

PISTIA stratiotes, "Water-lettuce" small floating plant,
sometimes rooting along the edges of water in shadow:the light
green, velvety, fluted leaves originate from a common center in
the way of head lettuce, a beautifully formed rosette that will be
of interest in a small pool....turns yellow in a too-hot sun.

## AUSTRALIAN LAUREL

PITTOSPORUM---sturdy shrubs and trees, general purpose plants
of first importance for subtropical regions, some of the species
being among the most dependable throughout the area for substantial use in the landscape. There is much to recommend in them
for general hardiness and obstinacy under adverse conditions,
when they always flower well and berry consistently. The bloom
will be deficient for color, but is unusually effective in the
wide spread of fragrance. In general, these plants favor the
heavier soils, but with exceptions....must have drainage....all
take exposure on the ocean.
     -crassifolium, a large shrub of very open, sparse growth
or a slender tree 25', of slim, erect lines and thinly foliated
if not pruned to consolidate growth:the tough, thick, grey leaves
are little affected by salt wind and spray:small, reddish-brown or
chocolate-colored flowers in spring, show only by reason of contrast against the pale leafage:this one for sandy ground:screen.
     -erioloma, "Hedge-laurel" smaller over-all and more re-
fined, the better one of the group to use as hedging, especially under shearing:foliage is naturally dense, the leaf very
dark, paler beneath, covering off more nicely to the ground:
flowers are small, yellow, in terminal umbels:choice and rare.
     -eugenioides, "Lemonwood" a very large and attractive
rounding shrub, but mostly grown as a tree, an oval at 40', the
slender vertical lines of the branches revealed partially by the
inadequate spread of yellowish green leafage....often disfigured by a blotch under poor growing conditions....go with purple twigs:insists on good drainage and good culture if it
is to appear at its best:variable, at times almost columnar, again broadly pyramidal, preferably used inland away
from the sea:limestone soils and light frost.
     -heterophyllum, "Pitchberry" half-reclining or near-
ly erect, a spreading shrub for bank planting:has very light,
shining, comparatively small leaves and tiny yellowish flowers that beget jet-black berries that are telling against the
foliage:growth very slow, normally effective at 3-4', but as
much as 10' with support or suspending downward:resists deep dryness in poor soils that bake out under the sun....almost
indestructible after having been established.
     -phillyraeoides, "Desert-willow" an erect, slender
tree 20', the branchlets bending over, elongating, streaming to the ground carrying the long and narrow, very pale
leaves and small yellow flowers of much fragrance late
winter and spring....ultimately the large yellow berries
set precisely like rosary beads:withstands extreme heat
and dry, stiff, unworked soils:may root-sucker.
     -rhombifolium, "Diamondleaf-laurel" an erect, sym-
metrical tree 40' or to 60' in a deep, rich soil with
moisture:has dark foliage, the leaf geometric, lozenge-
shaped and quite glossy:small whitish flowers that open
in generous clusters, are not conspicuous and hardly suggest
the effectiveness of the small, light yellow berries that fol-
low:an ornamental tree for more general use in the garden and in
the landscape where the going is good:lacks vigor in Florida.
     -tenuifolium, a large shrub, seldom an erect tree 25', with
thin, dull green foliage and black twigs that will hold fresh a
considerable time after having been cut....do not force growth
in interest of a long life:will not take a heavy soil and do
well, but an excellent tall and narrow hedge in well drained ground....a sandy loam that drains and feeds.

-tobira, sturdy shrub of rather slow growth 5-8', dense
and spreading under the shears or erect with distinctive
foliage, while the stubby heads of whitish flowers winter-
spring are most fragrant:withstands heavy frost, salt wind
and alkali, intense heat and considerable drought:good low
broad hedge.      var. variegatum, the less common "White-
spot tobira" has white in the leaf, the base color a peculiar whitish green, a vigorous plant and a bright patch in
shadow. These plants are known also as "Mock-orange".
    -undulatum, "Victorian-box" an open-headed tree to 60',
rising in rather definite whorled planes of growth, rapid and
very satisfactory in performance:very fragrant, light yellow flowers scent the evening air January-February:good broad hedge of
some height, a street tree if headed high, since it tends to grow
low to the ground....never a shrub, tortured to fit beneath windows
as so often found:best in a heavy soil that is not over watered.
    -viridiflorum, a generously molded shrub or an open-headed
tree with strong, irregular limbs to 25', more in very good
ground of satisfactory moisture, the dark leaves in large
tufts:tree for a narrow street or lane, handsome in deep,
fertile soils....otherwise must be fed for growth and color:
greenish flowers and old gold berries.

PLATANUS racemosa, "Sycamore" distinguished native of
Southern California, the preferred "Plane-tree" to use in
the south, a large tree of generous girth, the leaf very
large, subject to a fungous disease under domestication
causing drop in summer too soon....shows then the round,
button-like fruiting bodies clinging to their short stem:
greyish white or creamy bark peals off to disclose lighter tones of pristine green in a wide mottling:any soil will
do so long as it is deep and well supplied with water....other-
wise do not use. Here is abstraction served up as beauty for a
mature consideration, the heavy mottled bole and white, wierdly
twisting limbs writhing in lofty contortion under an open canopy.
They bend always and always they are picturesque....chief
value in planting is this quality. The species   -orientalis
"Oriental Plane", with probably only hybrids available, is
another too-large tree for general use, only where much
space is available such as is frequently found in public
places:straight stem to 75' and a huge top that may be
cut in any manner or degree to fit a situation.

PLATYCERIUM bifurcatum, "Staghorn Fern" striking specimen
for the large plant house or any other cool appropriate spot,
to be grown on damp moss or spagnum, attached to the rough
bark of a tree or other support:will take light frost while the
growth and ultimate size will regulate to the moisture it gets:
the great greyish structure will scale down an area....contempor-
ary stone walls, indoors or outside in shade.

PLATYSTEMON californicus, "Creamcups" an annual that is native in
good sandy loams of Southern California:the plant erect or sprawling
slightly:scant foliage, but many small, poppylike, light yellow
flowers in spring:warm, light soils, sun and sure drainage.

PLEIOGYNIUM solandri, "Burdekin-plum" an attractive, rapid-
growing tree 40' with a stout trunk and branchy, open-rounded
top, the dark foliage dropping easily in cold, normally ever-
green:fruit the size of a large plum, purple when ripe, used
in jams and jellies:dryish soils best.

PLUMBAGO capensis, "Cape Leadwort" a large sprawling
shrub, recumbent in a broad mass on the ground, piling
up to as much as 10-15' or a half-hearted climber:has pale
blue flowers in a phlox-like head, nearly continual, princi-
pally over summer:a warm place in a sandy or drained soil is
more than desirable, it is mandatory for results and the less
water it has, after a sufficiency, the more abundant is the
flowering:pinch back new growth for more color and cut out

stems to the crown and as near the ground as possible,
late winter or spring. This will control the spread of
the mass and should be begun early in life or it gets
out of hand.  --var. alba, is similar or vining to
15', somewhat less vigorous and the white flowers more
seasonal:may be twined. The species  -indica, with
handsome purplish-red to scarlet flowers and with the
leaf rolling over to clasp the stem:is too tender for
general use, wanting slight shade and protection. This
is subject to a root-knot, but is choice far south.

### BLUEGRASS

POA  common sod forming plants, used almost universally in cool
humid areas for lawns, grown far south under compulsion, playing a
part under difficulties, dryness and heat, and especially the ener-
vation of the climate until better plants are developed to take
their place. They make turf of satisfactory denseness and uniformity under varying conditions. There are several specific
kinds, each of which will be found suitable for some special
condition, such as wear from trampling and shaded or damp
ground. Sow during the calm of the day and as a mix if conditions are complicated, allowing the resulting turf to adapt as
of its own likes and capacity to serve.
    -nemoralis, "Wood B.G." makes a turf that will survive in
shade, but not for very long and must be considered as a special nurse grass for others that are slower to develop, but which
are more permanent as turf.
    -pratensis, "Kentucky B.G." so-called, the accepted stand-
ard, the best all round turf grass under average and ordinary conditions, sometimes used pure, always as a base of any mix designed
for special places....slow to come along and needs help.
    -trivialis, "Roughstalked B.G." soft-textured, flat-grow-
ing, spreading somewhat by means of runners above ground:a grass
for damp places in shade, the dank, sunless side of a building or beneath trees:has great possibilities in such places if fertilized well
and mowed regularly....cut it low:shining, glass-like in appearance:use
it pure where nothing else has survived and be surprised.

PODACHAENIUM eminens, "Daisy-tree" a likable, lusty plant, urgent,
bouncing into place with over-size, most ample proportions, a
dome-like shrub in the way of an elderberry, but simulating the
dombeya; or a tree 25' for very rapid service:great rough leaves
lay a solid ground for open clusters of small, daisy-like, white
flowers any time April onwards....combine in a flatish head.

PODALYRIA sericea, "Satinbush" a small spreading shrub with a
certain gracefulness and restraint to within the 3-4' range for
size:entire plant takes the light with a silken, silvery brilliance that submerges only in winter to a near smothering of
pink to purple flowers; but look to culture and every day care:
wants no coddling, little water....sharp drainage imperative:tender.

PODOCARPUS---handsome coniferous trees with characteristics of
both yew and pine, sometimes called "Yew-pine", having long yew-
like leaves, the tree developing an open pine-like structure.  They
are superior for ornamental qualities in texture and form and are
highly favored for places of refinement. Experiance with and
observation of other than with the juvenile stages, are wanting, so that descriptions and culture must be general until
more maturity in growing trees is reached. The fruit is green
with a stem that is surrounded by a deep red, fleshy, cherry-
like body, a Christmas bauble set  sparingly and infrequently in point of time. Another delightful and unusual character in all, is the delicate lighter tones of the foliage as
the leaves unfurl....tipburn under wind and frost. They seem
to do best under high humidity of atmosphere and in the soil,
but must not be over-watered. They appear to resent lime.
    -elongata, an irregular open head of supple limbs and a
rounded top of turbulent, weaving branches, always in some
movement:the slender branchlets droop with the bluish-green

leaves which are flat, narrow, soft and pliable:40' specimens in Southern California are an indication of effective
height as now propagated. The species  -gracilior, is probably synonymous or with longer leaves.
    -macrophylla, as tall as the preceding, rigid over-all
with short branches standing out horizontally from a central leader:larger leaves are also more stiff and of a
lighter shade of green, sometimes with a buffish cast:it
shears easily into columnar forms as a result, adapting to
semi-formal usage.   --var. maki, has smaller leaves, the
young plant less strict and probably shrub-like.
    -nagi, "Nagaea" shrubby at first, but probably in the end
the largest of the lot, the short, broad, sharply pointed leaves
like dammar-pine, with tintings of violet when new and long-tapering into the petiole. This is a graceful butchers broom in general
appearance and has been used for years as a hedge in Florida.
    -totara, as observed in these regions, a large, open bush of
quite irregular and very rapid growth, the leaves short-needle-
like to an inch long, dull, yellow green, tough and leathery.This
plant has a Japanesque quality and is very easily modified for form

PODRANEA---strong-growing vines for a good body of foliage, the
leaves rather finely divided, the plant becoming quite woody and
widely spreading in good garden soils. They require much pruning
if vigor and blooming is to be maintained and will be at their
best only in the sun. The flowers are short-trumpet-shaped in
the way of a bignonia, but larger and in definite heads.
    -brycei, "Queen of Sheba" the pale lavender-pink
flowers with a yellow throat, December-January, the fruity
fragrance most acceptable the time of year:prune in late
spring or early summer:rarely seen.
    -ricasoliana(Tecoma mackeni)with light, lacy leaves a
fine texture that builds up to considerable density and with
refinement....on the borderline, ready to drop at first sign
of frost:flowers in large, loose heads at ends of laterals,
June-August, but a rather shy bloomer unless cut for new wood.

POINCIANA---showy flowering shrubs for near tropical parts
or cooler, brilliant color set against such a light-textured
foliage that the flower seems almost suspended....bright yellow
with exserted crimson filaments. These plants make a delicate
background against which further flowering effects may be thrown
for the light shade afforded....perennials. They prefer a neutral
to acid soil, but perform surprisingly well in poorer ground.
    -gilliesi(Caesalpinia)somewhat straggling and of finest tex-
ture, affording fairly clear vision directly through the structure
where the flower clusters are poised like birds in mid-air....some-
times called "Bush Bird of Paradise" :light frost-hardy.
    -pulcherrima,  "Barbados Pride" the foliage heavier than
above and the flowers more conspicuous, larger, and at any time
during warmth:prune to improve the structure of the plant and
to remove developing seed heads which results in further flow-
ering:used as a large, untrimmed hedge or close-set screen:has
a poor root system and should be used out of the wind.

POLIANTHES tuberosa, "Tuberose" summer-flowering bulbs with
waxy-white, single or double, exceedingly fragrant flowers on
narrow, spiring stalks 2-3' in height:long associated with the
florists and not often seen in gardens, due possibly to time
worn funeral implications:wants a light, very rich soil, the sun
with its accumulated heat in the soil and constant if only a
little moisture. When planting, slice off the hard knotty base
of last years roots and set bulbs March-April or June at the
latest, last of the plantings flowering in autumn:cover bulb
proper with an inch of soil, or with the papery sheaths just
showing....8" between plants:leave in ground, but lift and
reset every second or third year, or store over winter, drying  out bulb in the sun....those coming through with green
tips to be replanted in spring. They are difficult to maintain in flowering condition over the years. The heavy scent

is too much indoors, but should not be objectionable out in
the garden unless much overplanted:single forms bloom earlier
and longer than doubles:choose medium-sized bulbs for blooming,
small ones must be built up, while the largest are liable to
split up, to flower another year:will flower in winter far south
in Florida if rested over autumn:no alkali in ground or water.

### MILKWORT

POLYGALA---bushy symmetrical shrubs, much grown south, especially
in California for the abundant bloom that is so difficult to handle
color-wise in the garden. The flowers are born at the ends of the
regularly spaced branches. The foliage tends also to crowd to the
ends and into an outer perimeter in such a way as to leave the
base of the plant bare....don't prune to correct; use a facing
plant to cover off. They resist drought and do in poorer soils.
   -apopetala, slender-stemmed, 5-8', seemingly always bare
of foliage below; above with very strong, purple, pea-shaped
flowers in the summer and weaker along its margins:extremely re
sistant to drouth and may be naturalized in dry regions....can
be a pest in too much moisture:seeds and reseeds.
   -dalmaisiana, regular-rounding, 2-3' or more, the larger
pea-shaped flowers a rosy-purple or magenta, tipped with a white
brush of stamens:doubly troublesome in color combinations because of the color first, and second because of the long period of bloom....one of the most constantly flowering:the pale
foliage notably free of insect pests and disease.

POLYPODIUM mandaianum, a large fern, very strong-growing,
too vigorous for most parts of the garden, better outside
where control may be more sketchy:frond simple but immense,
4-5' long and proportionately wide, the waving pinnae or
leaflets grey-green, suffer over winter:shade normally or
coolness with sun, moisture always:tender and belongs with the
tropicals for contemporary treatment of architecture....splendid
against grey stone.

POLYGONUM auberti, "Lace-vine" strongly woody, growing to 20'
in length, vigorously rooting, abundantly provided with material
for covering, but is deciduous, of second-rate quality:rustic in
feeling and fact, it is for places that will tolerate several
forms of litter, the flowers, the seed and capsules, the leaves
and a kind of bark drop:fleecy white flowers come along for June-
September, a sprightly and buoyant lift over heat:prune severely
in winter to lighten the over-full tangle of stems and head back the
leaders as mass gets out of hand:an untidy and inferior plant, but
will grow nearly anywhere to supply a need where need is greatest.

POLYPTERIS hookeriana, "Palafoxia" silver-touched, rosy-winged
petals to a ragged cone, then a mop of flowers:an annual plant
of some merit, but little known, growing 3-4' in very ordinary
dryish soils:a weedy plant, but rich in color all summer and
autumn....an everlasting of sorts if taken in fullness of bloom
and from where it is grown driest:native in the Southwest.

POLYSTICHUM---handsome ferns of considerable substance, mostly
from warmer regions, adapting to the subtropics for rather dense
shade, where a happy faculty for reflecting momentary motes
of light, enlivens dark places. The ground should be well
drained, with no standing water at any time; high in
humus as well as fibrous material breaking down....set
there very shallow, the rhizome barely covered, and that
mostly of mulch. The air should be reasonably quiet and
moisture uniform....self-reliant with all this.
   -aculeatum, "Bristle F." for full shaded places in
a moist, well drained place:fairly rigid fronds are 6-8"
wide and as long as 2', or more under best conditions.
   -adiantiforme(capense)"Leatherleaf F." the fronds are
roughly triangular, highly polished and very durable under
wear of movement....taking exposure:growing 2-3' in length
and very wide, they hold well when cut:striking.

385

SUBTROPICAL REGIONS

-tsus-simense, seldom more than 18" in height, to be
reserved largely for pots or used as a master-piece for a hanging basket or fern dish, a thin, very dark frond:frost-hardy.
-viviparum, lacy fronds that may be as much as 18-24" wide
and 3-4' in length, for large pots or a tub, producing young
plants very freely:tender.

## POPLAR
POPULUS---trees of very rapid growth, soft wood and brittle,
dangerous in the wind and in other ways not desirable about habitations or where people gather. They are planted almost exclusively
for quick shade or grouped for wind shelter. All are more or less
drouth resistant. The main differential lies in the form or in the
structure of limbs, with marked contrast, sometimes even within the
species. Some noble forms will be found in this group that is so
generally deprecated explosively....employ them, rather, intelligently. Prune with system in winter to strengthen the limb structure, keeping the weight as much as possible toward the center, or
toward a prevailing wind....always in balance. They are conspicuously short-lived; have a weakness for borers; root at the
surface and generally should be planted in masses for a
mutual protection in the wind. After all, they thrive
where more select trees will not grow and may be expected to make a better tree under hard going.
-alba, "Silver P." wide-spreading 50', used only
in a large planting for the excellent foliage....the
under side of the leaf being silvery-white, the entire mass quickens into sparkling animation with the
slightest movement of air:perpetually suckering, especially near worked ground:excellent salt resistant
thicket in sand near the sea.   --var. pyramidalis, a
columnar that is extremely narrow and sharply pointed,
known as "Bolles P.":subject to borers.
-fremonti, "Cottonwood" a very large and angular tree with a
great head of white branches and drooping branchlets, coming from
arid lands, frequenting the areas there of water holes and along
streambeds in deep soils:thrives in heat, accustomed to alkali,but
must have this deep moisture:picturesque.
-nigra italica, "Lombardy P." columnar, bluntly topped at
75', of some considerable favor in the rural landscape, but not
so highly regarded in town:used to line a highway or for exclamatory groups in space or with massive architecture:should
have fair depth of soil; adapts easily in dry ground or wet;
serves to accent and fairly cries aloud any mistaken placement....ask where the roots will go....they are formidable.
-simoni, "Chinese P." of the same general form as above
and somewhat in character, but only 35' high, the leaves smaller, of a lighter, more shining green and not so predatory in the
ground. The structure as a whole is more loose and active.

PORTULACA grandiflora, "Sun-moss" prostrate annual or the succulent
stems ascending, a cover for hot dry soils in the garden:blooms thru
summer, the flowers like small, single roses, too frequently in gaudy,
primary coloring, yellow, rose, scarlet, crimson and purple, and with
white forms of real value as a peace-maker:sow seed late, not
before April-June, since they require heat above all else
for germination:wants a light soil and all the sun, the
flower not opening fully on clouded days or in shade....no
feeding:seaside gardens in sand and under salt air.

PORTULACARIA afra, "Speckboom" a curious, meaty crassula-
like plant, roughly pyramidal for shape when young, finally breaking away to become an irregular and heavy mass,
gargantuan in looks and in the way it feeds:some of the
fleshy stems may reach 10' in height, not concealed by the
chubby, thickened leaves....all suffused with purple:tiny flowers, at first, clustered specks of wine-red, concentrate as they
open to rosy effusions of foam against the deeper color of stems
in summer:stands in contentment in any soil, with much water
or none, in hat sun or shade and alkali ground.

386

COMPENDIUM

## PRIMROSE

PRIMULA---herbaceous plants of gracious and intimate
charm, radiant with sparkling color, if not the typical
substance and stately form in the south. They flower over
winter and spring by species. Here they must have the good
shade, with morning sun or that of late afternoon or both
if at all possible. They must have a rich, porous soil that
is high in humus. A continual mulch of leafmould is most beneficial. They abhor drought and heat and quickly pass on in
a baked out soil or exposed to drying winds. Generally, they
are not to be divided....renew, rather, with strong fresh
plants derived from northern seed. They may be qualified for
the rock garden, the shaded border, bedding and damp-spot planting, and the gardener will be put on his metal culture-wise, considering diversity in form and origin. In fact, they are only for
those who will give thought to need and condition....and provide.

-kewensis, a hybrid with bright yellow flowers in winter,
reaching up, loose clusters on slender stems, to the sun here
with good timing and if not too hot....then shade:pots, bedding.

-malacoides, English or Fairy P." the more commonly seen in
the south, low dense tufts of light green crumpled leaves and
delicate lavender-rose flowers on slender, wiry stems, very
free-flowering late winter and early spring:may be used in
the garden as a border filler or at the foot of shrubbery:
reseeds when conditions are favorable.

-obconica, essentially a winter pot plant as generally
used, having generous heads of rather larger flowers in varying
shades of pink, rose and lavender to blue, held to 12" high:wants a
warm place to be at its best in winter, but coolness and shade if
pointed for summer bloom....left on its own, blooms anytime.

-polyantha, commonly known as "Polyanthus" a low, tight
tuft of wrinkled leaves, at times not much more than a flange
to the stout stalk and midrib:full open heads of white through
yellow, red and blue flowers in many shades and combinations to
fit the exuberance of spring. This is a more rugged plant that
is quite persistent in reasonable moisture and shade, carrying
over for awhile as perennial if watched over summer....divide in
late spring to make strong new plants by next spring....feed well.

-sinensis, "Chinese P." growing 6-8" high, a delightful little
spot of color, the leaves variously shaped, the flowers of many shades
from pink to much deeper, nicely fringed, sometimes double, the
flower stalk very short or almost without stem:pots or bedding,
or touches winter in the rock garden with bright green.

## ALGAROBA

PROSOPIS---among the more handsome of the spiny plants found
in the desert, for abounding interest and application to the arid
or barren landscape, coming easily and well under domestication all through the Southwest....too readily in soft, well-
watered lands, becoming a pest there. They go deep for moisture,
when they make their best appearance, growing shallow if forced,
but not nearly as typical. They are supple-branching with a film of
light, lacy foliage, a special beauty from the wild that is scarcely modified under cultivation. They bloom fully eight months of the
year, June-December, when taken into Florida; over winter in California, greenish yellow and not important except for time and place.

-glandulosa, "Mesquite" an erect, much-branched shrub or a
flat-topped tree at 25' with fluffy heads of green gold beginning in November:an attractive plant laboring, and with some
understanding, under a name of ill-repute:clothes efficiently
and well a dry rocky hillside....seed is best.

-pubescens, "Tornilla" viridian green, contrast and contra-
diction, cheer and invitation along the flat shores of the
Rio Grande, a shrub there 10-15', but farther north about
habitations and with a little more water, a tree 35', the
bean pod a curious winding affair like a compact and
tightly drawn corkscrew, a good yellow in color gathered together
in tight clusters that are seen late into winter decorating the
leafless woody structure of the tree.

387

*Primula malacoides*

*Primula obconica*

*prosopis*

*prosopis pubescens*

*glandulosa*

PROSTANTHERA nivea, "Mintbush" a soft-woody shrub 3-5',
with some refinement in the aromatic foliage, and either a
white or blue to purple flower from a nearly black bud April
to June:use lies in the median area of a perennial or shrubbery combination or as an element in either in coolness and
light shade, under dryness or slight moisture:tender and of
rather short life, but a lightsome, glowing little thing for
a time....cutting material of fair quality.

## THE STONE FRUITS

PRUNUS---bushy shrubs and small twiggy trees that are completely
deciduous, some having transient but showy flowers very early in the
spring, others featuring substantial evergreen foliage for a longer
service. Prune the first class to cut out old branches that are in-
terfering and reduce last years wood right after flowering, thus
developing bearing wood for the following year....the evergreen
species only shaped from time to time. They are all sun-loving
with the deciduous kinds too shallow-rooted to stand in much
wind. They thrive best in a medium weight soil that is heavy
enough to retain moisture, yet permeable for drainage....short
lived in clay, growing in sand with sufficient irrigation.
   -amygdalus, "Almond" deciduous tree of moderate size,
exceptionally clean, superb for shade, most attractive in
late winter or spring with flowers that will rival peach
bloom:nut-bearing under cross-pollination, only infrequently when out alone:best with heat in a light,substantial and
very well drained soil:drought resistant and frost-hardy.
   -campanulata, "Taiwan Cherry" an ornamental flowering tree 25' with clustered, single, light red flowers in
early spring or sometimes in late winter south, very freely
carried with or before the leaves:stands in considerable heat
and dry air for use in California and the Southwest, deciduo-
ous. The species    -cerasoides, is similar and evergreen, but
seldom obtainable.
   -caroliniana, "Laurimundi, Cherry-laurel, Southern or Carolina
Cherry" all these, serving to emphasize the esteem in which the
plant is held, a large evergreen shrub or slender, pyramidal to
columnar tree to as much as 40', low-branching, probably not as
large in California where the light green, clossy foliage will
fail to come through winter unscathed:a symmetrical plant of
quality that may be sheared further at any time of the year,
a good high narrow hedge....slow at first, vigorous when es-
tablished:no insects, but the leaves may become disfigured by
a sooty blotch that is not serious:wants a fairly moist, rich
soil with drainage and grows well into warm temperate regions.
   -ilicifolia, "Islay" large spreading dome, a shrub 8-12'
as grown in its native California under good culture, less and
straggling, in nature:dark, holly-like leaves an appropriate
setting for the white heads of flowers April-May:wants a coarse
deep soil with a minimum of moisture where it is rather slow to
take hold and grow:has a wide tolerance and many legitimate uses,
a fine serviceable plant in the right hands:hedges, clipped or
low and wide. Usually, better results follow when seed is placed
where the plant is to stand, especially in hedging....no time
will be lost:substantial soils only, in Florida.
   -jaquemonti,dense shrub or tree-like 10-12', an oval in outline from very close to the ground....better allowed its natural form:a haze of bloom in the spring, early and short-lived,is
light pink, the individual flower very small and delicate, thin
of petal and quite Japanesque:small edible red fruits are
real cherries of tradition, long stem and all:deciduous.
   -lusitanica, "Portugal-laurel" erect-shrubby as normally
used, a tree 20-40', whipped up and trained as such, and particularly handsome, having light, leathery leaves that are
remotelt shining, flowers in long racemes, white, May and
June....stand clear of the leaves:does in the heavier soils,
in moisture and in heat, when the leaf turns inward to reduce
transpiration....an identification:tubs, or a good standard,
pruning lightly to shape, using a knife to avoid mutilating the
large leaf....cut into hard wood in the winter.

388

-lyoni(integrifolia)"Catalina Cherry" large shrub
or slender, round-topped tree to 35' under cultivation in
deep soils:foliage is very light and lustrous, the long racemes of white flowers in May, followed by large red cherries
that lure, but with little meat to satisfy:growth is rapid and
continuous for a lively contrasting foliage all through warmth:it
takes moisture with drainage in almost any soil and can be formed
into a good tree for narrow streets:native to California islands.
    -persica, "Flowering Peach" a deciduous tree 15' with wide and
spreading limbs to a rounded top:has single to very double white,
pink or red flowers, but the semi-double forms are generally
more satisfactory south:grows in any reasonable soil in full
sun and are to be preferred in a cold exposed place over
other deciduous species:spray for leaf curl.

## GUAVA

PSIDIUM---erect shrubs, tender in frost, bearing edible
fruit, the foliage mass of considerable value in the
landscape. Other characters are appropriate, useful in
the garden, stem interest and flower. They may be kept
low or allowed to go up into a small tree of unusually attractive structure, normally branching close to
the ground to make the most of tortuous stems and the
flaking bark, the new skin with contrasting color and texture. They will be found growing best in loamy soils, that
may be either light or rather heavy, wanting moderate to generous moisture. The root structure is not demanding. The fruit
is eaten out of hand and quite generally used in preserves.
    -cattleianum, "Strawberry G." shrubby little tree 10-12',
sometimes only a medium sized bush, the shining foliage darkened,
shading the smallish red fruits that so often go into short-cake:
grown commercially, this is somewhat drouth resistant but
showing up in size of fruit, the better species for California: wants sun to produce crops and is the hardiest in
cold, when the leaves tend to thin out until almost, if not
all, have followed the dropping fruit....bare by spring
for line value....accented by systematic removal of the
superfluous twiggy growth and occasional water sprout. There
is little pruning otherwise except for those who know beauty
in line, and would guide.    --var. lucidum, a yellow-
fruited form with a more delicate flavor and larger size,
better eating out of hand:both for hedges, clipped or not.
    -guajava, slender tree to 30', probably better called
"Tropical G." on account of its extreme tenderness in frost, being too tender for California except in most favored spots, but
doing well south in Florida:brown scaling bark and somewhat
larger yellow fruits with musky fragrance:improved varieties.
    -guineense,"Castilian or Brazilian G." a shrub 6-8', erect-
rounding, the stems well clothed with large, slightly hairy
leaves, rectangular in shape, turning to dull shades of purple
with the lightest frost or only cold weather, pale orange by
spring:flowers are large, as are the elongated fruits which
are of much poorer quality for eating:will do with a minimum of
water late summer to develop firmer fruit and harden for winter.

PSORALEA pinnata(aphylla)"Scurfy Pea" straggling, formless
shrub 6-8', the very fine, needle-like leaf strangely roughened
for effect, uncertain with stems frequently bare in a check, such
as drought;the "Blue-broom" flowers are pale and wash out still
more after a time with the elements May-June; the wing white or
not, bloom starting along the stems, clustered at the ends:es-
sentially water-loving, for the sun and in sandy soils where
growth is very rapid and equally ragged....a filler thing.

## BRAKE FERN

PTERIS---rugged ferns, some of tropical origin, but all with
much to recommend for unusually difficult service in pots or in
other containers or in ordinary conditions of the border. As a
potted plant, they are used in decoration of tables indoors or
outside on a terrace, where a dryish, tenacious quality found

*Prunus persica*

*Psidium guajava*

*Psidium cattleianum*

*Psoralea pinnata*

in the foliage, arms the plant against wear and violence
found there. The long, linear, ribbony character of the
leaflets offers something of distinction that is acceptable in way of a fern. They do equally well in sunlight
or shade, but many of them will burn in reflected heat.
    -aquilina(Pteridium)"Bracken" forming dense patches of
dry harsh fronds rising from a very persistent, quite death-
less system of roots that spread out as a prime nuisance in
any but waste places....use there only:collect stock to plant.
    -cretica, a small plant that is supremely variable in the
form and cut and especially in the serration of the leaf, at
times curled or even colored on occasion:pots, as a choice
piece indoors or outside.
    -serrulata, a bushy plant some 12" in height for dryish
soils in the sun....dislikes heavy shade or any at all
and will be grown only in the open:hard rain will affect
or actually ruin the fronds, so that new growth is important in coming along:lime keeps in trim.
    -tremula, "Australian Brake" rugged and rather rapid
in growth to as much as 3', the polished stems an attractive brownish color for considerable line interest:may be
used in the border under conditions of heat and drought and
for the unusual textured mass of the foliage.

    PTEROCEPHALUS parnassi, a prostrate perennial, becoming woody
at the base, re-rooting there to make a more or less persisting
mass, a grey, rather dense 3-4" cover with short-stemmed lilac-
pink, scabiosa-like flowers, lowly pincushions over-spread-
ing the body of the plant in summer:must have drainage, as
it goes out quickly in a heavy soil....but serving for a
time:deep-rooted cover of refinement, containment and
discrimination in sandy soils that are not too rich:
sun in its entirety is important.

    PTEROSPERMUM acerifolium, a very large and commanding
tree, blooming mid-winter, or cut to the ground at that
time by frost, re-appearing multiple-stemmed, ranging outward as a great bush, immense in all its parts:rusty,
12" leaves are tough and leathery, the 6" pure white
flower a huge, star-like magnolia with fragrance:semi-
deciduous, with warmth and drainage indicated.

    PUERARIA thunbergiana, "Kudzu-vine" a vigorous perennial
with large, heart-shaped leaves and purple, pea-shaped flowers in the summer:very rapid growth, covering quickly in any
place where refinement is of no object:give it warmth in a
deep, well drained soil to allow the long, whip-like fleshy
roots scope....penetrate deeply for nutrients and to resist
drouth:pest-free, easy to grow and in other ways a commoner.

    PUNICA granatum, "Pomegranate" a large brushy shrub, normally
to be seen at 8-12' height, more under suitable conditions:the
showy flower is scarlet in crumpled flounces of orange-red, the
semi-fleshy basal parts developing into the dry, seedy and
scarlet fruits that are so striking:prune in late winter
to preserve any semblance of neatness, or reduce strong
growing shoots a third as they mature:quite resistant
to, and fruits satisfactorily only in heat:does especially well in heavy soils and takes some drought, surviving, but....leaves take on typical gold of autumn
as it begins to suffer and drop gradually until caught
by moisture, which will hold those remaining:makes a
rough natural hedge and good fruit only in a dry climate....use improved forms for ornament....sometimes doubtful in performance and may not set fruit unless grown
as above. A cooling drink is made from the fruit pulp
by adding sugar and water.   --var. nana, dwarf and
similar, tending to hold leaves over winter....only
tending:low ornamental hedge, or can be pinched in
for summer service in a tub.

390

PUTORIA calabrica, a low brittle branching little plant, woody at the base and extending into structure, having something of a daphne look in foliage and flower, used as a garden cover on a small scale or in the rock garden, growing 3-6" high and spreading much further; the brash, breakable branches re-rooting to carry on:elongated, quite narrow, meaty leaves glisten in the sun beneath the close-clustered, rosy-pink flowers spring and summer into early fall, or almost continuous during warmth:berries develop concurrently with the flowers and weigh down the weak stems with winey, Indian-currant clusters of red berries into early winter:must have sun, moisture and drainage:choice.

PUYA alpestris, a yucca-like plant that develops several low thick leafy stems, a clumpy thing but picturesque, a mass of long, grassy and spined leaves with a great close panicle of dull, steel-blue, flaring flowers accented by orange anthers, summer:adaptable in the matter of climate and soils....drier, colder parts best, but will take moisture and may even be grown indoors for awhile in a planter or other container:takes the most extreme exposure to weather and its vicissitudes....quickly made.

## FIRETHORN
PYRACANTHA---splendid evergreen shrubs, compact if not grown too rapidly, easily kept in hand, substantial in foliage, highly ornamental in flower and fruit. They prefer the heavier soils when drained, with a little lime added if there is any question as to sweetness....don't allow ever to get really souer. Prune in late winter or early spring and then only to re-new old wood or to correct branching. Limit digging about the roots as much as is good, since the scant system will be better not disturbed. The best plants are always propagated by cuttings rather than seed and a superior strain or variety is well worth the extra effort and cost....recognized in nursery catalogues as named varieties. Give full sun for complete crop of berries, that may last thru winter to mingle with the white flowers of spring, miniature appleblossoms. These shrubs can be sheared, but not too satisfactorily far south where dieback of stems is more marked. This results from a bacterial disease of all pomaceous or apple-like shrubs and trees manifest in blackening of leaf and stem. It is very contagious and the only cure is to cut out infected parts and burn....cut well back into sound wood....keep hand and knife out of contact with infected area....disinfect both from time to time. Specific forms are disappearing from use gradually in favor of selected hybrids. These are general purpose plants of considerable importance and everything possible should be done in the south to keep up the health-tone for longevity.
     -crenato-serrata(crenulata)rather compact and more easily kept under 5' than most, with dark foliage and with the red fruits carried generously among the leaves....the one to clip as a hedge, against all advice:good soil and moisture in moderation and uniformity. This species is the one most amenable to shade, also the better one to take south.   --var. yunnanensis, prostrate, a woody cover or grown over a bank, used nicely to face a broad slope that recedes or to pull high shrubs into the ground where it will build up 2-3' in height and good mass:foliage tends to drop in winter or in high wind to reveal orange to coral berries. This can be propagated with seed, prostrate forms indicating their character very early for selection.
     -koidzumi, shrub of rapid growth 10-12' or a slender tree with slim, tortuous stem and revealing feather of light green foliage, an outstanding ornamental:grow slowly as possible.
     -coccinea lalandi, very erect lines in the stems 15', a scraggly plant with scant dark foliage held close to the main stems on stiff, spur-like twigs:orange berries by mid-summer most effective in abundance....stands against a high wall where it will do everything a vine will accomplish and without support:hardiest one in frost.

391

PYROSTEGIA ignea(Bignonia venusta)"Flame-trumpet" striking color, a vigorous plant but wanting on foliage, the
long, narrow, orange-yellow tubes that scarcely open,
hang in massed, rope-like strands mid-winter:poor foliage and time of bloom suggest using with a summer blooming evergreen vine for its foliage in compensation:quite a
tender thing in frost,so that this magnificent flowering will
be available only in warm places:returns following year
after having been cut by frost, possibly with bloom.

PYRUS calleryana, a crooked tree 15-25' with a sturdy trunk
and strong branches horizontally spreading:dark shining leafage is persistent and white flowers of very early spring most
attractive and acceptable, nostalgic impulse with many new-
comers in subtropic regions:growing tips will burn back in
fire blight, but mature wood seems immune and damage is not
serious unless plants nearby are subject.     --var. kawakami,
may be grown as an espalier, but to be planned on the grand
scale, if considered permanent. This is because of the ultimate size and must be considered in light of the type above
for the long pull. Picturesque as shrub or tree....a pear.

### STAR GLORY
QUAMOCLIT---known generally as "Mina" in gardens; tender,
very slender little vines of refinement, annuals or perennial
far south, but always re-seeding rather freely to carry on
from year to year. They should have a warm sunny place,
one that is well protected, a little shade in extreme heat
and a comparatively light soil. Sow it early in spring because
of late germination.
  -lobata, "Flag o' Spain" of vigorous growth with large,
heart-shaped leaves that are three-lobed and terminal clusters
of tubular flowers that do not entirely open, but rich in color,
rosy-crimson at first, changing through orange to pale yellow
August-November....delightful to see....crimson and gold in
the cluster for light cutting:very late germination.
  -pennata, "Cypress-vine" dainty and delicate in all its
parts, a little plant of felicity that wins utterly....and
utterly fine, feathery foliage that attempts to conceal, failing
to obliterate the deep scarlet, long-tubular flowers....a star
at the mouth and fully opened only at sundown or early morning.

### OAK
QUERCUS---stately, wide-spreading trees for the most part, with
a massive bole and canopied head, otherwise erect and comparatively
slender. The group may be divided roughly into three designations,
the white and the black oaks and the evergreen....and with all,
one strives not to be too lyric. The first class is notably
difficult to transplant and should be brought up in the nursery with best fibrous rootage possible, and while they are
generally considered very slow in growth, one finds good
sized trees in a surprisingly short time under cultivation.
the white oaks as a rule prefer good moisture in the soil,
but stand better in dry air, and while the black oaks take
dry or gravelly ground, they flourish in a moist atmosphere.
The evergreen or liveoaks are ideally situated above a supply of free water, but survive on dry hillsides. These conditions are not invariable, however, and they are all found in
clay and humidity, adapting to drouth, reveling in an acid reaction of their own making or as of a granite base. They are
pest-free and of little difficulty in management after having been established....retain central leader in starting.
  -agrifolia, "California Coast or Live Oak" round of
head and wide-spreading, 75' or more with rough, black bark-
ed trunk and dull dark foliage to pendulous branches, the
leaf spined and turned under at the edge, cupped in reverse:
a clean tree for the lawn, very deep-rooting, wanting the
ground drained, but standing with the roots in free
moving water, as of a stream:growth more rapid than

people realize....expect one inch caliper per year in deep
grav ~ soils with moisture....a tree with a 15" diameter in
fiftt ∴ years. There are better oaks to grow for domestic
purposes as this one mildews badly in air humidity.

-chrysolepis, "Goldencup O." erect-rounding to somewhat spreading at 60', usually less:pendulous branches will
carry light, bluish green foliage that is yellowish powdery
in spring, the leaves entire or toothed, and spined according to stage of development. This is a mountain tree that may
be grown at lower levels, not available in the nursery trade,
so that one sets an acorn for the better kind of a start.

-douglasi, "Blue O." deciduous, a slender tree to 40',
and compared with the others, inconsiderable, only middling,
but unique for the blue foliage:an oval in outline or broader
with several stems from an early injury or fire:the stout leaf
is pale beneath and only slightly lobed or sinuate along the edge:
native in California on clay or rocky hillsides, thrusting deeply
through impossible structures for moisture....practically indestructible. This too, is worth a trip into the hills for a
handfull of acorns....there are many.

-dumosa, a "Scrub Oak" from the heights above the ocean
in California, a brushy little tree or dense, wide-spreading
shrub if the leader is cut out, invaluable in either case for
covering a hot dry hillside, the greyish leaves so sharply
spined as to be very uncomfortable to touch. To establish
this plant properly and quickly, with minimum attention
and irrigation....only germinate the acorn in a narrow
carton or other flimsy, so that the tiny new plant will have
to be set out soon, thus saving the inordinately long tap root
in place....secret of success with the acorn is the initial tapping for deep moisture before there is much top growth.

-ilex, "Holm or Holly O." a dome-like mass for seaside communities primarily, in the lighter soils of poor quality or sand,
where it will take full exposure to wind in the protection of other,
less rugged growth, or stand in its own right:difficult to move, must
be several times transplanted in the nursery or pot grown:an evergreen
tree, but losing leaves in extreme cold, growing to 60', the leaf flat
and dark greyish with enough luster for briskness in the sun, contrasting lighter underside to help with animation in the wind;
holly-like, partially so or entirely without serration. This
tree is being discovered now for these regions and will be
grown with much satisfaction in landscape and in only lesser
degree in the garden where it will be found less subject to
oak troubles and tribulation.

-laurifolia, "Laurel O." a shade tree for the South
Atlantic and Gulf areas, in California in high heat and far
north into warm temperate regions; half evergreen, growing
60' or more with slender branchlets to a glistening, rounding top, easily transplanted in sandy soils. The "Darling-
ton Oak" is a fully evergreen form to use south in Florida
and along the California coast....a white oak for streets.

-lobata, "Valley O." deciduous, very wide-spreading 100'
in the air, extremely open up there for a lightly cast shade
over a wide expanse:branches drooping, at times considered as
weeping, the leafage light green with suggestions of grey when
new, silvery beneath....colors up like a high beacon in autumn.
This is another one of the "most beautiful" of trees and lives up
such claim back in the hot interior valleys of California with a
litle frost and deep soils....not to be grown in character elsewhere unless with these conditions:a white oak.

-pumila, "Running O." spreading out from the base crown,
shrubby or prostrate 2-12' in height, half-evergreen, native
in the well drained, sandy soils of Florida....good cover
there from the ubiquitous acorn:thick leaf entire or toothed.

-suber, "Cork O." an erect, very open-headed tree 50'
for hot dry and gravelly soils in great heat....a better
tree in the Southwest....but resents lime....calliche. A
unique feature is the bark, which is the cork of commerce,
appearing in deeply gashed furrows, the ridges rounded and
rolling in thick layers....a shambles from small boys.

393

-virginiana, "Live Oak" a storied tree, the grand
old oak of the South, used in practically all sections, extensively along the gulf coast into Texas, with moisture and
now available in California....why the interchange of these
basic trees either direction....may not be known:head of this
one broadly rounding at 50', spreading out 100', the huge extended limbs magnificently buttressed at the base of a short trunk:the
tree rapid in growth comparatively, leaves dropping in the spring
but coming out again almost immediately:primary uses shade and
avenue planting, growing north into warm temperate regions.

QUILLAJA saponaria, "Soapbark-tree" growing to 75' in good
ground, round-headed, a good tree for wide streets and in lawns
with much soil beneath:foliage shines agreeably for a great highlight in mass plantings and the white clustered flowers are mostly terminal:to be grown in moisture and not exceptionally desirable. excepting the above.

## R

RANUNCULUS asiaticus, "Turban Flower" a fleshy-rooted plant,
sold and treated in the garden as a bulb, the flowers large and
poppy-like, semi or full double, embracing all colors excepting
blue, February-May:set in the fall, being sure to get the fang
of the claw downward, with only a sprinkling of soil or sand above:
ground should not be too heavy, never short of moisture during the
growing period....no fresh manures:be prepared to protect the leaves
against birds as it comes through and lift when thoroughly ripened:a
first rate cutflower. They are easily rotted out during the early
stages of growth....soak very lightly before planting, if at all and
don't over-water as the leaves are showing through....better established in a flat, being careful not to hold there too long so that
the roots must be cut in moving:best stored over summer in adhering
soil that is not allowed to dry out completely. The species
-repens fl. pl., known as "Button Buttercup" with flowers in the
summer, is vigorous, invasive, and tolerates considerable shade
but wanting sun....caterpillars denude:found repeatedly through
these regions as a partly prostrate perennial, straggling, running in growth and rooting at the nodes to make a high, thick mat:
small, shining, waxy-yellow flowers are very double.

RAPHIOLEPIS---hardy shrubs, general purpose plants of
quality, most serviceable, durable in foliage and frame, the
leaves of a dull metalic aspect, of particular interest and
value for places of refinement where control is important.
They are for all time low in stature, finely formed, almost
never over-grown, easily held in by pinching out soft growth.
They develop slowly, do well in heavy soils and are quite
at home within reach of salt winds....down to the surf
line with drainage. The retiring leaves turn purple or
pick out the weighty mass in crimson before they fall.
They tolerate some shade.
    -delacouri, a hybrid between the following species
that is typical of a new race of pink flowering shrubs
of various sizes and structure as well as bloom intensity
and timing....this one of many years standing, a shapely,
presentable little thing, dense in the sun or as it comes
of age:blooms December-March and the bronzy character of the
new foliage is marked and very attractive.
    -indica, "India-hawthorn" rather precise in growth 3-5'
with erect stems that are tipped with loose heads of white
or flushed flowers March-April, long-lasting blue berries later and for long:slow to get started, but long-
lived and thoroughly satisfying as a building material.
    -ovata, "Yeddo-hawthorn" rigid and uncompromising,
eventually massive and very heavy in feeling, a dome

to the ground, the round, leathery leaves a dull, livid
green and the new growth russet:white, spicily fragrant
flowers come late winter-spring, while the closely clustered,
larger round blue berries last out the balance of the year:
a useful and long-lived plant for the larger rock garden,
repeating rock form and substance, with shadings in many
vague and indistinct colorings:very hardy in frost.

REHMANNIA angulata, "Beverlybells" a short-lived perennial, or treated as biennial, re-seeding freely to produce the new plants in place, or root-suckering:long bell-
shaped flowers hang from near the top of a 2-3', erect
stem or spike on the order of foxglove, light carmine,with
markings in orange:well placed under high shade in a spot
sheltered from the wind and in good, mellow garden soil:
sow inside in autumn or spring and pot up before setting
out....something of a substitute for either hollyhock or
foxglove in the far south:cut spikes keep a week in
water, but not normally grown with the cutflowers.

REINECKIA carnea, liliaceous cover, a very persistent
leafy plant, a spreading 6" tangled mass of stout, stolon-
like, tight-rooting stems and narrow leaves:perennial
and very efficient in holding its ground or soil on slopes
in broken sun or in deep shade:flesh-colored to pink,
short-stalked flowers are not important:takes dryness or
moisture in average soil or below the mean, where it will
be invasive, jealous of its space, covetous of that of its
neighbors....right cover in heavy competition.

REINWARDTIA indica, "Winter-flax" a soft-woody perennial
12-18" high and with more spread, blooming in the pit of the
winter, frost permitting:difficult to bring along and flower
satisfactorily except in a warm, protected place of good
light, indirect if not in the sun....stumbles along in the
shade without much color:single, golden-yellow flowers will
appear in some profusion, a good year, November-February,
a warming touch for that time:shear back a good part of
the top after flowering or cut to the ground....don't
force following growth, and let come along slowly, drying
out somewhat in late autumn for matured wood:light, well
drained soils best, but will manage in heavier....only
average moisture and feeding:sulks in deep shade.

BUCKTHORN

RHAMNUS---worthy shrubs for domestication, natives
largely for the landscape rather than the garden proper,
some useful as hedging, others or all in the rougher part
of the shrubbery or any planting of a wild nature. While
the matter of utility seems always in the fore-front,color
in berry may not be overlooked here, nor can one forget the
many shadings available in the substantial and durable foliage. They will more generally be used in hot arid climates
and under extreme drought.
    -alaternus, "Italian B." erect 10-15" or clean-
cut as a small tree 25', if desired:dark, glossy foliage is persistent except under heavy frost and partially conceals the blue berries which become black at
the last:used as a hedge plant where sufficient stock is
available; in the shrubbery for solid service and is the one
exception that finds a place in the garden or to grow in a
humid climate:the variegation is well used in darkened places.
    -californica, "Coffeeberry" a large native shrub of loose,
yet rather precise, rounding habit, spreading 8-10' across,
not quite as high:large round berries lend an air in late summer and fall, due to various stages in coloring at any
given time and over-all, yellow, through reds and finally
dark purple to black:grows anywhere, best in a little shade.
    -crocea, "Redberry" usually very small, dwarfed 3-5'
or even less, rigid-erect in habit, but adapting nicely

395

in form to a bank, to vary a normal treatment:the small
round leaves are notched at the tip for identification, are
sometimes toothed, a dark slate-green with an over-laid or
superficial luster, on short, spur-like branchlets:flowers
are notable only for the fragrance which is mild but pleasing....bright red berries are most conspicuous:native in California in either intense heat or coolness, in soils that are
light or heavy or gravelly, so long as they are well drained.
--var ilicifolia, a larger plant, but the two with much in common,
the leaf more definitely spined, the plant less rigid, growing to
15' in good ground....prune for compactness when young, if that is
desirable:marked exhibit, a wealth of tiny, curiously glassy
berries that are strangely brilliant.

*Rhapis excelsa*

RHAPIDOPHYLLUM hystrix, "Needle Palm" a dwarf fan palm 3-4',
the stems prostrate to erect and from several in a crown to only
one, always covered inches thick with a black, fibery plush of
coarse hair from which the long black spine glares, giving the
plant its name:grows in nature in low places and transplants
easily in moist rich soils:rare in cultivation, available and to
be grown in Florida and neighboring parts.

### BAMBOO PALM
RHAPIS---slender, reed-like fan palms with a typical bamboo
stem in thick clumps, long used over the country in tubs for an
artificial kind of decoration for terrace, lobby or shown frankly in a conservatory. They are entirely practicable out of doors
in these regions as a material in patio or garden, but in a rich
moist soil out of extreme wind. There they will develop slowly
into tight bundles of stems, the fans split back practically
the entire distance. They are of peculiar interest and some
charm, with a rather fixed grace as found in a purely decorative
function. They adapt to full sun in comparative heat, but are
better in shade, wanting uniform, if little moisture.
    -excelsa(flabelliformis)"Lady P." stark-erect, hard
canes 5-8' in height, clothed with the tattered remnants
of leaf sheaths, the segments of the leaf long and comparatively wide, indented at the tips or roughly pointed.
    -humilis, "Ground-rattan" normally much smaller and
more refined all around, nearly stemless or growing in a tub
2-3' in full wide clumps, the very narrow leaf segments light
green. Outside in good soils, this plant, in time, will lift
up 10-15' in height in graceful, tenuous lines of varying
length, getting away completely from the fixed and rigid
structure of youth.

*Rhapis humilis*

RHODOMYRTUS tomentosa, "Rose-myrtle or Hill-gooseberry" a
downy-stemmed shrub 3-5' with rosy-pink, myrtle-like flowers
in May and edible fruit with a slight raspberry flavor by June
or July:thrives in almost any soil that can be kept moist, the
loose or sandy loams to be preferred:tender in frost. This is
difficult to propagate so that chance seedlings should be held.

*Rhodomyrtu*

### SUMAC
RHUS---deciduous and evergreen shrubs, those native in California grown only there. They are valued for the substantial
foliage and its ability to survive the wear of time and
weather; for the fruiting heads that carry considerable
color and structural interest; but mostly they are used
for the stubborn growing qualities that seem to run in
the blood.....dry, rocky ground, steep hillsides, any difficult condition of soil or micro-climate or the unthink-
ing carelessness of men. They are better not forced.
    -cismontana, deciduous, the type normally covered by
the term sumac, slender individual stems from the ground
2-3' or to 6', straggling, a stemmy mass that will sucker
into a colony effect:terminal clusters of greenish to off-
white or creamy flowers June-August carry through winter as
dark red fruiting heads. This plant is native on the
higher elevations of the Southwest:fall coloration.

*Rhus lancea*

   -integrifolia, "Lemonadeberry" coarse, spreading
or sprawling as a shrub, an erect san sturdy little
tree to 25' as found in deep canyon soils....gnarled,
heavy low trunk and top with a solid feel:has slate-green,
leathery, toothed leaves and close, sticky heads of flat,
orange berries that are so high in acid as to make a passable
drink:good bank cover, quite adaptable, flattening out to the
ground in wind against the sea in California....only a foot
through and five or six steps across.
   -lancea, "South African S." willowy shrub complete and
direct reversible of above, with hard, very slender-lobed
leaves, a cover that scarcely obscures the stems, the twiggy
structure dark, reddish in the sun, the whole effect that of
extreme airiness:makes a weepy, slender tree 25' and as much
across for rough going in heat and raw soils:new and rare,
with possible use in the garden as an unobtrusive screen.
   -laurina, "Laurel-leaf S." naturally an open, more or
less vase-shaped shrub, graceful, aromatic, enduring much
heat and dryness, adapting to rocky soils, but wanting better,
answerable to frost alone....killing to the ground in low
places, but recovering....size of existing plants is relative
to degree of past frosts and indication of future:new growth
reddish, followed soon by large plumes of whitish flowers.
   -ovata, "Sugarbush" a straggling shrub 6-10', of open habit
with clean, bright green smooth leathery leaves, the new growth
reddish, in winter:pink flowers in tight, dense heads are rather handsome in early spring, topping an ornamental spray that is
highly regarded to take indoors from mid-winter on:flattened berries
are dark orange to red in close roundish clusters:highest heat and
drought immaterial to this plant....good cover for the most exposed
and barren lands:native inland in California.
   -trilobata, "Squawbush" deciduous, spreading or procumbent,
bushy 1-5', a high mountain plant within these regions, excellent
cover there and lower, on open ground in hot places or in some
shade....just keep it away from habitations....evil odor:
deeply cut leaves turn crimson before falling.

   RIBES---more wildlings, shrubs that are infrequently used,
but most attractive in flower and deserving more consideration
at the hands of the plantsman. They are not so particular as
to exposure, wanting, however, slight to as much as half
shade or even more in heat....with soil that is moist in
season. These plants all tend to deteriorate in foliage,
or actually drop the leaves in late summer, to break out
again in the winter....sometimes in autumn with abundant
moisture....active in any event, all winter-spring. In pruning, hook out one or two of the older stems at the ground during dormancy, leaving the strong new shoots undisturbed. Do
not cultivate the soil. They appreciate much humus and leafmould as a continuing mulch. Late summer irrigation or early
rains may carry the foliage over so that it may become nearly
evergreen. Currants are unarmed, the gooseberries with weak spines.
   -echinellum, a gooseberry that is native in Florida, growing to 3' in height, the slender stems heavily spined and the
green fruits prickly:flowers are white or chartreuse, green or
something in between.
   -glutinosum, Pinkflowering Currant" scarcely waiting
for winter rains in California to burst into opulent bloom
on nearly bare 8-12' arching stems late summer or fall, very
fragrant:stands excessive irrigation, a good garden subject.
   -malvaceum, a winter-flowering currant, low and spreading
with some maturity, erect and unbent in early, vigorous youth,
having the typical leaf of the hawthorn, large and effective
individually:pinkish or rosy flowers are quite handsome and
have a spicy fragrance that carries on into spring:native in
the back country and highlands of California.
   -speciosum, a gooseberry, small, straggling, the gracefully arching stems completely
covered with fine spines....hung in row with
the fuchsia-like, intensely red flowers in late
397

winter:wants a cool soil that is rich and a place
protected from the wind:tolerates rather deep shade
in north-opening canyons in California:evergreen.
-viburnifolium, "Catalina Currant" an evergreen
shrubby plant with both prostrate and arching stems, the
lower ones rooting....or hanging as a curtain in a sunless place:aromatic, blunt-ending leaves are shallow-
toothed, a dull, dark green with contrasting brightness
in the red twiggs and rosy flowers February-May:grows in
the sun, but wants a little shade over noon when growing in
heat:leafmould or other humusy material in a well drained soil,
although it gets along in any reasonable situation:choice as a
landscape material, but rarely seen, even in its native California.

RICINUS communis, "Castorbean" a tree in the absence of frost,
growing rapidly from seed to 15' in the south, having a wide
spread of semi-woody branches from a thick, soft-woody trunk:the
very large, lobed leaves and furry-spined seed coverings lend a
decidedly tropical aspect. There are many other forms and possibly
another species, differential lying in coloring and veining of
the leaf, red stems or crimson leaves or veining picked out in
color or white. They grow anywhere, but in warm places in the
sun, typically and in good drainage:dependable under salt wind.

RIVINA humilis, "Rouge-plant" "Bloodberry" herbaceous, but shrub-
like 18-24", a tiny pokeberry standing in a pot for patio or indoors
for decoration:flowers white or rose-colored May-June, the tiny berries filling out a generous raceme with their blood-stained plumpness
the balance of the season:discard old plants and carry on with cuttings which strike easily:may be used in the garden in some shade.

ROCHEA coccinea, "Red-crassula" a leafy, shrub-like succulent, the
stems with thin, over-lapping leaves regularly spaced, the stem,
carrying the large heads of fragrant crimson flowers, nearly ob-
scured:pinching out tips of growth may be practiced from time to
time with advantages in over-all color effect:wet, poorly drained soils will almost surely cause crown-rot and death for this
plant which resists drought:use indoors in summer when in flower.

ROHDEA japonica, "Manchu-lily" substantial foliage plant the
year round, with most durable leathery leaves that show
wide variation in form and pattern and in the markings:
flowers not conspicuous, but the closely packed berries
which top a short stalky stem, turn scarlet in the fall
and keep fresh-looking until spring. The infinite modification of leaf place this as a collectors item with a background of much interest and labor of hand and mind to delight the hearts of oriental gardeners....many large collections attest:wants moisture and shade and will be grown in a
pot in a cool location:frost-hardy into warm temperate regions.

ROMNEYA coulteri, "Matlija-poppy" a large, semi-woody plant
with light bluish, silvered leaves and satiny, crumpled white
flowers 3-5" across, a tasseled yellow button at the center, May
into heat:warm place in the sun, where the soil is well drained and deep, not too rich and sandy....sensitive at both
root and crown, with transplanting a problem....divide
in late autumn:suckering when established, do not cultivate. This is too coarse for other than rough, out of
the way places:better flowers on new wood....hook out
old stems at the ground late summer or fall:grown north
into warm temperate regions as a perennial, mulched.

RONDELETIA cordata, an erect shrub 5-8' or more, with durable, wear-resistant foliage and full heads of flowers, December-April; buds color by mid-winter and open to deep pink, finally yellow-throated by March, in full bloom and gone by May....a
well grown plant a goodly demonstration of color:wants moisture,
a little shade in heat, but sparing since reduced vitality will
open way to mealybug or scale:requires considerable servicing

in removal of spent leaves which hang on,while flower
heads stand fixed interminably if not removed:resents
alkaline water, wants a warm exposure and is tender in
frost. The species amoena, is quite similar, blooming
later to extend the flowering season into May-June.

### THE ROSE

ROSA---inclusive here of the wild species and what may be
termed oldfashioned types, as apposed to the highly developed
hybrids usually associated with the name..These are the roses
used out in the landscape as against the cutting rose of the
strictly rose garden and will be single or only semi-double.
They will be grown surprisingly far south into the tropics in
good tilth. They carry and express a simple lovableness, an
appeal that is free of restraint or disclipine, something
that has been bred out of the marvelous creations now to be
found in gardens. Use them in the outlying shrubbery or to
cover widely over waste ground. Employ them freely and
naturally, but with discretion in view of the strong growth
and crowding tendencies. They will want the sun and a soil
that is retentive of moisture. They are free of pests.

   -banksiae, evergreen in the south, high-climbing and
practically without thorns, a splendid plant with a certain
refinement, if large and strong-growing:has small white or
yellow, very double flowers in great clusters, an old plant in
the garden....serviceable there if pruned to hold in and to
develop new wood for bloom.

   -bracteata, "McCartney R." another very old rose, an
evergreen climber with polished dark leaves and large single
flowers, white May-October. The rose Mermaid, along with Capt.
Thomas are varieties of this species, very resistant to all
disease, vigorous to require much space....very practical.

   -californica, the little roses of Castile of the early
padres, a wild rose growing in thickets in substantial soils
that do not dry out completely:single, pink or deeper flowers
over spring, and orange to red hips for summer:use locally.

   -laevigata, "Cherokee R." sprawling, or climbing to as much
as 15', the rambling streamers with white, pink or deeper single
flowers as early as March and as late as June, with a lesser bit
of bloom in the fall:flowers best along the coast in California
and has naturalized all over the South:makes a good hedge along
a wire, or an old fence that needs cover, or other support.

   -stellata, "New Mexican R." an erect, wiry little shrub 18-24"
the branchy stems covered with a fine felt:solitary flowers are a
deep rosy-purple April-June, laid down over the attractive and unusual grey-green foliage:native in the Southwest, used there and
in other areas of high heat as a landscape material:naturalize.

ROSMARINUS officinalis, "Rosemary" of old world fragrance
and association, untidy, as usual in the way of intimate
things, but never-the-less a charming little plant:shrub
2-3' with aromatic, slender, flattened needle-like leaves
and pale blue flowers over a long period....practically
everblooming in warm places near the sea:requires a dry soil
with drainage and to be grown slowly in the sun for good form
and close texture and further, to be pinched in from time to
time if always presentable....cut deeply to remove dead or
dying wood. This plant will serve better in poor soils and
should be starved for the gnarled, irregular stem that is the
hallmark of the picturesque as against merely slovenliness:the
clippings are used in cookery or will scent the house pleasantly as they dry out.   --var. prostratus, growing flat to the
ground, an excellent cover in the right place, re-rooting or hanging down the face of a low wall. A form that
was selected by Lockwood de Forest and named for him,
is in between these two extremes for height and seems
naturally to be more tidy for texture while the flower
is bluer and holds the color better in the sun. This
plant will lie flat, more or less against the ground,
but breaks the plane with interesting risings.

Rosa laevigata

Rosa bracteata

Rosa stellata

Rosmarinus officinalis
prostratus

SUBTROPICAL REGIONS

ROTHROCKIA cordifolia, a perennial twining herb with
woody lower stems, loosely growing, flinging about for
support, climbing to show axillary heads of white and or
yellowish flowers:native in the Southwest, used there.

ROYENA lucida, "Snowdrop Bush" a shrubby plant or
tree-like, growing anywhere from 3 to 15', having a smooth
whitish to light grey bark of much attraction:white flowers
are set close to the branches along with the small, glossy and
leathery leaves:harsh and rather dry conditions in culture:tender.

RUELLIA devosiana, low-spreading shrub 18-24" with soft wood,
the twiggy structure practically herbaceous through the outer
area:leaves are purple beneath, veined in white above while the
flowers come in lilac to much deeper....as virile as cerise:a
broken half shade is about right for exposure, with uniform
moisture and warmth....no bloom without warmth:soil should
be acid, or at least neutral, loose and fibery....can be
grown decumbent by forcing:continually flowering with sufficient warmth....no wind....no frost....better in a pot to
take indoors for winter flowering.

RUSCUS aculeatus, "Butchers Broom" an erect, very harsh,
tenaciously woody plant, a kind of shrub with dull, light
green leaf-like branches or bracts which serves as foliage:
tiny red, bead-like seedy berries are set on these strange
chiselings....the flowers having been colorless and probably not
noticed:may be used in salt-tainted ground, beneath a tree in the
darkest shade and in quite dry soil....thin out the built
up structure in the spring. The climbing butchers-broom is
Semele androgyna, high-climbing or sprawling, a shrubby mass
on the ground, or well used over a bank:tiny yellow flowers
along the edges of the so-called leaves give a sprightliness.

RUSSELIA equisetiformis, "Coralblow or Fountain-plant"
a low, semi-herbaceous, shrubby thing with squarish and
creased, sedge-like stems that reach out at a flat angle
to fabricate a rolling, irregular structure, more or less
indented or depressed at the top:bright red, tubular flowers,
flaring at the mouth, develop pretty much over the year, heavily
spring and summer....this with uniform moisture, otherwise more
intermittent:light, well drained soils in the sun or very slight
shade:masterplant for a very large basket, a tub, or blocked in
cement of a contemporary terrace....good for years of service
there, moved then into a deep planter for more:banks.

S

PALMETTO
SABAL---fan palms, low and apparently stemless or tall, tree-
like with stout, non-narrowing trunks. The fans are strongly
constructed to resist breakage in severe storms. They grow
in rich black soils or poor sandy ground, in the leached
sand of a Florida hammock, and on north into warm temperate
regions, but seldom seen in California. They require that an
attempt be made to keep up some fertility if the full beauty
of the fan be brought out and maintained.
   -bermudiana(blackburniana)"Bermuda P." the thick
stem to 40' in height and thickened at the middle, grown
in Florida, not unknown in California, but seldom seen.
   -minor(glabra)a dwarf palmetto, the stems buried,
creeping underground, the unarmed fans bluish, raised
2-3' high:good cover for reasonably fertile soils that
grade up in moisture content until near swampy condition
is reached for the most luxuriant growth, or grows
400

along the edges of swamps:may be transplanted as a bare
crown without benefit of leaf or root.
    -palmetto, "Cabbage P." an erect stem to 50' or more,
the most typical palm and the one most commonly found in
Florida and along the coast northerly, not grown in Calif-
ornia:hardy in 15 degrees of frost.

SAGINA subulata, "Pearlwort" perennial, with all parts
minute, a cover close to the ground, carpeting, a moss-mat
with fine but rough-cast, pin-pointed leaves:best in partial
shade and constant, if light moisture....not very persistent
in the south:may be used with flagging or makes a small snatch
of lawn under the right conditions:no mowing:pale evergreen.

SAGITTARIA---aquatic herbs, perennial with tuberous roots, the
leaf shaped like the head of an arrow or long and narrow in the
likeness of a lance head. They are strong-growing for ponds, but
require too much space and lack refinement and color to be desired
in a pool. They find their most appropriate place and best use in a
bog for Florida or a seepage for California.
    -graminea, the leaves nearly grassy, forming clumps to 2'
in height, a plant that is more in scale with normal operations
in the garden.        -lancifolia, growing to 6' high, repetition
of many vertical lines, the leaves narrow-lance-shaped to nar-
row-elliptic as a terminus:flowers white.        -montevidensis,
"Giant Arrowhead" growing 6' high and with more body, the
large white flower with a purple splotch at the base of
each petal:tender northerly in these regions.

SAINTPAULIA ionantha, "African-violet" a low, sappy perennial for pots indoors or a warm, cozy spot in the plant house
where there will be no drafts: soft hairy leaves are touched
with purple or remain green, the "violets" continuous or spor-
adic, according to warmth and the way of water....light better
filtered or indirect, with excessive heat or dryness undesir-
able:feeding is important, with special foods available for the
loose, sandy, leafy soil that they want:fragile and uncertain
for most people, but becoming more dependable year by year, in
more knowledge, definition and selection in the welter of var-
ieties:new plants may be kept coming along by means of the leaf
cuttings, side removals:are shallow-rooted and will reach to the
light and become one-sided....do not rotate, allow more of what
it wants. Basic is drainage,tepid watering, warmth, subdued
light and quiet, with no checks in growth or shock....challenge
to anyone, to get into the wallow of submerging varieties, blue,
purple, pink or white and unending combinations. This is a teem-
ing and rewarding field for the collector....and demanding.

### WILLOW
SALIX---lowland deciduous trees of interesting habit, with
some that are ornamental, but largely used for special purposes south. An airy grace marks all species. They are extremely rapid in growth and correspondingly short-lived,
to be used for temporary screens, quick shade or shelter
in exposed places for young plantings. A few of the more
commonly used species will be found in the nursery trade
while others, especially where large plantings are contemplated, will be obtained as branch or root cuttings and set
directly in place....moist time of the year. These trees are
curiously unconventional, gypsy-like, adapting to cold or dry
climates, luxuriant in humid countries.
    -babylonica, "Napoleon W." "Weeping W." growing to 35',
the head somewhat open-spreading, branches drooping and the
long, cord-like branchlets hanging vertically....sweeping the
ground when doing well:usually set in conjunction with water,
but satisfactory anywhere under average conditions of soil
and moisture.    --var. crispa, "Ringleaf W." with the typical but more refined long-hanging tresses, the much
narrower leaves curled tightly into rings:bizarre.
    -discolor, "Pussy W." shrub or small round-

401

headed tree for wet places that may become fairly dry late in
the season:silky catkins are treasured for cutting in the
spring:do not place stems in water as taken indoors...touch
lightly with crayon for any color that may be desired.
   -lasiolepis, "Arroyo W." native in the west and growing
to 35', usually less, of especially rapid growth and reliably
hardy.....dependable in cold, dry regions.

   SALPIGLOSSIS sinuata, "Painted Glory" hardy root-tap-
ping annual 18-24" with wide-funnel-shaped flowers that
are notable for a brocade of prominent veining, the
flower ranging in color through pink, rose, carmine,
purple, bluish and yellow....unique in the marbl-
ing and penciling....dusky brocatelle, with just
the suggestion of gold showing through the velvety
surface:sow indoors very early and in the ground
as soon as may be in spring, in deep, light soils
which may go fairly dry after growth:requires to be grown
well, without any stunting checks....help with trace and
other mineral elements to bring out the rich coloring and
strong-textured character....hurry seedlings along after
late planting to strike the heat of the season:best not to
use same ground successive years:irrigate, don't sprinkle.

                    SAGE
   SALVIA---herbaceous perennials with a will and with marked
tendencies toward wood, sometimes almost shrubs.  They are
late blooming with a remarkable range in pure coloring
for the border or kinds of bedding. This color may be
brilliant to excess or softly toned, but usually retains
its identity and remains well defined when mixed in the same
flower. Results are highly gratifying when grown in poor
ground, with only enough moisture to keep in shape and
moving along. But generously provisioned, they quickly recede from this very satisfactory state, to become just another flower out of place....rank-growing and weedy. They
are mostly hardy into warm temperate regions.
   -argentea, "Silver S." biennial, or sometimes holding over
in light soils that are not over-watered, growing 18-24" high,
usually less, with most of the silvery grey foliage at the
ground:may be used in the better garden soils, since the foliage is the chief attraction....yet color is heightened in a
dry soil:may be sheared back to lower leaves for bedding:very
likely to die out quickly in a heavy soil.
   -carduacea, "Thistle-sage" a weedy Californian, an
annual for dry, sandy soils only:the whorled, cobwebby,
thistle-like floral leaves have a fantastic quality, and
function with the pale lavender flowers in dry heat after
rains when the ground begins to parch:not in the garden.
   -clevelandi, bushy, with a dry, very brittle-wood base,
2-3' in height, sprawling to as much as 10' across, the foliage
dark and greyish and the flowers dark blue, rich coloring May-
August and very fragrant....retained after having dried out,
that of honey and sage, more pronounced after rain or overhead
sprinkling:used in seasoning, the leafage may be cut dry and included inconspicuously in a corsage for the odor:short-lived.
   -columbariae, "Chia" from the Southwest, a trim little annual 10-12" height, the leaves deeply cut and wrinkled, largely
at the base of the plant, the stems passing through the button
of blue flowers:seed is ground by those who know and a soft
drink results....or may be taken further:naturalize.
   -farinacea, "Mealycup S." semi-woody, perennial, with a
slim, bluish stem to 24", the top few inches set with white,
blue or purplish flowers late summer and fall:a border plant
with more flowers and those of better quality if grown dry,
especially during early season:the plant mealy over-all
and does satisfactorily in fertile soils.
   -greggi, "Autumn S." a bushy shrub 2-3' with luminous carmine-red flowers more or less over the year
under cultivation, especially brilliant July-October:
                    402

COMPENDIUM

native in the Southwest, a shrub for a dry spot in the gard-
en, shapely and permanent there, growing and surviving in
excessive drought but showing much dead wood.
-leucantha "Mexican Bushsage" makes a strong, spreading clump 24" in height and somewhat more across, woody at
the base, too weedy for the refined garden:violet-purple flowers August-October, with a thick white down of added floral
effect and value:cut to the ground in winter, divide or replace when it deteriorates:good color for little effort.
-officinalis, "Garden Sage" a compact, shrubby plant
less than 12" high, with pale greyish bark and aromatic
foliage....leafage variable to include markings in yellow,
gold, white rose or red, plain or crisped:still widely used
in domestic medicine and seasoning....gather the leaves as
the blue or white flowers appear, and afterwards shear.
-patens, "Gentian S." select as to form, but more particularly as to color, growing 18-24" in height with somewhat arrow-shaped leaves and large, richly colored blue
flowers:a garden plant wanting a slightly acid soil, fair
moisture and partial shade:choice.
-sessei, a great gangling shrubby plant of very quick development to 10-15', essentially a filler in the shrubbery due to
uncontrollable habit:brilliant orange-red flowers in irregular,
erect heads September-October or as early as July, carry far as
color....cut hard after bloom:a striking plant but without any
discipline....used in the border behind lower planting.
-splendens, "Scarlet S." an old plant in gardens, used as
an annual in bedding....a woody shrub 3-4' as grown on:brilliant
scarlet flowers enter their full show in July and carry steadily
into winter, nearly continuous far south:use to fill in between
early flowering plants, later to carry color alone, with white
or pale blue....intensity varies, so that anyone sensitive to
color will do well to find a subdued value.

SAMANEA saman, "Rain-tree" growing to 75', a spreading, umbrageous dome of yellowish green foliage, very rapid-growing:a
dirty tree, littering the greenish white flowers, the opening
pods in season and then the leaves:an immense and welcome spread
of light shade, however, in badly exposed places:will not
reach full proportions in California unless in a deep soil
where it can tap and have available constant moisture.

ELDERBERRY
SAMBUCUS---large deciduous shrubs done in pithy sticks
and pale greens, coarsely formed, usually dilapidated and
without definition, good for mass but not for outline unless
kept up with the shears. They are better used in the distance
in native or cover plantings where the gross character is not
so obvious and where their desirable qualities may still be
available, if diluted. They will want a deep soil.
-caerulea(glauca)"Blue E." of tree-like proportions
in lowland soils with a water-table within reach, producing great panicled masses of yellowish flowers June-July
followed by white-bloomed, blue-black berries which by
custom go to the birds....humans next, for the wine
they make.   --var. neo-mexicana, a greyish green,
and a little short on leafage as a whole, but standing
up under dry heat:native in the Southwest.   --var.
velutina, with hairy leaves comes from Southern California.
A form  -simpsoni, "The Sauco" from Florida and along the Gulf
Coast, is lower as to size and more shrubby, to be used east and
far south into the tropics:white flowers and black berries.

SANGUISORBA minor,"Burnet" a culinary herb, perennial
some 18-24" with notably handsome oval leaflets, nicely and precisely notched all around the edges;used to
impart a cucumber flavor to salads, taken fresh and at height
of growth. This little plant is very attractive and quite
distinctive for the foliage and the unusual texture it
brings to a dry spot in the garden or border.
403

BOWSTRING HEMP

SANSEVIERIA---stiff, harsh-leaved plants that may be
classed with the succulents actually, being bulbous, with
liliaceous flowers in slender, erect and loose heads. They
are grown, however, for the durable, very distinct foliage
character and almost entirely in containers, planters for
the house, porch or patio and in pots to carry about for
difficult areas. Some shade is desirable but not necessary
in a coolish climate and the soil should be built for good
body, but just ordinary fertility....feed with a liquid as
indicated. Otherwise they demand little attention.
     -parva, the 12-15" leaves narrow, recurved, channeled,
with a narrowly and sharply pointed tip:flowers freely, pale
pink or orchid and chartreuse to a dark green, banded scape,
July or November, depending, evidently on feeding....may break
in January, warm winters:stoloniferous growths reach out to
carry a new plant to fresh ground or hang it from a basket
where it grows upright to bloom over the side. This will repeat until several years growth will be suspended in line....a
plant of many cascading stems in time.
     -zeylanica, "Snakeplant" the rigid-erect, narrow sword-like
leaves have transverse grey or whitish markings:pots for a sharply
delineated line, or may be grown in the ground for the same purpose on a small scale....a little shade good; cooks in full sun.

SANTOLINA chamaecyparissus, "Lavender-cotton" low, expanding, semi-woody, a plant with dense grey foliage of a fine,
pleasing texture and buttony, dull gold flowers on very long
stems June-July:grows 15-20" in height and will spread out
much more, fitting nicely to a slope, or shears up into the
straight lines of a hedge in the garden....for awhile:rugged
in cold and drought and poor soils; losing grace in old age,
the nicely molded form breaking away to show the dead, chalky
parts of the interior; parts dying out and wanting the shears
to keep presentable:flower heads will be removed after bloom,
when the entire plant may be gone over as a matter of rejuv-
enation....best accepted as short-lived and not carried too
long in point of time. The species, -virens, is similar, but
a bright green, not so commonly found.

SANVITALIA procumbens, trailing annual 6" in height generally and for summer primarily, but lasting and blooming
late into autumn:little sunflowers are rich in color and
having a contrasting dark purple disc:light sandy soils in
the sun and as hot a spot as can be found:rock garden.

SAPINDUS saponaria, "Soapberry" a slow-growing tree 30',
erect, dense, round-headed, with rough greyish bark, to be
grown in poor, dryish or rocky soils:the white flowers in a
full head....not as important as the shining, orange to brown
berries:tender in frost, but survives alkali ground, and other
uses are practical in the very nature of the tree....not one
for beauty.

SAPIUM sebiferum, "Tallow-tree" for Florida and the Gulf
Coast in a moist soil, much dwarfed in California, more so in
the typical Southwest climate and scarcely worth growing:poplar
leaves change through the season from a light shining green to
many tones of orange to red as they age:grows to 40 ', a handsome spreading specimen, the trunk dividing, usually into
several slender branchings that are not symmetrical:nearly
evergreen, formalized for streets, standing in somewhat dryish
ground:durable whitish berries are lasting indoors.

SARCOCOCCA hookeriana, formless shrubs for the foliage
under rather special conditions related to heat or sour
soils in the shade, of general utility for other trying
places so long as the moisture is available and sun not
too direct in heat:grows 3-5' with neat stems set precisely to dark leaves that are good for heavy wear:
404

flowering is inconspicuous, so that it will be difficult to
place the special winter fragrance....the blue berries that will
carry into summer are of more consequence. This is a plant of
solid beauty for a difficult place.   --var. humilis, the foliage
lighter and of a yellowish cast, the leaves long and narrow:will
spread out wide as a ground cover by means of slowly running roots
that pretty well occupy the soil:pinch out the stem tips to hasten
progress:a shrub 2-3' when held in. These plants are both subject
to scale and suffer in high heat and reflected sun.

   SASA---small, shrubby, running bamboos that may be used in the
garden for the usually fine-textured foliage and grass-like
sheaths which help with the execution of an effect. They are tenacious, persistent, quite hardy in frost and probably less littering than other, larger kinds under cultivation. They are good
feeders, size not-with-standing, and should not be transplanted
late in the year. Keep them in hand.
   -disticha(Pleioblastus)"Fernleaf Bamboo" delicate structure but strong growth 2-3' or sometimes more, responding to a
very rich soil that has moisture, a good garden subject with
dark slender stems that are feathered to the ground....good
hedge either clipped or casually headed in:choice and very
much refined for a bamboo.
   -humilis, growing 3-4' and a little weedy, even for the
company it keeps, but reasonably easy to keep within bounds,
the pale green leaves nearly an inch wide and to 6" in
length:grow in a tub or box for containment.
   -palmata, with large, spreading, finger-like leaves,
three and twelve inches,from a purple petiole:unexpectedly
neat and contained....very effective, unusually hardy in considerable frost:growing 4-6' in slender height, a plant for
a prominent place on terrace or in a patio.
   -pygmaea, the terrible fingerling, small fry, only
inches high to a foot....but potent, inextinguishable, re-
lentless in taking over ground, resolute in its occupation:
use as a cover where competition is violent and the end a
complete subjugation. This little runagate walker must be
kept headed in desired direction or firmly confined.

### SAVORY
   SATUREJA---aromatic herbs or neat little shrubs for the
border, rock and kitchen gardens. They are best grown in
the lighter soils that are rich and mellow for thrift. Of
further importance, and frequently over-looked, is drainage,
both above and below ground in the matter of surface get-away
and in the soil itself for thorough aeration.
   -hortensis, "Summer S." slender annual 10-15" for purely
culinary purposes, although the white, pink or purplish flowers
of summer may be mentioned and do make a point in selection and
placement:green parts are used in seasoning meats and dressings
and should be taken for drying as the plant comes into flower:
sow seed in the spring in a warm sunny spot.
   -intricata, perennial, or slightly woody at the base, even
shrubby as it builds up:a densely tufted little plant with closely packed, dark tiny leaves appressed against the stems that
twist, and curl, and turn  back on themselves:white flowers
are considerable, very pure and effective against a dark
background, the general area of September:rock garden in the
sun or a cover to 3" in height....delightful roughened texture.
   -montana, "Winter S." a compact sub-shrub 6-12" with the
leaves closely set, aromatic, used in cookery....in the garden
or with rock for the form and the pale blue to purple spikes
of flowers:low hedges from seed....germinates best in fall.

   SAXIFRAGA sarmentosa, "Strawberry-geranium" ground cover for cool places in shade, spreading by reddish runners
in right combination of light, shadow and moisture:grey
green, round leaves are marked with white, red beneath:
tiny white or pink flowers, high in lacy heads:takes
total shade, burns in full sun:lath-house, baskets.

*Sarcococca humilis*

*Satureja intricata*

*sasa pygmaea*

*Saxifraga sarmentosa*

### SCABIOUS

SCABIOSA---flower garden annuals and perennials or used in the
border as fillers. They prefer a light sandy soil in the sun, but
tolerate heavier ground if drained. They will appreciate some
lime worked in from time to time. All are desirable for cutting,
with some of them among the best material from the garden for
this purpose. A long season of bloom, together with continuing hybridization are points to note.

-atropurpurea, "Sweet S." common annual in many forms
and colors from white to crimson and purple and from a low
dwarf to as much as 24", erect-growing or sprawling proper-
ly:seed sown from November until June will give flowers
from April through October.

-caucasica, "Mourning Bride" status variable, perennial
or biennial and probably best used as an annual in warm climates, certainly in places of excessive heat....blooms first
year from seed, with a long season:foliage greyish, sometimes
nearly white, but with a silvery cast and not mealy:flattish
heads of lilac, lavender or blue flowers on long slender stems
keep coming June-October, frequently until December....and
very profusely:many hybrids with marvelously delicate tintings, fully apparent and appreciated only in the sun.

-columbaria, "Pincushion Flower" more definitely perennial than above, with broader leaves and the head not nearly as flat, the flower with more blue to go with the clearer green of the foliage:fairly dependable for bloom in the
winter. Where a choice may be made, this will be used in
the border for the more correct form and full body, while
the other will be grown primarily for the flowers and
very likely with the cutflowers.

-graminifolia, typical perennial that holds long in
the south, the silvery, low-matted leaves bedding down the
long slender stems of pale blue flowers July-August:a smaller
plant that is somewhat drouth resistant, but not very freely
flowering....in character and scale for the rock garden.

SCHINUS---dependable trees for heat and dryness in the extreme,
growing and serving under many other adverse circumstances,in
fact, almost any visitation an arid climate has to inflict.
There are many desirable qualities for general planting, but
these trees must be selected for special and definite purposes and with certain limitations always held in mind.
There is a great deal of litter and the root system ranges
far and wide in its own interest alone. The soil beneath
becomes highly acid from tannic substances which exude and
any object there-under likewise takes a plastering.

-dependens, shrubby and wide-spreading, with all
the pepper-tree characteristics, or a crooked-drooping
little tree 15' with a short trunk, the branchlets loosely hanging, or the whole plant prostrate, fitting to any
large bank with a little help....or with none:flowers are
yellow and the parchment-like berries dark purple:very rare.

-molle, "Pepper-tree" an open, full-rounded top at 50'
with wide-spreading, thick and gnarled limbs from a short knotty
trunk:pendent branches plentifully supplied with the much refined, light green leaves....sometimes trailing to the ground:the
generous clusters of rose-colored, rattling berries are
taken indoors:utterly rugged and hardy, thriving on neglect, littering interminably and not for a lawn:subject to
scale and prime source for further infestation:best trees
in deep soils, ideal for shade there where the earth is
hard-packed from trampling:Tucson termination easterly.

-terebinthifolius, "Brazilian P."smaller, with less
grace, but picturesque with crooked, winding stems, never
quite decided where to go:branches erect-spreading from a
short trunk, 25' over-all, larger and darker leaves and
larger and more deeply colored berries for Christmas:may
be grown throughout these regions, wanting and taking more
moisture, less subject to spot droughts and so, less
littering:handsome trees to be seen in Florida.

SCHIZANTHUS wisetonensis, "Butterfly Flower" "Fringe Flower"
an annual, 18-24" in rounding height, bearing lightly the soft-
tinted, delicately formed flowers, playthings of the air, white
or pink and carmine suffused with yellow any time April-October:
probably best used in pots, urns or baskets or as a filler in the
planter, moved always with a good ball of earth, pinching out top
from time to time and probably staked at the last if well grown:the
scant foliage suggests its use in the garden with other plants of good
leafage and a fuller flowering results from crowded roots:wants the
sun and a soil that is heavy enough to retain moisture that must
be supplied:sow in fall or early spring and bring along in
pots is best procedure or sow in the ground in spring, or
for extra desirable strains and due to brittle character of
the stems, it may be found desirable to go to the nursery for
setting-out stock:moist air and takes low temperatures.

SCHIZOCENTRON elegans, a ground cover of some elegance, a
delicate mat on the flat or trailing tentatively, probing,
groping for just the right combination of light and shade and
moisture....too often fumbling, always on probation....a pot
or basket that can be moved about experimentally before it
is set permanently:green foliage modified slightly with red, a
low rest in summer for the single, rosy-purple to magenta flow-
ers:moist, well drained soils that are high in humus, with shade
as well as a certain light, seem to indicate principal wants:will
benefit in close proximity of rock for equalized temperature,but
no high heat:spreads widely when well situated....floor of lath-house.

SCHIZOPETALON walkeri, an annual, the seed sown in the spring and
blooming by mid-summer:stems erect to 12" carrying white, fringed
flowers that are noticeably fragrant in the evening:rock garden
or pots or only touching the border, near a seat or other spot
where it may assert its special claim for attention and dis-
charge its singular service to a moon-lit evening.

SCHIZOSTYLIS coccinea, "Crimson-flag" of slender stems
and narrow, iris-like leaves, the flowers large, bright,
exceptionally clear in color, pink to crimson October-
November or later:grows 18-24" in height, vigorous in a
moist, light soil with drainage, or survives in a rather
wet spot of some fertility in the sun....spreads to make a
considerable patch....rhizome never allowed to dry out completely whether in ground, in storage or potted....when it may
be taken indoors for winter flowering:an attractive cutflower in
a vase, invasive in the garden when happiest.

SCHREBERA swietenioides, a neat tree 40', quite dark as
to foliage which is very substantial, tough in the wind
and to feel, the tree slender erect, fairly dense and
round of top:thrives under considerable wind and the infiltration of salt, making a typical growth:streets, windbreaks.

SQUILL

SCILLA---bulbous plants of spectacular and rather pure color
for casual uses; of unusual ease in culture, tucked away, as they
should be, beneath or out in front of shrubs or against a rock
where they can have either heat or the cool side and not be lost.
They will last for years when they find the right spot, blooming
in the spring and along the early edge of summer. Set bulbs in
the fall of the year in fertile, well drained ground and allow
good time after bloom for the curing leaves and the drying out
of the bulbs for as much rest as they will take. They cut.
        -hispanica, "Spanish Bluebell" a small bulb, but throwing
a stout stem 10-15", bearing bell-shaped flowers in lilac, pink
or blue January-April:the head is irregularly formed and the
flowers few but welcome:rock garden or beneath deciduous shrubs.
        -hyacinthoides, "Hyacinth S." the purple to blue flowers of
exquisite daintiness in an open head on 2-3' stems from a well
fed bulb April-May:an absolute necessity that the bulb be rested
dry over summer....even to digging with adherring soil and baking

407

*Schizocentron*

*Schizostylis*

*Scindapsis*

*Scilla hyacinthoides*

out in the sun:well used in a pot for sure control of rest.
•    -peruviana, "Jacinth" the bulb much larger than any
of above, with white, lilac or purple, but mostly blue
flowers in heads that are flattened into a cone-like figure
to 8" across, the hundreds of flowers very small, in May, and
likely to bloom alternate years:evergreen, but makes a quick
exchange of foliage in June, the disheveled mass of leaves
always dominant, effective in a way:may be taken indoors
in a pot or used in the border:hardy into warm temperate
regions.

SCINDAPSIS(Pothos)aureus, "Ivy-arum" for decoration indoors on
a totem-pole, or high climbing on trunks of trees far south:large
to very large leaves are simple and usually variegated, size depending on culture, degree of sun and cold the plant must endure;
half sun to deep shade is desirable:a rare flower is like calla.

SCIRPUS cernuus, "Ornamental-sedge"  a grassy plant 10-15' high,
the foliage mass when growing lush, more or less broken, reclining to form a desultory mat, turf-like:use at the edge of a
pool in moist soil, in a pot plunged in shallow water or set
on the flat coping, the erect hair-lines of the foliage breaking and drooping gracefully to meet their reflection on the
plane of the water....should not be allowed to dry out.

SECURIDACA diversifolia, "Easter Flower" a climbing shrub
of considerable merit and needless rarity, having substantial
medium green leafage and narrow, racemed clusters of pink to
lavender and purple flowers January-March:wants to be grown in
coolness and good moisture and with some guidance....makes a
bushy, tumbling mass with consistent pinching out of terminal
growths or under the little drouth it will take or will climb
high for light, or just to be climbing.

STONECROP
SEDUM---perennial herbs that are invariably succulent in
character, rarely sub-shrubby, but frequently woody at the base
with leaves that are beady or flattened and sappy or somewhat
leathery and hard. They are easy to grow, wanting a light and
sandy soil with no excessive moisture....but doing a job almost anywhere. While they thrive best in a cool, often shaded
spot, they are, as a class, of value for considerable heat and dryness in the sun and in ground of scant fertility that would support little else. They are generally evergreen, used mainly as
ground covers or sealing in rock or flag-stone; to fill out
the cup of a pot or tub; in a basket or small planter on
occasion. They have special qualities of advantage at the
seashore where gardening is attempted and survive varying
degrees of salt up to and including the spray line.
    -adolphi, a little bush for the rock garden, erect and
low-woody-branched, the upper portions very succulent with
leaves that are large comparatively, thick and fleshy:light
golden yellow through winter, bronzy under summer sun....a white
blooming in the spring:must have drainage to survive.
    -album, mat-forming 3-5' through, with closely set, bright
green, beady leaves all year and a good showing of white bloom
for a month mid-summer:vigorous in poor ground, but becoming less
lush as it deteriorates, down to less than an inch of tight-textured mat to the earth:has many varieties, based on color in the
leafage, white through yellow and pink to purple.   --var. brevifolium, carpeting, fitting a white-mealy, finely textured mat to the
ground, literally covered in spring with white to pinkish flowers:
drainage and a little moisture gives a tight-stretching antimacassar
to micro-topography....closer still in a poor soil:cooks in heat.
    -altissimum, "Love-entangle" prostrate, with somewhat woody stems
that ascend at the tips, which will be succulent....end sections drop
off to start new plants:greenish yellow flowers and slightly bluish
foliage that becomes reddish in heat....stands in moderate heat.
    -dasyphyllum, growing in low tufts, eventually an undulating
carpet, a nap of less than 2" for better ground:color is clearly

408

Scilla
peruviana

Scirpus
cernuus

Securidaca
diversifolia

Sedum
adolph

Sedum
brevifolium

and permanently a soft blue which sets off the white flowers in
a striking, very simple and effective plan:chink in rock.

-guatemalense, "Christmas-cheer" very succulent, spreading, the bright green, turgid, pickle-shaped leaves tipped with
a lurid red in winter suns, furnishing yellow flowers for summer:
the rock garden or parterre bedding.

-hispanicum, difuse, widely spreading to make a low matting
of greyish green touched with mauve:pinkish white flowers are
carried on slender red stems:carpeting, rock work, flagging.

-lineare, trailing, neatly built, the leaves elongated
and flattened, the flowers greenish or tinged with pink in
the shade....smelling faintly of rose water.  --var. variegatum, the more commonly seen and more erect, the narrowed
leaves lined with white or yellow:boxes or baskets.

-pachyphyllum, for bedding, quite succulent, the little
pickles short, pale green, the tips only, touched with pink
or rose:pale yellow flowers in summer, sometimes in winter.

-prealtum, practically a shrub, bushy, growing 2-3' high,
the newer growth and foliage succulent:long, flattened, shining and pale green leaves build rather good body for the very
bright yellow flowers June-July:garden or border for color.

-sieboldi, decumbent, with short stems of flat, wavy-
tipped bluish leaves in wide threes and daphne-like heads of
pink flowers late summer or autumn:choice pot plant in a bit
of shade:deciduous.

-spurium, trailing, the naked stems reddish, rooting at
the joints, the wedge-shaped leaves few and partaking of the
red coloring under neglect or in drought....flowers June-
September in baskets, crevices in rock work.

-stahli, another trailing form, the branched, pinkish
stems strung with roundish, bead-like dull red or brownish
leaves....the color more pronounced in the sun:yellow
flowers are raised above the reclining mat summer and
autumn:pots, boxes,  or grown in the rock garden.

-treleasei, a pale bedding succulent with a vigorous
growth of light green, long-beady leaves faintly washed at
the tips with pink:wants shade or a north exposure.

SELAGINELLA---flowerless herbs, fern-like plants with
feathery or mossy leaves, very select bits, oddments left
over from another age for planting in moisture and shade. They
are grown in such places supplementary to other growth, and for
the attractive, sometimes highly colored fronds, used by species as cover in beds, small planters or in pots to set there,
sometimes for table decoration. These are tropical things, but
related to and similar in kind to the club moss of the north.

-brauni, the stems erect 15-18" the foliage not dense, the
small leaves widely spaced and straw-colored, running into
bronzy shades.

-denticulata, carpeting in deep shade, used to fill
out over the soil in a tub or box:scale-like leaves are
crowded, rope-like, surrounding thin stems:close-matting.

-uncinata, a taller plant with running root-stems, the
raised, thin, blue-green leaves variable, but with added
splendor in color, a kind of "peacock" irridescence.

SEMPERVIVUM tectorum, "Houseleek" lowly rosettes of sharp-
pointed succulent leaves. with a hard, unfeeling hide, stemless,but throwing a stalk of showy, clustered flowers:grows
in neat, starry clumps of high decorative value, comfortable with
plain fare, efficient in development, serviceable in hot dry soils
but flowering better in good air humidity:primary uses include the
old-new idea of carpet bedding or open block cover in contemporary
work; ideal for a high crevice and hanging masses of truly
marvelous complications of delicate coloring....jade, shell
pinks, amethyst, rose-quartz, the greens that come with oxi-
dized copper and bronzy browns....a multiplicity of hybrids that usually work back to the above species.  Two
regional forms to use in the south are    -atlanticum,from
Morocco, with pale green rosettes and red flowers for

wide patches in dry ground and    -calcareum, from southern
Europe, with variations of green in the 2" rosette, dusty
over-all, the tip of the leaf a reddish brown, piling up in
broad mounds:flowers light red or pinkish, touched with some
shade of green....color in both leaf and flower coming out
stronger in the sun.

### GROUNDSEL

SENECIO---a widely dissimilar group of plants that may be
herbaceous or shrubby or even succulent in character or in
some combination of same. A tendency to segregate the succulent
types in other genera is marked. In common they bear yellow flowers of more or less importance....usually less. Generally, they
are persistent growers and strong, profusely blooming and somewhat resistant to drouth in poor soils. They will want full sun
and some moisture to help along dry seasons and with a dressing up of the disorderliness left by the flowering....cut the
straggle back hard in the fall.

-cineraria, a "Dusty Miller" and well formed plant,
bushy 2-3' or less with white-dusted leaves and yellow-heads
of flowers at any time, but mostly in the summer:may be used
in bedding, with the crowns pinched out to compact for foliage or grown in the border in way of a perennial and allowed
to flower:strong-growing, satisfactory under a wide range of
conditions, an old plant in gardens.

-confusus, "Glow-vine" an untidy plant of great unruli-
ness, but grown for the brilliant coloring, orange and red
to go with the heavy meaty leaves:neither shrubby nor vining,
it merely flops around and over and will be trained as either,
but with little success:full sun and heat, with moisture early
season, dryness later to accent color, and a sterile soil to
help hold into late fall or winter:limestone....practically
everblooming in a warm enough exposure.

-mikanioides, "German-ivy" a perennial with succulent
leanings, the twining, twisting runners carrying bright green
ivy-like leaves and cone-like heads of light yellow flowers
which tend quickly to break away from form....early winter:
a foliage plant for banks or slopes of some extent; to base
a plant box or to be used in rather poor ground where it will
survive pretty rough treatment....can be a nuisance in moist,
rich soils, easily kept under control by pinching in or pulling
out herbage:re-roots in high glee and effectiveness.

-petasitis, "Velvet G." an erect woody perennial, practically a shrub, used as such south:makes a considerable mass of stems
that are obscured by the large, downy, rumpled leaves, growing
6-8' in moist, fertile soils:showy purple flower buds are out
in large heads by late winter, long before they open to the
bright display of golden yellow flowers in the spring:while
impatient of a very dry soil, abundant moisture will force a
growth out of scale for the average garden:takes any amount
of heat with moisture to support.

SEQUOIADENDRON giganteum, "California Bigtree" probably the
most massive of the trees, closely related to redwood, but the
more successfully grown  in the south in heat, and in
deep soils only, where it develops very slowly as a
close, comparatively broad pyramid at first, a great
column later, the foliage massed tight about the immense
trunk:not good east, seen only occasionally in Southern
California, but the one to use there.

SERENOA repens, "Scrub-palmetto" prostrate and slowly creeping, the thick and branching stems almost stoloniferous, but normally obscured by the low mass of the foliage....great saw-toothed masses that become impenatrable
in time:a fan-palm for cover primarily in wet ground,
but this is not invariable and one finds these palms
in low ground that dries out periodically. This a
popular plant used in decoration, the fans used
or crowns set in water:native east and south.

410

Senecio
petasitis

Senecio
confusus

senecio
repens

Senecio
mikanioides

Serenoa

# COMPENDIUM

SERISSA foetida, an erect shrub 18-24" and rounding, but
open to light for the tiny white flowers which stud the dull
green body of the plant like summer stars, never profusely,
but effectively:forms with the leaf edged in white or yellow are more sprightly in appearance and should be given
preference when obtainable:shallow rooting for erosion
control in the garden or near landscape:deciduous.

SETARIA palmifolia, "Palm-grass" perennial, growing
4-6' in height, a clump grass for spotting the border or
grown in a tub for a certain livliness for a stagnant sit-
uation:holds the juvenile palm leaf indefinitely to show
against a plain surface, as from a planter:rare.

SEVERINIA buxifolia, "Box-orange" a low spiny shrub with
short, sharply pointed thorns among the dark, box-like leaves:
dwarf and spreading in habit, it almost reclines at times, as
used free in the shrubbery....more often seen as a boxed hedge
where it will require minimum shearing:has small white flowers,
not too conspicuous but sweetly scented, followed by black,
cherry-like berries:hardy into warm temperate regions.

SIDALCEA malvaeflora, "Checkerbloom" an erect, semi-woody perennial 2' for the rear of a dry border or grown with shrubs,used
with the wild flowers most appropriately, native in California:
large, satiny pink to purple flowers overflow spring into summer,
the flowering of longer duration in a light warm soil with scant
moisture late season....the plant itself longer lived:variety
forms will be found for the garden.

SIDERITIS(Leucophai)candicans, subshrubby, 12-18" with thick,
rounded leaves soft with a white felt, the greenish basic of
the structure showing through, but faintly:edges of this leaf
are scalloped or marked in a stitch-like manner....a plant
to observe and to touch for creature comfort:use in the
house or on a terrace in the sun:pots or boxes in some dryness, or at least with very sharp drainage and do not
water from over-head. This plant is rare and quite select
and will be found more commonly in the florist trade, or
seed may be planted in early spring while cuttings taken in
late summer and rooted, may be carried over.

SILENE laciniata, "Indian-pink" perennial, erect 2-3' or partially sprawling, with nicely fringed flowers in summer, pink to
purple or bright carmine:difficult to establish but of no trouble in
growing afterwards....start with well ripened seed, in sun and heat
and not too much water, even in germination:native in California and
will be grown dryish in the border, in the rock garden, probably more
at home with the wildflowers. The species  -schafta, persists with
rock far south in as much as half shade, while the rare
annual,  -noctiflora, is fragrant by night.

SIMARUBA amara, "Paradise-tree" rare and beautiful, a
tall and slender tree that will be sought out in the far
south as a substitute for,and much more select tree than
ailanthus or tree of heaven:evergreen, this, the tough leaflets dark and glossy, paler beneath, the bright yellow of
the flowers intermingling, a modifying cast or livery, but
telling as color:branching is open to display this blending
and to throw a light shade:thrives under secondary exposure to
the wind and salt near the sea.

SIMMONDSIA californica, "Brushnut" a native shrub, growing
naturally as a low and very dense mound of some regularity when
in the sun and in heat or exposure, less so on a north slope
in coolness or in rich soils....sized there at 4-8':should
make a good clipped hedge in dry ground....started from the
nuts in place....leaf roundish, elongated, leathery and dark
grey. The meat of the nut has a filbert flavor, bitter until with time to cure, the shell thin and easily hulled.

411

SINOCALAMUS(Dendrocalamus)oldhami, "Giant Bamboo" a magnificent growth that is suitable for a large windbreak or tall
dense screen of precise, aggregate line:a clump form, with
straight and very slender but sturdy stems 25-30', sometimes
more, exacting toll of the soil to the extreme detriment of
nearby planting....and to exclusion of the weaker ones. A similar species, -beechyanus, has a more open, spreading top that
is notably active, the stems twisting, squirming in the wind,
rolling to the punch of a gale.

SIPHONOSMANTHUS delavayi, a finely textured, twiggy shrub
3-5', the small white flowers of March-May narrow-tubular and
very fragrant:foliage off-green toward yellow, a fairly dense
back of small, rounded, leathery leaves for flower and scant crop
of bluish-black berries:could be a small general purpose shrub if
entirely understood....sun or shade, partial or rather deep and
with other conditions at least favorable as generally understood:
will not take green manures and is at best.....temperamental, a
term that may be used, looking at a subject through a glass
darkly and finding no complete answer.

## RUSHLILY
SISYRINCHIUM---grassy perennials with strong fibrous roots and
small flowers of satiny sheen, grown in the border or rock
garden in damp soils, or reaching deeply for moisture in dryness. They flourish in medium weight, rather fertile ground
and must have moisture during the growth period. All may be
naturalized in their respective regions, some, however, more
suitable for the garden as will be brought out below. They
will flower properly only in the sun.
    -bellum, "Blue-eyed-grass" slender growth to 12", little
standing tufts of iris-like leaves and deep blue flowers
with a golden eye held to 18" in good ground and in wet
years....coming up with the California rains, disappearing
as heat develops, retiring then into the somewhat tuberous
root system:essentially a wild plant that may be taken into
the garden successfully only with proper alternation of
moisture and dryness.
    -bermudiana, a taller plant that may be known as "Golden-
eyed-grass, the flattened, leaf-like stems to 18" carrying the
disappointingly small flowers....lavender with a yellow center
or full yellow over-all:growing anywhere in the garden, to be
naturalized in Florida and along the Gulf coast.
    -californicum, growing 6-10" in height, the bright yellow
flowers in the likeness of tiny iris, the petals lined with
brown:may be used throughout these regions and into warm temperate regions, doing best with continual moisture, the flowering cut off sharply in drouth:mass in forepart of the border.
    -macouni, low clumps 6" or less that spread, each to its
neighbor so that an attractive mat develops in the garden or
more particularly with rock:short stems of flattened and up-
facing dark purple flowers May-July, a sheet of color:choice
    -striatum, a border plant, strong-growing and quick to
develop a good neat body of 12-15", iris-like narrowing
leaves to an acute point:the rigid-erect flower stalk 2-3'
with pale yellow, short-stemmed flowers May-July....cut, with
the appressed, flattened leaves are outstanding for arrange-
ments:reseeds discreetly and not of much color intensity in
the garden:two-year old plants may best be discarded in
favor of last years seedlings that have been allowed.

## CHALICE VINE
SOLANDRA---coarse, high-climbing vines that make a great
deal of soft wood, so that strong support is required in
maturity to carry the load, a roof or other well-built
structure. The immense, solitary, white, yellow or
gold flowers are spectacular against the large,
shining, bright green leaves, normally
September-May in near tropical places
but modified in California to read

412

Siphon-
osmanth
u

Sisyrinchium
betmudiana

Sisyrinchium
striatum

Sisyrinchium bellum

fall and spring or September-November and March-May, due to cold
and heat, in season. Frost will perform like service in Florida.
A poor soil will bring on better flowering and tends to hold the
fabulous growth in check. In pruning, cut back laterals to stubs,
which will mass up the foliage and develop flowering wood. Do not
force growth ever, and allow these plants to go dryish over late
summer if possible, or any time the plant seems to want rest or
even hesitates....ripe wood the answer for flowers. They are tender, want warmth and sun for satisfaction, both plant and planter.
    -grandiflora, very high-climbing, as much as 40', the frag-
rant white or creamy flowers open-trumpet-shaped and as long as
10", the leaf smooth and shining.... a large plant.
    -guttata, "Cup of Gold" climbing to 20' or more, the
great, wide-cup-shaped flowers a dull, golden yellow, deepening as they fail, the four broad purple bars within becoming more pronounced. This is completely out of scale with
a small house or detail of any refinement.
    -longiflora, a smaller plant, leaf and flower, less
vine-like, a standing shrub under control and support,
as of a building or other bolstering shrubs:the 2"
flower is long-narrow-tubular to 12" in length from
a purplish bud, creamy white September-November and
on into winters of low temperatures:use in a planter
or as a large espalier.

## NIGHTSHADE
  SOLANUM---an important group of free-flowering
plants that are widely used in these regions, making
rank herbage, mostly vining, some few in the definition and nature of a shrub or even small trees, with
others piling up on themselves to serve as shrubs.
Most are tropical in origin, very tender under frost,
dropping leaves quickly in cold weather, suffering in any
wind. They are not very substantial plants in the sense
of form and body and dependability for a part in the primary or structural scheme and will be used with a kind of
expediency in mind. They will be found at their best in a
light, moist soil of some fertility and in the sun for the best
flowering. Much wood may be cut out in the interest of vitality
and longevity....and color.
    -giganteum, "African-holly" a shrub, heavily armed with short
broad prickles that are little more than a bluff, the plant erect
to 15' in rich soils, usually less, the leaf very long and white
beneath:lilac or blue flowers are early enough to bring the red
fruits into color by september....held erect in broad, rigid heads.
    -jasminoides, "White Potato-vine" a half-deciduous climber to
15' with neither the foliage nor the flowers of outstanding significance, but commonly found in use:flowers in spring will be
white, or with an uncertain bluish tinge; not for color, but
enough to impair the white....get plants in flower to be
sure of purity....handsome enough then.
    -laurifolium, straggling, a slender shrub 6-8' high,
having light greyish foliage of substance and quite handsome flowers, a clear dark purple over summer, the surrounding parts with a mealy texture that serves as good protection in salt winds....but hopelessly suckering over a wide
area....waste places or the roots boxed in.
    -montanum, for contrasting masses of pale, textured fol-
iage in the modern concept, shrubby and spreading in habit
5-6' across and as high....must be pruned regularly to have
in good shape and vigor....very rapid growth:full sun for
the pre-chalk-white branches, mealy-white flowers and the
strange white to pale green, spined leaves which set this up
as a fit subject for pot and tub:keep this moving, but at any
time under forced draft it breaks down....short-lived:keep
young plants coming along from seed.
    -muricatum, "Pepino" a vining shrub 3-5', requir-
ing support for the soft-woody matrix of stems:the
bright blue flowers are continuous as are the hard-
shelled fruits which are round or flattish, yellow

Solandra
longiflora

Solandra
guttata

Solanum
wendlandi

Solanum xanti

413

streaked or splashed with violet-purple. They
are juicy to eat, slightly acid and fragrant, a
strange flavor between banana and rhubarb, a help.
The fruit is prime on the plant for a considerable period
and is best harvested early , rather than late.
    -pseudo-capsicum, "Jerusalem-cherry" a shrubby plant to
a single stem normally, practically herbaceous, certainly so
under frost; growing 12-18" high in the garden, less in pots
as they are taken indoors:large, orange-red fruits begin to
color by midsummer and are in full display for Christmas:
tips should be pinched out during growth, starting early,
a compact plant resulting....will need replacement the
second or third year....have young plants coming along.
    -rantonneti, "Blue Potato-vine" a vining shrub as
ordinarily used, with a fairly dense foliage and quantities of blue to purplish flowers more or less throughout
the year in warmth, greatest during summer:leaves are lost
easily in any sudden check such as drought or disease or in
high wind and in particular does it falter in a drafty spot
or where a surplus of water fails to move on:of merit in the
right environment; less than ordinary otherwise:espalier.
    -seaforthianum, "Tomatillo" slender, rather weak-
growing plant with sprawling stems 3-5', or vining to
as much as 10' far south out of frost....does in some
shade:blooms very early in life, even with the leader
only 12-15", the beautiful, clear lavender flowers in
large loose heads....red berries follow:tips tend to die
back in cold weather, entire plant in frost:pots.
    -warscewiczi, coarse, thorny shrub or an umbrag-
eous tree 15-20', the mammoth leaves dull green, rather deeply cut, rusty haired:whitish flowers turn out
yellowish berries which become brown and disintegrate
on the tree:striking plant of very rapid growth, desired
for the large leaves and not much else:suckering.
    -wendlandi, "Great Blue Potato-vine", high-climb-
ing, definitely and completely deciduous, having very
large trusses of pale blue flowers July-October, later
in warmth:slow-starting in the spring, but quickly catching up with a remarkable growth....sometimes measured in tens
of feet per year:used with other vines, the bare stems are concealed both in and out of season:wants full sun and feeds well
although not requiring a rich soil....better not on account
of tenderness:winter pruning, heading back and reducing
laterals to spurs, induces greater heads of bloom and tends
to thicken the foliage cover:no frost for this.
    -xanti, "California Nightshade" a native cover in the
west; shrubby, with clear blue flowers that are typical
and few:wants full sun and fairly good soil for a good
spread as ground covering:takes water or gets along
without....let up in late spring:seed.

    SOLENOMELUS chilensis, "Goldflower of Chile" hand-
some and personalized, a bulb that throws a comb-like head of
yellow flowers May-June, a one-sided raceme at once teasing,
irritating, fascinating....a novelty that opens only 2-3 hours
of late afternoon:sun, coolness, moisture where it will have difficulty policing itself of spent stalk and leaf which hold:rare.

    SOLLYA heterophylla, "Bluebell Creeper" vining low or twisting
on itself, shrub-like, a compact, rippling mass of wiry stems,
leaping into shrubs or other support:clean, very bright green
foliage that holds all year and under all conditions, the prim
little bells only partially stifled, so that the blue enters
in with the fast green for a rich effect....all summer:takes
abundant moisture with drainage, but does without under com-
pulsion:roots attractive to nematode and gopher and from
that standpoint may be considered short-lived. This
will re-seed freely and does to carry a planting
along:has many good uses that are performed
willingly in garden and landscape.
                414

# COMPENDIUM

SOPHORA secundiflora, "Mescalbean" shrubby 6-8', infrequently, or with guidance, a narrow-headed tree to 35',
the blue flowers with the scent of violet, spring-summer:
silvery grey or whitish pods open to show the hard red
seeds late in the fall....an espalier of merit:grows in
dryish soils, but requires moisture, late rains or irrigation, for a proper blooming and the fragrance that
is there:outstanding, hardy into warm temperate regions.

SPARAXIS tricolor, "Wandflower" spring bulbs for light or sandy
soils where drainage is without reproach:set either in the fall
or very early spring and lift....or leave in ground that may
be allowed to dry out over summer....where they will expand
in permanent clumps, ultimately large patches:flowers upheld on
some 6-10" wiry stems, are good for cutting, color ranging
through white, rose, carmine, crimson and purple, all with a yellow
center....less pleasing variations occur from seedlings, splotchings
and stripes out of place, spots and other irregular breakings:colon-
ize readily in the south, hardy into warm temperate regions, but do
not persist....cover:give all heat possible.

SPARMANNIA africana, a bulky, brushy shrub 8-10'in height,
arching to as much or more across, rounded in the feeling and
form of an elderberry, but with more definition:shallow
lobed leaves on the order of maple are rough and heart-
shaped at the base, 8-10" across:flowers appear October-
March, loose heads that are not punctual in point of time,
but fitful and capricious....white, with a central splash of pale
red and yellow or dull rosy-purple over-all....can weigh side
stems to the ground:heavy wood should be kept in hand and a
partial elimination made each year or so while the spent
flower heads will make a not too presentable subject even more
unkempt if not removed....dry up brown on the stem. This is an
old plant in use, gone out of favor and fashion, attributable to
above....careful culture will prevent this lumbering habit and
untidy aspect, otherwise....use in some out of the way place
with room for an appropriate thicket of strong growth.

SPARTIUM junceum, "Spanish Broom" a shrub, very erect to 10',
with practically leafless, quill-like green stems or branches and
bright yellow, pea-shaped, very fragrant flowers April-June and
scattering:resists all drought, takes any exposure in sun, but may
be grown well only in a light soil where drainage is good:heavy
ground will lessen effectiveness, increase dieback and shorten the
life materially....but lasts indefinitely by re-seeding when grown
dry and less subject then to arch enemies, aphis and genista worm:
pruning consists largely of removing dead wood....do not head it
back; face off with lower shrubs:naturalize.   --var. nanum, an
identical form that reaches only 3-5' in height.

SPATHODEA campanulata, "African Tulip-tree" for dependably
frost-free areas, a showy tropical tree it is hoped will adapt its
way further into these regions; erect to 50' with a strong buttressed trunk to spreading branches of soft wood that is damaged in the wind:young plants are particularly sensitive in cold
with multi-stemmed trees usually resulting:foliage heavy and of
a yellowish green, carried outwardly against the terminal truss
of upturned scarlet flowers, winter, summer or any time:deep,
rich soils where it will be evergreen in the south of Florida,
dropping the leaves in California, grown there with no satisfaction unless in the warm foothills with good air drainage.
The species,  -nilotica, "Nile Tulip-tree" is similar,
smaller all around, with much lighter foliage, and
only 20' high. It is wasted time trying to flower
these trees unless wood carried over winter has been
matured....with-hold water and fertilizer late summer on until danger from frost is over.

SPHAERALCEA ambigua, "Globe Mallow" from the deserts
of the Southwest, with an open shrubby growth 2-3', hav-

415

ing rose-colored to apricot mallows strung with the greyish
leaves the length of a slender swaying stem:wants a dry or
starved place in the sun where it will not over-grow:cut
back to the ground from time to time:naturalize.

SPIRAEA cantoniensis, probably the most amenable and long
suffering of the "Spireas" for the far south, managing to
hold its foliage most of the year, its health and vitality
for many years:a bushy, well formed shrub 3-5' in the vase
analogy:has the leaf and flower of the better known vanhoutte
and its wide-spreading grace for which it might well be substituted, even in lower temperate regions:blooms March-April,
with considerable value for arrangements.   --var. lanceata,
the leaves dark, narrow-elongated, the flowers full double in
tight little umbels for a precise head.

SPREKELIA formosissima, "Aztec, Jacobean or St. James-lily" and
not a lily at all, but in the gorgeous character and relationship of amaryllis:evergreen, however and the segments of the
curiously orchid-like flower not so regular, less conventional,
a dark velvety crimson, the lower segments glinting with the gold
of spilled pollen from above, May-June....may be flowered again
by resting and forcing:use in a pot or in the border, to be moved any time out of flower, taking all roots....rich or poor soil
but always with drainage. This is hardy into warm temperate regions, but flowered successfully only when the bulb mass is dried
out some time and thoroughly....lift, dry out, replant, crowd.

### BETONY
STACHYS---herbaceous perennials in the main, more or less
woolly-leaved, used largely in bedding, for edging or in the
rock garden for the sharp contrast in foliage. The flowers are
white or softly tinted pink or pale purple and are of little importance except to heighten the effectiveness of the rather lifeless neutrality of the summer foliage. They are best planted
in dryish places that are sunny and well drained. Watch
closely for mealybug and give up when it appears.
     -coccinea, "Hedge-nettle"  growing 18-24", a perennial
that is native in the great Southwest:has scarlet flowers
for a dry spot in a remote border.
     -corsica, an annual for warm dry places, creeping to
form a carpet for the time....disappearing, reappearing
only where conditions are right for germination of the seed
left....if any:leaves tiny, held closely to the earth, an
off green:flowers comparatively large, creamy white or
pale pink, sometimes purple June-August:ground cover for
a restricted area, chinks or in flagging where surplus water
gets away quickly and surely....cherish the soil where it
stood and use it, with its seed to further a planting.
     -floridana, a tuberous-rooted perennial that will be
found growing wild in Florida:takes more water, along with
the usual drainage to develop the whorled lilac flowers.

STAPELIA divaricata, "Carrion Flower" a low-clumped succulent with curious and fleshy, finger-like leaves that in reality are leafless stems ascending directly from the earth....and
an earthy thing, but evil-smelling, dull-toned and altogether
disagreeable at times:flowers also of the flesh, interesting,
bizarre, star-shaped, in smoky shades of yellow with red or
purple to brown markings, tucked in at the base of the stubby
stem:does have some place on the floor of the rock garden or
planted as a curio by the collector:any soil with drainage and
just average moisture, but in the sun and kept dry over winter
or grown in a pot and carried away at mating time.

STENOCARPUS sinuatus, "Firewheel-tree" open-headed, with
erect lined stems to 25' or more, wanting particularly sun
and heat for good growth:leaves are large, a dull dark
green, long-oblong and cut deeply into lobes like an
oak, scarcely concealing the stems:
     416

display is the curious and spectacular crimson flowers
June-August and later, a study in the pageantry of color
in nature, a singular unfoldment and manifestation....these
strange circular umbels:growth slow but substantial in
reasonable protection, better in good moisture with an
acid soil....mulch in extreme heat.

STENOLOBIUM stans, "Yellow-elder" an erect, somewhat spreading
shrub or brushy little tree to 25' as an extreme, wanting particularly dressing with the pruning shears:rapid growth will be
irregular and without control unless by the thinking hand of the
gardener....keep body open, free of dead wood and of the forming
seed pods to prolong bloom:reacts decidedly to climate, being a
smaller plant under arid conditions, but adapting to dryness and
some shade:clear yellow flowers September-January in large terminal clusters:quite tender, but recovers from killback rather
quickly.   --var. velutina, similar but with a more velvety
foliage, and other habits of blooming, being profuse over April
and June, scattering the balance of summer. This is an unusual
combination with and crowning glory under jacaranda.

STENOMESSON luteo-viride, an amaryllid with yellow flowers,
probably better grown in a pot for the crowding and possibil-
ity of resting dry over winter:set bulb February-March for
blooming April-June, water in growth, sun but not in extreme heat:feed well and do not allow offsets to take over:
flowers in scant or rather full umbels raised 2',primrose
yellow with tips of segments washed in green, the long,
strap-shaped leaves concurrent, a pale bluish green.

STENOTAPHRUM secundatum, "St Augustine-grass" a coarse
perennial for lawns, thriving farther south than any grass
generally used for turf....but a pest used in the wrong place or
out of control:competes with roots of trees in dense shade or out
in full sun and seems better off near the sea than inland,where
it will survive inundation of salt water:similar in habit to
bermuda-grass, a more vivid green which holds over winter:
texture is so heavy it may be considered in nature of a
ground cover other than lawn and probably better so, due to
difficulty in mowing the terrific thatch:renovate as required and use only with discretion and after thought.

STEPHANOTIS floribunda, "Madagascar-jasmine" a heavy
fragrance for tropical moonlight, a twining vine 10-15' with
leathery, shining, very thick leaves and perfuming, waxy and
pure white flowers to use in a corsage, late summer....stirs
a quiet patio for strange emotions of an evening:wants a west
or south exposure for warmth, but shade to protect from a too
direct sun; good feeding in the spring, a lesser one in mid-
summer and to be pruned knowingly for flowers....stop terminal growth before its completion to activate laterals which
carry the bloom:long flowering streamers may be taken inside
for very special occasions in decoration....but not for any
ordinary function:starts very slowly and a small plant will
be years coming into crop, and more reaching the stage of production contemplated above:subject to mealybug and scale.

STERNBERGIA lutea, called "Winter-daffodil" due to late
flowering, suspected of being the "Lily of the Field of the
Scriptures; bulbous, having yellow crocus-like flowers of
burnished aspect, blooming in the fall concurrently with
the abundant narrow leaves, an upstanding clump in support
of the flower:wants a middling heavy soil with drainage, a
place in the sun to bring out the gold, one that is dryish
over summer if possible and gritty with gravel:small, inferior
bulbs are very slow to come into flower and are very late paying
dividends....move in the summer and set shallow, working a complete fertilizer into the soil above....repeat each spring:the
north slope is the preferred exposure where it will make the
place all its own:choice and practical for the south.

Stenolobium stans

Stephanotis

Sternbergia

Stenomesson

417

STIGMAPHYLLON---twining woody vines with delicate, almost
orchid-like flowers in yellows any time during warmth. Growth
is slender and the foliage sparse, a garnish so to speak, in
pattern and grace for garden structures or a dress for architectural detail. They are clean and pest-free.
   -ciliatum, "Amazon-vine" comparatively weak-growing, but
sufficient for tenuous lines and mellow tones in the warmer and
more protected places....slight shade in heat:lacy, light yellow flowers are profusely produced when the plant is doing
well, the leaves long and narrow, heart-shaped at the base,
fringed with surprisingly coarse hairs, a very light green.
   -littorale, rampant, a much more vigorous vine, but still
a thin over-lay, the leaf oval in outline, tough and leathery,
more durable, to be used under considerable exposure seaside:
flowers are dark, a yellow gold, dull, in compact heads.

   STIZOLOBIUM deeringianum, "Velvetbean" an annual twining vine, primarily for Florida and the Gulf Coast with
soil building implications for sand....evidently not as yet
found in California:produces streamers of great length and
much herbage high in nutrients, quickly covering the ground
or climbs with support to show the purple, pealike flowers
and black, velvety pods:sow as early in the spring as is
convenient for a long season:heat and warm soils.

   STOKESIA laevis, "Cornflower-aster" choice perennial for the
far south, of irregular form 12-18" high or sprawling beneath
the large, fairly full blue or purplish flowers, infrequently
white, pink or yellow, July-October:possible to grow well only
in light soils and in the sun....mildews in shade:a comparativ-
ly dry slope ideal, otherwise use ashes or gravel around crown,
freshened season of rain....divide every two or three years:avoid
low spots and don't coddle otherwise.

### BIRD OF PARADISE FLOWER
   STRELITZIA---large herbaceous plants, mostly tree-like with
the typical banana leaf, but leathery and more substantial
in the wind, the flower with an exotic generosity, form and
brilliant coloring....suggestive of the head of a cockatoo
and so realistic as to require little of the imagination
in accepting the vernacular. They thrive in any fertile
soil with moisture and reasonable sunlight and require no
special attention to produce flowers, but will be treated
each year in most soils with gypsum and soil sulphur for top
production. They may be subjected to as much as ten degrees of
frost without serious injury....but prepare them.
   -augusta, growing 10-15' in height, the pure white
flowers with purple bracts on stalks of similar color:rare.
   -nicholai, similar to above but larger, the white flower with a blue tongue and continually produced in warmth:ulti-
mately develops a woody stem 25', the very large leaves two-ranked, inversely heavy in feeling toward the top for a strong tropical aspect:an over-abundance of moisture brings on a flow of sweet-
ish juices which ruins the flower:warm places and rich soils.
   -reginae, the more commonly seen and the more colorful, a
robust, stemless plant 3-4' normally, the heads in orange, blue
and purple, carried on a long stout scape for cutting from
August through May or continually....always a feature plant
in a tub or set near a pool....important to keep the crown
in same relation to the soil when transplanting:survives
neglect, but performs better under good care.

   STREPTANTHERA cuprea, bulbous, a dense clump of narrow,
pleated leaves to 6" that must be preserved for the new bulb
attached to the base of the stem....cut, don't pull, unless
for the bulblet to reset;an extremely colorful plant from
February through March into April, the type a deep
copper-purple, black at the throat, pink
to crimson in hybrids:keep reasonably
dry in summer rest:choice.

418

COMPENDIUM

STREPTOCARPUS hybridus, "Cape-primrose" fibrous-rooted
herbs with showy flowers for cool, shaded places as bedding, or with forms for a proper spot in the rock garden:
luxuriant leaves are clumped at the ground, with slender
stems raised for narrow, gloxinia-like flowers, white, pink,
rose, purple, lavender and blue:use new plants each year,
transplanting in own soil to a mix of loam, peat, sand and leafmould from seed sown in boxes February-March....sometimes the year
previous:blooms normally in late summer, but old plants may be
flowered in pots in winter....divide June-July, earlier being
best, retaining all leaves possible and washing soil out to reveal
best cuts to be made....feed regularly during growth with a liquid.

STREPTOSOLEN jamesoni, a small, very select shrub of grace-
full flowing lines and attractive foliage, normally 3-4' or
less, but growing into trees with the help of a plantsman and
support of other shrubs:exuberant in bloom in warm, sunny
places in moist ground....flurries or full-flowering of the
two-toned orange trumpets at any time of the year, depending
largely on this combination of heat and moisture:prune lightly each spring after a flowering to assure wood for more of
the good color that then may last into winter, warm seasons:
tender in frost and may be killed to the ground, but returning quickly....susceptible to nematodes:short-lived
at best, so that one makes the most of its youth.

STROBILANTHES dyerianus, "Burma Conehead" low shrubby
plant for the lath house or protected garden in some shade,
wanting essentially a warm spot, grown satisfactorily far
south:leaves are purplish beneath, irridescent above with
much blue and an all over silvery sheen:wants to be grown in
a moist, rich soil, with at least one yearly going over with
the pruning shears....this to preserve size of the leaf and a
generally attractive appearance:morning sun intensifies the
coloring....shear close in early spring for a kind of bedding.

STROPHANTHUS speciosus, an interesting shrub which is seldom
seen, probably because of lack in color appeal:foliage, however,
a rare soft green, medium with just enough highlight and depth in
the structure to place it among the prime plants for shadow as well
as that indefinable something we look for in the unusual:large occasional flowers open star-like, the petals elongating into a
tail-like appendage, creamy and just touched with orange:may
be rambling, or just erratic in growth, but closes quickly
and nicely under the shears and has no essential cultural requirements that ordinary good gardening will not serve:tender.

STRYCHNOS spinosa, "Natal-orange" short and tree-like,
with nearly round leaves, the branchlets with half-inch
spines and accompanying, strangely greenish flowers:fruit
the size of a small orange, leathery-skinned and yellow,
the pulp aromatic and of the consistency of ripe bananas:
very tender in frost, but with hardier strains to be had:tubs.

STYLOPHYLLUM orcutti, a native California succulent with cylindrical, long-tapering, finger-like leaves that reach up tentatively into the sunlight from lower growth; a test for the curiously wrought white or rose-colored, red-antlered flowers in the
spring:use with rock or to under-spot shrubs on a dry hillside.

SWAINSONA galegifolia, "Darling-river Pea" shrubby, but almost
herbaceous, spreading 2-3' or climbing to light when supported, herb-like:pea-shaped flowers in loose clusters,
white, pink or in deeper reds to purple, open by mid-summer
and continuing, or nearly everblooming south....color never
very strong, but the flower long-lasting when cut:used as
a filler with shrubs and kept under control or planted in
the herbaceous border....in either case cut to the ground
in winter or replaced with seedlings.

419

SYAGRUS weddelliana, a dwarf, slender-stemmed palm that may
grow to 6' in height where conditions are found suitable:
has a pleasing top and graceful spread that will be in
scale with the patio or house interior:growth is very
slow in a pot and as carried along in tubs....not often
found in the ground. This little plant is difficult to
establish and somewhat uncertain in maintenance, but will
be found hardy in light frost if hardened off:choice.

SYRINGA persica, "Persian Lilac" the only true lilac
grown with any satisfaction in these regions:built of slender
lines, arching stems 5-8' with narrow, lobed leaves or entire, and
white or pale lilac to reddish, rather small open trusses of typical
flowers April-May, or sometimes completely out of season:shade part
of the day in very hot climates will be beneficial, and it will
be found doing best in warmth:deciduous.

SYZYGIUM cumini, "Jambolan-plum" eugenia-like tree, but with
larger, much more individualistic and interesting leaves:endures
more dryness after having become well established, but does
not fruit satisfactorily in California:fruits are comparatively large, purple and edible:makes a good windbreak.

T

TABEBUIA umbellata, probably the hardiest of the "Trumpet-
trees" which are so extremely spectacular in flower and ornamental otherwise, even to the pod. The flowers are held erect in large
clusters of white, pink, purple or yellow and drop quickly in dryness or too much cold, as does the foliage. They are not significant as trees in these regions, but are planted in the
south of Florida for the bloom; may be planted in Southern
California in the warmer sections where they can be flowered, but not proven for general use. They like a rich, moist
soil, but must be grown in less fertility as used northerly if
wood is to survive winter. The species generally used are
-argentea, a gnarled, spreading tree 25', the foliage silvered, the
flowers yellow and the seed pods grey, lined with black.    -pallida,
with intermittent flowering over the year, white with red veining, a
better tree for adverse conditions and in wind.   -serratifolia,
spreading, frequently multi-stemmed with a close top of bright
green, while yellow flowers fill in a definite leaf drop in winter.

MARIGOLD
TAGETES---brightly colored annuals for the flower garden and
for bedding in the sun, blooming long and late, with a smell that
is haunting and pleasant to some, acrid and sharply disagreeable to
others, according to early associations with them. They may be grown
in heat, better somewhat cool; make good cutflowers, carrying into the
home the glitter of the sunshine that means so much to their thrift in
the garden. They are strong-growing, deeply and widely rooting
and have a wide tolerance, even to a little thrown shade.
    -erecta, "African M." an erect, branchy plant growing
to 24" high, used for summer bedding or as a filler in the
border for late color:large, double and ruffled flowers
with the original shades of orange and yellow....char-
acteristic scent the only object of out-breeding:wants
root-room in a fertile soil for the better bloom, and
space for the top which should not be crowded.
    -patula, "French M." a spreading, bushy structure
to 12" high and seldom more, probably the better bedding subject:foliage is darker and the flowers are more
freely born, ranging in color from yellow to almost

pure red, but usually with red markings of some kind:
serves better in a deficient soil and will bush out more in
a root-filled soil.
-signata pumila, less than 12" high, with some very dwarf
kinds:has small, bright yellow, single flowers all summer and
fall from an early spring sowing:used almost entirely in bedding,
the dwarfs as edging and all of them in the rock garden.

TALAUMA hodgsoni, a large tree of exceeding beauty all
along its 60' height, leaf, flower, and clean, straight
bole:great elongated leaves are medium green, deeper in
tone with shade where it is well to start out the young
tree:six inch flowers are ivory-white and fragrant,at
times in the summer:coolness....no extreme heat:rare.

TALINUM paniculatum, "Fame Flower" a low, meaty-leaved
little plant 18-24" of sturdy woody base, quiet, substantial
purpose in decoration, calm, placid and unruffled for patio
or terrace and in the house in a pot, outside in the rock
garden:persistent in dry gravelly ground or anywhere with
sure drainage, a subject for heat and high sun:wide panicles of tiny round buds open to red, stiff-erect and well
above the succulent leaves July-September....wait for heat
to sow seed:deciduous.

## TAMARISK
TAMARIX---shrubs of very rapid growth, the slender branchings set closely with tiny scale-like leaves while feathery
clusters of rose-pink flowers are spaced along the terminal
shoots....very responsive to and eager for a breeze. The
typical beauty in form and structure will be qualified in
the end by ungainly wood that develops at the base. This may
be anticipated and lower growth placed in front or the top
cut to the ground every few years to entirely re-new. These
are plants for windswept places, to grow in drouth and in alkali
ground or under salt spray on the ocean; standing anywhere in
practically pure sand with roots in tainted water. They are
not so well adapted to regions of high rainfall.
-africana, somewhat erect and more or less rigid at 10',the
foliage a vivid green:blooms in the spring and should be pruned
immediately after having finished:tender in frost.
-aphylla(articulata)"Athel-tree" an erect tree of slender and
loose growth to 35', used in very dry countries to break the force
of the wind or does equally well near the sea:remarkably
resistant to the action of alkali salts in dry ground:the
naked green branch and twigs have winter value to the eye:
set hard-wood cuttings where the tree is to stand, but not
near a damp open-tile line....roots will fill quickly:will
make an excellent large and narrow hedge with attention.
-chinensis, with the typical form , but usually with a
more graceful structure; in flower during the summer in
weak terminal sprays.
-juniperina, "Salt-cedar" a large, ill-favored shrub
that drops its foliage easily and surely, even in the
warmest areas:leaves are a clear green, the flowers in
a large, plumy head....excess debris that catches in the
crotches for a grotesque winter appearance:an ugly plant
that will be used only under the bite of alkali in the
ground or push of the wind above....and usually inland.
-pentandra(aestivalis)a spreading structure, easily kept
growing outwardly to occupy space as a filler, growing to 15' if
allowed its head:typical blue-green foliage and late flowering, the
last one in summer and on into autumn.

TANACETUM vulgare, "Tansy" strong-growing, very leafy,
one of the bitter herbs, the weedy herbage aromatic,
the leaves used to season puddings and omelets:grows
2-3' high with loose heads of buttony, yellow flowers July-September. The species    -capitatum, is
a five inch cover for dry ground:rare.

TAXODIUM distichum, "Bald-cypress" deciduous tree,
strictly pyramidal in early stages, eventually becoming
very large, but not in the south of California, the light
green foliage effect is much that of the redwood; the
tree splendid in its new leafage in spring:moist to very
wet or swampy ground or adapts to fairly dry, but always
wanting some moisture for thrift:becomes picturesque in
age with warm, red, very heavy buttresses that lead the
eye upward into the spent grey bark of the trunk and on
into a round top of spreading, recurving branches:lime.
The species,  -mucronatum, "Montezuma-cypress" is a better
tree for the far south, but seldom available:very large, the
leaves persisting to become nearly evergreen, reddish brown over
winter, dropping with their branchlets in the second year....is
littering, but allow lower limbs of the tree to splay out over
the ground to accept and conceal the fall:choice

TAXUS baccata, "English Yew" coniferous evergreen of high
quality and elegant simplicity, usually multiple-stemmed
8-10', shrubby in the south, a tree 60' far north, of
very slow growth and long-lived. The foliage is somber,
yellowish, the needly leaves short and flattened. They
will grow in any soil that is drained; benefit with occasional manuring; free of insect pests or disease:will
thrive in full sun and almost as well in deep shade:grows
in heat, but should not be subjected to reflected light, as
of a white wall....coolness indicated for long service and
best eye appeal.   --var. stricta, "Irish Yew" a dark, close
grained column when young, held so under a starvation diet,
the vertical stems inclined to break away after many years:may
be held to form by a little pruning, or shearing lightly:a plant
for emphasis.   --var. repandens, low-spreading and easily
kept at 2-3' as cover:bluish green.

BUSH TRUMPET
TECOMA---tender shrubs with great ornamental value in garden
and landscape....exceptionally well adapted to massing in the
open, with detail and color for that closer inspection of the
garden. With an erect growth of graceful stems, good foliage set
to much color in season, they fill a very real need in the
subtropical shrubbery. A loose, well drained, fertile soil is
desirable, and while they want moisture, they will endure some
dryness after having been established....but show it. They require rather drastic pruning, with properly placed cuts if the
native grace is to be retained. All are very tender in frost.
    -capensis(Tecomaria)"Cape-honeysuckle" of stout growth,
erect as a shrub under the shears or vining, in either case
with pliable, cane-like stems that will reach out in length:
foliage is dark and glistening, the flowers bright scarlet or
yellow October-May:stands in considerable drought, in tempered winds off the ocean and in heat, but will not make a good
growth in poor ground or in deficient drainage:may be grown in
a tub or other restricted ground and the canes led some distance
for an effect:prune early in summer for prolific flowering....an
impenetrable high, narrow hedge that flowers freely under the
shears:an adaptable plant all around.
    -garrocha,graceful,5-8' high, the supple stems with large
clusters of narrow trumpets in yellow and dull scarlet July-
September:cut away seed pods immediately after bloom and
prune lightly each year, never into deep wood:the hardiest.
    -smithi, erect, stiff-stemmed 5-8' high, with light
foliage and terminal heads of yellow flowers flushed with
orange January-March:leafage does not weather cold very
well and the plant should be kept out of drafts.

TECOPHILAEA cyanocrocus, "Blue-crocus" unusual and
attractive low bulbous plants for coolness, but in a
soil that will go dry late summer and fall:growing
only some 6-8" in height, the channeled, linear leaves
somewhat more:sweet-scented, clear blue flowers have a large

area of white at the center, February-April:wants good moisture in growth, but to be allowed rest when indicated and
that in reasonable dryness:rare.

TEMPLETONIA retusa, "Coralbush" a low branchy shrub 3-5',
without definite shape, but taking its goodly share of salt
and sand and spray:has scant foliage, but that leathery, close
grained and durable:resents a heavy or undrained soil, wants
lime and stands considerable cutting, but to little effect.
This is an old plant gone rare, probably because of its generally disheveled condition and short life.

TERMINALIA catappa, "Myrobalum" an erect-spreading tree 75',
with whorled horizontal branches at right angles with the trunk,
the foliage in the outer areas:large, smooth leaves, dark and with
a high gloss....turn red in drought, and falling, will renew in
moisture....falling again in dryness or cold....the tree seldom,
however, entirely bare:greenish-white flowers autumn-winter are
not important and litter the ground noticeably:fruit is almond-
like, edible but not much used or desired:streets and
used for shade in frost-free areas.

TERNSTROEMIA japonica, exceptionally handsome shrub of
very slow growth, the leathery leaves in a bold and telling pattern, unusually lustrous, washed with purple and
tinged bright orange-bronze when new:creamy flowers on
short, stubby stalks are inconspicuous, but very fragrant
July-August:does best in a loamy soil of mild acidity:prune
lightly or pinch out to develop character or to thicken for
a tub:best in broken shade where the leafage is very active
in reflecting light:choice.

TETRAGONIA expansa, "New Zealand Spinach" spreading, semi-
succulent herb that makes a wide mat on the earth, the individual plant as much as 6-8' across and 4-6" through:has little
ornamental value except used as a rolling cover....but outside
the garden where it re-seeds to become a nuisance:juicy, pale
green leaves may be used as a substitute for spinach and
make a relish when grown rapidly and taken young:no color.

TETRAPANAX papyriferum, "Ricepaper Plant" gangling, woody
stems 10-12' to a canopied top of immense downy leaves, a plant
to use out of the wind for a super-tropical effect:the great
panicled head of greenish-white flowers enter November-December
with promise....but with slight fulfillment, doing little more
important than to fix the season and decline on the stem:suckers
widely, but not too much of a pest.

GERMANDER
TEUCRIUM---semi-shrubby plants, or with considerable
wood, to be grown in the rock garden or very dry border.
They want the sun and to be set in a light, rather sterile
soil if they are to serve well and for very long. The best
drainage is important, almost a necessity. Heat and drouth
they take in moderation or extreme, according to species.
They thrive particularly in California.
     -chamaedrys, procumbent and more or less slowly run-
ning, the bearing stems ascending 10-15", set closely with
the dark, glossy leaves:mint-like rosy or reddish purple
flowers July-September:a border plant if the soil is thoroughly drained:boxing for a garden bed or used as a low mass
in the rock garden.    --var. prostratum, only 3-4" in height
and wide-spreading for effective cover:pink flowers
     -fruticans, a brushy shrub 3-5' with very light grey
foliage and pale blue flowers in some moderation over the
year, mostly summer....silvered stems:dry, rocky or gravelly soils in the sun, with the least fuss and bother,
is where it survives long and where the best color in
leaf and flower will be found:filler in the right place.
     -marrum, a tiny shrublet for only comparatively
                         423

dry soils in the rock garden or fore-part of the
border, well placed at the top of a dry wall:has a
hoary grey leafage and pink to purple flowers:cats
will maul this for the foliage aroma and ruin for a time.

THALIA dealbata, "Water-canna" robust aquatic herb for wet
soils or to be used in a shallow pool, a stately plant to be
used informally, but naturally formalized to the plane of
the water, marking a spot with delicate, slender lines:
reddish violet flowers begin in May and continue thru
summer:stems are covered with a white powder.

THALICTRUM dipterocarpum, "Meadowrue" manifestation
and quintessence of delicacy, an herbaceous perennial
3-6' for the border in any place that does not suffer
in heat....a little protecting shade good, but the sun
in coolness:commanding, as of stem and thin leafage,
the tiny flowers more apparent by reason of the fine-
spun structure....most of the foliage toward the ground:
wants a moist, rather heavy soil with minimum fertility,
but with humus and rather sure drainage:graceful sprays of
pale rose or to violet-lavender, June-October:choice.

THEA sinensis, the "Tea" plant of commerce, an ornamental
with essentially the same culture as camellia, usually grown
as a shrub, but making a small tree in its time and in the right
culture....moisture with drainage, a mulch of leafmould and fed
a phosphate, possibly, in the spring:leaves are dark and
wavy-elongated, the single flowers a pearly white, or at
times, a pale pink, cupped about conspicuous tufts of gold-
en anthers November-February:difficult to transplant, but does
take to the pruning shears in adapting to formal purposes....a
hedge in deep shade:grows northerly beyond these regions.

THENARDIA floribunda,slender woody vine of average climbing
capacity, decorative in line, thinly foliated, yet thickening
nicely as a ground cover:light purple flowers are clustered and
most notable for the fragrance of ripe apples....nostalgic of
an old-time cellar:wants full sun to bloom freely, summer.

THESPESIA populnea, "Portia-tree" tropical evergreen tree 50',
dense, round-headed, spreading out in humidity, close and formalized otherwise, as in California where it adapts after a manner:
has leaves of the poplar, the flowers mallow-like, clear yellow
with a darker yellow center, or reddish becoming purplish as they
fail, April-June and scattering:moisture and heat as accepted in
Florida and along the Gulf Coast....not for general use else-
where:litters rather badly.

THEVETIA nereifolia, "Yellow-oleander" grown normally as
a medium to large-sized shrub, but makes a small tree far
south with no discouraging cold weather, everblooming in
moist warmth there:long, narrow leaves of the oleander are
very light, a milky-green, the rich, clear yellow flowers
satiny and also pale, of the general character of oleander:
grown satisfactorily only in a moist, rich and warm soil,
surviving very light frost....but the touch quite light,
when the plant will take most of the next season getting
back into shape....and but little time left for flowering. There
is a peach-colored form of this and the species  -thevetioides, is
much more spectacular in bloom, with a larger flower earlier and
with narrower leaves having a deep-set veining that gives the edge
a stitched appearance:said to be hardier, but evidently requires
the same heat to break out the bloom. The milky juice is poisen-
ous internally, toxic in the eye of contacting an abrasion:grow
the foliage high or the plant within enclosing plantings.

THOMASIA purpurea, "Wrenflower" a low-spreading cover,
shrubby for use with rock, a plant that must prove of
value when its wants are discovered....probably favored

424

by heat, dryness and drainage, the sun and alkalinity:elongated,
rather small roughened leaves lie flattened along the nearly prostrate stems and the tiny purplish flowers are scarcely to be seen,
but do leave the impression of having thoroughy peppered the
plant:studied acclimatization probably the answer.

THRYALLIS glauca, "Fluvia de Oro" flowing gold, which aptly
describes this plant in flower and for form:a shrub 3-5' high
with willowy, pliable stems in slender, flowing lines that are
easily modified, a plant for heat, some drouth and sterile soil,
bushy to make an attractive flowering hedge:yellow flowers July-
October or nearly continuous far south, are sometimes tinged with
red:foliage is lighter in the shade, dulls to olive tones in more of
the sun which it likes, turns to dark purple in cold weather:no
frost here as this plant probably won't come back after a freeze.

THUJA orientalis, "Arbor Vitae" a narrow pyramidal tree of dense
texture, the ascending branches with rigid sprays of scale-like
leaves, held in vertical planes....may be sheared to further
thicken the mass:adaptable in the matter of soils preferring them
cool, moist and loamy, heavy rather than too light....decidedly
out of place in the extremes of drought or smog and sand or grav-
el:always used for accent or in some formal relationship and
has many accepted varieties, some of which follow. --var.
aurea nana, growing to 5', the tips of growth tinted with
bright yellow the year round. --var. beverlyensis, pyramidal to 15', the sprays very distinct and very rigid:the
sun will bring out the new growth in rich yellow. --var.
bonita, very broad-cone-shaped to 3' high and flattening out
more with the years:good green all year. --var. elegantissima,
typically bushy at the base, narrowing sharply toward the top
at 12-15' in height:touched with bright yellow in the spring,
settling down to a bronzy, golden green the balance of the
year. --var. pyramidalis, growing to 15', a narrow column
of permanent and very bright green:dependable in matter of size.

## CLOCK VINE
THUNBERGIA---perennial twiners or infrequently shrubby,
greatly favored in warm quiet localities for the abundant
and effective color, together with the refining influence
of foliage and line in stem. They are too tender northerly
in these regions, but begin re-growth immediately after
having been frosted back. They are for rapid coverage in
the garden and may be used in boxes and in a pot, although
better when not restricted at the root. Prune in winter to
thicken or thin out as the case may be, but lightly since
cutting bears down heavily on the production of flowers. They
will take a little shade, must be protected from the wind,
want a fertile soil and abundant moisture.
   -alata, "Black-eyed Susan" vining to 5-6'; of a fine,
satiny texture, leaf, bud and flower, mostly yellow to orange with a dark purple center July-September, blooming the
more profusely in moisture:wants space in a permanent location of good moisture and fertility if it is to establish and flower satisfactorily....a cover where there is
nothing to climb while a willingness to grow downwards fits
it for basket or box:renew there each year from seed:annual.
   -cordata, an herbaceous perennial; trying, but only
flopping in its attempt to climb:flower a deep, royal purple
with yellow throat and tube, sparingly late spring over summer in flushes....more profuse with feeding:the really superior flower suggests use in large pots to tubs, which it will
take gracefully, but wanting support:place this against a
light background for full color value.
   -fragrans, climbing or a running ground cover,
used as a screen on wire, not as rampant and rather
more tender in cold, the dark leaves good contrast
for the slender-tubed and pure white flowers of
July-August, or longer far south....fragrant
in sufficient warmth.

425

Thryallis

Thunbergia gibsoni

Thunbergia fragrans

Thunbergia grandiflora

-gibsoni, the rich, true orange flowers are sometimes touched with crimson, in flower any time in the
year except deep winter:a cover or climbing 20', seemingly the most useful in California, cut to the ground in
frost. The species   -gregori, is a more substantial plant,
less powerful in mass color, but more pure, possibly less persistent in growth, hardier and less invasive as a cover:choice.
    -grandiflora, "Skyflower" robust evergreen climber,the
large pale green leaves intermingling with the light blue,
white-throated, short-tubed trumpets, fall, winter and i-
the spring or continuous far south:the woody shoots are
quite brittle and should be tied if subjected to much wind:
allow space and root-room for a very vigorous plant:choice.
The variety   --albus, is carpeting for cover:very dark foliage and contrasting white flowers.

THYMOPHYLLA tenuiloba, "Dahlberg Daisy" "Golden Fleece" an
annual for bedding, normally 6-10" through the pack, a fleecy,
finely cut body of foliage and cup-shaped flowers, half-inch
daisies all summer and fall from early seed:sun and sandy soil.

### THYME

THYMUS---aromatic material of the first order, low woody plants
that may be erect as shrublets, semi-prostrate or creeping, re-
rooting....so well known in garden literature, not so well as
of the place itself. They will be encountered in old gardens
since they are long-lived and had their past with people who
gardened....for the love of a garden. They will be found to be
persistent under neglect as well as in poor ground that may
dry out periodically. They bloom freely in the sun over the
general period of May-September. They may be transplanted at
any time and will not be affected by any frost that may be
expected in these regions.
    -broussoneti, prostrate, and woody at the crown with the
flowering stems ascending to 8", almost shrub-like but weak:a
large head of rosy-red flowers is distinctive, come and go all
summer:well-grown plant a bright spot of color:rock work.
    -nitidus, a little shrub at 12-15" height with primary
uses in the rock garden:tiny leaves are rather close-set, shining in the sun, the rosy-lilac flowers April-May backed by a
purple-tipped calyx for appreciable color.
    -serpyllum, "Mother of Thyme" perennial, for a wide accept-
ance as cover of the carpeting type, semi-prostrate or creeping,
with a dense, dark leafage of very fine texture, the mat an
inch or less through:has many uses with rock or in the
garden proper, but never in wet or even moist soils, if
it is to function in perfect freedom, and for long.
--var albus, carpeting, a very fine, thin mat of very
dark green, covered in early summer with a sheeting of
white.   --var. -coccineus, tightly creeping, a little
more difficult to establish and hold:use between flagstones or as bright color over a rock, the grey in the
mass of foliage in sympathy with the neutral tones of
the stone....strong crimson or pink.   --var. lanuginosus," Woolly T."flat, surging grey carpet, a throw of
mouse-eared, downy leaves for the border or hanging on
the face of a low wall.   --var. minus or minima, are miniature forms that will be used in chinks in concrete or a
narrow crevice in rock....any small scale study.
    -vulgaris, an erect-spreading shrub 6-8" or more, with
stems crowded and the foliage whitish(argenteus), a number
one subject for hot, dry soils, clay or sand or gravel
and all known manifestations of neglect. This is the common "Thyme", one of the sweet herbs with lilac or purple flowers May-June, to be used as cover in a difficult soil complex, as an edging or low garden boxing.

TIBOUCHINA semidecandra, "Glorybush" reluctant
shrub of straggling growth 8-10', of doubtful
beauty as such, but with superb flower color

426

where they thrive. Directions for their growing are all too
uncertain, so that of hundreds planted few servive....accept,
if need be, as transient, the dark royal purple 2" flower, and
try again:growth is slender and open, the leaves deeply ribbed and covered with a pile of silvery hair, turning red as
they fall:the flower August-November or until April far south
in Florida or mild winters in California:sprouts from the base
when cut by frost, or reduce with the knife when it appears to
need revigoration....a moribund bush comes to life quickly when
cut in spring:wants warmth, drainage, good feeding into late
summer and probably an acid reaction from much humus in the
soil....continued with a balanced acid fertilizer:will be
seen most frequently in thrift and content against the east
or west exposure of a wall. The species   -elegans, is similar,
smaller, to 3-5' high, the flower only an inch across.

TIGRIDIA pavonia, "Tigerflower" summer flowering bulbs of
straggling growth, the 12-15", sword-like leaves at their
best during hot weather....flamboyant color and exotic
form, flowers of extravagance July-October in yellow, orange, pink and scarlet to crimson, spotted or blotched.
They are strangely three-parted and lasting but a day,
but each repeating at intervals of from three to four
days for continuity:wants a rich, porous soil in a warm
sunny place protected from wind and with plenty of water
from above....never wet or soggy:set out April-May, or
when the ground has warmed; cut tops green or dried out and
lift after bloom; store humid or allow to remain in stand until next planting when bulblets are removed and clumps re-set:
not a cutflower since buds coming on do not open.

TIPUANA tipu, "Tipu-tree" very rapid growth to 40' with all
of a 60' spread, the branches tending to droop with the or-
ange-gold flowers June-July....the petal-fall a field of old
gold beneath....could be litter and a nuisance:somewhat of
a tenderling in frost; appreciative of a deep soil; taking
some drought, but much better in moisture:head in for shape
desired and cut side limbs for good head room:foliage is off-
green toward grey, nearly holding south in Florida, out of
leaf two winter months in California:deciduous.

TITHONIA rotundifolia, "Mexican Sunflower" a plant that becomes shrub-like, although only an annual, very coarse to the
eye and touch, growing to 6' in height:large, zinnia-like
flowers are colorful, if sparse, orange-scarlet or vermilion, blooming in late summer until cold weather:resists a
drought, but with the leaves withering on the stem and the
flowers stranded on bare ugly stems....reviving with moist-
ure:harsh and weedy for garden use, it may well be planted
for cutting or in the far background where the brilliant coloring will show above lower growth....topping a low wall or a
fence. The form in common use re-seeds very freely.

TORENIA fournieri, an annual with bloom of especially high
order for bedding, for a box or pot or edging. It is not easy
to grow, wanting a light, rich soil of good moisture, damp to
the point of wetness in dry heat....and much humus-forming
material:grows in the sun if not too hot, preferring afternoon shade:continued fog or high humidity is conducive to
mildew which suggests pointing for the drier season....re-
seeds at times of good moisture, but the plant not overly
rugged and suffers under neglect:bushy, it is 8-10" high,
the flower two-toned, a light velvety blue and dark royal
purple, sometimes a white self. The species   -flava, has
mostly yellow flowers, more spreading or stems creeping.

TUMION

TORREYA---obscure native trees of these regions that could
well become better known and more widely planted....and it is
a knowing public on the rummage that puts the netherside heat

on the nurseryman. The fir-like foliage is glossy, almost
glazed in its brightness, the leaves or needles in a tous-
eled, two-ranked arrangement, flattened like redwood, the
individual leaf as in yew, rigid, bristle-pointed and
comparatively long. They are found in cool, protected
places in moist, loamy to rather heavy ground and are
hardy far into warm temperate regions, although but seldom used, even within their own locale. They may be
heavily shaded....up to total.
    -californica, "California-nutmeg" found growing to 70'
in central California out of the wind, but with considerable heat and dryness in the air, reaching to moisture be-
low:becomes picturesque in age, with a rounding top and irregular drooping limbs:deciduous north.
    -taxifolia, "Stinking-cedar" very much localized in
nature in western Florida, growing to 40' in height and,
as found in Tallahassee, an excellent body of darkened
foliage:grows in heavier soils than above and more
humidity:choice, despite the name.

    TRACHELIUM caeruleum, "Throatwort"  perennial 18-24", but
not positive and better treated as biennial:becomes woody at
the base when held over, with an inferior flowering....set new
plants each year for sumptuous color:large, flattened to nearly
round heads of filmy blue or white flowers arrive late in the
summer or autumn:when sowing the fine seed, melt into the soil
with a fine spray:superior pot plant.

                    STAR JASMINE
    TRACHELOSPERMUM---twining vines, clambering or used as cover,
when they should be headed back from time to time....makes a knee
height hedge at the crest of a bank, fitting overside to the
slope. The salver-shaped flowers are twisted in the way of a pinwheel, forming open clusters in early summer. They like a good
soil, one that is cool, moist, and with humus to keep up life.
Slow-starting, they continue a liesurely development for a most
satisfactory service under an average garden environment. The
flower is very fragrant and the plant frost-hardy, but not
well used in the wind. There are no pests.
    -asiaticum, has pale yellow flowers; is not as vigor-
ous in growth as the following and not naturally as close
covering, but probably the hardiest in frost.
    -fragrans, is much more rapid in growth than the others
and higher climbing, with much larger dark green leaves that
are leathery and creased:white flowers are long-tubed, fragrant
    -jasminoides, "Confederate-jasmine" by all odds the more
commonly found in gardens, an old plant there:shrubby, but
mostly climbing, the dark mass of thick, tough leaves concealing a dense stemmy tangle of wiry, winding wood:white
flowers of April-July are intensely fragrant:a tub plant
with support, or forms a long-lasting, 12-15" ground cover
in the shade....peg stems down. There are red and white variegations of attraction but less vigorous than the type.

    TRACHYCARPUS fortunei, "Windmill Palm" the slender stem
quite fibrous, matted with long hair, inversely tapering to
a compact mop of dark fans at 25':grows almost anywhere and
satisfactorily under all conditions except in extreme heat
and in the sandy soils of Florida:exceedingly dramatic, picturesque in groups of slanting stems....disturbed at the
crown in early life, it develops same effect:very
hardy in frost.

    TRAGOPOGON porrifolius, "Salsify" a tall, sturdy
biennial, growing as high as 4' from a strong and
deep-tapping root:has rather showy light purple
flowers which are open only in the morning:ornamen-
tal points scarcely warrants its use in the border
and less so in the garden....suitable with the wild
flowers or culinary herbs for the root:naturalize.

428

# COMPENDIUM

TREVESIA palmata, "Tropic Snowflake" extraordinary,
a plant with a strange pattern in the leaf, compounded in exact mimicry of an immense snowflake....to 18"
across, the lobes sub-lobed and turning to gold when
they go....surely an eccentric, in the aralia matrix
and reminder, stout, stubby stem of thorns and bizarre
leaf:should have a loamy, leafy soil with filtered sunlight or sun in coolness, shade in heat....grown in a
tub, but not for long:reaches 12-15' in height or to as
much as 20' for distinct line value, especially if multiple
stemmed....for which, head in when young.

TRICHOCEREUS candicans, in appearance an erect cylindrical cactus
with narrow stems or joints in slender lines, a clump to 3-4' high:
large, waxy-white flowers of a summer night is an inspiring thing
to behold....pit and essence of awareness in the garden....at its
best and fully opened in the morning:appear in quick succession
around the tip of the vertically ridged and heavily spined stem,
surely a revelation of the meaning in nature....underlying.

TRICHOLAENA rosea, "Ruby-grass" very pleasing and most ornamental when naturalized in out of the way places, or covering
distant ground with alternating waves of color in the wind:
plumy heads are silvery over a base of winey rose or purple,
all of a silken quality that intensifies as summer spends
itself and runs out:requires a little water in California
to extend the growing period and mature seed, but is wide
spread in Florida with lively and distinctive effects....a
weed there in cultivated fields..

TRICHOSPORUM(Aeschynanthus)pulchrum, "Blushwort" or sometimes
called "Basketvine" from the major use; trailing with short woody
runners, but only in warmth....not heat, for which shade must be
provided:short leathery leaves are dull, dark green, the scarlet
flowers marked with yellow at the wide-thrown lips:wants a loose,
fibrous soil that has been enriched, and to be kept uniformly in
moisture, certainly in growth, better at all times:pots or a
master plant for a basket with the hanging tips pinched out
for the form desired:cut back when through bloom:summer.

TRICHOSTEMA lanatum, "Romero" or latterly known as "Woolly
Bluecurls" a low spready shrub from low hills in California, the off-green leaves narrow like rosemary with the
edges rolled back, pleasant to smell:dark blue, very soft
woolly flowers collect as little round buds about the stems,
to become the flowering spikes of spring-summer:dry and poor
soils or rocky ground is best....will die out under cultivation if over-watered in summer:pinch in late season for form.

TRIFOLIUM repens, "White Clover" a creeping perennial grass
for lawns where it is valued most for winter and early
summer growth while the nodules and content together with
the deep-rooting are beneficial to the soil:becomes patchy if
not kept in vigorous growth and is short-lived at its very best
in the south:frequently used in a bluegrass mix for turf,
but should be sown separately to insure a uniform stand.

TRIPHASIA trifolia, "Limeberry" citrus-like, a brushy shrub
or small tree to 15', sharply spined and sometimes used for
hedging:has rather scant dark foliage and fragrant, inch-wide
white flowers while the greenish to dull red berries make a
tart, lemon-like drink or go into preserves to spike the
flavor:endures frost, drought and some salt in the soil.

TRISTANIA conferta, "Brisbane-box" an erect tree 50',
with a warm reddish orange trunk and a crimson area at
the base of new growth:round-headed and of open structure,
the vertical lines of the branches are multiple and the large
light green leaves are dropping all year:white or yellow,

star-like, eucalyptus type of flower will litter pavement, but
vanish into grass....they and the fruiting capsules of no imp-
ortance:quite resistant to heat, wanting moisture to get started, drought resiatant after having become established:should
be kept in hand, held back the early years to erect stems desired and branches stopped to hold foliage which tends to
outer perimeter:a tree for an average width street if maintained properly. The appearance of this tree is much that
of the madrone, which may not be grown in these regions excepting at higher elevations in the moist acidity it craves.

TRITONIA crocosmaeflora, "Montbretia" choice bulbous material, hybrids, corms with iris-like grassy leaves and
slender, 18-24" arching or irregularly twisting stems of
curved, trumpet-shaped flowers, flaring widely at the mouth in
summer, orange to scarlet to dull brick-red:wants deep, open
ground in the sun where they will receive moisture up until bloom,
drying out more or less afterward for a long rest period....the
patches may be divided then, usually fall:hardy into warm temperate regions, but do not establish permanently....lift and store.
There are several obscure species of singular beauty, sometimes
available, to be used as above.   -hyalina, the most beautiful
of the lot, closely clumped with upraised bells:translucent,
peach-colored April-May, the nodding bud stem straightening
out to accomodate the opening flowers.   -lineata, a running
mass at the ground, the flowers to one side of the diverging,
straggling stem, straw-colored, strongly veined with purplish
brown in April, sometimes washed with a kind of orange.
-squalida, low and weak-growing, not persisting unless well fed
and maintained, but colorful with flowers, freesia-like,shatter-
ing in like manner, pink, salmon to orange, April-May.

### NASTURTIUM
TROPAEOLUM---common garden annuals of soft succulent nature, to
be grown in boxes, for bedding, as cover in the garden or climbing
there. The color of the flowers is superior and the flowers themselves more abundant in poor ground, where the plant takes to hot
dry places, growing in soils and under conditions not capable
of producing results with the average plant. The flower is
single or double, cream-colored or orange to deep scarlet.
They re-seed freely and are not subject to insect pests and
disease....ask mostly for drainage and deliverance of the fertility that goes so much to foliage.
    -majus, vigorously climbing, sprawling in the garden or
over waste places, having a strange preference for dumps
where it masks the crumbling debris and thrives with its
roots deep in the relaxing chaff:young flowers and leaves
are used in soups and salads and the nearly full green fruits
are pickled to substitute for capers.
    -minus, a dwarf, smaller in all ways, otherwise with
many similarities with above, a little bushy clump that is
earlier to flower and more free in its offering:each will
flower from early spring through summer and into autumn,
where moisture holds....and if little seed is allowed to
set:grow in a pot for the herbage against a hot back.
    -peregrinum, "Canarybird Flower" a climbing annual or in-
corrigibly rambling:of very rapid growth, the odd, clasping gems,
the flowers, yellow and quite irregular as to form and somewhat
scattering in arrival:blooms in the summer and tends to become perennial in the south....do not feed.
    -speciosum, "Flame N." trailing, or climbing 10-12', to be
used in a cool, shady place where moisture can be controlled:the
dark leafage goes with the brilliant red or vermilion flowers June
October....then the blue berry:perennial and tuberous-rooted.

TULBAGHIA---perennial bulbous plants for quite general use in
the outer environs of the garden or massed in the border for
color....which fails to carry very far. They are of simple
culture, demanding only the sun for an exceptional and extended flowering. They are hardy in

Tristania

Tritonia hyalina

Tritonia lineata

Tritonia crocosmaeflora

frost, but will lose the strap-shaped leaves in as much as
ten degrees. They are vigorous to the crowding point, but not
weedy and they may be transplanted at any time.
  -fragrans(simmleri)with lax or sharp-bending, inch-wide,
grey-blue-green leaves that will cook in a hot sun or discolor
at the break in drought:has large umbels of handsome rose-laven-
der flowers over winter, October-April:of intense and pleasing
fragrance:may be potted and used indoors.
  -violacea, "Society-garlic" narrow leaves and smaller heads
of lilac-lavender flowers for a prolific period, March-November,
with vagrant heads appearing warm winters:foliage has an oder of
turnip or onion, may be used in cookery, hung to dry for winter;
develops a tight clump that is best divided after four or five years
or when appearance becomes unsatisfactory....done in winter.

                    TULIP
  TULIPA---for subtropical regions, where only the botanical
species may be expected to persist and give any satisfaction;
better grown in the Southwest than in the East, since they come
from like climate. Set them deep and where they will be dry as
possible over summer, among rocks or in competition with roots
of trees or shrubs, preferably those which drop their foliage. They will increase from year to year when they find
the right place to rest from their labors. Set them in
December and feed bonemeal. They are difficult to bring
along under garden conditions and are not commonly seen.
  -clusiana, "Lady T." the 10-12 outer petals crimson,
the inner ones white with shadings of violet or deeper
purple at the base:the better one in the garden where it
must be free to make growth in the fall:good cutting.
  -fosteriana, a very large flower in strong crimson that
deepens at the base....sometimes lavender there.
  -kaufmanniana, "Waterlily T." generally the first one to
flower in the spring, the large flowers opening nearly if not
quite flat:leaves lie on the ground, with or after the flowers.

  TUPIDANTHUS calyptratus, shrubby, or a small, side-branch-
ing tree, almost identical in appearance with brassaia, but
more contained like a clump-bamboo:typical large, shining
leaves are palm-like and of extra-tropical feeling:may be grown
in the sun or will tend to climb for light in shade:distinctive in
a tub and for places where tubs are used....planters:somewhat cold
resistant which is valuable in this type of plant.

  TURRAEA obtusifolia, "Starbush" a handsome shrub 2-3' high and
spreading, the deep, shining, lively fabric of the foliage an excellent transition between the conifers and broadleaved ever-
greens....a plant of sleek refinement for many uses and odd
places about the garden:a ribbon and a well developed blooming terminal constitute a full, complete corsage:a broad flowering hedge or one that is clipped, the flaunting white petals
submerged or breaking away from the cut plane June-November and
into winter, late seasons:wants good drainage and a cool exposure.

  TYPHA latifolia, "Cat-tail" tall and slender water plants, perennial and very strong-growing in heavy, invasive masses, restricted
only by deep water on the one hand and dry ground on the other:
suitable for marshy places or a large pool when held in a box:
soft brown, cylindrical seed heads are taken indoors for decoration, tinted or not:can be a menace in the wrong spot.

U

## ELM

ULMUS---shapely deciduous trees, coming from colder climates,
not completely in sympathy with these regions, but useful under
special conditions related to hardship and difficult growing
conditions. They are surface feeders with roots spreading out
to complicate lawn maintenance and other growth in the garden,
but in tough places of alternating heat and cold, their value is
very real. Prune if necessary, but be careful, when or if topping
these trees as the beauty out of leaf lies in the structure and
branching, at which time any man-made deformity is exaggerated.

-alata, "Wahoo or Winged E." an erect, slender tree 35-50',
regular in outline, cylindrical with short horizontal branches,
the darkened leaves oblong, downy beneath, dressing the corky-
winged branchlets:does not make a heavy shade and by the very
nature and figure of the tree, suited to streets.

-crassifolia, "Cedar E." native in the Southwest, growing
to 40' in height with scaling branches and leathery leaves in
a rigid-erect posture, dark above and lighter beneath, blooming in the fall. This is an unusually pest-free species that
will do in mild alkali ground and out in salt wind somewhat
back from the surf-line:limestone.

-parvifolia, "Chinese E." slender-erect, a tree of many
faces and all rather pleasant, growing from 20' to as much as
50' in deep, fertile soils, rather dense-rounding or loose
in structure and spreading high up, sometimes with branches
drooping, even weeping, the pendulous branches reaching the
ground....a tree that is confusing in its variation of habits
and form....some being completely deciduous without frost,
others holding foliage through frost....the illustration
being of   --var sempervirens, the "Evergreen E." taken from
a tree that has held true for persistence of leaves through
more than thirty years in Southern California:flowers in the
fall are messy and serve only to distinguish this tree casually
from the one which follows:must be grafted to be sure of expected character:leaves are very small compared to the others.

-pumila, "Asiatic or Siberian E." a small tree, probably
not more than 50' high at the most and under best conditions
sometimes actually shrubby:graceful and of very rapid growth
seemingly rugged and hardy in any extreme of heat, frost and
alkali or drought, while all soils are acceptable....a valuable plant for the arid Southwest.

UMBELLULARIA californica, "California-laurel" a tree to
some 20-30' under wind exposure, becoming dense-rounding
there, but more open to 75' and somewhat spreading as grown
in the protection of canyons with underground water:sometimes
it is shrub-like and low or a multi-stemmed tree of considerable height....always there is a marked tendency toward several competing stems:aromatic foliage of long, leathery leaves
that are dark, shearing to make a hedge, or works up nicely
in a tub for formal purposes....try to find the plant as it
comes into growth for the shears:develops rapidly under favorable circumstances to make an acceptable street tree in deep
soils out of the wind and with sufficient moisture:subject
to scale south, better used northerly in these regions and
in humidity....particularly resents hot dry air.

UMBILICUS(Sedum)chrysanthus, a low and spreading little
plant of dryish succulent character, to be used in the
rock garden with slight shade and considerable heat:the
downy leaves are flattish, in rosettes and the yellow
flowers are striped with red:resists heat and drought
when it becomes very in-drawn and compact and later
blooming than the related sedums.

UNGNADIA speciosa, "Spanish, Texan or Mexican-
buckeye" a slender-stemmed, formless shrub, sucker-

432

*Umbel-lularia*

*Ulmus parvifolia*

*Utrechites*

*Ursinia*

*Ulmus alata*

ing in patches, or a tree 30' in bottom land:deciduous, the foliage drying up in early heat, departing in haste along with the
rosy-pink blooming that some years scarcely gets out of the bud
stage:flowers sometimes before the leaves, when they develop a
small buckeye to intrigue the northern botanist:available in
Texas, does along the humid Gulf Coast and may be collected
in arid lower California.

URECHITES lutea, "Wild-allamanda" from far south in Florida,
to be tried only in frost-free areas in loose, open ground in
the sun, with moisture:will be used prostrate, or twining high
as a vine to show the gorgeous flower that is 2" across with a
mandevillian twist of the petals....but a rich yellow instead
of white:an intermediate range in temperature is best.

URSINIA anthemoides, "Jewel-of-the-Veldt" an annual for bedding
or for a pot, a bushy little plant with bright green, finely cut,
feathery foliage and wiry stems carrying yellow or orange flowers
as much as 2" across, the purple disc melting into a dark, glistening zone following around the base of the ray petals:wants the
sun and must have a well drained, preferably light soil. This is a
South African that will remain open without direct sunlight and will
serve on the shadowed face of a dry stone wall.

## V

VACCINIUM virgatum, "Rabbiteye Blueberry" native in Florida
and northerly, to be used in wet acid soils, or will grow in a
drier place, the white or pink flowers April-May, the edible blue
berries by July or August:a deciduous shrub 10-12' in moist ground,
less in dry soils, the foliage turning brilliantly to color in the
autumn....most valuable in the landscape at that time, with a touch
of frost to help out.

VALLISNERIA spiralis, "Eel or Tape-grass" submerged, an
aquatic plant that roots at the bottom and sends long,
springing stems in spirals to the surface of the water
where a tiny flower rests for the sun and observation:
more curious than ornamental, but a good oxygenator for
pond or pool:a natural for an aquarium of glass where
the parts may be observed.

VALLOTA speciosa, "Scarborough-lily" stout, robust, stubborn,
an oldtime garden plant with short scapes from a closely packed
mass of bulbs, topped by many shallow, funnel-formed, bright
scarlet flowers August-September, or any time under extra-
seasonal influence:used in the border or in pots and placed in
tubs when the clump enlarges, but wherever used, the bulb mass
must not be disturbed....blooms better with crowding, breaks
easily into vegetative growth and smaller, non-flowering bulbs
which should not be removed:wants full sun, good fertility,
best dryish as blooming time approaches, dependable for flowers when established and held....have an unpleasant odor:the
foliage tends to go in the fall, but may hold under cultivation....liquid manure and no complete drying out. This is
temperamental as to flowering, but is long-lived and serviceable when local secrets in growing are worked out.

VELTHEIMIA viridifolia, rare but very easily grown bulb, a
striking plant for the handsome, vivid-green, undulating leaves
that arch and spread out in generous mass for a novel effect,
as much as 2-3' across, building up in mass nearly as
much:large, closely packed bulbs tend to push out of the
ground....best left so, with neighboring plants to shade
the dormant mass over summer:the tight, conical head of

Valisneria

Vaccinium

Vallota

Veltheimia

flowers is held rigid at 18-24" December-April, a mild lilac
pink to purple:likes a rich, sandy loam in slight shade and
moisture, but not very demanding....can be over-done:goes down
in May, with new growth by August and resting completely in dryness....less thorough in dampness, so that spikes may be raised by
Christmas:large bulbs pay dividends....a spectacular set-in for a
large planter or can be moved indoors for an occasion.

### MONARCH DAISY
VENIDIUM---robust, straggling, herbs with as much width as height
in the untidy grey-green foliage mass. The great flowers fairly
dazzle with a brilliance seldom found in the garden, magnificent
daisies done in pure gold or orange, of a burnished lustre, zoned low with black in startling contrast. They must have a warm,
drained or sandy soil and in the sun, else flowers may be deform-
ed....pinch out growing points to hold in. Old seed is best, sown
any time after mid-summer and generously since germination is most
uncertain....best under natural conditions where the matured seed will
fall to a hot soil and bake over a period, eventually to germinate
in its own good time. They are subject to stem rot and should not
be watered heavily at any time.
     -decurrens(calendulaceum)silky stems and leaves, spreading out
and up 2-3', the smaller flowers golden-yellow, 2-3" across. This
is a perennial and really something to have in a rough place.
     -fastuosum, cobwebby over-all, only 18-24" in height,
but the bright orange flowers 3-4" across....an annual that
will re-seed in reasonable dryness:naturalize.

### VERVAIN
VERBENA---annual or perennial herbs, the stems prostrate or
lax, rooting to form a loose mat in any good garden soil in the
sun. The full heads of brilliantly colored flowers on long, raised stems give constant succession throughout the year, slowed up
only by winter. Sow seed indoors November-March for early flowering
plants, or outside in early spring for later bloom. All are best
treated as annuals excepting the tuberous kinds, and renewed each
year. The many named varieties are gradually superseding specific
forms in the garden, but this is not true in same degree for the
border or rock garden. Mostly they are subject to mildew....sulphur
in the soil will fume in heat for some protection....always in the
sun when grown in humidity.
     -hortensis, the hybrid "Garden Verbena", reclining, with much
good color in white, pink, rose, lilac, crimson, purple and blue,
wanting fairly good soil and scant watering after having establish-
ed:streamers may be pegged down for close cover or the tips pinch-
out in the interest of compactness:best used as cover in the gard-
en, for filling boxes, renewing each year from cuttings, or layer
to retain desirable colors.
     -peruviana(chamaedrifolia)subshrubby in the south, but
with long runners for good spread in short order:perennial
with flat clusters of scarlet, very brilliant flowers all summer and later....dependable in the matter of color as grown on
from seed:resists mildew seaside.
     -pulchella(erinoides)"Moss V." perennial, becoming some-
what woody, permanent cover for sandy ground, very persistent
and constantly in flower, the lilac, bluish or purple heads a
close structure like clover:withstands some drouth, but requires
some water California summers to be at its best:baskets.
     -rigida, tuberous-rooted and spreading underground, the
heads of lilac-purple or light blue flowers on 12-15" stems
June-September....verge on magenta and must be placed careful-
ly:tubers may be lifted to clear ground for winter, but used
correctly, the plant will occupy the ground permanently:bushy in
form, tenacious, requiring little attention:naturalize.

VERBESINA encelioides, "Butter Daisy" an annual "Sunflower" for
the far south, having notched, glistening yellow rays in a delightfully unconventional head that fades to a pattern, wilts in drouth:
snip first flowers as they fail and the laterals lower on the
stem will take over for blooming all summer and

434

successively lower to the ground....or take entire stem for the
grand bouquet at height of the blooming:native in Florida and
re-seeding in California in a garden.

### SPEEDWELL

VERONICA---herbaceous perennials, usually somewhat woody at the
crown, essentially border plants, the lower ones adapted as cover
or grown in the rock garden. They are not especially showy and not
very free-flowering, but with some very pure blues in the flower
that do quiet the turbulent spirit of a warm day. Any ordinary
garden soil will be suitable, one that is on the heavy side and
retentive of moisture.....take full sun or partial shade. A
little discreet heading in may be necessary to keep some of
these plants in hand, especially in the rock garden. They
are not to be used far south, and in great heat, with shade.

   -incana, "Hoary S." erect 18-24", a distinct tuft of
whitish foliage and deep blue flowers in terminal heads in
June-September:a border plant in mild heat.

   -nummularia, slender creeping stems, intricate for a
flat, carpeting mat, good cover in the garden, with an extremely flattened nap of tiny leaves....a stand-in for a
dichondra turf, mixing, joining to carry the similar texture into more shade than the dichondra likes:very small
flowers of pink or blue May-June, which become more scant as
a blooming as the species is taken south:rock garden or with
flagging, in the lighter, but moist drained soils.

   -pectinata, creeping, rooting only superficially at the
joints in dryish soils under light shade, a velvety, hairy or
plushy mat there of greyish foliage, the flowers raised as
much as 6", rose-colored or blue with a white eye:will be
sheared a little to maintain good body  and to bolster
condition since it is inclined to run out early, south.

   -repens, doing better south, prostrate, forming a
dense, lustrous fabric an inch through, viridian back
for heads of white, but mostly blue flowers May-June,
held just above or reclining:wants very slight shade, will
grow in moderately dry soil, but requires constant moist-
ture for a flourishing condition:may be grown in spots
where grass will not hold permanently.

   -tourneforti, a tiny annual with weak stems, casual carpeting for a moist, shaded place in sandy or loamy ground:the
flowers not abundant, light blue with a white eye March-October:
disappears quickly in drought or heat and retreats with shade,
re-seeding under conditions for germination for a rather
thorough occupation of a neighborhood.

VIBURNUM---substantial, strictly evergreen shrubs, mostly
general purpose plants grown in one case for the handsome flowers, in another for the handsome fruits, always for the foliage
They have considerable value for the garden, with many material
offerings out in the open landscape; appearing at their best under
light shade. There is preference here for cool, deep or rocky
ground, loam that is well drained, otherwise with no whims
or fancies, taking exposure by species in stride. They
offer much variety in form and height, considerable
in color of the fruit, but with less in that of the
flowers....some with a delightful habit of forming
buds in the fall, holding them with color over the
winter and ready to break with the new season. The
stark, continuous drouth of mid-summer is not to be
tolerated and may be fatal, but don't pamper. They
will benefit with pruning, in thought and good execution. They like much humus in the soil and all
will grow far north into warm temperate regions.
Most of them are happier there.

   -burkwoodi, for cool places in rather deep shade,
the flowers a pure waxy white in a full-rounded head tinted pink in the bud December-March....fragrance remarkable
for heaviness and as penetrating as gardenia:culture
is important; pinch in for good body to correct
thin foliation and do not allow any serious

*Veronica nummularia*

*Viburnum odoratissimum*

*Viburnum tinus*

*Viburnum carlesi*

*Viburnum suspensum*

435

drying out:an excellent espalier for the proper exposure, the leaves standing out dark, by the count, telling against a light wall and holding for winter, but
thinning out:very choice.

     -carlesi, spreading, flat-topped bush for more sun
than above, of considerable refinement 3-4' high and as
much across, less open in structure:tough foliage is a lead-
green, the fruiting blue-black, while the pinkish flowers
of March-May have a delicious fragrance that has been variously interpreted and compared with everything nice from
trailing arbutus to gardenia:must be on its own roots for
permanence and is better south, distantly exposed to cool
sea breezes....small plants only, on account of cost and
for other reasons:no very heavy soils.

     -fragrans, deciduous with a serious touch of frost,
growing to 10' in height, the abundant white flowers in
late fall, after or as the foliage begins to thin out,
continuing until February-March with an increasing fragrance that is pleasing, welcome the time of year that is
so scentless:has purple berries into summer.

     -japonicum, a sturdy, clear-cut, totally evergreen,
stemmy shrub  10-12' or to 18' under duress and compulsion
of crowding, becoming leggy and devoid of foliage below to
a tree-like structure:large, very smooth,pale green leaves
of some distinction and slightly fragrant white flowers,
April-June in terminal heads that serve up red berries by
autumn:a vigorous plant, but subject to thrip and spider.

     -odoratissimum, "Sweet Viburnum" an evergreen shrub
that will compete with rhododendron in nobility of leaf, a
bright, clear medium green and dependable:erect 10', but at
times a cone-shaped little tree in the south, 15-18' in rich
moist soils:white, very fragrant flowers April-June are closely followed by bright red berries that gradually darken:will
stand in rather deep shade....wanting some in heat:choice.

     -suspensum, "Sandankwa" medium-sized, inclined to
bushiness, 3-5'in height:white flowers February-April,
may retain a pinkish cast from the buds....only suggestive of the berries to come:benefits with a little shade,
succeeds under a wide range of conditions:pest-free.

     -tinus, "Laurestinus" erect and fairly dense 6-8'
ordinarily, but as much as 10' in time, growth being
rather slow:reddish flower buds begin coloring in the
winter,gradually opening to rosy-white masses of bloom
February-April....blue-black berries all summer:an excellent natural hedge without shearing....pruning will
thicken but flowers are largely lost, so pinch out terminals before new growth:thrips and red spider work havoc
with the foliage....repeats of strong contact solutions
in spring and hard, deep hosings from time to time later:
air circulation very important:may be grown far north in
dryish ground.  --var. lucidum, a better plant from the
health point of view, splash of white in winter:resists
mildew.   --var. robustum, larger, less compact and with
coarser leaves:flowers in large white heads fall-winter.

  VICIA atropurpurea, "Vetch" annual vine, forage cover or
filler in the shrubbery the first few years:deep-rooted
and drought resistant, it opens and builds up the soil for
following growth:blue to purple flowers are attractive and
abundant over the tangled mat of herbage.

  VIGNA marina, "Beachbean" vining herb, a kind of runner bean,
a cover crop for soil conditioning to be used far south in beach
sand or other, a rambling creeper or climbing into shrubs:light
yellow, pea-shaped flowers are quite ornamental, short-wisteria-
like:sow seed in warmth.

  VIGUERIA tomentosa, "Bush-sunflower" spreading shrub, a wide
mass some 6-8' in height, broad, ruffled fluff of soft, greyish green foliage that falls just short of being

silvery....but with highlights and depth:small,
golden-yellow daisies in full round clusters, more
or less all year, strong winter and summer:wants
sun and reasonable moisture in heat:lower California.

VIMINARIA denudata, "Goldenspray" a broom-loke shrub
or slender-tree-like 15-20', the wythe-like branches tending to
weep....and do in good growth:pea-shaped, golden-yellow flowers on
streaming, rush-like branches, attached with leafy-cylindrical petioles November-January or, any time:takes moisture.

## PERIWINKLE

VINCA---herbaceous plants for the garden or for strictly
decorative purposes about the house, planters, window or
porch boxes and hanging baskets. They make the best of
any or all soils that are within any reason....allow
for a little moisture to keep fresh. They grow in the
shade, but take heat and flower more freely in the sun.
They are entirely immune to insect pests and disease.
   -major, a trailing evergreen perennial with soft but
firm and durable leaves that shine in the sun and come alive
in the shade as spotted by sunlight:forms a loose, running
fabric set sparingly with large blue flowers:good cover for
low banks in the sun or deepest shade in sand, clay or loam,
at the same time competing under and over-ground with the roots
of shrubs and trees....a very excellent material.
   -rosea, "Madagascar P." bushy perennial 18-24", woody at the
base after a time, the rather scant but effective, phlox-like
flowers rosy-purple or white, all summer or more or less thru
the year south:an attractive thing and practical in a pot for a
spot of color, largely used as an annual for bedding down hot or
exposed places:best in poor, sandy soils, but with enough moisture
for thrift:tip-pinching in early stages will induce an extra and
desirable bushiness and more color.

## VIOLET

VIOLA---heartsease, that touches the imagination of
childhood with thoughts that carry over into the lives
of the gardening fraternity....low, lovely little herbs,
with some one to furnish a bit of color, or solace for
most any day in the year. General considerations in the
garden are a cool, rich and well drained soil with moisture, especially in summer or in heat. Shade through the
middle of the day is usually beneficial and protection
from drying winds a necessity. This is all generic;
specifically, some come from the woods while others
are from the edge of a swamp, bog or very wet ground,
or from a crevice on a high, mountain ledge:still others
come from dry plains and want naturally to go dormant over
summer as well as winter. Fortunately it will not be necessary to simulate these various circumstances in the garden
to suit individual species, except as found....horticulture
has accepted, developed and passes on forms suited to the
norm in gardening so that growth may be satisfactory and the
flowering....special food for far-flung thought.
   -cornuta, "Horned V." a tufted, ultimately spreading
plant for bedding or edging in the garden or border:large
violet and yellow flowers are born in profusion in warmth,
with some flowers any day in the south:a fertile soil of
good body is best for growth and longivity. Improved
forms are available under the term Viola, that must
not be confused with the type because of the annual
blood in their breeding. They are erratic in blooming
and lack permanency, used in bedding alone.
   -gracilis(calcarata)a "Johnny-jump-up" for the
south, having slender, creeping stems, easily grown for
the blue and yellow flowers, concentrating May-June, but
more or less throughout summer:the wildflower garden or
tucked in around the more intimate places about the
house....for more heat and dryness.

-odorata, "Sweet V."  a low clumpy plant, ultimately
spreading to form a loose patch of everything we have come
to expect of the term violet, and the long-stemmed, supremely perfumed flowers....usually dark violet, but frequently a
rose color, pink or purple or white:wants the usual coolness and
shade and fertile ground to one that is a little lean but having
a high humus content:renovate and build up with leafmould and well
rotted manure when a planting begins to run out. This is the parent of the florists violet, the one that comes to mind with the
name violet and the one most often found in gardens:blooms from
February until May or longer if one cares enough to pick.
     -pedunculata, "Yellow V." native Californian, almost
trailing, the flowers very small in the wild, larger under
domestication, veined with purple within, brownish outside:
rather thinly foliated, spreading rapidly from seed or from
underground runners in good garden soils.
     -tricolor, the "Pansy" of high horticultural development,
purely a bedding plant, the seed sown in August to transplant in
the fall, sowing again in October to carry over for spring plant-
ing:a flower of marked character and sentimental appeal from its
time over the years with lovers of flowers, the flat pixie-face of
the bloom having come to signify thought of another or remembrance:
develops a good root system and transplants willingly, even while in
flower:cultivate lightly, or better, mulch as the season turns hot
ending spring....then the matter of taking the crop or disbudding
or in some way removing the flower before the seed becomes
viable, is important as an item of culture all along the line
of blooming....so that flowering which normally may be expected to fail with heat, can be carried on further if bloom
is picked in its prime:plant burns out quickly in high sun.

VIRGILIA capensis, an open-headed, medium-sized tree of
rapid growth in deep fertile soils:an over-all coarse ferny
character in the rather scant foliage may be improved with
pruning or lightly shearing the young plant immediately after
flowering:pea-shaped, lavender-pink to rosy-purple flowers in
the spring are somewhat unique for color:rarely planted.

VISNEA mocanera, shrubby 6-8' or a small tree of compact and
rather dense growth of leathery, very dark, shining leaves:the
flowers are solitary, white and hanging beneath the foliage:not
too significant except for the excellent green of the cover and
extreme fragrance of the flower:used like ternstroemia or camellia for select places:very rare.

VITEX---a diverse group of woody plants, shrubs, trees, evergreen or deciduous and tropical to sub-tropical, some surviving
far north into much colder climates....others adapting as well
in arid places as in humid climates. In common, they have
foliage of striking and unusual charm, with no pests or
serious diseases to mar their special beauty. They want
only to be found and known....known to be more rugged and
persevering than appearances would indicate.
     -agnus-castus, "Chaste-tree" a large deciduous
shrub 8-10', precise in growth in youth, especially
with a little late winter pruning, otherwise inclined to
brushiness in the way of an elderberry and going into old
age prematurely:late-starting in the spring, the aromatic leaves are light greyish green, more or less deeply
cut, digitate or finger-shaped while the spike head of the
flowers, lilac to blue, appear over July-October:takes heat
in poor or dry soils in the sun and better performing there
than with an over-plus of the good things so often forced
upon an unwilling plant.
     -lucens, "Puriri-tree" a round-headed, rather dense
growth at 40-60', the pale green leaves exceptionally
handsome, deeply creased  at first, relaxing in later
growth from the corrugation, an oval in shape but fold-
ed down the middle and shining toward the center:flowers

438

of March-May carry over winter in the bud tinted,
open to pale rose or deeper red, with a following elongated cherry-like fruit of like color:will not prosper
in poor shallow soils or dry....give it the best and set
up for good dividends in satisfaction and pleasure:tender
when young and should have some help until it gets up off
the ground and the frost that may collect there.

-trifolia, shrubby 10-15', very fast-growing to fill in
between other, slower-growing materials, covering off low at
the ground to face down trees or leggy shrubs:leaves in threes,
the blue flowers in terminal clusters, indeterminate as to time
tender.   --var. unifoliolata, prostrate, reaching out 5-20'
on beach or other sands or well drained soils:short-stemmed
leaves are rounded, downy, and curl up to light from the
stoutish runners while inch-long clusters of blue flowers rise with the leaves:hold in for good cover:rare.

### GRAPE

VITIS---the Vine literally, the term used to denote
the climbing plant at large or individually. Robust and
high-climbing, twining and using tendrils, these vigorous
plants are scarcely excelled in rough beauty and in service
ability of the foliage as well as in the job they do in overhead covering or screening....always on support. These below
are mostly native forms of localities where they are recommended to be used, exceptions being noted as suitable for the
garden. See Cissus for most of the evergreen species.

-arizonica, "Canyon G." growing low, in the nature of a
shrub or slightly climbing, the grey-green leaves narrowed, usually to a single point and more full along one edge as in elm
or hackberry:the stem takes on an interesting line, usually with
a bend to earth in carrying the top:has character in silhouette
against a wall or floppy for a bank. This is native in the
Southwest where it will be found for use.

-girdiana, the wild grape of Southern California, very
rapid in growth, to be used in rustic places for overhead
shade where the sun is desirable in the winter, but too punishing in the summer:fruit is acid to taste, dark purple.

-munsoniana, "Bird G." native in Florida, continuously
fruiting, the leaves somewhat smaller than above and the
stems more slender:prefers to run along the ground in dryish
sandy soils or topping shrubs:nearly evergreen.

-vinifera, the wine grape of California, coming from
Europe and not used ornamentally nor planted for other than
the ultimate lift it affords:has many full-meated varieties
for which consult the nurseryman. They want heat.

-voinieriana, large scale vines with great five-parted,
leathery leaves, the new growth coming in with a flourish and
magnificence seldom to be seen, great mealy-white or golden feel-
ers that settle down finally to a low, olive green when mature.
The term  -vomerensis, appears frequently with the above and
may refer to the golden form, or the species itself may belong
to the genus Cissus....known in nurseris, however, as Vitis.

W

WACHENDORFIA thyrsiflora, "Redroot" dominating plant, a
tuberous-rooted perennial with a wealth of accordian-plait-
ed leaves 2-3' long and a loose spike of yellow flowers at
4-6' height May-June:must have continual and unsparing
irrigation or natural water and plenty of root room in
the sun, wet places or standing in water....a disappoint-
ment elsewhere:leaves turn black unaccountably at the
tip, probably due to to hot sun or dryness.

WAHLENBERGIA saxicola, a carpeting perennial, making a dark
spreading 2" mat in moist, well drained soils or gravelly
ground and sending up small, neatly uplifted blue bells
over May-June:best use probably with flagging or low in
the rock garden for the uniformity in moisture that is
found there:re-seeds about when happily situated.

WASHINGTONIA---hardy palms with strong character in line,
commanding wherever grown in a strict manner and with some
ostentation; dashing, yet solemn, stately, statuesque.
They are equal to nearly any situation that may arise in the
matter of soil or climate, frost, heat, alkali, murder or
fire. The spent fans hang naturally and indefinitely as a
drab, ash-colored mantle and it would appear the tree might
be permitted the protection of this beard up to old age or
until it begins to disintegrate. Then the extending naked
bole will show in an undressed state to serve as a finer
line in the landscape. This may be less gratifying, if in-
dulgent, than where the fan material is continually removed
in a mistaken call for neatness.
    -filifera, "California Fanpalm" a thick, very heavy
bole, a monstrous trunk to 80', ponderous at its very best,
smooth and inclined to lumpishness without the thatch:the
better tree in high heat, not so clean and healthy in
a humid atmosphere, as of the immediate coast in California....not to be used in Florida and the Gulf Coast
at all....not a handsome tree anywhere.
    -robusta, "Mexican Fanpalm" an extremely slender
stem to as much and more than 100', abruptly enlarged at
the base and well anchored....has not been known to blow
over in the wind:the shaggy thatch holds in place many
years, ultimately rotting away in ugly worn patches like
the fur of a mangy dog....the time to clean up:as fans are
removed in growth, the column is crossed and re-crossed by
the decurrent lines of the leaf-boots in a regular pattern.
There is some reason here in taking the fans. It grows rapidly and the small, compact head leaves the ground in haste,
soon to become inaccessible to other than simian curiosity:the
better one at the seashore, a prime subject in salt wind.

WATSONIA iridifolia, "Bugle-lily" large bulbous plants, very like
gladiolus, having erect 3-4' sword-shaped leaves and a flat head of
curved, trumpet-shaped flowers April-May, pure white to scarlet,
with gradations between:the type species is normally dormant over
June-August, but with evergreen varieties which tend to bloom in
the summer:best lifted over summer unless the ground can be permitted to dry out a little....re-set September-October or later.
This may be grown into warm temperate regions and lifted, stored
dark in soil in order that growth may be held back until the ground
opens:flowers smaller than gladiolus, but many more and over a
longer period of time....side shoots coming after the main
spike has blossomed:a good cutflower that favors an arid soil
for best flowering and full crops.

WEDELIA trilobata, a low cover for sandy ground at the seaside
or sterile, well drained soils anywhere out of frost:trails
to form a deep-rooted mat, a bright green and considerable
back for the small, yellow, daisy-like flowers in as much
as three-quarters shade.

WEIGELA florida(rosea)deciduous shrub 6-8' in height
or less, quite showy in flower, ornamental and serviceable in the foliage, spreading in habit with handsome
arched stems clustered with the rosy trumpets April-
June:dislikes heat and dry air, but manages in polluted
atmosphere of the city and in heavy soils:one of best of
flowering shrubs beneath trees and blooms proudly at the
seashore with a little protection:prune in summer to
promote flowering, but lightly since the life of the
plant can be shortened by excessive wood reduction.

# COMPENDIUM

WESTRINGIA rosmariniformis, "Victorian-rosemary" a
small bushy shrub 3-4', having rather dark, olive-
green, almost needle-like leaves that are silvery beneath and arranged in scant whorls about the silvered stems:
a low, tight mound in dryish ground, loosely formed and in
little character in too much moisture....with-hold everything in moderation and pinch back tips before it is necessary to go into deep wood....yet cut sprays will outlast
several weeks in water if handled right:good hedge seaside
under rather heavy exposure, but in soil....not sand:the sun
is to its liking, but tolerates broken shade.

WIGANDIA caracasana, a large, very coarse shrub 10-15', tree-like,
erect-straggling, of no particular shape or form and interminably at
suckering....having enormous rough leaves and loose, curving heads
of splendid blue flowers March-June:rejoices always and always ex-
uberant, either in heat and dryness or moisture and coolness while
the roots will surely outmanouver the neighbors and master the top
indignities the most impervious soil has to offer....literally:not
a garden subject, yet with points for consideration where the root
system can be contained....a large planter box with bottom....and
re-inforcing steel....again literally:tender in frost and disappointing when grown toolush.

WISTERIA---immense climbers with coiling, tightening, rope-like
lianas bearing the remarkably beautiful and well-known trusses
around March of a spring....reaching to heights or out to lengths
measurable in city blocks in the end, for a proper showing of the
flowers. The plant is deciduous, the pale green leaves breaking,
usually with the flowers. Almost any soil will do, but with good
depth; with moisture and substance and with light to produce the
full truss and herbage in support. In planting, dig out a deep
wide pit and fertilize generously with rotted manure to quickly
build up the frame of the plant. As this is consumed, the roots
reach out into poorer ground so that a balance is reached gradually and without checks nutritionally....an important bearing on
blooming and the time. If this condition can be maintained in all
further rationing, being careful not to over-feed, the plant comes
into its own freely and naturally. This is believed to be the
answer to delayed blooming, subsequent crops depending largely on pruning....spur canes in by shortening long growths of
secondary stems immediately after flowering, cutting to within
5 or 6 buds of the base. Do this again if necessary and still
again in the winter if growth has been very heavy. An old plant
can be encouraged to flower by root-pruning, done preferably during October, with April second choice. Close-twisting of stems a-
bout each other promotes flowering, also horizontal growth after
the full vertical has been reached or simply the whacking and cutting the plant must undergo when it outreaches its space and that
of the neighbors....gets down to business when there is no further
place to go. Grafted plants will bloom sooner when cions are tak-
en from flowering wood, but set the graft low in the ground.
Remember always that these plants become enormous in the south,
with the trunk of an ordinary tree; that an over-abundance of
wood costs flowers; that sun is essential and that the plant
will not be denied. Stems may lie on the ground the first
year or two, but require stout support later, standing alone
if hard-pruned to make a standard of exceeding interest. The
species    -frutescens, may be used as a smaller plant.
    -floribunda(multijuga)"Japanese W." the plant commonly
used in the south with trusses to 24", vertical lines in white
or delicately tinted, lilac, lavender, pink or bluish, single
florets or double:raceme so long south, the opening florets
may be failing at the top as lower ones are opening:best to
start with a large plant of proven color.
    -japonica(Millettia)"Winter W." evergreen in absence of
frost, the pure white or purple flowers in 12" racemes, in
the winter and over with by spring. This rare
plant will not be readily found, is not
secure botanically....but a known plant.

441

X

XANTHISMA texanum, an annual from the great Southwest, a
biennial on occasion or from a late sowing, growing 18-24" in
height with good soil and moisture:wants full sun and other
good things, but does nicely in heat and dryness and in poor
sandy, windswept ground:slender, wand-like stems carry long-
stalked yellow daisies in summer, all of 2" across.

XERANTHEMUM annuum, "Immortelle" erect herbaceous plants
with sparse silvered foliage and double, button-like chaffy
flowers that are the everlasting type to point up all everlastings in this particular character:flowers are white,
with shades of pink, rose, purple or violet from May until November, according to time sown:normally grown as a
cutflower, but may be used to advantage in certain kinds
of bedding, pinched out and sheared for body:sow where the
plants are to stand and in the cutflower garden; but for
bedding, the plants should be grown in a flat and set out
April-May....later for fresh fall bloom....likes heat.

XYLOSMA senticosa, a general purpose shrub for foliage, a
good mass of yellowish-green, shining in the sun, soaking in heat,
mellowing in shade; growing 6-8' and more, rounding or tree-like
with pliable but strong branchings that will stiffen in place for a
free-standing espalier of sharp contrast in shadow on a wall:notable
for withstanding heat and cold, a wide range of soil conditions and
moisture content....but no soggy ground:pestfree, with no pruning
required excepting growth direction where that is perti-
nent:splendid clean shrub for many uses.

Y

YUCCA---conspicuous, bristling, harsh to sight and touch,
altogether aggressive, storming the senses, typical of the
arid subtropical flora. These plants are effective grouped,
but are better used to pick out a normal planting in startling contrast. The leaves, like sharp and narrow spear-heads,
are set in dense spiky clumps at the ground and ultimately will
be seen as such in the branching of some species. The floral effort is truly magnificent, the pure white or greenish, sometimes
creamy tinted bells of the massive flower head are more or less
closed by day....open at night, especially one of a bright moon.
They do not like ground that is continually damp, otherwise offer
no complications in culture.
    -aloifolia, "Spanishbayonet" grown in Florida and along the
Gulf Coast, a tree to 25' with a woody trunk and branches, rigid
leaves that are needle-pointed, the creamy flowers sometimes
tinged with purple spring or early summer:frost-hardy far north
into warm temperate regions.
    -brevifolia, "Joshua-tree" the old man of the desert,
supremely grotesque, with a feeling of gracelessness that becomes character compounded.... fantastic, ghost-like, unbeliev-
able....difficult to duplicate in all the queer things in nature:
use only in dry barren places away from any ordinary kind of development for practical considerations of culture as well as for
the substantiality of the mind....and thinking.
    -elephantipes, "Guatamala Y." this one wanting a more
moist situation, to be used in very opposition to above:
rapid-growing as an erect, suckering mass of wide, lax
leaves, bright green with purple over-tones in winter:
442

immense full spikes of pure white flowers are dependable
for spring and grace the season with something of the im-
ponderable in beauty....etherial;should have moisture and a
fertile soil:gophers will come to the knotty crown and roots.
    -tenuistyla, a low stemless plant in repeated rosettes or
clumps of very narrow, rather rigid leaves that are a bright
green with purplish tinges in winter if taken too far north:comes
from Texas, with a flowering spike raised to 3' from an unleaven-
ed, deckle-edged mass of leaves at the ground:long-lived subject
for a tub within the domestic realm or seed is sown to cover
rough ground out in the open.
    -whipplei(Hesperoyucca)the"Lords Candle", a native Califor-
nia yucca, the plant stemless, with clustered, thick and sharply pointed narrow leaves, the one large spike crowded with the
drooping, waxy-white bells late spring into summer:dry rocky
slopes, steep hill-sides against the sun or the wildflower
garden:unlawful and immoral to dig up plants in the wild, but
seed germinates readily to keep stock coming along....plant
will die after one supreme flowering.

*yucca brevi-folia* (illustration label)

## Z

ZALUZIANSKYA capensis, "Night-phlox" an annual plant growing 12-15" high with small heads of phlox-like flowers, long-
tubed and very dark purple without, white within, June-August:
give of their fragrance in darkness and closed until late of an
afternoon or evening:sow inside in early spring to transplant
or outside after the ground has warmed, or use in a pot to
place wind-wise for the spread of odor....just as well
that this is obscured by day.

ZAMIA floridana, "Coontie" a simple, fern-like cycad 12-18"
grown in the moist atmosphere of lower Florida and warm spots
along the Gulf Coast in the company of palms, having something
in common in the sprightly foliage mass:leaves leathery and
somewhat fern-like from a tuberous root or trunk-like
body beneath or low above the ground, the frond recurving, very dark and glistening, the leaflets blunt-tip-
ped....fruit red, in an irregular, cone-like head:makes
a handsome, rather regular low mound with some shade in a
medium weight soil....light to fairly heavy and from fairly dry to very wet:good cover in the right spot.

*Zantedeschia rehmanni* (illustration label)

### ARUMLILY
ZANTEDESCHIA---tuberous-rooted plants of tropical flavor,
the flower a spathe in pink or yellow besides the well-known
white. The foliage is lush, the leaf that of a spear-head or
shaped in the likeness of an arrowhead or halberd, dark against
the severely plain but striking flower. They are tremendous
feeders, liking strong manure, but as a mulch so as not to
contact the tubers directly; wanting moisture but tolerating
considerable dryness at times; taking shade, but always with
indirect light and good air circulation....dry as may be in rest.
They may be left in the ground indefinitely, but for superior
bloom, will be lifted and the tubers broken apart, rather
than cut, to be packed away in coolness over the normal
resting period, holding there as long as they can be kept
down....re-set September-October for vigorous growth.
They are tuber-hardy into warm temperate regions, but
with more complications than above in establishing.
    -aethiopica,"Calla-lily" the leaves arrow-like,
the plant 18-24" high with fragrant, cold-white flowers
creamy yellow low inside December-May, sun or deep in
the shade....half shade probably best under most con-

*Zantedeschia elliottiana* (illustration label)

443

*Z. aethiopica minor* (illustration label)

ditions.    --var. godfreyana, practically everblooming
in the ground and out of frost and not nearly as large
as the type.    --var. minor, is very dwarf, only some 6"
high with comparable spathes. The little plant known as
childsi probably belongs here.

   -elliottiana. "Golden Calla" growing to 24", the lighter
green leaves heart-shaped at the base, nearly or quite the form
of an arrow and marked with light spots or blotches, the spathe
a rich golden yellow June-July:not as easily brought into flower
as above and must be kept active to see it through a full blooming period:tuber does not keep well out of the ground, probably
best not lifted from most soils except to be immediately re-set:
must have sun and good drainage....no wet feet through any long
period, summer or winter.

   -rehmanni, "Pink Calla" growing 12-18", the typical spathe
pink, or sometimes in deeper shades or nearly white shaded
with rose April-May:flowering will be more satisfactory in
plants that are continually, but gently forced:the light
green, narrow lance-shaped leaves will show pale dots:gets
along with less water in the garden than the others and
will be the better one to use northerly.

ZAUSCHNERIA californica, "Hummingbird-trumpet" a low,
straggling, semi-woody plant with foot-long stems of
greyish foliage and scarlet flowers late in the summer and through autumn:untidy at best, the plant must be
sheared for any semblance of form suitable for the normal
garden....especially ragged in seed:remarkably resistant
to drought, spreading underground in hard, baked soils,
a natural for a rough dry-wall or barren banks that
wither under a hot sun, liking to delve deeply among and under
rock:should be grown in poor soils and as much heat as is available when brought into the man-made landscape:a native.

ZEBRINA pendula, "Wandering Jew" a highly colored ground cover
or used in the planter, other box or basket:sappy stems will
root at the joints when in contact with the earth in support of
the mat of glistening foliage:leaves striped in bright red or
dark purple, green, white and sometimes blue....reverting or
some forms entirely green:wants moisture and some shade, but
with enough light to bring out full color capability:has an extremely artificial aspect in early or juvenile stages.

### ZEPHYR FLOWER
ZEPHYRANTHES lowly little bulbs with neat, self-kept
foliage for the rock garden or border in a damp place or
one that is fairly wet. They want a rich soil that never
becomes quite dry and the bulbs will be set closely for
best flowering. They will bloom in light shade. The leaf
is long and narrow, thick and a little succulent in some,
flat and less meaty in others, grassy as it will appear in
mass in a well grown patch. The flowers are comparatively
large and crocus-like, raised well above the foliage. The
more vigorous species will require dividing on depletion of
the clump or within a few years, according to strength of soil.

   -candida, "La Plata-crocus" developing strong clumps in
the wet border, or will grow at the edge of a swamp or in other
marshy ground:pure white flowers are freely born September thru
October or later in a warm sunny place....sometimes tinged with
pink outside:leaves frequently longer than the flower stem at
some 12" and concurrent:dense clump for a pot.

   -grandiflora(carinata)"Fairy-lily" the more common one
to be found and very attractive, the rosy or light pink flower as much 3" over-all, across and length, May-August, individually long-lived:not too vigorous, this is something to
cherish and sustain....feed discretely.

   -rosea, comparatively weak-growing in thin, uncertain
masses and groupings of falcate or curling flat leaves, the
smaller rosy-red flowers an inch or less across August-
November:allow every advantage in culture.

*Zephyr-anthus*

*Zingiber*

*Zauschneria californica*

*Zebrina*

COMPENDIUM

ZINGIBER officinale, the true "Ginger" with tropical,
cane-like stems, straight-erect from a hard, knotty root
crown, decorative in line 3-4' high:purple or white flowers
that are spotted in yellow, terminal and difficult to bring
into flower....very tender:wants are warmth, humidity, a moist
fertile soil and some shade in heat:root used in cookery, the
plant of ornamental value in the garden.   --var. darceyi, will
grow some 2-3' in height, the leaves vari-colored, white or pink
as stripes or in marginal coloration:flowers late summer and fall,
down and in complete rest over November-December:flowering spike
consists of over-lapping bracts from a base of leaf-stalks, the
flower orchid-like, the petal transparent, short-lived;rich mucky
soils are best, where strong clumps will develop.

ZINNIA elegans, annuals for summer flowering, best in a dry
atmosphere away from fog and dampness:sow seed generously indoors over March-May for extended plantings through the heat
of the year. These are old-time flowers become modern in a
large way and with many strains from dwarfs to giants; with
coloring blended beautifully, yellow through red to violet, a
pageant....diorama in the garden:thrives under good feeding in
warm, non-acid soils, but with no over-head sprinkling, which
fosters mildew. The species   -linearis, is a dwarf with particularly good forms for bedding and edging.

ZIZYPHUS jujuba, "Jujube" a small deciduous tree with
hanging branches, sometimes suckering badly in a fruit
planting where the ground is cultivated:date-like fruits
are produced early in life of the tree, rather surely in
partial shade and warmth:takes heat, drought and some alkali,
preferring soils of substance....heavy but reasonably drained.
The species   -obtusifolia, native in the Southwest will be used
for planting in extreme heat when available.

ZOYSIA tenuifolia, "Velvet-grass" thread-like leaves forming a
dark, dense mat that moves out in waves of interesting form, but
settling down eventually to an area of low hummocks....bas-relief
in plan....shear for a repetition:does with little water and no
mowing, tolerates considerable shade and should be set out only
in warmth....may show brown in cold weather, burns under a
strong fertilizer:has great possibilities as a turf
specialty:do not irrigate during spells of heat.

ZYGOCACTUS truncatus, "Crab-cactus" inevitably ending any
ordinary alphabetical plant accounting; an interesting and a
striking plant with pendulous stems and branchings from a
woody crown, the bright carmine flowers in mid-winter
attached to the curiously moulded joints or leaves:un-armed,
as opposed to the true cactus and will be used in pots in summer shade and, possibly, winter sun....or baskets where it
becomes a single plant feature to impress the eye and mind
of the incredulous:wants a fibrous mix, but of some body, and
on deterioration, remove and re-pot, retaining all roots. Firm
buds result from the right amount of shade through summer and
the correct amount of sun over the rest of the year....study
this for the plant is long-lived and should serve well. Let it
go reasonably dry late summer and through autumn, fertilizing
only in early season. An ordinary mix of loam, leafmould and
rotted manure with some moss or other fiber, should satisfy
the plant for several years. There are a number of varieties
 of which   --var. bicolor is very powerful for color,
and blooms in the fall.

445

C

INDEX

Phoenomeria magnifica, 190.
Phormium colensoi, 22, 29, 60,113
116,136,185,377.   -tenax,11,34,46
47, 53, 60, 72, 74, 76, 90,93,107,111
113,120,129,136,147,156,160,162,
377.   veitchianum, 132,377.
Phoradendron flavescens,120,133.
Photinia serrulata,4,24,33,38,41
53, 60, 69,74,89,93,102,120,127,129
131,133,134,137,145,186,188,377.
Phygelius capensis, 42,54,84,111
113,140,148,154,156,168,187,377.
Phyllanthus acidus, 12, 101, 128
159,162,378.
Phyllostachys aurea,10,34,35,120
135,157,159,161,378.
Physalis alkekengi, 157,192.
Physostegia virginiana, 14,29,42
49,71,72,93,106,141,147,148,165.
Phytolacca dioica, 18, 32, 41,44
56,71,80,82,101, 129, 137, 143, 159
168,378.
Pickeringia montana,13,22,98,104
105,145,378.
Pickle-plant, 367.
PICTURESQUE PLANTS, 163.
Pigeon, beak,341;berry,279.
Pigmy Date, 377.
Pilea microphylla, 40,43,101,116
119,121,160,171,183,378.   -nummu
laraefolia, 102,378.
Pimelea ferruginia, 24, 32, 38,48
51, 58, 63,67,89,90,127,130,140,145
152,153,184,379.   -coarctica,96
100,170,379.
Pimpernel, 213.
Pimpinella anisum, 117,166,379.
Pinckneya pubens, 14, 39, 59, 120
184,379.
Pin-clover, 285.
Pincushion Flower,406.
Pine, 379;Australian,244;Cypress
238;Bunya,216;Dammar,206;Norfolk-
island, 216.
Pineapple, Guava;-lily,292.
Pink, 274;ball,277;Ground,304;
Indian, 411;Shower, 244;-vine,215;
Waxflower, 318.
Pinus attenuata, 35, 44, 49,53,55
57,62,68,96,98,108,156,163,379.
-canariensis, 2, 16, 33,34,51,57,62
76,79,93,94,101,108,130,136,379.
-caribaea, 2, 14, 41,49,51,53,57,59
62,76,80,93,94,98,108,130,379.
-cembroides,120,156.   edulis, 35,
41,44,49,51,53,55,62,68,98,108,379
-coulteri, 13,41,51,57,65,68,80,93
94,98,108,187,379.   -halepensis,2
18, 19, 33, 41, 44,46,49,51,53,57,62
67,68, 76,81,93,94, 98,103,108,125
128,130,185,380.   -mugo,2,171,191
-patula,23,51,57,76,89,108,128,130
156,380.   -pinea,2,18,19,32,41,44
52,53,57,62,65,68,76,82,94,108,127
130,156,158,163,168,187,380.
-radiata,2,13,17,19,32,52,59,62,66
68,73,75,79,80,81,82,93,94,98,108,
127,130,158,380.   -sabiniana, 13,
17, 18, 33, 34, 41,44,49,51,53,57,62
68,80,93,94,98,108,130,135,187,380

-torreyana,13,18,42,44,49,51,53,55
62,75,79,94,98,108,125,130,158,163
Pipe-hyacinth, 257.
Piqueria trinervia, 28, 109, 113
115,122,138,179,380.
Pistache, 380.
Pistacia chinensis,3,18,33,41,46
53,69,79,81,89,119,133,163,185,380
-simaruba,41,53,158,185,380.
-texana,15,41,53,185,380.   -vera
11,41,53,185,380.
Pitcairnia xanthocalyx, 190.
Pitchberry, 381.
Pithecoctenium cynanchoides, 27,
186,381.
Pistea stratiotes, 173,381.
Pittosporum crassifolium,4,20,44
47, 49, 51,56,62, 66, 70, 75, 133,136
381.   -erioloma, 44, 56, 66, 70, 77
133,381.   -eugenioides, 19, 33, 51
56,66,77,79,81,93,131,135,158,381.
-heterophyllum, 17, 21, 23,34,41,44
45, 49, 53, 55, 56,66,70,71,77,85,98
99,102,128,130,131,165,186,381.
-phillyraeoides, 3, 19, 44,47,49,53
56,68,77,88,98,101,104,107,130,133
138,143,156,161,185,381.   -rhom
bifolium,3,17,18,23,32,48,51,63,65
77,79,81,82,89,120,127,131,133,161
381.   -tenuifolium, 4,16,34,56,66
70,77,90,91,92,118,119,158,381.
-tobira, 5,21,23,24,32,39,44,45,53
56, 62, 65, 69, 70,74,75,81,85,89,92
107, 121, 127, 129, 131, 133, 137,143
150,157,158,188,382.   -variegatum
116,132,382.   -undulatum, 3,18,32
44,45, 48, 52, 56, 66, 70, 71, 73, 76,
77,79,80,82,93,107,118,128,133,150
382.   -viridiflorum,44,52,55,56,
66,75,77,79,81,127,133,382.
PLANT HOUSE, 183.
PLANTS TO ABUSE, 71.
PLANTER BOX, 112.
PLANTING CALENDAR, 193.
Platanus orientalis, 3, 13, 17,45
52,59,66,79,80,82,128,129,159,382.
-racemosa, 17,18,35,46,56,59,66,81
128,129,133,158,163,182,382.
Platycerium bifurcatum, 10,183.
Platycodon grandiflorum, 192.
Platystemon californicus, 14,97.
Pleiogynium solandri, 11,18,66.
Plum, Burdekin,382;Coco,253;Jam-
bolan,420;Kafir,311;Natal, 242;
Pigeon, 259.
Plumbago capensis, 6,21,23,32,37
41, 45, 51, 66, 70,74,99,125,128,141
148,149,152,186,382.   -alba,83,84
87,94,138,382.   -indica, 382.
Plume-acacia, 208.
Plumeria emarginata, 35, 83, 107
137,163,190.
Poa species, 124,383.
Podachaenium eminens, 18, 67, 103
129,383.
Podalyria sericea, 6, 75, 106,135
140,150,383.
Podocarpus elongata, 2, 18, 33,42
45, 51, 66,68,69,73,77,79,81,89,119
127,156,161,163,187,383.   -macro

ACACIA saligna, "Goldenwreath W." a coarse tree 15', rounding shrub
like, of extremely rapid growth in meager soils;the leaves are long
and unusually wide, undulating;massed large flower balls are nearly
orange, open April-May and scattering;a filler type.

COBAEA scandens, "Cup and Saucer-vine" perennial,developing fairly dense foliage with amazing speed, normally used for temporary effects;the flowers are yellowish green at first, changing to a violet-
purple, later;an annual north or in frost, growing 10-20', the flat,
winged seeds to be planted in early spring set individually on edge;
there are no pests that are serious.

CRASSULA corallina(nana)an Orpet introduction into Southern California, prostrate, spreading, only some 2" through the mat of closely
crowded, pale green leaves....stems will root-in sparingly.  This is
a diminutive for a fissure in half-shade and moisture, to be used in
carpet bedding, or more largely spread for choice texture in a floor
block;tiny white flowers rise 3-4" in summer.

MICROLEPIA platyphylla,  a large fern, 3-4' over-all, in good mass
of exceedingly handsome, delicate fronds of medium cut and graceful
sway;wants shadow, drainage and moisture;does not spread unduly  and
will be used more generally when better known.

OLIVERANTHUS elegans, a low, shrubby succulent, with bright color
over summer, the five-angled, short-tubular, red flowers tipped in
yellow when opened;wants a loose soil of good drainage and some fertility with warmth to prosper;does poorly over winter, but will  be
found frost-hardy into warm-temperate regions:pots, a basket which it
will fill in time or used with rock.

PLECTRANTHUS australis, "Cockspur Flower"  patio plant for a basket
or pot or used as quick cover in fairly deep shade, the foliage of an
unusual texture, due to various sizing of the meaty remotely toothed
leaves:slender lilac flowers in summer, or warmth. The small roundish
leaf is dark green and pales-out as it becomes of size, contrasting in
the spreading, open mass....pinch in to compact.

SEDUM caeruleum, an annual to have in odd corners and places of the
naturalistic garden:growing 3-4" in height, blooming in the  summer,
the blue flowers white at the back:a casual for the rock garden.

THUNBERGIA laurifolia, climbing as  high as 60 ft., a woody twiner
with a leathery, laurel-like leaf and a light blue flower with a white
eye:dependable for winter bloom where warmth holds.

# 1998 NOMENCLATURE INDEX

The science of taxonomy is constantly striving to clarify
our understanding of the natural world through the proper
classification of living animals and plants.  As a result,
many plant names have changed since Roland Stewart Hoyt
first wrote this book in 1938.  The whole book was surveyed
to determine which names were no longer valid.  To assist
the reader in finding information on a particular plant,
this book includes  an index of modern botanic names to
supplement the original index.  This index contains the
most recent botanical name cross referenced with Hoyt's
nomenclature and relevant page numbers.

| MOST RECENT BOTANICAL NAME | HOYT NOMENCLATURE | PAGE |
|---|---|---|
| Bougainvillea buttiana 'Mrs. Butt' | Bougainvillea 'Crimson Lake' | 7,26,27,32,37,41,46, 56,70,70,74,77,85,87, 98,105,159,186,231 |
| Bougainvillea glabra 'Sanderana' | Bougainvillea Sanderiana | 7,26,27,32,37,41,46, 56,70,85,87,98,105, 145,154,159,168,186,231 |
| Bougainvillea spectabilis 'Lateritia' | Bougainvillea lateritia | 231 |
| Bouvardia alexanderae | Bouvardia alexanderiae | 21,57,63,105,107,109, 119,152,154,169,183,231 |
| Bouvardia longiflora | Bouvardia humboldti | 3,40,44,50,56,63,65,69,79, 81,82,89,128,129,140,146, 153,159,162,168,185,232 |
| Brachychiton acerifolius | Brachychiton acerifolium | 3,19,31,40,44,46,50,56,68, 79,90,93,119,128,185,232 |
| Brachychiton populneus | Brachychiton populneum | 1,23,45,55,65,71,81,90, 125,136,163,286 |
| Brahea armata | Erythea armata | 34,71,90,286 |
| Brahea brandegeei | Erythea brandegeei | 2,16,45,55,65,71,76, 79,90,286 |
| Brahea edulis | Erythea edulis | 5,21,38,51,91,92,104, 132,184,233 |
| Breynia disticha | Breynia nivosa | 233 |
| Breynia disticha 'Atropurpurea' | Breynia nivosa var. atropurpurea | 233 |
| Breynia disticha 'Roseo-picta' | Breynia nivosa var. roseo-picta | 51,59,129,272 |
| Brugmansia sanguinea | Datura sanguinea | 4,52,59,67,85,90,103, 118,129,145,155,162, 168,273 |
| Brugmansia suaveolens | Datura suaveolens | 143,153,234 |
| Brunfelsia pauciflora 'Eximia' | Brunfelsia calycina var. eximia | 151,234 |
| Brunfelsia pauciflora 'Floribunda' | Brunfelsia calycina var. floribunda | 234 |
| Brunfelsia pauciflora 'Macrantha' | Brunfelsia calycina var. macrantha | 23,39,42,48,57,59,60, 63,127,183,184,234 |
| Brunfelsia pauciflora var. calycina | Brunfelsia calycina | 4,20,33,34,36,52,59,67, 78,93,103,125,186,235 |
| Buddleia asiatica | Buddleja asiatica | 4,22,23,36,52,59,67,68, 73,78,105,107,141,146, 149,153,186,187,235 |
| Buddleia davidi magnifica | Buddleja davidi magnifica | 22,33,36,48,52,59,78,89, 92,141,147,153,186,235 |
| Buddleia lindleyana | Buddleja lindleyana | 21,36,52,67,78,97,103, 117,122,186,235 |
| Buddleia madagascariensis | Buddleja madagascariensis | 33,36,52,59,67,78,118, 134,147,186,235 |
| Buddleia nivea | Buddleja nivea | 5,20,22,36,52,59,67, 76,78,103,107,186,235 |
| Buddleia salviifolia | Buddleja salvifolia | 41,53,158,185,380 |
| Bursera simaruba | Pistacia simaruba | 5,38,235 |
| Buxus harlandii | Buxus harlandi | 15,22,34,35,37,41,49, 51,57,60,62,69,78,98, 100,102,103,130,139, 146,152,161,163,165, 168,186,384 |
| Caesalpinia gilliesii | Poinciana gilliesi | |
| Caesalpinia pulcherrima | Poinciana pulcherrima | 5,20,37,41,47,78,92, 93,103,139,153,159,384 |
| Calathea roseopicta | Calathea roseo-picta | 109,112,113,116,132, 135,160,183,236 |
| Calliandra haematocephala | Calliandra inaequilatera | 20,23,35,41,66,73,83,89, 130,140,143,149,150,237 |
| Calliandra tweedii | Calliandra tweedi | 35,66,68,70,130,140, 143,144,237 |
| Callistemon citrinus | Callistemon lanceolatus | 4,20,33,36,41,44,45, 46,51,56,66,68,70,76, 80,101,125,140,143,144, 153,186,237 |
| Callitris preissii | Callitris robusta | 16,19,34,44,66,90, 127,155,156,238 |
| Calocedrus decurrens | Libocedrus decurrens | 13,16,33,45,51,65,69, 80,81,94,108,130,156, 158,163,187,335 |
| Calocephalus brownii | Calocephalus browni | 21,22,24,28,32,36,41, 70,91,92,104,114,121, 134,168,169,170,186,238 |

NOMENCLATURE INDEX

| MOST RECENT BOTANICAL NAME | HOYT NOMENCLATURE | PAGE |
|---|---|---|
| Camellia sinensis | Thea sinensis | 38,43,58,90,92,127,150, 157,183,424 |
| Camissonia cheiranthifolia | Oenothera cheiranthifolia | 14,37,45,47,50,52,54, 57,61,70,97,123,363 |
| Campanula isophylla 'Mayi' | Campanula isophylla var. mayi | 24,38,46,48,51,78,86,109, 114,116,138,148,188,240 |
| Canarina canariensis | Canarina campanulata | 43,111,151,160,169,183,240 |
| Cardiospermum grandiflorum Forma hirsutum | Cardiospermum hirsutum | 7,15,27,41,84,106, 120,152,241 |
| Carica pubescens | Carica candamarcensis | 242 |
| Carissa bispinosa | Carissa arduina | 92,105,133,242 |
| Carissa macrocarpa | Carissa grandiflora | 12,20,22,23,32,41,60, 62,66,73,75,88,92,105, 107,127,131,132,133,137, 151,158,182,186,242 |
| Carissa macrocarpa 'Minima' | Carissa grandiflora var. minima | 91, 242 |
| Carissa macrocarpa 'Prostrata' | Carissa grandiflora var. prostrata | 21,64,86,94,98,242 |
| Carpobrotus chilensis | Mesembryanthemum aequilaterale | 14,37,47,50,54,55,72, 76,96,97,145,350 |
| Carpobrotus edulis | Mesembryanthemum edule | 37,47,50,54,72,74, 75,95,96,98,102,351 |
| Cassia didymobotrya | Cassia nairobensis | 36,54,60,70,103,128, 149,150,151,244 |
| Cassine orientalis | Elaeodendron orientale | 32,62,79,111,133,282 |
| Castilleja exserta | Orthocarpus purpurascens | 14,117,366 |
| Casuarina cristata | Casuarina lepidophloia | 33,40,44,46,50,59,69,76, 93,97,104,130,163,244 |
| Catharanthus roseus | Vinca rosea | 6,14,29,37,42,50,57,61, 71,72,93,112,113,115, 138,141,147,148,149,152, 187,437 |
| Cedrus atlantica 'Glauca' | Cedrus atlantica var. glauca | 136, 246 |
| Centaurium scilloides | Centaureum massoni | 30,38,51,58,100,165, 181,182,247 |
| Centaurium venustum | Centaureum venustum | 13,37,51,106,144,247 |
| Cephalophyllum anemoniflorum | Mesembryanthemum anemoniflorum | 12,37,47,50,54,55,72, 76,95,96,187,350 |
| Ceratostigma griffithii | Ceratostigma griffithi | 6,21,52,68,75,97,98, 141,149,248 |
| Cercidium floridum | Cercidium torreyanum | 15,33,98,105,136,158,248 |
| Ceropegia woodii | Ceropegia woodi | 34,40,86,114,249 |
| Cestrum elegans | Cestrum purpureum | 22,36,45,48,52,59, 66,103,140,150,152, 153,159,182,184,249 |
| Chaerophyllum tainturieri var. dasycarpum | Chaerophyllum dasycarpum | 28,107,121,122,138, 165,179,250 |
| Chamaecyparis funebris | Cupressus funebris | 17,19,33,50,66,68,90, 108,128,130,156,161, 163, 267 |
| Chamaedorea elegans | Collinia elegans | 39,84,99,111,113,116, 183,260 |
| Chamelaucium uncinatum | Chamaelaucium ciliatum | 5,21,33,35,36,44,54, 55,67,99,105,108,120, 143,150,186,250 |
| Chasmanthe aethiopica | Antholyza aethiopica | 10,141,144,150,179,181,215 |
| Chiranthodendron pentadactylon | Chiranthodendron platanoides | 120,129,135,146,159,251 |
| Chlorophytum comosum | Chlorophytum elatum | 40,55,86,95,109,114, 132, 251 |
| Chonemorpha fragrans | Trachelospermum fragrans | 27,84,85,88,129,130, 160, 428 |
| Chrysanthemum mawii | Chrysanthemum mawi | 37,44,50,53,55,58, 78,95,104,106,123, 146,152,179,188,252 |
| Chrysanthemum parthenium 'Aureum' | Chrysanthemum parthenium var. aureum | 29,114,167,253 |
| Chrysophyllum cainito | Chrysophyllum caineto | 11,113,119,135,160,253 |
| Cibotium schiedei | Cibotium schiederi | 10,60,63,111,159,184,253 |
| Cissus adenopoda | Cissus adenopodus | 7,27,68,70,113,114, 134,135,254 |
| Cistus hybridus | Cistus corbariensis | 5,21,22,36,41,44,45,49, 51,54,55,56,60,67,68, 71,73,76,97,98,99, 137,144,146,169,186, 188,255 |

NOMENCLATURE INDEX

| MOST RECENT BOTANICAL NAME | HOYT NOMENCLATURE | PAGE |
|---|---|---|
| Delosperma pruinosum | Mesembryanthemum echinatum | 37,47,50,54,72,75, 96,99,187,351 |
| Dianthus gratianopolitanus | Dianthus caesius | 30,37,42,50,53,51,61,74, 77,95,96,118,121,141, 170,171,182,186,188,274 |
| Dichelostemma capitatum | Brodiaea capitata | 10,31,53,106,123,142, 144,165,180,186,188,233 |
| Dichelostemma ida-maia | Brevoortia ida-maia | 13,31,141,145,180,188,233 |
| Dichondra micrantha | Dichondra repens | 124,182,275 |
| Dieffenbachia maculata | Dieffenbachia picta | 40,109,113,114,116, 132,160,183,185,275 |
| Dierama pulcherrimum | Dierama pulcherrima | 24,29,37,59,123,141, 145,161,174,275 |
| Dietes bicolor | Moraea bicolor | 29,42,44,50,70,74,77, 124,157,180,355 |
| Dietes vegeta | Moraea catenulata, Moraea iridioides | 11,29,42,44,46,50,54, 70,72,74,77,86,98, 102,110,114,123,124, 147,153,157,151,170, 180,187,355 |
| Dimorphotheca pluvialis | Dimorphotheca annua | 37,42,44,50,51,70,102, 122,123,145,165,186,276 |
| Dimorphotheca sinuata | Dimorphotheca aurantiaca | 8,37,42,44,47,50,51, 70,102,114,151,122,123, 139,149,151,165,171, 181,186,276 |
| Dioon edule | Dion edule | 2,35,33,36,41,44,49, 69,70,71,74,87,89,92, 108,118,130,137,143, 171,186,276 |
| Diplacus puniceus | Mimulus puniceus | 13,22,55,59,60,71, 139,168,354 |
| Distictis buccinatoria | Phaedranthus buccinatorius | 7,24,26,32,46,48,53,67, 70,74,75,85,87,88,90, 127,140,149,152,154,374 |
| Distictis laxiflora | Distictis lactiflora | 25,27,67,70,78,82,88, 95,142,144,145,146, 148,149,154,277 |
| Dodonaea viscosa 'Purpurea' | Dodonaea viscosa var. purpurea | 135,277 |
| Dombeya tiliacea | Dombeya natalensis | 36,129,137,150,159,277 |
| Dracaena surculosa | Dracaena godseffiana | 110,113,120,132,278 |
| Drosanthemum floribundum | Mesembryanthemum floribundum | 12,30,37,47,50,54,55, 72,74,76,86,95,96,98,99, 102,124,141,145,187,351 |
| Drosanthemum speciosum | Mesembryanthemum speciosum | 37,47,51,54,55,72,74, 76,86,96,99,141,144, 154,169,170,352 |
| Dudleya attenuata subsp. orcuttii | Stylophyllum orcuttii | 14,110,115,170,172,419 |
| Dudleya pulverulenta | Echeveria pulverulenta | 12,13,39,43,49,61,76, 134,170,280 |
| Dyckia brevifolia | Dyckia sulphurea | 12,101,110,116,149,172,279 |
| Dyssodia tenuiloba | Thymophylla tenuiloba | 8,15,37,42,52,115,147,426 |
| Echeveria derenbergii | Echeveria derenbergi | 12,43,49,61,78,95,101, 115,121,172,280 |
| Echeveria gibbiflora 'Metallica' | Echeveria metalica | 43,49,61,110,280 |
| Echeveria harmsii | Echeveria harmsi | 43,49,61,115,172,280 |
| Echinocactus grusonii | Echinocactus grusoni | 12,25,105,113,280 |
| Echinocereus pectinatus var.rigidissimus | Echinocereus rigidissimus | 15,105,117,280 |
| Elaeagnus pungens 'Fruitlandii' | Elaeagnus pungens var. fruitlandi | 120,282 |
| Elaeagnus pungens 'Reflexa' | Elaeagnus pungens var. reflexa | 85,87,282 |
| Elymus arenarius | Elymus arenarious | 282 |
| Emilia javanica | Emilia sagittata | 8,107,109,147,148,154,181,282 |
| Endymion hispanicus | Scilla hispanica | 31,102,108,118,122, 142,151,166,169,172, 181,182,187,189,407 |
| Ensete ventricosum | Musa ensete | 19,63,129,159,357 |
| Epilobium californicum | Zauschneria californica | 6,13,32,37,45,49,51, 54,55,72,86,95,98,99, 100,104,117,125,136, 140,148,166,170,171,444 |
| Epipremnum aureum | Scindapsis aureus | 25,27,40,116,119,132, 160,183,408 |

# NOMENCLATURE INDEX

| MOST RECENT BOTANICAL NAME | HOYT NOMENCLATURE | PAGE |
|---|---|---|
| Eranthemum pulchellum | Eranthemum nervosum | 39,42,48,63,141,143, 150,159,183,283 |
| Erigeron karvinskianus | Erigeron karvinskyanus | 9,28,30,44,50,55,70, 72,74,77,95,96,100, 121,152,170,186,284 |
| Eriogonum grande var. rubescens | Eriogonum rubescens | 36,49,54,76,86,96,97, 100,107,125,169,285 |
| Erythrina bidwillii | Erythrina bidwilli | 40,59,69,83,99,120, 140,146,287 |
| Erythrina corallodendrum | Erythrina corallodendron | 18,40,59,66,82,120, 140,159,184,287 |
| Escallonia bifida | Escallonia montevidensis | 4,33,42,52,69,62,66, 69,70,71,76,81,128, 137,143,152,184,288 |
| Escallonia glasneviensis | Escallonia glasniviensis | 5,24,34,42,552,59,62, 66,69,70,74,76,88,92, 128,152,184,287 |
| Escallonia laevis | Escallonia organensis | 33,42,52,59,62,69,70,74, 76,128,137,146,184,288 |
| Eucalyptus blakelyi | Eucalyptus blackeleyi | 56,59,69,71,184,288 |
| Eucalyptus camaldulensis | Eucalyptus rostrata | 3,40,44,46,52,53,56, 62,68,69,71,73,79,80, 93,94,127,185,291 |
| Eucalyptus citriodora | Eucalyptus maculata citriodora | 18,32,40,76,81,89,108, 128,290 |
| Eucalyptus globulus 'Compacta' | Eucalyptus globulus var. compacta | 103,136,290 |
| Eucalyptus lehmannii | Eucalyptus lehmanni | 3,18,40,44,45,46,55, 56,62,69,71,73,75,93, 98,103,119,135,158, 163,290 |
| Eucalyptus sideroxylon | Eucalyptus sideroxylon rosea | 3,17,33,40,45,52,55, 56,62,68,69,71,73,76, 79,81,82,98,132,140, 143,185,291 |
| Eucalyptus stricklandii | Eucalyptus stricklandi | 40,44,56,69,71,103, 150,185,291 |
| Eucomis autumnalis | Eucomis undulata | 48,121,147,162,292 |
| Eugenia supra-axillaris | Eugenia supraaxillaris | 4,14,52,62,71,128,161,293 |
| Euonymus japonicus 'Albomarginatus' | Euonymus japonicus var. albo-marginatus | 293 |
| Euonymus japonicus 'Aureo-marginatus' | Euonymus japonicus var. aureo-marginatus | 293 |
| Euonymus japonicus 'Microphyllus' | Euonymus japonicus var. microphyllus | 6,91,100,171,293 |
| Euphorbia clavarioides var. truncata | Euphorbia truncata | 30,53,70,86,95,101, 132,156,172,186,295 |
| Euphorbia lathyris | Euphorbia lathyrus | 53,70,132,155,186,294 |
| Euphorbia milii var. splendens | Euphorbia splendens | 12,21,35,53,55,70,99, 105,110,116,149,150, 151,157,186,295 |
| Felicia bergerana | Felicia bergeriana | 8,24,37,55,61,70,142, 145,154,171,297 |
| Felicia fruticosa | Aster fruticosus | 5,22,33,36,55,70,71, 87,101,109,144,153, 164,187,222 |
| Ferocactus cylindraceus | Echinocactus cylindraceus | 105,280 |
| Festuca ovina var. glauca | Festuca glauca | 10,28,95,114,121,136, 182,186,188,297 |
| Ficus microcarpa | Ficus retusa | 3,17,18,32,45,19,52, 56,62,65,69,71,73,76, 79,90,111,127,130,298 |
| Fragaria vesca | Fragaria californica | 39,299 |
| Fraxinus velutina | Fraxinus velutina var. coriacea | 3,15,17,18,32,46,47,56, 66,79,80,81,94,127,185,300 |
| Fraxinus velutina 'Modesto' | Fraxinus velutina var. glabra | 3,15,17,18,32,46,47, 56,66,79,80,81,94,127, 185,300 |
| Fremontodendron californicum | Fremontia californica | 13,20,33,54,66,71,98, 105,139,143,182,300 |
| Fremontodendron mexicanum | Fremontia mexicana | 54,145,153,168,300 |
| Furcraea foetida | Furcraea gigantea | 76,111,301 |

# NOMENCLATURE INDEX

| MOST RECENT BOTANICAL NAME | HOYT NOMENCLATURE | PAGE |
|---|---|---|
| Malacothamnus fasciculatus | Malvastrum fasciculatum | 15,22,35,41,44,54,70,<br>96,98,103,128,133,134,<br>140,151,346 |
| Malephora crocea | Mesembryanthemum croceum | 12,30,37,47,50,54,55,<br>74,76,86,95,96,97,99,<br>102,141,183,351 |
| Malosma laurina | Rhus laurina | 13,22,53,54,357 |
| Malvaviscus arboreus var.<br>mexicanus | Malvaviscus grandiflorus | 5,21,59,66,103,140,<br>146,346 |
| Mandevilla laxa | Mandevilla suaveolens | 7,24,26,33,37,43,48,<br>51,57,66,70,84,104,<br>108,138,146,185,346 |
| Manettia inflata | Manettia bicolor | 26,100,110,113,130,<br>140,152,169,183,346 |
| Manilkara zapota | Achras zapota | 11,31,35,44,52,62,65,<br>76,82,93,94,159,204 |
| Marah macrocarpus | Echinocystus macrocarpa | 68,117,122,281 |
| Matthiola incana | Mathiola incana | 9,29,48,52,77,108,112,<br>115,141,167,169,179,<br>187,347 |
| Matthiola longipetala subsp.<br>bicornis | Mathiola bicornis | 118,347 |
| Medicago polymorpha | Medicago denticulata | 117,124,347 |
| Melaleuca huegelii | Melaleuca huegeli | 4,35,41,47,62,66,70,71,<br>77,81,89,127,130,137,<br>145,156,186,348 |
| Melaleuca hypericifolia | Melaleuca hyperiscifolia | 5,21,41,44,47,49,55,<br>62,67,70,71,74,125,<br>128,135,140,186,348 |
| Melaleuca quinquenervia | Melaleuca leucadendra | 17,41,45,46,47,49,52,<br>55,59,62,70,76,79,81,<br>93,101,104,133,158,<br>162,184,348 |
| Melia azedarach<br>'Umbraculiformis' | Melia azedarach var.<br>umbraculiformis | 19,32,162,349 |
| Mentha requienii | Mentha requieni | 43,61,86,100,102,108,<br>119,182,349 |
| Mertya sinclairii | Mertya sinclairi | 102,129,134,135,350 |
| Metrosideros excelsus | Metrosideros tomentosa | 3,17,18,19,35,40,51,<br>59,62,65,69,75,79,<br>81,52,91,136,140,144,<br>153,158,163,184,352 |
| Michelia figo | Michelia fuscata | 4,24,38,43,52,65,69,<br>78,81,83,85,88,89,<br>100,107,111,131,135,<br>145,157,184,188,353 |
| Microcoelum weddellianum | Syagrus weddelliana | 63,100,111,116,130,<br>183,420 |
| Mina lobata | Quamoclit lobata | 7,37,51,61,68,129,148,<br>169,188,392 |
| Mindium campanuloides | Michauxia campanuloides | 9,29,138,154,162,353 |
| Moraea neopavonia | Moraea pavonia | 29,42,50,70,77,141,<br>180,355 |
| Moraea ramosissima | Moraea ramosa | 31,60,70,77,139,145,<br>157,180,185,188,355 |
| Moraea tricuspidata | Moraea glaucopis | 24,42,50,70,77,138,<br>171,180,355 |
| Morisia monanthos | Morisia monantha | 30,42,50,102,124,169,<br>171,356 |
| Morus alba 'Kingan' | Morus rubra var. kingan | 356 |
| Mucuna deeringiana | Stizolobium deeringianum | 7,58,68,88,95,117,134,<br>142,185,418 |
| Muehlenbeckia axillaris | Muehlenbeckia axillare | 55,86,95,98,124,170,<br>182,188,356 |
| Murraya paniculata | Murraea paniculata | 5,20,85,356 |
| Musa acuminata 'Dwarf Cavendish' | Musa cavendishi | 100,159,357 |
| Musa paradisiaca | Musa sapientum | 11,159,168,357 |
| Myosotis sylvatica | Myosotis alpestris | 9,28,40,43,60,61,64,<br>70,74,115,118,119,155,<br>167,181,183,188,357 |
| Myriophyllum aquaticum | Myriophyllum proserpinacoides | 97,173,357 |
| Myrtus communis | Myrtus communis var. italica,<br>Myrtus communis var. romana | 16,90,111,358<br>358 |

# NOMENCLATURE INDEX

| MOST RECENT BOTANICAL NAME | HOYT NOMENCLATURE | PAGE |
|---|---|---|
| Osmanthus heterophyllus 'Aureus' | Osmanthus ilicifolius var. aureo-marginatus | 366 |
| Osmanthus heterophyllus 'Purpureus' | Osmanthus ilicifolius var. atro-purpureus | 366 |
| Osmanthus heterophyllus 'Variegatus' | Osmanthus ilicifolius var. argenteo-marginatus | 366 |
| Osteospermum ecklonis | Dimorphotheca ecklonis | 37,42,44,50,51,70,72, 76,92,102,104,122,123, 142,153,165,186,276 |
| Othonna capensis | Othonna crassifolia | 12,49,55,78,95,101, 112,115,139,147,149, 151,159,170,187,368 |
| Oxalis bowiei | Oxalis bowieana | 10,31,43,61,70,72,74, 78,102,115,119,122, 123,149,165,172,180, 182,187,188,367 |
| Oxalis herrerae | Oxalis hererei | 39,43,61,70,78,100, 110,113,114,165,180, 181,187,367 |
| Oxalis pes-caprae | Oxalis cernua | 31,43,61,70,72,78,102, 119,123,139,144,165, 180,187,367 |
| Palafoxia hookerana | Polypteris hookeriana | 15,28,45,61,123,147, 154,179,385 |
| Parthenocissus tricuspidata 'Lowii' | Parthenocissus tricuspidata var. lowi | 26,40,70,121,142,144, 145,180,185,370 |
| Parthenocissus tricuspidata 'Veitchii' | Parthenocissus tricuspidata var. veitchi | 370 |
| Passiflora alatocaerulea | Passiflora alato-caerulea | 26,37,50,68,74,78,87,90, 108,145,146,152,162,370 |
| Pellaea andromedifolia | Pellaea andromedaefolia | 10,14,42,50,55,57,61, 64,72,78,104,158,165, 169,170,171,187,372 |
| Peltophorum pterocarpum | Peltophorum inerme | 3,55,62,63,66,81,82, 89,106,107,138,146,148, 152,161,372 |
| Peperomia argyreia | Peperomia sandersi | 109,132,160,183,373 |
| Phacelia minor | Phacelia whitlavia | 14,37,45,61,115,122, 123,142,144,179,374 |
| Philodendron domesticum | Philodendron hastatum | 40,66,85,113,116,160, 183,375 |
| Philodendron scandens subsp. oxycardium | Philodendron oxycardium | 25,26,40,84,85,116, 160,375 |
| Philodendron wendlandii | Philodendron wendlandi | 40,113,116,183,375 |
| Phlox drummondii | Phlox drummondi | 8,15,28,30,37,42,49, 61,74,77,112,115,122, 165,181,188,376 |
| Phoenix roebelenii | Phoenix roebelini | 34,41,48,65,69,76,84, 88,100,111,113,116, 130,377 |
| Phormium tenax 'Variegatum' | Phormium tenax var. Veitchianum | 132,377 |
| Photinia serrulata 'Nova' | Photinia serrulata var. nova | 4,24,33,38,41,53,60, 69,74,89,93,102,120, 127,129,131,133,134, 137,145,186,188,377 |
| Phyla nodiflora | Lippia canescens, Lippia nodiflora | 42,50,77,86,122,124,338 |
| Pilea nummulariifolia | Pilea nummulariaefolia | 102,378 |
| Pimelea prostrata | Pimelea coarctica | 96,100,170,379 |
| Pithecellobium flexicaule | Ebenopsis flexicaulis | 15,81,158,279 |
| Pittosporum tobira 'Variegata' | Pittosporum tobira var. variegatum | 116,132,382 |
| Platycladus orientalis | Thuja orientalis | 2,17,19,32,52,65,70, 78,81,111,130,135,161, 187,425 |
| Platycladus orientalis 'Aureus' | Thuja orientalis var. aurea nana | 65,81,90,425 |
| Platycladus orientalis 'Beverlyensis' | Thuja orientalis var. beverlyensis | 2,65,81,90,425 |
| Platycladus orientalis 'Bonita' | Thuja orientalis var. bonita | 2,65,81,90,425 |
| Platycladus orientalis 'Elegantissimus' | Thuja orientalis var. elegantissima | 2,65,81,90,425 |
| Platycladus orientalis 'Strictus' | Thuja orientalis var. pyramidalis | 425 |
| Pleiogynium cerasiferum | Pleiogynium solandri | 11,18,66,382 |

# NOMENCLATURE INDEX

| MOST RECENT BOTANICAL NAME | HOYT NOMENCLATURE | PAGE |
|---|---|---|
| Pleiospilos bolusii | Mesembryanthemum bolusi | 37,47,50,55,72,149, 162,172,187,351 |
| Plumbago auriculata | Plumbago capensis | 6,21,23,32,37,41,45, 51,66,70,74,99,125, 128,141,148,149,152, 186,382 |
| Plumbago auriculata 'Alba' | Plumbago capensis var. alba | 83,84,87,94,138,382 |
| Podocarpus gracilior | Podocarpus elongata | 2,18,33,42,45,51,66, 68,69,73,77,79,81,89, 119,127,156,161,163, 187,383 |
| Podocarpus macrophyllus | Podocarpus macrophylla | 2,17,32,42,51,68,77, 111,119,128,156,384 |
| Podocarpus macrophyllus var. maki | Podocarpus macrophylla var. maki | 384 |
| Polianthes geminiflora | Bravoa geminiflora | 144,150,169,180,181,233 |
| Polygonum aubertii | Polygonum auberti | 7,27,34,44,46,50,51, 58,67,72,74,78,85,87, 104,106,130,138,148, 149,161,188,385 |
| Polypodium aureum 'Mandaianum' | Polypodium mandaianum | 10,104,119,160,385 |
| Populus alba 'Pyramidalis' | Populus alba var. pyramidalis | 17,386 |
| Populus fremontii | Populus fremonti | 17,46,53,56,67,94,128, 129,158,161,185,386 |
| Populus nigra 'Italica' | Populus nigra italica | 3,17,34,45,56,66,73 79,93,94,104,128,129, 131,133,161,163,386 |
| Populus simonii | Populus simoni | 45,56,67,79,93,128, 161,386 |
| Poterium sanguisorba | Sanguisorba minor | 157,166,403 |
| Prunus dulcis | Prunus amygdalus | 3,11,17,18,23,41,51,78, 81,82,89,106,107,388 |
| Prunus ilicifolia subsp. lyonii | Prunus lyoni | 4,13,20,43,45,48,54, 57,66,74,77,79,81,98, 128,131,164,137,182, 389 |
| Prunus jacquemontii | Prunus jacquemonti | 6,51,78,85,88,100,121, 156,182,388 |
| Pseudosasa japonica | Arundinaria japonica | 45,72,156,159,161,220 |
| Psidium cattleianum 'Lucidum' | Psidium cattleianum var. lucidum | 133,389 |
| Pteridium aquilinum | Pteris aquilina | 10,55,58,64,71,72,98, 104,117,123,189,390 |
| Pteris multifida | Pteris serrulata | 57,71,116,189,390 |
| Ptychosperma macarthurii | Actinophloeus macarthuri | 1,34,111,128,159,205 |
| Pueraria lobata | Pueraria thunbergiana | 7,26,41,50,68,94,95, 142,148,157,186,390 |
| Punica granatum 'Nana' | Punica granatum var. nana | 6,23,65,91,100,110, 157,171,390 |
| Puya berteroniana | Puya alpestris | 12,25,37,45,54,71,91, 102,111,120,142,149, 162,391 |
| Pyracantha coccinea 'Lalandei' | Pyracantha coccinea lalandi | 4,5,20,34,45,47,53, 57,66,69,71,74,77,92, 105,120,127,133,137, 158,182,186,188,391 |
| Pyracantha fortuneana | Pyracantha crenato-serrata, Pyracantha crenato-serrata var. yunnanensis | 5,21,23,32,35,45,53,55, 57,55,59,74,77,86,88, 89,92,105,120,130,133, 134,137,182,186,188,391 |
| Pyracantha koidzumii | Pyracantha koidzumi | 4,33,35,45,53,55,57, 67,69,74,77,84,88,105, 120,128,133,137,163, 182,186,188,391 |
| Pyrostegia venusta | Pyrostegia ignea | 7,25,26,27,33,37,50, 53,67,70,74,85,88,128, 139,150,154,392 |
| Pyrus kawakamii | Pyrus kawakami | 83,392 |
| Quercus douglasii | Quercus douglasi | 3,13,17,41,44,66,71,79, 91,119,136,187,393 |
| Rehmannia elata | Rehmannia angulata | 29,39,49,53,71,102, 106,395 |
| Rhamnus ilicifolia | Rhamnus crocea var. ilicifolia | 13,131,395 |

| MOST RECENT BOTANICAL NAME | HOYT NOMENCLATURE | PAGE |
|---|---|---|
| Rhaphiolepis delacourii | Raphiolepis delacouri | 24,38,48,53,62,69,71,75, 87,130,134,143,150,153, 157,158,188,394 |
| Rhaphiolepis indica | Raphiolepis indica | 5,20,21,23,33,38,43, 45,58,53,60,52,58,59, 70,74,81,85,87,89,90, 92,134,145,150,157,158, 171,188,394 |
| Rhaphiolepis umbellata | Raphiolepis ovata | 6,21,23,32,39,48,92, 127,133,134,143,150, 157,158,171,188,394 |
| Rhododendron austrinum | Azalea austrina | 14,42,51,57,58,64,78, 107,139,143,184,223 |
| Rhododendron indicum | Azalea indica | 5,23,39,42,51,57,63, 64,78,87,89,92,107, 109,140,149,150,153, 183,184,187,223 |
| Rhododendron kaempferi | Azalea obtusa var. kaempferi | 223 |
| Rhododendron obtusum | Azalea obtusa | 6,39,42,51,57,64,78, 100,107,109,156,170, 184,223 |
| Rhododendron obtusum 'Amoenum' | Azalea obtusa var. amoena | 233 |
| Rhododendron serrulatum | Azalea serrulata | 42,51,57,64,78,107,131, 137,146,184,223 |
| Rhoicissus capensis | Cissus capensis | 26,27,44,50,70,72,74, 77,85,129,132,134,155, 168,254 |
| Rhus glabra var. cismontana | Rhus cismontana | 15,49,53,55,57,62,66, 98,100,104,125,182,396 |
| Rhynchelytrum repens | Tricholaena rosea | 10,25,117,120,121,166, 185,429 |
| Ribes sanguineum var. glutinosum | Ribes glutinosum | 38,43,48,53,61,64,66,78, 89,140,143,150,188,397 |
| Rosmarinus officinalis 'Prostratus' | Rosmarinus officinalis var. prostratus | 399 |
| Rosularia pallida | Umbilicus chrysanthus | 102,115,149,170,172, 182,432 |
| Rumohra adiantiformis | Polystichum adiantiforme | 10,24,64,119,131,385 |
| Ruschia uncinata | Mesembryanthemum uncinatum | 6,37,47,50,54,55,72, 76,99,145,187,352 |
| Sabal bermudana | Sabal bermudiana | 184,400 |
| Salix babylonica 'Crispa' | Salix babylonica var. crispa | 33,93,158,162,401 |
| Salvia clevelandii | Salvia clevelandi | 37,50,54,61,67,78,107, 118,146,149,187,402 |
| Salvia greggii | Salvia greggi | 5,15,21,37,49,50,60, 61,71,72,77,88,89,99, 102,106,110,140,148, 149,152,165,179,187,402 |
| Sambucus mexicana | Sambucus caerulea var. neo-mexicana, Sambucus caerulea var. velutina | 13,14,15,22,48,67,129, 130,188,403 |
| Sambucus simpsonii | Sambucus simpsoni | 14,22,48,67,403 |
| Sarcococca hookerana | Sarcococca hookeriana | 5,22,23,24,39,42,44, 45,48,64,65,69,70,74,88, 98,127,134,150,188,404 |
| Saritaea magnifica | Arrabidaea magnifica | 24,27,70,78,85,88,140, 149,153,154,219 |
| Satureja douglasii | Micromeria chamissonis | 14,30,40,59,64,95,104, 108,166,174,185,335 |
| Saxifraga stolonifera | Saxifraga sarmentosa | 30,40,43,64,95,114, 132,136,157,170,171, 183,185,189,405 |
| Schefflera actinophylla | Brassaia actinophylla | 34,111,113,120,129, 131,135,159,162,232 |
| Schinus polygamus | Schinus dependens | 21,35,44,56,83,98,99,406 |
| Schlumbergera truncata | Zygocactus truncatus | 7,12,25,40,49,101,110, 114,116,141,151,156, 160,162,184,445 |
| Schlumbergera truncata 'Bicolor' | Zygocactus truncatus var. bicolor | 149,445 |
| Sedum album 'Brevifolium' | Sedum album var. brevifolium | 30,43,86,101,102,115, 182,184,408 |
| Sedum dendroideum subsp. praealtum | Sedum prealtum | 45,71,77,139,145,170, 187,409 |

## NOMENCLATURE INDEX

| MOST RECENT BOTANICAL NAME | HOYT NOMENCLATURE | PAGE |
|---|---|---|
| Sutera hispida | Chaenostoma hispidum | 5,28,37,91,137,145, 151,250 |
| Syzygium jambos | Eugenia jambos | 44,52,118,133,135,293 |
| Syzygium paniculatum | Eugenia paniculata, Eugenia paniculata var. myrtifolia | 3,16,17,34,52,55,63,67,73,77, 80,81,90,93,128,134,137,293 |
| Tabernaemontana divaricata | Ervatamia coronaria | 5,20,23,48,58,63,70, 89,99,100,111,118,128, 129,131,137,146,147, 149,184,286 |
| Tagetes erecta | Tagetes patula [now included in T. erecta] | 29,37,50,52,71,78,108, 139,167,169,179,182,420 |
| Tagetes tenuifolia | Tagetes signata pumila | 37,38,71,70,101,108,103, 115,121,171,179,182,420 |
| Talauma hodgsonii | Talauma hodgsoni | 3,42,107,129,421 |
| Tamarix chinensis | Tamarix juniperina [now included in T. chinensis] | 35,41,44,47,54,62,69, 96,98,125,421 |
| Tamarix ramosissima | Tamarix pentandra | 4,22,34,35,41,44,45, 47,49,51,54,62,67,69, 70,74,92,93,96,98,103, 106,125,130,140,148, 188,421 |
| Taxus baccata 'Repandens' | Taxus baccata var. repandens | 2,23,35,88,136,422 |
| Taxus baccata 'Stricta' | Taxus baccata var. stricta | 17,23,32,34,52,65,88, 89,127,156,422 |
| Tecoma alata | Tecoma smithi | 5,20,37,48,67,70,89, 106,139,143,150,422 |
| Tecoma stans | Stenolobium stans | 4,14,22,53,54,59,103, 120,128,135,138,148, 150,153,184,417 |
| Tecomaria capensis | Tecoma capensis | 6,22,26,33,37,38,44, 45,48,54,67,70,72,74,84, 89,92,98,102,103,106, 127,140,144,148,149, 150,165,186,422 |
| Ternstroemia gymnanthera | Ternstroemia japonica | 24,38,43,58,63,65,83, 87,90,107,113,116,121, 125,127,131,136,146, 156,157,161,423 |
| Tetragonia tetragonioides | Tetragonia expansa | 76,99,117,166,423 |
| Tetranema roseum | Allophyton mexicanum | 164,209 |
| Tetrapanax papyriferus | Tetrapanax papyriferum | 35,54,72,104,129,136, 159,162,423 |
| Tetrastigma voinieranum | Vitis voinierana | 26,27,38,50,51,58,68, 85,87,88,129,158,439 |
| Teucrium chamaedrys 'Prostratum' | Teucrium chamaedrys var. prostratum | 30,95,170,423 |
| Thevetia peruviana | Thevetia nereifolia | 33,41,47,48,53,57,59, 61,63,67,70,90,103, 130,135,139,146,148, 149,152,184,424 |
| Thunbergia grandiflora 'Alba' | Thunbergia grandiflora var. albus | 426 |
| Thunbergia gregorii | Thunbergia gibsoni, Thunbergia gregori | 37,41,48,53,68,94,95, 99,104,139,144,145, 146,152,185,426 |
| Thymus broussonetii | Thymus broussoneti | 30,45,57,61,77,95,108, 141,147,169,170,187, 189,426 |
| Thymus praecox | Thymus serpyllum | 42,45,50,55,57,61,74, 77,86,95,96,108,166, 169,171,181,182,187, 189,426 |
| Thymus praecox arcticus 'Albus' | Thymus serpyllum var. albus | 30,102,426 |
| Thymus praecox arcticus 'Coccineus' | Thymus serpyllum var coccineus | 30,102,426 |
| Thymus pseudolanuginosus | Thymus serphyllum var. lanuginosus | 86,136,426 |
| Thymus richardii subsp. nitidus | Thymus nitidus | 45,47,61,77,100,108, 169,171,182,189,426 |
| Tibouchina urvilleana | Tibouchina semidecandra | 58,60,63,103,142,148, 149,154,159,184,426 |
| Triteleia bridgesii | Brodiaea bridgesi | 24,31,43,53,106,123, 144,165,186,188,233 |
| Triteleia hyacinthina | Brodiaea lactea | 31,43,53,59,106,123, 138,144,165,180,186, 188,233 |

## NOMENCLATURE INDEX

| MOST RECENT BOTANICAL NAME | HOYT NOMENCLATURE | PAGE |
|---|---|---|
| Triteleia laxa | Brodiaea laxa | 31,43,53,61,106,123,144, 165,180,186,188,233 |
| Tulipa fosterana | Tulipa fosteriana | 31,102,123,144,180, 187,189,431 |
| Ugni molinae | Myrtus ugni | 12,24,58,62,66,92,358 |
| Ulmus parvifolia | Ulmus parvifolia var. sempervirens [now included in species] | 18,19,131,432 |
| Verbena hybrida | Verbena hortensis | 9,30,37,42,47,51,61, 74,78,86,95,108,112, 142,187,434 |
| Verbena tenera | Verbena pulchella | 30,37,42,47,55,57,61, 95,96,142,151,152,157, 181,187,434 |
| Veronica tournefortii | Veronica tourneforti | 30,39,122,142,181,435 |
| Viburnum burkwoodii | Viburnum burkwoodi | 5,38,43,48,53,57,61,69, 83,90,127,150,188,435 |
| Viburnum carlesii | Viburnum carlesi | 6,21,38,48,53,61,69,78, 88,90,106,107,125,134, 140,188,436 |
| Viburnum farreri | Viburnum fragrans | 5,6,107,150,188,436 |
| Viburnum tinus 'Lucidum' | Viburnum tinus var. lucidum | 120,150,436 |
| Viburnum tinus 'Robustum' | Viburnum tinus var. robustum | 149,436 |
| Vicia benghalensis | Vicia atropurpurea | 113, 117, 436 |
| Vigna caracalla | Phaseolus caracalla | 7,27,37,50,57,68,87,88, 108,142,152,162,375 |
| Westringia fruticosa | Westringia rosmariniformis | 5,33,44,45,62,70,75, 88,90,92,119,125,130, 135,441 |
| Xanthisma texana | Xanthisma texanum | 9,15,37,45,50,52,61, 72,139,145,187,442 |
| Xylosma congestum | Xylosma senticosa | 5,20,24,33,35,39,41, 45,62,65,69,70,74,78, 83,84,85,87,90,105, 119,130,131,135,150, 186,188,442 |
| Yucca constricta | Yucca tenuistyla | 15,47,50,54,69,84,100, 111,117,118,156,160, 187,443 |
| Zantedeschia aethiopica 'Childsiana' | Zantedeschia aethiopica var. minor | 172,444 |
| Zantedeschia rehmannii | Zantedeschia rehmanni | 49,58,78,121,144,160,444 |
| Zephyranthes drummondii | Cooperia drummondi | 10,15,31,37,41,51,72, 108,118,147,148,153, 165,172,180,186,261 |
| Zingiber darceyi | Zingiber officinale var. darceyi | 132,445 |
| Zinnia angustifolia | Zinnia linearis | 45,101,109,121,445 |
| Ziziphus jujuba | Zizyphus jujuba | 11,19,41,44,46,49,98, 104,133,154,156,161,445 |
| Ziziphus obtusifolia | Zizyphus obtusifolia | 15,47,105,445 |